Irish voters decide

Voting behaviour in elections and referendums since 1918

Richard Sinnott

Manchester University Press

Manchester and New York

Distributed exclusively in the USA and Canada by St Martin's Press

Published by Manchester University Press
Oxford Road, Manchester M13 9PL, UK
and Room 400, 175 Fifth Avenue, New York, NY 10010, USA

Distributed exclusively in the USA and Canada
by St. Martin's Press, Inc., 175 Fifth Avenue, New York, NY 10010, USA

British Library Cataloguing-in-Publication Data
A catalogue record for this book is available from the British Library

Library of Congress Cataloging-in-Publication Data
Sinnott, R. (Richard)
    Irish voters decide : voting behaviour in elections and
referendums since 1918 / Richard Sinnott.
        p.   cm.
    Includes bibliographical references.
    ISBN 0–7190–4036–1 (cl). — ISBN 0–7190–4037–X (pbk)
    1. Elections—Ireland.   2. Voting—Ireland.   3. Ireland—Politics
and government—1922–   I. Title.
JN1541.S57   1995
324.9417′082—dc20   93–49042

ISBN 0 7190 4036 1 *hardback*
     0 7190 4037 X *paperback*

Typeset in Great Britain
by Servis Filmsetting Ltd, Manchester

Printed in Great Britain
by Redwood Books, Trowbridge

Contents

Tables

Note: Census data are taken from relevant publications of the Central Statistics Office and electoral data from Gallagher, 1994; Walker, 1992; and, from 1948 on, from the relevant volumes of election and referendum results published by the Stationery Office.

Figures and maps

Note: Census data are taken from relevant publications of the Central Statistics Office and electoral data from Gallagher, 1994; Walker, 1992; and, from 1948 on, from the relevant volumes of election and referendum results published by the Stationery Office.

Acknowledgements

The debts I have incurred in writing this book are extensive and I happily take this opportunity to thank all those who have given time and thought in response to my enquiries or in reaction to my ideas. First, there are the debts to those who have provided or assisted in locating the data that is the basis of the research: Tim Sexton of the Franchise Section of the Department of the Environment who has always responded to intricate enquiries with care and courtesy; Brian Walker who made available a pre-publication draft of his Royal Irish Academy book of Irish election results at a time when it was the only source of detailed reports of first preference votes in elections prior to 1948; Brendan J. Whelan for providing census data for the 1980s in a way that could be easily matched to electoral data and for his involvement in our efforts in collating transfer data since 1948. For access to opinion poll data in either raw or report form I am indebted to the Economic and Social Research Institute, the Gallup Poll, Irish Marketing Surveys, Lansdowne Market Research, Market Research Bureau of Ireland, National Opinion Polls, Research Services Ireland, the Surveys, Research, Analyses Unit of DG X of the European Commission and the Zentral Archiv at the University of Cologne. In particular, Charles Coyle of IMS, Jack Jones of MRBI and Roger Jupp of Landsdowne were always most helpful in their response to requests for and enquiries about data collected by their respective companies. Grateful acknowledgement is also made to the various initiators and sponsors of these surveys and opinion polls – Radio Telefis Eireann, the European Commission, the European Parliament Election Study Group (co-ordinated by Hermann Schmitt), Fine Gael, Independent Newspapers, *The Irish Press*, *The Irish Times*, the Labour Party and Stein Larsen of the University of Bergen – for permission to use the data.

Secondly, for help in analysing the data I am indebted principally to James P. McBride and Brendan J. Whelan: to James P. McBride for the endless patience with which he computerised the data and ran and re-ran statistical analysis of all shapes and sizes and then turned his virtuoso computer skills to the task of making the results accessible in well designed tables, graphs and maps; to Brendan J. Whelan who not only co-operated in collecting the transfer data but wrote the computer programme to analyse it, who is still rewriting parts of that programme in our on-going project on transfer patterns and with whom I have worked closely on the ecological analysis of voting patterns since 1981. The assistance of Joe Brady and Tony Parker in adapting computer-generated maps is also gratefully acknowledged.

Thirdly, there are my debts to those who have read all or parts of earlier drafts of the book or who have otherwise inspired, advised on or criticised various aspects of it. On circulating an early draft, I encountered remarkable encouragement and collegiality and lots of constructive criticism, for all of which I am deeply grateful. With explicit disavowal of any responsibility on their part for remaining imperfections in the book, I record my thanks to John Baker, John

Bowman, Ian Budge, John Coakley, Brian Farrell, David M. Farrell, Peter Feeney, Michael Gallagher, Tom Garvin, Brian Girvin, Patrick Honohan, Kieran A. Kennedy, Michael Laffan, Michael Laver, James P. McBride, Moore McDowell, Peter Mair, Maurice Manning, Michael Marsh, Hermann Schmitt, Brendan M. Walsh, Brendan J. Whelan and the late John H. Whyte.

Finally, for vital assistance in producing the book, I wish to thank Clodagh Murphy, Dolores Burke and Ricki Schoen who, in addition to typing drafts and inserts, locating missing files, resurrecting apparently perished ones and assembling the references, at various times helped to keep the show on the road. On the editorial and production side, I am also grateful to Richard Purslow, Jane Hammond Foster and the staff of Manchester University Press and to MUP's readers for encouragement and many helpful suggestions.

In acknowledgement of the most important debts of all, this book is for Margaret, Gillian and Daniel.

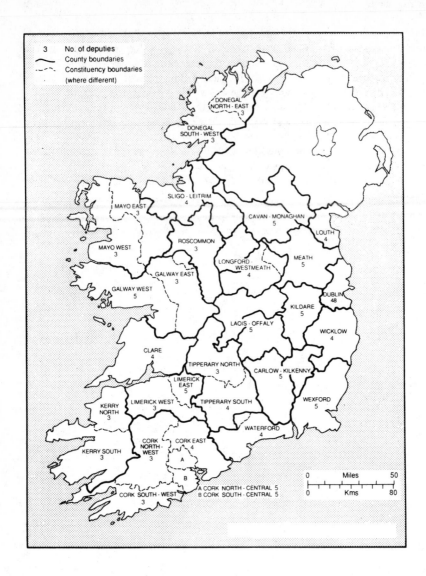

Map 1 Dáil constituencies 1980

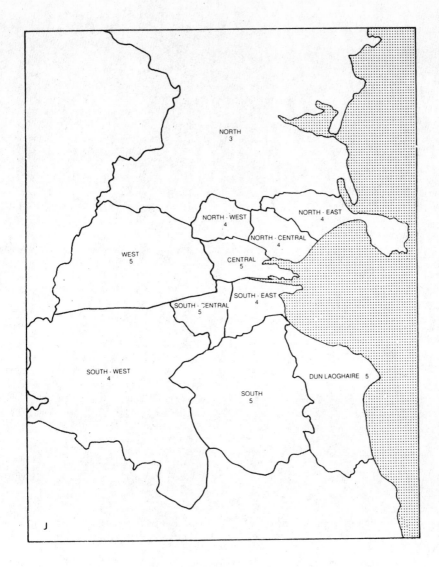

Map 2 Dáil constituencies (Dublin) 1980

Chapter 1

Analysing Irish electoral behaviour

The agenda

In the recent past Irish voters have been confronted with an exceptionally full agenda. Between 1981 and 1994 there were six general elections, eight referendums, three European Parliament elections, two country-wide local elections and a presidential election. All of the general elections either overturned governments or produced new and unforeseen coalitions. The 1987 election witnessed a remarkably successful début by Ireland's first avowedly liberal party. Then in 1992 came a significant recovery in the vote for the Labour Party, after a dismal twenty-year decline, a result that led to an historic first – the formation of a coalition between Fianna Fáil and Labour. The termination of that coalition in November 1994 was even more dramatic than its inception. The ensuing political crisis produced another historic first – the formation of a new government involving a different combination of parties without the intervention of an election. This development did not occur, however, without electoral intervention. The narrow Dáil majority of the Fine Gael–Labour–Democratic Left combination which took over in December 1994 had been created by a net gain of three seats by these parties in four by-elections in June and November of that year.

Several of the eight referendums mentioned above also had a major impact. One of them put Irish voters briefly in the European spotlight and provided an antidote to the Danish 'no' to the Maastricht Treaty. Referendums on abortion (1983) and divorce (1986) roundly reasserted the conservative position. In stark contrast, the presidential election (1990) put into office a feminist, a reformer and a radical individual rights campaigner who had been closely identified with the liberal side on the divorce and abortion issues. Three further abortion referendums in 1992 established that the constitutional prohibition of abortion did not restrict the right to freedom of information or the right to travel,[1] and showed a wide divergence of views on the circumstances in which abortion could be permitted, effectively throwing the issue back into the legislative arena. European Parliament elections have reduced Irish socialist representation in Strasbourg to zero (in 1984) and have backed independents at the expense of

---

[1] Based on the 1983 amendment, restrictions on the dissemination of information relating to abortion had been secured from the courts by anti-abortion campaigners. It is estimated that some 4,000 to 5,000 women travel to Britain each year for abortions.

the larger parties. Even local elections have had national significance, the 1985 local elections providing a portent of the collapse of a thirty-year-long recovery by the second largest party in the state.

Taking a longer historical view, many of the issues that have confronted Irish voters are of considerable relevance in the transition to democracy in Central and Eastern Europe and elsewhere, i.e. the questions of separatism and sovereignty; the problems of holding elections in a situation of impending civil war and in its immediate aftermath; the challenge to the legitimacy of the state caused by abstention from the elected assembly by more than one-quarter of the elected members; the crucial first transfer of power from defeated incumbents to the victorious opposition, and, subsequently, the threats posed by extreme nationalism on the left and by an embryonic fascism on the right.

Coping with these issues left its mark on the Irish party system and Irish electoral alignments and the existence of this historical legacy poses a number of puzzles. The first is what does this division between the parties that were formed in this early period mean? Is this pro- and anti-treaty division something unique, something peculiar to a given set of historical circumstances? Writings on Irish politics and, indeed, on comparative party systems are littered with references to the peculiarity of Irish political parties. Concern with this issue arises not just from a desire to pigeon-hole Irish parties; it arises more because, if the party divisions are unique, then general frameworks of explanation of the development of party systems and electoral alignments are likely to be of little use in attempting to understand the Irish system.

The second puzzle is the weakness of socialism as an electoral force. It is clear why socialism did not flourish in the immediate context of an overriding nationalist struggle, but why did this weakness persist? Ireland has had, by far, the lowest left-wing vote in Western Europe. Socialist optimists may hope that 1992 is the longed-for breakthrough, but a total left vote of 23 per cent is still a long way off the average Western European left vote and the left vote in the 1994 European Parliament elections did not provide any assurance that the breakthrough would endure. Even if 1992 proves to be the socialist dawn in Ireland, the electoral failure of socialism over a seventy-year period demands explanation.

The third puzzle is what happens when the historical legacy encounters a changing demographic, social, economic and political environment? The Irish party system and the pattern of electoral behaviour associated with it have persisted through a period of fundamental change in the demographic and socio-economic characteristics of the Irish electorate. These changes have been occurring since independence but have been especially noticeable over the last thirty years or so. In addition, the role and scope of government – what elections are ultimately all about – have been transformed. Yet, over most of the same thirty years, continuity was the dominant feature of electoral politics. The same parties competed; they garnered much the same proportions of the vote; minor parties waxed and waned; realignments were mooted but did not materialise; referendums confirmed the status quo on fundamental issues. From the late 1980s on there were signs of change, in the success of the Progressive Democrats in 1987, in the victory of Mary Robinson in the presidential election of 1990 and in the outcomes of the general election and of the referendums in November 1992. The issue of change, therefore, involves a threefold question: how substantial are the current signs of change? When did change really get under way? And how do we account for the persistence for so long of generally stable electoral patterns in a society undergoing rapid transformation?

The particularities of the institutional context add to the complexity and fascination of the Irish electoral agenda. The Irish constitution provides expanded opportunities for the expression of the views of the voters. It does so first in the obvious way, by creating extra occasions for voting – in referendums and in the direct election of the head of state. It does so in a more subtle way via the electoral system. This allows voters to emphasize either candidate or party criteria, or some combination of both, in making up their minds and enables them to express not just a categorical choice but their order of preferences for candidates and parties. As far as the study of electoral behaviour is concerned, the existence of referendums and preference voting means that there is much more behaviour and much more evidence out there to be analysed. It also means that the analysis must take into account both the interaction between preference voting and basic party choice and the interaction between the referendum process and the party system.

In summary, whether viewed from the perspective of a practical interest in Irish politics or from that of comparative political analysis, Irish electoral behaviour presents an impelling research agenda. And these are not only intellectual concerns. Irish government is party government. Governments act within the constraints set by the past decisions of the electorate and, even more, by the anticipation of future electoral reward or retribution. The top personnel of government are selected, confirmed and moulded by the electoral process. Beyond these general effects on policy and decision-making, highly specific issues with very real and tangible consequences (e.g. the issues of divorce and abortion, or the issue of articles 2 and 3 of the constitution)[2] are decided by majority vote in referendums. It is a truism that electoral behaviour reflects the society in which it occurs. But voting also shapes the society and influences the effectiveness of society's response to the problems it faces.

It is important to emphasize that the focus of this book is on electoral behaviour, that is, on what the voters did and why they did it. It therefore treats only tangentially such important topics as the organisation of political parties, election campaigning, the role of the media, and the actual distribution of seats that is the end result of an election. On the other hand, electoral behaviour is understood comprehensively as includ-

---

[2] Article 2 reads 'The national territory consists of the whole island of Ireland, its islands and the territorial seas'. Article 3 reads 'Pending the reintegration of the national territory, and without prejudice to the right of the Parliament and Government established by this Constitution to exercise jurisdiction over the whole of that territory, the laws enacted by that Parliament shall have the like area and extent of application as the laws of Saorstát Éireann and the like extra-territorial effect'. In the Joint Declaration issued by the British Prime Minister and the Taoiseach on 15 December 1993, the Taoiseach acknowledged the existence in the constitution of 'elements which are deeply resented by Northern unionists' and he confirmed that '. . . in the event of an overall settlement, the Irish Government will, as part of a balanced constitutional accommodation, put forward and support proposals for change in the Irish Constitution which would fully reflect the principle of consent in Northern Ireland'.

ing, not just, as is often the case, voting in general elections, but also voting in local elections, in European Parliament elections, in presidential elections and in referendums. It also includes the complex patterns of political behaviour that arise from the workings of the electoral system.

The book has two main objectives. The first is to give an account of Irish electoral behaviour in its various manifestations, both describing what happened and, where possible, offering an explanation, in the sense of identifying the proximate correlates and causes of particular patterns of behaviour. Potential correlates and causes include the social and demographic characteristics of voters, in particular their social class position. They also include voters' loyalty or lack of loyalty to party, their issue preoccupations, their preferences (or aversions) for individual political leaders and the weight they attach to national or local concerns.

The second objective is to build on these accounts to provide an interpretation of Irish electoral alignments and electoral behaviour that addresses the issues raised above – the underlying significance of the original division between the parties, focusing especially on the issue of peculiarity versus comparability; the related questions of the weakness of socialism as an electoral force and the role or, as many would argue, the none-role of social class in determining party choice; the implications of preference voting in multi-member constituencies and, finally, the issue of stability and change as manifested in party choice and referendum voting and in the interaction between these two expressions of voter opinion.

The target audience of this book is a wide one. Elections exercise a certain fascination and do so across a broad spectrum of people – from the partisan activist to the election–night spectator, from the punter, to the pundit, to the political scientist, from the citizen as 'rational actor' calculating the effect of the outcome on his or her interests or values, to the citizen as philosopher ruminating about democracy, participation and the distribution of power. And these points on the spectrum overlap, for, when it comes to politics, we are all, or almost all, partisans and punters, spectators, expert analysts, citizens and philosophers. The focus on electoral behaviour will at times require the use of statistical techniques that are essential in the systematic study of mass behaviour of any kind. The approach to these techniques is, however, strictly instrumental and minimalist. They are used only when absolutely necessary and they are presented with as little technical jargon as possible. Readers interested in the technical aspects are referred to the relevant literature.

This chapter seeks to lay the foundation for what follows by describing the changing context of Irish voting, by examining the institutional framework that structures the voters' expression of their opinion and, finally, by introducing and evaluating the available sources of evidence and methods of analysis.

The changing context: the electorate

Changes in basic demographic forces – marriage rate, fertility and migration – allied to late but rapid economic modernisation have had fundamental effects on who and what the Irish people, and therefore Irish voters, were and are. The first forty years of

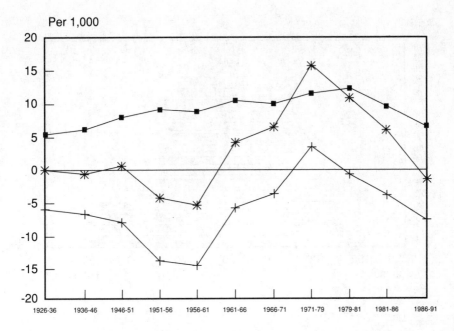

Per 1,000

■ Natural Increase + Net Migration ✳ Population Change

Figure 1.1 Population trends 1926–91: natural increase, net migration and population growth (average annual rates). (*Note*: All figure sources are given on pp. ix–xi.)

the state's existence were characterised by a combination of low marriage rate, high fertility of marriage and a high, at times extremely high, rate of emigration. This was followed in the 1960s by a high marriage rate with moderate fertility plus, for a short period in the 1970s, net in-migration. More recently still, this has given way to a return to high emigration, lower fertility and a reversal of the rising marriage trend (Kennedy *et al.*, 1988, pp. 140–1). The overall effect of this changing pattern was a static or declining population until the 1960s, followed by a period of rapid growth in the 1970s, a lower but still positive rate of growth in the early 1980s and slight population decline between 1986 and 1991 (see Figure 1.1).

Emigration was particularly pronounced in the 1950s, when for several years 'annual net emigration amounted to over 2 per cent of the country's population' (Walsh, 1980, p. 4). The result was that by 1961 net emigration had 'accounted for just over 100,000 of [the cohort that was aged 10–14 in 1951], a loss of almost 40 per cent in a decade!' (*ibid*.). The scale of the emigration of the 1950s helped to generate a sense of crisis that had very far-reaching consequences for public policy. Emigration also had potentially important electoral consequences. Losses through emigration among the 1950s cohort meant that the electorate of the early and mid-1960s was pronouncedly middle-aged. While there is no certainty that the 'missing' 100,000 who would have been eligible to vote in the early 1960s would have voted differently from their elders, by stripping the electorate of such a large proportion of its younger cohort, the emigration of the 1950s may well have had

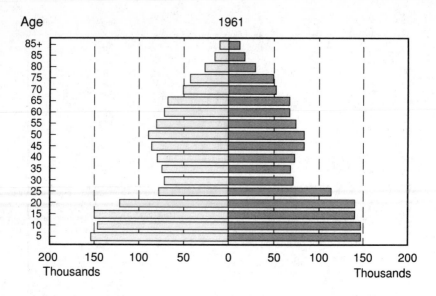

□ Males ■ Females

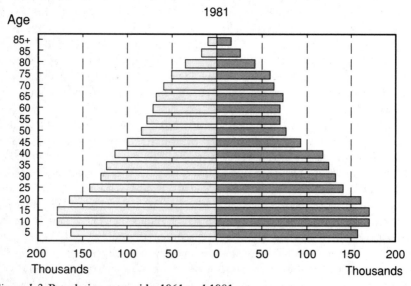

Figure 1.2 Population pyramids, 1961 and 1981.

a conservative effect on electoral politics.[3] The reverse effect might have been expected in the early 1980s when fully one-quarter of the electorate were under 25 years of age. This suggestion will be examined later. At this stage it is sufficient to note that, as is clear from the different shapes of the age pyramids shown in Figure 1.2, the voters of the 1980s differed from those of the 1960s in a quite fundamental way.

Migration, whether internal or external, was mainly a rural phenomenon. Its effect on rural areas was related to and reinforced by a decline in agricultural employment and a growth in industry. The combined effect of the three trends considerably altered the balance between town and country and between one region and another. In 1926 two-thirds of the population were rural dwellers according to the standard Census definition of the term, i.e. they were living in the countryside or in towns or villages of less than 1500 people. This balance had shifted substantially by 1961 and by 1981 a majority of the population were living in towns. A considerable part of this change was the growth of the Dublin region (from 17 per cent of the population in 1926 to 29 per cent in 1986) and a concomitant decline in Connacht-Ulster (from 29 per cent in 1926 to 19 per cent in 1986).

Part and parcel of these demographic shifts was a radical alteration in the kinds of things that voters were doing to earn their living. Thus the percentage engaged in agriculture declined from 52 per cent in 1926 to 36 per cent in 1961 and down to 15 per cent in 1986. At the same time the percentage engaged in industry expanded at a fairly steady rate, from 13 per cent in 1926 to 24 per cent in 1961, to 29 per cent in 1986. The increase in the services sector, from 35 per cent in 1926 to 56 per cent in 1986, has occurred mainly since the early 1960s (see Figure 1.3).[4]

It is not just that people shifted from one job to another. The changes involved added up to a transformation in the class structure of the society. Breen *et al.* argue that this vital change occurred in the period 1961–81 and conclude that 'by the 1980s, the new class structure was fully in place' (Breen *et al.*, 1990, p. 58). Based on a re-categorisation of Census data and focusing on post-1951 trends in male employment, they identify the main developments as a significant increase in the number of non-agricultural employers (indicating that 'Ireland has clearly ceased to be *petit bourgeois*'); a tripling of the proportion of employed professionals (from 5 per cent in 1951 to 17 per cent in 1985); a doubling of the proportion of skilled manual employees (from 10 to 20 per cent) and an increase in the proportion of lower middle-class workers, from 14 to 22 per cent. The main areas of decline were among self-employed farmers and their 'relatives assisting' and among semi- and unskilled manual workers, the decline among the latter being again concentrated in the agricultural sector. The main changes occurred between 1961 and 1981 and these are illustrated in Figure 1.4. Of course, changes of this kind have significant effects on social mobility and on the make-up of

---

[3] It has also been argued that emigration, by 'removing pressures to reform a conservative and conformist social structure' and by holding down the scale of the home market, may have had adverse economic consequences (see Kennedy, 1992, p. 28). The retarding role of emigration is also a key factor in the analysis of Irish economic performance in Mjoset (1992).

[4] See Franklin, Mackie and Valen, 1992 (pp. 33–46) for a summary account of these and other sociodemographic changes across a range of sixteen countries, including Ireland.

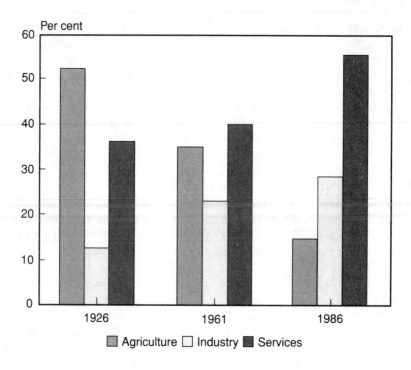

Figure 1.3 Workforce in agriculture, industry, and services: 1926, 1961 and 1986.

the various classes in terms of class origins. This in turn has implications for the relationship between class and voting, because individuals may be as much or more influenced in their voting decisions by their class origins as by their current class. Thus, it
is important to note that by 1987 the professional, administrative and managerial class
was quite heterogeneous in respect of origins. In contrast, the industrial working class
tended to be homogeneous in terms of class origins, even allowing for the substantial
inflow into this group from agriculture (Whelan, Breen and Whelan, 1992, p. 115).

If the average voter in the 1980s was much more likely to be young, urban, and
middle class, he or she was also likely to be considerably more educated than the voter
of the 1950s or even the 1960s. Beginning with the implementation of the free education scheme in 1967, a substantial rise in participation rates in post–primary education
occurred. In the early 1960s only half of all 15–year–olds were still at school; by 1970
this had risen to 70 per cent, by 1975 to 82 per cent and by 1985 to 94 per cent (Breen
et al., 1990, p. 128 and Department of Education Statistical Reports, various years).
The impact of these changes in school participation rates on the educational level of
the electorate was enhanced by the fact that the age cohorts involved were a dispropor-
tionately large segment of the population, and by the fact that the voting age was
lowered from 21 to 18 years (though the referendum to approve this change was passed
in 1972, the change did not become operative in a general election until 1977).

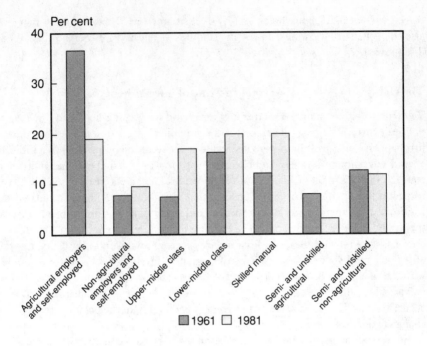

Figure 1.4 The evolution of the class structure (occupational class of males at work).

In the light of all this change – industrialisation, urbanisation, change in the class structure and a virtual revolution in rates of educational participation – one might have expected a concomitant process of secularisation. In fact the evidence up to 1988–89 suggests that 'secularisation is taking place in Ireland at a considerably slower pace than had been expected' (Fahey, 1992, p. 258). For Catholics, the basic measure of religious practice (attendance at Mass at least once a week) declined from 91 per cent in 1974 to 87 per cent in 1984 to 82 per cent in 1988–89 (*ibid.*). Other evidence indicates that change in religious beliefs has also been modest. All of this has two implications for the analysis of voting. First, it is a reminder that economic, social and demographic change is not necessarily and automatically followed by changes in behaviour and outlook. Secondly, it raises the question of whether such change in religious practice as has occurred is reflected in any way in voting patterns, a question taken up in chapter 7.

Of the many other changes affecting the Irish voter that could be documented, one in particular deserves mention because of its direct relevance to elections and electioneering. A national television service was established in 1961. By 1967 almost 60 per cent of households had a television set, though there was a considerable contrast in television ownership between urban and rural communities (only 39 per cent of the latter having a set). By 1971 the figure for ownership had increased to three-quarters of all households and by 1979 it stood at 90 per cent. By that time also the urban–rural contrast in the distribution of television ownership had almost disappeared.[5]

The changing context: the scope and role of government

Television was not simply a matter of a new window opening up on an unchanging political world. The post-1960 social and economic changes described above did not just happen – many of them were instigated by or were the by-product of a radically altered government strategy launched in 1958. It was noted above that the rate of emigration was a measure of the depth of the crisis that characterised the 1950s. In retrospect it is easy to see that only a crisis of that magnitude could have stimulated and legitimised the turn-round in government and party policy – from protectionism to free trade, from self-sufficiency to welcoming foreign investment, from a strategy of minimal state intervention to at least indicative economic planning and a conception of the state and state bodies as agents of economic development. Chapter 2 will deal with the role of the political parties in this and subsequent economic policy developments. The concern here is simply to indicate the extent of the changes that were occurring in the scope and role of government and highlight the potential for electoral change that this involved.

Surveying the period since the foundation of the state, Kennedy *et al.* summarise a basic indicator of the growth of government as follows:

> The extent of the change can be seen most succinctly in the fact that total expenditure of public authorities (including transfers) has risen relative to GNP from less than 25 per cent in the mid-1920s to nearly 70 per cent in the mid-1980s. . . . the really large increase in the ratio has taken place since 1960, when it was 32 per cent, and more particularly in the period 1973–85 when the ratio rose from 42 per cent to 67 per cent.
>
> (Kennedy *et al.*, 1988, p. 87)

This growth was not just due to the post-1958 emergence of government as an agent of economic development or to the concomitant expansion in its role of welfare provider. As the timing of the most dramatic growth indicates, much of the expansion was due to the response of government to the economic recessions induced by the two oil crises of the 1970s. The problem was that Irish governments sought to maintain growth levels and living standards that had been achieved on the basis of expansionary policies in the more favourable international economic climate of the 1960s. The dramatic expansion of public expenditure in the mid- to late 1970s was funded partly out of substantial increases in taxation. Prior to 1960, tax revenue was a fairly stable 20 per cent of GNP. By 1973 it had risen to 31 per cent and in 1985 it was 43 per cent (Kennedy *et al.*, 1988, pp. 88–9). The other basis of the expansion in government spending was borrowing, which, from 1974 on, increasingly meant foreign borrowing. On the debt front, 'the net result was that in the 13-year period between 1973 and 1986,

---

[5] Figures from Chubb, 1982, p. 27.

the national debt/GNP ratio rose by nearly 90 percentage points . . .' (Kennedy *et al.*, 1988, p. 91).

The gap between the state's resources in terms of taxation and borrowing capacity and its obligations in terms of public expenditure commitments was the clearest indication of governmental overload. Some would add that this aspect of overload was exacerbated by political and institutional factors, such as the apparently irresistible pressure of sectoral interests of all kinds, the failure to implement or enforce policy decisions in certain areas and a declining sense of the legitimacy of political institutions, and perhaps of the political class (Chubb, 1987, p. 228). Be that as it may, there was a consensus by the mid-1980s that existing levels of both taxation and borrowing were unsustainable and that government had reached the limits of growth. Eventually, a severe process of budgetary retrenchment was initiated in 1987.

Both the expansion and retrenchment of government were deeply enmeshed in electoral politics. This is true in the sense that expansionary policies were explicitly put before the electorate in the 1977 election and that, subsequently, perceived electoral pressures inhibited all parties from effectively tackling the problem for too long. It is also true in the sense that the adverse fiscal consequences of the expansion affected the voter in a most direct way. First there was the very considerable increase in taxation. Secondly, the politics of retrenchment figured prominently in electoral campaigning once the magnitude of the crisis became apparent. Of course, the impact of economic problems on the voters was not confined to what government did or did not do in terms of fiscal policy.

Two basic indicators of the changing but very real economic problems directly affecting voters in the period since the early 1970s are presented in Figure 1.5. The elections of 1965 and 1969 took place against a background in which unemployment was a steady 5 to 6 per cent and inflation, though rising, was moderate. The period from 1974 to 1982 witnessed very steep fluctuations in inflation and substantial increases in unemployment. Since the early 1980s, inflation has fallen dramatically but unemployment has continued to rise, presenting an overriding challenge to the society and political system alike. When these issues are combined with the issues of government spending and borrowing described above, it is apparent that, in so far as elections are about what governments attempt to do and the problems they face in the economic and social realm, the context of electoral competition has changed in very far-reaching ways.

The changing context: relations with the external environment

Irish governance and the context of Irish voting have also been affected by changes in the external environment. The first and most obvious of these was the change in Anglo-Irish relations. Preoccupation with Anglo-Irish relations was a dominant feature of the context of Irish political life and Irish elections in the early years of the state's existence. As time passed and the more tractable aspects of the relationship were sorted out, the assumption seemed to develop that all a government had to do was to reiterate its commitment to the recovery of 'the fourth green field' and the need for

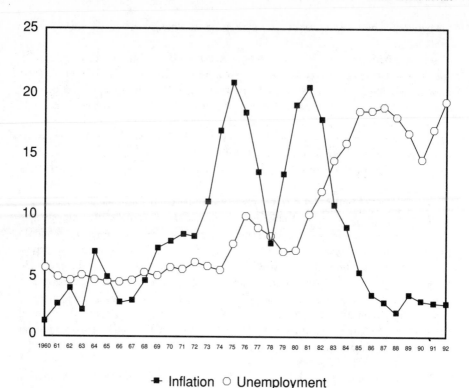

■ Inflation ○ Unemployment

Figure 1.5 Inflation and unemployment, 1960–92.

both an effective electoral appeal and a policy *vis-à-vis* Northern Ireland was *ipso facto* met. Both the preoccupation and the assumption changed gradually and, by the mid-1960s, there were signs of a more relaxed and realistic attitude to the issue. This was interrupted by the outbreak of the Troubles in 1969, and a longer, slower and more painful process of re-evaluation began. Eventually, a new relationship, in which both Dublin and London recognised their mutual interdependence in managing the Northern Ireland problem and in searching for a solution, was reflected in the Anglo-Irish Agreement of 1985 and in the Downing Street Declaration of 1993. Given that the party system had been founded on divisions over nationalist principles, this contextual change, beginning in the 60s and continuing through to the mid-80s and early 90s might be expected to have a discernible electoral impact.

Changes in relationships with the broader external environment were also evident. Accession to the EC in 1973 confirmed the trend away from the relative isolationism of the first forty years of independence. In certain areas, it has shifted the balance of policy initiation and in some cases policy determination from Dublin to Brussels. It has also introduced new perspectives and new issues in foreign policy and has exposed politicians to ideological traditions and institutions beyond the Westminster models to which the state had been so bound in the early years. While the potential effect of these environmental changes on the electoral context is indirect and difficult to assess, it should not be underestimated. It has been reinforced by the cycle of opportunities for electoral involvement in this area in referendums on EC constitutional issues and in European Parliament elections.

Stability and change

In summary, there has been a dual transformation in the context in which Irish voting takes place – on the one hand, social and demographic change and, on the other, change in the political and governmental environment, both domestic and external. There are two obvious ways in which this transformation might affect voting. Voters could change their allegiance or their preference as a result of their changed situation or parties could change the nature of their appeal in order to adapt to the changed circumstances and, by assumption, the changed attitudes of the voters. There is also a third alternative, which is that voting decisions proceed on some set course impervious to the changes in the social, demographic and political context. Determining which of these alternative descriptions, or which mixture of all three of them, best fits the Irish voter will be a recurring theme in the chapters that follow.[6] There are, however, still some necessary preliminaries to consider – first, the institutional context of voting, i.e how the rules of the game affect the choices the voters make, and secondly, the matter of evidence and method.

The institutional context

As already noted, in structuring the voter's choice, the Irish constitution expands rather than restricts the voter's opportunities. Firstly, there are the provisions for referendums. Ireland has had two constitutions (1922 and 1937) and both have provided for the referendum as the normal method of constitutional amendment. Both have also provided for the possibility of referral of a bill to the people on the initiative of the Seanad (the upper house of the legislature). In the case of the present constitution, this provision is hedged about with considerable conditions and qualifications.[7] In addition, the 1922 Constitution provided for the possibility of a referendum as a result of popular initiative. Despite the more generous provisions for a referendums under the 1922 Constitution, no referendums were held in the period 1922–37.[8] In contrast, despite the restrictive provisions of the 1937 constitution, events have conspired to create, between 1937 and 1992, no less than seventeen occasions for direct popular

---

[6] The question of the relationship between change in party support and demographic, social and cultural change is subjected to systematic comparative analysis by Franklin *et al*. They describe their central research question as 'If electoral change is consequential upon social change, then why did the effects arise so late?' (Franklin, Mackie and Valen, 1992, p. 9). This comparative perspective will be considered in the concluding chapter.

[7] See chapter 9.

[8] See chapter 9 for discussion of the referendum provisions in the 1922 Constitution and the reasons for their non-use.

participation in political decision-making (this number includes the 1937 referendum to approve the constitution).

Not only has there been a relatively large number of referendums, the issues involved have traversed a broad range of political controversy. In a comparative study of referendums, Butler and Ranney note that they have tended to be either about constitutional issues, in the sense of the basic rules of the regime, or about territorial issues, and that, with some exceptions, 'the great moral issues seem by general consent to have been avoided' (Butler and Ranney, 1978, p. 10). Ireland is one of the exceptions, having had five referendums on moral issues (divorce and abortion) in recent years. Categorising Irish referendums as either regime-related or religious/moral, chapter 9 examines the behaviour of the voters in this, the most direct and clear-cut opportunity the electorate has for exercising a decisive voice.

The second way in which Irish institutions expand the opportunities for electoral choice is in the particular form of proportional representation adopted. In comparison to most other electoral systems, proportional representation by means of the single transferable vote (PR-STV) allows for the expression of a more complex range of voter preferences. This is because it allows for the expression of preferences between parties *and* candidates and, unlike many of the other systems that incorporate both elements, it allows the voter to move from party to party in choosing candidates and puts no restriction on the number of preferences expressed. All of this considerably complicates the task of analysing Irish electoral behaviour.

In order to tackle the complications, an understanding of the electoral system is essential. There are three distinct senses in which one can have an understanding of PR-STV: in terms of what is involved in the act of voting, in terms of the basic logic of the system and in terms of the mechanics of the count. The first is quite simple and the instructions (shown in the facsimile of a ballot paper in Figure 1.6) are self-explanatory. It is perhaps worth emphasizing that this is so because a frequent objection to the system is that voters will not be able to understand it. If one had in mind the second or third kind of understanding of the system mentioned above this might well be so. The bulk of the voters probably have, at best, only a hazy notion of the logic of the system and almost certainly do not understand its 'mechanics'. They do not need to. All that is needed in order to use the system to the full is an understanding of the notion of ranking a set of candidates according to one's preferences. Understanding the mechanics of the system is undoubtedly somewhat difficult, particularly as one gets into the detailed aspects of transfer of surplus votes. While it will be necessary to get into these details in order to interpret transfer behaviour, the task can be postponed to chapter 8. At this point it is sufficient to understand PR-STV in the second sense indicated above, that is, in terms of its basic logic.

The key problem for all electoral systems is how to translate votes into seats. The simplest and crudest solution is the first-past-the-post formula, i.e. giving a seat to the candidate who is ahead of any other single candidate when all the votes have been counted. The kind of problem to which such a system gives rise can be seen in the 1992 general election in Britain, when the Liberal Democrats won 18 per cent of the vote, but got 3 per cent of the seats at Westminster. With 42 per cent of the vote, the

Marcáil ord do rogha sna spáis seo síos. Mark order of preference in spaces below.	Marc Oifigiúil Official Mark →
	ABBOTT — FIANNA FÁIL (Henry Abbott, of Monilea, Mullingar, Co. Westmeath. Senior Counsel, M.C.C.)
	COONEY — NON-PARTY (Benny Cooney, of 128 Auburn Heights, Athlone, Co. Westmeath.)
	DUNNE — NON-PARTY (John Dunne, of Streete, Mullingar, Co. Westmeath. Publican.)
	GERAGHTY — NON-PARTY (Declan Geraghty, of 9 Park View, Athboy, Co. Meath. Sales & Marketing Consultant.)
	HUMPHREYS — NON-PARTY (Mary Humphreys, of 11 Retreat Park, Athlone, Co. Westmeath. Teacher.)
	McFADDEN — FINE GAEL (Brendan McFadden, of Dunard, Athlone, Co. Westmeath. M.C.C. & Retired E.S.B Employee.)
	McGRÁTH — FINE GAEL (Paul McGrath, of Carna, Irishtown, Mullingar, Co. Westmeath. Public Representative & Teacher.)
	O'ROURKE — FIANNA FÁIL (Mary O'Rourke, of Arcadia, Athlone, Co. Westmeath. Public Representative.)
	PENROSE — THE LABOUR PARTY (Willie Penrose, of Ballintue, Ballynacargy, Co. Westmeath. Barrister-at-Law, M.C.C.)
	PRICE — NON-PARTY (Stephen Price, of Station Road, Moate, Co. Westmeath. Retired Driver.)
	ROGERS — SINN FÉIN (Peter Rogers, of 255 Dalton Park, Mullingar, Co. Westmeath.)

TREORACHA

I. Féach chuige go bhfuil an marc oifigiúil ar an bpáipéar.

II. Scríobh an figiúr 1 le hais ainm an chéad iarrthóra is rogha leat, an figiúr 2 le hais do dhara rogha, agus mar sin de.

III. Fill an páipéar ionas nach bhfeicfear do vóta. Taispeáin *cúl an pháipéir* don oifigeach ceannais, agus cuir sa bhosca ballóide é.

INSTRUCTIONS

I. See that the official mark is on the paper.

II. Write 1 beside the name of the candidate of your first choice, 2 beside your second choice, and so on.

III. Fold the paper to conceal your vote. Show *the back of the paper* to the presiding officer and put it in the ballot box.

Figure 1.6 Ballot paper, constituency of Westmeath, 1992.

Conservatives got 51 per cent of the seats. All very well if you are a Tory, but not very satisfactory if you are a Liberal Democrat and, in general, far from satisfactory from the point of view of fairness.

The system used in French presidential elections introduces a refinement on the above procedure. In order to win a seat a candidate must cross a certain threshold, in this case, 50 per cent plus one, or an absolute majority. A problem, of course, is that, with more than two candidates, no one may reach the threshold. When this arises, all but the top two candidates are eliminated and the voters troop back a second time to choose between the remaining two. This amounts to asking those who voted for eliminated candidates to register a second preference.

The underlying logic of the Irish electoral system is best approached by first considering its operation in a single-seat situation, when it operates not as a proportional system but as a sophisticated version of the majority system just described. This is not an entirely hypothetical example – it is the situation that obtains in a presidential election and in by-elections. Though usually thought of in the Irish context as still being PR-STV, in such situations it is in fact what is known as the 'alternative vote' system.

PR-STV imposes a threshold, called a quota, which a candidate must achieve in order to win a seat. The formula for calculating the quota is:

$$\text{Quota} = \frac{\text{Total number of valid votes}}{\text{Number of seats}+1} + 1$$

This may look somewhat obscure until it is considered in the single-seat situation, in which it is identical to the threshold used in the French system, i.e. 50 per cent + 1 or the absolute majority principle. The system used in an Irish presidential election or by-election has been described above as a version of the majority system. The sophistication lies in how it deals with the problem of no candidate reaching the threshold. It does not, as it were, waste the voters' time by asking them to come back later and register their second choice. Instead, it collects both this information, and information on third, fourth, fifth, etc. choices, all in one economical operation. Then, rather than disposing of all but the two leading candidates in one fell swoop, PR-STV eliminates them one by one, reassigning the votes of the eliminated candidate according to the next preference they contain. The advantage is to preserve as wide a range of choice of candidates for as long as possible, while the process moves by successive eliminations towards the goal of one candidate reaching the vital threshold.

PR-STV is not, however, merely a refined version of the majority-rule procedure – it has the all-important additional feature of multi-seat constituencies. This feature is essential in achieving the objective of reducing the disproportionality between votes and seats for any group or party. The multi-seat constituency introduces two new elements. The first is a lowering of the quota or threshold of election. In the single-seat situation the quota was half the votes plus one. A quick look at the formula shows that this principle can be easily extended as follows: in a two-seat constituency, the quota is one-third plus one, in a three-seater, one fourth plus one, in a four-seater, one fifth plus one, and so on. Thus, as the number of seats is increased, the threshold or proportion of votes required to win a seat is progressively lowered.

The second feature introduced by moving to multi-seat constituencies is the transfer of the surplus votes of elected candidates, i.e. the number of votes by which an elected candidate exceeds the quota. If this were not done, those who voted for such a candidate would not get the full share of representation to which they are entitled. For example, suppose that, in a three-seat constituency, 50 per cent of the voters vote for one particularly popular candidate. Since the quota is 25 per cent and since this is sufficient to elect the candidate, without such redistribution the second 25 per cent of voters who voted for the candidate in question would achieve no representation and their votes would be, as it were, wasted. This problem is solved in PR-STV by transferring the surplus votes to continuing candidates in proportion to each such candidate's share of second preferences in the elected candidate's set of votes. This is the point at which the mechanics of the counting procedure become somewhat complex. For now, however, it is sufficient to note the general principle, leaving detailed discussion to chapter 8. The essence of the system is that it ensures proportionality by (a) lowering the cost of a seat by transforming the fixed majority threshold (50 per cent plus one) into a variable and lower threshold by the addition of extra sets per constituency and (b) taking into account and using extra information on the voter's choice, i.e. his or her order of preference among the competing candidates.

Every electoral system structures the choice that faces the voter and in that way affects voting behaviour. This can be thought of in terms of whether the system restricts choice to general issues (a choice between fixed regional or national party lists) or allows for the expression of particular issues (a choice between local candidates representing national parties). The plurality (first-past-the-post) system enables the voter to pick either on the basis of party or candidate, but in the case of conflict between these two, the voter must decide on one basis or the other. PR-STV, on the other hand, allows the voter the luxury of employing both criteria at once. The voter can choose on the basis of general criteria first (i.e. choose a party) and then, within that choice, go on to record a preference for whichever of the individual candidates of that party he or she would like to see elected. Alternatively, absolute primacy can be given to the candidate criterion in making the first preference choice, and this can be followed by a return to a mix of general and particular criteria in expressing subsequent preferences. A third possibility is to give exclusive attention to choice of party, voting the party ticket without consideration of the order of particular candidates.[9]

The implications of this electoral system for the analysis of electoral behaviour are twofold. In the first place, it complicates the task of analysing first preference votes. Secondly, the system enriches electoral analysis by providing unparalleled data on how voters behave, not just in relation to their own party but also in relation to the other parties in the system. These data consist of the transfer patterns that result from the redistribution of the votes of eliminated and elected candidates. Chapter 8 takes up the complexities of this aspect of Irish voting behaviour.

---

[9] This gives rise to the phenomenon of alphabetical voting identified by Walsh and Robson, 1975.

Sources and methods

Aggregate data: national trends and regional analysis

Because of the absoluteness of the principle of the secrecy of the ballot, published electoral results only tell how relatively large geographically-defined groups or aggregates of individuals have voted. This is a major limitation. Even taking it into account, however, the officially published results – aggregate data in the academic jargon – can be quite useful in the analysis of electoral behaviour. The most obvious use of national results as a whole is to show the trend in voting behaviour over time (see chapter 4). Such trends represent the net outcome and it is entirely possible that there may have been much greater underlying but self-cancelling movements of voters between the parties than the trend in national results reveals.

Moving from national- to constituency-level results gives a better handle on the question of movement of voters between the parties but it does not eliminate the problem of net change. Moreover, moving to the constituency level introduces the problem of generalisation. It is undeniable that a general election consists of (in the Irish case) forty or so individual contests, each with its own special circumstances and conditions. It is equally true that these help to explain the overall outcome (see, for example, the various series of Dáil directories and election commentaries initiated by Nealon, 1974; Browne, 1981; Kenny and Keane, 1987; Donnelly, 1993). Accounting for the results by reference to events, or situations, or personalities in individual constituencies does not, however, answer the need to have a general picture that makes sense of what happened on a national scale. It is essential to be able to talk not just about forty individual constituencies but about overall patterns. It is essential to be able to generalise.

One way of attempting to achieve this is to group the constituencies by province and to compare the changes in voting in each. Basing comparisons on the provinces has the advantage of familiarity based on a mental image of the areas in question. However, the whole rationale of regional comparison is to group similar constituencies together in order to generalise about the common underlying causes of changing voting patterns. For this purpose, provincial boundaries may not be the most appropriate. For example, the westernmost constituencies in Munster (West-Cork, North and South Kerry and Clare) have much more in common with areas of Connacht than with Cork city. Yet they are lumped together with Cork city if Munster is used as a region. One can attempt to deal with this problem by juggling with the regional boundaries and by attempting to use smaller and more homogeneous regions. The subdivision of Leinster into Dublin and 'the rest of Leinster' in fact takes a small step in that direction. Nealon's comment on the use of provincial boundaries captures the nub of the problem:

> The regions used were chosen as convenient geographical areas within which, for economic, social, or historical reasons, the electorate might be expected to react in a fairly uniform way to major political developments at national level. However, it is impossible to get fully satisfactory, clear-cut divisions, whatever the basis chosen.
>
> (Nealon, 1974, p. 117).

Rather than seeking endless – and still ultimately unsatisfactory – refinements of regional groupings, it is worth re-examining the logic of regional analysis to see whether there is not a better means of achieving the same objective. The idea of regional analysis is to group similar constituencies together and the implicit inference is that the attributes (degree of urbanisation, level of prosperity, degree of industrialisation, size of farm holdings, etc.) that characterise each region explain the differences in voting behaviour between the regions. Rather than embarking on modification of regional groupings the question must be asked: why remain tied to the regional notion at all, with its restrictive assumption of geographical contiguity? Why not simply compare groups of constituencies that have similar characteristics, regardless of where in the country they happen to be situated? Taking this step is the decisive move from regional analysis to ecological analysis, that is, to the systematic search for relationships between voting and the characteristics of the basic units for which voting results are reported.

Aggregate data: cartography

The first attempts at ecological analysis were undertaken by geographers and consisted of drawing maps of party support and comparing these with maps of a variety of social, economic and even physical characteristics of the areas (Taylor and Johnston describe the aim of Andre Siegfried, the pioneer of this approach, as being to 'trace aspects of social and economic milieu back to the physical environment' Taylor and Johnston, 1979, p. 27). Subsequent cartographic studies have been less concerned to go all the way back to the physical environment and have rather tended to use the basic method (comparison of maps) simply to relate voting to any relevant social or economic characteristics.[10]

One of the earliest systematic studies of Irish electoral behaviour made extensive use of the cartographic method.[11] Both the advantages and disadvantages of the approach stem from the same basic fact – the approach depends essentially on the visual inspection of patterns in maps. This has the advantage of keeping the analyst of electoral behaviour as close as possible to the original data and may lead to the discovery of unexpected patterns. The accompanying disadvantage is that the visual comparison of patterns lacks precision and the assessment of the relative strength of the relationship between voting and various social and economic factors is necessarily subjective. If, however, the question is rephrased to read 'which of the several variables portrayed in a given set of maps is most closely related to support for a particular political party?', an appropriate statistical technique can be employed to provide a more precise answer.

Aggregate data: statistical analysis

At this stage a brief non-technical explanation of the relevant statistical tool may be in order. Multiple regression analysis takes a dependent variable (in this case support for

[10] More recently, this 'rampant empiricism' in electoral geography has been criticised and efforts have been made to marry the method to a more theoretical approach (see Johnston, Shelley and Taylor, 1990).

[11] The reference is to the work by Erhard Rumpf, which is discussed extensively in chapter 4. See Rumpf, 1959 and Rumpf and Hepburn, 1977.

a particular party) and seeks to explain the variations in it from one constituency to another as a function of the combined influence of a number of independent variables (in this case, the social, demographic or other characteristics of the constituencies). The outcome of a multiple regression analysis is an 'equation', sometimes also referred to as a 'model', with the dependent variable on one side and, on the other side, a series of independent or explanatory variables. Each explanatory variable is multiplied by a weight (the regression coefficient) which indicates that variable's contribution to the explanation. The weight or regression coefficient is either positive or negative, and hence it indicates not only the size of the contribution of the independent variable but also its direction – if the coefficient is positive, the variable causes an increase in the dependent variable, if it is negative, it causes a decrease. The overall success of the equation is indicated by the R^2 value. This runs from zero to one, zero indicating that none of the variation in the independent variable has been explained; one indicating that all of the variation has been accounted for. Finally, the technique has the advantage of taking the effects of each independent variable into account while controlling for the effects of each of the others. In subsequent chapters, frequent reference will be made to the equation or model for this or that party in one election or another. While the statistical technicalities behind the equations or models are very complex, all the non-technical reader needs to grasp are the relatively simple elements just described.

The ability of multiple regression analysis to assess the relationship between several variables on a simultaneous basis is a major advantage over the cartographic approach, which is inevitably limited to looking at variables in pairs. Like most statistical techniques, however, it has its limitations. It assumes that any relationship that might exist between the variables is a linear one. It assumes that there is not an excessive level of interrelationship between the independent variables. It is also limited in the number of variables it can cope with relative to the number of cases available for the analysis. Finally, when used in this context, it raises in a particularly acute form the general problem associated with aggregate data referred to at the outset, namely, that the observations refer not to individuals but to aggregates or collectivities.

The problem to which this gives rise is usually referred to as 'the ecological fallacy'. This, in a way, is a bit of a misnomer, because it is a potential fallacy that can be avoided and is, therefore, a limitation rather than an inevitable source of error. The fallacy would occur if, from the correlations between variables uncovered at the aggregate level, one inferred that identical correlations or relationships obtain at the individual level. As Robinson, in the classic article on the ecological fallacy, has shown, relationships between variables look much stronger when measured at the aggregate level and the higher the level of aggregation the greater the apparent strength of the relationship (Robinson, 1950). Moreover, even if this were not the case, one could not conclude that the same relationship obtains at the individual level. For example, analysis shows a correlation between proportion of the workforce engaged in agriculture and support for the anti-Treaty side in the 1923 election. This cannot be used as proof that farmers voted Sinn Féin. It is possible that this was the case but one cannot rely on such an inference.

One approach to the problem is to rigidly confine inference to the aggregate level, drawing conclusions simply about the kinds of areas that tend to support one party rather than another and bearing in mind that the strength of the relationships identified will be somewhat inflated. Even this will provide a significant step forward on the cartographic approach (which itself is subject to the ecological fallacy). Some would argue that one can go further than this. Thus, Allardt defends the practice of using ecological correlations for arriving at statements about individuals as 'a fruitful way to proceed' (Allardt, 1969, p. 44). In doing so, he shifts the ground of the debate away from the narrow issue of logical inference to a more general interpretative approach that uses every available clue and draws conclusions on the basis of a cumulation of bits of evidence and supporting theory.

Ecological analysis is particularly important in certain circumstances. At a minimum, it is often all that is available. In fact, in the Irish case, because opinion polling started relatively late, the analysis of electoral behaviour prior to 1969 is dependent on aggregate data and therefore on ecological analysis. More positively, ecological analysis can be valuable in its own right if what is in question is the impact of some genuinely collective characteristic, that is, a property not of the individual but of the area or context in which individual behaviour occurs. Linz gives examples from the analysis of rural society – patterns of land tenure, settlement patterns, types of crops, and so on (Linz, 1969, p. 95). An example in the Irish case would be the correlations to be found between traditions of agrarian unrest in an area in the late nineteenth century and voting patterns in the early twentieth century. The advantages (and disadvantages) of ecological analysis are best appreciated in the context of considering actual research results in later chapters. For the moment enough has been said for a comparison to be made between ecological analysis and the other approach to electoral behaviour – opinion polling and survey data.

Opinion polls and survey data
Linz succinctly identifies the point on which survey research scores most heavily: 'The direct rather than the inferential linkage between individual social position and behaviour is the great advantage of survey research over ecological analysis' (Linz, 1969, p. 102). In addition, survey research enables one to bring subjective factors (attitudes and perceptions) directly into the analysis. Thus, in place of the constituency characteristics of the aggregate data tradition, this approach collects data on the socio-economic and demographic characteristics of the individual voter – his or her social class, education, age, family background, type of employment and employment status, organisational affiliations and memberships. Then, over and above everything that can be measured at the ecological level, it adds the voters' perceptions, evaluations, and feelings towards politically relevant groups, candidates, parties, and issues.

This focus on the individual is also a potential source of weakness. Individual-level data on electoral behaviour is based on vote recall or stated voting intention, and more generally, on the willingness and ability of those interviewed to give accurate responses, in relation to both attitudes and behaviour. Furthermore, data collected directly from individuals are only as good as the questions asked. So often, in dealing with opinion poll and survey results, one wishes that the question had been formulated in a different way. These particular methodological problems will be dealt with as they arise in practice in subsequent chapters. In the meantime, this survey of sources and methods would be incomplete without some consideration of the implicit distinction between 'opinion poll' data and 'survey research' data.

One version of this distinction is that the former monitor trends in opinions and attitudes while the latter are aimed at arriving at an understanding of voting behaviour (Taylor and Johnston, 1979, pp. 93–6). Niemi and Weisberg go further and, in answering their own question 'why not use Gallup and Harris type polls?', argue that explanation 'requires separate polls' (Niemi and Weisberg, 1976, p. 8). It is undoubtedly the case that significant differences between the two exist; it is also the case that the differences can be exaggerated. The differences are attributable to different sponsorship and sponsors' purposes. What are described as opinion polls are typically conducted for political parties or the media, and their form is determined by the particular needs of such organisations. One such need is for fast results. This leads to one of the most obvious differences between opinion polls and survey research: the former usually employ a mainly quota-sampling approach, the latter normally adheres to the more rigorous but slower and much more expensive procedure of full-scale probability sampling. Even this is not, however, an essential difference; a survey research project could well decide on a mixture of probability and quota sampling as a legitimate way of making scarce financial resources go further. In terms of substantive content, the difference tends to be one of degree rather than of kind. Thus, custom-built survey research has the time and resources to employ more sophisticated measures of voting history, party identification, social class and various attitudinal variables, and to pursue theories and hypotheses more systematically. This does not, however, imply that measurement employed in opinion polls is necessarily naive or that it cannot be guided by theory. In sum, while there are some practical grounds for drawing the distinction, it should not be allowed to blind the analyst of elections to the merits of data collected for practical purposes, or to the potential triviality of data collected for 'academic' purposes. This has comforting implications in the Irish case because specialised survey data are rare and it is necessary to rely to a very great extent on media-commissioned opinion polls. At the same time, the fact that Ireland, unlike most advanced democracies, has never had a full-scale election survey means that there is a significant gap in the evidence on which we can draw.

Outline

Before analysing voting behaviour, we must have at least some idea of what choices the voters were being presented with. We can think of parties as packages, each package consisting of the party's policies or programmes, personnel and past performance. The appearance of the package is only partly determined by the policies that the parties explicitly put before the voters in a given election, or by the image of the party leader that the parties seek to project. Equally, if not more, important is the imprint of the party's origins and of both its successes and failures as it responded to events, especially when in government. It is essential, therefore, to have some appreciation of the way in which the policy-programme-personnel-performance package that is each party has taken shape and developed,[12] hence the need for a brief history of the parties, or a set of 'party portraits' (chapter 2).

Historical portraits are inevitably partial and impressionistic. Accordingly, in chapter 3 some more systematic and quantitative evidence on party identities, party images and party differences is presented. The second part of chapter 3 completes the groundwork by examining voter turnout and its variations over time and across different kinds of electoral contests.

Chapters 4 to 8 focus on general elections. Chapter 4 presents a periodisation of Irish elections and examines trends in voting behaviour within and across periods. In reviewing the sources of evidence and the question of aggregate-level data versus individual-level data, it was evident that each has its particular strengths and limitations. Accordingly, they are treated here as complementary approaches to be used as the nature of the research question indicates and the limitations of data availability dictate. Chapter 5 takes up those issues relating to first preference voting behaviour in Irish general elections that pre-date the arrival of opinion-poll data, and then applies this technique to the six elections held between 1981 and 1992. Chapter 6 turns to the evidence contained in opinion polls and voter surveys examining voter volatility, loyalty and the location of the parties as seen by the voters. Chapter 7 continues with this body of data, looking at the voters' criteria, their issue preoccupations and the socio-demographic contrasts among supporters of different parties. Chapter 8 deals specifically with transfer patterns, prefacing the discussion of the evidence with an explanation of the intricacies of the transfer process that have a bearing on the interpretation of the evidence. Chapter 9 focuses on referendum voting and chapter 10 deals with second-order elections, paying particular attention to the 1990 presidential election. Finally, chapter 11 seeks to draw the various strands of evidence together and to address the overall interpretative issues.

[12] Personnel in this context means national leaders. Local candidates are also part of the 'personnel' element in the package but they are a part that cannot be readily summarised in a historical portrait of the parties. The influence of local candidate considerations on voting will be examined briefly in ch. 7.

Chapter 2

Party portraits

Ancestry

Any account of the origins of Irish political parties and electoral alignments must begin before the founding of the state in 1922. How far back to go is a matter of dispute. A classic comparative study of the development of party systems and voter alignments offers some guidance, namely analysis should begin at the point of political mobilisation, usually the point at which the right to vote was extended to the mass of the population (Lipset and Rokkan, 1967). The question is, when did this combination of franchise extension and mass political mobilisation take place in Ireland? There are two contending dates – 1885 and 1918. One study argues that the temporal frontier must be 'pushed back to the threshold of mass politics: the 1885 election, the first after the electoral reform of 1884, from which distinctively modern forms of party political activity date' (Coakley, 1986, p. 29). Attention is drawn to the fact that the 1884 reform gave voting rights to the majority of adult males and political mobilisation in the 1880s is described as 'massive' (Coakley, 1986, p. 89).

The effectiveness of this mobilisation is, however, open to question. Thus, the 'modern mass political organisation' produced by this wave of mobilisation is acknowledged to have become 'emaciated' and 'moribund' by the early 1890s (*ibid.*). Doubts about the degree of mobilisation in this early period are reinforced by the observation that the Irish party system in the 1890s and early 1900s was 'profoundly non–competitive. . . . in 1892 eighty-three of 103 territorial Irish seats had been contested; this figure fell to forty-two in 1895 and reached a nadir of twenty-one in 1906' (Garvin, 1981, pp. 89–90). In fact the decline in political competition was even more marked in the area that was to become an independent state – of the 78 seats in the South, 69 were contested in 1892, 30 in 1895, 21 in 1900 and a mere 5 in 1906. Garvin summarises the 1890s as: 'a period of political stagnation. The agrarian question had been substantially settled, and the Church had set its face against political adventure. The great nationalist machines of the 1880s crumbled. . . . A wholesale political demobilisation occurred' (Garvin 1981, p. 98). If the mobilisation of the 1880s crumbled so quickly and so decisively, it is difficult to see it as the main source of the modern Irish party system.[1]

---

[1] A recent study emphasizes the importance of the occurrence of uncontested seats throughout the nineteenth century: 'Most striking are the data on competitiveness for they indicate just how uncompetitive much of nineteenth-century Irish politics actually was' (Carty, 1993, p. 28). The data reveal a cyclical pattern

A second reason for preferring 1918 as the point of departure is that the absolute size of the franchise extension in 1918 was much greater. Whereas in 1884 the electorate increased from 8 to 31 per cent of the population aged 20 and over, in 1918 it went from 26 per cent to 75 per cent.[2] The 1918 franchise came far closer to creating the conditions for mass participation and thus for mass mobilisation than did the much more partial reform of 1884.

The third reason for starting with the 1918 election is that not only did it involve a far greater extension of the suffrage, but, unlike its 1885 predecessor, it was followed by a decade and a half of intensive political activity. The partial nature of the independence granted in 1921 and the consequent split over the treaty ensured a continuing intense competition around the issue of Anglo-Irish relations and a reinforcement of the mobilisation of 1918. Obviously, it would be a mistake to ignore the party activity and electoral mobilisation of the late nineteenth century. Both undoubtedly played an important role in the development of democratic politics in Ireland. However, in terms of tracing the origins of the party system and voter alignments, the foregoing arguments suggest that it would be best to begin with the 1918 election and the party that dominated it – Sinn Féin.

Sinn Féin

The party which became part vehicle and part instigator of an aroused public opinion in 1918 had been founded in 1905. However, apart from managing to publish a regular nationalist journal, Sinn Féin had not been a particularly prominent or successful political organisation. The post-1916 party was as much a new creation as a direct successor, and it encompassed a wide variety of groups and views; it was self-consciously a national front party. From its new start in 1917, it strove incessantly to overcome differences between Irish people, whether in the form of differences within the nationalist camp[3] or within the country as a whole, as in its successful efforts to persuade the fledgling Labour party to stand down in the 1918 election (see below). By the time that election came (December 1918), public opinion had been thoroughly roused by the execution of the major leaders of the abortive 1916 rising and by the enactment of the legislative basis for conscription in Ireland in April 1918. These two events antagonised a wide range of southern Irish opinion and consolidated it behind the separatist option. The result was that Sinn Féin won a dramatic victory – in the island as a whole, it won 73 of the 105 seats. More importantly, from the point of view of tracing the ancestry of the present Irish party system, in the area that was eventually to secede, it swept the board, winning 70 of the 75 seats. The consequence was the virtual

---

with electoral mobilisation alternating with periods of quiescence, leading to the identification of four party-building episodes between 1832 and 1918 (Carty, 1993, pp. 26–40). The argument emphasizes both the need to trace the roots of the Irish party system back in time and the definitive nature of the mobilisation begun in 1918.

[2] Electorate figures for 1884 from Hoppen (1984, pp. 87–8); for 1918 from Lyons (1973, p. 399). Population figures from Census of Ireland, 1881 and Census of Ireland, 1911.

[3] On these see Laffan, 1971, pp. 360–77.

elimination of Sinn Féin's main rival for the role of representative of Irish nationalist opinion – the Irish Parliamentary Party, which had pursued a moderate nationalist line, seeking Home Rule (essentially, devolution), and had brought the country to the verge of that objective in 1914.

The fact that 25 of the 70 seats taken by Sinn Féin in the South were won without a contest complicates the task of determining the precise rate and extent of nationalist mobilisation. One can summarise the situation as follows: in those Southern constituencies that were contested, Sinn Féin won 65 per cent of the votes cast; in areas that corresponded approximately to seven of the 25 uncontested constituencies, it had won 59 per cent of the vote in by-elections in the previous two years.[4] In the remaining eighteen constituencies in which seats were handed over to Sinn Féin without a contest, it is unlikely that the Irish Parliamentary Party would have conceded such seats unless it had known that Sinn Féin had overwhelming support in the areas in question, and it is scarcely credible that the electors would have been unaffected by the sea-change going on all around them.

In immediate political terms the importance of the 1918 election was that it conferred a degree of democratic legitimacy on the demand for total separation from Britain that had been voiced manifestly without such legitimacy in 1916. In the longer term, its significance was that it was a crucial moment in the foundation of the modern Irish party system. In the first election that even approximated to universal suffrage, Irish voters were mobilised into a nationalist consensus in which the 'constitutional axis' (Farrell, 1971), or the issue of centre-periphery relations (Lipset and Rokkan, 1967), predominated over all else, including over the considerable potential conflict between capital and labour.[5] Thus the party system of what is now the Republic of Ireland began in 1918 with an overwhelmingly dominant single party – Sinn Féin. The Irish Parliamentary Party was reduced to two seats and the Labour Party, having stood on, or been pushed to, the sidelines, had no representation. From this stark beginning a complex party system developed. Given the complexities, Figure 2.1 provides a rough reference guide to the development of the parties to be described in this chapter, indicating, in an approximate fashion, their relative sizes and identifying which parties were in government at any given time.

The salience of the nationalist issue was reinforced by the War of Independence (1919–21). For the neophyte Sinn Féin party, however, this phase carried considerable risks. On one side, its activities were hampered and disrupted by British repression; on the other, it was marginalised, even despised, by those directly engaged in the military struggle with the British.[6]

[4] These by-elections were of course conducted on the old, more restricted franchise. By-election figures are from Walker, 1978.

[5] In fact, the setting of the mould of Irish electoral politics and in particular the establishment of the basic cleavage spanned the period up to at least the second election of 1927. The relevant events are summarised in what follows and the long-term significance of electoral mobilisation and its relationship to the prevailing cleavages is taken up again in chapter 11.

[6] For a full account of these difficulties and how Sinn Fein coped with them, see Laffan, forthcoming, chapter 7.

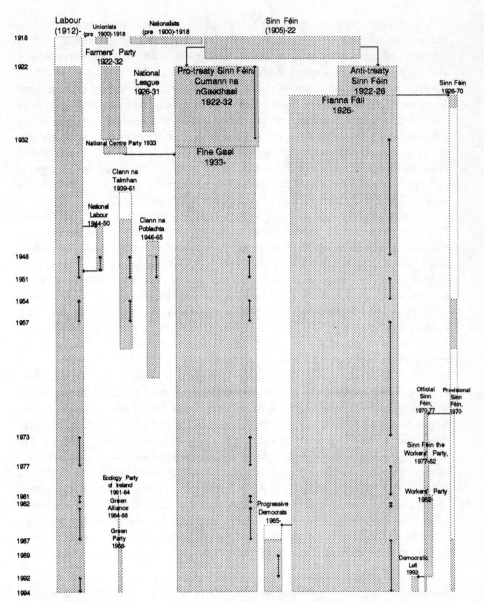

Notes Shaded columns are proportional to the size of each party as measured by share of the first preference vote in all elections contested (see Figures 4.2 and 4.3 for variations in vote shares). Vertical arrows within columns indicate that the party was in government in the period in question.

Figure 2.1 Irish political parties 1918–94: development, approximate size and participation in government.

Urban local elections in January 1920 showed considerable heterogeneity of electoral opinion, the expression of which was facilitated by the introduction of proportional representation by means of the single transferable vote as the electoral system. In the island as a whole, Sinn Féin obtained only 27 per cent of the vote, to 15 per cent for other nationalists, 18 per cent for Labour, 27 per cent for Unionists and 14 per cent for independents (most of whom were unionist with a small 'u').[7] Because these elections were based on a more restricted franchise, because they were purely urban elections and because Sinn Féin was a proscribed organisation, one should not, however, make too much of this apparently poor showing by Sinn Féin: 'The 1920 elections should not be taken to indicate growing nonconformism among Irish voters but rather, as will be seen, the residual tendency for urban nationalism to be less efficiently organised and disciplined than rural nationalism' (Fitzpatrick, 1978, pp. 113–44).

The pattern in the rural and county elections of June 1920 was very different – Sinn Féin took control of 338 of the 393 boards of guardians, rural district councils and county councils (including those in Ulster). However, in most instances outside Ulster these victories were won without a contest. It is difficult to say whether this was because Sinn Féin was overwhelmingly strong in rural areas or because it was simply determined to avoid contests where possible and, with the guerrilla war conducted by the military wing of Sinn Féin at its height, this was certainly possible in June 1920. Uncontested seats were even more a feature of the general election held under the Government of Ireland Act in 1921. In this case all seats in the South were uncontested, Sinn Féin taking all but four.

The nationalist consensus that had been concocted in 1918 was well and truly shattered by the reactions to the compromise settlement which terminated the guerrilla struggle. The issues were crystallised in the Dáil debate on the ratification of the Anglo-Irish Treaty that took place from December 1921 to January 1922. When the debate finally closed, the treaty was accepted by sixty-four votes to fifty-seven. Looked at with over seventy years of hindsight, the concessions made in the treaty – dominion status, the oath of allegiance,[8] the concession of naval defence facilities to the British at certain ports – may appear to have been relatively minor. Viewed from the perspective of those involved, both those against and those in favour of the treaty, the issues at stake were neither minor nor reconcilable. The reason was simple – both sides could be said to have had a valid case. Mansergh succinctly summarises the core of validity in the argument of each side: on the one side 'Dominion status, despite the

[7] Excluding the province of Ulster, the figures were Sinn Féin 41 per cent, Labour 17 per cent, Nationalists 14 per cent, Independents 21 per cent and Unionists 7 per cent. Percentages here and in text calculated from figures given in Martin (1921, pp. 212–18).

[8] The Treaty and the 1922 Constitution required those elected to Parliament in the new state to take the following oath: 'I . . . do solemnly swear true faith and allegiance to the Constitution of the Irish Free State as by law established and that I will be faithful to H.M. King George V, his heirs and successors by law in virtue of the common citizenship of Ireland with Great Britain and her adherence to and membership of the group of nations forming the British Commonwealth of Nations.' Partition did not figure as a crunch issue, not because it was not regarded as important, but because it was to be dealt with by a Boundary Commission and it was assumed on the Irish side that the outcome of this would create the conditions for a satisfactory resolution of the problem (see discussion in Foster, 1988, p. 507).

fears of some of its critics and, perhaps even more important, despite the forms with which it was still enshrouded, conferred a substantial measure of freedom and opened the way for complete independence'; on the other side

> There are times when constitutional forms express things that for many men matter most and this was one of them . . . Ireland, for the most part, was not a country of settlement. It was one of the historic nations of Europe. It was not extra-European but European national symbolism to which it aspired. . . . The countries that were dominions in 1921 might seek independence, but Ireland was seeking something more as well – independence and recognition of a separate national identity. (Mansergh, 1966, pp. 137–8)

As the country edged with seeming inevitability towards civil war, some on each side sought a means of preventing the catastrophe. Part of this process was the arrangement of an electoral pact between the feuding sides for the election due under the terms of the treaty. Michael Collins, one of the two main leaders on the pro-treaty side, and Éamon de Valera, the leader of the anti-treatyites, hoped to recreate the pre-truce unity of Sinn Féin by agreeing to eliminate competition between the factions by means of an agreed panel of candidates, drawn up in proportion to their existing Dáil strength. Despite considerable opposition in many instances, the Labour Party, the Farmers' Party and a number of independents went forward for election and only seven constituencies – all of them in the west – went uncontested.[9] In the event, the pact election, as it became known, failed to contain the conflict within the political arena and in fact precipitated the full withdrawal of the anti-treatyites from the Dáil and their repudiation of the legitimacy of the pro-treaty government. This highlighted what was for many on the pro-treaty side the most fundamental issue at stake – the right of the people to decide matters through the ballot box.[10] The conviction of each side that it and it alone was right was powerfully reinforced by the fact that in the ensuing conflict men killed and died for their beliefs. A brief, small-scale, but bloody civil war ensured that the split in Sinn Féin between pro-treatyites and anti-treatyites would not only result in two competing parties but that the division between them would be intense and bitter.

Anti-Treaty Sinn Féin

Despite the fact that he had been President of Sinn Féin since 1918 and President of the Republic and of the Executive Council from January 1919 until December 1921, de Valera was relatively powerless as long as civil war continued. The initiative on the anti-treaty side lay with those running the military campaign and, as late as March 1923, de Valera was 'kept waiting outside while those he deemed political illiterates pondered whether to even admit him to their primitive counsels' (Lee, 1989, p. 150). It was only after the death of the IRA commander-in-chief, Liam Lynch, in April 1923,

---

[9] The pact greatly complicates the task of interpreting the results of the 1922 election – the first election in the new state. The issue is taken up in detail in chapter 4.

[10] See Lee, 1989, p. 67.

an event that seemed to symbolise the hopelessness and futility of further military opposition to the Government and the treaty, that de Valera's appeals for a cease-fire and for the pursuit of the struggle by political means carried weight.

The first step in the political struggle was the 1923 election. The anti-treatyites had appropriated the Sinn Féin label. The party's performance in that election (just over one-quarter of the vote)[11] could be interpreted as a considerable achievement in the wake of civil war defeat and with many of its activists in jail. The performance was impressive, given the party's abstentionist policy; the fact that, because of its refusal to recognise the legitimacy either of the ratification of the treaty or of the government or parliament established under it, it was committed to not taking up any seats it would win. From the point of view of Sinn Féin's immediate objective of undoing the treaty, however, the performance was a decisive defeat. In the wake of it, Sinn Féin vigorously set about the task of recovery. In line with its abstentionist policy, part of its plan was to set up a virtual counter-state, with the full panoply of institutions – a parliament, courts and even alternative educational institutions. The futility of this effort soon became apparent (Pyne, 1969). In terms of the more mundane political activity of forming party branches and contesting by-elections, the early signs seemed somewhat more hopeful. However, in a set of by-elections amounting almost to a mini general election in March 1925, the apparent advance did not yield any real gains. Cumann na nGaedheal won seven of the nine seats vacated by those who had resigned their Dáil seats because of dissatisfaction with the way in which a potential mutiny in the army had been handled. The only reason Sinn Féin won two seats was that, in two constituencies, two TDs (Teachta Dála) had resigned, and under PR-STV, these constituencies presented a much lower electoral threshold. Overall, anti-treaty Sinn Féin won only four of the twenty-one seats contested in by-elections between 1923 and 1927.

The electoral débâcle of March 1925 reinforced a growing realisation in Sinn Féin circles that a radical departure in political strategy was required. The process of self-criticism that had been developing within Sinn Féin from mid-1924 on and that now moved into high gear was characterised by two themes – the need to get off the hook of abstentionism and the need to put forward practical and radical policies that would address the prevailing serious social and economic problems. The former theme was very much the preserve of de Valera himself. The latter was articulated most clearly by Seán Lemass, who, although one of the youngest of the prominent anti-treatyites, was emerging as a key political figure. Lemass argued his case trenchantly in the pages of *An Phoblacht* and in the party's various committees (Farrell, 1983, pp. 8–15). It was a case that had its origins in part in an instinctive identification with the 'men of no property', but perhaps in equal part in a shrewd electoral calculation. Whatever its cause, it was to become the root of Fianna Fáil's much vaunted socio-economic radicalism.

De Valera's revisionism was tested in an internal party debate on the proposal that, if the oath of allegiance demanded by the Treaty were abolished, abstentionism would

---

[11] The details of the levels of support for each party in each election are discussed in chapter 4.

be a matter of tactics rather than principle. De Valera's motion was rejected. As in the Dáil in January 1922, so too in the Sinn Féin extraordinary Ard Fheis (party convention) of March 1926, De Valera found himself outvoted by a narrow margin (223 votes to 218 on the crucial amendment). And again he formed the nucleus of a break-away group. The difference this time was that he was leading the dissidents towards rather than away from legitimate politics and ultimately towards political power.

Fianna Fáil from de Valera to Lemass

Fianna Fáil was launched on 16 May 1926, committed to 'isolating the oath for attack', to participation in 'the common assembly' once the oath had been removed, with the 'reassertion of the nation's sovereignty' and the achievement of the 'freedom that our people may live happily and rightly, freedom to make this nation of ours great in well-being and noble doing' as the ultimate objectives (Moynihan, 1980, pp. 133–43). The new party was equally committed to the view that organisation is the key to electoral success and the founding members put in an enormous effort establishing the countrywide network of branches that was to become the hallmark of the Fianna Fáil party.

Fianna Fáil entered the election of June 1927 still encumbered by the policy of abstention but at the same time clearly signalling its search for a way out of this cul-de-sac, even to the extent of creating ambiguity about its intentions regarding entry to the Dáil after the election (Moss, 1933, pp. 150–1 and 160–1). While much of the Fianna Fáil argument in the campaign centred on the evils of the oath of allegiance, it also emphasized both wider aspects of the nationalist issue and its policies on concrete economic and social problems. Notwithstanding the ambiguity of its election slogans, after the election Fianna Fáil was still committed to abstention, as long, that is, as the oath remained in place. The final and crucial step towards a full role in legitimate politics came, however, a mere two months later and was a result not of a Fianna Fáil initiative but of the Government forcing the issue. Following the assassination of Kevin O'Higgins, who was Minister for Justice, Minister for External Affairs and Vice-President of the Executive Council (the Cabinet), the Government introduced a series of law and order measures that included the requirement that candidates agree at the time of nomination to take the oath and assume their seats if elected. In a sense, this provided de Valera with an alibi and, subscribing to the oath as 'an empty political formula', Fianna Fáil entered the Dáil on 11 August 1927.[12]

Its arrival in the Dáil transformed the parliamentary arithmetic and the Government barely survived a vote of no confidence in mid-August. A week later William T. Cosgrave, leader of Cumann nGaedheal and President of the Executive Council, called an election for 15 September. This was to be a particularly important

[12] Fianna Fáil's uses of the 'empty political formula' stratagem was not the end of the matter. In November 1927 it organised a petition directed at using the constitutional provisions of initiative and referendum to remove the oath. The strategy was blocked, however, by the government's abolition of the relevant provisions in June 1928 (see chapter 9 for details).

election in the evolution of the party system. Fianna Fáil was now competing on equal terms, that is, as a party that accepted the rules of the game.[13] Furthermore, given the proximity of the two elections, there were far fewer independent and minor party candidates to distract attention from the main contest. Both major parties made substantial gains. Fianna Fáil's gains put it in a dominating position on the opposition benches, overshadowing the Labour Party, which had conscientiously and constructively performed the task of opposition in the absence of the anti-treatyites since 1923.

By 1932 the appeal of Fianna Fáil's nationalist, welfarist and protectionist programme was enhanced by the Government's ultra-conservative response to the world economic crisis. Fianna Fáil was careful to allay fears that it might be about to do anything extreme in Anglo-Irish relations. As its manifesto for the election put it: 'We shall not in the field of international relations exceed the mandate here asked for without again consulting the people' (Moss, 1933, p. 208). The Fianna Fáil mandate related to the oath of allegiance and the non-payment of land annuities, de Valera having 'with some deliberation limited the mandate he sought from the electorate to these two issues' (Bowman, 1982, p. 110). Even taking this caution into account, however, the electorate was offered 'a clear choice between a party campaigning in defence of the status quo, and a party proposing sweeping constitutional, economic, and social changes' (Lee, 1989, p. 170).

The result was a remarkable recovery from defeat and demoralisation in the civil war and a mere one-quarter of the vote in 1923 to conquest of office (with the assistance of the Labour Party) in 1932, followed by a resounding victory in a snap election in 1933. The 1933 election inaugurated for Fianna Fáil a period of domination of Irish government which lasted, with only two relatively brief breaks, for the next forty years.

In office, de Valera set about abolishing the oath and generally dismantling the Treaty settlement. The government also relaxed the coercive security policies of its predecessor. However, nothing was done in haste and de Valera's progress towards his constitutional objectives in 1932–37 was 'crablike' (Fanning, 1983, p. 112). In line with its specific election promises, Fianna Fáil implemented improvements in pension provision, unemployment assistance and house-building schemes and proceeded to withhold the land annuities. The immediate result of the latter measure was a protracted 'economic war' with Britain. Though the issue at stake was primarily political rather than economic, that is, a matter of the assertion of Irish independence, the consequent deterioration in Anglo-Irish economic relations was reinforced by the global shift to protectionism and the government's leanings towards the goal of economic autarky. Protectionist measures had in fact been introduced before Fianna Fáil assumed power. These measures had been forced on the Cumann na nGaedheal government by the growing international economic crisis, and especially by the threat of dumping (Meenan, 1970). When Fianna Fáil assumed office this policy was intensified and was pursued as a matter of nationalist conviction.

---

[13] If we were to take at face value Lemass's reference to Fianna Fáil as a 'slightly constitutional party', the thoroughness of Fianna Fáil's conversion to constitutionalism might be questioned, but see the discussion in Farrell, 1983.

The culmination of Fianna Fáil's efforts to assert Irish sovereignty and independence came with the adoption in 1937 of a new constitution that gave full expression to nationalist aspirations. At the same time, Fianna Fáil had considerably tempered its early radical social and economic rhetoric and pursued a careful middle path. The government's ameliorative social legislation was counterbalanced by enshrining in the new constitution a conservative property clause. On religious and moral issues and in church-state relations generally, de Valera pursued the conservative Catholic policies of the Cumann na nGaedheal government. When it came to the new constitution, while he resisted the more extreme demands for a constitutional expression of the concept of a Catholic state for a Catholic people, he did create a special, albeit symbolic, position for the Catholic Church and, in terms that were far more than symbolic, the new constitution contained a clear-cut prohibition of divorce[14] (see Whyte, 1971, pp. 51–6).

The party's efforts over its first full term of office were somewhat hesitatingly rewarded in the simultaneous election and referendum of 1937. In the plebiscite on the new constitution, the voters said yes, but by a modest margin. In the election, Fianna Fáil was returned to office but only as a minority government, dependent on the support of the Labour Party in the Dáil. However, in the following year, in an election that followed hard on the heels of the highly successful Anglo-Irish Agreement, which settled both the economic war and the remaining contentious issues in the treaty (partition excepted), it achieved the rare feat of topping 50 per cent of the vote.

Fianna Fáil did not get the opportunity to enjoy the fruits of its diplomatic and electoral achievements, as the approach of World War II put the extent and nature of Ireland's newly consolidated independence to a severe test. De Valera's policy of neutrality was an assertion of Ireland's national independence in two senses. First, there, was the simple fact of acting independently of the former colonial power – 'Neutrality was not an end in itself, but a means to an end: the means whereby the end of sovereignty might be freely expressed in the form of an independent foreign policy – a policy independent, above all, of British policy' (Fanning, 1983, p. 121). Secondly, the immediate pretext for the policy of neutrality was partition. The policy was thus both an assertion of independence gained and a reiteration of the demand for complete independence. In practice, there was a sharp disjunction between appearance and reality in the implementation of the policy – the appearance was of a punctilious observation of the forms of neutrality, the reality was extensive co-operation with the Allies (Fanning, 1983, p. 124).

The initial domestic political effect of the policy of neutrality was a closing of ranks and a reinforcement of the nationalist consensus (on Fine Gael's response to neutrality see below). However, as the Emergency, as it was known, entered its fourth year, discontent with war-time stringency and especially with the rigours of wage control grew and, in the mid- to late 1940s, Fianna Fáil faced a series of challenges to its electoral supremacy. Two surfaced in the 1943 election – one from an apparently resurgent

[14] Both features of the constitution came up for reconsideration in referendums a generation later – see chapter 9 for details.

Labour Party and the other from a new agrarian party, Clann na Talmhan (see below). Fianna Fáil barely held on to office. However, in a third example of de Valera's snap election tactic, Fianna Fáil saw off both challenges in the following year.

The immediate post-war years were not propitious times for an incumbent government. Rationing and the scarcities of the war period continued, and in 1946 there was a series of strikes as workers sought to recoup the losses suffered in the wages standstill imposed during the war. The 1948 election was precipitated by the rise of the third challenge to Fianna Fáil – the emergence of a new party that originated in part from these discontents and in part from nationalist dissatisfaction that, with everything else more or less out of the way, now focused on partition. Clann na Poblachta was an almost look-alike Fianna Fáil party, claiming to be the true inheritor of the radical republicanism that was said to have animated Fianna Fáil in the '20s and '30s. Despite the abysmal performance of Fine Gael in the 1948 election, the electoral impact of the newcomer created the conditions for a five-party coalition. In opposition for the first time in sixteen years, Fianna Fáil did little more than sit back and wait for the inter-party government to collapse, aiding that collapse by judicious silence on the most controversial issue of the period – the Mother and Child scheme (see page 62 for details). The party did devote some energy to the Northern Ireland issue – de Valera embarked on an international propaganda campaign against partition and the party participated in the Mansion House anti-partition committee. The evidence suggests that both these efforts were motivated by the latest twists in inter-party competition and by de Valera's belief that such measures were 'necessary if he was to retain his leadership of mainstream Irish nationalism' (Bowman, 1982, p. 175).

With the collapse of the coalition government in 1951, Fianna Fáil found itself back in what it regarded as its rightful position in government. Despite the rationing and the industrial unrest, the immediate post-war period had in fact been a period of modest economic growth, as Ireland benefited to at least some extent from the post-war recovery in the international economy. In the early 1950s, however, external economic conditions were more difficult and 'the domestic fiscal response compounded the external difficulties' (Kennedy *et al.*, 1988, p. 61). There followed five years of very tough economic conditions in which growth slumped and unemployment and emigration (as we saw in chapter 1) soared.

Looking at the course of the economy in the 1950s from a party-political perspective, both alternative governments – Fianna Fáil in 1952 and the second inter-party government in 1956 – committed deflationary errors that exacerbated the problem. Each received electoral retribution in its turn, Fianna Fáil being put out of office in 1954, after a mere three-year return, and both Fine Gael and Labour suffering an electoral hammering in 1957. Thus, after sixteen years of government by the same party (1932–48), the country now saw the alternation of government at four successive elections in the space of ten years (1948–57). The warning signs to the politicians could not have been clearer. To be fair, politicians of all hues heeded the warnings and groped towards solutions to the problem represented by the failure to develop economically. Commissions were established and several state development agencies – the Industrial Development Authority, An Foras Tionscail, the Capital

Investment Advisory Committee – were established. The real work, however, was being done in the Department of Finance by a group of civil servants under the leadership of T. K. Whittaker, who was promoted to the position of Secretary of the Department in 1956.

Fianna Fáil had the good fortune to be in government when these policy developments saw the light of day, with the publication of a *Programme of National Economic Development* and of the report on which it was based (Whittaker's *Economic Development*) in November 1958. One may debate the issue of the source of the policy shift to free trade, encouragement of foreign industry and planning and of the precise contribution of these changes to the economic growth registered in the 1960s. In electoral terms this almost doesn't matter. Fianna Fáil was in office and, as Murphy puts it, 'they could plausibly claim that it was *their* programme for economic expansion that had *created* the new prosperity' (Murphy, 1979, p. 4).

The plausibility of the first part of the claim was increased by the genuinely important role played by Seán Lemass, de Valera's long-time second in command, in the gestation and implementation of what was after all a major U-turn for the party of protectionism and economic nationalism.[15] For Fianna Fáil, the U-turn was facilitated by the elevation of the objective of economic growth into a fundamental tenet of nationalism. It was also facilitated by the way in which the government, and Lemass in particular, sought to involve all the relevant sectional interests in a neo–corporatist-style common national effort. Both of these emphases were eminently compatible with Fianna Fáil's image of itself as a national movement rather than just another political party.

The centrality of Lemass's role throughout this period of change was finally institutionalised when he more or less automatically succeeded de Valera on the latter's retirement as party leader and Taoiseach in 1959.[16] After a somewhat shaky start – barely surviving the 1961 election to form a minority government – Lemass led Fianna Fáil to a substantial increase in its vote and a stable parliamentary situation (though not an outright majority of seats) in 1965.

Lemass was also central to a process that was of vital importance given Fianna Fáil's domination of the system for so long, that is, the succession to the revolutionary generation. Under his direction, organisational renewal and personnel recruitment were begun in earnest following the defeat of the party in the 1954 election. Accompanying this was the gradual appointment of younger politicians to positions of responsibility. Not surprisingly, the generational change was marked by a change in style, particularly after de Valera's retirement. Lemass was a more activitist Taoiseach than de Valera had been, and he gave scope for and expected similar activism from his ministers – a classic example of this activism was the announcement of the free educa-

---

[15] For details of Lemass's role see Farrell, 1983, pp. 91–7. For another interpretation, see Bew and Patterson, 1982, pp. 189–90.

[16] De Valera ran for the office of President while still Taoiseach. However, he resigned as Taoiseach before the result of the presidential election was known, indeed 'before the ballot boxes were collected' (Longford and O'Neill, 1970, p. 448).

tion scheme by Minister for Education, Donough O'Malley (Lee, 1989, p. 362). There were also changes that were not quite policy changes, but were more than matters of style. This has been characterised as a shift from ideology (nationalist) to pragmatism (Cohan, 1972). Although this was more a matter of emphasis than a clear dichotomy between an ideological past and a pragmatic future, it was not any less real for that. Even the approach to the Northern problem emphasized practical issues, a change of approach perhaps best symbolised by the visit of Lemass to Northern Ireland in 1965, with its implied recognition of the Northern Ireland state and its more than implied revisionist approach to the traditional tenets of Irish nationalism.

A change in Fianna Fáil's style in the literal, sartorial sense was also widely perceived and commented on, as 'the men in the mohair suits' came to symbolise a whole new image of politics in the popular mind. For some, the image was far from positive – it carried connotations not just of materialism but of too cosy a connection between the world of politics and the world of business. This was to become a criticism levelled at Fianna Fáil in both inter-party debate and in the media in the years ahead. The attacks by the party's critics were bolstered at the time by a Fianna Fáil effort to establish a support group (TACA) among the business community (an effort that was subsequently abandoned), and by lack of effective controls on the receipt of financial contributions by political parties. The issues were eventually tackled when a commitment to 'ethics in government' was made part of the Fianna Fáil–Labour Programme for Government in 1993. Bills to implement this commitment were published in May 1994 (Ethics in Public Office Bill) and in October 1994 (Electoral Bill).

Fianna Fáil from Lynch to Ahern

It is appropriate to label the first forty years of Fianna Fáil's existence as 'Fianna Fáil from de Valera to Lemass' because of the extent to which these two men dominated the party in that period. It is equally appropriate to label the period since then in terms of the succession of party leaders, not because they personified the party in the way their predecessors had done, but because of the extent to which the issue of leadership dominated much of the life of the party. The leadership contest that followed Lemass's resignation in 1966 was shaping up to be highly divisive when Jack Lynch, a quiet-spoken and not obviously ambitious, but highly experienced, minister, emerged as a compromise candidate and the 'reluctant Taoiseach'. Both of Lynch's predecessors as leader of Fianna Fáil had been involved in the nationalist movement from the beginning. Lynch's only apparent connection to nationalism was cultural, that is, his outstanding record in inter-county hurling, one of the two main Gaelic games, the early development of which had been closely intertwined with the nationalist movement.

In his first electoral test Lynch managed to lead Fianna Fáil to the majority of seats that had eluded Lemass. This was, however, on the basis of a somewhat reduced popular vote, and detailed examination indicates that 1969 was the one Irish election in which it can be demonstrated that the redrawing of the constituency boundaries had the intended effect on the outcome (Gallagher, 1975). Lynch's electoral success did not undo the fact that the contest for the leadership of the party had opened deep divisions and eroded the authority of the party leader. Both factors were to play a significant role in the 1970 'Arms Crisis'.

Revisionism in Dublin and reformism in Northern Ireland had been severely challenged by the recrudescence of communal conflict and violence in Northern Ireland in 1969. It was against this background that the Arms Crisis broke on an unsuspecting Irish public. The episode involved the sudden dismissal from the cabinet of two senior ministers (Charles J. Haughey and Neil Blaney) on suspicion of illegally importing arms for use in Northern Ireland. At the same time the Minister for Justice was relieved of his office on health grounds and another minister (Kevin Boland) resigned in sympathy with those who had been fired. Blaney and Haughey were arrested and tried for conspiracy but the case against Blaney was dismissed and Haughey was found not guilty.

The crisis was of epic proportions and has yet to be satisfactorily explained.[17] The significance of the event in terms of a portrait of Fianna Fáil is that it crystallised differences over policy towards Northern Ireland and sharpened those differences by entangling them with issues of personal probity and responsibility, and with an underlying challenge to the party leadership. Thus, it fuelled the factionalism that, in particular from 1979 on, was to plague the party, with serious adverse consequences for both its performance in government and its electoral appeal.

It was characteristic of Fianna Fáil discipline that, with the exceptions of Blaney and Boland, the party closed ranks for the duration of the immediate crisis and carried on. The major event of the remainder of its term of office was entry to the EEC in January 1973, following a referendum held in May 1972 (see chapter 9). When the government finally faced the electorate in February 1973, it lost office more because of the coming together of the opposition parties in a pre-election coalition arrangement (see below) than through any adverse retrospective judgment by the voters on the events of 1970.

Once it recovered from the shock of being in opposition after its second sixteen-year term in government, Fianna Fáil used the time to modernise its organisation, revamp its policies and renew its appeal. Policies were treated as products to be updated, packaged, and marketed and voters were consumers to be captured with all the techniques of marketing – specific policies for specific market niches, loss leaders, brand image, and general media razzmatazz. The approach appeared to pay dividends electorally, though it will be necessary to take up the issue of the specific impact of the manifesto promises in more detail in chapter 7. In any event, the party swept back into office in 1977 with its second highest share of the vote ever.

As a strategy for dealing with economic problems in the wake of the first oil shock, the Fianna Fáil approach (a strong stimulus to the economy financed by means of heavy foreign borrowing) turned out to be the disaster many of its critics

---

[17] One eminent contemporary historian sidesteps the issue in a footnote that refers the reader to three books where 'various viewpoints may be sampled' (Lee, 1989, p. 459). Some light is thrown on aspects of the affair by the report of the inquiry carried out by the Committee of Public Accounts into the expenditure of the Grant-in-Aid for Northern Ireland Relief (Committee of Public Accounts, 1972).

predicted. By massively increasing foreign indebtedness, it contributed significantly to the crisis in the public finances that dominated politics for much of the next decade.[18] The post-1977 policies must, however, be seen in context. The seeds that were to produce a luxuriant crop of overspending and overborrowing were sown in the early '70s by both Fianna Fáil- and Fine Gael-led governments (Lee, 1989, pp. 466–73).

In electoral terms too, the 1977 achievement quickly came undone and, in simultaneous European and local elections in June 1979, Fianna Fáil performed calamitously. Partly as a result of this performance, and partly as a result of by-election defeats the following November, Lynch came under severe pressure from a section of the Fianna Fáil parliamentary party and retired prematurely. The factionalism which had its roots in and before 1970 came out in the open in a very divisive election of party leader (and Taoiseach), and remained in the open in the sense that the defeated group refused to give full allegiance to the newly elected leader, Charles J. Haughey. The sense of controversy engendered by the leadership contest is not surprising. Haughey had been a highly active and effective minister in the 1960s, whose ministerial career had been, to all intents and purposes, terminated by the Arms Crisis. However, he had tenaciously fought his way back, first to a front bench position (1975), then to a ministerial position and, finally, to the position of party leader and Taoiseach. The Arms Crisis had inevitably associated him with the more nationalist wing of the party and, after a decade of the 'Troubles' in Northern Ireland, such an association was bound to be divisive – highly positive for some, but equally negative for others. The fact that Haughey had substantial self-made wealth also led to divided views. For some it was a significant plus – the skills that had enabled him to amass a fortune might be turned to effective management of the economy. For others, it was entirely negative, the innuendo being that political office might have been used for personal gain. Haughey's accession also saw a transformation in relations between the leaders of the government and the opposition, previously amicable and co-operative relations being replaced by highly personalised conflict.[19]

In January 1980, in a specially televised broadcast, the new Fianna Fáil leader promised radical economic retrenchment . The promise (or threat) was not acted on; the government appeared to vacillate, presumably in the hope of postponing the unpalatable measures until after an election victory. As chapter 6 will show, Haughey had in fact inherited a disastrous position in the public opinion polls and the question of timing must have seemed crucial. Ultimately, events deprived Fianna Fáil of the advantage of choosing its own time for the election and the party waged a defensive campaign on the issues of job creation and inflation, whilst, according to its critics, withholding the bad news on the economy that had been hinted at in the January 1980 broadcast.

---

[18] Part of the reason for the failure was that the strategy was explicitly predicated on co-operation with the unions in arranging low-wage settlements, a co-operation that the party could not deliver.

[19] For accounts of Haughey's controversial career in politics see Murtagh and Joyce, 1983; Arnold, 1993.

Fianna Fáil under Haughey may have vacillated on economic policy; the same cannot be said of policy on Northern Ireland or Anglo-Irish relations. A decisive change from previous policy was signalled in Haughey's speech to the 1980 Fianna Fáil Ard Fheis (party convention). He based his analysis of the problem on the premise that Northern Ireland was 'a failed political entity'. This was a radical departure from the line pursued by the previous Fianna Fáil administration, which had favoured an internal settlement of the problem. In line with the analysis, there followed an attempt to make the search for a solution a matter primarily for 'the two sovereign governments'. Seen from the perspective of Haughey's policy aims, much was achieved at the December 1980 Anglo-Irish Summit (see the discussion in Downey, 1983, pp. 170–99). However, the achievement was jeopardised, partly by excessive Irish government claims as to the significance of what had been agreed, and partly by the deterioration in Anglo-Irish relations and in the Northern Ireland situation itself following a prolonged and bitter hunger strike by IRA and INLA prisoners in Northern Ireland. The H-block hunger strike, in which ultimately ten hunger strikers died, loomed large in the election of June 1981, following the decision by the group co-ordinating the protest to nominate candidates in nine constituencies and their success in winning two Dáil seats. Fianna Fáil ended up six seats short of an overall majority and with two seats less than the combined strength of Fine Gael and Labour.

A minority Fine Gael–Labour coalition government took power and there followed a period of considerable political instability that saw three elections in the space of eighteen months. Added to parliamentary instability was the reopening of dissension in Fianna Fáil, which led to no less than three challenges to Haughey's leadership between February 1982 and February 1983. After the indecisive outcome of the February 1982 election, Fianna Fáil achieved office by means of an expensive deal (the 'Gregory deal') that involved a package of measures targeted at a deprived inner-city constituency, the purpose of the package being to secure the support of the independent TD representing the area. There followed a seven-month period of minority Fianna Fáil government, during which the party was bedevilled by a series of political embarrassments that were at least partly of its own making (B. Farrell, 1987, pp. 17–20).

On the economic front, Fianna Fáil showed signs of serious intent to tackle the borrowing and spending problem, but was under severe pressure from sectional interests and from its perilous position in the Dáil. On suffering a Dáil defeat on a motion of no confidence on 4 November 1982, Fianna Fáil went to the country with a manifesto based on the programme the government had been about to implement in order to deal with the fiscal crisis. Fianna Fáil's conversion to a policy of austerity did it no good electorally and a coalition of Fine Gael and Labour took over. Back in opposition, Fianna Fáil appeared to reverse itself again on economic policy, attacking the government's austerity programme at every turn. The period in opposition was also notable for the line the party took on the Northern Ireland problem, and on the question of constitutional provisions governing moral issues. On the former, the party pursued a strongly nationalist line in the New Ireland Forum, in its interpretation of the Forum

Report and in its reaction to the 1985 Anglo-Irish Agreement.[20] On a number of moral issues it either explicitly or implicitly took a conservative stand. It opposed the government's liberalisation of legislation governing the availability of contraception.[21] In the referendums on abortion and divorce the party deliberately stayed on the sidelines of the campaign, but party leader Haughey had supported the holding of the abortion referendum in the first place, and argued strongly in favour of a 'yes' vote – to insert an anti-abortion clause in the constitution. In addition, many Fianna Fáil activists and some Fianna Fáil Deputies sided with the majority conservative position on both the abortion and divorce issues (see chapter 9).

In the 1987 election Fianna Fáil took care not to be explicit on the economic measures it would take, reserving its position and then proceeding, as a minority government, to implement the strategy first outlined by Haughey in January 1980. In this it had the support in parliament of both Fine Gael and the Progressive Democrats. Equally importantly, in terms of the legitimacy and the effectiveness of the policies being pursued, it had the support of 'the social partners'. This represented a renewed resort by Fianna Fáil to the neo-corporatist-style arrangements it had first pursued in the 1960s. This time around, however, the agreement negotiated with representatives of the trade unions, the employers and the farmers was much more conservative than earlier agreements in its implications for both fiscal policy and wage levels.

In the 1989 election Fianna Fáil had to defend its record of retrenchment and, according to participants in the campaign, it got a rude shock when faced with virulent voter discontent, on the health cuts in particular.[22] Emerging from that election still without a majority, Fianna Fáil reversed an attitude to government formation that it had long prided itself on and entered a coalition government. The move was extremely controversial, particularly among rank and file members of the party, as it was seen as abandoning a 'core value' of the party that had almost defined its stance *vis-à-vis* the other parties over five decades.[23] The change was indeed historic, as one commentator put it '[Fianna Fáil] is now just another party, hoping to govern alone but willing to bargain should there be a post-election impasse'.[24] The change perhaps illustrates the ultimate core value of the party – pragmatism. Fianna Fáil is 'the party of reality', dedicated to the exercise of power in pursuit of the national interest as defined, with appropriate flexibility, by Fianna Fáil itself.

This same pragmatism and, in particular, the concern of many of the party's Dáil Deputies that the leadership of Charles Haughey was becoming, or had become, an electoral liability ultimately led to the ousting of Haughey in January 1992 and to the election of Albert Reynolds as party leader and Taoiseach. A successful self-made

[20] On the New Ireland Forum and subsequent developments in Anglo-Irish relations see below p. 50.

[21] The official party line on the contraceptive issue and on Northern Ireland provoked renewed dissent within the party, dissent that ultimately led to the establishment of a new political party, the Progressive Democrats (see below).

[22] The impact of the health cuts issue on voting is discussed in chapter 7.

[23] For many of the party's supporters, the strategic U-turn was all the more difficult to accept because the alliance was with its offshoot and arch-rival, the Progressive Democrats.

[24] John Bowman, 'Haughey can't live on slogans', *The Sunday Times*, 28 July, 1991, pp. 2–3.

businessman and former holder of the Industry and Commerce and Finance portfolios, Reynolds had been dismissed from the Cabinet in November 1991 when he indicated support for a motion of no confidence in the leadership of Taoiseach Charles Haughey. When Haughey resigned in January 1992, Albert Reynolds was elected Fianna Fáil leader by a large majority. Given his lack of previous involvement in policy-making on Northern Ireland or Anglo-Irish relations, he surprised many observers with the degree of priority he accorded to the search for peace in Northern Ireland in his first statements as Fianna Fáil leader and Taoiseach. His single-minded pursuit of this objective contributed substantially to the developing peace process in Northern Ireland and to the calling of a cease-fire by the Provisional IRA in August 1994.

Determined from the outset of his tenure as Taoiseach to face down the Progressive Democrats in cabinet, Reynolds precipitated an election in November 1992 by a personal riposte to Progressive Democrat leader Desmond O'Malley, delivered in the course of Reynolds' evidence to the Beef Tribunal. This was a public enquiry established by the Dáil and conducted under the chairmanship of the President of the High Court, the purpose of which was to investigate allegations made in a television programme and in the Dáil in regard to the beef-processing industry. The allegations included tax evasion, abuse of European Community subsidy schemes, and claims of political favouritism by senior Fianna Fáil politicians, including Albert Reynolds, towards one beef-processing company (the Goodman Group) in the allocation of state-backed export credit insurance and general state support to the industry. As already noted, suspicions of political corruption had circulated on and off without corroboration for more than two decades. The political importance of the tribunal lay in the fact that it was the first major investigation into a specific set of allegations. The report of the tribunal revealed considerable fraud in the meat industry. It was also highly critical of aspects of government and ministerial decision-making. Furthermore it obtained information on substantial contributions made by companies and individuals in the food processing industry to political parties. However, on the issue of political corruption, the tribunal concluded that 'such contributions were normal contributions made to Political Parties and did not in any way affect or relate to the matters being inquired into by the Tribunal' (Beef Tribunal, 1994, p.12). It also concluded that 'there is no evidence that either the Taoiseach at the time [Mr Haughey] or the Minister for Industry and Commerce at the time [Mr Reynolds] was personally close to Mr Goodman or that Mr Goodman had any political associations with either of them or the Party that they represented' (*ibid.*, p. 321). In regard to Mr Reynold's controversial decision on export credit insurance, it concluded that 'the decisions were made by him having regard to his conception of the requirements of the national interest and there is no evidence to suggest that his decisions were in any way based on improper motives either political or personal' (*ibid.*, p. 232). Not surprisingly, spokesmen for Taoiseach Albert Reynolds emphasised these aspects of the report. Their presentation of the findings was hotly contested by the other political parties, including the Labour Party. The issues were debated in a special three-day Dáil sitting in early September, 1994 (Dáil Debates, Vol 445, Nos. 3–5, 1–3 September 1994).

The outcome of the 1992 election was a drastic shock for Fianna Fáil – a drop in the party's support to a level below that in any of the elections in the previous sixty years. Equally significant was the particular governmental alliance (Fianna Fáil and Labour) that emerged as a result of the parliamentary balance of forces after the election. In terms of understanding the nature of Fianna Fáil, the alliance with Labour underlined the party's adaptability and put a definitive seal on the availability of Fianna Fáil as a coalition partner, first tentatively signalled by the coalition with the Progressive Democrats in 1989. For many, it also highlighted, or was at least compatible with, an important aspect of the party's multifaceted image, that is, its interventionist approach to problems of economic management, industrial development and social welfare. A poor European Parliament election performance in Dublin in 1994 and the simultaneous loss of two seats in by-elections reminded the party that adaptation and availability for coalition would be likely to continue to be necessary elements in the party's strategy.

Even so , coalition did not appear to come easily to Fianna Fáil and certainly not to its leader, Albert Reynolds. The Beef Tribunal and its aftermath had undermined relations between the government parties and had created an atmosphere of considerable distrust. This finally exploded with the withdrawal from the cabinet and subsequent resignation from government of the Labour ministers in November 1994. The immediate issue was the appointment of the Attorney General to the position of President of the High Court but this became entangled with the issue of the accountability of the Attorney General's office for a seven month delay in extraditing a priest accused of paedophile offences in Northern Ireland and with the withholding of information from the Dáil in the debate on the issue. In the dramatic government and political crisis that followed, Albert Reynolds was forced to resign, first as Taoiseach and then as leader of Fianna Fáil. He continued as acting Taoiseach pending Dáil agreement on the nomination of a successor but was replaced as leader of Fianna Fáil by Bertie Ahern. Ahern was Finance Minister at the time and had been a successful Minister of Labour in previous administrations and the broker of several national pay agreements. The fact that he was seen as a consensus politician and a conciliator was an important factor in accounting for the sustained and almost successful attempt to rebuild the shattered Fianna Fáil-Labour coalition. The deal was on the point of being signed when a story in the *Irish Times* of 4 December, 1994 reopened the issue of the extent to which the Dáil had been deliberately misled and by whom. As a result, Labour walked away from Fianna Fáil for the third time in as many weeks and talks with a view to forming a government between Fine Gael, Labour and the two smaller opposition parties began (for the outcome see below). Back in opposition, Fianna Fáil faced the immediate challenge of repairing the damage it had suffered in the collapse of the government and the medium term challenge of devising an opposition strategy that would position it effectively for the next election.

Cumann na nGaedheal

The pro-treaty side of the split that tore Sinn Féin apart in 1922–23 emerged in April 1923 as Cumann na nGaedheal (see Figure 2.1). The party was established by those

Sinn Féin deputies who, in virtue of their shared commitment to the Treaty settlement, found themselves in control of a parliamentary majority and governmental power. They also found themselves facing an election and in need of organising electoral support. These circumstances had several important consequences. The first was that, on many issues, the party encompassed a wide variety of views. This is as true of attitudes to the national question (see, for example, the events surrounding the Army Mutiny in 1924) as it is of attitudes to economic policy. The most obvious example of the latter was the difference between the protectionist views of J. J. Walsh, Minister for Posts and Telegraphs, and the more conventional free trade views of the bulk of the cabinet, especially of the Minister for Agriculture, Patrick Hogan. The one area where there was consensus was on religious and moral issues. Government ministers were 'products of the same culture as the bishops, and shared the same values. There was only one Protestant in the government, Ernest Blythe, and his austere Ulster outlook seems to have fitted in well enough with the Catholic puritanism of his colleagues' (Whyte, 1971, p. 36). This consensus led to a series of measures – the Censorship of Films Act 1923, the removal of the possibility of obtaining a divorce by means of a private bill in parliament (1925) and the Censorship of Publications Act 1929. The latter measure, in addition to introducing a rigid system of censorship of books, made the publication and distribution of literature advocating birth control an offence (Whyte, 1971, p. 37).

The second consequence of the circumstances of the party's establishment was the adoption of an organisational form more reminiscent of nineteenth-century conservative parties than of the newly emerging disciplined mass parties that were to prove highly successful in electoral competition in the first half of the twentieth century (Moss, 1933, p. 54). A third consequence of the fact that Cumann na nGaedheal was, as it were, born in office, was that, from the outset, it suffered the electoral disadvantages of incumbency. This applied across the board – in Anglo-Irish relations, in security policy and in regard to the economy.

On a specific and highly salient issue in Anglo-Irish relations, it had to take responsibility for the dashing of the excessive expectations many nationalists had invested in the Boundary Commission. More generally, its progress in enlarging the area of freedom conferred by the treaty, though in the long term very significant, appeared in the short term very modest. On the security front, it bore the odium of the draconian steps taken by the government during the Civil War and of the continued policy of stern measures in support of public order which it felt obliged to take.

In the economic realm, the immediate task facing an incumbent government was to manage the adjustment to post-war economic conditions, conditions that, with the ending of the wartime boom in agricultural prices, were none too favourable to a primarily agricultural economy. The primacy of agriculture was more than a statistic. That it was the basic engine of economic growth was a fundamental assumption of orthodox political and economic thinking, and this led to the policy of keeping agricultural costs at a minimum through low state expenditure and low taxes. In all of this, Cumann na nGaedheal politicians were receptive to the advice proffered by the Department of Finance. The major theme of the Department was 'the most rigid economy and retrenchment' and it appears that little or no discussion, let alone criticism, of the Finance viewpoint occurred (Fanning, 1978, pp. 105–8). The most celebrated instance of the implementation of this approach was the cut of one shilling a week in the old age pension in 1924. This must be seen in the context of the heavy burden of pension payments due to the structure of the population. It should also be noted that the cuts were across the board – cuts in the army estimates being of such a magnitude as to have been a contributory factor in the army mutiny of March 1924 (Fanning, 1978, p. 117). All that having been said, the cut in the old age pension was not the stuff of which election popularity is made and it damaged the image, not just of Cumann na nGaedheal, but by entering the popular mythology of Irish politics, the image of its successor, Fine Gael, as well.

Having suffered through the immediate post-war economic adjustment, Cumann na nGaedheal faced the crisis brought on by the Great Depression. The innovativeness which had characterised its policy in specific sectors (for example, the Shannon hydro-electric scheme and the establishment of the Electricity Supply Board) was notably lacking in its approach to general economic policy and, except when forced by external factors to do otherwise, it stuck rigidly with the inadequate nostrums of free trade and budgetary cut-backs. Despite the economic crisis, it approached the 1932 election on its record, adding to that record in the last year of the government's term a tax-raising supplementary budget and security legislation which allowed for the setting up of military tribunals which could impose the death penalty. To encourage its supporters in the face of all this, the party issued dire and improbable warning of the consequences of letting Fianna Fáil get its hands on the levers of power. Conjuring up the notion of a Fianna Fáil onslaught on the institutions of the state, Cumann na nGaedheal warned:

> With your state institutions will disappear the Stability, Religious, Economic, and Financial, which, through ten years of State experience, is becoming a characteristic of the organised Irish People. Its place will be taken by sporadic Revolution, Irreligion, Poverty and Chaos – the chief and well-known marks of those countries which experiment in Constituent Assemblies and changes of regime . . . our Country, once become a prey to Disorder and Chaos will be transformed into a free field for the cultivation of those doctrines of Materialism and Communism which can so effectively poison the wells of Religion and National Traditions.[25]

Whereas at an earlier stage, Cumann na nGaedheal had lost members and spawned break-away parties with alarming frequency, now it began to act as a pole of attraction for independents, for members of the Farmers' Party, with which it had been allied, and for the remnants of the Redmondite National League, including Redmond himself. Fianna Fáil described these adhesions as 'the alliance of a dog with its fleas' (quoted in Moss, 1933, p. 180). With greater objectivity, Moss draws the implication: 'By taking into its ranks the farmers, independents and members of the National League, Cumann na nGaedheal has given up its identity with Sinn Féin. This formerly moderate wing of Sinn Féin has now become the party of the conservative elements in

---

[25] Party statement appearing as an advertisement in the *Irish Independent*, 7 February 1932. Quoted in Moss, 1933, pp. 203–4.

Irish society . . . all their acts are studied with due consideration for their conservative supporters' (Moss, 1933, p. 30).

It may be argued whether Cumann na nGaedheal's conservatism was a product of these additions or whether these additions occurred because of its increasing conservatism. In any event that conservatism was clear and unmistakable in its appeal to the voters in 1932. Neither the nature of that appeal nor the party's new-found friends appeared to have done it much good. Its vote dropped sufficiently to bring about the crucial handing over of power from civil-war victors to civil-war vanquished, from those whose primary commitment had been to upholding the institutions of the state to those who had held those same institutions in contempt and had sought to undermine them. The actual handing over of power in 1932 was relatively, one might even say remarkably, smooth. This was both absolutely vital for the establishment of stable democracy and, at the same time, a tribute to the firm roots democracy had put down, beginning in the period well before the foundation of the state. It was arguably the most important legacy of Cumann na nGaedheal.

Although the handing over of power in 1932 went smoothly, the practical working out of the transition over the next few years was not without moments of considerable tension, moments that were marked by some violence and a good deal of both genuine apprehension and some posturing on both sides (Manning, 1972). Part of the response on the pro-treaty side was the establishment of the Army Comrades Association to protect Cumann na nGaedheal meetings from alleged danger of attack by republican supporters. This association developed into the National Guard and adopted some of the more ephemeral physical and intellectual trappings of continental European fascism, including a military style of organisation and the wearing of a uniform, in this case the blue shirt by which the movement became known.[26] In the wake of defeat in the highly charged election of 1933, Cumann na nGaedheal entered into merger talks with the like-minded National Centre Party. An entirely unexpected result of the talks between Cumann na nGaedheal and the Centre Party was that the merger which formed Fine Gael included the Blueshirts.

Fine Gael, 1933–77

What was even more surprising than the inclusion of this extra-parliamentary political force, however, was that the man chosen to lead the new party was the volatile and politically inexperienced leader of the Blueshirts, General Eoin O'Duffy. In the event, O'Duffy's tenure as leader of Fine Gael was short. He resigned amid controversy in September 1934 and Cosgrave was restored to leadership of the party at the Ard Fheis in March 1935. While the leadership change did not end the party's relationship with the Blueshirts as such, it did do away with the danger of direct confrontation with the government and closed off whatever slight risk there might have been that the main opposition party in the state might have developed along fascist lines. The Blueshirt movement was finally disbanded by the leadership of Fine Gael in October 1936.

[26] On the Blueshirts and fascism see Manning, 1987b.

Thus Fine Gael had been born with an odd pedigree. Among the important consequences of this were that the first three years of its life were marked by uncertainty, both as to the leadership of the party and the direction it might take. With hindsight we can see that this was but an interlude. As Manning puts it 'to all intents and purposes Fine Gael resumed in 1936 where Cumann na nGaedheal had left off in 1933' (Manning, 1972, p. 196). However, the Blueshirt episode was undoubtedly damaging to the image of the party and distracted it from its main task – that of presenting the electorate with a credible alternative to Fianna Fáil.

War-time neutrality made further difficulties for Fine Gael, facing it with an impossible choice. Realistically, there was no alternative but to row in behind de Valera's policy and accept the sop of participation in the National Defence Conference that de Valera offered in lieu of an all-party coalition government (Fisk, 1983, pp. 160–2). On the other hand, in one vision of the party's identity, this stance robbed it of the key elements of its claim to distinctiveness. James Hogan, a professor of history and a prominent Fine Gael activist at the time argued that:

> for Fine Gael to accept and endorse the logic of neutrality would be tantamount to abandoning the Commonwealth idea, which would be to forfeit the main ground of its individuality as a party. For, once it ceased to stand for a Commonwealth policy, no simple and fundamental issue would remain to distinguish the Fine Gael party from its former rival. (Hogan, 1945, p. 33)

Hogan's view was a minority one that, in the face of Fianna Fáil successes in dealing with Britain, probably had little chance of forming the basis of an effective electoral appeal. In any event, the party's mind on the issue of neutrality was clear and when the deputy leader of the party, James Dillon, suggested in 1942 that Ireland should align itself with America, he was promptly expelled from the party.

In the wake of a disastrous performance in the 1943 election, W. T. Cosgrave stood down as Fine Gael leader. He was replaced by General Richard Mulcahy, a divisive choice in terms of inter-party relations, as he was the figure most closely associated with the hardline internal security policies pursued in the 1920s. Organisationally there were significant signs of decline, with the party having a difficult time finding candidates and with a number of former deputies and candidates opting to stand as independents in the 1944 election (O'Leary, 1979, p. 35 and see discussion in chapter 4).

The party underwent what might be described as artificial resuscitation in 1948. Its fortunes recovered not by virtue of its own performance, which was in fact a shade worse than in 1944, but by virtue of the accident of being the largest single party in an unlikely combination of parties that outnumbered Fianna Fáil and brought about a change of government for the first time in sixteen years. Though it was by far the largest party in the new alliance, Fine Gael paid a high price for participation in that coalition government. Because of the objections of Seán MacBride (leader of the new Clann na Poblachta party), the leader of Fine Gael was obliged to stand aside when it came to choice of Taoiseach and allow John A. Costello, a prominent barrister, party spokesman and former Cumann na nGaedheal Attorney General, to assume the position.

The episode reinforces the impression of a contrast between the leadership of Cumann na nGaedheal/Fine Gael and that of Fianna Fáil. While Cosgrave's record as a government leader in the difficult first ten years of the state is impressive, it is unlikely that he would ever have become leader had it not been for the deaths in quick succession in 1922 of Michael Collins and Arthur Griffith, who were the joint leaders of the pro-treaty side and would have been the obvious candidates for the leadership of the new party. Then there was the débâcle of the leadership of O'Duffy, followed by a six-month interregnum when the party was led by a directorate of four, representing the different strands of the party. This was followed in March 1935 by the return of Cosgrave, who had been judged to lack the dynamism required to lead the new party a mere two years earlier. Cosgrave was followed by Mulcahy, who was regarded with such disfavour by republicans that he had to be bypassed as Taoiseach in 1948; Fine Gael ended up in the 1950s in the peculiar situation of having a party leader who was not Taoiseach and a Taoiseach who was not party leader. Meanwhile, throughout the entire period up to 1959, Fianna Fáil enjoyed the unquestioned leadership of someone who had the aura that attached to being the most senior surviving officer from the 1916 rebellion, and whose role was encapsulated in the frequent reference to him, even by close associates, as 'the Chief'.

Because Fine Gael had office thrust upon it in 1948, it did not enter government with a new political programme. Its policy tended to be reactive, either *vis-à-vis* events or the initiatives of its more proactive partners. This was certainly true in the case of the famous Mother and Child Scheme (see below p. 63). Fine Gael's reaction to this highly controversial episode confirmed that it had inherited the conservative approach to church-state relations that had characterised Cumann na nGaedheal in office.

Fine Gael's reactive approach was also evident in the case of the declaration of the Republic, the impetus for the measure coming from Clann na Poblachta and especially from its leader, Seán MacBride. Though the announcement of the decision to repeal the External Relations Act (the legislative basis of Ireland's links with the Commonwealth) was made by Costello during an official visit to Canada, the evidence suggests that, while Costello was sympathetic to the idea, he was not its initiator (Fanning, 1983, pp. 172–6). Whatever the details of the circumstances of the decision, it certainly put an end to adherence to 'the Commonwealth idea' as the defining mark of Fine Gael.

The 1948 government's tentative exercise in economic planning was also reactive, being required by the terms of an offer of Marshall Plan aid. On the other hand, some economic policy initiatives were undertaken, for example, the establishment of the Industrial Development Authority, which was subsequently to become an extremely important agent in the development of industrial policy, and the land rehabilitation programme, undertaken, with Marshall aid support, by the Minister for Agriculture, James Dillon. By 1951, however, none of these or the other measures taken by the government could hide the fact that the economy was in difficulty and that the recovery taking shape in Europe was likely to pass Ireland by. Given the political débâcle of the Mother and Child scheme and the economic difficulties, the government was vulnerable on two fronts. However, the defeat of the government in 1951 was certainly not a defeat for Fine Gael. In fact, Fine Gael managed to consolidate in electoral terms the recovery that had been initiated by the party's unexpected assumption of office in 1948. A further increase in support in the 1954 election put Fine Gael back in office at the head of a more compact coalition government that included Labour and Clann na Talmhan, with external support from the remnant of Clann na Poblachta.

Faced with a severe budgetary crisis in 1956, Fine Gael's conservative Finance Minister, Gerard Sweetman, introduced a highly deflationary budget that arguably exacerbated the economic crisis. It certainly exacerbated the Government's unpopularity. Fine Gael was not only put out of office in 1957, it received a severe check to its electoral recovery. Despite this, over the period as a whole, Fine Gael had done well out of participation in coalition government and it entered the 1960s in bullish form. It also entered the 1960s under a new leader, the duo of Mulcahy and Costello being replaced by James Dillon. Dillon was the son of the last leader of the Irish Parliamentary Party. He had been an independent Deputy in the 1920s, and co-founder of the National Centre Party in 1933. Expelled from Fine Gael in 1942, he rejoined it in 1952 and was Minister for Agriculture in both the inter-party governments of the 1950s. His political style was both old-fashioned and highly individualistic. The result was that, in a period when Ireland was experiencing a sense of development and change, the search by Fine Gael for a new policy identity occurred in spite of rather than through the party leadership.

The outcome of this search was a mildly social-democratic policy document ('The Just Society'), which a ginger reform group pushed through as the substance of the party's manifesto in the 1965 election. This was perhaps more important as a setting of the stage for another coming together with Labour than as a source of immediate electoral gains. In the short term, such an alliance was unlikely, given that Labour was strongly committed to a go-it-alone policy and given yet another leadership succession in Fine Gael. James Dillon retired after the 1965 election and the party chose Liam Cosgrave to replace him. If Mulcahy and Dillon were rooted in the politics of an earlier era because of their generation and experience, Liam Cosgrave was steeped in the same traditions through family connection (he was the son of William T. Cosgrave, the Cumann na nGaedheal leader), and through the fact that, though only forty-five when elected leader, he had already served for twenty-two years as a Fine Gael Dáil Deputy.[27]

The failure of Labour to make the anticipated breakthrough in 1969, and the sense of political crisis engendered by the Arms Crisis and its aftermath, paved the way for a pragmatic compromise between Fine Gael and Labour, expressed in a fourteen-point programme for government put forward by an alliance of the two parties in the run-up to the 1973 election. When it assumed office in 1973, the Fine Gael–Labour coalition was seen as having 'a gloss of imagination, vigour and reform . . . impressive

---

[27] See the discussion of the link between Cosgrave's background and outlook and the lack of organisational or strategic development in Fine Gael in Manning, 1978, pp. 88–91.

looking ministers and considerable liberal, trade-union and media support' (Downey, 1983, p. 155). It proceeded to introduce a wealth tax, gender equality legislation (though much of this was in response to EEC initiatives) and a programme of expansion of the social welfare services. Within its first year of office the government had participated in the apparently highly successful Sunningdale negotiations on Northern Ireland. The political settlement established at Sunningdale admittedly proved short-lived, but the government continued to pursue a consistent low-key policy of moderation and conciliation that contrasted with the simmering controversies on the subject of Northern Ireland in the Fianna Fáil party.

If there was a contrast with Fianna Fáil on Northern Ireland, there was continuity in a basic aspect of economic policy. The Fianna Fáil Minister for Finance had introduced a current budget deficit in 1972. The approach was repeated by Fine Gael's Richard Ryan in 1973 and was to prove particularly significant when the oil shock hit the economy, and government borrowed more and more in an effort to simultaneously protect living standards and control rising unemployment (Lee, 1989, pp. 464–73). As we have seen above, this deficit spending approach was pushed even further by the Fianna Fáil government elected in 1977. The economic effects have already been noted in chapter 1, and the political consequences were the domination of elections by the issue of government spending and borrowing for the next decade.

The 1973–77 Fine Gael–Labour coalition's reforming image was dented when a government bill to liberalise Ireland's highly restrictive legislation on contraception was defeated by Fine Gael defections, defections that included the Fine Gael Taoiseach, Liam Cosgrave and his party colleague, the Minister for Education, Dick Burke. The image was further undermined by the introduction of draconian internal security measures in 1976, and by the handling of a crisis in relations between the Government and the Presidency that arose when the Fine Gael Minister of Defence criticised the President in very robust terms for referring the Emergency Powers Bill to the Supreme Court. The crisis led to the resignation of the President 'to protect the dignity and independence of the presidency as an institution'.[28]

Despite these difficulties, the coalition approached the 1977 election in a highly confident, even complacent, mood and appeared to have addressed very little attention to either timing, tactics or campaign preparation. A good part of that confidence resulted from the belief that the redrawing of the constituencies in 1974 almost guaranteed a coalition victory. In the event the 1977 election was, from a Fine Gael point of view, both mistimed and mispredicted. The results were a débâcle for Fine Gael and they led to an immediate change of leadership.

Fine Gael since 1977

Unlike all previous leadership changes in Fine Gael, the change effected in 1977 did mark a significant break with the past, both in terms of political outlook and in terms

[28] Quoted in Lee, 1989, p. 482.

of approach to party organisation. The new leader was Garret FitzGerald, a major figure in the leftward shift of a section of the party that took place in the mid-1960s. FitzGerald immediately set about reorganising the party, bringing about major changes in structure and personnel and using the 1979 local and European Parliament elections as a proving ground for both. In policy terms the new look Fine Gael was very much in FitzGerald's image – liberal and pluralist, while being cautious in taking the steps necessary to bring about change; social democratic, while being very anxious about the mounting evidence of severe public indebtedness and, in line with party traditions, moderately nationalist, emphasizing in particular the need to effect a reconciliation of nationalist and unionist traditions.

Having done very well in the local and European elections of 1979, and with a thoroughly revamped organisation and a supply of both new candidates and keen young activists, Fine Gael approached the 1981 election intent on winning power. Its only handicap, one that was not publicly acknowledged, was its dependence on the co-operation of Labour in order to achieve that objective. In the event, it did achieve power, or rather, a shaky grip on power, in the form of another coalition with Labour that was sustained by the votes of several independent deputies. The government immediately set about tackling the acute fiscal problem by introducing a severe supplementary budget within months of winning office. This set the trend for its efforts in this area over the ensuing months, efforts that concentrated on raising revenue as the solution rather than cutting public expenditure. And it was a revenue-raising measure – extension of VAT to children's shoes – that led to the withdrawal of independent support and the fall of the government in the vote on the Budget in January 1982. In the ensuing election Fine Gael stuck to its guns and fought the election essentially on the 'harsh' budget that had been defeated in the Dáil. In the circumstances, Fine Gael did quite well. It increased its vote marginally and lost only two seats. However, the finely balanced electoral arithmetic put Fianna Fáil back in office and returned Fine Gael to the opposition benches after a mere seven months' taste of power. Given the outcome of the February 1982 election, one might infer that there was considerable public support for a serious approach to tackling the debt problem. As we have seen above, Fianna Fáil was edging towards this position when it was defeated on a motion of no confidence in early November 1982. The result was that in the second election of 1982, the budgetary issue was effectively neutralised and the election was fought mainly on the basis of such broad themes as stability and credibility (B. Farrell, 1987, p. 23).

Undoubtedly, Fine Gael's intention on being elected was to implement its austerity programme and to phase out the current budget deficit over a four-year period. In order to form a government, however, the party had to negotiate with the Labour Party and this led to the following formula: 'The phasing of the elimination of the current Budget deficit between now and 1987 will have to be undertaken with due regard to prevailing economic conditions, and in particular, to the importance of achieving economic growth and dealing with unemployment' (quoted in B. Farrell, 1987, p. 25). In the circumstances of continuing recession, rising unemployment and a renewal of emigration, a balancing of the twin aims of eliminating the budget deficit and at the same time emphasizing the 'importance of achieving economic growth and dealing with unemployment' was a gargantuan task. When it was being undertaken by two parties who, as time went on, increasingly interpreted every policy initiative and every economic statistic from different perspectives, the task became impossible:

> Within the Cabinet there was a growing rift between those whose first priority is a commitment to fiscal rectitude and those seeking to soften the impact of harsh measures; there was also disagreement in regard to the role of public and private enterprise. In time these disagreements would harden into a partisan division that would split the coalition.
>
> (Farrell and Farrell, 1987, p. 233).

In other policy areas, in which the two coalition partners either agreed or in which Fine Gael was freer to go its own way, significant policy initiatives were undertaken. The most significant was undoubtedly that in relation to the Northern Ireland problem and Anglo-Irish relations. FitzGerald launched inter-party talks encompassing all the constitutional nationalist parties in the island. The New Ireland Forum, as it was known, produced a report that in part glossed over and in part reconciled the conflicting approaches of Fianna Fáil and Fine Gael to the Northern Ireland problem. Its most important effect was to give FitzGerald a mandate to negotiate with the British Government in a new round of Anglo-Irish talks. The talks began with near disaster as Margaret Thatcher peremptorily ruled out all three options put forward in the Forum report. Rather than being put off, FitzGerald persisted and, marshalling an intense diplomatic effort, succeeded in bringing about a new relationship between the British and Irish Governments in a joint approach to the Northern Ireland problem, embodied in the Anglo-Irish Agreement of November 1985. Looked at from an Irish Government and Irish nationalist perspective, this was a major achievement. It was not, however, to be the basis for improving the electoral performance of Fine Gael.

Fine Gael, or rather FitzGerald, also embarked on a pluralist initiative. In a radio interview in October 1981 he announced a 'constitutional crusade', part of the purpose of which was to rid the constitution of its 'confessional' aspects. This crusade ran into severe difficulties when it came face to face with the insistent pressure for an anti-abortion amendment to the Constitution. Fine Gael, having initially, in an extremely tight electoral situation, committed itself to such an amendment, repeatedly attempted to defuse the issue and minimise the set-back to its pluralist programme. Its failure to do so culminated in the 1983 abortion referendum, which inserted a conservative anti-abortion clause into the Constitution. This experience increased both FitzGerald's and Fine Gael's caution in approaching the other pluralist issue – divorce. Under pressure from Labour, it eventually took on the issue in 1986, and again its reforming intentions received a decisive set-back. In the politics of both referendums, the conservatism of a section of the Fine Gael party played a significant role.

These were, however, diversions from the underlying preoccupation of government with the economy and the state of the public finances. On this issue the inevitable split between the two sides of the coalition government came in February 1987, when the Labour Party exercised its veto and withdrew from the government rather than accept an essentially Fine Gael-dictated retrenchment budget. Following a crushing electoral defeat for Fine Gael, FitzGerald resigned and was replaced by Alan Dukes, a former

Minister for Finance and for Justice, and FitzGerald's preferred successor. Dukes shared FitzGerald's commitment to social democracy and fiscal responsibility. With the Fianna Fáil minority government aggressively pursuing a policy of retrenchment, he adopted the logical strategy of conditional support for the government. The approach was not only adopted in practice, it was publicly articulated and defended by Dukes, most notably in a speech in Tallaght in September 1987. Responsible and logical as the Tallaght strategy may have been, it did not endear the new leader to Fine Gael activists in the constituencies, nor to his critics within the parliamentary party. However, the Tallaght strategy was balanced by an aggressive effort on Dukes's part to assert the primacy of Fine Gael over the Progressive Democrats. While Dukes's strategy may have been right in principle and even inevitable in practice (in so far as another general election was scarcely an attractive prospect for Fine Gael), it did not bring any benefit in terms of immediate support in the opinion polls or of significant gains in votes in the 1989 election. Consequently, when the party's candidate did disastrously in the 1990 presidential election (see chapter 10), Fine Gael unceremoniously dumped its newly acquired leader, replacing Dukes with John Bruton. This change was clearly designed to reverse the party's electoral fortunes. However, the results of the 1992 election suggested that either the party's problems went well beyond the issue of leadership or John Bruton was not the answer. In the wake of that election, the party, emulating a Labour Party tactic of the mid-1980s, established a commission to undertake a root and branch review of the party and its prospects. Though the report and recommendations of the Commission did not appear to have any immediate effect, the party's fortunes received a boost in a good European Parliament election performance and in by-election victories in Mayo West and Cork North Central in 1994. However, on the very day of the second of these by-election victories, a political crisis over the appointment of the President of the High Court rocked the government (see above). Throughout much of this protracted crisis, Fine Gael appeared unable to capitalize on the disarray in the government and, as noted above, it seemed as if the Fianna Fáil–Labour alliance would be patched up. However, as soon as Labour finally rejected going back into government with Fianna Fáil, three options, all of which included Fine Gael and Labour, opened up. The options were a right-of-centre three party coalition including the Progressive Democrats, a left-of-centre three party coalition including the Democratic Left instead of the Progressive Democrats, or a four party coalition that would have covered the entire political spectrum and so straddled the centre. Preliminary talks involving all four parties quickly resulted in the exclusion of the Progressive Democrats from the coalition equation, and a government consisting of Fine Gael, Labour and Democratic Left and led by Fine Gael's John Bruton was formed. As in 1948, the political fortunes of Fine Gael and, in this instance, the political fortunes of its leader, John Bruton, were given a significant boost by the imperative of forming a government that would exclude Fianna Fáil.

The Labour Party

The origins of the Irish Labour Party are a matter of some dispute. It has been argued that, contrary to the conventional wisdom, the Labour Party cannot claim to have been founded in 1912 (Gallagher, 1985, p. 68). According to this view, all that happened in 1912 was that the Irish Trades Union Congress passed a motion to the effect that 'the independent representation of Labour on all public boards be and is hereby included among the objectives of this Congress' (*ibid.*). In the turbulent decade that followed, little practical organisational work was undertaken, though there was some planning and programme writing. Gallagher concludes that 'Even by 1922, when Labour first contested a general election, the party still really existed only on paper . . .' (*ibid.*). The issue is partly a matter of terminology. It depends on what is meant by party. The fact is that there was a labour movement and it had spelled out its aspiration to elective political office as early as 1912. When the first significant opportunity to run for such office arose (the 1918 election), a decision to enter the contest was taken, a manifesto was drawn up, and a plan to put forward candidates for a significant number of the seats was envisaged. In the local elections of 1920, a large number of candidates ran under the Labour banner. According to one minimalist but widely accepted view, this is the defining activity of a political party. The fact that, under considerable pressure, Labour stood aside in 1918 to 'let the national issue be decided first' merely means that the party withdrew from that particular contest, not that the party did not exist.[29]

Labour's general election début occurred under the somewhat artificial circumstances of the 1922 'pact' election. Its achievement in winning 21 per cent of the vote was impressive. Whether one should regard this performance as a genuine good start that subsequently went wrong, or as an artefact of the peculiar circumstances of the pact election will be considered in chapter 4. In the meantime, there is no denying Labour's electoral marginalisation over the next decade and a half. At first, however, this was not accompanied by political marginalisation. For the first four years, Fianna Fáil's abstentionist policy made Labour the official opposition. Under the leadership of Thomas Johnson, the party put forward cautiously reformist policies and, while supporting the treaty, sought to redirect the agenda of politics towards social and economic issues. After Fianna Fáil's entry into the Dáil in mid-1927 it continued on its cautious path, its leadership refusing, for example, to support Fianna Fáil on the issue of withholding land annuities.

A symptom of the party's underlying electoral weakness was the defeat of two Labour leaders in two successive elections (Thomas Johnson in September 1927 and Thomas O'Connell in 1932). Following O'Connell's defeat, however, Labour chose a leader of remarkable durability – William Norton, who was to lead the party for the next twenty-eighty years. Norton was less conservative than his predecessors but his radicalism took the form of aligning the party with nationalism and with the newly

[29] The significance of that withdrawal is another aspect of the early history that has been hotly debated. Was it the cause of subsequent Labour weakness, or only a symptom? The answer to this question hinges on one's understanding of both the party system and its associated electoral alignments, and will be considered in the final chapter.

elected Fianna Fáil government, the votes of Labour Party deputies actually being essential to the formation of that government. The contrast is clear in Norton's attitude to the land annuities question, which he described as 'having been a millstone around the necks of the Irish people' (quoted in McKay, 1986, p. 33). Thus Norton's political rhetoric had more in common with a nationalist-inspired socio-economic radicalism of the Fianna Fáil type, rather than with socialist theory. The problem for the Labour Party was that 'if the party could identify with de Valera, then there was no reason why the ordinary Labour voter could not do likewise' (McKay, 1986, p. 33).

The party's origins made it a 'party of trade unionists for trade unionists',[30] and this limited its horizons and inhibited it from seeing itself as having either a majority vocation or a crusading role. Alignment with the trade-union movement also had the disadvantage of drawing the party into the bitter splits and rivalries that developed in the trade-union movement following the return to Ireland of James Larkin in 1923. These rivalries had a particularly adverse effect on Labour Party performance in Dublin in the 1920s and again after 1944. Following the separation of the Labour Party from the ITUC in 1930, there was a renewed organisational effort with a large number of branches being formed. The problem was that these branches were formed almost exclusively in constituencies with incumbent Labour TDs, and little or no effort was made to broaden the base of the party (McKay, 1986, p. 32).

In 1936, following the entry into the party of a number of leading socialist figures previously associated with minor left-wing parties (Coakley, 1990, p. 286), the party did include some radical phraseology in its new constitution and stated the aim of the party to be the 'establishment in Ireland of a Workers' Republic'. However, opposition from within its own ranks, combined with clerical pressure mediated by a union affiliated to the party, led to the removal of the offending matter and the party withdrew into caution and platitude again (Gallagher, 1982, pp. 12–13). A significant Labour recovery in the 1937 election brought it back to the level of support it had in 1923, and Fianna Fáil was again dependent on Labour to form a government. This was the last time for almost sixty years that such support was to be either offered or accepted, and in May 1938 Labour sided with Fine Gael to bring about a government defeat.

The early war years provided an opportunity for Labour in the form of rising prices, rising unemployment, wage control and anti-strike legislation. The 1943 election proved a dramatic success for the party but the hopes raised were short-lived. They were dashed in considerable part by an internal party squabble that actually led to the formation of a break-away party, the National Labour Party. The split had its origins in the inter-union dispute that had been going on since the 1920s, and it was exacerbated by a personal feud between William O'Brien, the General Secretary of the Irish Transport and General Workers' Union, and James Larkin. In the 1944 election the combined vote of the two parties was substantially down on Labour's 1943 vote.

Though Labour's performance in 1948 was no better than in 1944, circumstances offered the opportunity of participation in government, an opportunity which, despite the dominant position in the proposed coalition of the conservative Fine Gael party,

[30] Quoted in Gallagher, 1982, p. 4.

Labour had no difficulty in accepting. In the ensuing government, individual Labour ministers successfully pursued Labour objectives, for example, in the area of government-supported house building (Lee, 1989, p. 309). Labour as a whole, however, played a conservative role, particularly in relation to the major controversial issue that confronted that government – the Mother and Child Scheme. The option of participation in government was again available after the 1954 election, in which Labour had campaigned on its own policies while advocating the return of the coalition government (Gallagher, 1985, p. 77). The circumstances of that government were quite different from those of the first inter-party government. The country was in the middle of an acute economic crisis. Labour's acquiescence in the Government's severe austerity measures in 1956 alienated the trade unions and brought severe electoral retribution in the 1957 election. In the wake of the defeat, the party overwhelmingly rejected future participation in coalition government. This was more than an immediate reaction to an electoral drubbing: 'This decision . . . was the starting point of the policy which was to culminate in the 1969 election campaign . . . it was a conscious decision . . . to pursue an independent line' (Gallagher, 1982, p. 161).

If an independent line were to be pursued, new leadership would be required. Norton's conservative leadership has already been noted. After twenty-eight years, it was a tired leadership and in early 1960, in the wake of recent leadership changes in both Fianna Fáil and Fine Gael, Norton resigned. His successor was the forty-one-year-old Brendan Corish, TD for Wexford and a former Parliamentary Secretary. Over the next decade it was not just the party that changed; the leader changed with it. As one participant observer has put it, Corish 'might almost be regarded as a late developer', nudging his party towards positions 'one would not have expected from someone of his background' (Horgan, 1986, p. 37). The party broadened its membership, professionalised its headquarters, radicalised its programme and succeeded in recruiting a new type of candidate, including a number of prominent left-wing intellectuals. This process can be seen as having occurred in two phases – tentatively between 1960 and 1965 and more aggressively between 1965 and 1969. Labour's performance in the 1965 election was the best for more than twenty years. At its 1967 Conference the slogan was 'The Seventies will be Socialist' and the expectations invested in the 1969 election were so high that there was talk of a Labour government. Relative to these high hopes, the results in 1969 were 'a shattering disappointment' and were a major factor in the reversion to a coalition strategy in 1973 (Gallagher, 1985, p. 78).

From Labour's point of view, the policy balance sheet at the end of the 1973–77 period in office was mixed. The party could claim modest progress in the general area of redistributive policies and measures to protect workers against the effects of the recession of the early 1970s, but it failed to make any progress on its liberal agenda and it was unable to do anything to control the recession-induced problems of inflation and unemployment. Moreover, there was a price to be paid in terms of party unity. Very much a minority in the '70s, the anti-coalition faction, which feared a threat both to the socialist identity of the party and to the party's long-term electoral interests, became stronger as the decade-and-a-half of coalition politics begun in 1973 unfolded.

The debate between pro-coalitionists and anti-coalitionists was only one of many controversies that wracked the party in those years. The changes initiated in the 1960s had given the party a sense of mission and attracted controversial personalities, among them Noel Browne, Conor Cruise O'Brien, Justin Keating and David Thornley.[31] On the other hand, the changes did not make the party's conservative rural wing disappear. When this underlying conflict was combined with close relationships between the media and the party, the scene was set for searching – and at times searing – public debates, not just about socialist economics, but about political strategy, about church–state relations and about nationalism and the Northern Ireland problem. The latter debate, between traditional nationalists and revisionists, ended in victory for the latter and a significant shift away from the strongly nationalist position that had characterised the party since the 1930s.[32]

Following the defeat of the coalition in 1977, Labour consoled itself that, of the two coalition parties, Fine Gael had fared worse. Like Fine Gael, Labour elected a new leader, Frank Cluskey, but it did not radically alter its policies or organisation. It defused the issue of coalition by deciding to fight the next election on independent policies, authorising the party leader to negotiate a coalition arrangement, to be ratified by a special conference of the party in the event of no party having an overall majority. To its own surprise and disappointment, the party lost ground again in 1981. But so too did Fianna Fáil, and a coalition with Fine Gael was again on the cards. However, the Labour leader had lost his seat and the coalition negotiations were the responsibility of the new leader, Michael O'Leary. The government thus formed was short-lived and, given the austerity budget which was the occasion of the government's fall in February 1982, Labour was lucky to incur a vote loss of less than one percentage point. Michael O'Leary's tenure of office was also short-lived – he resigned in October 1982 and joined Fine Gael, following an annual conference decision that was in conflict with his preferred approach to the coalition question. Dick Spring, the new leader, immediately faced the November 1982 election and was rewarded with the opportunity to participate in what augured to be a stable coalition government. In this government, as we have seen, the Labour Party played a restraining role and when, at the end of 1986 and during the first weeks of 1987, it became obvious that Fine Gael would brook no further restraint on its plans to reduce public indebtedness, the Labour ministers resigned *en bloc*, precipitating the 1987 election.

Free of the constraints of government, Labour campaigned against public expenditure cuts, especially in the health services. It also reiterated its commitment to government intervention in the economy and to 'borrowing for productive investment' (Girvin, 1987, p. 23). As we shall see in chapter 4, Labour recorded its second lowest vote ever in February 1987. However, it managed to hold on to twelve seats, compared to fourteen at the dissolution of the Dáil. Given that there had been speculation that the Labour Party would 'return to the Dáil after the election in the back of a taxi', the

---

[31] On the intertwining of issues and personalities in the party in the period 1960 to 1985 see Horgan, 1986.

[32] For evidence of the impact of this on public perceptions of the party see ch. 6.

outcome in terms of seats was a significant consolation. On the other hand, the outcome confirmed the predictions of those in the party who had always opposed coalition and, after the election, Labour settled happily into an opposition role. The potential of this role was enhanced by the co-operation that Fine Gael was extending to the government. At times it seemed as if Labour was the real opposition and Labour Party leader Dick Spring capitalised on this opportunity, emerging as a strong presence in the Dáil.

Behind the scenes, a concerted effort to rebuild and reorient the party was under way. The 1985 Annual Conference of the Labour Party had approved the establishment of a 'Commission on Electoral Strategy'. This produced a wide-ranging report in September 1986, which, though too late to affect the party's approach to and performance in the election of February 1987, undoubtedly contributed to the sense of direction and purposefulness that was apparent in Labour's performance after 1987. In the 1989 election campaign, Labour could advocate its policies regarding the role of the state and its opposition to health cuts in particular, with the credibility derived from its spell in opposition; the fortunes of the party were restored to the level of November 1982. Spring's leadership image was further enhanced by his decision to promote the candidacy of Mary Robinson for the Presidency in 1990 (see chapter 10).

At the time, most observers expressed scepticism that the Robinson victory would translate into support for the Labour Party. The dramatic rise in support for Labour in the 1992 election might be seen to have confounded the sceptics. The relationship between the two outcomes is an interesting and important question which will be addressed in later chapters. What is undoubtedly the case, however, is that there was a continuity in style and approach between the Labour campaign in 1992 and the role played by Labour in the Robinson campaign. There was also continuity in another sense – the part played by Labour Party leader, Dick Spring, in the Robinson victory considerably enhanced his stature as a leader and that stature proved to be significant in the 1992 campaign. However, the 1994 European Parliament and by-election results put the party on notice that the durability of the swing to Labour in 1992 was by no means guaranteed. Some commentators took the view that the main threat to Labour's 1992 gains was the party's decision to go into coalition with Fianna Fáil after that election. Whether or not the problem was a real one, it was solved in December 1994 when, as a result of the political crisis over the appointment of the President of the High Court, Labour broke with Fianna Fáil and joined in forming a government with its erstwhile coalition ally, Fine Gael, and with its adjacent rival, Democratic Left.

The Progressive Democrats

The establishment of the Progressive Democrats was a direct result of the divisions in Fianna Fáil described above. Desmond O'Malley, a leading member of the dissident minority that developed within Fianna Fáil following the election of Charles Haughey as party leader, was expelled first from the Fianna Fáil parliamentary party (May 1984) and subsequently from the Fianna Fáil party organisation (February 1985), for articulating his dissent from the party line on two issues – the party's stance on the Report of the New Ireland Forum and the party's decision to vote against the government's Family Planning Bill. O'Malley linked the two issues in his speech in the Dáil debate on the Family Planning Bill, emphasizing the relevance of pluralism in the Republic to the search for a solution to the Northern Ireland problem, and proclaiming a renewed republican credo. The speech anticipated the new party's approach to these issues and was to define a significant proportion of the party's identity. The party was launched in December 1985 and the two founding TDs, O'Malley himself and another Fianna Fáil dissident, Mary Harney, were quickly joined by two other Fianna Fáil TDs and by a defector from Fine Gael. The latter – Deputy Michael Keating – was a particularly important recruit at the time in that he helped reduce the initial impression that this was simply a Fianna Fáil splinter group. Moreover, in terms of the make-up of the quickly swelling ranks of party activists, it became evident that the new party was much more than a disaffected rump of Fianna Fáil, as it drew members from Fianna Fáil and Fine Gael and especially from the ranks of those who had never been involved in party politics. At the voter level, too, it soon became evident that the party was in fact attracting more Fine Gael than Fianna Fáil support.

To the themes of a moderate approach to Northern Ireland and a pluralist approach within the Republic, the policy documents issued at the time of the party's first national conference in mid-1986 added an emphasis on the need for legal, institutional and bureaucratic reform, and spelled out specific programmes for controlling public expenditure and cutting taxation (Lyne, 1987, pp. 107–14). The latter were the policies with which the party became most clearly identified.

Popular support shortly after the foundation of the party was at a remarkably high level – 21 per cent in an opinion poll taken in February 1986 (Lyne, 1987, p. 109). The party performed very impressively (but below its own expectations) in its first general election (1987). Despite a poor showing in 1989, the parliamentary arithmetic created the option of coalition government with Fianna Fáil. This may not have been the mould-breaking exercise the Progressive Democrats originally promised but it was mould-breaking nonetheless, fundamentally altering the rules of government formation by forcing Fianna Fáil to abandon a 'core value' and agree to a coalition. The Progressive Democrats emerged from the 1992 election as a significant minor party, given the relative Dáil strengths of the various parties, but their coalition potential was reduced by greater policy compatibility between Fianna Fáil and Labour than between the Progressive Democrats and Labour. In early October 1993 Desmond O'Malley resigned as leader and was succeeded by co-founder and deputy leader Mary Harney. Her first challenge was to pull the party together after considerable internal division in the course of European Parliament elections of June 1994. In the political crisis of November 1994 she strengthened her leadership of the party by playing a significant role as an opposition leader in the Dáil. Despite this role, the Progressive Democrats were not included in the government formed as a result of the crisis. However, the fact that the government so formed was a left of centre coalition may serve to recreate the space which the Progressive Democrats had emerged to fill in the mid-1980s.

The Workers' Party/Democratic Left

Like so many Irish parties, the Workers' Party is the product of a split. In this case the split was that which took place in the IRA and in its political wing, Sinn Féin, in 1969–70. The overt issue was the movement's attitude to the legitimacy of the parliaments in Dublin, Belfast and Westminster, but underlying this was a division over both social and economic issues and, most ominously, over the relative emphasis on constitutional versus terrorist tactics. The respective camps became known as Official IRA/Official Sinn Féin (the majority and more pragmatic group in 1970), and Provisional IRA/Provisional Sinn Féin. In the course of the 1970s, Official Sinn Féin moved further and further away from militant nationalism and its associated campaign of violence, and more and more towards a purely political strategy based on a radical socialist approach and on a critique of traditional nationalism. The change was symbolised in 1977 by the alteration of the party's name to Sinn Féin The Workers' Party, the symbolism being completed in April 1982, when the party became simply the Workers' Party.

In the late 1970s the party adopted an orthodox Marxist-Leninist approach that became increasingly evident both in internal party decision-making and in its policies (Dunphy, 1992, pp. 22–4). The focus of the party's efforts was the urban industrial working class, and it was prepared to countenance some rather non-socialist measures, for example the policy of attracting multinational companies to invest in Ireland in order to build up the industrial base that was seen as a necessary precondition of the development of this class, and hence, of socialism. The strategy also involved the cultivation of close links with Eastern European regimes and with the Soviet Union. At the same time, successful participation in parliamentary politics was creating pressures towards the adoption of a democratic socialist approach. With the collapse of Communism in Eastern Europe, the conflict between the extra-parliamentary Marxist-Leninist elite and the parliamentary leadership of the party inevitably intensified.

The issue came to a head at an extraordinary party congress in February 1992, which was called to debate and decide on a motion proposing that the Workers' Party should be reconstituted as 'an independent democratic socialist party', repudiating 'any vestiges of "democratic centralism" as a method of organisation and . . . "revolutionary tactics" as a means of advancing the party's aims'.[33] The motion had been put forward by party leader Proinsias De Rossa, with the backing of the bulk of the party's parliamentary representatives. It failed to secure the necessary two-thirds majority and six of the seven TDs and the majority of the party's activists established a new party – the Democratic Left. As Dunphy puts it, it is Democratic Left 'which inherits the radical and permanent revisionism which has been a feature of the WP's political culture for two decades' (*ibid.*, p. 38). As we shall see in Chapter 4, it also inherited the major part of the support of the Workers' Party in the next (November 1992) election, though the combined support for the

---

[33] Quoted in Dunphy, 1992, p. 36.

two parties was considerably down on Workers' Party support in 1989. The revisionism of the new party was certainly radical is so far as, within three years of its foundation, the party was to be found sharing government with Fine Gael and the Labour party. In electoral terms, the potential benefits of this move were twofold: it represented the final step in the incorporation of the onetime revolutionary party into normal democratic politics and, at a more basic level, presented an opportunity to establish the new party's name and image in the minds of the voters.

The Green Party

The Green Party began in 1981 as the Ecology Party of Ireland. It went through something of a metamorphosis in 1983–84, emerging as Co-Aontas Glas/ Green Alliance. In the course of this change it took on a de-centralised, participative decision-making style associated with Green politics elsewhere (Farrell, 1989). However, by 1988, the underlying issue of the extent of the organisation's commitment to electoral politics was resolved in favour of electoral participation. The organisation was then renamed the Green Party/Co-Aontas Glas (Whiteman, 1990, p. 51). Its 1989 manifesto covered the full range of issues in addition to the environment – the economy, European integration, social issues and political issues and structures. Up to June 1994 the high points of its performance had been its 3.7 per cent in the 1989 European election, and its winning of a seat (not the same seat) in the 1989 and 1992 general elections. Then, in June 1994, it took two seats in the European Parliament elections, signalling that on the European front at least, it was a force to be reckoned with.

Other parties and independents

Under the label 'other' can be gathered a number of parties, varying considerably in size, whose common characteristic is that they have passed off (or never reached) the parliamentary stage. In addition to these, there is the important category of independents, important for their sheer size in the early years of electoral competition and important at various subsequent stages when, although reduced in number, they have played a vital role in the formation of parliamentary majorities. In between genuine minor parties and genuine independents there is a grey area, where we find little more than a label under which an individual or a number of individuals have contested elections.

Sinn Féin   When de Valera split from Sinn Féin at its 1925 Ard Fheis and went on to establish Fianna Fáil, he took with him a substantial number of the party's elected representatives and party activists, but by no means all. In the June 1927 election, Fianna Fáil emerged as the decisive winner in the contest with Sinn Féin, leaving the latter with only 3.6 per cent of the vote and five seats. That was the last election Sinn Féin contested until the mid 1950s. For much of the intervening period, Sinn Féin led a shadowy existence and maintained only a tenuous relationship with the IRA. However, in the early 1950s the IRA took the political initiative and the party reverted to the status of political wing of a military movement. Then in the 1957 election, in the midst of an IRA campaign of violence, mainly along the border with Northern Ireland, the party won just over 5 per cent of the vote and four seats (seats it did not take because of its continuing adherence to the policy of abstentionism).

Following the split of 1969–70, the main elements in Provisional Sinn Féin's stance were unqualified commitment to a terrorist campaign and opposition to any recognition of parliament. Sinn Féin was drawn into electoral politics in the Republic in support of the H-Block candidates in the 1981 election, and it followed up its relative success in this by contesting the February 1982 election in its own name. However, in the election of February 1982, with no emotive issue to stir up support, Sinn Féin won only 1 per cent of the vote. In 1986 the annual conference of the party formally ended the policy of abstention. In the light of the IRA's continuing campaign of violence and Sinn Féin's support for it, this move had little or no electoral impact. It remains to be seen whether the IRA cease-fire announced at the end of August 1994 and Sinn Féin's stated commitment to the peace process and to constitutional politics will improve the electoral prospects of the party.

The Farmers' Party   A party of the 1920s, the Farmers' Party was a classic 'sectional party'. It was a direct offshoot of the farmers' employer organisation, the Irish Farmers' Union. Despite this narrow base, it was a significant political force in the early 1920s. Apart from its commitment to the interests of larger farmers, or perhaps because of that commitment, it was unambiguously pro-treaty. A merger with Cumann na nGaedheal was proposed in 1927 but was vetoed by the Farmers' Union; the party leader thereupon joined Cumann na nGaedheal. Following the September 1927 election, the Farmers' Party supported the Cumann na nGaedheal government. In return, its new leader was made a parliamentary secretary. In the 1932 election the party was not much more than a loose federation of independent deputies, operating under the title National Farmers' and Ratepayers' League (Coakley, 1990, p. 282). This group formed the nucleus of the new National Centre Party in 1933 (see below).

The National League   The National League appeared at first sight to be a reincarnation of the Irish Parliamentary Party. It was founded by two former Irish Parliamentary Party MPs, one of whom was a son of John Redmond, the former leader of the Irish Parliamentary Party. The impression was reinforced by the fact that nine of its candidates in June 1927 'were former Irish Parliamentary Party Westminster MPs, another four had stood unsuccessfully for the Irish Parliamentary Party or one of its splinters, and at least nine others had been "associated with" the party' (Gallagher, 1985, pp. 100–1). The party was pro-treaty but it also emphasized cutting public expenditure and lowering taxation, while at the same time calling for spending on housing, transport and the development of natural resources. It acted for a time as the representative of two interest groups – town tenants and publicans.

The party's parliamentary performance did not match up to the promise of its gains in the June 1927 election. When Fianna Fáil entered the Dáil, Redmond, the National League's leader, undertook to support a Labour motion of no confidence in the government. This caused confusion in his own ranks and he was unable to deliver the promised support. At the election the following month it was evident that the League had disintegrated electorally as well, as it put forward only six candidates and was reduced to 1.6 per cent of the vote and two seats. The party was wound up in January 1931 and Redmond went on to stand as a Cumann na nGaedheal candidate in 1932. Ultimately five of the eight TDs elected for the National League in June 1927 went on to win seats for Cumann na nGaedheal/Fine Gael (Gallagher, 1985, p. 102).

The National Centre Party   The Centre Party was transitional, not just in the sense that it lasted for only one election, but more particularly in the sense that it facilitated the absorption of a number of politicians (from the Farmers' Party, from the ranks of the independents and from the National League) into Cumann na nGaedheal/Fine Gael. Though its origins were complex, it was in essence little more than 'a revival of the old Farmers' Party, with the addition of a few nationally-minded politicians such as Dillon and MacDermot' (Gallagher, 1985, p. 104).

Clann na Talmhan   The name literally translated means 'people of the land'. Clann na Talmhan, the first entirely new political party to arise since the foundation of the state, grew out of the felt grievances of small farmers in the west of Ireland. Though talks were held with representatives of the larger farmers and a link was formed with the eastern-based National Agricultural Party, the party remained the representative of the small farmers of the west, a role that was clearly perceptible in its programme. Its performance in its first election in 1943 was a very creditable 10.3 per cent, and unlike all other minor parties in snap election situations, it actually increased its vote in 1944. However, having survived that particular hurdle it succumbed on the long haul – its vote halved in 1948 and halved again in 1951. Ironically, it was when its vote had started to decline that it had most impact, participating in both inter-party governments in 1948–51 and 1954–57. It came to an end in the mid-1960s, with the death of one of its TDs and the decision of the other to stand down.

National Labour   National Labour was the product of a schism in the Labour Party that had its roots, as noted above, in a dispute within the trade-union movement. The immediate occasion was the readmission of James Larkin, leader of one side of a bitter inter-union conflict, to the Labour Party in 1941 and his election to Dáil Eireann in 1943. The other participant in the conflict, the ITGWU, attempted to have Larkin expelled from the party and when this failed, five out of the eight TDs who were members of the ITGWU rejected the party whip and went on to form their own party – National Labour. The split lasted through the 1944 and 1948 elections, National Labour campaigning on a conservative Labour platform, alleging that the Labour Party was under Communist influence. However, a process of reconciliation began when National Labour, contrary to the expectations of some, supported the formation of, and participated in, the inter-party government of 1948–51. The reconciliation was formally completed in June 1950 (Coakley, 1990, p. 286).

Clann na Poblachta   The origins of Clann na Poblachta lay in republican or extreme nationalist circles, drawing especially on their resentment at the treatment of republican prisoners and their sense that Fianna Fáil had reneged on its nationalist commitments. It also emphasized the egalitarian and radical aspects of Irish republicanism, attacked alleged political corruption, raised general economic issues and focused on some highly specific issues, such as the appalling tuberculosis problem and proposals for a massive programme of afforestation. Founded in mid-1946, it had reasonable time to organise before an election was due and it even had a dry run in the form of three by-elections which fell due at the same time and were held at the end of October 1947. Surprisingly, Clann na Poblachta won two of the three contests, in each case helped substantially by transfers from other opposition parties. De Valera responded by calling an election within just three months of the by-election defeats, the election being held in early February 1948. Perhaps the new party was made over-confident by its by-election successes, perhaps it simply became a victim of its own propaganda. Whatever the cause, Clann na Poblachta was over-ambitious in its approach to the election, with the result that a reasonably good performance (13.2 per cent of the vote) had all the appearance of a failure. (Admittedly, its share of the votes was not matched by even a nearly proportionate share of the seats – it won 10 of the 147 seats, i.e. 6.8 per cent.) Despite self-induced disappointment, Clann na Poblachta had the compensation of sharing in the formation of the government.

The role of Clann na Poblachta was notable for a number of reasons. In the first place, it was the intervention of Clann na Poblachta in the election that created the opportunity for a change of government for the first time in sixteen years. Secondly, it played an important part in one of the major policy initiatives of the period – the declaration of the Republic. Thirdly, in the person of Noel Browne, it spearheaded an effective campaign against tuberculosis. Fourthly, again through Noel Browne, it sought to introduce a 'Mother and Child Scheme', which proposed to provide free health care and health education to mothers and their children. The absence of a means test in the scheme was vehemently opposed by the medical profession. The Catholic hierarchy objected both to the provision of a universal scheme by the state and to the fact that the educational aspects of the scheme 'could cover topics, such as birth control and abortion, on which the Catholic Church has definite teaching' (Whyte, 1971, p. 214). Because of the prevailing conservative consensus on church–state relations and because of on-going conflicts between Browne and other members of the government, including Browne's party leader, Seán MacBride, the issue did not so much split the coalition, as isolate Browne from the other members of the government, who were happy to ensure that the features to which the

Catholic hierarchy objected were removed. The crisis erupted in a very public manner, with the forced resignation of Browne and the publication by him of the entire correspondence between members of the government and various bishops and spokesmen for the Catholic hierarchy in the three main national newspapers.[34] The fact that Seán MacBride, the leader of Clann na Poblachta, sided with Fine Gael's conservatism rather than with his radical, if troublesome, party colleague undermined the party's *raison d'être* and 'ruined whatever chance existed of an opening to the left in postwar Ireland' (Lee, 1989, p. 318).

Micro-parties and independents In the micro-party category there have been several notable cases on the left of the political spectrum. The Irish Workers' League, a grouping of ex-Communist Party members centred around the *Irish Worker* news-paper, edited by the militant trade unionist James Larkin, succeeded in winning a seat in Dublin in September 1927 (Coakley, 1990, p. 285). The National Progressive Democrats won two seats in 1961 (however, the two successful candidates – Noel Browne and Jack McQuillan – were already incumbent Independent TDs and the party merged with the Labour Party in 1963). The Socialist Labour Party won one seat in 1981 (Noel Browne again); and the Democratic Socialist Party, which was formed by independent Limerick socialist Jim Kemmy in 1982, won one seat in 1987 and 1989. It was disbanded when its TD, Jim Kemmy, rejoined the Labour Party after the 1989 election. Minor parties representing business interests had some success in the very early years of the state and performed the function of inte-grating ex-unionist and Protestant interests into the political process.

All of the parties mentioned above have succeeded in winning at least one seat in Dáil Eireann in at least one election. In addition to the parties so far mentioned, there have been a large number of other political affiliations, not counting the cat-egories of independent and non-party. Examples are Christian Democrat, Progressive Association, Ratepayers' Association, Town Tenants' Association, Clann Éireann, Ailtirí na hAiséirghe, Aontacht Eireann, and the Irish Republican Socialist Party.

In a sense the category of 'independents' is a residual and shifting one, its size depending on how much substance one attributes to ephemeral party labels. Chubb suggests two defining characteristics of the genuine independent: 'that he does not have behind him at election time the resources of any political party worth the name; and, second, that he does not take a party whip in the House' (Chubb, 1957, p. 132). While the latter is capable of precise measurement, the former is capable of wide variations in interpretation. Whether defined as micro-parties or as inde-pendents, elected representatives of this type played an important role up to and including the 1961 election. In the first ten years of the state's existence, inde-pendents were a relatively coherent group in the Dáil (Chubb, 1957, p. 136). By the early 1930s, however, they had either dropped out of political life or been absorbed, via the Centre Party, into Fine Gael. From 1933 on, independents appear as a less

---

[34] The correspondence is reproduced in full in Whyte, 1971, pp. 399–428.

distinctive group, though in the late 1950s Chubb identified four categories – Independent Farmers, Business Candidates, party dissidents and political oddities (Chubb, 1957, pp. 134–5). To these categories one might now add that of ideological (left-wing) independent. Acknowledging that they are a rather disparate category, it is nonetheless essential, given their size, particularly at certain periods, to take them into account in assessing trends in voting choice in chapter 4. First, however, it is necessary to take a more systematic look at what the parties have stood for, and at variations and fluctuations in the extent to which voters turned out to vote for them.

Chapter 3

Parties and voters: some quantitative evidence

In many theories of democracy, political parties play a crucial role by providing alternatives from which voters choose. But what if there are no differences between the parties? Carty, among others, has argued that this is precisely the situation in Ireland: 'The Irish party system is unique. In no other European polity does a small number of programmatically indistinguishable parties, each commanding heterogeneous electoral support, constitute the entire party system' (Carty, 1981, p. 85). One could argue the issue of the existence or non-existence of inter-party differences either way on the basis of the impressionistic evidence presented in the historical portraits of the parties in chapter 2. Perhaps the evidence for the early decades would be more conclusive and would point to the existence of differences in terms of constitutional and nationalist issues and, more intermittently, in terms of economic and social policy. In more recent times, the differences might seem to be reduced to the partisan allegation that Fianna Fáil has a 'political culture' that is averse to openness, transparency and democratic accountability and is prone to engage in 'strokes', backroom deals and generally unprincipled behaviour. In most political systems these kinds of allegations are levelled from time to time by all sides at all sides. Where, as in Ireland, one party has dominated government for substantial periods of time, that party is more often the target and some of the mud may stick. But are there any policy differences between the parties or are they indeed programmatically indistinguishable?

In order to answer this key question, it is necessary to turn to some systematic quantitative data on party images and inter-party differences. Such data derives from three sources – from samplings of expert opinion, from analyses of party manifestos, and from an examination of the perceptions and attitudes of party elites. In dealing with this evidence, it must be first of all be emphasized that it relates to different time points and, in so far as party images change, the images that emerge from these data will not be fully comparable. Secondly, the evidence relates to particular aspects of the parties, for example how they choose to present themselves in particular elections, or the attitudes and outlook of the party elite at a particular time. There is no guarantee that inter-party differences that may become apparent from these various sources of evidence will be consistent with one another. Acknowledging these difficulties and potential discrepancies, it should still be possible to piece the bits of evidence together in a way that fills out our understanding of the choices that have faced the voters.

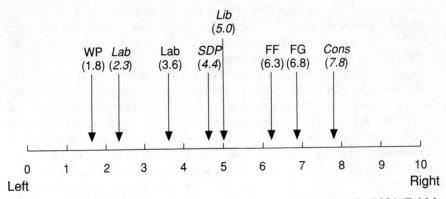

Figure 3.1 Placement of Irish and British parties on a left-right scale, 1984 (British parties in italics).

Before proceeding to the evidence, a few brief remarks are necessary regarding methodological assumptions and techniques. Discussions of party differences using the kinds of evidence mentioned above tend to be dominated by a spatial metaphor. The basic question is how close or far away the parties are from one another, and the very question implies that they can be located in a spatial framework. The most popular spatial metaphor is that of left and right, with the implication that parties can be placed along a single dimension – a straight line between two points or poles. Attractive as this simplification is, reality often seems to resist such procrustean treatment. There is no inherent reason why the space inhabited by parties should be one-dimensional, though, from the point of view of interpretation, there is an advantage if the number of dimensions is low (three or less), because they can then be visualised and graphically represented. Ultimately, the number of dimensions of inter-party difference in any party system is a matter to be empirically determined and in order to do this, political scientists have resorted to a variety of complex statistical techniques, such as factor analysis, discriminant analysis and multidimensional scaling. The discussion that follows adheres to the general approach to statistical techniques used in this book, i.e. presentation of the results in as straightforward a manner as possible, referring the reader interested in the technicalities to the source of the research.[1]

Expert judgements

If we want to know what, if anything, distinguishes one party from another, then one obvious way of going about the task is to ask a group of experts. In this case the experts are usually taken to be the political scientists specialising in the politics of the country concerned. The method involves using pre-defined scales on which the experts are asked to locate the parties. A comparative study conducted in the early 1980s focused exclusively on the left–right scale defined as follows: Ultra-Left (0); Moderate Left

[1] See Sinnott, 1986a for a review of different approaches to the spatial representation of political parties.

(2½); Centre (5); Moderate Right (7½); Ultra-Right (10). It was found that the Workers' Party had a mean score of 1.8, the Labour Party 3.6, Fianna Fáil 6.3, and Fine Gael 6.8. The results are presented graphically in Figure 3.1, which also includes the placings of parties in the United Kingdom.[2]

Important features of the Irish case are that the centre is unoccupied, that there is an almost complete lack of differentiation between the two largest parties in the system and that, in comparative perspective, the Labour Party is exceptional among European social democratic parties in its relatively right-wing scoring (Castles and Mair, 1984, p. 79). The comparison with parties in the United Kingdom is striking – there the gap between the two main parties is 5.5 points. Given such a range, it is not surprising that there are parties located in the centre – the main ones being the Liberals and the then newly-established Social Democratic Party. As noted above, this kind of left–right ordering of the parties has the merit of simplicity. Moreover, the picture of the Irish party system that it presents is plausible, though the unidimensional assumption involves the danger of leaving something essential out. The fact that the approach fails to differentiate between Fianna Fáil and Fine Gael suggests that this may well be the case.

The problem arising from the imposition of a single *a priori* scale can be overcome by presenting the experts with a variety of scales on which to place the parties, and then asking them both to place the parties and to rate the salience of these various scales, or policy dimensions, in the system in question. This approach has been adopted in a wide-ranging comparative study by Laver (Laver and Hunt, 1992; Laver, 1994). The study has the additional merit of obtaining responses from a much larger number of experts and of having been carried out twice (1989 and 1992).[3] The first study used eight pre-defined policy scales, allowing the respondents in the survey (the experts) to introduce additional scales specific to the country in question if they felt this was necessary. The two most salient dimensions in the majority of countries surveyed were 'Promote raising taxes to increase public services versus promote cutting public services to cut taxes' and 'Promote versus oppose permissive policies on abortion and homosexuality' (Laver and Hunt, 1992).[4] Although these two dimensions also figured prominently in the Irish case, a further dimension was added by the Irish experts, a dimension defined as 'Promote versus oppose permanent British presence in Northern Ireland'. This dimension – referred to as 'Northern Ireland policy' – was rated as considerably more salient than the abortion/homosexuality dimension that was one of the two dominant features of party differences elsewhere in Europe. As there is a close correlation between the placing of the parties on the Northern Ireland policy and the abortion/homosexuality dimensions, Laver argues that, for the purpose of comparing the structure of the policy spaces within which parties operate in Ireland to that in other countries, one can drop the Northern Ireland policy dimension and

---

[2] In examining the placing of parties cross-nationally, Castles and Mair emphasise that such comparisons must be tentative (Castles and Mair, 1984, p. 83).

[3] There were thirty-two respondents in the second Laver survey, compared to six in the Castles and Mair study.

[4] This abortion and homosexuality policy scale is referred to as 'social policy' by Laver and Hunt. In order to avoid possible confusion, it will be referred to here as 'policy on abortion and homosexuality'.

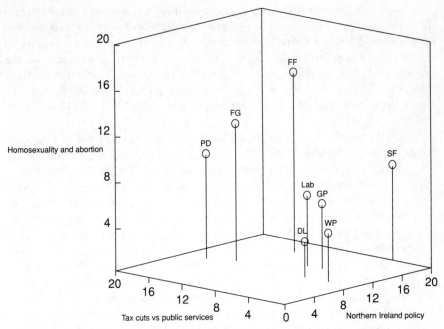

Figure 3.2 Placement of Irish political parties on three policy scales, 1992.

concentrate on the tax cuts versus public services and abortion/homosexuality dimensions which are common to all systems.[5] However, for the purpose of building up a picture of the actual differences between the parties, it is preferable to retain the three separate dimensions. Accordingly, the positions of the political parties are plotted on three dimensions in Figure 3.2.

Opposite points of the tax cuts versus public services scale (20 = promote cutting public services to cut taxes; 0 = promote raising taxes to increase public services) are occupied by the Progressive Democrats and the Workers' Party. Grouped fairly close to the Workers' Party position are Labour, the Democratic Left and the Green Party. Fine Gael is located close to the Progressive Democrat position and Fianna Fáil occupies a more or less centrist position. Predictably, on the Northern Ireland scale (20 = oppose permanent British presence in Northern Ireland; 0 = promote permanent British presence in Northern Ireland), Sinn Féin is at the extreme end, ranged against the Democratic Left at the opposite end. Fianna Fáil is relatively close to Sinn Féin on this dimension, and all the other parties are towards the less nationalist end, not too far from the Democratic Left position. Note that the positioning of the parties on the

[5] On the basis of such a comparison, Laver concludes that 'there seems nothing particularly peculiar about the ideological configuration of the Irish parties. They seem to fit very well with one of the major European party constellations – the Mediterranean type that is characterised by the confrontation between a divided left, on the one hand, and a powerful pole of populist nationalism, on the other – a constellation that is typically found among the catholic countries of southern Europe' (Laver, 1992, p. 376). This view will be considered when the question of comparability is addressed in chapter 11.

scale is somewhat lop-sided, as no party is seen as strongly promoting the British presence in Northern Ireland. On the homosexuality and abortion scale (20 = oppose permissive policies on abortion and homosexuality; 0 = promote permissive policies on
abortion and homosexuality), Fianna Fáil is at the conservative end and the
Democratic Left at the liberal end. The other 'left' parties and the Greens are fairly
close to the Democratic Left; the Progressive Democrats are in the middle and Fine
Gael is in between the Progressive Democrats and Fianna Fáil, but closer to the
Progressive Democrats.

In summary, while there are individual political scientists who argue that there are
no differences between the parties, the consensus among political scientists specialising in Irish politics seems to be that significant differences do exist. In terms of
groupings of like-minded parties, the left-wing parties plus the Greens form a fairly
tight grouping on all three issues, in a position that is distinguishable from the
Progressive Democrats and Fine Gael on tax cuts versus public services, and from
Fianna Fáil in terms of both Northern Ireland policy and policy on homosexual-
ity/abortion and, to a lesser extent, on tax cuts versus public services. Fianna Fáil
tends to be distinctive *vis-à-vis* all groups on all three dimensions, though the main
difference between it and the Fine Gael/Progressive Democrat pairing is, firstly,
Northern Ireland policy and, secondly, homosexuality and abortion.

We must remember that these conclusions are based on a consensus among experts.
There is always the danger that such a consensus is self-sustaining – the experts talk
to the experts, read one another's books and academic articles and so the consensus is
generated and reinforced. It is essential to turn therefore to more direct evidence of
party differences for confirmation of these conclusions.

Party manifestos

One source of direct evidence is the way in which the parties have presented themselves in elections. The evidence comes from an analysis of party manifestos and quasi-
manifestos for the period 1948–82 focusing mainly on the period 1961–82 (Mair,
1987a). The methodological approach in this case is to subject the party manifestos or
surrogate manifestos for each election in the period covered to a form of content analysis, in which key themes are identified and their frequency of occurrence is measured.
Resort to surrogate manifestos is necessary because, until relatively recently, Irish
parties did not produce single documents that could be regarded as the definitive party
manifesto. Surrogate manifestos are party leader's speeches, radio broadcasts, newspaper reports, and so on.

The picture of Irish party competition that emerges from this analysis is notable first
of all for the considerable overlap between the appeals of the parties. Thus, it emerges
that seven of the ten most frequent themes in Fianna Fáil and Fine Gael election manifestos were common to both parties. The seven themes were social group interests, productivity, expansion of social services, government authority, governmental efficiency,
enterprise and national effort. Furthermore, five of the above themes also occurred in
Labour Party manifestos. Does this mean that Irish political parties are all identical? No,

but it does mean that the differences are differences of degree and of emphasis rather than outright conflict. The differences arise both because the parties put a different order of priority on the themes they share, and because there are themes that are specific to each party. The themes emphasized by Fianna Fáil and not by Fine Gael were defence of the Irish way of life, law and order and Irish unity. In their place Fine Gael emphasized social justice, economic orthodoxy and a controlled economy. The two Labour themes not shared by either of the other two parties were freedom and democracy and quality of life.

If the use of a single left–right scale risks excluding too much detail and oversimplifying the differences and relationships between the parties, the content analysis of manifestos runs the opposite risk, that of overwhelming us with detail. This problem can be overcome by means of a factor analysis of the data, leading in this case to the reduction of the wide range of particular differences to seven dimensions, ranked in terms of their importance. The most important dimension to emerge from this analysis was the opposition between a social democratic appeal on the one hand, and a corporatist appeal on the other. The social democratic appeal emphasizes egalitarianism, social justice and interventionism in economic affairs. The opposite, corporatist end of the dimension is defined by three themes: an appeal to the national interest and social solidarity, a stress on economic growth and productivity and an emphasis on strong government. Although party positions on this primary dimension varied somewhat from election to election, a consistent pattern can be discerned and plotted over time (see Figure 3.3). The three parties start out on the corporatist ideology side of the dimension in 1961 but from there on a clear contrast emerges between Fianna Fáil on the one hand and Fine Gael and Labour on the other. Fine Gael in fact moved earlier and further than Labour. On the basis of the 1965 manifestos, it was substantially further towards the left than Labour and, surprisingly, was still to the left of Labour in 1969, albeit only slightly. In 1973 and 1977, the two parties shared the same manifestos but it is interesting to note that these were located at quite different points on the spectrum (see Figure 3.3). In 1981, the trajectories of the parties diverge, until in February 1982 Fine Gael actually appears to the right of Fianna Fáil. However, in its manifesto for the November election of that year, it crossed back over to a left of centre position, not far from that of the Labour Party.[6]

In terms of the objective of understanding the context of electoral choice and, in particular, of tackling the question of whether there are any significant differences between the parties, the picture in Figure 3.3 is extremely useful. Unfortunately we do not have similarly detailed content analyses of party manifestos for elections after 1982. However, the manifestos in the 1987 election have been impressionistically examined from the same analytical perspective, and the results suggest that in 1987 Fine Gael did shift to the right again, advancing a platform that was different only in degree from that advocated by the Progressive Democrats (Mair, 1987b). Simultaneously, Labour shifted to the left, in part in reaction to the coalition experience with Fine Gael and in part in order

---

[6] Mair, 1987a, pp. 189–92; see also Mair 1987b, pp. 30–34, which provides a convenient summary of the argument.

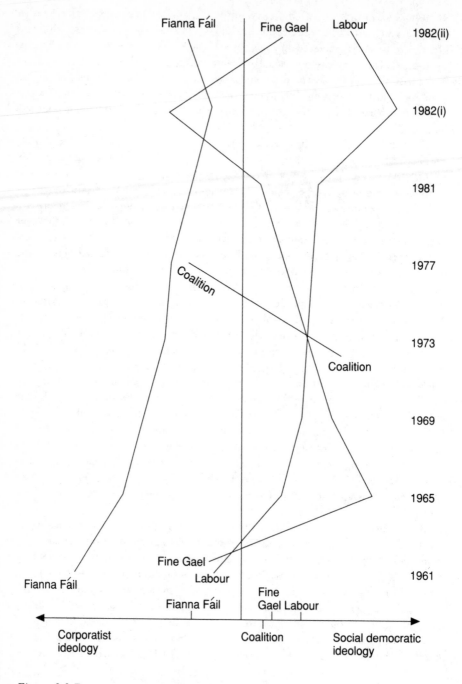

Figure 3.3 Party movements along the corporatist/social democratic ideological dimension, 1961–82.

to compete with the advancing Workers' Party. In the case of Fianna Fáil, the analysis argues that in the mid-1980s the party attempted to 'resurrect the ghost of de Valera and to revive its traditional shibboleths in an effort to compensate for the declining appeal of Lemass style corporatism' (Mair, 1987b, p. 41). In the actual election, however, the party reverted to its platform of the 1961–82 period, emphasizing in particular a cross-class corporatist appeal. Overall, the situation in 1987 confirms the trend of the previous twenty years as far as Fianna Fáil is concerned, but indicates a fragmentation of the social democratic pole of the dimension that had dominated electioneering from 1961 to 1982. Fine Gael and Labour did not just break up as a coalition government in 1987 – they parted company in policy terms, one moving to the right and the other to the left. This put Fianna Fáil in the centre of the political spectrum.

Somewhat surprisingly, in view of the 1987 Programme for National Recovery and the 1991 Programme for Economic and Social Progress,[7] Mair's analysis of the party positions in and after the 1989 election does not identify a corporatist appeal on the part of Fianna Fáil. Rather, it portrays the main dimension of party competition as a straightforward left/right socio-economic dimension, with the Workers' Party on one end, Progressive Democrats on the other, Fine Gael in the centre, Labour left of centre and Fianna Fáil right of centre (Mair, 1990, pp. 214–16). Note that, in contrast to the party positions on the corporatist-social democratic dimension in 1987, the centre position in this analysis of the 1989 election was occupied by Fine Gael. The analysis of the 1989 election suggests that one other, subordinate, dimension exists in the system, that is, traditional religious and nationalist values on the one hand versus secularist and pluralist values on the other. This dimension pits the Workers' Party at one end against Fianna Fáil at the other, with the Progressive Democrats in the middle (*ibid.*).

Two general conclusions can be drawn from this analysis of the nature of the appeals that the parties put before the electorate. First, the findings 'cast doubt on the notion that the parties are programmatically indistinguishable' (Mair, 1987a, p. 169). Secondly, it is clear that economic issues predominate over traditional nationalist issues or over the problem of Northern Ireland in the appeals of the parties. The explanation of this relative lack of emphasis on nationalism or the Northern Ireland issue lies in the distinction between the dimension or domain of identification and the dimension or space of competition (Mair, 1987a, p. 141). The domain of identification refers to the terms in which certain voters identify with a party. The dimension or space of competition, on the other hand, refers to the dimension along which 'lie the non-identified partisans or floating voters for which it is rewarding to compete' (Sani and Sartori, 1983, p. 330). For obvious reasons, manifestos are likely to be dominated by items in the domain of competition. However, the dimension of identification is an integral part of each party that contributes to defining how it differs from the other parties and is an essential element in the maintenance of the loyalty of its core supporters. It may not be much talked about during campaigns and there is not

---

[7] These were comprehensive agreements covering not just pay but also aspects of broad policy areas such as taxation and public expenditure, which were negotiated between government, the employers' and farmers' organisations and the trade unions.

much point in putting it in a prominent place in the manifesto, but, for the party stalwarts, it is part of what the party is and is a vital element in their voting choice. Of course, if all voters took their cues as to what the parties stand for from the manifestos, and only from that source, the question of what the parties put in or leave out for tactical reasons would not matter – the party manifesto would be the party image for the purpose of electoral choice. But parties are more than their manifestos. Behind the manifesto there is a complex reality that is to some extent reflected in the portraits in chapter 2, that in part finds its way into the manifestos and that can be further probed by looking at the attitudes of the party elite.

The attitudes of party elites

Here again we encounter a limitation of the data – the party elite will always be a particular body of individuals and, unless we have recurrent elite surveys, the evidence of their outlook will be time-bound. The available evidence relates to two time points: 1974–75 and 1983. The methodologies underlying the two sets of evidence differ considerably. The 1983 evidence comes from a mail survey of all TDs, to which 72 (i.e. 43 per cent) responded (Gallagher, 1985, pp. 143–4). The survey used a scale somewhat similar to that used by Castles and Mair (see above) and asked the TDs to place themselves and the other parties on it. The self-placement results, which are shown in Figure 3.4, show some similarities to those in the comparable expert survey (see Figure 3.1) – Fianna Fáil and Fine Gael place themselves quite close to one another on the ten-point scale (Fianna Fáil 5.8 and Fine Gael 5.1). Note, however, that the left–right positioning is the reverse of that in the expert survey (i.e. Fianna Fáil is to the right) and both parties place themselves significantly closer to the centre in comparison with the placement by the experts. Similarly, Labour deputies place themselves slightly further left on the scale (2.8) relative to where the experts place the party. In addition to the self-placement shown in Figure 3.4, the survey asked the respondents to place their own and the other parties on the scale. The interesting finding here is the tendency for Fianna Fáil respondents to place Fine Gael well to the right of their own party, and for Fine Gael respondents to do precisely the

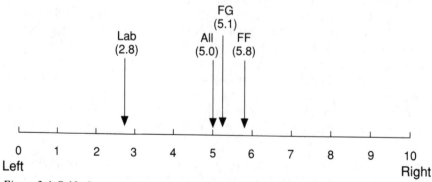

Figure 3.4 Self-placement of members of the Dáil on a left–right scale, by party, 1983.

reverse, that is, to claim that the Fianna Fáil party is well to the right of Fine Gael. The Labour Party respondents in the survey took a rather nuanced view, placing the Fine Gael party as a whole to the right of Fianna Fáil, but reversing the ordering in the case of the parliamentary parties. Labour was in coalition with Fine Gael at the time.

These findings are of considerable interest but they suffer from the two weaknesses of the left–right scale – the imposition of a single dimension, and the fact that we cannot be certain what respondents have in mind when they use the term. A more exploratory and comprehensive investigation of elite perceptions and attitudes in the mid-1970s, involving lengthy oral interviews with a stratified sample of seventy-five members of the twentieth Dáil (1973–77), goes some way towards solving the problem.[8] Transcriptions of the interview tapes provide rich contextual material, firstly, on politicians' perceptions of party differences (in response to the question 'What do you see as the major differences between the parties in Ireland today?'), and secondly, on the actual differences that emerged when the politicians were asked to discuss substantive problems (e.g. economic problems and Northern Ireland). As a third measure of inter-party differences at elite level, the interviews included a question asking respondents to rank twelve prominent politicians (four from each of the three main parties) in terms of closeness to their own political outlook. This question was designed to produce data suitable for multidimensional scaling and, as will be explained below, it provides an opportunity for an open-ended exploration of the dimensions of inter-party differences. In sum, these data provide three measures of inter-party differences as exhibited by the political elite in the mid-1970s – perceptions of difference, attitudes to issues and rankings of leading politicians from the three main parties.

In describing party differences, two-thirds of the politicians interviewed gave accounts that implied at a minimum the existence of important differences between the parties. The proportion positing significant differences between the parties rises to three-quarters if we include those who took the view that there were important differences between the parties, but there were also some exceptions in the form of parties or sub-groups within parties that were similar. Four main features dominated these accounts of inter-party differences. The first was group representation. This frequently embodied the claim to cross-sectional representation, as in the case of the Fianna Fáil TD who said 'my own party . . . would be the most broadly based. Would have a wider viewpoint, the collective wisdom of a broadly based party that caters for every single section of the community'.[9] The second feature is nationalism, often referred to in terms of the notion of 'national outlook'. National

---

[8] The sample was a disproportional stratified sample, designed not to be representative of the Dáil as a whole but to focus on the parliamentary elite. It consisted of all current and former government ministers and opposition front-benchers, 15 notable back-benchers (identified as such by the political correspondents of the main national newspapers), and 18 deputies randomly selected from the remaining back-benchers. The response rate was 83 per cent among government and opposition front-benchers and 94 per cent among back-benchers. Interviews lasted on average one-and-a-half hours. For a fuller discussion see Sinnott, 1983, 1986a, 1986b.

[9] This quotation and those that follow come from the interviews with the sample of TDs described in footnote 8.

outlook is a subtle sort of term, the flavour of which is captured in the following excerpt from a Fianna Fáil TD: 'I would say, I don't know whether I said this earlier on, but the reason why I joined Fianna Fáil was because I saw in it a party which has a tradition . . . I saw in it the party which by tradition, by aim, was the one which would best cater for my aspirations as an Irishman, having what I would regard as a national outlook and I think that Fianna Fáil has that, more so than any of the other parties'. A Fine Gael TD, while rejecting the validity of 'national outlook' as a basis of party difference, confirmed that it is resorted to as such:

> I honestly think that Fianna Fáil is the party of shamming and humbug, affecting if you like a special kind of Irishness, it is not only skin deep but in fact is a film on a glass – leave it for a moment and it is blown away and disappeared. They set up to be more nationally minded, and attach great importance to the word 'republican' and all that arid stuff. In fact it means absolutely nothing, they have done no more than anybody else . . .

Thirdly, in the discussion of what differentiates the parties, there were references to general socio-political attitude (left versus right; radical/liberal or progressive/ reform-ist versus conservative). These terms are not necessarily used in an ideological sense, at least not in the specific ideological sense of, for example, socialism versus capitalism. In fact one Fine Gael TD, who used the terms left and right to apply both to class-related issues and to nationalism, concluded by saying 'having said all that, at the end of it all, Irish people are non-ideological, anti-ideological and the parties are non-ideological because they reflect the Irish people who don't want ideology anyway'. Fourthly, and finally, there was the category of named ideology–most often socialism versus capitalism.

Broadly speaking, these differences identified by the political elite tend to confirm conclusions drawn from the manifesto analysis for the same period, with Fianna Fáil emphasising cross-sectional representation (a notion quite compatible with the corporatist emphasis in its manifestos), Fine Gael emphasizing broad socio-political attitude (compatible with the social-democratic appeal in its manifestos) and Labour most likely to mention ideological differences. However, in contrast to the results of the manifesto analysis, nationalist differences emerge much more prominently in polit-ical elite discourse. This is presumably because, while they do not figure prominently in direct electoral appeals, for tactical reasons, they are in fact quite fundamental to the identities of the parties.

These inter-party differences, elicited in response to the direct question: 'What do you see as the main differences between the parties?', could perhaps be discounted as the self-serving rationalisations of individuals whose professional identity is bound up with the notion of distinct and competing parties. It is important to emphasize, there-fore, that when the politicians were asked to discuss the problems of the economy and Northern Ireland, consistent patterns of difference emerged between them. In order to identify these patterns, the transcribed recordings of the interviews were content-analysed with a view to producing measures of the frequency of occurrence of symbols or themes. These data can then be used either to provide a detailed item by item description of party differences in a given issue area,[10] or as input to a statistical tech-

[10] See, for example, Sinnott, 1986b.

nique designed to reduce the multiplicity of themes to some common dimensions. The latter approach is the most relevant here. The technique in this case is discriminant analysis, which both 'predicts' the party affiliations of individual respondents, on the basis of the symbols and themes that occur in their discussions, and produces a plot of the positions of the individual party politicians and the average positions of the parties along the dimensions that emerge (Sinnott, 1986a).

The first point to be made about the outcome of the analysis is that the success rate in predicting party affiliation solely on the basis of the themes occurring in the discussions is considerable. Prediction was successful in 97 per cent of cases, that is, in the vast majority of cases, it was possible to tell which party a politician belonged to solely on the basis of analysing the way he or she discussed the problems of the economy and Northern Ireland. This adds considerably to the mounting evidence against the view that there are no policy-related or programmatic distinctions between the parties. This predictive success is based on placing the respondents on two dimensions. The first is a left–right socio-economic dimension, identified in terms of five variables or themes – socialist economy, economic orthodoxy, social justice, incentives and group benefits. The second is best described as a less nationalist versus more nationalist dimension, in which the key variables are the tendency to prefer a solution to the Northern Ireland problem based on co-operation and reconciliation within Northern Ireland, the policy of laying less emphasis on the demand for a United Ireland in public utterances, and an approach to the problem that gave high priority to taking action against the IRA.

Figure 3.5 shows the position of the respondents from the three main parties and the average position of each party in the two-dimensional space. It shows that Fine Gael respondents were distinguishable from Fianna Fáil mainly along the vertical, i.e. the nationalist dimension. Looked at in terms of the horizontal (left–right) dimension, the two groups occupied very similar positions, with Fianna Fáil slightly right of centre and Fine Gael in the centre. The Labour Party parliamentary elite was located mainly in the lower left-hand quadrant, distinct from Fianna Fáil along both the nationalist and left–right dimensions, and from Fine Gael just in terms of left and right. There is also evidence, however, of a considerable spread of Labour deputies along the left side of the spectrum, from the two deputies who were almost indistinguishable from Fine Gael, to their two party colleagues who were quite far to the left.

The data on which this analysis is based was derived from explicit questions put to political elites regarding the problems of the economy and Northern Ireland. Such a procedure involves the danger that some other dimension of difference that is not relevant to these two issues might exist, and might fail to be identified by this particular approach. There is some evidence that this may have been the case because the more exploratory technique of asking politicians to rank-order a set of twelve prominent political figures, and then subjecting the data to multidimensional scaling analysis, reveals a dimension that otherwise did not emerge in the interviews – the confessional–non-confessional dimension. The twelve politicians chosen as stimuli for this exercise were all prominent politicians, and were either ministers or former ministers and members of the Opposition front bench. They were chosen because of their prominence and because they were thought to represent a range of political positions

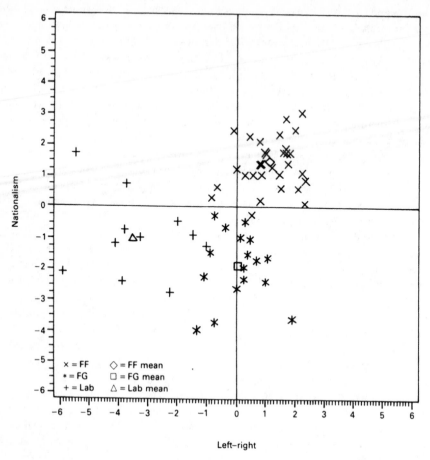

Figure 3.5 Plot of party elites on discriminant functions derived from analysis of discussions on the economy and the Northern Ireland problem (1974–75).

and views. The list of names is: Dick Burke (FG), George Colley (FF), Brendan Corish (Lab), Liam Cosgrave (FG), Conor Cruise O'Brien (Lab), Garret FitzGerald (FG), Charles Haughey (FF), Justin Keating (Lab), Jack Lynch (FF), Dessie O'Malley (FF), Richie Ryan (FG), and Jimmy Tully (Lab).

The respondents in the elite survey were handed twelve cards (eleven, if the respondent was one of the politicians named above), each card having the name of one of the 'stimuli'. Respondents were then asked to 'arrange the cards so that the top one is the one closest to your own political outlook, the next one the next closest and so on'. On the basis of these rankings, multidimensional scaling produces an n-dimensional spatial representation that reflects the proximities and distances expressed in the data. In this case the statistical analysis produced a two-dimensional space. The statistical analysis does not, however, indicate in substantive terms how the dimensions of the

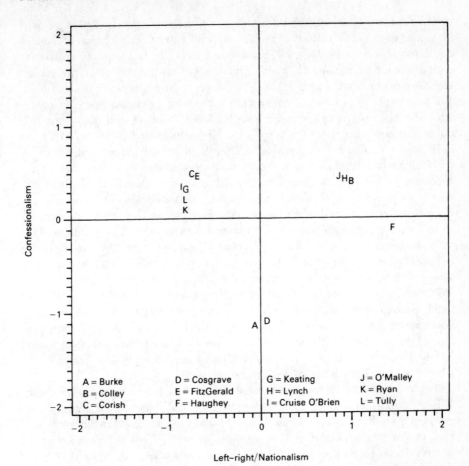

Figure 3.6 Multi-dimensional scaling of party elite preference rankings (1974–75): stimulus configuration.

spatial representation ought to be interpreted. Interpretation depends on the positions of the twelve politicians in the space, and on what is known about what each of them stands for. This kind of interpretation obviously involves considerable contextual knowledge of the political situation at the time, as well as a certain element of subjectivity. The space that emerges as a result of the dimensional analysis of the rankings of these twelve politicians by the political elite is shown in Figure 3.6.

The horizontal dimension in Figure 3.6 contrasts the positions of the four Fianna Fáil politicians on the right-hand side with the positions of six of the prominent politicians (four Labour plus FitzGerald and Ryan of Fine Gael) on the left. The other two Fine Gael politicians (Burke and Cosgrave) are located in the middle of this dimension. At first sight this looks very much like a conventional left-right arrangement. The proximity of FitzGerald to the Labour politicians is understandable in terms of his involvement over the years in the effort to move Fine Gael to the left, and in terms of his role as one of the architects of the alliance with Labour. The location of Ryan in this group is also intelligible – as Minister for Finance he had been responsible for capital taxation legislation, which, though comparatively mild in intent, had earned him the nickname 'Red Richie'.[11] On the other hand, the horizontal dimension could also be interpreted in terms of nationalism – contrasting the positions of Haughey, who, since the 1970 Arms Crisis, was associated with those in Fianna Fáil advocating a more strongly nationalist policy *vis-à-vis* Northern Ireland, with that of Cruise O'Brien, the Labour Party spokesman on Northern Ireland and an acerbic critic of nationalism. In sum, the horizontal dimension cannot be given a single clear inter-pretation – it appears to be a combination of left–right and nationalist differences, and thus to incorporate the two dimensions that were separately identifiable on the basis of the more issue specific data derived from the discussions of contemporary problems.

In contrast to the ambiguity of the horizontal dimension, the interpretation of the vertical dimension in Figure 3.6 seems clear and self-evident. It pits Burke and Cosgrave of Fine Gael against the other ten politicians. This presumably reflects the distinctive stance of Burke and Cosgrave, which was dramatically and publicly signalled in July 1974 when, on a free vote, both voted against legislation designed to liberalise Ireland's highly restrictive laws on the availability of contraceptives, legislation introduced by the government of which one was Taoiseach, and in which the other was a minister. On the basis of this, combined with the generally conservative and traditional views expressed by both Burke and Cosgrave on a range of related issues, the vertical dimension can be labelled 'confessionalism versus non-confessionalism'.

Figure 3.6 extends our understanding of the issue space of Irish politics in the mid-1970s. It confirms the existence of the left–right and nationalist differences that emerged from the analysis of the substantive discussions, and it adds a further dimen-sion, that of confessionalism and non-confessionalism. Of course, Figure 3.6 merely points to the existence of these dimensions. In order to see the extent to which they dif-ferentiate the parties, it is necessary to examine the location of the individual members of each of the parties. This is done in Figure 3.7, which places the individual respon-dents in the space defined in Figure 3.6. An individual's location is determined by the proximities and distances underlying his or her ranking of the stimuli. The *horizontal* left–right/nationalist dimension does separate the parties, with Labour on the left and/or less nationalist end of the spectrum and Fianna Fáil on the right and/or more nationalist end. The bulk of Fine Gael deputies interviewed lie slightly to the right of centre, in a position that is distinguishable from both Fianna Fáil on the one side and Labour on the other. It is notable that very few Fine Gael deputies are to be found in the Labour-FitzGerald-Ryan area defined in Figure 3.6. The *vertical* (confessional) dimen-sion divides Fianna Fáil and Labour, on the one hand, from a section of Fine Gael iden-tified with the Burke-Cosgrave position. It is apparent, however, that Fine Gael was internally divided, with a majority of Fine Gael respondents closer to Labour and Fianna Fáil on this dimension than to the confessional wing of their own party.

[11] For a brief description of this measure and the political background to it see Sinnott, 1989.

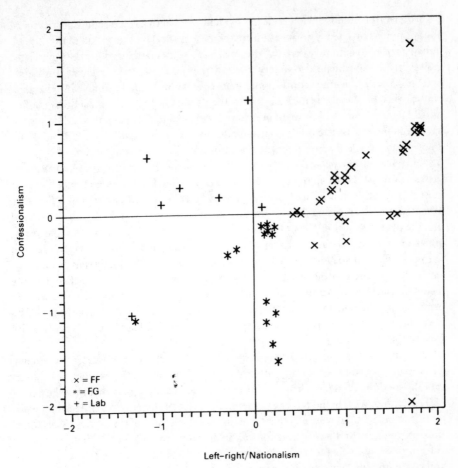

Figure 3.7 Multi-dimensional scaling of party elite preference rankings (1974–75): subject configuration.

In summary, evidence of the perceptions, attitudes and orientations of party elites in the 1970s points to considerable inter-party differentiation along three dimensions – left versus right, less nationalist versus more nationalist and confessional versus non-confessional. The differences identified can be seen to have been at work in relation to the capital taxation issue in the 1970s, in relation to policy on Northern Ireland in the late 1970s and early 1980s, and in relation to the issues of divorce and abortion in the early to mid-1980s (Sinnott, 1989).

The question arises as to whether these differences are permanent features of the party system or simply reflect the situation at the particular time at which the data were collected. Confirmation of the continued existence of the three dimensions is to be found in the Laver surveys of experts. The taxes versus spending dimension in the expert survey can be seen as corresponding to the left–right dimension in the elite data;

a Northern Ireland dimension is clearly evident from both sources, and Laver's 'social policy' dimension (policy on abortion and homosexuality) is closely akin to the confessionalism dimension revealed by the analysis of the rankings of the politicians. However, the expert data also suggest that, by the late 1980s, the particular configuration of parties on the confessional–non-confessional dimension had changed. Underlying this change is the fact that by then Fine Gael had lost most of its confessional faction through retirement or electoral defeat, and Fianna Fáil could be seen as having adopted a tacit confessional position in the referendums of 1983 and 1986. These changes would account for the positioning of the parties on the abortion/homosexuality scale in the expert judgment study, i.e. Fianna Fáil is placed well to the conservative end of the social policy scale, and though Fine Gael is judged to be the next most conservative, it is located a substantial distance from Fianna Fáil and quite close to the centre. In assessing the significance of this change it should be borne in mind that the evidence of the 1970s identified Fianna Fáil, not as a crusading secular party, but as a non-confessional party relative to the confessionalism of a conservative faction in Fine Gael. This suggests that the position of the party on the confessionalist dimension is relative and contingent. This interpretation would fit with the conclusion of the historical portrait of Fianna Fáil, which suggested that it is, above all, a pragmatic party, happy, when in opposition, to seize political advantage in the discomfiture of the government and quite prepared to adapt its positions to what it sees as the majority view of the electorate.

We can conclude that the quantitative evidence derived from expert judgments, party manifestos and interviews with political elites points to the existence of significant distinctions between parties while, at the same time, emphasizing that the extent of these differences should not be exaggerated. These findings help to fill out and make more systematic what we can gather from historical portraits of the parties. A key question, of course, is do these distinctions mean anything to the voters? This will be considered in detail in chapter 6. In the meantime, enough has been said to establish that voters are presented with a choice in general elections and, drawing on both the historical and quantitative data, to give some sense of what those choices have been. The next chapter attempts to provide an overview of how the voters have responded to these choices over seven decades. Before doing so, however, it is important to remember that there is a difference between the voters and the electorate. Varying but significant proportions of the electorate have responded to the choices offered in general elections with an implicit 'no thanks' by not turning out to vote. Larger proportions have declined to participate in the various other voting opportunities that the system offers. The remainder of this chapter considers these variations in voter turnout.

Voters and non-voters

The popular view has it that Irish people are exceptionally political. There are various aspects to the image – for instance, that the emigrant Irish have formed the nucleus of political movements and parties in several countries abroad, and that there is an exceptional degree of interest in politics at home. Verification of the latter view would require a comprehensive definition of interest in politics, but if we take turnout in general elections as a measure and place Ireland's record in this respect in comparative perspective, the popular image turns out to be something of a myth. Ireland ranks fourteenth in a list of fifteen Western European democracies in terms of turnout in national elections between 1945 and 1978 (Dittrich and Johansen, 1983, p. 97). Of course, cross-national comparisons such as these must take into account different institutional settings, especially the fact that in certain countries (four of the fifteen countries in the above comparison) voting has been compulsory or quasi-compulsory in all or in part of the period surveyed. However, even taking this into account, it appears that the Irish are not, in this respect at least, as political as the popular myth would have it. Some, even many, of those who do vote may be very interested in politics and, as will be shown in chapter 6, may be very well informed, but in each general election there appears to be, relative to other Western European democracies, a fairly sizeable section of the population that does not play any part. There is, moreover, some evidence that a substantial proportion of this group of non-voters may consist of the same people from election to election and contest to contest. A study of voting behaviour in the period 1969–73 points to 'the apparent stability in the behaviour of the non-voting group' and suggests that 'a large minority of the Irish electorate, somewhere around 20 per cent of all those enfranchised, never voted during this period' (the period included two general elections, a presidential election and a referendum) (McCarthy and Ryan, 1976).

While the explanation of variations in turnout between different countries is complex and difficult, Ireland's position in the ranking is consistent with the most important single cause that has been identified in comparative studies of turnout. This cause is the strength of the link between the party system and the major group cleavages in the society. For example, Crewe concludes that there is 'a strong positive association between a country's turnout rate on the one hand and, on the other, the closeness of fit between its party system and major social cleavages' (Crewe, 1981, p. 252). In similar vein, Powell refers to the 'consistent and robust conclusion' that 'strong linkages between citizens' cleavage group memberships and their party preferences are a powerful predictor of voting turnout across nations' (Powell, 1980, pp. 18–19). The issue of the relationship between the party system and the cleavage system in Ireland will be considered in the final chapter. However, enough has been said so far to indicate that this is a weak relationship. Thus, the relatively low turnout in Ireland is not surprising. It should be emphasized, of course, that while empirical expectations in regard to turnout should not be very high, the matter is quite different when looked at from a normative perspective. Voting is not the only form of participation in a democracy but it is a particularly important form: 'Elections based on a full adult franchise encapsulate more directly than any other means of participation the two core democratic principles of universality and equality – that every individual, whatever his social or economic circumstances, should have an equal say' (Crewe, 1981, pp. 216–17). In the light of this, the level of turnout in general elections in Ireland should not be viewed with complacency.

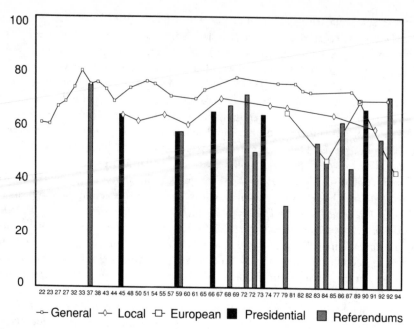

Figure 3.8 Turnout in general, local, presidential, and European Parliament elections and referendums, 1922–94.

Trends in turnout, 1922–92

The top line in Figure 3.8 traces turnout in general elections between 1922 and 1992. The most obvious feature is the dramatic increase between 1923 and 1933. Understandably, this has been much commented on and will be considered in detail in a moment. The 81 per cent turnout in 1933 was in fact to be the peak of general election turnout – turnout fell back five percentage points in 1937 and never subsequently went above 77 per cent. It is, perhaps, not surprising that turnout was down somewhat in 1943, given wartime censorship and rationing of both petrol and newsprint. However, assuming that these constraints did not intensify over the following months, it is difficult to account for the further sharp decline in 1944. Turnout did not recover to pre-war levels until 1951, and almost no sooner had it done so, than it fell quite significantly again (in 1957 to 71 per cent, a level repeated in the following election). Turnout again returned to what might be described as normal levels in the late 1960s and early 1970s. Thereafter, significant declines in turnout occurred in 1982 and again in 1989. In the latter year the decline was quite sharp, and 1992 saw a repeat of this level of 68.5 per cent.

Turnout and voter mobilisation, 1923–32

The apparent sharp increases in turnout in the 1920s have been cited as a factor that helps to explain trends in party support in that crucial first decade of the state's existence. Thus, taking account of increases in turnout in mainly western areas in the period 1923–32, it has been argued that Fianna Fáil won over the bulk of the newly mobilised voters and that the mobilisation of this new western electorate was due to the party's impressive organisational efforts (Garvin, 1974). Lee also sees the increases in turnout as favouring Fianna Fáil. He attributes the increases between 1927 and 1932 (and between 1932 and 1933) to the conversion of previous non-voters to Fianna Fáil due to the popular enthusiasm generated by the new party newspaper, *The Irish Press*, which was founded in 1931 (Lee, 1989, p. 169). More generally, Carty sees Fianna Fáil's national organisation carrying the party to power in 1932 'in a final mobilization wave, achieved by a dramatic and permanent increase in voter turnout' (Carty, 1993, p. 39).[12] Increases in turnout were recorded in particular in some western seaboard counties. The low turnout in these areas in the very early years has been attributed to the fact that 'the mountainous terrain and the scattered nature of the communities make communications difficult' (Chubb, 1970, p. 334). However, before drawing any far-reaching conclusions from the variations in the published turnout figures, it is worth taking a closer look at the data and in particular at the figures for the registered electorate, which form the basis for the calculation of turnout.

Table 3.1 presents turnout by county in 1923, 1927 and 1932. It also provides a measure of the accuracy of the electoral register by indicating whether, for each county, the register shows a surplus or a deficit relative to an estimate of the population aged 21 and over in the county in question. In each year the counties are arranged in ascending order of turnout. It is immediately apparent that there were quite fundamental problems with the electoral register in certain counties in 1923. Thus, for example, Mayo had well over 15,000 more people on the electoral register than existed in the adult population. Lesser, but still substantial, electoral register surpluses occurred in Galway, Donegal, Leitrim-Sligo, Cavan and Kerry. Several of these counties are western seaboard counties, and the ordering of these counties in ascending order of turnout in 1923 indicates that these were generally the counties with low turnout. Thus, the turnout in Mayo, with its 15,000 surplus on the electoral register, was 51 per cent, the turnout in Galway, with its almost 8,000 surplus, was 46 per cent, in Donegal (over 6,000 surplus) it was 54 per cent, in Leitrim-Sligo (3,500 surplus) it was 56 per cent. Both Cavan and Kerry had somewhat higher levels of turnout (60–61 per cent), but this is still relatively low and might well have been much higher but for their 4,000 and 6,500 surpluses on the electoral register.

Considerable improvements were effected in the electoral register between 1923 and 1927. However, it was still flawed and there were substantial surpluses on the register in Galway, Donegal, Cavan, and Mayo.[13] Much smaller surpluses occurred in Roscommon, Kildare, Wicklow and Monaghan. The effect of the improvement in the

[12] Carty had earlier taken a more sceptical view of the extent of this late mobilisation – see the exchange of views in Carty (1976) and Garvin (1976).

[13] One should also note that throughout this period Dublin appears to have had a very significant deficit on the electoral register (some 34,000 in 1923, 23,000 in 1927 and 39,000 in 1932). This suggests a substantial under-registration of the adult population in the capital city. The other area with a major urban centre (Cork county) showed a deficit of almost 9,000 in 1927 and almost 15,000 in 1932. If we focus on Cork city, which we can do for the electorate/population comparison in 1927, it appears that the 1927 deficit was concentrated in Cork city.

Table 3.1: Electoral register surplus/deficit and levels of turn-out (in ascending order) 1923, 1927 and 1932

	1923 Electoral register surplus/deficit	Turnout 1923 (%)		1927 Electoral register surplus/deficit	Turnout 1927.1 (%)	Turnout 1927.2 (%)		1932 Electoral register surplus/deficit	Turnout 1932 (%)
Galway	7,977	46	Galway	3,696	57	59	Dublin	-39,511	70
Mayo	15,646	51	Donegal	1,699	57	60	Kildare	-1,272	72
Donegal	6,397	54	Roscommon	472	62	66	Galway	-7,720	72
Leitrim-Sligo	3,684	56	Cavan	5,224	62	63	Longford-Westmeath	-1,330	73
Cork	-1,643	56	Kildare	474	64	63	Roscommon	-1,124	73
Longford-Westmeath	-969	59	Mayo	1,812	65	66	Donegal	-899	74
Cavan	4,018	60	Cork	-8,795	65	67	Meath	-1,490	75
Roscommon	523	60	Longford-Westmeath	-1,609	65	66	Mayo	-3,468	75
Dublin	-34,182	60	Dublin	-23,112	66	67	Leitrim-Sligo	-2,818	76
Kerry	6,752	61	Limerick	-2,730	67	71	Kerry	-4,570	76
Meath	-650	61	Meath	-470	68	69	Cork	-14,953	76
Wicklow	1,847	62	Clare	-891	68	71	Wicklow	-1,047	76
Wexford	1,094	63	Carlow-Kilkenny	-1,874	68	70	Louth	-2,216	76
Tipperary	-172	63	Leitrim-Sligo	-3,531	69	71	Wexford	-2,796	77
Leix-Offaly	-210	63	Kerry	-4,554	69	71	Clare	-3,416	77
Louth	1,112	64	Wicklow	281	69	70	Cavan	-1,356	77
Kildare	274	64	Waterford	-2,746	70	71	Waterford	-4,301	77
Monaghan	133	64	Wexford	-1,334	70	68	Carlow-Kilkenny	-3,060	78
Limerick	-2,802	64	Leix-Offaly	-1,670	70	71	Leix-Offaly	-3,454	78
Carlow-Kilkenny	-4,200	64	Louth	-700	73	72	Limerick	-7,083	80
Clare	-64	67	Tipperary	-4,098	73	72	Tipperary	-4,786	80
Waterford	-1,693	70	Monaghan	142	79	75	Monaghan	-1,755	84

Note: All table sources are given on pp. vi–viii.

electoral register was very noticeable. Thus, turnout in Galway increased from 46 to 57 per cent, in Donegal from 51 to 57 per cent and in Mayo from 51 to 65 per cent. In Cavan, where the surplus was actually worse than in 1923 (5,224 in 1927, compared to 4,018 in 1923) turnout only increased from 60 to 62 per cent.

By 1932 surpluses on the electoral register had been completely removed. Presumably as a result of this improvement, the range of variation in turnout narrowed very considerably. The range had been 46–70 per cent in 1923 and 57–79 per cent in the first election of 1927; it was 70–84 per cent in 1932. More relevantly, from the point of view of the current discussion, it is evident that the constituencies with the largest increases in turnout were precisely those which had suffered a surplus on the electoral register in 1927. Turnout in Galway between September 1927 and 1932 increased from 59 to 72 per cent, in Donegal it went from 57 to 74 per cent, in Roscommon from 62 to 73 per cent, in Cavan from 62 to 77 per cent, in Kildare from 64 to 72 per cent and in Mayo from 65 to 75 pr cent. In summary, a substantial part of the increase in turnout between 1923 and 1932 and, in particular, the variations in the rate of increase between different counties and between the western and northwestern region and other areas of the country, are more apparent than real, being very significantly affected by defects in the electoral register up to 1927. There was undoubtedly some mobilisation of previous non-voters, but close inspection of the evidence suggests that it was a much less potent factor than appears at first sight. The increase in recorded turnout between 1932 and 1933 can, however, be taken to be genuine.[14]

Turnout in referendums and second-order elections
Apart from indicating the variations in the level of turnout in general elections, Figure 3.8 draws attention to the multiplicity of occasions on which Irish voters have been asked to go to the polls and to the considerable variation in the levels of their response to such invitations. Including four of the early local elections, which are not in the graph because turnout figures are not readily available for them, there have been fifty occasions for turning out to vote in the seventy years since 1923 (there have, in fact, been sixty-three opportunities for casting a vote, as on many of the days on which voters were called to the polls there have been two or more issues to be decided, e.g. a combination of a general election and a referendum (1937 and 1992), of a presidential election and a referendum (1959) or of a local and a European Parliament election (1979)).

Turnout in referendums is indicated by the shaded bars in Figure 3.8. The first and last of these can be discounted because the referendums in question coincided with general elections.[15] Apart from these two, referendums have drawn turnouts of very

---

[14] The fact of this increase does not in itself lend any support to the thesis that turn-out increase or the mobilisation of new voters was responsible for the increase in the Fianna Fáil vote between 1932 and 1933. In fact, the correlation between change in the Fianna Fáil vote 1932–33 and change in turn-out 1932–33 was negative (–0.29).

[15] Note, however, that 10 per cent of the votes cast in the 1937 referendum on the constitution were spoiled votes. Some of these were undoubtedly due to voter error or to deliberate spoiling of the vote. A substantial proportion, however, may have been blank papers. Accordingly, the real level of turn-out in the first referendum may have been much lower than the 75.8 per cent recorded.

different levels, presumably reflecting the electorate's estimate of the importance of the issues (these issues are discussed in chapter 9). The highest turnout has been the 71 per cent in the 1972 referendum on EC membership, and the lowest has been the 29 per cent in the referendums on adoption and university representation in 1979. The second referendum on PR (1968) elicited substantially higher turnout than the first (1959) (66 per cent compared to 58 per cent), despite the fact that the first coincided with a presidential election. Given the political controversy generated by the issues involved, it might have been expected that turnout in the 1983 abortion referendum (54 per cent), and even that of the 1986 divorce referendum (61 per cent), would have been higher.[16] Finally, it is worth noting that the referendum with the second lowest turnout was the referendum on the Single European Act (1987). It was 27 percentage points lower than in the original referendum on EC entry. This low level of involvement may have been due to the circumstances in which the referendum came about, and to the considerable degree of confusion in the debate (see chapter 9). At any rate, turnout in the referendum on the Maastricht Treaty (1992) made up about half the 27 point discrepancy.

The remaining electoral contests for which turnout is shown (Figure 3.8) are what have been described as 'second-order' elections. This concept is explored in some detail in chapter 10. It is sufficient to note here that the main feature of second-order elections is that they do not determine the distribution of power at the level that really matters – the national level. This leads to the general expectation that turnout in such contests will be considerably lower than in general elections.

Given this, and given the relative powerlessness of Irish local government even at its own level, turnout in Irish local elections may be considered to be quite high. As discussed in chapter 10, this may partly be accounted for by the importance of local elections to the political parties, both in terms of the recruitment of candidates for Dáil elections and because those elected to county and borough councils constitute the bulk of the electoral college for Senate elections. Turnout in local elections peaked in 1967 and has been on a slight downward trend since. In line with the trend in general election turnout, the decline was more substantial in 1991.

The four European Parliament elections up to 1994 have been held on the same day as other electoral contests – the first in combination with local elections (1979), the second with a referendum (1984), the third with a general election (1989) and the fourth with partial local elections (1994). In the first and third of the four, we can assume that turnout was determined essentially by the non-European contest. Since the 1984 referendum issue – a proposal to extend voting rights in certain elections to non-citizens – was neither of very great moment nor particularly controversial, it is unlikely that it raised the turnout. Consequently, the 1984 figure of 47.6 per cent is probably an accurate estimate of turnout in the European Parliament elections of that year. It is also unlikely that the 1994 urban district council elections of June 1994 did much to boost turnout and so the 44 per cent figure for 1994 can be taken as confirma-

---

[16] The analysis in chapter 9 of the determinants of voting in the 1983 abortion referendum will take up the issue of the significance of the low turnout.

tion that less than half the electorate are moved to vote in a European contest. Looked at from the point of view of the European Parliament, and in particular from the point of view of the Parliament's potential to contribute to a solution to the problem of the democratic deficit, this proportion must be regarded as disquieting (see Sinnott and Whelan, 1992).

We have noted the intermittent nature of the cycle of presidential elections. In theory, they should occur every seven years but, for reasons discussed in chapter 10, only two contests (1966 and 1973) have taken place at the prescribed seven-year interval after the previous one. The most recent interval has been seventeen years. There have been five presidential elections – 1945, 1959, 1966, 1973 and 1990. Figure 3.8 indicates that, with one exception (1959), turnout in these elections has been in a fairly constant range of between 62 and 65 per cent. In view of the recent tendency for turnout to decline somewhat, it is, however, notable that turnout in the 1990 presidential election was higher than turnout in the presidential election prior to that (1973), and was close to the highest recorded (1966).

In suggesting that there may be a constant group of non-voters, McCarthy and Ryan comment that 'It would be interesting to know more about [its] demographic and socio–economic composition' (McCarthy and Ryan, 1976, p. 287). Despite this pointed call for research in the area, there has until recently been relatively little systematic study of the determinants of turnout. Such evidence as exists will be considered when analysing the determinants of voting choice in later chapters. However, before proceeding to the question of what are the sources of voting behaviour, we need an overview of the outcomes of general elections and of the choices the voters have made since the foundation of the state.

Chapter 4

General election outcomes: periods, trends and change

Introduction

The party portraits in chapter 2 touched on the performance of individual parties in particular general elections. However, in order to obtain an adequate view of election outcomes, each party's ups and downs in support must be examined over time and must be seen in relation to what is happening to the other parties. For example, the significance of Fianna Fáil's gain of 9 per cent in the September 1927 election must be assessed in the context of an even greater increase for Cumann na nGaedheal (11 per cent), and of losses among all the minor parties and particularly among independents. Similarly, Fianna Fáil's gain of 5 per cent between 1932 and 1933 may appear to be simply matched by the 5 per cent loss suffered by Cumann na nGaedheal, until we take into account the complication of the arrival on the scene of the Centre Party, which was contesting an election for the first and only time in 1933, and which took 9 per cent of the vote, a substantial part of which must have come from Cumann na nGaedheal. The implication is that both individual party performance and election outcomes as a whole must be assessed in the context of whether the competition for votes is concentrated among a small number of fairly large parties, or fragmented across a broader range of parties of various sizes. It also means that we need to consider whether the movement of voters tends to occur within each side of the political divide or across it.

There are, in fact, three variables involved here. First there are the two variables that define the notion of party fragmentation – the number and the size of the parties. A more fragmented party system is one with a relatively large number of parties, with the vote more or less evenly spread between them; a less fragmented system is one with either relatively few parties, or with a few dominant parties and some other parties of very small size. The third variable is the location of fragmentation relative to the main dividing line in the party system. The significance of this variable is that it has a bearing on the extent to which votes are lost to or gained from adjacent parties on the same side of the cleavage line, rather than to or from opponents on the other side of the cleavage. In the discussion of trends that follows, the location of party fragmentation will be a recurring theme and the final section of the chapter will address the issue more directly and systematically.

It is remarkable how much Irish election outcomes have varied in terms of the number and size of the parties. Counting the number of parties is not without problems, but, broadly speaking, the number of parties has fluctuated from six, plus a large group of independents, in June 1927, down to three plus independents in 1938, back up to six in 1948, down to three with almost no independents in 1965 and back up to five in 1987.[1] The relative size of parties, as measured by the combined size of the two largest parties, has also varied very considerably. The largest two parties have at times come close to monopolising the vote between them, as in 1938 and 1982, when they accounted for around 85 per cent of the vote. At other times their combined vote has been in or around the 60 per cent mark, for example 54 per cent in June 1927, 62 per cent in 1948 or 64 per cent in 1992. The question is whether there is a coherent pattern to these changes. If there is, could that pattern be used to identify sequences of elections sharing similar competitive characteristics? If so, we would have a useful periodisation of Irish elections that would facilitate the task of setting individual party performances and the outcomes of individual elections in their appropriate competitive context.

Periodising the party system

The problem encountered by any attempt to periodise election outcomes in this way is how to take into account both the number of parties in the system and their relative size, giving adequate weight to the large parties, and at the same time not excluding the small parties by use of an arbitrary cut-off point. The problem is not unique to the analysis of party systems. Taagepera and Shugart point out that economists have faced a similar problem in assessing the degree of concentration in foreign trade or in industrial sectors, and they go on to adapt the index of concentration devised by economists to the task of measuring concentration and fragmentation in party systems (Taagepera and Shugart, 1989, pp. 77–81).[2] If one party had 100 per cent of the vote, concentration would be total and the index would equal one. When all shares have extremely small values the index tends towards zero. Taagepera and Shugart note that a two-party system with equal vote shares for each party would give a value of 0.5, a three-party system with equal vote shares would yield a value of 0.33, a four-party system

[1] For a discussion of the difficulties involved in counting parties and deciding what counts as a party see Bartolini and Mair, 1990, pp. 131–2.

[2] Each party is weighted in terms of its size by squaring its fractional share of the vote, i.e. a party with 40 per cent of the votes would receive a weighted value of $0.40 \times 0.40 = 0.16$. Similarly, a party with a 10 per cent share would receive a much smaller weighted value ($0.10 \times 0.10 = 0.01$), and a party with only 1 per cent of votes would be almost discounted, its weighted value being 0.01×0.01, i.e. 0.0001. If such weighted shares are added up for all parties in a particular vote or seat distribution, the result is an index of concentration that varies from zero to one. The index is called the Herfindahl-Hirschman concentration index, after the authors who developed it in the economic literature, and its formula is:

$$HH = \sum pi^2$$

where p is proportion of the vote won by party i. Fragmentation is the obverse of concentration and can be calculated by simply taking $1 - HH$. This is, in fact, the Fractionalisation Index or F devised by Rae (Rae, 1967, p. 54).

would have a value of 0.25 and so on. The significance of this is that, in these hypothetical examples of exact two-, three- and four-party systems, taking the inverse of the index of concentration yields the precise number of parties in the system, i.e. the inverse of 0.5 is 2, of 0.33 is 3, and so on. On this basis, they propose that the inverse of the index of concentration be used as a measure of the number of effective parties, that is 'the number of hypothetical equal-sized parties that would have the same effect on fractionalisation of the party system as have the actual parties of varying sizes' (Taagepera and Shugart, 1989, p. 79). This has the advantage over the concentration index of enabling us to visualise the party system in familiar terms of two-party, three-party, four-party, and so on, or points in between.

One problem that arises in applying an index of this sort to published election results is that such results frequently treat small parties as a residual category, and report their vote shares together under the heading 'other' or 'independents and others'. In arguing that one of the advantages of their measure of the effective number of parties is that this treatment of independents does not greatly affect the results, Taagepera and Shugart give an example based on a residual category in the 1975 New Zealand election that encompasses 5.4 per cent of the vote. Over the range of Irish elections, however, the residual category has been as high as 14.1 per cent, and in four of the five elections up to and including 1932 it exceeded 10 per cent. There are, therefore, good grounds for arguing that the impact of such small parties and of independents on the fragmentation of the system should be measured as accurately as possible. This means including all independents as if each was a distinct competing entity or 'party'. If we do this, however, is there not a danger that we will exaggerate the fragmentation of the system? No, because the whole value of the weighting system involved in the formula for the number of effective parties is that it discounts the impact of small 'parties' (the smaller the party, the greater the discount), while still taking them into account.

A useful complementary measure of the degree of fragmentation in the system is the two-party concentration ratio. This is a straightforward measure obtained by simply summing the share of the vote of the two largest parties, and it conveys one important aspect of fragmentation, that is the extent to which two parties dominate, regardless of the absolute number of parties in the system. One could, of course, also calculate a three-party and even a four-party concentration ratio. However, the purpose here is to obtain a rough periodisation and, with this in mind, Figure 4.1 simply presents the effective number of parties and the two-party concentration ratio. Note that the former is calibrated on the left axis of the graph and the latter on the right.

Figure 4.1 does offer some help in periodising electoral outcomes. It is immediately evident that there were three peaks of party fragmentation as measured by the effective number of parties – June 1927, 1948 and 1992. The elections immediately before and after June 1927 and 1948 and before 1992 had relatively high numbers of effective parties or levels of fragmentation. The low points on the index are 1938 and a series of low points between 1965 and 1982. Beyond this, a precise demarcation between periods is difficult to establish. A tentative periodisation can be suggested by drawing

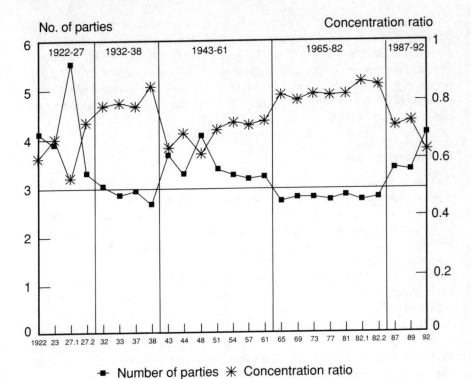

Figure 4.1 Number of effective parties, two-party concentration ratio, and periodisation of elections, 1922–92.

a horizontal line through the graph to distinguish between outcomes with three or more effective parties and those with less than three. Allowing that 1932 is marginally above the line, this suggests five periods of greater and lesser fragmentation, designated by the vertical lines in the graph: 1922–27, 1932–38, 1943–61, 1965–82, 1987–92. The periodisation is confirmed by the consideration that if one were to draw a horizontal line at 0.8 on the two-party concentration scale, the arrangement of points above and below the line would give exactly the same periods.

The system starts out with a fairly high level of fragmentation in 1922, a situation that continues up to and including the second election of 1927. In 1932 the number of effective parties falls to just a fraction over three, and this situation of low fragmentation continues until 1938. In 1943 there is quite a dramatic jump, checked somewhat by the snap election of the following year but reconfirmed in 1948. The four elections from 1951 to 1961 see a levelling off of the effective number of parties at a point significantly above three. In 1965 the system again undergoes significant concentration, ushering in a long period (1965–82) in which there is very little fluctuation in the number of effective parties in the system. The 1987 and 1989 elections mark a return to a larger number of effective parties (3.4), and the number increased again in 1989 and 1992.

Without going into the complex literature on the categorisation of party systems, one can describe these alternating periods approximately as periods in which a multi-party format has prevailed (1922–27, 1943–61 and 1987–92), and periods in which the format of the system has approximated to the 'two-and-a-half party model'.[3] Whatever terminology is used, the important point for the present purpose is the identification of periods of greater or lesser fragmentation that enable us to see each particular election in its systemic context.

Election outcomes: an overview

The periods identified in Figure 4.1 have been superimposed on the graph of party support between 1922 and 1992 (Figure 4.2). Within each period one can see fairly clearly the reflection of the greater or lesser degrees of fragmentation of the party system, that is, more or fewer parties successfully competing for the vote. Before looking at each period in detail, it is worth taking an overview of the long-term performance of each of the main parties.

Once it established itself as the leading party in the state (1932), Fianna Fáil showed a remarkably consistent pattern of gains in one election, followed by losses in the next, followed by recovery in the next and so on. The 1987 election was the first in which its vote declined in two successive elections and, rather than producing the bounce-back that had been such an integral part of the pattern of Fianna Fáil performance, the 1989 election merely confirmed the 1987 situation – Fianna Fáil's share of the vote in both elections was identical. However, it was 1992 that really broke the spell, pushing Fianna Fáil to a level (39 per cent) below anything it had experienced since before it first took office in 1932. The entry for 1992 in Figure 4.2 still shows Fianna Fáil as clearly the largest party in the system, but the graph equally clearly shows that its ability to maintain a really dominant electoral position is under severe threat and has been eroding since 1982.

In contrast to Fianna Fáil bumping up and down on its 40-per-cent-plus plateau for so long, Fine Gael has had several runs of elections in which its vote has gone either consistently up or consistently down. Oversimplifying somewhat, one can see the Fine Gael vote as having two peaks – in the 1920s and in the early 1980s, with a deep valley – the 1940s – in between. From 1948 the party began the gradual climb back to real major party status. That progress was checked twice on the way, on both occasions (1957 and 1977) after participation in coalition government during periods of severe economic difficulty. On both occasions, however, the party recovered immediately and sustained that recovery over at least three elections. This marks out what has been different about the Fine Gael performance since 1987, compared with the rest of the post-war experience. The 1987 election saw the biggest vote drop in the party's history. True, there was some recovery in 1989, but it was half-hearted and, most seriously of

---

[3] See the discussions of the problem of categorisation in Farrell, 1971; O'Leary, 1979; Mair, 1979; and Sinnott, 1984. It is worth noting that the periodisation suggested in the text corresponds very closely to the periodisation that emerges from Farrell's application of Blondel's two-and-a-half party model to the Irish case up to the 1969 election (Farrell, *ibid.*, Blondel, 1969, pp. 153–76).

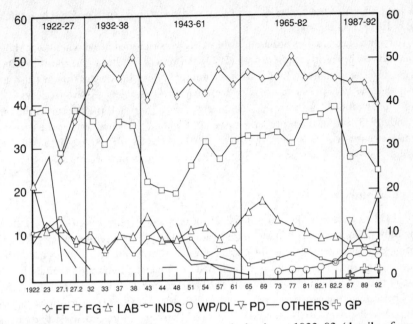

Figure 4.2 Party share of the vote in general elections, 1922–92 (details of party support below 30 per cent are shown in Figure 4.3).

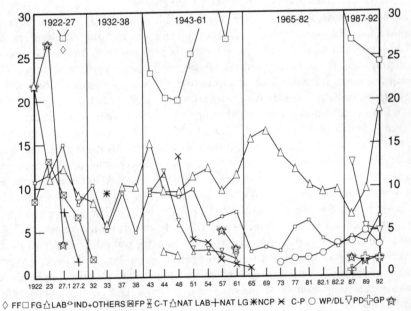

Figure 4.3 Party share of the vote in general elections, 1922–92 (parties under 30 per cent).

all, not only was it not sustained in 1992, it was in fact more than negated by a further fall of five percentage points.

Labour has also had its peaks and valleys. As will be argued in a moment, one should discount its apparently highest peak (1922) and regard 1992 as the summit to date of its electoral achievement. Evidence of the number of candidates put forward also suggests that the 1992 performance is even more impressive than its previous peaks (1943 and 1969). Labour has, however, deep troughs in support and they occur in the early period (1933) and in the quite recent past (1987). The 1987 low came at the end of an almost twenty-year slide that was only really checked in 1989. That slide makes the Labour vote at the point at which Figure 4.2 ends all the more dramatic.

Election outcomes, 1922–27

The 1922 election was of vital importance in terms of determining the future direction of Irish politics and of Anglo–Irish relations. Despite an attempt on the part of the Sinn Féin elite to arrange that the outcome would simply reflect the status quo ante in the Dáil, the anti-treaty position was rejected by a much larger margin than in the Dáil vote of the previous January. The anti-treatyites received 21.3 per cent of the vote, to 38.5 per cent to the pro-treaty party and 39.7 divided between three groups who were all effectively pro-treaty (Labour, the Farmers' Party and independents). The election was also important as a milestone in the establishment of a stable democracy. However, it is of considerably less importance, indeed it is downright unsatisfactory, as a benchmark from which to measure subsequent electoral change.

In the first place, it was not until 1923 that full adult suffrage was introduced. Secondly, the 1922 election took place in the context of an impending civil war. Thirdly and most importantly, with civil war imminent the pro- and anti-treaty factions actually attempted to fix the election outcome in advance by making an electoral pact. The attempt was partly successful. The plan was that each side would run candidates corresponding exactly to their existing strength in the Dáil, and that afterwards they would form a coalition government. The hope was that this would avoid exacerbating the conflict and might avert civil war. Thus, if it had been left to the treaty parties there would not have been an election at all. It was only where third parties intervened, often despite considerable pressure to stand aside, that contests occurred. The result was that over one-quarter of the constituencies were uncontested. In the constituencies that were contested, the campaign was lop-sided, as the pro-treatyites showed a marked reluctance to become involved (Hoppen, 1989, pp. 109–10). In short, the different franchise, the lack of contests over a considerable area of the country, the half-hearted nature of the campaign by the government party, and the inevitable tendency for voters, already weary after two-and-a-half years of guerrilla war and British government reprisals, to say to the now-quarrelling Sinn Féin factions 'a plague on both your houses' makes comparisons of voting strength between the 1922 election and later elections hazardous.

The difficulty of using 1922 as a yardstick is particularly evident in the case of the Labour Party. As Figure 4.2 shows, Labour seemed to make a splendid start in the first election in the new state with a vote of 21.3 per cent. From this starting point, its 10.6 per cent in the 1923 election looks catastrophic, and it appears that it was not until seventy years later that Labour even came close to matching its achievement on its first outing. But was that 21 per cent a real Labour vote that could have been expected to persist in a more normal election?

What was to become the core of Labour Party support – the votes of farm labourers in large farming areas – was certainly in evidence. The constituencies in which the party got over 25 per cent of the vote (seven of the fourteen constituencies it contested), were all predominantly rural constituencies with significant large-farming areas (Laois-Offaly, Wexford, Louth-Meath, Kildare-Wicklow, Carlow-Kilkenny, Tipperary-Waterford, and Tipperary North, South and Mid). Even in these constituencies, however, it is evident that there was more to the Labour vote than farm-labourer support. Closer inspection of the results suggests that an important additional factor in many instances was the lack of any alternative. Thus there were five constituencies in which Labour offered the only alternative to a vote for either the pro- or anti-treaty party. In a further four constituencies, voters alienated by the divisions over the treaty or fearful of their consequences had a choice of voting Labour or Farmer, though a vote for the latter would hardly have been much of an option for many voters, since the Farmers' Party was clearly identified with the large farmers. The average Labour vote in these nine constituencies, in which the treaty parties were challenged by Labour alone, or by Labour plus the Farmers' Party, was 31.1. per cent.

In the areas where there was an alternative in the form of an independent candidate, the Labour vote was substantially lower (22.7 per cent). This lends support to the intuitively plausible view that a significant source of Labour's success in 1922 was that it provided a way, sometimes the only way, of registering a protest against the Sinn Féin factions, whose squabbling over the Treaty was fast approaching civil war. Interestingly, there is some evidence of contemporary awareness that this was a crucial factor in such constituencies. Thus, in the Louth-Meath constituency, a newspaper article predicted that the Labour vote would be higher than it ever would be again because the Labour candidate was the only one 'who gave the electors a chance of breaking the cold chain of silence that has bound them since 1918' (quoted in Gallagher, 1979. p. 416). The Labour vote in the constituency turned out to be 38.3 per cent. This illustrates the point that neither Labour's spectacular performance in some constituencies, nor its total of 21.3 per cent in the country as a whole, should be used as a yardstick against which to measure subsequent Labour support.

For the reasons indicated, the real analysis of trends in this period of Irish electoral behaviour begins with 1923. The 1923 election produced five main groups – the pro-treaty Cumann na nGaedheal, anti-treaty Sinn Féin, and, bunched together, each just above the 10 per cent mark, the Farmers' Party, independents and Labour. The Sinn Féin vote in 1923 (27.4 per cent) can be interpreted in two ways. On the one hand it was a remarkable performance for a side that had just been involved in an unsuccessful rebellion against the established government, that had 1,200 of its activists, including its president, in jail and that was now, by its policy of abstention, refusing to recognise the legitimacy of the parliament to which it was seeking election.

The result indicated a solid base upon which a challenge to the pro-treatyites could be built.

The anti-treatyites may also have taken comfort from the fact that their main rivals – the government party, now organised as Cumann na nGaedheal – were, at 39 per cent, well short of having the support of a majority of the voters. However, Cumann na nGaedheal's modest performance must be seen in the context of an emerging multi-party system, and especially in the light of the fact that almost all the fragmentation in that system was on the pro-treaty side. All the other parties in 1923 – the Farmers' Party (12 per cent), Labour (11 per cent) and the independents (11 per cent) – were pro-treaty. Thus in a new and fluid political situation, Cumann na nGaedheal had a lot of competition within the area of its own principal appeal, that is, for the pro-treaty vote. And its immediate competitors had the advantage that they could pursue partic-ular interests while offering the voter much the same pro-treaty security by their support for Cumann na nGaedheal in the Dáil.

This fragmentation of the pro-treaty vote was even more evident in the June 1927 election. The outcome was a near disaster for the governing party, which was reduced to only a little over a quarter of the vote. Cumann na nGaedheal's problem was that, in addition to the existing competition for the pro-treaty vote, there was the new chal-lenge posed by the pro-treaty National League. Thus, while Cumann na nGaedheal was down almost 12 percentage points, Labour went up 1.9, independents 3.2, and the National League captured 7.3 per cent. The net result left Cumann na nGaedheal only 1.3 per cent ahead of Fianna Fáil, and actually with less votes than Fianna Fáil and Sinn Féin combined (see Figures 4.2 and 4.3).

Despite the dramatic split in Sinn Féin in 1926 and the consequent founding of Fianna Fáil, fragmentation turned out to be much less of a problem on the anti-treaty side. As Figure 4.2 shows, in June 1927 Fianna Fáil won approximately the same share of the vote as Sinn Féin had in 1923, and the latter was reduced to a mere 3.6 per cent. It should be emphasized, however, that the eclipse of Sinn Féin, while in part due to the fact that 'anti-treaty voters had come down clearly in favour of a practical and prag-matic line' (Gallagher, 1985, p. 12), had been effectively brought about prior to the election itself. Fianna Fáil had won the battle against Sinn Féin among the party activists well before the election had been called (Lee, 1989, p. 152). As a result Sinn Féin could only muster 15 candidates, compared to 87 for Fianna Fáil. Once it had dealt with Sinn Féin, Fianna Fáil was insulated from the existing fragmentation in the system by its opposition to the Treaty. Even when, as in the case of Clann Eireann, a new party emerged campaigning on an anti-treaty platform, Fianna Fáil had no diffi-culty fending off the challenge. Clann Eireann's eight candidates won a mere 5,527 votes between them in June 1927, and did not contest the September 1927 election.

Having successfully laid claim to the hard-core anti-treaty vote, Fianna Fáil faced the much more difficult task of winning over pro-treaty supporters. In this regard, Fianna Fáil's performances in the two elections of 1927 merit particularly close comparison. In the twelve weeks that intervened the most significant event in parlia-mentary and electoral terms was the ending of the policy of abstention and the entry of Fianna Fáil into the Dáil (in August 1927). The change in policy had dramatic electoral effect. Fianna Fáil's vote went up from 26 per cent to 35 per cent in the space of three months.

Fianna Fáil's arrival in the Dáil chamber also, however, concentrated the minds of its opponents. In September, Cumann na nGaedheal recovered all the ground it had lost in June 1927, actually increasing its vote by 11.3 percentage points compared to Fianna Fáil's increase of 9 points. Cumann na nGaedheal's recovery was aided no doubt by the sense of crisis created by the assassination of Kevin O'Higgins, and the government's stern security response to that event. In interpreting Cumann na nGaedheal's recovery, one must also bear in mind the simplification of the party system which was getting under way. First there was the near demise of the National League, which put forward only 6 candidates in September compared to 30 in June, and saw its vote drop from 7.3 to 1.6 per cent. As Figure 4.2 shows, independents also suffered heavy losses. This was no doubt partly due to pro-treaty votes turning to the government party in a time of crisis. However, it was also partly due to the simple fact that the number of independent candidates offering themselves for election more than halved (from 65 to 31).

Labour also suffered heavily in the process of party system consolidation in September 1927. After the false Labour dawn in the pact election of 1922, the real thing was a sobering experience – the party barely exceeded 10 per cent of the vote in 1923. June 1927 offered some encouragement (up two percentage points) but, once the battle between pro- and anti-treatyites began in earnest with the entry of Fianna Fáil into the Dáil, Labour support fell to 9.1 per cent. A further element in this process of simplification of the party system in September 1927 was the decline of the Farmers' Party. In common with all the minor parties, it lost substantially in the snap election of September 1927. Unlike the others, however, it was already in decline – 1923 had been its high point and it failed to blossom in the minor party springtime represented by the June 1927 election. By the late 1920s, it was clearly a spent force (see Figure 4.3). It fell to 6.4 per cent in September 1927 and to 3.1 per cent in 1932.

All of this meant that, though there was still considerable party fragmentation in September 1927 (the effective number of parties was 3.4), the trend was downwards and 1932 saw a further shake-out, as the two major parties faced one another in a contest that would decide not just the fate of the government but the nature of the constitutional settlement and the direction of Irish politics for almost two decades. Before going on to consider electoral outcomes in this next period of party competition (1932–38), it is worth developing a point made above in relation to support for independents, i.e., that support for any group or party is affected by the number of candidates that are put forward under the label in question.

Because, in PR-STV, a party can have multiple candidates in a constituency, the number of candidates put forward can have a significant effect on the party's first preference vote. The ratio[4] of candidates to total Dáil seats is shown for Fianna Fáil,

---

[4] It is necessary to express the number of party candidates or independent candidates as a ratio of candidates to total Dáil seats rather than just to give the number of candidates, because the number of Dáil seats has varied somewhat over the years.

Fine Gael, Labour and independents in Figure 4.4. It will be necessary to refer back to this graph and to some of the remarkable fluctuations in the ratios during discussion of the outcomes of elections. At this stage, three points should be noted. First, the number of independent candidates in 1923 was remarkable; the independent candidate to seat ratio was almost as high as that of Fianna Fáil and almost double that of the Labour Party. It fell somewhat in the next election (June 1927) but was still relatively high. In the light of the lower success rate of independent candidates, the occurrence of a gap of only three months between the two elections of 1927 and the intensification of party political competition resulting from Fianna Fáil entry into the Dáil, the substantial fall in the number of independent candidates in September 1927 was perhaps inevitable. It was also long-term. With the exception of 1943, it did not rise significantly again until 1977.

The second point to note is the tendency for the ratio of contestants to seats to fall in almost all instances of snap elections (i.e., an election called very soon after the previous one), with the fall being least for Fianna Fáil and greatest in the case of the independents.[5] The fact that Fianna Fáil was better than the other parties, and in particular better than the independents, at maintaining a high candidate to seat ratio in a snap election situation, combined with the frequency of snap elections in the 1930s and 1940s (1932–33, 1937–38, and 1943–44), was a contributory factor to the regularity of Fianna Fáil's recovery of votes in alternating elections in those years.

The third and final point relates to the number of constituencies contested. For the large parties, this is almost always 100 per cent; exceptions in the case of Fine Gael are noted in the discussion of particular electoral outcomes that follows. In the case of the smaller parties and independents, the number of constituencies contested can vary and can do so independently of the number of candidates put forward. The point is illustrated in the case of the Labour Party in Figure 4.5. The proportion of constituencies contested by Labour dropped quite sharply in September 1927 and in 1933. Figure 4.5 also includes the Labour share of the vote, and one can see the decline in the party's support in these two elections. The recovery in the Labour Party vote in 1937 to almost double its 1933 level is all the more impressive because it was based on contesting virtually the same proportion of constituencies and on only a slight increase in the ratio of candidates to Dáil seats. Clearly, this is also a graph to which reference will need to be made as the story of election outcomes and trends in party support unfolds.

Election outcomes, 1932–38

Lasting just four elections, all of which occurred within the space of seven years, this period saw Fianna Fáil rise to a position of remarkable dominance with 51.9 per cent of the vote in 1938. By 1932 Fianna Fáil had fully established its democratic credentials and, as indicated in chapter 2, Cumann na nGaedheal was suffering from the

---

[5] The only exceptions are the ratio for Fianna Fáil between June and September 1927 and for Labour between 1937 and 1938.

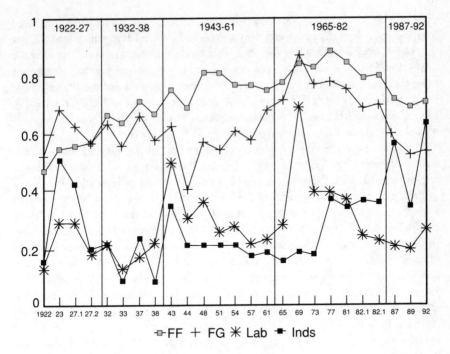

Figure 4.4 Ratio of candidates fielded to total Dáil seats, Fianna Fáil, Fine Gael, Labour (including National Labour), independents, 1922–92.

disadvantages of incumbency. As Figure 4.2 illustrates, 1932 was the decisive point at which the position of leading party swung from Cumann na nGaedheal to Fianna Fáil. The reversal of fortune opened a gap between the parties that was not even to be narrowed until the election of November 1982. The 1933 election, 'arguably the most bitter, turbulent and colourful in the history of independent Ireland' (Fanning, 1983, p. 114), confirmed Fianna Fáil's dominance with a vote that was within a hair's breadth of an absolute majority.

The normal difficulties for any party in government were compounded in this case by the economic war and the immediate adverse effects that had on specific segments of the voters. The Fianna Fáil vote fell by 4.5 percentage points in 1937. However, a combination of the snap election tactic and the surge in support due to the Anglo-Irish agreement gave Fianna Fáil an absolute majority of first preference votes in 1938.

Though Cumann na nGaedheal lost office in 1932, its loss of votes was not disastrous (down 3.4 points). However, in the following year it lost another 5 points. Both results illustrate again the importance of seeing what was happening to Cumann na nGaedheal in the context of gains and losses by adjacent parties. In 1932 it was buffered by the decline of the Farmers' Party, some of whose members actually joined Cumann na nGaedheal between 1927 and 1932, and by pre-election absorption of the remnants of the National League and some independents. In 1933, on the other hand, it suffered from the success of the newly established National Centre Party, which took 9.2 per cent of the vote and which had absorbed what was left of the Farmers' Party after the 1932 election. This challenge was taken care of by the merger of Cumann na nGaedheal and the Centre Party to form Fine Gael in the wake of the 1933 election. Despite a drop in Fianna Fáil support, and despite the merger with the Centre Party, Fine Gael support was 4.9 percentage points below the combined Cumann na nGaedheal/Centre Party strength in 1933.

We have seen that, following the entry of Fianna Fáil into the Dáil, Labour lost substantial support in the September 1927 election. Further losses occurred over the next two elections, Labour Party support going from 9.1 per cent in September 1927 to 7.7 in 1932 and to a record low of 5.3 in 1933. In the 1937 election, however, it recovered strongly, reaching its 1923 level of just over 10 per cent. Independents and micro parties had also hit a low (5 per cent) in 1933 and they too bounced back to 9.7 per cent. In both cases the decline registered in 1933 was partly explainable in terms of the reduced number of candidates fielded (see Figure 4.5). As compared to the 1932 election, Labour Party candidates were down from 32 to 19 and independents from 34 to 13. In 1937 Labour's stronger performance was less dependent on an increased number of candidates (up from 19 to 23) than was the performance of the independents (up from 13 to 36). Then, in 1938, Labour held on to its vote. This is partly explained by the party's decision, unusual in a snap election, to run more rather than fewer candidates and, in particular, to contest more constituencies (see Figure 4.5). However, the Labour vote was still only 10 per cent. At the same time, the vote for independents hit a new low. The fact that Fine Gael suffered only slight losses meant that the 1930s closed in a situation that was quite close to two-party competition. At that stage, there was little overt sign of the upheaval in the party system that was about to occur.

Election outcomes, 1943–61

As a glance at the middle period in Figures 4.2 and 4.3 will show, the shifts in electoral support in the more fragmented party system of 1943–61 were nothing if not complicated. The complexity is reflected in conflicting emphases that occur in interpretations of the early part of the period. These differences centre on the implications of the shifts in support for Fianna Fáil and on the significance of the challenges that led to those shifts. In one view 'the fruits of its efforts in the areas of social and economic policy became apparent at the 1943 election . . . even though it lost its overall majority' (Gallagher, 1985, p. 14). In similar vein, Fianna Fáil in the 1940s has been seen as moving 'into a central position in Irish society', as appearing to be in an 'unassailable' position and as having created 'an extraordinary electoral empire' (Garvin, 1981, p. 166). But the opposite view has also been argued, i.e. that the 1940s saw Fianna Fáil under threat from a new radical mobilisation involving a tripartite assault on its 'neglected have-not constituency'. In this interpretation, the 1940s contained the seeds of a potential realignment of the party system along left–right lines, which 'might have induced an alternative language of politics' (Mair, 1987, pp. 52–3). What then do

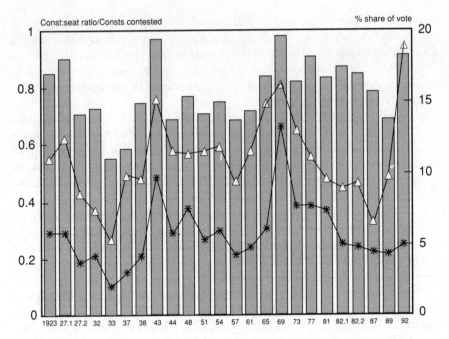

Figure 4.5 Labour Party ratio of candidates fielded to Dáil seats, proportion of constituencies contested, and share of vote, 1923–92 (including National Labour, 1944–48).

Figures 4.2 and 4.3 tell us about party fortunes and the unassailability or otherwise of Fianna Fáil in this period of renewed party fragmentation?

In the first place, 1943 did involve a precipitous fall of 10 per cent for Fianna Fáil compared to the 1938 outcome, and was one of the party's two worst performances in the fifty-seven-year period between 1932 and 1989 (significantly, the other low point was in 1948) (see Figure 4.2). The notion of 1943, or the 1940s in general, as the time when Fianna Fáil blossomed or became unassailable must therefore be treated with some caution. On the other hand, while Fianna Fáil may not have been unassailable, it was clear that Fine Gael would not be mounting an assault. Fine Gael support had held up reasonably well in the 1930s, partly through what might be described as a series of mergers and acquisitions. Between 1938 and 1948, however, the party went into a quite dramatic slide. As Figure 4.2 shows, its drop in 1943 was as steep as that of Fianna Fáil and, unlike Fianna Fáil, it did not recover in 1944. In fact, Fine Gael's weakness in the 1944 election must be taken into account in assessing the significance of Fianna Fáil's recovery to 48.8 per cent in that election. That recovery was facilitated by the very substantial drop in the number of candidates put forward and seats contested by Fine Gael, Labour and independents (see Figure 4.4). In 1944, Fine Gael's overall number of candidates was down from eighty-seven to fifty-five, and there were four constituencies in which it fielded no candidates at all – Cavan, Galway East, Kerry North, and Monaghan. In these circumstances, it is not surprising that, unlike Fianna Fáil, Fine Gael did not bounce back in 1944 following its severe drop in votes the previous year. On the other hand, the number of candidates put forward is not everything – despite the fact that the party fielded 82 candidates in 1948, its vote actually slipped again, this time to below 20 per cent.

If Fine Gael in the 1940s was not much of a threat, what of the three-pronged attack on Fianna Fáil from the left? The danger to Fianna Fáil in 1943 from Labour may be somewhat exaggerated by the dramatic jump in Labour nominations and constituencies contested by the Labour Party in the 1943 election (see Figure 4.5). In 1943 the number of Labour candidates more than doubled to 70 and the party contested all but one constituency. The artificially strong Labour challenge was short-lived. In 1944 Labour and National Labour combined contested 21 of the 31 constituencies with 40 candidates. Thus, if we accept that Labour's peak in 1943 was artificially high – boosted by an unrealistically high rate of nominations – it follows that, in 1943, there was less danger to Fianna Fáil and less prospect of a left–right realignment of the party system, at least one based on the traditional left, than appears at first sight.

The second element in the notion of a tripartite attack on Fianna Fáil was Clann na Talmhan. This new agrarian small-holder party won 10.3 per cent nationally in 1943 and was a considerably more formidable force in the western counties. Its western bias and small-farmer orientation immediately suggests that Clann na Talmhan was mainly a threat to Fianna Fáil. It did in fact contribute heavily to Fianna Fáil losses in the west in 1943, but the new party also made severe inroads on Fine Gael. Remarkably for a new arrival, it was not knocked off course by the sudden calling of another election in 1944 and managed to retain its share of the vote despite fielding a considerably reduced number of candidates. Four years later, however, its vote was halved and, despite participation in the 1948 government, it was downhill from there on.

The third element in the three-pronged challenge to Fianna Fáil in the 1940s was potentially more serious than the brief and unsustainable sally mounted by Labour in 1943, or the sectionally- and regionally-circumscribed Clann na Talmhan surge, which was evidently on the way out by 1948. De Valera certainly seemed to take the challenge seriously, as he brought the 1948 election forward in the hope of nipping Clann na Poblachta in the bud. Clann na Poblachta reinforced the fragmentation of the party system with an impressive 13.2 per cent in 1948. However, as noted in chapter 2, this did not come up to its own expectations and its decline between then and the next election (1951) was as sharp as its rise had been.

In summary, neither the unassailability of Fianna Fáil nor the strength of a tripartite left-wing challenge to it stand out as the main features of the 1940s. What is clear is that Fianna Fáil was vulnerable, but it is equally clear that its traditional opponents were weak and that the prospects of a new party or a number of new parties causing a fundamental upset in the system were ephemeral.

The remainder of this multi-party period (1943–61) was marked by a strong recovery by Fine Gael, a trend that was interrupted only once within the period – in 1957. Both Fine Gael's recovery and the one hiccup that occurred in it were closely related to the impact of the formation of the coalition government in 1948. This meant that for the first time since the early 1930s, voters could clearly identify a government seeking to be returned to office and an alternative government able and more than willing to take over. As long as this situation obtained, that is, in the elections of 1951, 1954, and 1957, the voters seized the chance and produced alternation of government on each occasion, perhaps blaming the 'ins' for the hapless state of the economy. Alternation would have been the result again in 1961, as Fianna Fáil confirmed its pendulum pattern by winning only 43.8 per cent of the vote and 70 of the 144 seats. However, there was no viable combination among the six parties and six independents holding the remaining seventy-four seats, and Fianna Fáil took office as a minority government.

Whereas Fianna Fáil's vote in the 1950s was a straightforward up–down pattern, depending on whether it was in opposition or in office, the movement of votes among the main partners to the coalition arrangement was more complex. Fine Gael was the undoubted gainer from the coalition arrangement – its vote rose 6 percentage points in 1951; the Labour Party gained 2.7 points but this was really a paper gain due to the reconciliation with National Labour, which had taken 2.7 and 2.6 per cent in 1944 and 1948 respectively. As the senior partner in a prospective alternative government, Fine Gael gained another 6 points in 1954, while Labour notched up a mere 0.7. Both were, however, punished for what was seen as the inept response to the economic crisis of 1956, Fine Gael losing 5.4 percentage points and Labour losing three.

The other main feature of the latter part of this period is the demise of the new challengers and a gradual reduction in the fragmentation of the party system. As Figure 4.3 shows, there was one brief exception to this declining fragmentation, with the electoral re-emergence of Sinn Féin in 1957. It took 5.3 per cent of the vote in that election but the challenge did not last, and its support declined to 3.1 per cent in the 1961 election, after which the party withdrew again from the electoral arena. In 1954 the independents suffered their biggest decline since 1938, and the significance of the decline was increased by the fact that it occurred after a three-year inter-election period, and not in a snap election situation as had been the case with all the previous substantial falls in independent support. The fall was due in part to a consolidation of the party system, as eight out of the fourteen incumbent independent TDs joined one or other of the main parties (Chubb, 1957, p. 133).

Election outcomes, 1965–82

All of the three main parties made simultaneous gains in the 1965 election, gains that set the scene for almost a twenty-year period (1965–82), characterised by what has been labelled two-and-a-half-party competition. The gains by the main parties were at the expense of Clann na Talmhan and Sinn Féin, both of which retired from the electoral fray, and particularly at the expense of the independents.

As Figure 4.3 shows, independent support fell in the 1965 election to its lowest level ever. In considering this, one must immediately note that the drop coincided with a quite significant change in the form of the ballot paper. In virtue of the 1963 Electoral

Act, and for the first time in an Irish election, party names could appear on the ballot paper. The increase all round for the main parties, and the substantial decrease for the independents, may well have been influenced by the fact that those voters who had only a marginal interest in politics, and who therefore may have been less well-informed about the party affiliation of candidates, now had clear and unambiguous information on the ballot paper as to which party the candidates they were voting for represented. Independent candidates may also have been adversely affected by the fact that the 1963 Electoral Act removed existing restrictions on constituency campaign expenditure (Farrell, 1992). However, within this period of two-and-a-half-party competition, the independent vote recovered substantially in 1977, peaked in 1981, after which it slumped in the two elections held in quick succession (February and November 1982).

The 1965 gain for Fianna Fáil was particularly significant, as it was the first time in the party's history that it gained votes as an incumbent government after a full term of office. The Fianna Fáil vote over the remainder of the period can be easily described. It was a steady state vote with smaller gains and losses than in any previous period, except, that is, for the 1977 election, when its vote shot up to above 50 per cent.

For Fine Gael the period was, with a single exception, one of a slow steady climb to the peak of November 1982, a result that put the party within 6 percentage points of Fianna Fáil. The exception was 1977, and Fine Gael's slump in that election was the inevitable corollary of the Fianna Fáil success. In some ways it mirrored the previous serious check in the post-war recovery of Fine Gael – that of 1957. Then also Fine Gael had been the dominant partner in a coalition government that had the misfortune to preside over a serious recession. This fact itself may bear as much responsibility for Fine Gael's losses as did the extraordinary Fianna Fáil campaign of that year (see the discussion of this point in chapter 7).

Labour's is the dramatic story of the period 1965–82. Under its new leadership, it had gained significantly in 1961 and it forged ahead in 1965, virtually matching its previous best result (that of 1943). In 1969 it advanced again, albeit by a small amount. However, this was its third successive rise. In fact, 1965 was the more impressive performance. Labour's 1969 result must, like that of 1943, be substantially discounted in virtue of the extraordinary increase in the number of candidates in that election (see Figure 4.5). The 1969 gains were also discounted in the minds of Labour strategists and activists, because, as noted above, after the leftward tilt in the party, they measured the gains against the expectation that the '70s would be socialist. Far from being socialist, the '70s saw a slump in the socialist vote that continued up to the end of this two-and-a-half party system period. This performance was made all the more agonising for the party by the fact that these were the years either of participation in coalition government (with Fine Gael), or of explicit or implicit coalition electoral strategy.

Finally, in this period of two-and-a-half-party competition, there was the emergence of the Workers' Party, previously Sinn Féin The Workers' Party. In absolute terms its vote in this period remained fairly paltry. What is impressive, however, was the steadiness of its progress over successive elections. That progress was such that, by 1987, it had become a contributory factor in the shift back to a multi-party system. The real and immediate agent of that shift, however, was the Progressive Democrat Party.

Election outcomes, 1987–92

As already noted, the Progressive Democrats burst on to the political scene in 1985 with a remarkable level of support in the opinion polls (in the region of 20 per cent). Their first real electoral showing was not as dramatic but – at 11.9 per cent – was impressive nonetheless. It was certainly enough to have a quite fundamental effect on the other parties and to shake the party system decisively out of the two-and-a-half-party pattern which had prevailed since 1965. Despite a halving of the Progressive Democrat vote in the 1989 election, the fragmentation of the party system continued and it was reinforced in 1992 by the simultaneous losses registered by the two big parties and the dramatic gains by Labour.

The parallels in Figure 4.3 between the graphs of support for the Progressive Democrats between 1987 and 1992, and that for Clann na Poblachta between 1948 and 1954, are striking. One should, however, be cautious about inferring that the Progressive Democrats will suffer the same fate as Clann na Poblachta. In the first place, the Progressive Democrats had not, by 1992, fallen as low as Clann na Poblachta in their third election. Secondly, the Progressive Democrat vote of 4.7 per cent in 1992 yielded ten seats, a number that is sufficient to enable the party to play a significant role in opposition.

.The arrival of the Progressive Democrats in 1987 had a small but crucial impact on the Fianna Fáil vote. If Fianna Fáil had followed its usual pendulum pattern, it would have swung back in 1987, after its loss in November 1982. The regularity of the swing of the pendulum for Fianna Fáil had been upset once before. As already noted, the Fianna Fáil vote had gone in the same direction in two successive elections in 1973 and 1977, but that upset to the pattern had been a positive one. In 1987, the trend was down for the second successive time – admittedly down fractionally, but down nonetheless. As Figure 4.2 shows, the Fianna Fáil vote stayed exactly on par between 1987 and 1989. The real change came in 1992. The fall from the dizzy heights of 1977 excepted, Fianna Fáil had not seen anything like a drop of 5 per cent in its vote since 1961. More significantly, it was a fall of 5 per cent from a relatively low point and, as a result, it put Fianna Fáil below the psychologically important 40 per cent mark. Fianna Fáil had not even had to contemplate such a figure since 1927, and in 1927 it was below 40 per cent and climbing.

Between 1982 and 1987 Fine Gael was again the senior partner in a coalition government in a difficult economic period. This time the fall was more than twice what it had been in 1957 and 1977. Figure 4.2 suggests that it was Fine Gael that was most affected by the arrival of the Progressive Democrats in 1987. Its vote loss

(12 percentage points) was even greater than its previous crash in 1943, and it was compounded by the failure to regain more than a fraction of the lost ground in 1989 and by a further fall in 1992. The rise and rise of Fine Gael, which had lasted, with only two blips, from 1948 to 1982, had been severely checked.

In 1987, the Labour vote fell to 6.4 per cent. The figure is extraordinary, even when one takes into account that there was another 4 or 5 per cent out there voting left, that is, for the Workers' Party or for left-leaning independents. What is even more extraordinary is that the party could come back in the space of two elections and five years to 19 per cent of the vote – its highest figure ever if we discount the 1922 result as not really a Labour Party vote. The party's level of support in 1992 was boosted by a jump in the number of constituencies contested (to the highest since 1969) (see Figure 4.5). On the other hand, it was not artificially boosted by a big increase in the number of candidates, as in 1943 and 1969. In sum, 1992 stands out as Labour's strongest performance to date.

In 1992, the combined vote for the Workers' Party and Democratic Left was 1.5 percentage points behind the vote for the Workers' Party in 1989. Thus, Labour's recovery plus the split in the Workers' Party put paid to the run of successive increases chalked up by the Workers' Party in its various guises over a series of seven elections since 1973. Finally, to complete the picture of the contemporary multi-party phase, it should be noted that the independent vote recovered in 1992 to the level last attained in 1981. It did so, however, on the basis of an all-time high in the ratio of candidates to seats (see Figure 4.4).

Voter volatility

With the trends portrayed in Figures 4.2 and 4.3 in mind, we can return to one of the basic questions raised in chapter 1, that is, what is the relationship, if any, between the extensive demographic, economic and social change which Irish society has undergone and political, or more specifically, electoral change? How much change in electoral support do the patterns in Figure 4.2 imply? How does the timing of electoral change relate to the timing of changes in society? In a word, how volatile has voting behaviour been and when has volatility been most evident?

It is essential to distinguish between aggregate and individual-level volatility. Aggregate volatility is the net change in support for the parties that is observable in the election results. It is called aggregate volatility because election results only tell us how aggregates of individuals, not individuals themselves, voted. The lowest level of aggregation at which election results are published is the constituency. In the discussion so far we have been considering results at a much higher level of aggregation, i.e. the national level. However, at any level of aggregation, the problem of net change, adverted to in chapter 1, remains. All we know about is the net effect of a host of individual decisions to switch to and from particular parties, that is, all we know is the overall effect of a possibly much larger level of individual volatility. Clearly, the two kinds of volatility are related but, because of the possible cancelling-out effect of movements of individual voters in opposite directions, individual-level volatility will always be greater than aggregate volatility. On the other hand, it may be reasonable to treat one as an indicator of the other. Bartolini and Mair argue strongly in favour of this approach, on the assumption that 'the measurable levels of aggregate volatility and changes in these levels over time reflect corresponding changes in levels of individual volatility' (Bartolini and Mair, 1990, p. 37). In support of this assumption they cite Denver's conclusion that there are reasonably high levels of correlation between individual and aggregate volatility in those cases where measures of both are available (Bartolini and Mair, 1990, p. 30). They also cite the results of a simulation which shows that the probability of a positive association between aggregate and individual levels of volatility is quite high. They conclude that these tests confirm 'the basic validity – given a sufficient number of cases – of considering aggregate volatility as one approximate indicator of individual volatility' (Bartolini and Mair, 1990, p. 34).

Though the interpretation of it may be somewhat problematic, aggregate volatility is easily measured, i.e. volatility is the sum of each party's gains or losses divided by two, or more precisely, it is the sum of the percentage point change in each party's share of the vote divided by two.[6]

When the average level of volatility is measured over the history of the state up to 1985, and placed in the context of a century of electoral outcomes in Europe (1885–1985), Ireland emerges as the third most volatile country, behind Germany and France (Bartolini and Mair, 1990, p. 73). If we restrict the comparison to contemporaneous or near contemporaneous periods, that is, Ireland from 1923 to 1985 compared to other European countries from 1918 to 1985, average volatility in Ireland is not quite so high relative to other countries, but is still in the upper half of the ranking – Ireland is the sixth most volatile out of fifteen countries.[7]

Turning to trends in volatility, there is evidence that volatility declined in the period 1948–82 – 'at five of the six elections between 1948 and 1965 net volatility was higher than at any of the six subsequent elections' (Marsh, 1985, p. 178). Just as the overall average level seems somewhat higher than one might have expected, this too seems contrary to expectations, that is, to the expectation that volatility would have increased as social change accelerated. It also sharpens the question of what happens to the pattern of volatility when the elections of 1987, 1989 and 1992 are considered.

Total volatility between successive pairs of Irish elections is traced by the top line in Figure 4.6. The first and, perhaps, obvious point is that volatility tends to be higher in the multi-party periods identified earlier in this chapter. This contrast is particularly evident when we compare the 1943–61 period with the period immediately following it, 1965–82. Thus the overall decline in volatility in the elections between 1969 and 1982 (the 1977 election being an exception) that was identified by Marsh can be seen to be related to the concentration in the party system that

---

[6] The formula is $\frac{\sum P_{it} - P_{i(t+1)}}{2}$ where P is the proportion of votes won by party i at time t. For a discussion of the index see Pedersen, 1979.

[7] My thanks to Peter Mair for providing the comparative figures for the 1918–85 period.

occurred during this period. The decline ended abruptly in 1987, when a steep rise in volatility accompanied the return of the multi-party system in that election. Volatility between 1987 and 1989 was somewhat lower but it rose substantially again in 1992.

At the outset of this chapter it was emphasized that there was a need to take account not just of the overall level of fragmentation in the party system, but of the location of such fragmentation. This is a crucial question because if there is more fragmentation on one side than on the other, there is likely to be greater volatility on that side. If this is so, then volatility across the political divide or cleavage line may be much less than the general level of volatility in the system. It can be argued that these considerations are particularly important in the Irish case because the process of alignment was asymmetric, that is, it was much stronger and more definite on the anti-treaty side than on the pro-treaty side (Sinnott, 1978, p. 39).

In dealing with this point on a comparative basis, Bartolini and Mair distinguish between total volatility (i.e. volatility for all individual parties) and block volatility (i.e. volatility across the political divide or between blocks of parties, the blocks being defined in terms of the prevailing cleavage in society). As they put it, 'by aggregating the parties into blocks, and by distinguishing between cleavage allies and cleavage opponents, we can move away from an emphasis on the individual party, and gain a real sense of the extent of change across the cleavage boundary' (Bartolini and Mair, 1990, p. 65). Bartolini and Mair analyse block volatility in terms of the cleavage that has dominated European politics for much of the last century – the class cleavage. Looked at in terms of this cleavage, Ireland moves from third most volatile in terms of total volatility to third least volatile. While it is interesting to see Ireland in this comparative class politics perspective, the key question is what has been the volatility across the dominant cleavage line in Irish politics, which at this stage can be defined simply in terms of the inherited divisions between Fianna Fáil (Sinn Féin in 1923) and the rest.[8]

We have seen that overall volatility in June 1927 was enormously high. Implementing the distinction just outlined shows that pro-treaty/anti-treaty block volatility was negligible (see Figure 4.6). This is because the main sources of volatility in that election – the decline of Sinn Féin and the emergence of Fianna Fáil on the one hand, and the success of the National League and independents at the expense of Cumann na nGaedheal on the other – were movements within each block. The approach also demonstrates that volatility in the second election of 1927 was mostly on the pro-treaty side, and hence that block volatility was also low in that election. Block volatility was, however, substantial in 1932, as Fianna Fáil replaced Cumann na nGaedheal as the dominant party, and again in 1943, as its extraordinary feat of winning over 50 per cent of the poll in 1938 was challenged

---

[8] The meaning of these inherited divisions and how that meaning may have changed over time is taken up in some detail in chapter 11. Using the term 'conflict area' rather then 'block' and defining the conflict areas in Ireland as Fianna Fáil versus the rest, Mair has examined the relationship between inter-party and inter-area volatility in Ireland for the period 1948–77 (Mair, 1983, pp. 408–14).

by Labour and Clann na Talmhan. After the relatively turbulent 1940s, block volatility gradually dropped to a low point in 1973, from which it was jolted by the dramatic Fianna Fáil victory in 1977 and the equally dramatic recovery of Fine Gael in 1981. Both total and block volatility were minimal in the elections of 1982. In 1987 and 1989, however, they diverge again – with high overall volatility, minimal block volatility, and with the drama of the 1987 election leaving Fianna Fáil, on aggregate, relatively unscathed. The final point on the graph brings out the significance of the 1992 election – the fact that it was not just a volatile election but that a substantial part of that volatility involved deep inroads on Fianna Fáil support.

Conclusion

The Irish party system has gone through five periods, alternating between a multi-party format and a two-and-a-half-party format: 1922–27 (multi-party); 1932–38 (two-and-a-half-party); 1943–61 (multi-party); 1965–82 (two-and-a-half-party) and 1987–92 (multi-party). One of the most remarkable features of Fianna Fáil has been its ability, prior to 1992, to maintain its electoral dominance in both types of competitive situation. Having made the breakthrough in two steps (September 1927 and 1932), its electoral performance up to 1982 has been a story of rise and fall,

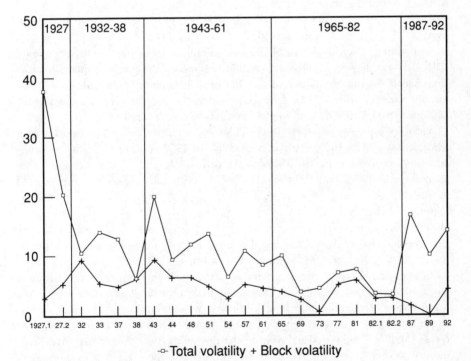

-□-Total volatility + Block volatility

Figure 4.6 Total and block volatility in Irish elections, 1927–92.

rise and fall in each successive election, no matter how many parties were challenging its dominance. Even with the new period of multi-party competition in 1987, Fianna Fáil seemed to be able to repeat its trick of remaining relatively immune to the changes going on all around it, although, for the first time ever, its vote fell in two elections in a row. Having failed to recover any ground in 1989, however, the party then continued the downward trend with a substantial drop in 1992 that took it to a level of support lower than anything since before it had first assumed office sixty years previously.

In contrast to Fianna Fáil's up-down pattern, Fine Gael support has tended to go through phases in which it has either been falling or rising more or less consistently. Its falls have been precipitous and its rises more gradual. Its low points (June 1927, 1943–48 and 1987–92) underline the party's vulnerability to the challenge of multi-party competition.

Labour has also had its peaks and valleys. The valleys have been widely separated in time – 1933 and 1987. The earlier peaks (1922, 1943 and 1969) need to be discounted somewhat in virtue of special circumstances (the 1922 'Pact' election) or in virtue of very large jumps in the number of candidates nominated. These considerations suggest that the Labour high points of real substance were 1965 and, most substantial of all, 1992.

The identification of periods of multipartyism emphasizes the importance at certain times of the presence of parties other than these three – in the 1920s, in the 1940s and 1950s and since 1987. Ireland's first period of multipartyism was short-lived (1922–27), though it did include four elections. It can be ascribed to a process of formation and settling down of the basic alignment. The next multiparty period (1943–61) was, however, a challenge to that alignment. Although the threefold challenge faded out, its occurrence in the first place has quite substantial implications for our interpretation of the Irish party system and Irish electoral alignments. Multipartyism returned again in 1987 and was reinforced in 1992.

Volatility was extremely high in the 1920s and remained fairly high over the next three decades. With the exception created by the 1977 election, volatility was substantially lower from the late 1960s to the early 1980s and it returned again with some force in 1987. Thus, in the period when social and economic change started to intensify, electoral change, at least at the aggregate level, decreased. It may be, therefore, that electoral change and social and economic change are quite unrelated. On the other hand, the possibility that they are related with a built-in lag effect, so that electoral change does follow social change, but only after a certain lapse of time, is suggested by the arrival of substantial volatility in 1987.

In assessing these trends, it is vital to distinguish between total volatility and block volatility, that is, volatility across the main cleavage line in the system. In the majority of elections, block volatility was substantially less than total volatility, indicating that, as between Fianna Fáil and its opponents, there was considerable stability. There is also, however, the possibility that change may have been more extensive at certain times than appears from the estimates of aggregate-level volatility presented in this chapter. In order to analyse this issue and, in order to probe the sources of various aspects of voting behaviour in general elections, it is necessary to pursue the analysis further, first to the level of the constituencies (chapter 5) and then to the level of the individual voters (chapters 6 and 7).

Chapter 5

Regions, cartography and correlations: evidence from aggregate data

It is a truism that an election is not one single contest, but forty-one (or however many constituencies there are), each with its own peculiarities and circumstances, each making its contribution to the overall result and each at the same time being influenced to a greater or lesser extent by national trends. From the point of view of analysing voting behaviour, these constituency variations generate a wealth of data, but this produces its own problems, i.e. how to piece the bits together into some coherent pattern, how to generalise and how to avoid becoming lost in the detail of the swings and roundabouts in the constituencies. Various approaches have been used to deal with the problem – looking at party support by region, examining the more detailed constituency-by-constituency results using maps and, finally, resorting to statistical analysis of voting and census data. The discussion that follows in this chapter uses all three approaches – regional analysis, cartographic analysis and correlational analysis – bearing in mind throughout that these are really all just different and complementary approaches to the same problem, that of trying to clarify the factors underlying the spatial variations in the vote.

Regional trends

Fianna Fáil

Two features stand out when one breaks the Fianna Fáil vote down by region (Figure 5.1). The first is the uniformity of the swings to and from Fianna Fáil across the four regions. The swings may vary in their extent but, in all elections between Fianna Fáil's first election in June 1927 and the election of 1965, all four regions moved in the same direction. The 1969 election broke the pattern, initiating a period (1969–92) in which Fianna Fáil was consistently lower in Dublin than in any other region. Such a gap had previously existed in the '20s and early '30s but had lasted only over a period of three elections.

The other obvious and related feature of the regional pattern of Fianna Fáil support is the party's strength on Connacht-Ulster, both in the 1930s and from 1965 on. Its position in the north-western region in the 1930s was extraordinary, being above 50 per cent of the vote in three successive elections. Extraordinary, but precarious, in that between 1938 and 1943 it plunged from 58 per cent to 43 per cent. Fianna Fáil's strength in

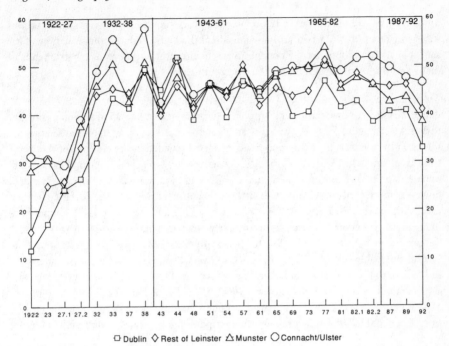

□ Dublin ◇ Rest of Leinster △ Munster ○ Connacht/Ulster

Figure 5.1 Anti-Treaty Sinn Féin/Fianna Fáil vote by region, 1922–92.

Connacht-Ulster has in fact been both more stable and more durable, though less spectacular, in the recent past then in the 20s and 30s. In 1965, it edged close to the 50 per cent mark in the region and remained at or above that point until 1989. Oddly enough, Connacht-Ulster did not participate in the otherwise nation-wide swing to Fianna Fáil in 1977. Fianna Fáil's exceptional performance in Connacht-Ulster would be even more evident were it not for the fact that, due presumably to the popularity of Cork-based Taoiseach Jack Lynch, the party's vote in Munster went against the swing of the pendulum in 1969 and remained high as long as Lynch remained Taoiseach, culminating in the remarkable level of 54 per cent in 1977. Support for Fianna Fáil in Connacht-Ulster fell in three successive recent elections (1987, 1989 and 1992), but this still left it substantially ahead of support for the party elsewhere.

A less obvious, but no less important, feature of the regional trends in the Fianna Fáil vote is the rapidity of the rise in the party's vote in Dublin in the early years. This is less obvious because it is overshadowed by the party's even more impressive performance outside Dublin, but, if one is to understand the Fianna Fáil vote in this period, it is vital to note that it had 43 per cent of the vote in Dublin (city and county combined) as early as 1933. The discussion in chapter 4 of the significance of the 1943 election for Fianna Fáil noted the need for caution in interpreting what happened in 1943 as a shift to a more promising support base, or as the achievement of nation-wide support by Fianna Fail. The present regional analysis confirms the point. The 1943 election was a negative experience for Fianna Fáil in all regions, and it resulted in a more even spread of support only because the party's losses in its western stronghold were so precipitous. Its real nation-wide breakthrough occurred much earlier. This aspect of the development of Fianna Fáil can be brought out more clearly by means of maps and the point is therefore taken up again below.

Fine Gael

The Fine Gael regional pattern of support is like that of Fianna Fáil in several important respects (see Figure 5.2). As Cumann na nGaedheal, it was quite strong in Connacht-Ulster in the 1920s, and that region has consistently turned in the best performance for Fine Gael since the 1960s. The Fine Gael success in Connacht-Ulster in 1965 is quite remarkable. Its vote was up 11 percentage points. The success was not further extended, however, and Connacht-Ulster made little or no contribution to the building up of Fine Gael support under Garret FitzGerald between 1977 and February 1982. Cumann na nGaedheal's other area of strength in the early years was Dublin, where it won over 50 per cent of the vote in 1923 and close to 50 in September 1927. Dublin ceased to be a Fine Gael stronghold in 1937 and has only once and very fleetingly filled that role since then, in 1982. With the benefit of hindsight, one can see that Dublin has not really been favourable terrain for Fine Gael since the early 1960s. Like Fianna Fáil, the party's current area of weakness is in fact Dublin, a situation brought about by its catastrophic fall from 43.1 to 23.7 per cent in 1987. The problem was compounded by a further slight fall in Dublin

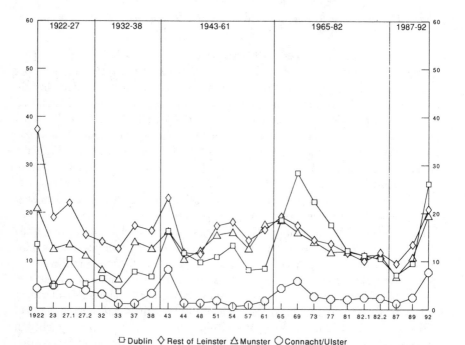

□ Dublin   ◇ Rest of Leinster   △ Munster   ○ Connacht/Ulster

Figure 5.2 Pro-Treaty Sinn Féin/Cumann na nGaedheal/Fine Gael vote by region, 1922–92.

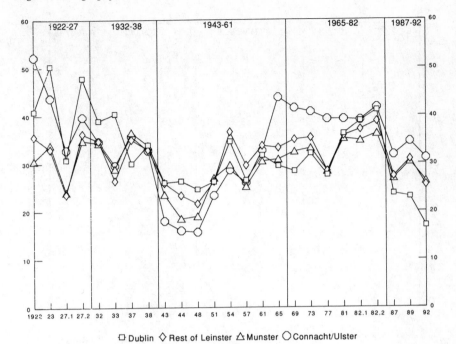

Figure 5.3 Labour vote by region, 1922–92.

in 1989 (against the trend elsewhere), and by a drop to its lowest vote ever in Dublin in 1992. The three elections of 1981–82, in which the party put in a strong Dublin performance, actually surpassing Fianna Fáil in the area in November 1982, appear as three exceptions crammed into a brief eighteen-month period.

Labour

Labour in the early years of the state presents a straight contrast with Fianna Fáil and Fine Gael – its strength was clearly and unambiguously located in the rest of Leinster and in Munster (see Figure 5.3). Dublin, which might have been expected to be a Labour stronghold, trailed the other two regions until 1943 and, after equalising briefly with them in 1943 and 1944, fell back into third position again between 1948 and 1961. Dublin appears, in fact, to be a remarkably volatile area for Labour. It has been as low as 3.6 per cent in 1933, 8.1 in 1957 and 7.1 in 1987. In between these lows, it has scored 16.2 per cent in 1943, 28.3 per cent in 1969 and 26.1 per cent in 1992. Note that in 1969 Labour's rise in Dublin was accompanied by quite significant losses in its two traditionally strong areas (rest of Leinster and Munster). In the light of this, it is no wonder that the party's public representatives and party activists from these areas were in a critical mood after the 1969 election (see chapter 2). However, Dublin followed suit in the next election, setting out on what was to be the downward path of the other regions with added alacrity and catching up with them in 1981. The volatility which has characterised Labour in Dublin was again evident in 1992 – the increase in support for the party was 16.6 percentage points.

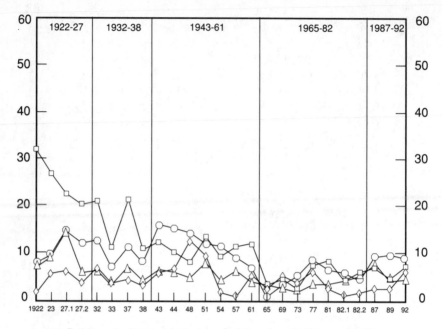

 ⊡ Dublin   ◇ Rest of Leinster   △ Munster   ○ Connacht-Ulster

Figure 5.4 Independent vote by region, 1922–92.

Independents

Independents have been a negligible quantity in Munster and, with the exception of 1948, in Leinster over the years (see Figure 5.4). Their presence was particularly marked in Dublin in the 1920s and into the mid-1930s, but declined to a moderate level there in 1938 and remained more or less at that level for the next two decades. In 1965 independent support in Dublin plummeted and, though it recovered somewhat in 1977, 1981 and 1992, it never reached the level it had maintained in the capital in the 40s and 50s. Since the early 1970s, the strength of independents has been in Connacht-Ulster, where, apart from the elections of February and November 1982, they have won over 5 per cent, and in the recent elections close to 10 per cent, of the vote.

In order to complete the picture of regional variations in general election voting behaviour, it is worth briefly considering the regional pattern of turnout over the years. Once we take into account the underestimation of turnout in Connacht-Ulster, in particular in the 1920s (see chapter 3), the main regional contrast has been that Dublin has had consistently lower turnout (see Figure 5.5). At certain times, by going against the national trend or by going with a downward national trend, except more sharply, Dublin showed very substantially lower turnout in comparison with the other regions. This occurred in 1938, in 1951 and, quite dramatically, in 1957. This latter dip might be thought to be explainable in terms of the same factor that accounted for much of the apparent low turnout in the 1920s, that is, in terms of a surplus on the electoral register. Such a surplus might have been thought to arise due to the very high levels of

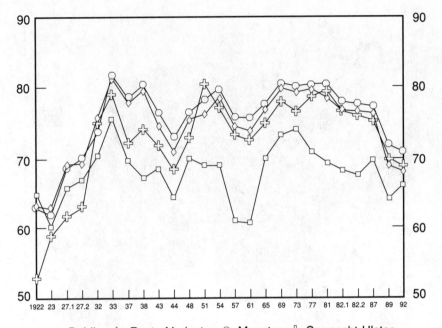

-□- Dublin -◇- Rest of Leinster ○ Munster -✛- Connacht-Ulster

Figure 5.5 Turn-out in general elections by region, 1922–92.

emigration in the 1950s. However, analysis of the electoral register does not indicate any such surplus and the decline would appear to be genuine. A decline against the trend elsewhere also occurred in Dublin in 1977 and 1981 (though turnout in the rest of Leinster also declined in the latter year). Some of the decline in Dublin in the late 70s and early 80s can be attributed to a change in the registration procedure in the Dublin borough that created a cumulating surplus of names on the register (Keogh and Whelan, 1986, p. 1). Even allowing for the register effect, however, Dublin continued to show a lower propensity to vote than the rest of the country.

This kind of regional analysis of voting behaviour raises rather than answers questions, the general form of the questions raised being 'what is it about region X that makes the performance of party Y different or that accounts for lower or higher levels of turnout?' One can immediately begin to speculate on the answers – the variations may be due to urban–rural differences, or to different historical experiences and traditions or to regional variations in social and economic conditions. To take a specific example, could the regional contrasts noted be related to the predominance of small farms in the north and west, and to the fact that 'only 12 per cent of the land of Ulster [3 counties] and 17 per cent of Connacht have a moderately wide use range, contrasting with 35 per cent of Munster and 54 per cent of Leinster' (Gillmor, 1985, p. 174)?

Such speculations as to the sources of the different voting patterns observed at regional level raise a fundamental question – are the regions homogeneous in respect of the key variables? Are they the best possible definitions of region? In fact, the ques-

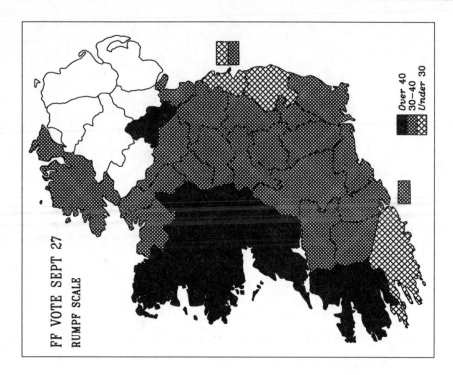

FF VOTE SEPT 27
RUMPF SCALE

Over 40
30–40
Under 30

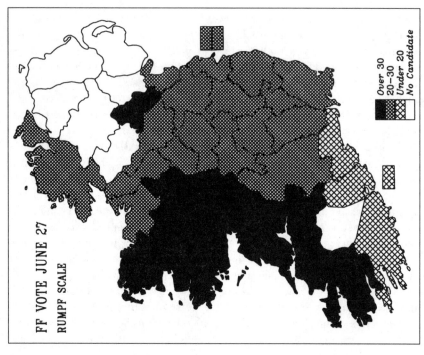

FF VOTE JUNE 27
RUMPF SCALE

Over 30
20–30
Under 20
No Candidate

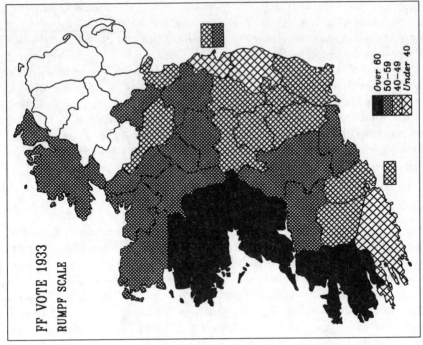

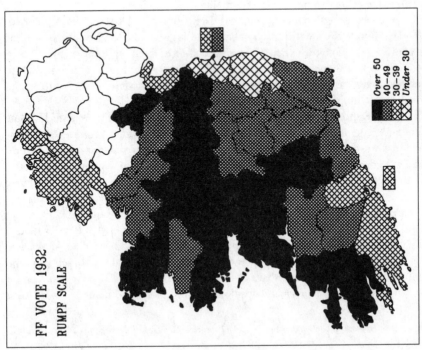

Figure 5.6 Rumpf cartographic analysis of Fianna Fáil vote, 1927–33.

tion suggests that the analysis should be conducted at the level of the individual constituencies rather than at a regional level. Once this is done, the problems of change and stability and of what variables or characteristics of localities 'account for' the variations in voting can be tackled much more systematically. There is a choice of approach – the analysis can be conducted by using maps or by an appropriate statistical technique. The mapping or cartographical approach can be used for either purpose – to analyse trends in spatial distribution of support for parties from election to election, or to search for relationships between support for a particular party and a variety of social, economic, demographic and historical variables. Both purposes were pursued in a remarkable pioneering study of Irish elections by Rumpf (Rumpf, 1959; Rumpf and Hepburn, 1977).

Mapping the trends: a centre-periphery conflict?

The issue of spatial contrasts in party support is of particular importance, because, if such contrasts could indeed be identified, the possibility of interpreting Irish party support in terms of a centre-periphery cleavage, and thus of fitting the Irish party system within one of the standard comparative schemas used in the analysis of West European party systems would be considerably enhanced.[1] The regional analysis already considered in this chapter has provided some conflicting indications. However, as the concept of centre-peripheral is essentially spatial but may not be adequately captured by standard definitions of region, cartography provides the ideal method of examining the centre–periphery interpretation.

The initial evidence is indeed promising. In the first place, Rumpf's cartographical method led him to the identification of 'an east-west gradient' defined in terms of the degree of anglicisation, the extent of the preservation of the Irish language and the proportion of non-Catholics in the population. Corresponding to this gradient, Rumpf found that there was a 'general gradient of increasing IRA activity from east to west of the country' (Rumpf and Hepburn, 1977, pp. 42–9).

Secondly, Rumpf's maps of the anti-treaty vote in 1923, and of the Fianna Fáil vote in June and September 1927, 1932 and 1933, seem to demonstrate an impressively consistent east-west political divide (redrawn maps using Rumpf's data and scales are presented in Figure 5.6). In interpreting these maps of Fianna Fáil support, however, it is vital to note that the scale used in shading the various levels of support varies from map to map. This means that a particular shading pattern, say the second darkest shading in Figure 5.6, signifies 20–30 per cent support for Fianna Fáil in June 1927, 30–40 per cent in September 1927, 40 to 50 per cent in 1932 and 50–60 per cent in 1933. Although Fianna Fáil's early successes outside the western area are adverted to in the text (Rumpf and Hepburn, 1977, p. 107), and although close inspection of each map, and examination of the percentage share of the vote for Fianna Fáil that was entered for each constituency in the original maps do reveal the extent of Fianna Fáil's progress

[1] The comparative approach in question is that of Lipset and Rokkan (1967). Its applicability to the Irish case is discussed in chapters 2 and 11.

outside the west, the overwhelming visual impression remains that of a stable east-west contrast. The problem is that while there were two aspects to electoral trends in the 1920s and early 1930s, Rumpf's cartography conveys only one of them. The one that is conveyed in the maps is the difference between the levels of support in the east and the west. Beyond that, the maps convey a static impression and certainly fail to capture the rapidity and comprehensiveness of Fianna Fáil's advance throughout the country.

Application of a constant scale to the four maps reveals a rather different picture of the development of Fianna Fáil support (see Figure 5.7). Thus in the three months between June and September 1927, Fianna Fáil support in almost every constituency moved up a level and, even at this early stage, the picture of Fianna Fáil as a party of the periphery begins to look questionable. In 1932, the same thing happens again – Fianna Fáil support moves up another notch on the scale almost everywhere and, with most areas of the country at least in the 40–49 per cent bracket of support, Fianna Fáil is already a national rather than a regional party. The only two exceptions to the widespread rise in support for Fianna Fáil between June 1927 and 1932 are the counties of Dublin and Wicklow. It is important to emphasize that it is the county constituency of Dublin that is in question here. In the two Dublin city constituencies (see inset on the map in Figure 5.7), the Fianna Fáil vote rose more or less in line with the vote in the rest of the country. By 1933, Fianna Fáil had an absolute majority of the votes in the south city constituency and was in the 40–49 per cent bracket (at 45 per cent to be precise) in the north city. Meanwhile, even county Dublin and Wicklow showed a significant improvement for Fianna Fáil and, in the rest of the country, Fianna Fáil consolidated its support, especially in the north-west and parts of the south.

In summary, there was an east-west gradient in support for Fianna Fáil but it was a moving gradient, more akin to an escalator than a hill. While the relative positions of Fianna Fáil in the east and west show a continuing contrast, the absolute position of Fianna Fáil in the east strengthened very significantly very early on. As noted already, there has been a strong tendency in analyses of Irish elections to identify 1943 as the turning point for Fianna Fáil. The present cartographic analysis reinforces the point made above that the decisive change occurred much earlier. The question of timing is crucial. If the evidence sustained the view that Fianna Fáil was a party of the periphery until the 1943 election and only then established itself in the east, one could perhaps argue that the party system in the early years was based on a centre-periphery cleavage. The pattern that becomes apparent in a redrawing of Rumpf's maps to a consistent scale makes this centre versus periphery interpretation difficult to sustain. Sustaining it becomes impossible when one considers the other half of the putative centre-periphery conflict, Cumann na nGaedheal. Simply put, there was 'no predominance of Cumann na nGaedheal votes in the south and east. Its support was fairly evenly spread across the whole country' (Rumpf and Hepburn, 1977, p. 75). In scotching the centre-periphery interpretation, this revised cartographic analysis simply sharpens the question: what were the factors underlying party conflict and the patterns of party support? In approaching this question, cartography can again be useful, at least as a starting point.

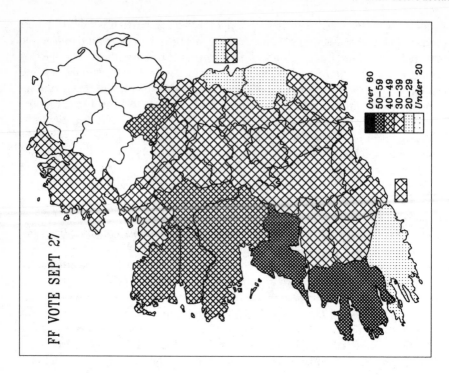

FF VOTE SEPT 27

Over 80
50—59
40—49
30—39
20—29
Under 20

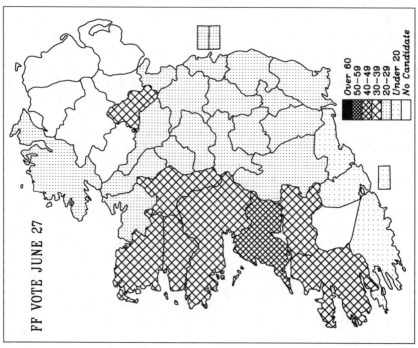

FF VOTE JUNE 27

Over 80
50—59
40—49
30—39
20—29
Under 20
No Candidate

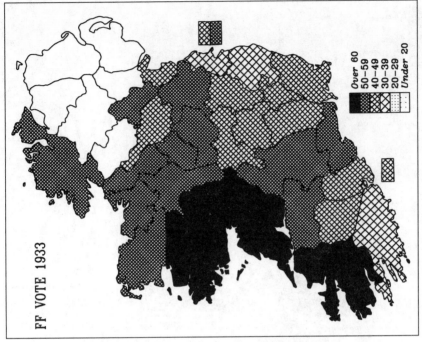

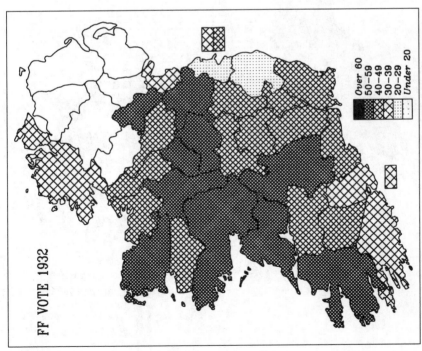

Figure 5.7 Revised cartographic analysis of Fianna Fáil vote, 1927–33 (standard scale).

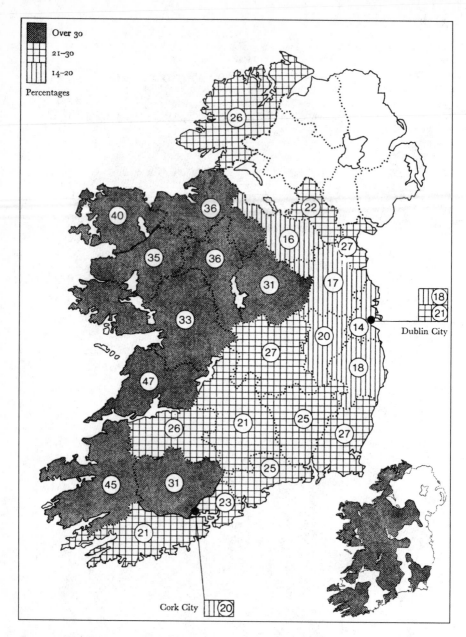

Figure 5.8 The anti-treaty vote, 1923, with inset showing the areas in which over 70 per cent of the working population were engaged in agriculture at the 1936 census.

Mapping the sources: explorations and limitations

The attempt to relate patterns of party support to some underlying independent or causal variables is central to Rumpf's use of the cartographical method. The range of independent variables he examines is quite wide, including, for example, the rate of reprisals carried out by British forces, 1919–21; the distribution of Irish language speakers in 1911; the non-Catholic population in 1926; the proportion of the working population engaged in farming and the main types of farming; agrarian outrages, 1880–82; the progress of land purchase to 1923; the number of farm labourers per 1,000 farmers. Rumpf seeks to link these socio-economic, structural and historical variables to two dependent variables: IRA activity during the war of independence and, the one that interests us here, 'republicanism', that is, the anti-treaty vote in 1922 and especially in 1923. His conclusion is that republicanism in this sense was related to farm size, the dominance of agriculture in the local economy, and the impact of traditional Irish culture as measured by the proportion of the population claiming to be Irish speaking in 1911 (Rumpf and Hepburn, 1977, pp. 57–68).

Rumpf's method and part of the basis of his conclusion can be seen in the map of the 1923 anti-treaty vote with an inset map of the distribution of the population engaged in agriculture in Figure 5.8. The basis of the conclusion drawn is, however, essentially impressionistic – it consists of a visual comparison of the spatial distribution of the dependent variable (anti-treaty vote in 1923) with the spatial distribution of the independent variable (population engaged in agriculture). This is both the advantage and the limitation of the technique. The advantage lies in its capacity to suggest relationships and to identify particular geographical areas that might be exceptions to the general rule. Thus, for example, there is a fairly close correspondence between areas where the anti-treaty vote was high and areas where over 70 per cent of the working population were engaged in agriculture. At the same time it is clear that there are areas (the south east and an area corresponding roughly to west Waterford and Tipperary) that were heavily agricultural but that do not show high anti-treaty sentiment. At this point one could turn to a map of farm size and seek to explain some of the anomalies by references to that. The problem is that within the bounds of the cartographical approach there is no way to be precise about the strength of the relationship between the independent and dependent variables, or about the interaction between a number of independent variables, and there is no way of eliminating a strong degree of subjectivity in making the interpretation. What the approach provides, then, is a suggestive exploratory tool for analysing voting patterns. If we wish to push the analysis beyond the impressionistic stage, we must turn to a statistical approach to the data.

Aggregate data: the statistical approach

Before plunging into the statistical analysis, it is worth cataloguing the hypotheses that have been advanced by a range of writers regarding the socio-economic and structural determinants of Irish voting patterns in the early years of the state. Far from the 'axiomatic attribution of voting patterns to attitudes towards the Treaty' which Lee criticises (Lee, 1989, p. 543), writers on Irish politics have frequently pointed to a socio-economic basis underlying party support. And this is so even without including those studies which specifically set out to analyse empirically the correlates of party support. In particular, two early studies strongly emphasized the socio-economic dimension. The earliest one was published in 1933 and was thus almost a contemporaneous account. It argued that the division was one between those within the modern economic system and those outside it. Stating forthrightly that 'the description of this division cannot be supported by statistical analysis, it arises chiefly out of the writer's observations', Moss maintained that the rift in Sinn Féin

> followed a fundamental division in Irish society . . . The prosperous farmers and graziers, the shopkeepers and townspeople and the skilled artisans had established themselves more or less securely in the modern economic system and were imbued with twentieth century notions. They had objected only to specific abuses. On the other hand, the unskilled labourers and small farmers, especially in the poverty-stricken West where barter continues to exist, remained outside this system and shared few of its benefits. To these people the Sinn Féin war had represented a battle against the whole existing order and its multitude of abuses.   (Moss, 1933, pp. 18–19)

In somewhat similar vein, a study completed in the late 1950s argued strongly that, originally, the social division between the two parties was clear-cut:

> the pro-treaty party which stood for peace and ordered government won the support of the conservative, propertied class in the country: the large farmers, the leaders in industry and commerce, and the well-established professional men. The anti-treaty party relied chiefly on the small farmers, the shopkeepers, and sections of the artisan and labourer classes.   (McCracken, 1958, p. 114).[2]

These points were developed by subsequent writers approaching the issue from a variety of perspectives. Thus Bew and Patterson refer to Cumann na nGaedheal as having 'the support of the more prosperous elements – the larger farmers, the higher bourgeoisie and the larger manufacturers'. Fianna Fáil's support came mainly from 'the smaller (and poorer) farmers, the small shopkeepers, the urban and rural petite bourgeoisie and even, in some measure, the urban working class' (Bew and Patterson, 1982, p. 3). Neary and O Gráda put a very explicit socio-economic interpretation on what they see as the growth of urban working class support for Fianna Fáil in the 1930s. Analysing economic policy and the pattern of economic growth in the period, they argue that the considerable hardship caused by the economic war to farmers was matched by increasing prosperity in the towns. The result is that 'cheap food and better job prospects go a long way towards explaining the substantial working-class support won by Fianna Fáil during the 1930s (which they have retained until the present day)' (Neary and O Gráda, 1991, p. 255). Lee advances what is perhaps the most explicit and comprehensive socio-economic interpretation of voting patterns in

[2] Note that, whereas Moss puts shopkeepers on the pro-treaty side, McCracken puts them on the anti-treaty side.

the early years of state. He argues that in order to fashion solid blocks of party support, party leaders had 'to appeal fundamentally to the socio–economic interests of the electorate' (Lee, 1989, p. 540). He takes the 1923 Sinn Féin vote as the 'ceiling of the undiluted anti-treaty vote', adding that even that number 'surely contained many voters opposing the government mainly on socio–economic grounds in the prevailing depression' (Lee, 1989, p. 543). Focusing on the jump in Fianna Fáil support between June 1927 and 1932 (see Figure 4.2, chapter 4), he argues that most of this 'can be reasonably assumed to have been attracted mainly by its policy on social and economic issues, once it began to seriously formulate a programme in this area' (*ibid.*). Lee paints a picture not just of have-not support for Fianna Fáil, but of a polarisation along class lines between Fianna Fáil and Cumann na nGaedheal/Fine Gael. He argues that the Fine Gael vote was really based more on opposition to the anti-treatyites than on support for the treaty itself, and that 'the division was one of socio–economic perceptions of status and self-interest' (Lee, 1989, p. 542).

Taken together these generalisations add up to a thesis that there was a significant class basis for party support. There are two propositions involved in the thesis. The first is that underlying the original treaty split there was a socio–economic conflict between the well-off, who favoured the status quo, and the have-nots, who, having no stake in the existing order of things, supported the anti-treatyites as an expression of their alienation and frustration. The second proposition relates not to the original conflict in 1922–23 but to the support bases of the parties as they developed in the late 1920s and early 1930s. In this case the argument is that socio–economic factors were the key to the growing support of the two major parties and to the polarisation of the party system. The question is: does the analysis of the aggregate data confirm these hypotheses?

The limitations attaching to statistical analysis of aggregate data that go under the general rubric 'the ecological fallacy' have been elaborated on in chapter 1.[3] In what follows, therefore, it will be important to remember that the evidence relates to constituencies and their characteristics rather than to individual voters. There is also the limitation that differences may occur within rather than between constituencies, and may not therefore show up in aggregate data analysis, and the further limitation that particular hypothesised relationships may be impossible to test simply because appropriate data are not available. These limitations can, however, be minimised and, as long as they are borne in mind, the effort is worthwhile.

In one of the first studies of this sort, Pyne analysed the votes for Sinn Féin and Cumann na nGaedheal in 1923. The correlates of the Sinn Féin vote can be summed up as follows: Sinn Féin support was stronger in constituencies with a high proportion of the work-force engaged in agriculture and in those with low average farm valuation, poor housing, a high rate of emigration in 1921, a low proportion of non-Catholics, and a high proportion of old-age pensioners. It was also related to the incidence of Land League meetings in 1879–80 and the number of agrarian outrages

---

[3] It should be noted that these limitations apply equally to the use of cartography to search for the correlates of party support.

between 1879 and 1882 (Pyne, 1970). Cumann na nGaedheal support in 1923 was not
the mirror image of support for Sinn Féin. Overall, the correlations for Cumann na
nGaedheal support tended to be low. Thus, it was not significantly stronger in areas
with high proportions of non-agricultural workers, nor in areas with better housing or
with high farm valuation. In fact, its vote was positively related to small farm size. Its
only other substantial correlation was with the density of rural population. The fact
that Cumann na nGaedheal support in 1923 was not the mirror image of support for
Sinn Féin but was of a somewhat indeterminate character both confirms Rumpf's
observation and points to the catch-all, rather than the class-based, nature of Cumann
na nGaedheal support in 1923.

In regard to the first summary proposition noted above, that relating to the pro-
treaty versus anti-treaty split, these results provide some evidence that the anti-
treatyites did receive disproportionate support from the less well-off, especially in
rural areas. At the same time, however, Pyne emphasizes that 'its support did not correspond too closely with any of the basic lines of social or economic cleavage. It drew
supporters from all sections of society' and that 'a purely socio–economic interpretation of Republican support is not altogether satisfactory' (Pyne, 1970, p. 243). In particular, there is little or no evidence that the urban working class offered
disproportionate support to the anti-treaty position. As Pyne himself puts it, the 'commonly held view that, along with the poorer farmers, the industrial workers formed
the backbone of resistance to the treaty' is 'open to doubt' (Pyne, 1970, p. 236).[4]

Verifying the second proposition, that suggesting a significant change in the social
bases of party support in the late 1920s or early 1930s, requires an analysis of the correlates of party support over several successive elections. One such analysis, extending
from 1923 to 1944, suggests a remarkable continuity in the social basis of Fianna Fáil
support up to and including the 1938 election (Garvin, 1981). The continuity was only
broken in 1943, though then the break was sharp indeed. Throughout the period,
Fianna Fáil support (and Sinn Féin support in 1923) was fairly strongly negatively
related to two variables – high land valuation and urbanisation. The land valuation
variable is the most interesting one in terms of the present discussion, but the correlation with urbanisation is worth noting. One interpretation of this is that it reflects a
centre–periphery conflict (Garvin, 1981, p. 166). However, given that Fine Gael does
not show a consistent positive correlation with urbanisation, and given the difficulties
involved in the centre–periphery conflict revealed by the cartographic analysis above,
it is probably better to avoid imposing the centre–periphery interpretation on the
finding and simply to record that Fianna Fáil support had a pronounced rural bias up
to and including the 1938 election.

The relationship with high land valuation is interpreted as indicative of agrarian
class conflict (Garvin, 1981, p. 162). It confirms Pyne's findings in regard to the anti-

[4] The lack of relationship between the proportion in the urban working class and opposition to the treaty
may be due in part to the apparent disenfranchisment of substantial sections of the urban population of
Dublin and Cork (see discussion of the state of the electoral register in the 1920s in chapter 3). On the other
hand, there is no substantial evidence to indicate that, once the electoral register was brought into line with
the population, there was any disproportionate surge of working-class support for Fianna Fáil.

treaty vote in 1923, and shows that such a relationship continued beyond 1923 and through the elections of the 1930s. On the other hand, there is no evidence of a strengthening of this aspect of the class basis of Fianna Fáil in the late 1920s. More importantly, the Cumann na nGaedheal vote does not show a corresponding positive relationship to high levels of land valuation, even in the election of 1932, by which time the party had had ample opportunity to establish its conservative credentials.

A major problem of the analyses reviewed so far is their bi-variate approach and their consequent inability to sort out the relative influence of a range of independent variables. An attempt to overcome this problem can be made by employing multiple regression. This uses a number of independent variables simultaneously and shows the effect of each, taking into account the effect of all the others.

Determinants of party support, 1927–65

Ten variables were included in a multivariate and longitudinal analysis of the determinants of voting covering general elections between June 1927 and 1965 (Gallagher, 1976). The variables were (1) the proportion of the gainfully employed population occupied in the agricultural industry; (2) the proportion of the gainfully employed population out of work; (3) the proportion of employers and managers, excluding farmers, in the gainfully employed population; (4) the rateable value of land per acre; (5) the proportion of farmers in the gainfully employed population; (6) the proportion of farm labourers in the gainfully employed population; (7) the ratio of farm labourers to farmers;[5] (8) the average annual rate of emigration; (9) the proportion of Irish speakers; and (10) the proportion of non-Catholics. This analysis makes it possible to examine the socio-economic determinants of support for the main parties in fourteen elections over a forty-year period.

Table 5.1 presents selected results from this study, the selection being determined by the fact that the equations presented either bring out persistent features of the support for the party in question or indicate significant changes in the structure of that support. The selected votes (the dependent variables) are those for Fianna Fáil and Fine Gael in 1933, 1943 and 1965, and that for Labour in 1965. The first line in the table is the equation for Fianna Fáil support in 1933.[6] It seeks to explain the Fianna Fáil vote as a function of three independent variables: the proportion of Irish speakers in a constituency, the proportion of farmers in the gainfully employed population and the proportion of non-Catholics. The R^2 shows that, taken together, these three variables explain 64 per cent, or almost two-thirds, of the variance in the Fianna Fáil vote. Individually, the contribution of each variable is indicated by the coefficient. Variation in the proportion of farmers across constituencies makes the largest contribution (coefficient 4.39). The other two variables make lesser contributions, both of which are of the same magnitude

[5] Farmers are owner-occupiers; farm labourers are hired labour. High numbers of farm labourers tend to be found in areas with large farmers and therefore relatively fewer farmers. High numbers of farmers are found in small-farming areas with farms that employ little or no outside labour.

[6] For a brief introduction to regression analysis and to the interpretation of the statistics it produces see chapter 1, pp. 19–20.

Table 5.1: *Aggregate data analysis of party support, 1933, 1943 and 1965.*

	Irish speakers	Farmers	Farm labourers	Non-Catholics	Employers & managers	R^2
Fianna Fáil						
1933	2.92 (4.21)*	4.39 (10.76)***	–	–2.92 (5.01)**	–	0.64
1943	3.27 (7.46)**	–1.89 (2.77)*	–	–0.23 (0.04)	–	0.31
1965	2.41 (5.19)*	–2.02 (3.76)*	–	0.19 (0.05)	–	0.23
Cumann na nGaedheal						
1933	–	–	–2.69 (3.68)*	–1.97 (1.85)	3.74 (6.57)**	0.36
Fine Gael						
1943	–	–	–	–	3.19 (5.22)*	0.19
1965	–	4.41 (12.57)***	–2.77 (5.09)*	–	–	0.46
Labour						
1965	–	–4.44 (8.94)**	5.07 (17.75)	–	–	0.61

Note: The main entry in each cell of the table is the semi-standardised coefficient (Gallagher, 1976, footnote 4) for that variable in the regression equation. t-values are given in brackets. Significance levels are indicated by asterisks (*0.05, **0.01, ***0.001).

but operating in opposite directions – a high proportion of Irish speakers increases the Fianna Fáil vote; a high proportion of non-Catholics decreases it.

The equation for Fianna Fáil in 1933 and the level of explanation it produces hold good for most of the elections between 1927 and 1938. In other words the structure of Fianna Fáil remains fairly constant in this period and its vote can be predicted with a moderate degree of success on the basis of the three variables – proportion of farmers (positive), proportion of Irish speakers (positive) and proportion of non-Catholics (negative). In 1943, however, the structure of the Fianna Fáil vote changed substantially. In the regression analysis, the levelling out of Fianna Fáil support through the disproportionate losses in the west, noted above, is registered in the effective disappearance from the equation of the variable measuring proportion of non-Catholics, and in a change from positive to negative in the impact of the proportion of farmers in an area. It is also registered in the substantial decline in the amount of variance in the Fianna Fáil vote that can be explained (from 63 per cent in 1938 to 43 per cent in 1943). In general this lower level of explanation persisted over the remainder of the period.

Contrary to several of the hypotheses outlined above, Fianna Fáil did not acquire a more identifiable class base during the ten years or so in which it progressed from winning one quarter of the vote (June 1927) to over one-half of the vote (1938).

Throughout these years the best set of predictors remained farmers, Irish speakers and non–Catholics. It should, however, be noted that other variables, including class variables, did show some relationship to the Fianna Fáil vote. Fianna Fáil support was negatively related to the main indicator of social class, that is, the proportion of employees and managers in an area. However, the relationship was relatively weak and was not very robust in the sense that it does not figure in the equation when other, more powerful predictors are introduced. It is worth noting also that the Fianna Fáil vote was negatively related to the level of unemployment in an area (Gallagher, 1976, p. 19).

Two features of Gallagher's analysis of the Cumann na nGaedheal/Fine Gael vote are particularly significant. First, by comparison with the analysis of the Fianna Fáil vote, there is a considerably lower level of R^2, that is of association between the independent variables and the Cumann na nGaedheal/Fine Gael vote, or of variance in the Fine Gael vote explained. On only three occasions does the R^2 for Fine Gael/Cumann na nGhedheal exceed 0.40, that is, in June 1927, in 1938 and in the last election of the series, 1965. Other than those elections, the analysis succeeded in explaining, at best, one-third the variance in the Fine Gael/Cumann na nGaedheal vote and in most cases much less (Gallagher, 1976, pp. 29–38). The second feature is the lack of consistency in the pattern of influence on the Fine Gael vote. Unlike the case of Fianna Fáil, the equation for Fine Gael support in 1933 shown in Table 5.1 is not typical; there is in fact no typical pattern for Fine Gael.

Having said that, however, the Fine Gael equations are informative, even when they lead to the conclusion of a lack of structure. In particular, the role of the employer/manager variable is of interest in the light of the various hypotheses outlined above. The evidence suggests that it was not until 1932 and 1933 that the class composition of the constituencies became a factor in the Cumann na nGaedheal vote (Gallagher, 1976, p. 32), and that this relationship was moderate at best and quite transient. It disappears in 1937 and 1938, reappearing in 1943 and in a number of the elections thereafter, but often possessing minimal explanatory power. In 1965 the Fine Gael vote became somewhat more predictable (R^2 0.46), and the pattern changed significantly. The variables having an impact on the vote then were the proportion of farmers, in this case a positive impact, and the proportion of farm labourers, a negative impact. This change in the basis of the Fine Gael vote in 1965 confirms and throws light on the regional analysis of Fine Gael discussed above.

The equation for the Labour Party for 1965 shown in Table 5.1 is typical. In the forty-year period stretching from the mid-20s to the mid-60s, the Labour vote was the most predictable of all the party votes. The relationship was a simple one. Labour votes were higher in constituencies with high proportions of farm labourers and lower in constituencies with high proportions of farmers. This set of relationships held up, election after election, in a remarkably consistent and stable pattern. They help to explain the equally consistent pattern in the regional analysis of Labour support above, that is, the relatively greater strength of Labour in the rest of Leinster and in Munster. These regions include the main large-farming areas, which, particularly in the early years of the state, would have had significant levels of farm labourer employment.

In summary, the analysis of party support in the period 1927–65 has shown, in the case of Fianna Fáil in the first two decades and Labour throughout the period, quite stable and pronounced support bases and, in the case of Fine Gael, a remarkably varied, shifting and generally weakly patterned support base. Fianna Fáil had a clear underlying pattern of support up to and including 1938; thereafter its support was much less predictable. However, there is no substantial evidence to support the kind of comprehensive class interpretation of Fianna Fáil support put forward in much of the literature. The most that can be said is that its strength in areas with high proportions of farmers is consistent with the party having a particular appeal among smallholding owner-occupiers. Class interpretations of electoral alignments are further weakened by the limited and intermittent role that class plays in determining Cumann na nGaedheal/Fine Gael support. There is, however, a class basis to the pattern of Labour Party support, but it is a very specific and circumscribed class basis, Labour support being related to the proportion of farm labourers. The fact that areas with high proportions of farm labourers tended to show high support for Labour rather than Fianna Fáil underlines the limits of even an agrarian class interpretation of the Fianna Fáil vote.

Determinants of party support, 1981–92

The complexities of the constituency boundaries as redrawn in 1968 and 1974 have meant that this kind of statistical analysis of the results of the 1969, 1973 and 1977 general elections has not been undertaken. Fortunately, the constituencies defined in 1979 and used, with minor changes, throughout the 1980s are much more closely related to the boundaries of counties and of census sub-units within counties. Accordingly, multiple regression analyses can readily be applied to the elections of the 1980s and 1990s. One such analysis of the Fianna Fáil vote in the November 1982 election concluded that 'there is a much clearer link between Fianna Fáil voting and the socio-economic factors' and that Fianna Fáil support 'appears to be more consistently predictable from aggregate data' than previous studies had suggested (Laver, 1986a, pp. 124 and 128). The key to this reinterpretation is a composite variable (agricultural structure) that was uncovered by means of factor analysis.[7] This new variable combines data on land-use patterns (proportion of land devoted to certain types of crops, to pasture, to rough grazing, etc.) with variables describing farm size. The effect is to draw a contrast between areas devoted to tillage/horticulture on the one hand and areas where livestock rearing and a pattern of small and medium-sized holdings are predominant on the other. Use of this variable in a series of two-variable equations explains about 60 per cent of the variance in the Fianna Fáil vote in November 1982. This compares well to the level explained by Gallagher for the period 1944–65 (see the discussion above). In all of the equations tested the crucial influence comes from the

[7] Factor analysis is used in this context in a preliminary data reduction technique, the purpose of which is to simplify the very large number of independent variables that are potentially relevant to an explanation of voting patterns. In this case the analysis yields ten factors or composite variables from the 66 individual variables used as input. The most useful of these is the agricultural variable described in the text.

agricultural structure variable. The Fianna Fáil vote increases substantially and consistently with increases in the level of livestock farming and small to medium-sized agricultural holdings in a county. In the case of Fine Gael, the analysis concludes that 'variations in the Fine Gael vote are impossible to predict using aggregate data' (Laver, 1986a, p. 126). The Labour vote shows only weak relationships to socio-economic variables and the conclusion is drawn that local and candidate factors appear paramount.

In evaluating these findings, certain limitations of the study, which are fully acknowledged, must be borne in mind. The limitations all stem from the choice of the county rather than the constituency as the unit of analysis. This involves, first, the elimination of Dublin from the analysis on the grounds that it is 'such a large unit that a distorted and potentially invalid set of data points would be generated by including Dublin on equal terms with other counties' (Laver, 1986a, p. 110). Secondly, it involves a reduction of the number of cases available for analysis from 41 to 26,[8] making for a considerably less satisfactory base for the statistical analysis. Finally, it involves the problem that five constituencies are made up of pairs of counties, and so the combined two-country vote for each party has to be apportioned to each of the counties using the 1979 local election results. This assumes that the swing from election to election is constant across the two counties of a joint constituency.[9]

The crucial test of the agricultural structural interpretation of Fianna Fáil support would be to use constituencies rather than counties, and to include all of the elections of the 1980s. The test would also require replication of the factor analysis carried out by Laver, as this is a central feature of the approach. Finally, for the purpose of strict comparability, the test should focus on the non-Dublin constituencies. When all of this is done, the results show that the structure of agriculture (tillage/horticulture versus livestock) has some impact on the non-Dublin Fianna Fáil vote in November 1982, and to a lesser extent in 1987, but that the impact is neither stable enough over time nor strong enough to warrant the conclusion that this variable is the major determinant of Fianna Fáil support, or that there is evidence for a 'politics with an agricultural basis thesis' (Laver, 1986a, p. 126).[10]

Does this mean that support for Fianna Fáil in the 1980s was as indeterminate as it had been between 1943 and 1965? And what of Fine Gael? Does the conclusion that it cannot be predicted by reference to the aggregate data hold when the Dublin constituencies and all of the elections of the '80s are included in the analysis? And then there is the question of what was the impact on the structure of support for each party of the considerable swings in votes that occurred in 1992. In particular, did the transformation in the level of Labour support also transform its structure? These questions

---

[8] There are 26 cases because the subdivision of one county – Tipperary – into two administrative units provides an extra case.

[9] The plausibility of this assumption is examined in Sinnott, Whelan and McBride, forthcoming.

[10] It is arguable that a fairer test would be to also eliminate other predominantly urban constituencies, on the grounds that the structure of agriculture in them cannot be thought of as the prime determinant of party support and that they may be diluting the relationship. However, a test along these lines offers even less support for the thesis. For this and the non-Dublin test see Sinnott, Whelan and McBride, forthcoming.

suggest the need for a comprehensive aggregate or ecological analysis of support for each of the parties in all six elections from 1981 to 1992, using all constituencies, both Dublin and non-Dublin.

In analysing the Fianna Fáil vote in this period, one constituency poses a particular problem. The constituency is Donegal North-East and the problem is the vote of the sitting independent deputy, Neil Blaney. As indicated briefly in chapter 2, Blaney was a prominent Fianna Fáil minister who resigned from the party in 1970 following the Arms Crisis of that year. Since then he has been elected as an independent TD for Donegal North-East (or for Donegal as a whole when the county was one constituency). The problem is that Blaney's presence greatly reduces the Fianna Fáil vote in the constituency. Since Donegal North-East scores particularly high on many of the variables one would wish to examine as possible determinants of Fianna Fáil support, the reduction of the Fianna Fáil vote due to the Blaney factor distorts the statistical analysis. One could treat the Blaney vote as if it were a Fianna Fáil vote or one could omit the case from the analysis. The former risks overstating the Fianna Fáil vote; the latter is undesirable both from the view of the loss of a case and from the point of view of the comprehensiveness of the analysis. The third alternative is to incorporate the Blaney effect into the model by including a variable measuring the impact of the Donegal North East case. This 'dummy variable' approach is the one pursued here.

The regression equations or models for Fianna Fáil support in the six elections from 1981 to 1992 are presented in Table 5.2. In all six elections, the one constant factor is that the proportion of farmers had a significant positive effect on Fianna Fáil support. However, the degree to which the vote can be explained in socio-demographic

Table 5.2: *Aggregate data analysis of Fianna Fáil support, socio-demographic variables, 1981–92*

	Constant	Proportion farmers	Proportion middle class	Donegal NE	Adjusted R^2	N
1981	41.09	0.30	0.00	−8.46	0.33	41
		(4.02)	(0.02)	(−1.62)		
1982 Feb	48.78	0.27	−0.58	−16.13	0.49	41
		(3.67)	(−2.29)	(−3.20)		
1982 Nov	45.03	0.35	−0.53	−13.19	0.54	
		(4.72)	(−2.10)	(−2.59)		
1987	49.14	0.30	−0.89	−15.06	0.48	41
		(3.11)	(−3.03)	(−2.39)		
1989	41.44	0.36	−0.20	−6.63	0.27	41
		(3.31)	(−0.63)	(−0.96)		
1992	34.73	0.51	−0.21	−4.96	0.58	41
		(6.27)	(−0.85)	(−0.97)		

Note: The main entry for each variable is the B coefficient, the figure beneath in brackets is the *t*-value. *T*-values in excess of 2.02 are significant at $p = 0.05$. In this and all subsequent aggregate data analysis tables, 'middle class' refers to professional middle class (groups 2 and 3 in the census classification of socio-economic groups).

terms is far from constant. Taking the elections of the 1980s first, the degree of structure in Fianna Fáil support was relatively low in 1981 and 1989 and relatively high in the three intervening elections (February and November 1982 and 1987). The difference is accounted for by the fact that, from 1982 to 1987, the middle-class variable also played a significant (negative) role in explaining Fianna Fáil support – the higher the proportion of middle class in a constituency, the lower the Fianna Fáil vote in those three elections, but not in either 1981 or 1989. The situation in 1992 was quite different again. The only significant influence on the Fianna Fáil vote was the proportion of farmers but, unlike 1981 and 1989, the effect this time was very substantial – the coefficient or weight attached to the variable went up to 0.51 and the model, in which this is the only significant variable, explains 58 per cent of the variance (see Table 5.2). Thus, as Fianna Fáil dipped below 40 per cent for the first time in 60 years, there was a considerable accentuation of its reliance on support in predominantly rural areas.

As we have seen, Fine Gael support has been found, in various studies, to be the most unstructured of that of any of the parties. Indeed, in respect of the November 1982 election, Laver found that 'none of the multiple regressions used to predict the Fine Gael vote were statistically significant' (Laver, 1986, p. 126). In contrast, the equations in Table 5.3 show two variables having statistically significant effects in all but one of the six elections between 1981 and 1992. It is true that the variance explained is quite low for the first three elections (those in 1981 and 1982), but it increased substantially in 1987 and again in 1992 (see Table 5.3). The two variables in question are the proportion in the professional middle class and the proportion of farmers. This suggests that Fine Gael had a more catch-all character in the elections of 1981–82, showing some limited dependence on support in areas with high proportions of either farmers or middle-class professionals, but that such dependence became much more pronounced as the vote for Fine Gael vote shrank in 1987. In 1987 also the impact of the proportion of farmers grew relative to the impact of the middle-class variable (compare the coefficients for each variable in Table 5.3). This process culminated in 1992 with the disappearance of any Fine Gael advantage in middle-class areas and the development of an even more pronounced dependence on areas with high proportions of farmers. In statistical terms, the farmer variable explains virtually on its own 58 per cent of the variance in Fine Gael support in 1992. We have seen a similar rural dependence in the case of Fianna Fáil in 1992. Clearly this is an issue that requires further analysis, and will be taken up again in chapter 9.

If Fine Gael support became more predictable in the 1980s, the reverse happened to Labour. Whether we try the model which explained so much of the variance in the Labour vote in the 1927–65 period (a negative effect for farmers and a positive effect for farm labourers) or revise the model, replacing farm labourers with the working class, the outcome is the same – zero variance explained in the four elections from 1981 to 1987 and some degree of explanation in 1989, but on the basis of a somewhat puzzling positive effect for the proportion of farmers. However, this finding is consistent with the regional analysis of the Labour vote (Figure 5.3). The Labour recovery in that election was significantly stronger in Munster and in the rest of Leinster than in Dublin, where it was held back in all but one or two constituencies by the success of the Workers' Party.

Table 5.3: *Aggregate data analysis of Fine Gael support, socio–demographic variables, 1981–92*

	Constant	Proportion farmers	Proportion middle class	Adjusted R²	N
1981	25.03	0.23 (2.52)	0.93 (2.95)	0.17	41
1982 Feb	24.34	0.22 (2.49)	1.11 (3.63)	0.23	41
1982 Nov	25.44	0.23 (2.54)	1.19 (3.85)	0.25	41
1987	13.59	0.51 (5.73)	0.74 (2.80)	0.44	41
1989	14.47	0.64 (5.96)	0.70 (2.21)	0.46	41
1992	13.64	0.65 (7.05)	0.28 (0.98)	0.58	41

Note: The main entry for each variable is the B coefficient, the figure beneath in brackets is the *t*-value. *T*-values in excess of 2.02 are significant at $p = 0.05$. In this an all subsequent aggregate data analysis tables, 'working class' refers to semi-skilled and unskilled manual workers (groups 9 and X in the census classification of socio-economic groups).

The absence of any pattern in Labour support at the constituency level between 1981 and 1987 reflects the declining level of Labour support and the fact that much of that reduced support was dependent on the personal following of a diverse group of incumbent Labour deputies. This supposition is supported by the fact that, when the Labour vote recovered, tentatively in 1989 and substantially in 1992, the predictability of that vote also increased. But there is a significant contrast between the pattern of Labour support in the two elections. In 1989 there was some slight evidence of

Table 5.4: *Aggregate data analysis of Labour Party support, socio-demographic variables, 1981–92*

	Constant	Proportion farmers	Proportion working class	Adjusted R²	N
1981	14.31	−0.03 (−0.31)	−0.16 (0.44)	−0.06	34
1982 Feb	13.21	−0.10 (−0.92)	−0.12 (−0.30)	−0.03	36
1982 Nov	12.09	−0.07 (−0.60)	−0.03 (−0.07)	−0.05	35
1987	10.95	0.01 (0.06)	−0.24 (−0.81)	−0.05	32
1989	7.97	0.39 (2.64)	0.18 (0.45)	0.16	28
1992	27.16	−0.47 (−5.16)	−0.07 (−0.21)	0.41	39

Note: The main entry for each variable is the B coefficient, the figure beneath in brackets is the *t*-value. *T*-values in excess of 2.02 are significant at $p = 0.05$.

greater support for Labour in constituencies with high proportions of farmers. In 1992, the impact of the proportion of farmers variable was negative and powerfully so (see Table 5.4). In that election there was, yet again, no evidence of a pro-Labour working-class effect at the constituency level. Thus, virtually on its own, the negative farmer effect accounted for some 40 per cent of the variance in the Labour vote. This confirms the signs of urban-rural polarisation evident in the analysis of Fianna Fáil and Fine Gael support in the same election.

Because of the relatively small number of cases (i.e. constituencies contested) available for analysis in the case of the Workers' Party/Democratic Left, caution must be exercised when drawing conclusions about the basis of its support. However, from November 1982 on, at least 20 cases are available and the results of the regression analyses are presented in Table 5.5. In November 1982 and in 1987, the equations produce only limited degrees of predictability and that rests almost exclusively on the positive effect of the proportion in the working class in a constituency. In 1989, this effect strengthened and was joined by a negative farmer effect (see Table 5.5), producing a moderate level of variance explained (40 per cent). However, following the split in the Workers' Party and the formation of the Democratic Left, the structure of the combined vote for the two parties collapsed entirely, with neither the farmer nor the working-class variables having an impact and with the level of variance explained dropping to 5 per cent. This suggests that the combination of the break-up of the Workers' Party and the substantial recovery by the Labour Party undermined the structure of support for the more left-wing grouping, a structure that had been painstakingly built up over the previous decade.

Mention of the competition between the Labour Party and the Workers' Party/Democratic Left for the left-wing vote suggests the possibility that the lack of structure in Labour support in the 1980s may be due to the division of the left vote between the two parties. If this were so, then the combined left vote should be much more predictable than the vote for either the Labour Party or the Workers' Party/Democratic Left on its own. Up to 1992, Table 5.6 offers no support for this hypothesis. However,

Table 5.5: *Aggregate data analysis of Workers' Party/Democratic Left support, socio-demographic variables, 1982–92*

	Constant	*Proportion farmers*	*Proportion working class*	*Adjusted R^2*	*N*
1982 Nov	−1.36	−0.11 (−1.00)	0.66 (2.18)	0.20	20
1987	−0.91	−0.19 (−1.85)	0.64 (2.40)	0.24	26
1989	−1.77	−0.46 (−2.52)	1.09 (3.12)	0.40	21
1992	3.83	−0.19 (−1.54)	0.25 (0.90)	0.05	23

Note: The main entry for each variable is the B coefficient, the figure beneath in brackets is the *t*-value. *T*-values in excess of 2.02 are significant at $p = 0.05$.

Table 5.6: *Aggregate data analysis of Left (Labour & WP/DL & Kemmy) support, socio-demographic variables, 1981–92*

	Constant	Proportion farmers	Proportion working class	Adjusted R^2	N
1981	10.82	−0.09 (−0.91)	0.35 (0.96)	0.01	34
1982 Feb	10.02	−0.21 (−1.96)	0.43 (1.08)	0.12	38
1982 Nov	11.62	−0.27 (−2.44)	0.51 (1.28)	0.19	36
1987	11.69	−0.35 (−3.00)	0.33 (0.97)	0.19	34
1989	10.88	−0.15 (−0.88)	0.85 (2.02)	0.09	29
1992	25.65	−0.69 (−6.24)	0.25 (0.95)	0.57	39

Note: The main entry for each variable is the B coefficient, the figure beneath in brackets is the *t*-value. *T*-values in excess of 2.02 are significant at $p = 0.05$.

in 1992 the combined left vote was more highly structured (variance explained 56 per cent) than the vote for either party on its own, and it is notable that the structure was due entirely to the negative impact of the proportion of farmers (see Table 5.6). This reinforces the point already made regarding the need for further probing of the nature of the urban-rural polarisation of voting in the general election of 1992.

Determinants of turnout, 1981–92

This analysis of the ecology of voting must tackle one remaining and sometimes neglected question – what distinguishes areas of high and low turnout? At a minimum, an examination of the determinants of non-voting is essential in order to make the account of the relationship between social structure and constituency voting patterns as comprehensive as possible. But there is more than just comprehensiveness involved. As shown in chapter 3, non-voters are a relatively large group in the Irish case. Consequently, our understanding of the relationship between voting and the social structure could be significantly affected if, for example, it transpired that turnout was substantially influenced by the class composition or urban-rural balance of the constituencies.

The regional analysis of voting patterns at the beginning of this chapter showed a persistent contrast in levels of turnout between Dublin and the other regions. As with any regional characteristic, the question is can the underlying variables that account for this contrast be identified? There are several possible explanations – the character of rural communities as such, the concentration of people in younger age groups in the Dublin area, or lower turnout in urban working-class areas. Table 5.7 explores these possibilities in relation to turnout in general elections between 1981 and 1992, and

Table 5.7: *Aggregate data analysis of turn-out, general elections 1981–92*

	Constant	Proportion farmers	Proportion working class	Proportion 20–29 yrs	Adjusted R^2
1981	91.79	0.16	0.09	–1.24	0.70
		(2.86)	(0.56)	(–5.19)	
Feb 1982	93.77	0.08	–0.20	–1.21	0.66
		(1.54)	(–1.26)	(–5.20)	
Nov 1982	97.06	0.11	–0.29	–1.44	0.73
		(1.86)	(–1.72)	(–5.89)	
1987	96.49	0.00	–0.35	–1.21	0.63
		(–0.04)	(–2.24)	(–5.42)	
1989	75.46	0.22	–0.16	–0.49	0.57
		(3.18)	(–0.92)	(–1.98)	
1992	80.77	0.05	–0.35	–0.55	0.42
		(0.88)	(–2.34)	(–2.38)	

Note: The main entry for each variable is the B coefficient, the figure beneath in brackets is the *t*-value. *T*-values in excess of 2.02 are significant at $p = 0.05$.

shows that, at the constituency level, age is the only variable to have a significant effect, turnout being consistently lower in areas with high concentrations of young people. The general indicator of rural society – the proportion of farmers – had a spasmodic effect, raising the level of turnout in 1981 and 1989 in particular. The effect on turnout of the working-class composition of constituencies was negligible, except in 1987 when it had a small negative effect. Overall, the level of variance explained is high for the elections of the 1980s but significantly lower in 1992.

Of course, as with any of the ecological analyses discussed in this chapter, there could be a relationship between turnout and other social structural variables that does not appear because the areas under consideration are too large and too heterogeneous. The hypothesis is that if we had data for much smaller units, the contrasts in class or other social and demographic characteristics of the units would be much clearer and we would have a much better chance of detecting relationships between such variables and voting if they exist. The point is emphasized here because it is possible to obtain turnout data for relatively small units, that is, at a level of aggregation much lower than the officially published returns. The data in question provides recorded turnout on a ballot box by ballot box basis, and is a by-product of the counting process.[11]

[11] The first step in the count in an Irish election is the checking of the ballot papers. This is done on a ballot box by ballot box basis and the number of ballots in each box is recorded by the returning officer. On average, there are three or four boxes, of approximately 800 potential voters each, per polling station or section of the electoral register. From the point of view of statistical analysis of the pattern of turn-out, a crucial consideration is that the polling stations coincide with or are sub-sections of the most basic unit for which census data are reported. These units are known as wards or district electoral divisions. The official record of turn-out per box is kept throughout the election count and for a short period afterwards by the returning officer. It is not officially published and indeed appears to be disposed of by the returning officer after it has served its immediate purpose of checking the vote against the number of ballot papers distributed.

It can be supplemented by the tally records kept by the parties.[12]

Data of this kind have been analysed so far only for the Dublin area for the 1989 general election and the 1984 European Parliament election (Sinnott and Whelan, 1992). The analysis accounts for about 40 per cent of the variation in turnout in the Dublin area in the 1989 election. Areas of low voting in Dublin are characterised by relatively high proportions of the electorate in the age-group under forty and over sixty-five; a lower degree of electoral competitiveness[13] and, most of all, by a pattern of social disadvantage, i.e. low levels of education, high unemployment and higher numbers of people in lower status occupations (for details, see Sinnott and Whelan, 1992). The latter finding has disquieting implications when viewed from the perspective of the democratic criterion noted in chapter 3, 'that every individual, whatever his social or economic circumstances, should have an equal say' (see above p. 81).

Conclusion

Given that all of the analyses in this chapter have dealt with the same phenomenon, the spatial pattern of voting, it is not surprising, indeed it is reassuring, that the various approaches used – regional analysis, cartography and statistical analysis – tend to reinforce each other. However, the concurrence raises an ominous question – is the statistical analysis simply a re-description of the regional analysis that does not therefore make any additional contribution to the task of explanation? The answer is no. This can be shown statistically in so far as replacing the substantive variables with a set of variables identifying the various regions produces a much lower level of explanation. In any event, identifying region as a source of difference simply raises a question – what is it about the various regions that makes the vote different? The first gain then is clarification of the factors underlying the regional contrasts. The second gain in moving beyond regional analysis arises from the fact that the statistical approach makes possible the testing of specific hypotheses about the relationship between voting and social class (or other social structural variables). The main findings of this chapter can in fact be summarised in terms of these two themes – firstly, the clarification of what lies behind regional patterns of voting and, secondly, the test of the social class hypothesis. In doing so, it is useful to concentrate first on the period up to 1989 and then take into account the impact of the 1992 election.

[12] Tally data consist of records of the vote from each particular area of a constituency that are made by party officials as the ballot boxes are opened and checked prior to the actual count. Their purpose it to give the party an accurate and detailed picture of the distribution of its support. Collecting the tally data has been developed into a fine art, often involving cooperation between the parties. They can and have been used to study sub-constituency electoral politics, demonstrating bailiwick and 'friends and neighbours' effects in Donegal (Sacks, 1970) and in Galway West (Parker, 1982, 1983) and, in the Galway case, also demonstrating patterns of determination of the vote that, in general, confirm the picture obtained through analysis at the constituency level (Parker, 1984).

[13] This is measured by the marginality of the constituency in which the ward or DED is located. The calculation is based on the results of the previous (1987) general election; see Sinnott and Whelan, 1992 for details.

The cartography of Fianna Fáil in the 1920s and early 1930s confirms the regional contrasts, while, at the same time, dramatically illustrating the rapidity of Fianna Fáil gains outside the periphery and the fact that it was well on its way to becoming a national party as early as September 1927, and had definitely become such by 1932–33. Then, in 1943, the effect of prior nationwide gains, combined with exceptional losses in Connacht-Ulster, gave Fianna Fáil a remarkably even balance of support, which lasted until 1965. In 1969 the party suffered a sharp decline in Dublin, creating a gap which has not been made up since. The statistical analysis clarifies the forces under-lying these contrasting patterns by showing the positive impact of the proportion of farmers in an area on Fianna Fáil support in the early years, the disappearance of this influence in the 1943–65 period and its reappearance in the early 1980s.

Cumann na nGaedheal's strongest areas of support in the 20s were Dublin and Connacht-Ulster. Dublin ceased to be an area of strength for Fine Gael in 1937 and was to play that role again only very intermittently. The party's support in Connacht-Ulster collapsed in 1943 but recovered dramatically in 1965, and the area has remained the bedrock of Fine Gael support since then. It was matched briefly by Dublin in the two elections of 1982, but the 1987 election saw a very substantial decline in Fine Gael support in the Dublin area. Again all of this is evident in the ecological analysis – the lack of consistent patterning in the early years, the sudden emergence of the farmer variable in 1965, a variable that was again in evidence when the same kind of analysis could be carried out (in 1981 and after) and which became a very powerful factor in Fine Gael support from 1987 on.

In the case of Labour, the contrast between higher support in the rest of Leinster and Munster, and lower support in Connacht-Ulster and Dublin through most of the party's history prior to 1969, is based on support in areas with high proportions of farm labourers and low proportions of farmers. That pattern was, however, well and truly gone by 1981 and the party's support showed no discernible patterns in the 1980s, pre-sumably reflecting the fact that the lower level Labour vote was very dependent on per-sonalised support for individual incumbent Labour deputies.

Turning to the second theme – the social class hypothesis – there is very little evi-dence to support a comprehensive class interpretation of party support in the 1920s and 1930s. Class does not show up as an independent effect for Fianna Fáil and only appears as a relatively weak and intermittent effect for Cumann na nGaedheal/Fine Gael in that period. Thereafter, evidence of a moderate but fairly consistent social class effect on voting in respect of either Fianna Fáil or Fine Gael only appears in the 1980s. Then the effect took the form of a negative middle-class impact on Fianna Fáil in three elections – February 1982, November 1982 and 1987. For Fine Gael, the middle-class effect was positive in all elections of the '80s but especially in Fine Gael's electoral heyday of 1981–82. As already noted, there is considerable evidence of a rural class effect on aggregate level Labour Party support up to 1965 but neither in that period, nor since, is there any evidence that the urban class structure, as this manifests itself at constituency level, had any effect on the Labour vote.

This brings us to the 1992 election. For both Fianna Fáil and Fine Gael, the pattern changed considerably in 1992. The predictability of the Fianna Fáil vote jumped substantially, especially when compared to the election that immediately preceded it. The degree of patterning in the Fine Gael vote also increased, despite the fact that it lost the middle-class boost that it had enjoyed throughout the 1980s. In the case of both parties, a single variable – the proportion of farmers in a constituency – dominated the pattern. This constituency characteristic accounts for almost 60 per cent of the variation in each party's support. There was a corresponding development in the structure of Labour Party support. From having had virtually no pattern at all in the 1980s, support for the Labour Party in 1992 became negatively and substantially related to the proportion of farmers in a constituency. If support for the Democratic Left plus the Workers' Party is added in as a measure of the combined left vote, the picture is even clearer – the underlying pattern of support for the left is the mirror image of the pattern of support for Fianna Fáil and Fine Gael. Thus, the 1992 election did see a degree of polarisation of voting patterns at constituency level but it was an urban–rural rather than a class polarisation. Clearly this has implications for our understanding of the significance of the 1992 election. The most obvious hypothesis must be that it points to the impact of the liberal–conservative issue on party support, an impact that might have been more likely given the concomitant referendums dealing with abortion. The issue requires further analysis but this is best postponed until the analysis of referendum voting is taken up in chapter 9. In the meantime, however, it must be emphasized again that there is a real and substantial limitation to this kind of ecological analysis. The limitation is that it is not possible to make direct inferences about individual voters. Despite the limitation, the approach is a useful way of exploring voting patterns. It will be used again in the analysis of referendum voting (chapter 9) and of voting in the 1990 presidential election (chapter 10). Continuing the focus on general elections for the moment, the next task is to move to the individual level and to take up some of the issues raised by the ecological analysis and to explore a range of questions that cannot be tackled via aggregate data.

Chapter 6

The voters: volatility, loyalty and party perceptions

Introduction

The last two chapters had to cope with the difficulty that, while there was plenty of hard data, the data did not relate directly to the behaviour of individuals. It might seem that survey and opinion poll data, based as they are directly on individual voters, provide the perfect solution to this problem. However, as emphasized in chapter 1, and as will become apparent throughout this chapter, surveys and opinion polls have their own limitations and bring along their own problems of interpretation and of validity of evidence. In the Irish case, these difficulties are compounded by the fact that there has never been a full-scale national election study and we must rely for the most part on data collected for other purposes, i.e. data collected on behalf of the media, on behalf of political parties, on behalf of the Commission of the European Communities,[1] or on behalf of academic researchers who were primarily interested in topics other than electoral behaviour. This means that the data-sets are not informed by an election-study research design. Many of the questions asked are only imperfect indicators of what we would really like to be able to measure. Questions that seem to be particularly fruitful often turn out to have been asked on only one or two occasions. Despite these limitations, the opinion poll data collected over the years provide invaluable evidence on Irish voting behaviour, and close inspection of the data indicates that there is more there than one might have expected. This chapter uses this evidence to take up again the question of voter volatility, and goes on to examine the relationship between the voters and the parties in terms of voter loyalty and in terms of voter perceptions of parties and party differences.

Voter volatility

By now it is evident that a crucial issue in the analysis of Irish voting behaviour is change – the extent of it, its timing and its implications for the parties and the party

---

[1] The Eurobarometer surveys are regular (for the most part twice-yearly) surveys of public opinion in the member-states of the European Community, carried out since the mid-1970s on behalf of the Commission of the European Communities.

system. Chapter 4 showed that some indication of the stability or instability of voting can be gleaned from published election returns, while noting that the conclusions to be drawn are subject to considerable qualification. Using data on individual voters means that the problem of stability can be looked at from another vantage point and, in some respects, in a much more systematic way. In particular it provides a way of overcoming the net change problem, that is, that small aggregate changes may mask much more extensive and self-cancelling change at the individual level. Volatility can be analysed at an individual level by comparing each respondent's voting intention in a given election with his or her reported vote in the previous election. It must always be borne in mind, however, that these data are subject to the error involved in remembering an event over an extended lapse of time, and are affected by the fact that, in all countries, a significantly greater number of people claim to have voted than actually voted according to the recorded turnout figures (see chapter 3).

Interpretations of the extent of individual-level volatility in Ireland and the timing of its onset vary quite considerably. A study of voting consistency at four pairs of successive elections (1965–69, 1969–73, 1977–81 and 1981-February 1982) concluded: 'In general then there is little evidence of volatility in Ireland. Rather, there is considerable stability . . ., the case for stability is more easily made and stability, rather than change, is what must be explained' (Marsh, 1985, p. 183). However, on the basis of the very same data series, another study identified 'unequivocal evidence' of a decline in the consistency of voting. This latter inference focuses on the figures for the electorate as a whole rather than the figures for each party, and points out that in 1969, according to the data, some 90 per cent of voters indicated a preference for the same party as in the previous election. This fell to 78 per cent in 1973 and to 75 per cent in 1981. Admittedly, the trend was reversed in the February 1982 election (with a consistency figure for all voters of 84 per cent), but it is argued that this could be accounted for by the short gap between the two elections (Mair, 1987b, p. 78).

A decline in inter-election voting consistency from a high of 90 per cent in 1969 does seem to provide very telling evidence in favour of the thesis that volatility is not a recent arrival in the Irish electoral scene but can be traced back some twenty years or more. However, the figure of 90 per cent may exaggerate the extent of voting consistency for the 1965–69 pair of elections. This is because the data on which the figure is based are taken from a study that was conducted in the summer of 1971. Thus the consistency figures are based on the respondent's memory of two events – how he or she had voted 18 months previously (i.e., in June 1969) and four years previous to that (1965). It would not be surprising if memory tended to lead to an exaggerated account of the consistency of the two choices. That this may have happened is suggested by evidence from the 1969 Gallup poll, which makes it possible to relate 1969 voting intention (as of April 1969) to remembered 1965 vote and which suggests an overall voting consistency figure for 1965–69 of 76 per cent. As Table 6.1 shows, this is quite in line with voting consistency in subsequent elections.[2] On this re-reading of the figures, it

[2] With the exception of 1965–69 and 1973–77, the figures for all other pairs of elections are taken from opinion polls conducted during the campaigns immediately prior to the second election in the pair, and the comparison is between remembered vote in the previous election and voting intention in the forthcoming

Table 6.1: *Consistency of party support, 1965–92*

Party	Percentage voting for the same party at consecutive elections								
	65–69	69–73	73–77	77–81	81–82	82–82	82–87	87–89	89–92
Fianna Fáil	84	77	86	72	91	79	75	74	60
Fine Gael	74	82	64	85	81	85	45	76	60
Labour	59	71	59	64	65	71	40	63	78
Workers' Party	–	–	–	–	–	67	44	71	33
Progressive Democrats	–	–	–	–	–	–	–	47	49
All Parties	76	78	82	75	84	79	59	72	60

appears that consistent support for the parties in general was not severely dented until 1987. Of course, consistency in respect of individual parties waxed and waned in particular elections; for example, it was down for Fine Gael in the 1977 débâcle and down for Fianna Fáil in 1981 as the party returned to its normal level of support following its 1977 high. The 1987 election was different. Voting consistency as a whole was down to 59 per cent. Less than half of Fine Gael and Labour voters in November 1982 voted for the same party again in 1987 (see Table 6.1). The main, though not the sole, source of this increased volatility was the arrival of the Progressive Democrats.[3] Although voting stability recovered somewhat in 1989, considerable instability was still evident, especially in the case of the new party, which managed to retain the support of less than 50 per cent of those who had voted for it some two years previously. Given the outcome of the 1992 election, the extent of individual level volatility displayed in the final column in Table 6.1 is not surprising. Only 60 per cent of voters voted in the same way as in 1989, and this volatility hit all parties except, of course, Labour. Labour retained 78 per cent of those who had voted for it in 1989; Fianna Fáil and Fine Gael stability or consistency was down to 60 per cent in each case;[4] the Progressive Democrats continued to show a high level of volatility and the Workers' Party showed the lowest level of stability of any party in any of the elections considered – only one in three 1989 Workers' Party supporters indicated an intention to vote either for the Workers' Party or the Democratic Left in 1992.

---

one. The proportions of consistent voters are calculated on the basis of all of those voting in the first election of the pair who indicate an intention to vote (or, in the 1973–77 pair, indicated having voted) in the second election. Because of different ways of handling non-voters in different surveys, abstention and therefore the possibility of differential abstention are not taken into account. For some evidence on the latter, see Marsh, 1985, pp. 179–81.

[3] See the discussion of 'defectors and loyalists' in Laver, Marsh and Sinnott, 1987, pp. 109–11 for an account of the origin and destination of vote switching in 1987.

[4] For an analysis of the class composition of consistent Fianna Fáil, Fine Gael and Labour supporters and of the key groups who switched between these parties, see Marsh and Sinnott, 1993, pp. 110–13.

Intergenerational voting stability

Another way of looking at the stability of party support is to examine evidence of inter-generational stability. Part of the folklore of Irish elections has been that experienced party activists could identify the voting of entire families and could say with some certainty that a particular house was a Fianna Fáil or a Fine Gael house (Sacks, 1976). It is sometimes assumed in Ireland that this kind of family preference and intergenerational voting stability is unique to Ireland. In fact, the intergenerational transmission of party preferences is not unusual (see, for example, Butler and Stokes, 1974). Table 6.2 compares the extent of such transmission in the Irish case in 1969 and in 1990. Carty's comment on the 1969 data is that they confirm 'that the continuing stability of the Irish voter alignments is rooted in the persistence of family partisan allegiances' (Carty, 1981, pp. 81–2). The 1990 evidence suggests that this familial voting persistence had weakened considerably some twenty years later. Among those with a Fianna Fáil father, Fianna Fáil voting had dropped from 78 per cent to 64 per cent. Starting from a lower level (65 per cent), Fine Gael family loyalty had fallen less (to 58 per cent). The continuity of voting in Labour families, which was weak enough to begin with (53 per cent) became almost negligible (30 per cent) in 1990, voters from a Labour background drifting away to Fianna Fáil (24 per cent), to Fine Gael (14 per cent) or to the Workers' Party (13 per cent). In sum, intergenerational continuity in voting had declined substantially by 1990, but it had not disappeared – it still obtained at a rate of almost two-thirds for Fianna Fáil families and almost three-fifths for Fine Gael families.[5] It must be emphasized, of course, that this was the situation in 1990. Family continuity could look quite different, especially for Fianna Fáil, if the evidence included voting in November 1992.

Party loyalty

The increase in voter volatility at the individual level and the increased tendency for the voting behaviour of one generation to differ from that of the previous one may well reflect something more fundamental than just a decision to switch from one party to another at a particular election. It may in fact reflect a decline of people's sense of loyalty or attachment to the political parties. It is possible indeed that a decline in such attachment precedes actual voting volatility, as voters continue to vote for the same party but with less commitment and with a greater potential to switch to another party.

A sense of attachment or loyalty to a political party is commonly defined as party identification, that is, depending on the party system, individuals think of themselves in politics as Republican, Democrat or Independent; Conservative or Labour; Fianna Fáil, Fine Gael, Labour or whatever. This is, in fact, the way in which the question measuring party identification has been asked in the United States over the years, that

---

[5] The evidence of family voting continuity is based on the father's vote. If the mother's vote is taken as the base in 1990, the same trends appear, though in a slightly weaker form. In the case of voters with both parents voting for the same party, continuity is slightly stronger than that evident in Table 6.2.

Table 6.2: *Respondent's vote by father's vote, 1969 (vote recall) and 1990 (voting intention) (%)*

	Fianna Fáil	Fine Gael	Labour	Other/DK
		Father's partisanship		
1969 vote				
Fianna Fáil	78	24	31	—
Fine Gael	9	65	5	—
Labour	7	6	53	—
Other	1	1	1	—
Refuse/DK	6	5	9	—
N	(407)	(245)	(77)	—
1990 voting intention				
Fianna Fáil	64	13	24	17
Fine Gael	9	58	14	19
Labour	7	9	30	9
Workers' Party	2	2	13	5
Prog. Democrats	4	6	5	4
Greens	3	2	5	3
Sinn Fein	2	1	4	3
Other	3	2	1	9
No party/Don't vote	7	7	5	33
N	(480)	(248)	(84)	(193)

being the country in which the concept was first developed.[6] In the American context it is quite common to be a Democrat, for example, and to vote for the Republican candidate in a particular presidential election without changing one's fundamental party allegiance. Only if significant numbers decide not just to vote for a different party, but to switch their loyalty or identification to another party, is a realignment said to occur. Of course, individuals may lose their loyalty to one party without transferring it to another. In this case, dealignment takes place (see Beck, 1984 and Särlvik and Crewe, 1983).

On the face of it, the concepts of electoral alignment and party identification fit quite readily into the Irish context. For one thing, 'breaking the mould' and 'bringing about a new political alignment' (usually, but not always, a left–right one) are part of the stuff of day-to-day political discussion. Secondly, down the years, the notion of individuals having a long-standing commitment to the parties ('being Fianna Fáil' or, less frequently, 'being Fine Gael') has always been widely acknowledged. On the other hand, it is also currently assumed that such commitment has been on the wane for some time. Unfortunately, this is another key area of Irish electoral behaviour where the available data fall well short of what we would need for a comprehensive account

[6] For a general discussion of the origin of the concept and of its cross-national applicability, see Budge, Crewe and Farlie, 1976.

of the changes in individual behaviour, which the notions of realignment and dealignment, and the waxing and waning of party identification, imply.

Assessments of available evidence differ sharply. One study infers the existence of strong party loyalty or allegiance from evidence of stability of voting and the solidarity of transfers: 'There is little doubt that Irish electors are party voters; their voting behaviour reflects strong and persistent partisan allegiances' (Carty, 1981, p. 68). Analysis of party identification data for 1976, 1981 and 1982 lends support to this view:

> two things are evident from these data. First, the majority of Irish voters have clear party
> attachments. Whilst levels of 'no identification' are about twice those found in Britain in
> the mid-1960s, they seem lower than those of several other European countries. There is
> no dealignment in Ireland. Second, there is some sign that the electorate is more aligned
> now than in the mid-1970s.   (Marsh, 1985, p. 194)

On the other hand, Inglehart and Klingemann noted that Ireland recorded the lowest level of partisan identification of nine European Community countries in 1973 (Inglehart and Klingemann, 1976). Consistent with this, a comparison of levels of attachment to party in the European Community in the late 1970s and early 1980s showed that Ireland had a lower level of partisan identification than all countries other than Belgium or France (Mair, 1984). In tackling the problem of the discrepancies between the various bits of evidence, Mair argues that 'while a similar or even greater proportion of the electorate may now think of themselves in terms of a particular party, this does not necessarily imply that they feel as close to that party as they once did'. He cites Eurobarometer data for Ireland between 1978 and 1985 that show 'an unmistakeable [downwards] trend' in the intensity of party identification, with an index designed to measure this intensity declining steadily from 38.2 in October 1978 to just 26.1 in 1984 (zero would indicate that no voters have any sense of attachment to party and one hundred would indicate that all voters have a 'very close' sense of such attachment) (Mair, 1987a, p. 78). Finally, using Eurobarometer data over a considerably longer period, Schmitt describes the Irish situation as follows:

> Eurobarometer data suggest that if there is dealignment somewhere in the European
> Community it is to be found in Ireland (and . . . in the United Kingdom). Irish party
> attachment decreased from slightly below 60 per cent in the late 1970s to around 50 per
> cent in the early 1980s and fell again to about 40 per cent in more recent years.
>   (Schmitt, 1989, p. 134)

What are we to make of these divergent views? The key to the differences would appear to lie in the varying ways in which the concept of party attachment or party identification is being measured. The data leading to the conclusion of persistent party identification up to 1982 are based (with minor variations) on the question 'In politics do you usually think of yourself as Fianna Fáil, Fine Gael, Labour or what?'. The data set reported in Marsh (1985) can be filled out to cover five separate time points by the addition of data for 1977 and 1978. On the face of it, the results of this more extended data set confirm the conclusion regarding the existence and stability of party

Table 6.3: *Party identification (%)*

	1976	1977 (Feb)	1978	1981	1982
Fianna Fáil	39	37	48	42	39
Fine Gael	23	23	23	23	32
Labour	14	12	9	8	8
Other	1	4	4	3	3
None	20	20	13	21	14
Ref/DK	3	4	3	4	3

identification up to 1982, and to that extent, conflict with the conclusions based on Eurobarometer evidence cited above. As Marsh noted, more people showed up as having a party identification in 1982 than in 1976, the main source of the increase being a growth of identification with Fine Gael, though this was partially offset by a decline in identification with Labour. This increase in identification with Fine Gael coincided with the peak of Fine Gael electoral support in the November 1982 election. Table 6.3 also shows that party identification increased for Fianna Fáil shortly after its 1977 electoral success. These two increases suggest that party identification as measured in this way may be picking up not just long-term party identifiers, but also those who attach themselves to the parties on a more short-term shifting basis. This implies that what is being measured includes a weak or minimal degree of party loyalty or attachment which fluctuates with the ebb and flow of support for the parties.[7] This is quite different from what is being measured in the Eurobarometer question.

As implemented in Ireland, the Eurobarometer has used no fewer than four different ways of asking about party attachment.[8] As an element in a time series, the first form of the question can be discounted in that it was asked on only one occasion – October 1975. It is worth noting, however, because it shows just how subject to question wording the responses are. The question was 'Do you feel affinities with any particular party? If so, do you feel yourself to be very involved in this party, fairly involved or merely a sympathiser?'. As Figure 6.1 indicates, party attachment measured in this way was evident among only 35 per cent of Irish respondents (note that, in the calculations underlying Figure 6.1, the don't knows are excluded). In the very next survey, party attachment in Ireland rose substantially, due, one must assume, simply to the change in question wording from 'feel affinities with any particular party', to 'consider yourself a supporter of any particular party'. In October 1978 the Eurobarometer party

[7] This makes this particular operationalisation of the concept of party identification less analytically useful, because one of the main purposes of examining party identification is to be able to distinguish between long-term loyalty and short-term voting decision. For similar difficulties with the measurement of party identification in the German case, see Kaase, 1976, pp. 81–9.

[8] For a discussion of the variations in measurement of party identification in Eurobarometers in all member states, see Katz, 1985.

attachment question changed again, this time from 'Do you consider yourself a supporter of any particular party? If so, do you feel yourself to be very involved in this
party, fairly involved or merely a sympathiser? etc.' to 'Do you consider yourself to be
close to any particular party? If so do you feel yourself to be very close to this party,
fairly close or merely a sympathiser?'. This version of the question has been used since
then with one exception – the Eurobarometer of autumn 1981 (see below). Though the
alteration in wording in autumn 1978 produced no change in the overall level of party
attachment in Ireland (see Figure 6.1), it produced considerable change within the
three levels of attachment – the 'merely sympathisers' fell 20 percentage points and the
two higher levels of attachment ('fairly involved/close' and 'very involved/close') rose
10 points each.

   The foregoing demonstrates clearly that evidence regarding party attachment is
very subject to variability in question wording. In considering the discrepancies
between Table 6.3 and Figure 6.1, the point to note is that one set of evidence does not
disprove the other. The discrepancies reflect the fact that different things are being
measured. As suggested above, the 'party identification' question used in Table 6.3 is
a minimal measure. The Eurobarometer question is more demanding. As implemented
from autumn 1978 on, it distinguishes at the outset between those who are close to a
party and those who are not (or in earlier versions between supporters and non-sup-
porters), and then measures degree of closeness or involvement. It is quite conceivable
that a respondent would answer with the name of a particular party when asked 'In

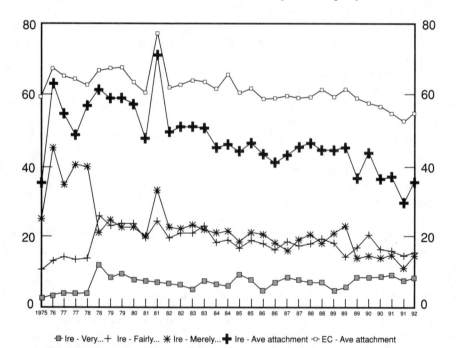

Figure 6.1 Party attachment in Ireland and in the EC, 1975–92.

politics do you usually think of yourself as Fianna Fáil, Fine Gael, Labour, or what?' and, at the same time, answer 'no' to the question 'Do you consider yourself to be close to any particular party?'. Such a person has a sense of party identification alright, but it is a weak identification and the person baulks at acknowledging being 'close to a party'. On the basis of the Eurobarometer question, individuals in this position would not even be classified as having a party identification because the initial question rules them out by eliciting a 'yes' or 'no' response to the question regarding closeness to a party. The matter can be put another way by saying that the Eurobarometer question excludes any respondent who is not 'close' to a party to begin with, and then measures just how close to a party the remaining respondents are. The identification question starts with those who have any degree of connection to a party, no matter how tenuous, and, in some but not all versions of the question, only then seeks to measure whether that connection is strong or weak.

An altogether different question asked in the 1969 Gallup poll tends to confirm the foregoing interpretation. The question was 'In deciding how to vote do you really sympathise with the party you've chosen or do you feel that you're having to choose between poor alternatives?'. On this measure 53 per cent turned out to be 'real sympathisers' (Gallup, 1969). This is consistent with the subsequent Eurobarometer data on 'Do you feel close to any party?'. Both questions identify the proportion of the population that feels quite positive about a party. In addition to such respondents, there are those who side with a particular party more or less as the best of a bad lot and who may, therefore, turn up as party identifiers in the question 'In politics do you think of yourself as . . .?', but who do not appear on the screen, as it were, when the question is 'Do you consider yourself to be close to any particular party?'.

The argument is further reinforced by the effect of the change in wording in the Eurobarometer taken in the second half of 1981. Eurobarometer 16 asked as the opening question on this topic: 'Generally speaking, do you feel closer to any of the parties on this list than to the others? If yes, which one?'. The second half of the question was altered to 'Do you consider yourself to be very close to this party, fairly close, etc.' The effect was for party attachment in Ireland to leap to 70 per cent (see Figure 6.1). Note that party identification in the member states of the European Community as a whole also increased substantially. The Irish figure is quite out of line with the figures in previous and subsequent Eurobarometer surveys, but reasonably consistent with the data for June 1981 shown in Table 6.3. The reason is simple. The question asked in autumn 1981 was a question not about an absolute level of attachment to party, as in 'Do you feel yourself to be close to any particular party?'. Rather, it was a question about relative closeness to any of a set of parties ('Generally speaking do you feel closer to any of the parties on this list than to the others?'). There should be no surprise that the latter question elicited a much higher positive response – any degree of closeness to one party rather than the others should lead a respondent to answer 'yes'. This interpretation is borne out by the fact that all of the increase occurred at the lower levels of attachment (i.e., 'fairly close' and 'merely a sympathiser').

All of this helps to clarify the nature of what has happened in Ireland between 1980 and 1992. Overall, there has been a 20 to 25 percentage point drop in the number of respondents reporting that they are 'close to a party' (see Figure 6.1). The drop seems to have occurred in particular in 1980–81 and between 1983 and 1986. This general period was one of considerable difficulty for party government in Ireland. The problems became apparent in 1979 with the evident failure of the very ambitious plans contained in the 1977 Fianna Fáil election manifesto. The failure led directly to a very serious problem in the level of government borrowing. At the same time, there was a change of leadership in Fianna Fáil, a change followed by continued internal.party dissension about the leadership, which was accompanied by both a heightening of the conflict between the parties and a significant personalisation of that conflict. There then followed a period of approximately eighteen months that saw very considerable governmental instability, three general elections and more internal Fianna Fáil leadership conflict and intrigue, including the apparently essential ingredient of all modern political intrigues – a number of phone-tapping episodes.

The period 1982–87 saw stable government but there was a continued and manifest failure to solve the government borrowing problem. This was also the period of a protracted and complex political struggle on the issue of inserting an anti-abortion amendment into the constitution. The struggle culminated in a divisive referendum in 1983, in which, according to many of the partisans on both sides of the issue, but in particular on the anti-amendment side, the parties did not acquit themselves well. This religious/moral divide emerged again in the divorce referendum of 1986, when the change to the constitution proposed by the government was defeated, again to the chagrin of liberals and to a chorus of complaint directed at all of the political parties. It is not surprising, therefore, that the number of people feeling close to a party should have declined during this period of political turbulence and widespread pessimistic assessments about the capacity of the political system in general, and the party system in particular, to cope with a number of fundamental problems.

While the decline in closeness to parties is interpretable in terms of specifically Irish political developments, it is worth noting that there are some parallels between the Irish trend and the average trend for the member states of the European Community as a whole (see the top line in Figure 6.1). In the European Community, the rate of attachment to political parties declined from a level close to 70 per cent in the late 1970s to 60 per cent in 1981. It stayed at about that level until 1989, after which it declined again over several surveys. Thus, Ireland's decline in party attachment more or less reflected a general trend in 1979–81, was against the Community norm in the mid-1980s and, towards the end of the period examined, coincided with general trends again. Obviously, this very broad comparison does not establish that there was a common cause at work; it does, however, serve to put Irish developments in a wider perspective.[9]

In summary, there has been both continuity and change in party identification in Ireland. The change is in the proportion feeling close to a party. This is not incompatible with the continuation of a minimal level of party identification, such as

---

[9] For a country-by-country comparison of the European trends see Schmitt, 1989.

Table 6.4: *Certainty of voting intention (general election) and reported vote in 1989 European Parliament election by voter type (attached/unattached) (%)*

(a) *Certain to vote for party*

	Attached party voters	Unattached party voters
FF	75	58
FG	62	44
Lab	77	44

(b) *Voted for candidate of party in European Parliament election*

	Attached party voters	Unattached party voters
FF	79	59
FG	78	54
Lab	63	50

that evidenced up to 1982 in Table 6.3. Fewer people are close to the parties but this does not necessarily amount to wholesale abandonment of them.[10]

Does it matter that the electorate's sense of closeness to the political parties has been declining, and that it is now down more than 20 percentage points on what it had been in the late 1970s? Are there any grounds for the assumption that this decline may have been a precursor of electoral change? We do not have the data that would allow a definitive answer to this question. However, research carried out in connection with the 1989 European Parliament elections confirms that party attachment does make a difference, both to the certainty of people's voting decisions and to the consistency of their support for their preferred party in different kinds of elections. Those intending to vote for a given party can be divided into the attached (those who say they are close to the party) and the unattached (those who intend to vote for the party but are not close to it).

In the case of each of the main parties, Table 6.4 compares attached and unattached voters in terms of (a) their certainty of voting for the party in question and (b) their reported vote in the European Parliament election. Whether a party's voters are attached or unattached makes a considerable difference. For each of the parties, attached voters are considerably more likely to be absolutely certain that they will follow through on their stated voting intention and considerably more likely to have voted for the party's candidates in the European Parliament election (see Table 6.4).

[10] Unfortunately, the absence of comparable data makes it impossible to assess the extent of change in minimal party identification after 1982. However, a modification of the standard Eurobarometer question on party attachment inserted in the June 1994 Eurobarometer showed that, in addition to the 36 per cent 'who consider themselves close to a particular party' a further 13 per cent considered themselves 'a little closer to one of the political parties than the others'. This confirms that some degree of party identification is more widespread than the data from 1978 onwards in Figure 6.1 suggest. For details of the 1994 data see Sinnott, 1995.

Note that Fianna Fáil tends to have an advantage in translating support into votes. Its attached supporters are more likely than Fine Gael attached supporters to say that it is certain that they will vote for the party, and more likely than Labour Party attached supporters to have voted for their own party in the European Parliament election of 1989. Even in the case of unattached voters, Fianna Fáil has an advantage, both in terms of certainty of voting for the party and, to a lesser degree, in terms of reported European Parliament vote in 1989.

Fianna Fáil voters in 1989 were also more likely to be very close or fairly close to their party and less likely to be merely sympathisers or unattached voters (see Table 6.5). All of this is consistent with several indications already noted, that volatility has been greater and has developed earlier on the non-Fianna Fáil side of the political divide. In summary, then, it is clear that the existence of party attachment makes a considerable difference and the fact that there has been a decline in the extent of party attachment (understood in the strong sense of 'feeling close to a party') since the early 1980s can indeed be assumed to have paved the way for the increased volatility of the late 1980s and early 1990s.

Among those who are unattached to a party there is, of course, the further very large difference between those who vote more or less regularly, and those who do not. Chapter 5 considered some aggregate evidence on voter turnout at constituency level for the country as a whole, and at sub-constituency level for Dublin. The conclusion drawn was that there was some evidence of a relationship between turnout and the age profile of an area at a constituency level, and between turnout, age and a combination of high levels of unemployment, low levels of education and large proportions of individuals in low status occupations at a sub-constituency level. Opinion poll data provide a means of overcoming the problems of ecological inference involved in the aggregate analysis of turnout. On the other hand, opinion poll data on turnout are particularly sensitive to the problems of survey data noted in chapter 1. The difficulty arises in particular because voting tends to be regarded by many people, at least in some vague way, as a civic duty. Consequently, a question asking whether the respondent turned out to vote in an election is subject, in the jargon of survey research methodology, to 'social

Table 6.5: *Attachment to party by party support, 1989 (%)*

	FF	FG	Lab	PD	WP	Other
Very close to party	8	2	3	0	4	8
Fairly close to party	18	15	15	10	4	11
Party sympathiser	26	29	24	21	24	27
Unattached voter	48	54	58	69	67	53
N	372	234	88	29	67	62

desirability response set', that is, some respondents are likely to report having voted, even though they have not done so, because they regard voting as a socially desirable activity. Survey research over-estimated turnout in the 1989 European Parliament elections by 13 percentage points for the member states of the European Community as a whole, and by amounts as high as 19 points in the United Kingdom and 18 points in Denmark (Schmitt and Mannheimer, 1991, pp. 34–5). The problem is not confined to reported voting in European Parliament elections – the average over-estimation of turnout in national elections in surveys in seven countries reported by Budge and Farlie is 10 per cent (Budge and Farlie, 1976, pp. 112–13).

The tendency for survey research to exaggerate the extent of turnout is confirmed in a recent study of turnout in Ireland using opinion poll data (Marsh, 1991). In the two data sets used in that study only 13 per cent of respondents acknowledged that they did not vote in the 1989 election; in fact 31.5 per cent of the registered electorate did not vote. Part of the discrepancy may be accounted for by the fact that the opinion polls are quota samples of the population as a whole, whereas turnout is measured on the basis of the registered electorate.[11] Even taking this into account, however, it is apparent that the data considerably underestimate non-voting. Nonetheless, provided we bear in mind that the data relates to a portion, rather than all, of the non-voters, the findings from research of this sort are of considerable interest.

Survey research enables a distinction to be drawn between short-term non-voters, or non-voters 'by accident', and long-term non-voters, or non-voters 'by design' (Marsh, 1991, pp. 3–6). Short-term non-voters are more like the active electorate, and appear to have been prevented from voting by some particular circumstance in the election in question. Long-term non-voters, on the other hand, differ from the active electorate and from short-term non-voters in that they have less interest in politics and a greater degree of dissatisfaction with political institutions. They are also less likely to be middle class, they are less well-educated and more likely to be unemployed (Marsh, 1991, p. 10). This picture of long-term non-voters is broadly in line with the findings of the aggregate study of turnout reported in chapter 5, and reinforces the point made there regarding the failure to provide all citizens, in practice and not just in theory, with an equal voice in the representative process.

While the analysis of non-voting is important and arguably deserves greater attention than it has hitherto received, our main interest lies with those who do vote. The waning of party attachment has implications not just for voter volatility but for our understanding of the basis of the voting decision. The problem is: do issues determine party choice or does prior party choice determine both current voting intention and issue preferences? A strict rational choice model of issue-voting assumes the former account – voters, having considered all the issues, make their voting decision by picking the party which is closest to them on the issues that are most important to them. The alternative explanation is that voters, armed with a prior commitment to party, that is, the party identification or party attachment notions discussed above, see

[11] For this and other reasons for discrepancies between official and reported turn-out in the 1987 British general election see Swaddle and Heath, 1989.

the political world, the issues it presents and the policy options selectively. They look through party-tinted glasses that have the advantage of simplifying an over-complex world. Thus it is their prior party commitment or choice that determines where they themselves stand on particular issues, and even how they see where the parties stand.[12] If party attachment has been declining for some time, does this mean that issues and what the parties stand for are playing a larger role in voting decisions? Even with an ideal data set, answering this apparently simple and obvious question would be very difficult because it raises complex methodological and theoretical problems. Far from there being an ideal data set, the available data in this area are fragmentary; this observation applies as much or more to the data on what the parties stand for and what the election issues are, as it does to the data on party identification or attachment that have been reviewed above. However, even if a comprehensive answer to the underlying question cannot be given, some progress can be made by describing how the voters see the parties and how they see the issues in particular elections. The rest of this chapter tackles the first problem, that of the voters' perceptions of inter-party differences. The role of specific issues in specific elections is taken up in chapter 7.

Party location

On the basis of the historical record, chapter 2 suggested that there have been and still are at least some differences between the parties. Chapter 3 reviewed some evidence supporting the view that significant inter-party differences exist: the parties are judged to be different by 'experts'; analysis of the party manifestos shows that they project different images in election campaigns; evidence from interviews with party elites shows differences in party image and in attitude and approach to problems. In terms of the analysis of voting behaviour, the key question is whether these differences register with the voters? Or are they just subtle nuances perceptible only to those directly involved, as actors or observers, in the game of party politics? Do ordinary voters see any differences at all between the parties?

One of the early systematic studies of Irish political parties is quite categorical that they do not: 'party identifications in Ireland persist despite a lack of any perceived differences in the parties themselves' (Carty, 1981, p. 80). The evidence is summarised as follows: 'Only one-third of the Irish respondents claim that they believe that there are any important differences between the parties; a majority see no difference at all' (*ibid.*, p. 80). The data referred to are taken from the Gallup poll of 1969. The specific finding was that 56 per cent saw the political parties as the same and only 31 per cent saw them as different (see Table 6.6). Carty highlights this finding by comparing it with data drawn from the Butler and Stokes study, *Political Change in Britain* (1974). Sixty-eight per cent of the British sample are reported as perceiving the political parties as different, with 29 per cent seeing them as the same. In assessing the significance of this apparently striking contrast, however, it is necessary, yet again, to take into account differences in the wording of the questions. The Gallup poll question

[12] See, for example, the discussion in Budge and Farlie, 1983.

asked in Ireland in 1969 was 'Do you think there is any really important difference between the parties or are they all much of a muchness?'. Thus, the question presented a stark dichotomy ('really important differences' versus 'much of a muchness') to the respondent. The Butler and Stokes question, on the other hand, specifically named three graded response categories, posing a much less extreme choice.[13] In fact, the 68 per cent figure quoted by Carty as indicating the proportion in Britain who see the parties there as different consists of 42 per cent saying 'a good deal of difference' and 26 per cent saying 'some difference'. Moreover, these figures reflect the situation in Britain in the spring of 1966. When the same question had been asked in 1963, however, the response was 36 per cent 'a good deal of difference', 20 per cent 'some difference' and 34 per cent 'not much difference' (there were 10 per cent 'don't know' responses) (see Table 6.6). One could argue that the 1969 Irish Gallup poll category of 'really important differences' (which drew a 31 per cent response) is comparable to the Butler and Stokes category of 'a good deal of difference' (42 per cent in 1966; 36 per cent in 1963). This suggests that there was not such a large gap between the perceptions of party differences in Britain and Ireland in the 1960s.

The question regarding perceived party differences was asked in Ireland in 1976 in the more satisfactory trichotomous form used by Butler and Stokes. According to this evidence, the perception that party differences do exist is not a minority view; the population at that point was, in fact, evenly balanced between the 45 per cent who saw at least 'some difference' and a similar proportion who saw 'hardly any difference'. If we use this evidence to compare perceptions of party differences in Britain and Ireland, a considerable contrast is still evident, but this contrast relates most especially to the extent of the perception of major differences, that is, the perception of 'a good deal of difference' (see Table 6.6). Given that the British party system has traditionally been regarded as a prime example of consistent inter-party differences, and given that one would expect the differences in the Irish case to be a matter of degree and of nuance, it is not surprising that there should be a contrast in the perception of the extent of major differences between the parties. Rather, what is surprising is that the aggregate perception of party difference in Ireland in 1976 (45 per cent) comes as close as it does to even one of the similarly aggregated British figures (56 per cent in 1963).

The question asked in the 1976 survey was not subsequently replicated. However, during the November 1982 election campaign, respondents were asked to what extent they agreed with the statement 'There is little or no difference between Fianna Fáil and Fine Gael'. Twenty per cent 'definitely agreed' with the statement and a further 25 per cent were inclined to agree. On the other hand, a total of 49 per cent disagreed (22 per cent were inclined to disagree and 27 per cent definitely disagreed) (RSI, 1982). Given that this question focuses on differences between only two of the parties and that these two are the parties most likely to be regarded as similar, the fact that 49 per cent disagreed with the statement that there is little or no difference between them tends to bear out the findings of the 1976 survey. Thus, though the evidence is not as

[13] The precise wording in the Butler and Stokes study was 'Considering everything the parties stand for, would you say there is a good deal of difference between the parties, some difference, or not much difference?'.

Table 6.6: *Perception of party differences in the Republic of Ireland and Great Britain, 1963–76*

Response categories Ireland 1969	Percentage of respondents Ireland 1969	Response categories Ireland 1976 Britain 1963 Britain 1966	Percentage of respondents		
			Ireland 1976	Britain 1963	Britain 1966
Really important differences	31	A good deal of difference	18	36	42
–	–	Some difference	27	20	26
Much of a muchness	56	Hardly any differences	45	34	29
Don't know	13	Don't know	10	10	3
Number	1580	Number	2038	2009	1874

extensive as one would wish, it suggests that Ireland is not as exceptional in regard to the perception of inter-party differences as might at first sight appear, and that the conclusion that there is a lack of any perceived differences between the parties would seem to be unwarranted.

If there are at least some perceived differences between the parties, what are they? In seeking to answer this question, we can examine perceptions of the positions of the parties on a left–right scale (in 1976 and 1989) and on a Northern Ireland policy scale (1978). In addition, there are data from the MRBI 1987 election polls, which, while they do not set out to measure party placement on a policy scale, can be used as indirect evidence of party positions on a number of issues.[14]

Left versus right

An early comparative analysis of the use of the left–right concept provides some preliminary evidence. In regard to Ireland, the study concluded that 'The left–right dimension seems to have a relatively unclear meaning for the Irish public. Both the partisan and the ideological component are weak in Ireland, our persistent deviant case' (Inglehart and Klingemann, 1976, p. 270). On a 10-point scale ranging from left (1) to right (10), the Irish sample turned out to be decidedly to the right in terms of self-placement (mean value 6.30), and the supporters of the two major parties had

[14] The 1987 data can only be treated as ancillary because the question does not ask the respondent to place the parties on a scale. Instead, it asks which party has the best policy on a particular issue, and one can then relate this choice to the respondent's own position on the same issue. This involves the risk of conflating perception and evaluation. Thus, party loyalists might well instinctively answer with the name of their own party when asked which party has the best policy, and this response might not correspond to how they would have answered if they had simply been asked, in a neutral way, to place each of the parties on a policy scale.

mean scores that were virtually identical (Fine Gael 6.68; Fianna Fáil 6.59). Moreover, the distance between their supporters and those of the Labour Party (mean score 5.03) was considerably less than the distance covered by any of the other eight party systems analysed. It is also noteworthy that the Irish parties had the largest standard deviation found in any party system, suggesting that 'Irish . . . party-identifiers are relatively widely scattered on the left–right continuum: and we suspect that this is true because cultural cues concerning the meaning of left and right are less clear in [Ireland]' (*ibid.*, p. 252). Similar comparative data from almost twenty years later confirm that, in comparison to a European sample drawn from nine West European countries, 'The Irish are distinctively less left-wing' (Hardiman and Whelan, 1994, p.153). Further analysis of the latter data identifies the attitudes associated with left–right self-placement and examines the distribution of these attitudes among party supporters. The conclusion confirms the closeness of Fianna Fáil and Fine Gael: 'Fianna Fáil and Fine Gael supporters, by and large tend to be right-wing in terms of self-assignment, economic values, views on sexual morality, confidence in establishment institutions and postmaterialism' (*ibid.*, p. 183). These two sets of findings – from the 1973 Eurobarometer study and the 1990 European Values Study – give some pointers to what the parties stand for. However, because in each case the data deal only with how the supporters of each party place themselves on a left–right scale, or with the views or policy preferences the party supporters espouse, the findings do not get at what we are really concerned with – where the voters locate the parties on such policy or issue dimensions.

The IMS 1976 survey already referred to contains not only a measure of self-placement on a left–right scale, but also a direct measure of perceived party placements. The first point to note about the responses is the high 'don't know' rate – 30 per cent for self-placement and 36 to 37 per cent in the case of party placements (IMS, 1976). The more than one-third 'don't know' in the case of party placement in particular indicates that a sizeable section of the public could make no use at all of a left–right dimension in differentiating between the parties. It might have been expected that, in the case of the two major parties, voters would have difficulty placing them on a left–right scale. Given the lack of historical differentiation between the parties in terms of traditional left/right concerns, and the definition of their electoral appeals in terms of limited and contingent competition along a dimension defined as corporatism versus social democracy (see chapter 3), it is little wonder that the voters fail to distinguish Fianna Fáil from Fine Gael in left–right terms. However, though the Irish Labour party has never been very far to the left, it is surprising and significant that the 'don't know' response was equally high for the question seeking the location of the Labour Party on the scale (the 'don't know' responses for placement of each party were Fianna Fáil 36 per cent, Fine Gael 37 per cent, Labour 37 per cent).[15]

---

[15] The 'don't know' figure for self-placement in the study by Inglehart and Klingemann was 20 per cent. While still high, this is less than that registered in the 1976 survey because the Eurobarometer actively discouraged non-responses. Commenting on the treatment of 'don't know' responses, Inglehart and Klingemann write: 'If the respondent hesitated, the interviewer was instructed to note that fact and ask him to try again' (Inglehart and Klingemann, 1976, p. 247).

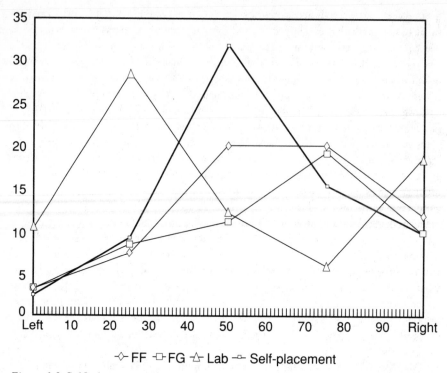

Figure 6.2 Self-placement and perceived party placement on a left–right scale, 1976.

Acknowledging that in this particular survey almost one-third of voters could not place themselves on a left–right scale, and over one-third could not place the parties, what of the remaining two-thirds? Where did such voters place themselves and, in particular, where were the parties seen to stand in terms of left and right? As Figure 6.2 shows, the plurality of the voters were positioned in the middle of the spectrum. However, the overall balance was tilted a little towards the right because somewhat more voters opted for the two right-wing positions on the scale ('slightly right of centre' and 'very right wing') than for the corresponding positions on the left side of the scale. Thus, if we take the scale as extending from 0 (very left wing) to 100 (very right wing), the average position for all voters placing themselves on the scale is 57.3.[16] Fianna Fáil and Fine Gael were placed by the voters on the right of centre and very close to one another (average placement 60.0 and 62.5). Their similarity is confirmed by the shape of the graph for each party (see Figure 6.2). Labour, on the other hand, was seen as occupying a moderate left position. Its average placement was 34.0 and the

[16] The format of the actual question used a 5-point scale ranging from –2 (very left wing) to +2 (very right wing). Other scales discussed in this section used either 7 or 10 points, and all have been standardised to a common scale of 0 to 100. It should be noted that while this procedure makes the scales numerically comparable, the comparability is not exact because of the different descriptions of the anchor points at the ends of the scales, and because of the different numbers of steps along the scales.

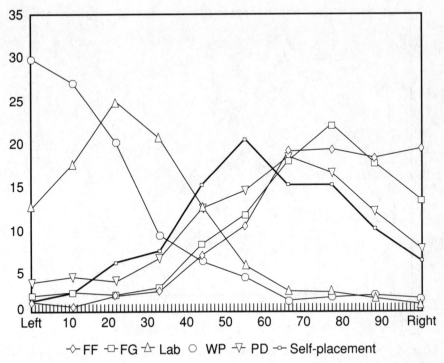

Figure 6.3 Self-placement and perceived party placement on a left–right scale, 1989.

graph of its distribution on the scale shows a decided contrast to those of Fianna Fáil and Fine Gael. Thus, using the more direct and satisfactory measure of party placement on the left–right scale, these data confirm that the two main parties in the system were seen to be basically alike in left–right terms, and that the only differentiation on this scale related to the position of the Labour Party. By registering such a large proportion of 'don't knows', it also confirms the limited utility of the left–right spectrum in the Irish case, at least among the public at large.

Data on perceived party placement on a left–right scale are not available again until 1989, and between 1976 and 1989 much had happened in Irish politics. On the face of it, it appears that not much had changed in terms of the voters' placement of themselves. It is true that in 1989 the electorate as a whole was located a fraction further to the right of centre (average position 64.1). However, because the 1989 scale used 10 points, in comparison to the 5 points used in 1976, it is difficult to say whether this slight shift to the right in the average voter self-placement and the less obvious peaking of the distribution of this measure in the centre in 1989 (see Figure 6.3), as compared with 1976, is due to a substantive change or simply reflects the difference in methodology. It is fairly clear, however, that the left–right span of the party system was greater in 1989 than it had been in 1976, a not surprising finding given the emergence of a multi-party system documented in chapter 4. The occupation of the space on the left

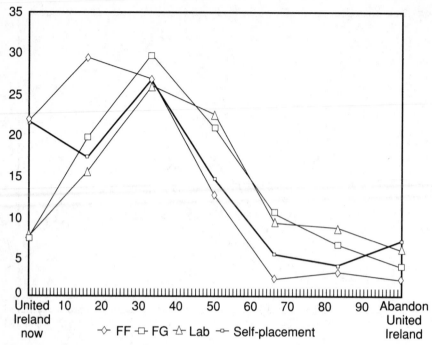

Figure 6.4 Self-placement and perceived party placement on the issue of a United Ireland, 1978.

of the spectrum is attributable mainly to the Workers' Party, which had an average score of 21.8;[17] Labour was seen to occupy a position (34.7) very close to its position in 1976. On the other hand, the Progressive Democrats (65.0) were not seen as the most right-wing party; in fact, they occupy the position previously occupied by Fine Gael and Fianna Fáil, and their presence pushes the latter two parties somewhat further to the right (76.5 and 72.7 respectively).

Nationalism

The evidence of elite attitudes and expert judgments in chapter 3 suggested that nationalism does serve to differentiate one party from another, especially Fianna Fáil from Fine Gael, and indicated that the parties can be located at different points on a nationalist or Northern Ireland policy dimension. How voters placed themselves and the parties on a scale measuring attitudes to the Northern Ireland problem in 1978 is laid out in Figure 6.4. The mean score for all respondents (34.17) on the scale was clearly on the nationalist side of a scale on which 0 indicates the most nationalist position ('insist on a United Ireland to be implemented immediately'), and 100 the least

[17] Also perceived to be located on the left were the Green Party (29.7) and Sinn Fein (16.2).

nationalist ('abandon the aim of a United Ireland altogether'). Unlike the distributions of self-placement on the two left–right scales considered above, which taper off at either end, the distribution on the nationalist scale in Figure 6.4 rises at both ends, suggesting a certain polarisation of attitudes. As is clearly evident from Figure 6.4, however, the polarisation is not equally weighted – more than one in five voters placed themselves at the nationalist extreme, whereas less than one in ten were to be found at the non- or anti-nationalist extreme.

The perceived placements of the parties were also skewed towards the nationalist end of the scale. However, they were not all equally skewed. The placement of Fine Gael and Labour was rather similar – both peaking just on the nationalist side of the centre point, both being seen by further substantial proportions of the electorate as occupying the exact middle position and both tapering off more or less equally on both sides. Fianna Fáil as seen by the voters showed quite a different profile. It peaked just one point from the end of the scale (point 6 on the original 7-point scale), and was seen by a very sizeable minority of the electorate (more than 1 in 5) to be positioned at the extreme nationalist end. The very considerable perceived differences between the parties on this issue were reflected in the average placement of the parties by the voters – Fianna Fáil at 26.3, quite distinct from Fine Gael and Labour at 57.0 and 60.5 respectively.[18]

Unlike the situation with the left–right scale, we do not have evidence from a later period that would indicate whether the perception of inter-party differences on the Northern Ireland issue that were evident in 1978 continued to obtain. However, the indirect evidence from the 1987 MRBI survey, while not precisely comparable to the 1978 data, does confirm the perception of considerable differentiation between Fianna Fáil and Fine Gael on this issue:

> On Northern Ireland, we see a clear distinction between Fianna Fáil and Fine Gael. Those who strongly agree that the British will have to withdraw before a lasting solution is found in Northern Ireland are quite a bit more likely to think that Fianna Fáil has the best policy on this issue. All others are more likely to think that Fine Gael has the best policy.   (Laver, Marsh and Sinnott, 1987, p. 121)

It is also clear from the 1987 data that the perceived differences between the parties on this issue are a matter of degrees of nationalism – the differentiation occurs between those who 'agree strongly' with the statement and those who 'agree' with it, not between those who agree and disagree (in fact, 60 per cent of respondents agreed with the statement compared to 26 per cent who disagreed) (Laver, Marsh and Sinnott, 1987, p. 118).

[18] It is worth noting that Labour Party supporters' average self-placement on this scale was quite nationalist, and indistinguishable from the average position of Fianna Fáil supporters (Fianna Fáil 32.0, Labour 33.17). The discrepancy between the position of Labour Party supporters on this issue and the perceived position of the party itself probably reflects both the fact that the party was in government with Fine Gael during a period that saw important developments in policy on Northern Ireland (1973–77), and more importantly, the fact that significant and controversial changes in the party's attitude to Northern Ireland occurred during more or less the same period (see chapter 2).

Confessionalism

As indicated above, the only evidence we have of where the parties are seen to stand on church–state issues is also indirect, being based on relating judgement of 'party with the best policy' to the respondent's own position. The data is obviously less satisfactory, but bearing in mind the qualification made above,[19] it suggests that Fianna Fáil is seen as the more conservative or confessional party. Of the approximately 20 per cent of respondents who held pronounced confessional views in 1987 (those who *strongly* agreed 'that the Government should make sure that the policies they adopt on matters such as divorce and contraception are in line with the teachings of the Catholic Church'), 49 per cent thought that Fianna Fáil had 'the best policy on such issues as divorce and contraception', whereas 16 per cent thought that Fine Gael had the best policy (see Table 6.7). In contrast, among the 13 per cent minority who took the polar opposite position (disagreeing *strongly* with the proposition), only 16 per cent thought that Fianna Fáil had the best policy, in comparison to 47 per cent thinking that Fine Gael had the best policy and 20 per cent looking to other parties. It is also worth noting that one-quarter of those who are moderately or strongly confessionalist regard none of the parties as having the best policy on the matter (see Table 6.7).

Conclusion

Though there has been much discussion over the years of voter volatility and electoral change, and though one might have expected that the economic and social changes initiated in the early 1960s might have brought about such volatility, the evidence considered in this chapter confirms the relative stability of Irish electoral politics from 1969 to 1982, and identifies 1987 as the year of the arrival of really substantial voter volatility. The proportion of voters voting for the same party as in the previous election dropped from an average of 81 per cent in the six elections of 1969–82 to 59 per cent in 1987. The rate of desertion was particularly high for Fine Gael and Labour, but Fianna Fáil was not entirely immune. The immediate occasion for this increased volatility was the arrival of the Progressive Democrats, but the scene had been set for a change even before the establishment of the new party. The volatility of 1987 had been preceded by a fall of some 20 to 25 percentage points in the proportion feeling close to a party, a drop that occurred between 1980 and 1986.

Is there any substance or policy content behind these (changing) alignments? The limited available evidence on voter perceptions does suggest that the inter-party differences that are identifiable at elite level (in expert judgements, in manifestos and in party elite attitudes – see chapter 3) are reflected in public opinion, though the reflection may at times be somewhat clouded. The basic similarity of Fianna Fáil and Fine Gael on left–right issues is confirmed, as is the distinction between these two (and the Progressive Democrats) on one side, and Labour and the Workers' Party (and the Greens) on the other. Nuances of nationalism distinguish Fianna Fáil from Fine Gael (and Labour) in the public mind, as in the judgement of experts and among the party elites. On the nationalist dimension, however, there is a discrepancy between the

[19] See footnote 14.

Table 6.7: *Party with best policy on divorce and contraception by confessionalism/non-confessionalism (%)*

Party with best policy on issues such as divorce and contraception	'The Government should ensure that the policies they adopt on matters such as divorce and contraception are in line with the teachings of the Catholic Church': Agreement/disagreement with the statement			
	Strongly agree	Agree	Disagree	Strongly disagree
Fianna Fáil	49	38	24	16
Fine Gael	16	32	53	47
Others	8	5	5	20
None	27	25	18	17
	100	100	100	100
N	218	262	277	131

evidence of voter perceptions of party differences in regard to Northern Ireland, and the evidence of the analysis of manifestos that this issue plays next to no role in the appeals presented to the voters by the parties. On the one hand, in terms of the identity of the parties, differences on the nationalist dimension are apparent to experts, party elites and voters. On the other hand, for a variety of reasons, not least of which is the intractability of the problem of Northern Ireland and the difficulty all Irish governments have faced over the years in attempting to do something about it, these differences tend not to emerge as central elements in the competition between the parties at election time. Finally, the existence of confessionalist differences between the parties receives some recognition in the more limited evidence of public perceptions that is available in this area. In regard to the contrast in party positions based on the confessionalist dimension, the elite evidence of the mid-1970s and positions based on the expert judgement data of the late 1980s, the 1987 public opinion data are in line with the more recent expert judgement evidence.

All of this gives us some hold on the question of what may underlie party choice. However, we are still a long way from answering the question. Most immediately, there is the problem of knowing which, if any, of the differences that are perceptible to the voters actually matter to them. And apart from this problem of the salience of these three dimensions, there are very many other potential issues that may affect voting decisions. Indeed, the term 'issue' has a variety of meanings. It may have a broad meaning, referring to the kind of ideological differences between the parties dealt with in the present chapter, or it may refer to the voter's general assessment that the country, the economy, the voter's own social group or the voter himself or herself has done, or would do, better under one party rather than another. On the other hand, it may refer to attitudes and preferences regarding specific policies, particular leaders, or local candidates. Within the limits of the available data, Chapter 7 seeks to give an account of the role of issues, in these varying senses of the term, in recent Irish elections.

Chapter 7

The voters: criteria, issue concerns and class contrasts

One way of tackling the problem of the basis of voters' decisions is to ask voters directly about what they see as the most important criterion in determining their vote. This chapter begins by examining various voting criteria, bringing in under each criterion mentioned by the voters any ancillary evidence that may help to fill out the picture of how the criterion in question might operate. However, voters' subjective interpretations of their behaviour do not necessarily provide an accurate, let alone a comprehensive, account of that behaviour. Accordingly, it is essential to take a more indirect approach, focusing on the problems or issues that are of importance or concern to the voters, and examining how they rate the political parties on these issues. An even more indirect approach is to examine differences in the voting behaviour of different socio-demographic groups. Social class is not the only factor likely to manifest itself in this way, although it is the most obvious one. Whether the basis be class or some other social or demographic factor, the existence of contrasts in voting behaviour between different segments of society gives some further clues as to the basis of the voters' decisions and takes us that bit further down the road towards understanding the determinants of voting.

Voters' subjective criteria

During the six elections between 1977 and 1989, opinion poll respondents were asked which of a series of criteria would be 'most important to you in making up your mind how to vote in the General Election?' The criteria, set out on a card presented to the respondent, were: choosing a Taoiseach; choosing ministers who will form a government; choosing between the policies of the parties; choosing a TD who will look after the local needs of the constituency, and (asked only in 1989) choosing a TD who will perform well on national issues in the Dáil. In 1992 this question was asked in a reduced form that presented three options: choosing the individual who will be good for your area, choosing the party whose policies you feel closest to, and choosing the party which you feel can form, or help form, a stable government.

Table 7.1 sets out the responses to this series of questions. There has been some movement back and forth between the various categories over the years. Thus, the salience of the choice of Taoiseach criterion increased noticeably in 1981–82 and, though it has fallen back slightly since then, in 1989 it was still greater than it had been twelve years previously (14 per cent as compared with 8 per cent). This undoubtedly reflects the heightened conflict between the party leaders, especially in the 1981–82 period. On this preliminary evidence, however, the system can hardly be regarded as a surrogate form of presidential-style electoral politics. It will be necessary to return to the leadership issue later in this chapter. At this point it is worth noting that individual leadership as a consideration has been equalled or outweighed on several occasions by a collective leadership criterion ('choosing the ministers who will form the government'). The policies of the parties have generally assumed a greater priority than either of these, though the proportion dropped significantly when the format of the question changed in 1989. It is also important to note that all of the three criteria considered so far imply a primary emphasis on *party* voting; that is, if a voter wishes to influence the choice of Taoiseach, or the choice of government ministers or the policies that the government will pursue, he or she must decide first and foremost between the competing parties. Thus the majority of voters profess to vote primarily on the criterion of party. However, this is a bare majority, and a very substantial plurality of voters indicate that their primary criterion is 'a TD who will look after the needs of the constituency'.

Table 7.1: *Voters' perceptions of most important voting criterion, 1977–92 (%)*

Criterion	1977	1981	February 1982	Election November 1982	1987	1989	1992
Choosing the Taoiseach	8	16	20	19	15	14	NA
Choosing the set of ministers who will form the government	18	16	17	15	18	9	NA
Choosing the party which you feel can form or help form a stable government	NA	NA	NA	NA	NA	NA	38
Choosing between the policies as set out by the parties	21	24	27	25	29	15	21
Choosing a candidate to look after the needs of the constituency	46	42	35	41	38	40	37
Choosing a candidate who will perform well on national issues in the Dáil	NA	NA	NA	NA	NA	16	NA
Don't know	7	3	1	0	0	12	5

Note: NA = not available

Localism

Between 1977 and 1992, approximately two out of every five voters named choosing a TD for the constituency as their primary criterion when voting. The 1989 figure underlines the significance of the local constituency factor, because in that year the question had an extra response category which also related to choice of TD, i.e. 'choosing a TD who will perform well on national issues in the Dáil'. Despite this additional response category, the choice of TD in the context of *constituency* needs remained constant as a criterion, and it would appear that those who emphasized the criterion 'choosing a TD who will perform well on national issues in the Dáil' came from the categories of those who had previously emphasized ministerial performance or party policy.

The extent of the emphasis on the service aspect of the TD's role is confirmed in responses to a question on the perception of the most promising contact when applying for state benefits that was asked in the IMS 1976 survey. The question was: 'If someone is applying for something from the Government, for example, a housing grant or some social or health benefit – which of the following do you think he or she would be best advised to contact in order to be sure of getting what they are entitled to'. Thirty-five per cent of respondents indicated that they would contact a Dáil deputy and a further 13 per cent indicated they would contact a local politician, i.e. a member of the local County Council or Corporation (Sinnott, 1978, p. 47). On this data, close to a majority of the electorate saw their elected representatives as having a brokerage role.[1]

Available evidence also suggests that Irish voters, particularly Irish rural voters, possess the knowledge that would be required in order to take brokerage or reputation for brokerage into account in deciding how to vote. When asked to name their local elected representatives, three-quarters of the adult population could name at least one local TD, and over half could name two (IMS, 1976). There was a substantial contrast between Dublin and the rest of the country in terms of knowledge of elected representatives, with only just over one half of Dubliners being able to name at least one local representative. Knowledge of local representatives increases substantially as one moves from the cities of Dublin, Cork, Waterford and Limerick to smaller urban areas, that is, areas with a town population of over 1,500 people and on to rural areas, that is, country areas and towns or villages with a population of less than 1,500. In the latter category, 87 per cent of the population could name at least one elected representative and 75 per cent could name two or more (IMS, 1976).

A comparison of ability to recall the name of incumbent elected representatives may help to put the Irish figures in perspective. A study of the constituency service aspect of voting in the United States and Britain found that only one-third of American respondents could identify the name of their incumbent Congressman (Cain *et. al.*,

[1]The term 'brokerage' is to be preferred to the perhaps more popular term 'clientelism', because the latter might be taken to imply a tighter and more structured relationship between the voter and the public representative than actually obtains (see the discussion in Komito, 1992).

1987, pp. 28–9). In Britain, ability to recall the name of incumbent MPs was double that in the United States, but, at 65 per cent, was still significantly lower than the ability of Irish respondents to name at least one of their elected representatives. There are two obvious qualifications to be made to this comparison. The first is that the ratio of population to elected representative in Ireland is very much lower than in Britain or the United States. Secondly, British and American respondents had to identify the one single representative, whereas Irish respondents could 'score' by being able to name one of three, four or five. However, even bearing these qualifications in mind, it is evident that ability to identify politicians in the Irish case is at an impressively high level.

The data on the voter's most important voting criterion must, however, be interpreted with care. In the context of PR-STV, asking 'Which of the following is most important in determining your vote?' involves a degree of ambiguity (Sinnott, 1978, p. 61). Given the party and candidate choices that can be made in PR-STV, it is quite possible for the local candidate factor that figures prominently in the various surveys to coexist in the voter's mind with an equal prominence given to either choice of Taoiseach, choice of ministers or choice of party policy. In other words, voters can pick their party on the basis of one of these three non-candidate criteria, and then, within party, can pick a candidate on the basis of constituency service. In querying the validity of the voting criterion measure, Mair argues that a 'prior question which asked the respondent to accord primacy to party or candidate would have proved more revealing' (Mair, 1987a, p. 92). Such a question was subsequently asked in a post-election survey on the 1989 election. The question read 'Still thinking of your first preference vote – which was more important to you, the candidate, himself or herself, or was it the party they were standing for?' Thirty-eight per cent said it was the candidate, 40 per cent cited party and 15 per cent said both equally. These figures tend to support the view that, while the voting criterion question asked since 1977 does not get over the problem of dual choice that is inherent in PR-STV, and so cannot be used to produce precise estimates of the extent of localist or brokerage voting, a focus on the individual elected representative, in combination with other factors, plays a prominent role.

Some confirmation of this mix of voting criteria that emerges from voters' subjective accounts of their decision is contained in a study of the impact of candidate attributes on electoral success in seven elections between 1948 and 1982. Brokerage considerations, legislative effectiveness and indifference to candidates (implicitly a concentration on party rather than candidate) all play a part in voters' decisions (Marsh, 1987, p. 74). The importance of the local candidate criterion is also reflected in the actual characteristics of successful candidates and in the candidate selection process. The typical successful candidate was born in the constituency, is resident there, has probably been an elected member of the local authority and will have built up a network of local contacts and supporters (Farrell, 1969; Farrell, 1984; Gallagher, 1983–84). Partly because of the personal power-base of incumbents and aspiring candidates, and partly because of the imperative of a local geographical balance in the slate of candidates, selection is ultimately locally dominated. The national party has considerable power on paper but in practice this is, for the most part, a right to consultation and a power to persuade rather than to decide (Gallagher, 1987).

Ministerial performance

Table 7.1 showed that approximately one in six voters cited choosing the ministers who will form the Government as their key criterion between 1977 and 1987, though this figure dropped to one in ten when the response categories in the question were changed in 1989. But how widespread is awareness of cabinet ministers and their performance? Respondents in the 1976 survey already cited were asked to give the names of the ministers of the then Government, other than the name of the Taoiseach. Eighty-four per cent of voters were able to name at least one Government minister. Fifty-four per cent named the incumbent Minister for Finance and between 30 and 50 per cent named one of six other ministers, most of whom held key portfolios, for example Health and Social Welfare, Labour, Foreign Affairs, Justice and Education (IMS, 1976). The minister who was the second most mentioned held a relatively minor portfolio (Posts and Telegraphs), but was very prominent due to his controversial views on the Northern Ireland issue.[2]

Of course, choosing ministers who will form the next Government implies knowledge also of Opposition politicians. The same survey asked respondents to name five leading politicians from the Fianna Fáil party. Jack Lynch, the former Taoiseach and then Leader of the Opposition, came out, not surprisingly, with the highest number of mentions (83 per cent). Two other prominent Fianna Fáil politicians, Charles Haughey, who was to become Taoiseach three years later, and George Colley, the main contender for the job in that leadership contest, came out with 55 per cent name recall and 41 per cent name recall respectively. Two other Fianna Fáil politicians also received fairly prominent mention, Desmond O'Malley with 24 per cent and Brian Lenihan with 24 per cent.

Obviously, evidence on the distribution of knowledge of ministerial names does not tell us anything about the assessment of ministerial performance. Again, we only have fragmentary evidence on this. A poll in April 1979 asked respondents to assess ministerial performance, the question having identified the Government department for which each minister was responsible. The results suggest that voters do indeed differentiate between the performance of one minister and another, or at least between what they see as good and bad performance in particular areas (for detailed responses to this set of questions, see Sinnott, 1987, p. 66). The differentiation partly takes the form that if the minister's responsibilities are not giving rise to problems, then a large segment of the electorate has no particular view on his or her performance. Thus in the spring of 1979, the Minister for Labour, Gene Fitzgerald, the Minister for Economic Planning and Development, Professor Martin O'Donoghue and the Minister for Industry and Commerce, Desmond O'Malley, produced 'don't know' responses

---

[2] The individual in question was Conor Cruise O'Brien (see discussion in chapter 2).

varying from 41 (O'Donoghue) to 48 per cent (Fitzgerald). The remainder of the electorate was fairly evenly divided on their performance.

However, in the case, of the Minister for Finance, George Colley, only just under a third of the electorate had no view and the remainder were divided: 22 per cent good performance, 47 per cent poor performance. The previous month had seen mass demonstrations in Dublin and in towns throughout the country protesting against the perceived inequities of the tax system. Lacking comparable data for other Ministers of Finance, one cannot be certain that it was this particularly salient tax reform issue that made Colley unpopular. Whatever the cause, it is clear that in this case voters did differentiate between one minister and another. And Colley was not alone in his unpopularity. Another problem for the Fianna Fáil Government at the time was a long-running postal strike (the strike started on 19 February 1979 and did not end until 25 June 1979). The Minister for Posts and Telegraphs, Pádraig Faulkener, ran a remarkable approval deficit. Only 27 per cent of the electorate had no view, a mere 8 per cent approved of his performance, 65 per cent disapproving. This supports the conclusion that when issues turn sour, it is not just the Government that is blamed but also individual ministers, and that voters may indeed be influenced in their voting choice in their own constituency by their evaluation of national politicians who will be part of the Government. However, in a cabinet system of government there is at least a prima-facie case that there is one individual who, either in decision-making terms or in electoral terms or both, matters more than all the others, i.e., the prime minister, in the Irish case, the Taoiseach.[3]

Choice of Taoiseach

Jack Lynch, Fianna Fáil leader from 1966 to 1979, and Taoiseach from 1966 to 1973 and 1977 to 1979, was widely regarded as a major electoral asset for his party. That may well have been so but, in 1977 at any rate, choosing the Taoiseach was not uppermost in the minds of the voters. Four years and a change of leader in both major parties later, the proportion preoccupied with this aspect of electoral choice had doubled. As we have seen, the proportion expanded further in 1982.

At the outset of this period of heightened concern with the issue of political leadership, Fianna Fáil and Fine Gael appeared evenly matched in terms of the attractiveness of Charles Haughey and Garret FitzGerald, their respective candidates for the position of Taoiseach (see Table 7.2). This net balance masked a considerable class contrast in support for the two men – FitzGerald being strongly preferred by the middle class and larger farmers, with Haughey favoured by working-class and small farmer respondents. In the next eight months, FitzGerald forged ahead to a lead of 23 per cent, a lead based on overwhelming support among the middle class, the large farmers and the skilled working class. This situation was repeated in November 1982, except that by then Haughey was running a substantial deficit in all classes except the unskilled working class. The final round in the electoral battle between these two was

[3] On the role of the Taoiseach in Irish government see Farrell, 1971.

the election of 1987. It ended as it had begun, that is, more or less in a tie (Haughey was, in fact, 5 percentage points ahead) and with class contrasts broadly similar to those in 1981. The middle class and large farmers favoured FitzGerald by about the same margin as in 1981, though by considerably less than in either of the elections of 1982. The Haughey lead among the working class and small farmers was firmer than in 1981.

In 1989 a degree of class contrast in leadership preferences persisted. Although Haughey's personal popularity made a remarkable come-back in 1987 and 1989, he did not succeed, even in 1989, in winning over middle-class voters. Only with his departure did the class differences in preference for Taoiseach disappear (see 1992 figures in Table 7.2). For a political system often noted for its apparent classless political alignment, the class differences in preference of Taoiseach evident throughout the 1980s, and especially in the elections of 1982, were quite remarkable.

The data in Table 7.2 all relate to a choice between candidates for Taoiseach from Fianna Fáil and Fine Gael. This is because these have been the largest parties and they have always provided the incumbents of the office of Taoiseach and, before 1937, of President of the Executive Council. Of course, it need not always be so and in 1992, for the first time, the possibility of a Taoiseach from another party was actively raised and became an issue in the campaign. In fact, as Table 7.3 indicates, when choice of Taoiseach from among four party leaders was put to respondents in an opinion poll during the campaign, the most popular choice was neither of the leaders of the two main parties, but Dick Spring, leader of the Labour Party and the one who had raised the issue in the first place. It is worth noting that he was as popular among the middle class as among the population as a whole, and that the only occupational contrast in his support was his higher than average support among the unskilled working class, and lower than average support among farmers. There was no class variation in support for Fianna Fáil leader Albert Reynolds, whereas John Bruton, the Fine Gael leader, showed the same limited class contrasts to those of Spring, only in the opposite direction.

While there is some evidence of an increased concern among voters with the issue of who should be Taoiseach, particularly during the elections of 1982, it is very difficult to prove that the popularity or unpopularity of leaders was a cause of any particular party's gains or losses in particular elections. The question of the relationship between the popularity of Dick Spring and Labour Party gains in 1992 illustrates the difficulty. Marsh and Sinnott point out that 'The limits of Spring's appeal . . . become apparent when we look at the voting intentions of supporters of the various leaders. . . . only 39 per cent of those who preferred Spring as Taoiseach were voting Labour' (Marsh and Sinnott, 1993, p. 104). Some further light can be shed on the matter by examining inter-election opinion poll data on the relationship between leader popularity and party popularity. Such data have the advantage of providing far more observations than are available when attention is confined to election campaigns and the polls conducted during them. The main conclusion of a series of systematic statistical tests on these data is that there is some evidence of a general connection in the case of Fianna Fáil, but only of an intermittent relationship in the case of the other parties (Marsh and Harrison, 1994). Interestingly, the connection was evident under the last two years of the leadership of Jack Lynch (1977–79), when, from early 1978 on, the popularity

Table 7.2: *Fianna Fáil lead or deficit vis-à-vis Fine Gael in preference for Taoiseach, by occupational class, 1981–92 (percentage points)*

Date	All classes	Middle class	Skilled working class	Unskilled working class	Farmers (fifty acres or more)	Farmers (less than fifty acres)	All farmers
June 1981 (Haughey–FitzGerald)	–1	–12	+4	+8	–18	+8	–3
February 1982 (Haughey–FitzGerald)	–23	–42	–33	–3	–38	–5	–20
November 1982 (Haughey–FitzGerald)	–25	–33	–24	–11	–51	–25	–35
February 1987 (Haughey–FitzGerald)	+5	–8	+18	+18	–28	+19	–4
June 1989 (Haughey–Dukes)	+3	–7	+4	+11	NA	NA	0
November 1992 (Reynolds–Bruton)	0	–2	+2	+2	NA	NA	–2

Table 7.3: *Preference for Taoiseach (choice of four 'candidates') by occupational class, 1992 (%)*

Preferred choice	All classes	Middle class	Skilled working class	Unskilled working class	Farmers
Albert Reynolds	20	21	18	18	22
John Bruton	13	14	12	9	23
Dick Spring	38	36	38	47	28
Des O'Malley	13	17	15	9	14
Don't Know	15	11	18	18	14

of both Fianna Fáil and its leader fell sharply.[4] The relationship between leadership popularity and party support in the case of Fianna Fáil is not limited, therefore, to the period in which Fianna Fáil was led by Charles Haughey, and in which the leadership issue became a matter of overt contention both between the main parties and within Fianna Fáil. Marsh and Harrison suggest that the reason for the existence of the connection in the case of Fianna Fáil may lie in the party's dominant position in the party system: 'The Fianna Fáil party, more than any other, offers leadership of the nation. Only Fianna Fáil can govern alone and has usually done so. Many marginal voters may be attracted to it because of this capacity and they may be particularly susceptible to the attractions or otherwise of the party leader' (Marsh and Harrison, 1994, p. 308).

The final voting criterion featured in Table 7.1 is party policy. From 1977 to 1987, approximately one-quarter of the voters claimed that, in deciding how to vote, they were most influenced by this factor. In 1989, reference to this criterion fell to one voter in six when the options presented in the question included 'a TD who will perform well on national issues in the Dáil'. The latter has, of course, substantial, if unspecific, issue overtones. Of course, as already emphasized, the proportion of voters influenced by party policy could well be far greater than the one-quarter to one-sixth indicated in Table 7.1. This is so both because voters could be operating with more than one criterion in mind, and because the electoral system actually encourages them to do so. In dealing with the role of issues in electoral behaviour, therefore, it is important to examine more specific evidence on what the voters have seen as the dominant issues in elections since 1969, and on how they have judged party stances or records on them.

Issue concerns and party capability

Important aspects of Irish economic and political development over the last twenty years or so can be seen reflected in the issue preoccupations of the voters during election campaigns between 1969 and 1992, as shown in Table 7.4. In 1969 voters had the luxury of worrying more about labour relations (which admittedly were not great) than about unemployment, which was then only about 5 to 6 per cent of the labour force.

---

[4] Because suitable data are only available from 1977 on, the study starts with that year.

Concern with rising prices outstripped both of these issues – inflation had risen from 2 or 3 per cent in 1966 and 1967 to 7 per cent in 1969.[5] In 1973, only 11 per cent of respondents in an IMS poll put unemployment as the top priority but there was considerable concern about inflation. Inflation took off over the next three years, a fact that was clearly reflected in the issue concerns of the electorate in 1977. At the same time unemployment went up substantially, and concern with the issue rose from one in ten voters in 1973 to almost one in three in 1977. Inflation dipped sharply but only briefly in 1978, and was raging again in 1981. By then, however, unemployment had taken over as the major issue in the public mind and, with inflation falling steadily, was, with the exception of one election, to remain the major issue up to and including the election of 1992. The exception was the 1989 election, when the issue of cuts in the health services dominated not only the campaigns of the opposition parties but, on the evidence in Table 7.4, the minds of the voters as well.

Chapter 3 showed that while the voters, the experts and the party elites see differences between the parties on Northern Ireland policy, the issue is not really raised by the parties in their election manifestos. The evidence in Table 7.4 bears this out, the issue being dormant except for the 1973 election, when it entered the list of important issues at 12 per cent. Then the problem was still new and, with the Arms Crisis of 1970 a very recent memory,[6] was close enough to the surface of party politics. Evidently, the problem's familiarity and, as suggested above, its intractability were to breed indifference – that is, at least, electoral indifference. After 1973 the problem only figured to any significant extent in the 1981 election, when the H–Block hunger strike in Northern Ireland was at its height, and when this very particular manifestation of the problem forced its way on to the electoral agenda in the Republic in the form of nine H–Block candidates (for details see Sinnott, 1987, pp. 93–4). Even then, however, as Table 7.4 shows, the Northern Ireland problem did not rate as a matter of concern for voters as a whole.

The earliest evidence we have on voters' assessments of the relative competence of the parties on the issues that figured in election campaigns comes from 1977. Given the frequent assumption that Fianna Fáil won its more than 50 per cent share of the vote in the 1977 election on the basis of give-away election promises and concessions, it is important to note that Fianna Fáil had a substantial lead over the coalition of Fine Gael and Labour on the salient economic issues in that election – it was 25 points ahead on the three most important issues of the campaign (see Table 7.5). Moreover, that lead went back at least as far as December 1976 (Sinnott, 1978, pp. 97). Fianna Fáil may have put forward policies that 'appealed primarily to the self-interest of consumers' (Walsh, 1986, p. 25), but the evidence suggests that the contest was won well before these blandishments were produced.[7]

That voters react to the government of the day on the basis of the performance of

---

[5] For the unemployment and inflation figures see Figure 1.5 in chapter 1.

[6] See chapter 2.

[7] Also contrary to the view that the voters judge issues primarily in terms of personal gain is the finding that in the case of preferences regarding the size and composition of public spending, 'with certain exceptions, it is clear that values other than narrow self-interest are the major determinants of expressed preferences' (McDowell, 1991, p. 49).

Table 7.4: *Perception of most important issue in elections, 1969–92 (%)*

	1969	1973	1977	1981	1982	1982	1987	1989	1992
Unemployment	20	11	30	48	46	45	59	30	53
Education and welfare	25	25	9	4	2	4	4	–	–
Labour relations	24	–	–	–	–	–	–	–	–
Health	3	–	–	–	–	–	–	39	8
Inflation	28	28	40	27	19	16	5	–	5
Northern Ireland	1	12	1	–	–	–	1	–	–
Tax	–	–	10	5	3	4	13	18	10
Stable government	–	–	–	–	7	17	3	–	8
Reduce govt spending	–	–	–	–	11	8	8	–	–
Other	26	25	8	17	11	7	8	12	16
Don't know	10	–	–	1	–	0	0	1	1

Note: Frequencies in 1969 add to more than 100 because of multiple responses

the economy as a whole is also supported by an analysis of the fluctuations in voting intentions during the periods between elections. Admittedly, when such voting intentions are considered, the swing against the incumbent government appears to be much larger than the swing evidenced during the campaign, government support tending to revive somewhat when an election is called. Presumably, the explanation is that voting intentions when there is no actual election in the offing are an expression of voter dissatisfaction, untrammelled by any qualms about actually bringing about a change in government. Accepting this inherent limitation in the inter-election voting intention data, it is nonetheless interesting that econometric analysis of the determinants of government popularity defined in this way show that in the period 1975–87 'there was a strong contemporaneous relationship between movements in the economy and movements in government popularity' (Borooah and Borooah, 1990, p. 87).[8] Such a relationship is quite consistent with the evaluations of economic policy performance at elections during the same period that are evident in Table 7.5.

The hopes for economic recovery that the voters invested in Fianna Fáil in 1977 evaporated rapidly, and, going into the next election, its massive lead on these issues had been transformed into a significant deficit (Table 7.5). Thereafter, assessment of the relative competence of the parties, or combinations of parties, on economic issues tended to follow an in-government, out-of-government cycle. Fianna Fáil was ahead if it was in opposition going into the election, and behind if it was in government. The issue of government borrowing, which arose for the first time in the February 1982 election, is, however, a clear exception to this rule. Fianna Fáil has been consistently judged to be weak on this issue, even in the 1987 election following which it imple-

[8] Borooah and Borooah regard this finding as 'contrary to the not uncommon belief that the divisions in Irish politics were frozen in the 1920s' (1990, p. 77). The point is an important one in terms of an overall interpretation of Irish electoral alignments, and the suggestion of an incompatibility between these particular findings and the 'freezing' thesis will be taken up in chapter 11.

Table 7.5: *Fianna Fáil's lead or deficit (vis-à-vis all other parties combined) in assessment of relative competence of parties on issues, 1977–89 (percentage points)*

Issues	1977	1981	1982	1982	1987	1989
Unemployment	+25	–6	+12	–7	+19	NA
Prices/inflation	+26	–2	+10	–12	–6	NA
Taxation	+27	–8	+5	–7	0	NA
Northern Ireland	–3	+9	–3	–2	–6	NA
Crime	NA	+4	+1	–15	+3	NA
Government borrowing/spending	NA	NA	–22	–24	–11	NA
Stable government	NA	NA	+21	–5	+21	NA
Health	NA	NA	NA	NA	NA	–16

Note: NA = not available

mented cuts that brought the problem under control. Unfortunately, we do not have data on assessment of capacity in this regard for 1989. The one policy assessment we do have, however, shows that Fianna Fáil may have paid a price for its handling of one particular aspect of government cut-backs between 1987 and 1989. As Tables 7.4 and 7.5 show, it was judged to be 16 points behind on the health issue, which was seen as the most important issue in the election by almost 40 per cent of the voters (see Marsh and Sinnott, 1990, for a detailed discussion).

Although for the most part Northern Ireland does not figure prominently on the electorate's agenda, it is worth noting that, with the exception of 1981, Fianna Fáil was at a slight deficit (–2 to –6 points) in terms of its ability to handle the issue over the period 1977–87. This is interesting in itself as an indicator of people's attitudes to the Northern problem (see the discussion of party policy towards Northern Ireland in chapters 2 and 3). It also suggests that there was very little mileage to be made by Fianna Fáil in raising the issue at election time.

Fianna Fáil has frequently resorted to the argument that it alone could provide stable government. Comparable data on the salience of this issue are only available for 1982, 1987 and 1992 (see Table 7.4). They show that in general the issue has been of limited salience, though it did register with one-sixth of the voters in November 1982. However, in that election, it told against Fianna Fáil in so far as that was the one election in which, as an incumbent minority government experiencing considerable buffeting on several fronts, the party was actually at a deficit on the issue. In the previous election (February 1982) and in the following one (1987) Fianna Fáil was some 20 points ahead, but then the issue seemed to matter to fewer people.

Evidence available for the 1987 election makes it possible to probe the question of the relationship between the salience of issues, issue preferences, perceived positions of the parties and voting intention a little more fully. The results are consistent with the evidence already reviewed that economic issues turned out to be the most salient and to have 'had the strongest effect on party fortunes' (Laver, Marsh and Sinnott, 1987, p. 126). However, for the electorate as a whole, the evidence suggests that a generalised assessment of the parties' performance on the economy may have been more important than precise preferences on particular economic issues. At the same time, there was greater consistency between policy preferences and evaluations of party position on the non-economic issues of Northern Ireland and church–state relations. However, the impact of these particular issues was limited by their low salience (Laver, Marsh and Sinnott, 1987, pp. 113–26).

It must be emphasized that the foregoing analysis of issue voting in 1987 applies to the voters as a whole. When attention is focused on subsets of the voters, a somewhat greater consistency between specific issues and voting choice is detectable. There is some evidence of this in the case of those who regard the issues in question as very important. In the case of those who switched party between 1982 and 1987, there is more substantial evidence of a consistency between evaluation of parties on a range of issues and declared voting intention (Bowler and Farrell, 1990, pp. 258–66). However, the problem of whether particular issues determine party choice, or whether prior party choice determines issue positions, remains. This is because the strongest evidence of a connection between party choice and issue position relates to those who switched vote between 1982 and 1987. The possibility that such switching was motivated by a generalised response to government performance, and that this in turn had an impact on the perception of party issue positions, cannot be ruled out. This reinforces Bowler and Farrell's conclusion that 'the fundamental requirement is for more data' (Bowler and Farrell, 1990, p. 266).

The need for a comprehensive election study is even more evident when it comes to analysing the issues in 1992. That election saw a greater turnaround in voting behaviour than any in forty years or more, yet we lack the data that would enable us to draw firm conclusions about what issues, if any, brought about the change. Table 7.4 shows that unemployment was back as the major issue, but we have no evidence of the voters' assessment of the competence of the parties on this or any other issue. Such issue-related evidence as we have suggests that there was no one issue that had a dominant impact. Rather, each of a series of particular issues – dissatisfaction with the incumbent government, the negative impact of the calling of the election, pessimistic economic expectations, the positive assessment of the Labour leader, the search for coalition options other than those on offer, and, finally, the liberal agenda – had a limited but cumulative effect in moving support from Fianna Fáil and Fine Gael to Labour. This 'particularisation of voter choice' corresponds to trends identified by recent comparative research, and supports the view that 1992 was part of a continuing dealignment of the party system, rather than a realignment.[9]

But the methodological point must be repeated: the opinion poll evidence on issues in the 1992 election is sparse, and there is a consequent danger of underestimating the role issues may have played in that election. In particular, using a 'yes' vote in the travel and information referendums of November 1992 as 'a crude measure of a more liberal outlook', and comparing those who switched parties between 1989 and 1992 with

---

[9] The relevant data are presented and discussed in Marsh and Sinnott (1993). The comparative evidence on the particularisation of voter choice is reviewed in van der Eijk, Franklin, Mackie and Valen (1992), pp. 406–531.

voters who voted the same way in both elections, Marsh and Sinnott note that 'the fact that switchers look more like voters of the party they are switching to than those of the party they are switching from . . . supports the view that the liberal agenda was probably more important than the figures [on perceived most important issue in the election] suggest' (Marsh and Sinnott, 1993, p. 102). The role of the liberal agenda in 1992 will be taken up again when referendum voting and voting in the 1990 presidential election are being analysed in chapters 9 and 10.

Class and other contrasts

As indicated at the outset of this chapter, in addition to the overt criteria and concerns of the voters there may well be underlying issues that do not appear in the salience or preference data collected in an opinion poll, but that are reflected in the social and demographic bases of the supporters of the different parties. Chief among the potential bases of party support is social class.

Class and voting

The question of the class bases of party preference has long been a preoccupation in analyses of Irish voting behaviour. The results of the first systematic survey of the issue were encapsulated in a memorable phrase by John Whyte when he argued that Irish party politics was 'politics without social bases' (Whyte, 1974). While a number of qualifications to this thesis have been suggested (Gallagher, 1984, pp. 134–5; Sinnott, 1978, pp. 44–5; see also Breen and Whelan, 1994), Whyte's analysis undoubtedly captured the most striking feature of the relationship between class and voting in Ireland in the late 1960s, that is, the cross-class nature of the appeal of the dominant party, Fianna Fáil.

The evidence for the politics without social bases thesis is clear from a glance at Table 7.6.[10] Fianna Fáil, at the time of the particular survey analysed by Whyte (i.e. 1969) certainly gave all the appearances of being a cross-class party, showing only slight variations in support across the urban class spectrum. It is true that there were contrasts in Fianna Fáil support between large and small farmers.[11] It is also true that both

[10] The individual-level analysis that follows is based on data from opinion polls taken during election campaigns (with the exception of the 1969 data, which in the absence of any opinion polls during the 1969 campaign, are taken from a Gallup poll conducted in April 1969). An alternative approach would be to combine a long series of inter-election opinion polls, using a mathematical smoothing technique to eliminate the random fluctuations typical of such data (Laver, 1986b). Laver argues for this approach on the basis that it overcomes the danger of reliance on the relatively small samples of particular social groups that are found in individual polls. On the other hand, inter-election polls relate only to hypothetical election situations. The advantage of campaign polls is that the measure of voting intention is reasonably close to the act of voting, and takes into account the circumstances of the calling of the election and much of the effect of the campaign. An opinion poll was conducted during the 1973 campaign but the cross-tabulations for voting intention are not available.

[11] The only exception to this pattern is 1977, when support for Fianna Fáil among larger farmers actually exceeded that for Fine Gael, and was equal to the level of Fianna Fáil support among small farmers. Laver's analysis of the inter-election opinion polls shows that this 1977 Fianna Fáil advantage among large farmers dates at least from 1976 (Laver, 1986b, p. 207). This suggests that it was more likely to have been the result of a reaction against the capital taxation measures introduced by the Fine Gael-Labour coalition than a swing to Fianna Fáil induced by the campaign promises of that election.

Table 7.6: *Voting intention by occupational class, 1969–92*

Party and year	All classes	Percentage of social grade supporting party					
		Upper middle and middle (AB)	Lower middle (C1)	Skilled working (C2)	Unskilled working (DE)	Farmers >50 acres (F1)	Farmers <50 acres (F2)
Fianna Fáil							
1969	43	37	48	40	43	38	53
1977	49	45	47	54	47	48	48
1981	44	34	48	46	45	35	49
1982 (Feb)	47	35	45	45	52	35	59
1982 (Nov)	40	32	38	42	40	37	51
1987	41	28	38	45	47	36	48
1989	40	32	42	39	41		43
1992	35	25	34	35	37	43	42
Fine Gael							
1969	25	37	26	21	14	46	26
1977	28	36	27	20	22	42	38
1981	33	46	31	29	24	53	36
1982 (Feb)	35	51	38	36	25	54	28
1982 (Nov)	37	58	42	31	28	54	35
1987	22	30	24	14	17	43	23
1989	26	35	30	21	14		39
1992	20	28	19	16	14	38	25
Labour							
1969	18	10	15	27	28	2	5
1977	9	6	7	11	16	1	5
1981	10	9	10	10	16	4	2
1982 (Feb)	7	3	7	6	10	3	4
1982 (Nov)	9	4	9	11	14	6	1
1987	6	3	6	9	5	4	3
1989	11	6	9	14	15		5
1992	16	16	18	18	19	3	8
Progressive Democrats							
1987	14	22	18	15	9	17	6
1989	6	10	6	8	10		4
1992	4	11	7	4	5	4	3
Workers' Party/Democratic Left							
1981	2	1	0	2	4	1	0
1982 (Feb)	2	0	0	3	4	0	0
1982 (Nov)	4	0	3	5	6	1	2
1987	3	1	3	3	4	0	1
1989	5	3	2	5	10		2
1992	3	2	3	4	5	0	1

Table 7.6 *(contd.)*

Party and year	All classes	Upper middle and middle (AB)	Lower middle (C1)	Skilled working (C2)	Unskilled working (DE)	Farmers >50 acres (F1)	Farmers <50 acres (F2)
Percentage of social grade supporting party							
Other/Don't Know/Refused							
1969	14	17	11	12	15	14	16
1977	14	13	19	14	15	8	8
1981	11	10	11	14	15	8	8
1981	11	10	11	14	9	6	12
1982 (Feb)	7	11	10	10	10	8	9
1982 (Nov)	9	6	8	11	12	2	12
1987	14	16	10	14	18	11	18
1989	12	15	11	16	13		7
1992	20	18	18	21	22	15	20

Notes: In 1969 the categories of farm size were 30 acres or more and less than 30 acres. In 1989 farmers were not differentiated as to farm size.

Fine Gael and Labour Party support were somewhat skewed in class terms; bracketing these two parties together, as was done in Whyte's main statistical analysis, does tend to lead to an underestimation of the role of social class in the system.[12] These observations, however, only require minor qualifications to be made to the 'politics without social bases' thesis. The dominant fact in 1969 was the cross-class nature of Fianna Fáil support.

In 1982 some dents were made in this image of Fianna Fáil class harmony and, in 1987, real cracks opened up. Then Fianna Fáil support among the middle and upper middle class fell to 28 per cent, creating a substantial gap *vis-à-vis* its 45 and 47 per cent support in the skilled and unskilled working class. As noted above, Fine Gael had always had a middle-class bias in its support. In November 1982, however, 'Fine Gael, from being a somewhat middle class party, edged towards becoming the party of the middle class' (Sinnott, 1987, p. 73). In that election, it had the support of 58 per cent of the upper middle and middle class, 42 per cent of the lower middle class and 54 per cent of the larger farmers. In the early 1980s, however, Fine Gael also made substantial progress among working-class voters, progress that had obvious consequences for the Labour Party. In 1969 Labour had obtained twice as much support from the working class as it had from the middle class. As its support declined, especially in the early 1980s, this class contrast became blurred and intermittent, and tended to reflect only a difference between the highest and lowest points on the class spectrum – the upper

[12] This point was, in fact, noted by Whyte (1974, pp. 645–6).

middle and middle class (AB grouping) on the one hand, versus the unskilled working class (DE) on the other. Labour's problem was exacerbated in that, among working-class voters, it was also losing ground to the Workers' Party.

Fine Gael's role as *the* party of the middle class was short-lived. As we have seen, the 1987 election was a serious set-back for the party, and the extent of its fall was greatest among the middle class. This was due to the intervention of the Progressive Democrats, who took middle-class support away from both Fianna Fáil and Fine Gael, but especially from the latter, thus contributing to the emergence of a significant degree of class polarisation. The 1989 election halted these signs of an emerging class politics. Fianna Fáil regained a substantial segment of the support it had lost among the middle class, and again began to take on the appearance of a cross-class party. The Progressive Democrats' losses were greatest among the middle class, and this considerably reduced the class distinctiveness of the party, which, in 1987, had seemed to promise most to those who saw a class-based realignment as a desirable development.

In 1992 the substantial gains and losses among the parties seemed to contribute to a further blurring of class-based political divisons. On the evidence in Table 7.6, Fianna Fáil appears to have been almost as much a cross-class party at the end of the 1992 campaign as it had been more than twenty years previously; the difference was that it was a cross-class party at a lower level of support. Fine Gael also showed much the same class pattern as in 1969. The most striking developments in regard to class and politics seemed to occur in the case of the Labour Party. On this evidence, Labour emerged in the 1992 election with equal support among middle-class, skilled working-class and unskilled working-class voters.

Before drawing final conclusions from this analysis, it is necessary to examine the possibility that the failure to find more pronounced class differences in voting in the individual-level data is a function of inadequate measurement of class stratification, rather than of the existence of genuinely classless politics. Issues arising in the measurement of social class have been widely discussed in Ireland, one review concluding that the market research scale, which is the one used to measure social class in the election opinion polls, is beset by 'a general conceptual and terminological confusion' as to whether the basis of the scale is class or social prestige (Hayes, 1987, p. 47). In Britain a similar scale has been criticised on the grounds that it is based on differences in income and lifestyle, and that it is questionable whether these 'are particularly relevant to politics' (Heath, Jowell and Curtice, 1985, p. 14).

A study of the relationship between social class and inequality suggested a scheme involving thirteen economic groups, these being reducible to four 'major cleavages' – the bourgeoisie, *petite bourgeoisie*, the middle class (i.e., non-manual employees) and the working class (Rottmann *et al.*, 1982). On the other hand, a new census-based social-class scale developed for Ireland has suggested a ranking of six social classes (O'Hare, Whelan and Commins, 1991). However, more important than the differences as to the precise number and demarcation of classes is the fact that these and other discussions of a revised class schema for Ireland draw on a common source and share some basic assumptions. In particular, they share Goldthorpe's emphasis on the need to take account not just of economic rewards attached to various occupations, but also of the

degree to which the occupation is exposed to market forces, and the amount of autonomy that characterises the occupation and the kind of experience of authority that this
implies (Goldthorpe, 1980).

This kind of re-evaluation of the concept of social class is likely to be particularly
important in the study of voting behaviour. Studies of British voting behaviour which
have used revised measures of social class have thrown considerable light on the relationship between class and voting in Britain (see Heath, Jowell and Curtice, 1985, pp.
13–27 and Robertson, 1984, pp. 107–25). A thorough application of a revised class
model and measurement procedure in Ireland would require a full-scale election study.
However, with the material to hand, it is possible to improve on the standard scale by
incorporating information on individuals' employment status. This gives at least an
approximation of the kind of class model implied by recent sociological research.

When this approach was applied to voting behaviour in an Irish general election for
the first time (the 1987 general election), it 'confirmed the suspicion that the particular way in which class has been measured in studies of voting in Ireland obscures some
of the differences that actually exist' (Laver, Marsh and Sinnott, 1987, p. 108). The
main new finding was the distinction that emerged within the middle class, between
the preferences of the bourgeoisie (defined as members of the AB occupational grouping who are self-employed) and those of the salaried middle class. In 1987, support for
Fianna Fáil was substantially greater among the middle class as compared with the
bourgeoisie (it was higher again among the *petite bourgeoisie*, i.e., the self-employed
among the lower middle class, skilled working class and unskilled working class). The
revised analysis threw light in particular on the nature of support for the Progressive
Democrats, which was 28 per cent among the bourgeoisie, making them the leading
party in that sector of the population. In terms of explaining the outcome of elections
or the sources of swings in voting support, the conclusions to be drawn from this
revised class analysis must be qualified by noting that the bourgeoisie as defined in this
way is a very small proportion of the population. Its distinctive voting behaviour has
only a limited effect on the parties' shares of the first preference vote. As long as this
is borne in mind, the revised analysis of the 1987 election, even in this fairly crude
operationalisation, throws some further light on the classless politics thesis, indicating
in particular that some of the apparent classlessness is due to the use of a very broad-
brush measure of social class.

The revised analysis of class and voting in 1987 was possible due to the insertion of
additional questions on class in all three MRBI surveys in that election. Unfortunately,
these were not repeated in 1989 and were used in only one MRBI survey in 1992.
Analysis of the relationship between class and voting in that one survey suggests that
differences in the preferences of the bourgeoisie and the middle class occurred in 1992
as well, and that the cross-class appeal of Labour may not have been quite as universal
as the data in Table 7.6 indicates. But these are no more than suggestions, because the
numbers involved in a single opinion poll are too small to sustain a breakdown of voters
into such detailed and refined class categories.

The suggestions are, however, supported by an analysis based on 1992 IMS data on
class and employment status (see Table 7.7). Because the questions used by the two

polling companies in this area are different, the social class categories derivable from the two sets of polls are not identical. Thus, it is not possible to put the data from 1987 and 1992 into a single table. However, the data are broadly comparable and provide a means of an approximate update of the Laver, Marsh and Sinnott analysis of 1987. Furthermore, the 1992 IMS data make it possible to treat the short-term and long-term unemployed as separate categories. The discussion of the changing class structure in chapter 1 noted that, by the late eighties and early nineties, unemployment had reached a level at which it becomes necessary to take it into account in any analysis of the relationship between occupational class and voting.

The first consequence of looking at class and voting in 1992 from this perspective is that the class basis of Labour Party support in that election was considerably more complex than the analysis based on the standard categories used in Table 7.6 suggests (see Table 7.7). The revised categorisation shows that Labour support was highest among the short-term unemployed (23 per cent), and that it was less than a third of this among the bourgeoisie (7 per cent). The bulk of Labour's middle-class support in 1992 came from the salaried middle class. In fact, its support among the salaried middle class (20 per cent) was higher than its support among the working class (15 per cent) (Table 7.7). Its support was also very low (9 per cent) among the long-term unemployed. One can conclude that the cross-class interpretation of Labour support in 1992 is sustained, but with significant nuances and qualifications.

Fianna Fáil emerges from this re-analysis of the 1992 evidence with a substantially more variegated social basis than that suggested by the data in Table 7.6. Its areas of strength were among the *petite bourgeoisie* (41 per cent), the working class (39 per cent) and the long-term unemployed (42 per cent). It was considerably weaker among the salaried middle class (29 per cent), and weakest of all among the bourgeoisie (22 per cent). It was also, however, quite weak among the short-term unemployed (26 per cent), most of whom, in terms of their former employment, would be categorised as working class. Again, therefore, the picture that emerges is a rather nuanced one. All in all, however, the evidence of a class contrast in Fianna Fáil support is almost as strong in 1992 as it was in 1987. (To this revised account of class contrasts in Fianna Fáil support one should add Breen and Whelan's finding regarding the impact of class origin on Fianna Fáil support among older voters; Breen and Whelan, 1994, pp. 129–30.) Indeed, it could be said that in 1992 Fianna Fáil had a more working-class basis to its support than the socialist party with which it formed a government after the election.

In 1987 the bourgeoisie were divided in their allegiance between the Progressive Democrats, Fine Gael and Fianna Fáil, in that order. In contrast, in 1992 a clear majority supported Fine Gael (48 per cent of declared voting intentions, which, if the 'don't knows' were excluded, would be well over 50 per cent). In the case of the Progressive Democrats, the change was striking – 28 per cent declared support among the bourgeoisie in 1987, 4 per cent in 1992. It is notable that, with the exception of the salaried middle class, each class category showed a predominant preference in 1992 – the bourgeoisie for Fine Gael, the *petite bourgeoisie* and the working class for Fianna Fáil. The salaried middle-class vote split, mainly between Fianna Fáil (29 per cent), Fine Gael

Table 7.7: *Voting intention by occupational class (revised measure), 1992 (%)*

	Bourgeoisie	Salaried middle class	Petite bourgeoisie	Working class	Short-term unemployed	Long-term unemployed	Students	Farmers	All voters (including retired, housewives, etc.)
Fianna Fáil	22	29	41	39	26	42	24	45	37
Fine Gael	48	21	41	39	26	42	24	34	20
Labour	7	20	17	15	23	9	20	5	15
Progressive Democrats	4	10	4	4	6	2	5	5	5
Democratic Left/ Workers' Party	2	3	3	6	8	3	5	2	4
Others	4	5	6	6	8	8	7	0	4
DK, etc.	13	12	16	15	18	28	15	12	16
N	54	371	139	506	301	67	99	286	3168

(21 per cent) and Labour (20 per cent), with the Progressive Democrats bringing up the rear at 10 per cent. Finally, it is worth nothing that student voting intentions were quite similar to those of the middle class, a finding that presumably reflects the fact that this is the class either from which a large proportion of students come or which they are destined to enter.

The account of the impact of class on voting given here broadly supports the aggregate data analysis of the support bases of the parties between 1981 and 1992 in chapter 5. Common elements in both analyses are the appearance of a negative middle-class effect for Fianna Fáil in 1982 and especially in 1987; the positive middle-class effect for Fine Gael in the three elections of 1981–82 that weakened in 1987; and the absence of a clear class contrast in the Labour vote, even when that vote recovered in 1992. Furthermore, the relationship between support for Fianna Fáil and Fine Gael and the proportion of farmers in a constituency, a relationship that increased substantially in the case of Fine Gael from 1987 through to 1992 and for Fianna Fáil in 1992, is confirmed by the strength of both parties among those with farming occupations.

In regard to the issue of voting and social class, we can note at this stage that, while there may not have been a consistent class-based politics in Ireland over the period since 1969, there have been some class constants; in particular, there is considerable evidence that class played a role in the shifting alliances and allegiances that occurred from 1987 on. But voting and social class is only one aspect of the overall issue of the potential impact of socio-demographic cleavages on voting. For one thing, chapter 5 indicated that the rural basis of party support requires further investigation. But there is more to it than that. There is a range of interrelated characteristics of voters that are relevant – the urban-rural contrast being related to age and to education and to rates of church attendance.[13] To the complications arising from the fact that all of these variables are interrelated is added the fact that we are interested in their influence on voting over time. In order to cut through the complexity, and at the risk of some over-simplification, the relationship between voting and each of the variables will be looked at individually over time.

Age and generation
In a period marked by the degree of economic, socio-demographic and cultural change documented in chapter 1, change in voting behaviour might be thought to be most likely among younger voters. For one thing, traditional processes of familial socialisation are likely to be less effective in an era with a distinctive youth culture. Secondly, because of the introduction of free secondary education in 1967 (see chapter 1), from the late 1970s younger voters have had considerably higher rates of educational participation than the older generation. The expectation that their voting behaviour might be different was heightened by the reduction in voting age to eighteen in the

---

[13] One might add gender to this list of potential cleavages, but the evidence indicates that gender differences in support for Irish political parties are, for the most part, negligible. A possible exception is a slightly higher level of female support for Fine Gael in the election of February 1982.

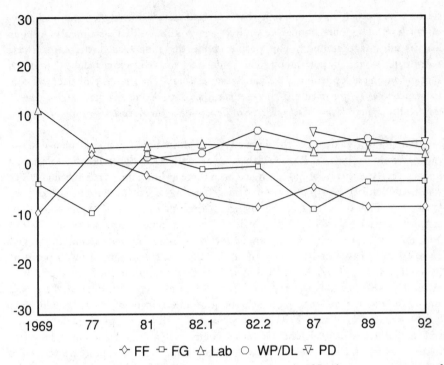

Figure 7.1 Party support and age: percentage aged under 35 minus percentage aged over 35 supporting each party, 1969–92.

1977 election, and by the size of the younger age groups in the population (see chapter 1). However, it must also be noted that the relationship between age and party support can be quite complex, as different combinations of generational and life-cycle effects are played out. An overall, and admittedly simplified, picture of trends in generational support for political parties can be obtained by examining the voting patterns of the younger and older generation, here defined as those under 35 years of age and those aged 35 and over.[14]

As Figure 7.1 shows, the differences between generations defined in this way are quite limited. The most substantial gap occurred at the beginning of the period for which we have this kind of evidence – 1969. This was the high point of the student radicalism of the late 1960s, both in Ireland and elsewhere, and the evidence suggests that the left-wing orientation of the students was reflected to some extent at least in the voting intentions of the younger generation as a whole. The difference in support for the parties in the younger generation was plus 12 percentage points for the Labour Party, and minus 11 and minus 5 for Fianna Fáil and Fine Gael respectively. In the 1977 election, Fianna Fáil's deliberate youth

[14] More detailed age breakdowns of party support for the elections of 1969, 1977, November 1982 and 1989 are presented and discused in Whyte (1973), Sinnott (1978) and (1987), and Marsh and Sinnott (1989).

strategy succeeded in eliminating that 11-point gap, achieving in fact a slightly higher level of support among the younger age groups. In that election also Labour lost its advantage among young people, while the Fine Gael age contrast was accentuated – its support among the under-35s was 10 points below that of its support among older people. Like much else relating to the Fianna Fáil electoral performance in 1977, the balanced inter-generational support for Fianna Fáil was transitory and the party reverted to a degree of dependence on older age groups from 1982 on.

Adding to the evidence of the distinctiveness of the Fine Gael performance in the three elections of 1981–82 is the fact that these elections saw the elimination of the age imbalance in the party's support that had been there in 1969, and that had been further accentuated in 1977. An examination of the detailed age breakdown of support for Fine Gael underlines the extent of the change evident in Figure 7.1. While Fine Gael support under FitzGerald went up in all age groups, the increase between 1977 and November 1982 was only 5 points among the over-65s and 7 points among those aged 35 to 64, whereas support among the under-25s went up from 19 to 38 per cent (Sinnott, 1987, pp. 96–7). With the drop in Fine Gael support in 1987, the age balance of the 1981–82 elections was replaced by a significant deficit in Fine Gael support among the younger generation. Some of this ground was made up in 1989 and in 1992, but Fine Gael, like Fianna Fáil, ended the period with an age imbalance in support very similar to that of 1969. The story of age contrasts in Labour Party support is easily told – 1969 was the only election in which Labour managed to capture a youth vote. Even with the recovery of Labour support in 1992, there was no real sign of the reappearance of a generation gap or of a particular Labour advantage among young voters.

While Figure 7.1 indicates different trends for different parties at different times, one consistent contrast is evident: Fianna Fáil and Fine Gael together tend to receive more support among the over-35s, and all other parties together receive more support among the younger generation. This contrast was reduced somewhat between 1977 and 1982, first by the success of Fianna Fáil among young voters in 1977, and then by the success of Fine Gael in the three elections of 1981–82.

Education

Part of the reason for thinking that voting might be different among the under-35s was that this was the generation that benefited from the introduction of free education in the late 1960s, and from the substantial rise in rates of participation in education over the next decade-and-a-half. But does level of education make any difference to how people vote? The evidence in Figure 7.2 suggests that it depends on which party and which period one is talking about.[15] In the 1970s there was a modest contrast between the voting preferences of those who had completed secondary education and those who had not – the former were more likely to be Fine Gael supporters, the latter more likely to support Labour or, more erratically, Fianna Fáil. In 1980 a substantial gap opened up between the voting preferences of those with more and those with less education, the main contrast now being between stronger support for

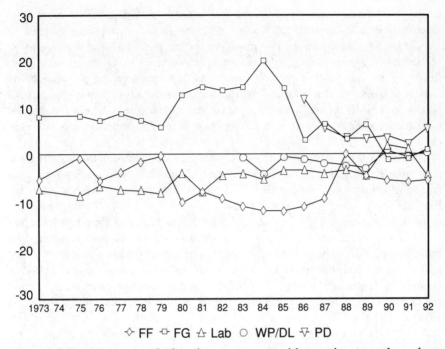

Figure 7.2 Party support and education: percentage with complete secondary education minus percentage with incomplete secondary education supporting each party, 1973–92.

Fine Gael among the former and stronger support for Fianna Fáil among the latter. A notable relationship between party preference and level of education persisted from 1980 to 1987. However, the relationship took on a new form in 1986, with a swing from Fine Gael to the Progressive Democrats among those with complete secondary education. In 1987, Fine Gael recovered some of the ground lost in the initial wave of enthusiasm for the newly-formed Progressive Democrats; then, in 1988, Fianna Fáil recovered support among those with more education, and educational level contrasts in party support became almost imperceptible. Though such contrasts strengthened somewhat in the following years, they remained much less noticeable than in the 1980–87 period.

Urban–rural differences

We have already seen indications of substantial urban-rural contrasts in support for the parties. These appear first in the post-1969 underperformance of Fianna Fáil

---

[15] Because respondents' level of education has not been asked for consistently in election opinion polls, Figure 7.2 uses Eurobarometer data to trace the relationship between level of education and party support on a year-by-year basis between the early 1970s and 1992. Likewise, it will be necessary to use Eurobarometer data in examining the relationship between church attendance and voting intention (Figure 7.4).

in the Dublin region; secondly, in the exceptionally strong performance of Fine Gael in Connacht-Ulster from 1965 to 1977 and in the same party's collapse in Dublin in 1987; thirdly, in the role played by the variable measuring the proportion of farmers in a constituency in predicting party support in various periods; and, finally, at the individual level, in the contrasts in support for the parties between those with farming and non-farming occupations. Another way of getting at these contrasts is to consider the area of residence of voters – whether they reside in mainly rural areas (countryside or villages with 1,500 people or less) or in urban areas (all other areas).

Moderate contrasts between urban and rural voters as defined in this way are quite clear from Figure 7.3. Fianna Fáil has always had more support among rural than among urban dwellers, though the extent of the contrast was relatively slight for Fianna Fáil in two of the elections considered – 1969 and 1987. It was more pronounced in November 1982, in 1989 and in 1992. Fine Gael had a stronger rural bias than Fianna Fáil in 1969, a fact that is consistent with its regional profile and with the positive impact of the proportion of farmers on its vote in 1965 (see chapter 5). Once again, the elections of the early 1980s marked a substantial change for Fine Gael – in the two elections of 1982 it was in fact slightly stronger among urban than among rural voters. However, in 1987 the rural bias reappeared, and was maintained in 1989 and 1992.

The case of the Labour Party is of particular interest. On the one hand, one would expect the party to be supported primarily by urban voters. On the other, the party has identifiable rural origins and, at the parliamentary level, has always had a 'rural wing'. When looked at in terms of the area of residence of its supporters, the Labour Party has not been, since 1969 at any rate, a rural party. In fact, Figure 7.3 shows that Labour support in 1969 was significantly more urban than rural.[16] Concomitant with the decline in the general level of support for the party, the Labour urban advantage declined and had disappeared altogether by 1987. With the recovery of Labour support, the urban-rural contrast in Labour support reappeared, especially in the 1992 election.

The urban–rural distinction just used is a crude one, including as it does in a single urban category both major cities and quite small towns. Likewise, the rural category includes both farmers and non-farmers. In fact, there are likely to be considerable distinctions in voting behaviour within each side of this broad urban-rural dichotomy. This is borne out by more detailed analysis of the data in the 1992 election. Thus, in 1992 Fianna Fáil support in the broad urban category was more likely to be found outside the major cities of Dublin, Cork, Limerick and Waterford. As between farming and non-farming rural residents, however, its support was quite evenly spread. The opposite was the case for Fine Gael. It had fairly even support across the various categories of urban residence, but its higher support in rural areas was significantly more likely to come from farmers than from other rural residents (for details see Marsh and Sinnott, 1993, pp. 111–12).

[16] It is worth noting, as shown in Figure 5.3 in ch. 5, that 1969 was the first occasion on which Labour support in Dublin outstripped its support in the other regions.

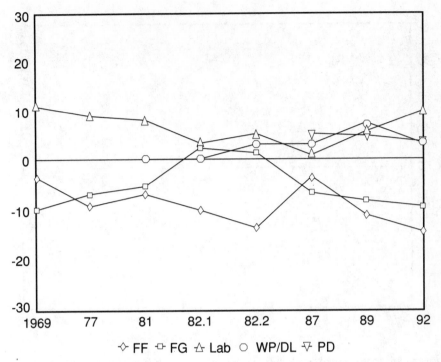

Figure 7.3 Party support and area of residence: percentage urban-dwellers minus percentage rural dwellers supporting each party, 1969–92.

Religious practice and voting

Historically, party differences on church–state issues in Ireland have been minor and variable, and Irish levels of regular church attendance have been extremely high. Taken together, these two factors have limited the potential for the emergence of a secular confessional divide in party support. On the other hand, chapter 3 presented some evidence that secular-confessional differences have manifested themselves in the past and are now seen by experts to be a definite feature of the party system. Moreover, evidence in chapter 6 suggested that such differences are to some extent perceptible to the public, and there is the undeniable fact of the politicisation of conflict on church–state issues in the abortion and divorce referendums (see chapter 9). At the same time, there has also been an incipient decline in regular church attendance. One might, accordingly, expect some evidence of the emergence of a religious factor in recent voting patterns.

In assessing the evidence on the relationship between church attendance and voting intention,[17] it is vital to bear in mind that the proportion of non-regular church-goers

---

[17] Unfortunately, the Eurobarometer asked a question on church attendance only on an irregular basis between 1978 and 1988. Given the religious/moral referendums that took place in Ireland in 1983 and 1986 (see ch. 9), one would wish to have had more frequent data on this topic during this period.

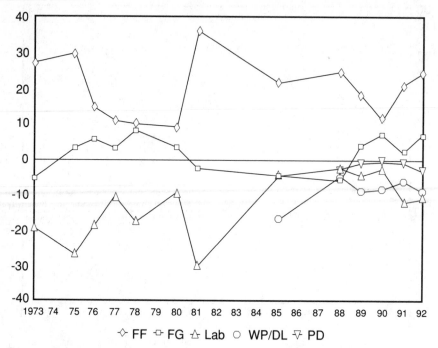

Figure 7.4 Party support and church attendance: percentage of regular church-goers minus percentage of non–regular church-goers supporting each party, 1973–92.

is very small, particularly up to the beginning of the 1980s (see chapter 1). This has two consequences. The first is that the measurement of the voting behaviour of the small samples of non-regular church-goers is subject to a greater degree of error. Secondly, because the vast majority of Irish people over the years have been regular church-goers, unless very great differences in the behaviour of the two groups are found, the impact on electoral outcomes will be limited.

In fact, there are quite substantial differences in the voting preferences of the two groups. Except for a brief period from 1976 to 1980, there has been a substantial difference between regular and non-regular church-goers in terms of their propensity to vote Fianna Fáil[18] (see Figure 7.4). Up to 1981, non-regular church-goers were more likely than regular church-goers to vote Labour, but at some stage between 1981 and 1985 that Labour advantage had disappeared, to be replaced by a

---

[18] With the data to hand it is impossible to say what might have caused the considerable drop in the Fianna Fáil advantage among regular church-goers as opposed to non-regular church-goers in the mid- to late 1970s. It is worth noting, however, that the beginning of the period saw the emergence of a clear confessional wing in Fine Gael, and it ended when Garret FitzGerald launched his constitutional crusade in the autumn of 1981, a crusade that aimed among other things to rid the Irish constitution of its confessional aspects, and when the abortion issue first emerged.

tendency for non-regular church-goers to prefer the Workers' Party. It was not until 1991 that a substantial Labour advantage among non-regular church-goers re-emerged. That advantage is also evident in the 1992 data in Figure 7.4, which, however, does not include the swing to Labour in the election of November 1992. The other change that occurred in 1989 was that, for the first time in more than a decade, Fine Gael obtained more support among regular church-goers than among non-regular church-goers.[19]

With the exception of some social class differences, the contrasts in party support are more substantial on this dimension than on any of the others that have been examined so far. Just as class differences in party support do not amount to a full-blown class cleavage, so these differences in the voting preferences of regular church-goers and non-regular church-goers do not amount to a secular-confessional cleavage. On the other hand, non-regular church-goers are a growing segment of the population. Thus, there may not be a secular-confessional polarisation in voting behaviour, but there are more indications than before that there is potential for such a polarisation to emerge. The matter is clearly related to how we interpret the urban-rural polarisation of party support in the 1992 election that was apparent in chapter 5. However the point made then still applies: further consideration of this issue must await the examination of referendum voting patterns (chapter 9), and of voting in the 1990 presidential election (chapter 10).

Conclusion

The evidence reviewed in this chapter can be briefly summarised in terms of what it reveals about certain persistent or general features of Irish voting behaviour, and secondly, what it tells us about the contingent aspects of voting behaviour, i.e. those that arise from the particular circumstances and shifting party campaigns and strategies of individual elections.

The first general feature is the *relative* weakness of the class basis of Irish voting behaviour. The term 'relative' is necessary and is italicised for three reasons: classlessness is mainly a characteristic of one party, i.e., Fianna Fáil, though it also applies to the Labour Party in 1992. Secondly, even on the basis of the standard measure of social class, the image of Fianna Fáil as a classless party is less satisfactory for the elections of 1982 and especially that of 1987.[20] Finally, it needs to be further qualified if we introduce a more nuanced and subtle set of class distinctions in place of the crude middle class versus working class division. The most important qualification introduced by this latter consideration relates to the distinctive voting behaviour of the 'bourgeoisie': this class offered only very limited support to Fianna Fáil in 1987 or in 1992; it supported the Progressive Democrats quite strongly in 1987 but subsequently deserted them, and it remained impervious to the otherwise widespread appeal of Labour in 1992. It must be emphasized, however, that because the bourgeoisie is a very small

[19] Regularity of church attendance appears to bear no particular relationship to support for the Progressive Democrats.

[20] However, the cross-class formula appeared to work for Fianna Fáil again in 1989.

group, the political implications of the revised class analysis are limited. Overall then, Fianna Fáil retains considerable cross-class appeal – in 1992 it had more or less equal levels of support among farmers, the long-term unemployed, the working class and the *petite bourgeoisie*, and it was the leading party among the salaried middle class. To the extent that there is a tilt in Fianna Fáil support, it is broadly towards the less well-off. In the case of the Labour Party, 'classlessness' remains the best summary description of its support in 1992, particularly in view of the fact that its support among the salaried middle class was greater than among the employed working class. Over the longer term, however, there has been a persistent, if rather weak, working-class basis to Labour Party support. In this sense there is a certain parallelism between the support bases of Fianna Fáil and Labour. However, there is also a persistent low to moderate difference in the support bases of the two parties in terms of age, level of education, urban-rural residence and regularity of church attendance. The impact of these related factors has varied from time to time, and it is notable that urban-rural and secular-religious contrasts were accentuated in 1992.

The second general feature of Irish voting behaviour is the balance of party and candidate considerations in the decisions of the voters. Candidate and local factors are cited by a plurality of voters as their most important criteria in deciding how to vote. Moreover, there is some evidence that voters have the knowledge required to vote on that basis, and such a focus would help to explain the relatively low impact of class and other socio-demographic factors just discussed. However, the importance of candidate considerations should not be exaggerated. Given the Irish electoral system, local candidate criteria of this sort are quite compatible with a concomitant emphasis on party related criteria. Moreover, the evidence suggests that considerations of party policy, party leadership and governmental leadership are the priorities of a majority of voters. Finally, there is evidence that the main inter-party differences identified in chapter 3 (the particular configuration of left–right differences, the nuances of nationalism and even the confessional-secular emphases of the parties) have some resonance with the voters.

This brings us to the second set of conclusions – those regarding the impact of circumstances or, the other side of the coin, regarding the contingency and responsiveness of Irish voting behaviour. The period between 1973 and 1977 marked a new phase in the history of Irish general elections. This was not just because of the novelty of a coalition government after sixteen years of Fianna Fáil rule. Nor was it only because of the innovative, and in some respects gimmicky, preparations that Fianna Fáil was making in its determination to return to power in 1977. What was new was the overwhelming preoccupation with economic issues. Inflation, unemployment and taxation accounted for the issue preoccupations of four out of five voters. Irish elections reflected international trends and pressures as the voters were confronted with the consequences of the international recession, induced by the first oil shock. Fianna Fáil was the party which responded to the public mood and this, rather than the auction politics which it also indulged in, led to it being rewarded with an absolute majority of first preference votes.

The longer term political and electoral consequences of Fianna Fáil's over-ambitious strategy were twofold. It raised expectations about what government could do in the economic realm, and simultaneously led to severe constraints on future government action because of the excessive borrowing for current expenditure that it entailed. Governments in the 1980s were put under intolerable pressure – expected to solve rising structural unemployment and faced at the same time with rising levels of public indebtedness. In 1981 and 1982 the preoccupation was with economic issues, at first with unemployment and inflation (in that order) and from February 1982 on with government borrowing. To these were added increased concern with leadership, a concern induced partly by the controversial choice of Charles Haughey as Fianna Fáil leader, partly by the Fine Gael strategy of emphasizing the leadership issue, but partly also by the sheer demands now placed on the leadership of whichever party was in power. It was not until the election of February 1982 that a substantial gap opened up between Haughey and FitzGerald, though the even balance between them in 1981 was based on a cancelling-out of pro-Haughey sentiment in the working class and pro-FitzGerald sentiment in the middle class. As the public mood in general swung against Haughey from February 1982 on, these class contrasts remained and undoubtedly contributed to the heightened role of social class in determining party support in these elections.

The knife-edge Dáil balance, created by the Fine Gael challenge to the dominant position of Fianna Fáil, raised the issue of government stability, particularly when it came to the third election within an eighteen-month period. This issue neatly illustrates the interaction between the salience or the importance of an issue and a party's rating on it. Fianna Fáil had a substantial lead on the issue of stable government in February 1982, but the issue was of relatively little salience. In the very next election, the importance of the stable government issue had increased by 10 percentage points, but Fianna Fáil's lead had been cut from a substantial 21 percentage points to a deficit of 5.

The extent of Fine Gael's achievement in coming to within 6 percentage points of Fianna Fáil (in November 1982) becomes evident when one considers that the climb to this height involved a turnaround for Fine Gael in relation to the younger generation, the urban sector and the more secular segment of the society. These successful appeals accentuated Fine Gael's existing advantage among those who had completed secondary school. The class gap in Fine Gael support remained, indeed widened, as the party forged ahead to over 50 per cent support among the upper middle and middle class and among large farmers. In another sense, however, the class gap narrowed – in November 1982 Fine Gael's support among the working class equalled the level the party had enjoyed among the middle class in 1969 and 1977.

This remarkable electoral coalition was short-lived. It was put together in three elections in under eighteen months. It did not survive the test of a full period in office. The reasons it did not are complex – ideological incompatibilities between the coalition partners, disappointment among liberals at the outcome of the abortion and divorce referendums, and the foundation of a new party competing directly with Fine Gael on part of its traditional patch all played a role. Then there was the economy – as unemployment climbed steadily to 18 per cent, concern with this single problem soared to 59 per cent, and the main opposition party had a 19 percentage point lead on the issue. In the circumstances, the collapse in Fine Gael support appears inevitable.

The ensuing minority Fianna Fáil government implemented the emerging economic policy consensus (without having acknowledged that consensus during the campaign). Government borrowing was brought under control and the rate of unemployment actually dropped. The government was doing well in the opinion polls and the calling of an election in 1989 was widely perceived to be unnecessary. In that election the voters again responded to the immediate circumstances, replacing unemployment with health at the top of their agenda. This enabled Labour and the Workers' Party to make significant gains among the working class. On the other hand, the proportion of voters voting against the health cuts did not match the proportion saying they were an important issue. The net result was that the voters stuck with the party that was seen to be performing well on the economic issues, and the middle class in particular returned to Fianna Fáil and restored the cross-class balance that had been shaken in 1982 and 1987. This accounts for the fact that, although Progressive Democrat support among the middle class was halved, Fine Gael only made a marginal recovery in that sector of the electorate.

The evidence suggests that 1992 was also an election highly influenced by the circumstances prevailing at the time. The controversial circumstances of the calling of the election, a prevailing mood of economic dissatisfaction, leadership popularity ratings favouring the Labour Party, a vague and unfocused desire for an alternative government combination, and aspects of the liberal agenda all seemed to play some role. All of this fits in well with the cross-class nature of Labour support in 1992, a support profile that cautions against interpreting the Labour performance as the beginning of a left–right political realignment. Could it be that there is some other polarisation underlying the 1992 election outcome? The accentuation of the urban-rural contrast in party support, and the strengthening of what has been a persistent secular-religious contrast certainly suggests that we should look at the relationship between these trends and voting in the moral referendums of 1983, 1986 and 1992, and in the presidential election of 1990 (chapters 9 and 10). In the meantime, there is one other vital bit of the jigsaw to consider – voting transfer patterns and what they tell us about the nature of party loyalty, and about the distances and the alliances between the parties.

Chapter 8

Transfer patterns and voting behaviour

Transfer patterns and understanding Irish voting behaviour

The Irish electoral process is information-rich. The combination of multi-seat constituencies and preferential voting, the logic of which was outlined in chapter 1, enables
voters to say much more about their preferences for candidates and parties than is possible in most other electoral systems. Filtered through a complex counting process,
these multi-faceted preferences are reflected in the records of the count in individual
constituencies (see the reproduction of the results of a constituency count in Figure
8.2 below). The evidence contained in these counts is a very useful resource in pursuing some of the questions raised in the discussion in previous chapters, in particular
questions about candidate and party voting and about the proximities and distances
between the parties. The first and most basic question is: To what extent do voters
make use of the opportunity to transfer votes? To what extent is the choice in fact, as
well as in form, ordinal (Katz, 1980, pp. 81–2)? Over and above this basic question, the
evidence of transfer patterns has been used as an indicator of partisan commitment,
i.e., the extent to which party voting prevails over voting for individuals (Carty, 1981,
pp. 67–8). In similar vein, it has also been used to measure the 'partyness' of lower
preference transfers (Mair, 1987b, pp. 70–4; see also Chubb, 1982, p. 153). An analysis of transfer patterns between 1923 and 1977 has focused on the solidarity and
exclusivity of the voting preferences of supporters of various parties, and the nature of
the voters' preference orderings as between the parties (Gallagher, 1978).

It is evident, therefore, that transfer patterns have potentially a lot to tell us about
Irish voting behaviour. The problem is that the procedures involved in the counting of
votes in the Irish system are quite intricate and, as a result, the recorded evidence of
the voters' transfer behaviour raises difficult problems of measurement and interpretation. In order to deal with these problems, it is necessary to complete the description
of the electoral system itself by dealing with what was described in chapter 1 as the
third level of understanding the system – the mechanics of the count.

The mechanics of the count in PR-STV

Explanation of the mechanics of the counting and transferring of votes is probably best
approached by considering the record of the count from an actual election. As with the

discussion of the logic of the system in chapter 1, it is worth starting with the simple situation – a single seat contest and the transfer of the votes of an eliminated candidate. The presidential election of November 1990 provides a good illustration. The detailed results of the election are displayed in Figure 8.1. Sixty-four per cent of the electorate voted and there was a small proportion of spoiled votes (0.6 per cent). This left a total valid poll of 1,574, 651, which when divided by the number of seats +1 (i.e., by 2) yielded 787,325.5. Disregarding the fraction and adding 1 to this number gives a quota of 787,326 votes.

After the first count, Brian Lenihan was leading the field with 694,484 votes or 44.1 per cent of the total. Mary Robinson was in second place with 612,265 votes (38.9 per cent) and Austin Currie had 267,902 votes or 17 per cent. Obviously no candidate had reached the quota of 787,326 votes or 50 per cent +1, and accordingly the returning officer proceeded to eliminate the candidate with the lowest number of votes (Currie) and distribute his votes in accordance with the second preferences indicated. On the second count 205,565 of Currie's votes were found to have second preferences for Robinson. This gave Robinson a total of 817,830 which was well in access of the quota. Robinson's share of Currie's second preferences was an impressive 76.7 per cent. Lenihan received only 13.7 per cent and 9.5 per cent contained no second preferences and appear in the table under the heading 'non-Transferable Papers'. The final result then was Robinson 51.94 per cent, Lenihan 46.44 per cent, with the balance of the votes being accounted for by the 1.62 per cent of the total valid poll that became non-transferable on the transfer of Currie's votes.

		TOTAL ELECTORATE		**2,471,308**
		VALID POLL		**1,574,651**
		QUOTA		**787,326**

NAMES OF CANDIDATES	First Count	Second Count		
	Votes	Transfer of **CURRIE'S** votes	Result	
CURRIE, Austin	267,902	- 267,902	—	
LENIHAN, Brian	694,484	+ 36,789	731,273	
ROBINSON, Mary	612,265	+ 205,565	817,830	
NON-TRANSFERABLE		+ 25,548	25,548	
TOTAL	**1,574,651**		**1,574,651**	

Figure 8.1 Count and transfer of votes in the 1990 presidential election.

The process of transferring the votes of eliminated candidates, i.e., the candidates with the least number of votes, is identical in a general election. The complications arise from the fact that general election contests are held in multi-seat constituencies. This leads to the necessity of not just transferring the votes of the lowest and eliminated candidate, but of transferring the surplus votes of candidates who have exceeded the quota while there are still further seats to be filled. The key aspects of the procedure can be illustrated by reference to the results in the Galway-West constituency in the 1989 election.

In 1989 Galway-West was a five-seat constituency and there was a valid poll of 49,339 votes. When this is divided by the number of seats +1 (i.e., by 6) and, disregarding the fraction, 1 is added to the result, the quota is 8,224 votes, i.e., a threshold of one-sixth plus one. One candidate (Bobby Molloy, Progressive Democrat) exceeded the quota on the first count by a margin of 693 votes. He was therefore declared elected and the next task was the distribution of his surplus (see Figure 8.2).

The destination of Molloy's surplus is determined by re-examining his entire set of 8,917 first preference votes. These votes are arranged in 'sub-parcels' according to the second preferences indicated on them, with votes indicating no further preference being set to one side. The total number of transferable votes is used as the base for calculating each continuing candidate's share of the transferable vote. These proportions are then applied to the 693 surplus votes that are actually available for transfer. Thus, if candidate X obtains 60 per cent of the transferable vote in the original 8,917 votes examined, he or she is entitled to 60 per cent of the 693 surplus votes. As Molloy had no party running mate to whom transfers could be made, the result in this case was that 48 per cent was divided between the two Fine Gael candidates, 26 per cent went to Michael D. Higgins of Labour, and only 20 per cent went to the three Fianna Fáil candidates, who, it may be noted, were former party colleagues of Molloy.[1]

---

[1] Once the number of surplus votes going to each candidate has been ascertained, the votes must be physically transferred and the question arises: which actual ballot papers should be transferred and which should remain with the elected candidate? In this regard, the rules state 'The papers to be transferred from each sub-parcel shall be those last filed in the sub-parcel . . .' (Electoral Act, 1992, section 121, subsection 7). Inherent in this process is the risk that the set of votes transferred may differ in terms of the next preferences they contain from the set of votes remaining with the elected candidate. Since the transferred votes may subsequently be examined for further preferences and determine the fate of candidates in contention, the issue of whether the set transferred accurately represent the entire set is of considerable potential significance. The defence of the procedure is that since the returning officer is obliged to 'mix together the whole of the ballot papers' (Electoral Act, 1992, section 114, subsection 3) when all the ballot boxes are opened at the start of the count, the set of papers taken from the top of any sub-parcel should be a random sample of the entire sub-parcel and should not, therefore, involve distortion or bias. The problem is that this involves a degree of reliance on the initial mixing process and on the accuracy of this kind of sampling that is probably excessive. Having constructed a probability model on the basis of the optimistic assumption that the sampling procedure is truly random, Gallagher and Unwin are still forced to conclude that 'the effect of sampling has probably been small overall, but that it has nevertheless surfaced too often for comfort' (Gallagher and Unwin, 1985, p. 352). There is a way around the problem, which is to transfer all the papers in the sub-parcel at the appropriate fraction of their value. This method is in fact used in elections to the Seanad. Gallagher and Unwin recommend that it 'should be regarded as a necessary feature of STV rather than as an optional extra' (Gallagher and Unwin, 1986, p. 352; see also Coakley and O'Neill, 1984).

Total electorate 77,178
Valid poll 49,339
Number of seats 5
Quota 8,224

Names of candidates	First count Votes	Second count Transfer of Molloy's surplus		Third count Transfer of O'Connor's and Shanley's votes		Fourth count Transfer of Brick's votes		Fifth count Transfer of Higgins' surplus		Sixth count Transfer of Ó Cuív's votes		Seventh count Transfer of Fahey's surplus	
BRICK, Jimmy (WP)	1,555	+ 30	1,585	+ 38	1,623	- 1,623							
COOGAN, Fintan (FG)	5,297	+ 204	5,501	+ 18	5,519	+ 204	5,723	+ 352	6,075	+ 253	6,328	+ 229	6,557
FAHEY, Frank (FF)	8,010	+ 44	8,054	+ 7	8,061	+ 68	8,129	+ 48	8,177	+ 2,152	10,329	- 2,105	8,224
GEOGHEGAN-QUINN, Máire (FF)	5,902	+ 39	5,941	+ 8	5,949	+ 47	5,996	+ 47	6,043	+ 2,272	8,315		8,315
HIGGINS, Michael D. (Lab)	7,727	+ 181	7,908	+ 67	7,975	+ 1,155	9,130	- 906	8,224		8,224		8,224
McCORMACK, Pádraic (FG)	5,987	+ 131	6,118	+ 12	6,130	+ 49	6,179	+ 152	6,331	+ 380	6,711	+ 211	6,922
MOLLOY, Bobby (PD)	8,917	- 693	8,224		8,224		8,224		8,224		8,224		8,224
O'CONNOR, Paul Ollie	84	+ 3	87	- 87									
Ó CUÍV, Éamon (FF)	5,733	+ 59	5,792	+ 25	5,817	+ 36	5,853	+ 63	5,916	- 5,916			
SHANLEY, Dermot (Non-party)	127	+ 2	129	- 129									
NON-TRANSFERABLE	-			+ 41	41	+ 64	105	+ 244	349	+ 859	1,208	+ 1,665	2,873
TOTAL	49,339		49,339		49,339		49,339		49,339		49,339		49,339

Elected

MOLLOY, Bobby (PD)
HIGGINS, Michael D. (Lab)
FAHEY, Frank (FF)
GEOGHEGAN-QUINN, Máire (FF)
McCORMACK, Pádraic (FG)

Figure 8.2 Count and transfer of votes in Galway West, 1989.

At this point we can note the first implication of the counting process for the interpretation of transfer patterns. It is based on the fact that the non-transferable votes in the original set of votes examined are set aside and not used in calculating the proportions of votes which should go to the continuing candidates. To be precise: the proportion of the set of votes with second preferences for candidate A that is actually transferred to that candidate is the ratio between the surplus and the number of transferable votes in the parcel examined. As the rules put it 'the number of papers to be transferred from each sub-parcel shall be ascertained by multiplying the number of papers in the sub-parcel by the surplus and dividing the result by the total number of transferable papers' (Electoral Act, 1992, section 121, subsection 6b). In so far as the recording and reporting of the results is concerned, the consequence is that non-transferable votes disappear, zero being consistently registered in the non-transferable column of the transfers of surplus votes unless the surplus exceeds the number of transferable votes in the parcel examined. This is highly improbable in the case of a first count because of the size of the parcel of votes being examined (i.e., the entire first preference vote of the elected candidate). However, it can and does happen when surpluses that accrue on subsequent counts are being redistributed. For now it is sufficient to note the key issue from the point of view of interpreting transfer patterns – a reported non-transferable vote of zero cannot be taken at face value; it is an artefact of the counting procedure.

Returning to Galway West in 1989, the transfer of Molloy's surplus did not result in putting any of the remaining candidates over the quota, and so the next step in the process (the third count) was the transfer of the votes of the lowest candidate. In fact, on this count, two candidates were eliminated in one operation. This is because the difference between the second last and third last candidates (Dermot Shanley, Non-Party and Jimmy Brick, the Workers' Party) was greater than the total vote of the last candidate (Paul Olly O'Connor). This being so, even if all of O'Connor's votes went to Shanley, Shanley would still have been the next to be eliminated. Accordingly, it makes sense to carry out both eliminations in a single count. This illustrates the point that what is being examined at this stage is what the rules call 'the next available preference'. For example, if some of O'Connor's votes had a second preference for Molloy, then, because Molloy has already been elected, it would be the third preference that becomes operative for that particular vote. If that third preference happened to be for Shanley, then, because he has been eliminated, the fourth preference is the one that would determine the destination of the vote.

The third count in Galway West in 1989 did not put any candidate over the quota, though Fahy and Higgins were getting close to it. On the fourth count, therefore, the next lowest candidate (Jimmy Brick, the Workers' Party) was eliminated. Over 60 per cent of Brick's votes transferred to Higgins, putting him over the quota by 906 votes. Accordingly, the next task (fifth count) was the distribution of Higgins' surplus. The approach to the distribution of a surplus that occurs at this stage of the count is the same as that described above for the second count, except that the proportions are determined not on the basis of a re-examination of Higgins' entire 9,130 votes, but on the basis of the 'last parcel received', that is, on the basis of the 1,155 votes he received from Brick. This procedure does involve substantial savings in time and effort. The rationale for the procedure is that the last parcel of votes in question is the set of votes that put the elected candidate over the quota and in this way created the surplus, and that therefore these are the votes that ought to determine the distribution of the surplus. It could equally well be argued, however, that the procedure involves a potential distortion of the process in that the distribution of next available preferences in Brick's vote may not correspond to the distribution of such preferences in the entire vote of Higgins, and that the logic of the system requires that all of the voters for an elected candidate should have a say in the destination of his or her surplus. Be that as it may, the point has considerable implications for the interpretation of transfer patterns. The surplus votes to be redistributed are those of Higgins, an elected Labour Party candidate. However, if our objective is to interpret the behaviour of Labour Party supporters, we should perhaps be careful about using the pattern that results from the transfer of this surplus. This is because the votes are not just Labour Party votes but a set of votes that went first to the Workers' Party and only then to Labour. To bundle them together with regular Labour Party votes would run the risk of distorting the picture of Labour transfers.

As it worked out in practice, the distribution of Higgins' surplus differed from the surplus distribution we have already considered in another way. This is because the last parcel received by Higgins contained a number of transferable votes that was less than the surplus to be transferred. When this happens, all votes that can be transferred are transferred (i.e., there is no need for the calculation of transfer ratios). However, since these transferable votes do not add up to the surplus, a number of non-transferable votes is reported that is sufficient to make up the discrepancy between the number of transferred votes and the surplus. In the words of the Act:

> Where . . . the surplus is greater than the total number of papers in the sub-parcels of transferable papers, the returning office shall . . . make a sub-parcel of a number of non-transferable papers equal to the difference between such total number and the surplus and set the papers therein aside as finally dealt with, such papers being, for the purpose of *section 127 (1)*, described as non-transferable papers not effective . . . .
>
>   (Electoral Act 1992, section 121, subsection 5)

Note the implication. In this situation the actual proportion of non-transferable votes is *not* the reported non-transferable vote as a proportion of the surplus; rather it is the reported non-transferable vote *plus* the vote remaining with the elected candidate (i.e., the parcel examined minus the surplus) as a proportion of the total number of votes in the parcel examined. In summary, if non-transferable votes are recorded in the distribution of a surplus we know that the reported figure is an under-statement of the number of non-transferable votes, but we can use the reported figure to calculate the actual number and thus to calculate the actual proportion of non-transferable votes in the parcel of votes examined.

We can now apply these two points – the under-reporting of non-transferable votes and the discrepant origin of the last parcel which determined the distribution of the surplus – to the case in question. If we were to take the distribution of Higgins' surplus at face value, we would conclude that 55 per cent went to Fine Gael, 27 per cent became non-transferable and 18 per cent went to Fianna Fáil. If, however, we correct these figures to take account of the extra information that can be inferred from the fact that some non-transferable votes are reported, we discover that 44 per cent went to Fine Gael, 43 per cent were non-transferable and 13 per cent went to Fianna Fáil. From this we might be tempted to conclude that there was an exceptionally high rate of non-transferable voting or plumping among Labour supporters in Galway West in 1989. Before going firm on this conclusion, however, we would need to take account of the other feature of this particular surplus distribution mentioned above, i.e., all of the votes examined were Workers' Party votes, a fact that goes a long way towards explaining the higher than average rate of non-transferability, and cautions against using data from this particular count in Galway West in 1989 as an element in inferring the transfer behaviour of Labour Party supporters in general.

The sixth count consists of a straightforward elimination and transfer of the next lowest candidate (Éamon O'Cuiv of Fianna Fáil). Seventy-three per cent of his vote transferred to his Fianna Fáil running-mates, Frank Fahy and Maire Geoghegan-Quinn. The fairly even distribution of the transfers between the two Fianna Fáil candidates was sufficient to put both over the quota, Fahy by a substantial margin of 2,205 votes and Geoghegan-Quinn by 91 votes.

At this stage of the count there were two candidates still in contention and one seat to be filled. The two candidates were Fintan Coogan and Padraig McCormack, both of Fine Gael. The final step in the count was the distribution of Fahy's surplus which, like that of Higgins' surplus in the fifth count, was done on the basis of examining the distribution of next available preferences in the parcel of votes received by Fahy from O'Cuiv on the sixth count. Again, as in the case of Higgins' surplus, the number of transferable votes was less than the surplus to be transferred. Accordingly, all the transferable votes were passed on. The result was the allocation of 229 votes to Coogan and 211 votes to McCormack, with 1,665 votes being reported as non-transferable. McCormack maintained his lead and, since these were the last two candidates in contention and since Geoghegan-Quinn's surplus of 91 was less than the difference between them, McCormack was declared elected without reaching the quota. Given that the difference between McCormack and Coogan going into the seventh count was only 383 votes and the surplus was 2,105, the outcome could well have been different had those voters who plumped for Fianna Fáil (four-fifths of the O'Cuiv voters who transferred to Fahy) expressed a further preference. The fact that McCormack fell short of the quota by 1,302, while there were 1,665 non-transferable votes in Fahy's surplus, also illustrates why the last candidate elected is frequently elected without reaching the quota.

From a research point of view then, it is of considerable benefit when non-transferable votes are reported on the distribution of a surplus. While such figures do not reflect the actual non-transferable vote, they enable one to calculate the correct figure. As we have seen, the possibility of doing so depends on the surplus being larger than the number of transferable votes in the parcel examined. When the surplus is equal to the number of transferable votes, all the transferable votes are re-allocated. In this case,

however, since the number of votes transferred adds up to the surplus, there is no discrepancy to make up and so no non-transferable votes are reported. All we can deduce
from the recorded results in such a case is the upper limit of the number of non-transferable votes. This upper limit will be the last parcel received minus the surplus. Again,
an example may help to clarify the point. The fourth count in the constituency of Dun
Laoghaire in the November 1982 general election involved the distribution of the 767
surplus votes of Liam T. Cosgrave. Barry Desmond of the Labour Party received 645
votes and no non-transferable votes were reported. If we were to take these results at
face value we would conclude that the terminal Fine Gael to Labour transfer vote in
that constituency was 84.1 per cent with zero non-transferability. It is of course possible that there were no non-transferable votes in the parcel of 940 votes examined (i.e.,
the parcel of votes received by Cosgrave on the third count from the distribution of
Sean Barrett's surplus). However, this is unlikely. What we can deduce with certainty
is that the number of non-transferable votes in this instance was not greater than the
difference between the surplus and the parcel of votes examined, that is, not greater
than (940–767) or 173 or 18.4 per cent. As a corollary of this we can also deduce that
the Fine Gael to Labour transfer on this count was not less than 68.6 per cent (i.e., the
number of votes received by Desmond as a proportion of the last parcel received). We
would be in a position to say definitely that the non-transferable rate was 18.4 per cent
and the Fine Gael to Labour transfer rate was 62.6 per cent, if we could be certain that
this was a case in which the surplus was equal to the number of transferable votes in
the parcel of votes examined. As it is we can only use these as limiting figures because,
on the basis of the recorded results, we cannot distinguish between those cases in which
the surplus is equal to the number of transferable votes in the parcel examined, and
those cases in which the surplus is less than this number.

All of this implies considerable limitations on our ability to identify the actual level
of non-transferability in the case of the transfer of surplus votes. If these limitations
are ignored, that is if the recorded numbers are taken at face value, then the effect is to
produce a systematic underestimation of the rate of non-transferability. The interpretative consequences of such underestimation will be different depending on the
variable one is dealing with and depending on the size of the party in question. To take
the latter point first: since the distortion only occurs in interpreting the distribution
of surplus votes, it will be greater for large and successful parties that have many surpluses, and it will be less for small parties that have relatively few surpluses. In terms
of substance, if the recorded results are taken at face value, intra-party transfers which
indicate the degree of party loyalty among a party's supporters will be overestimated
and party plumping, which, as argued below, is a somewhat irrational form of loyalty,
will be underestimated. In the case of inter-party relationships the distortion is less
consistent and is generally slight. There are notable exceptions to the latter observation, however, as in the case of the conclusion that the terminal Fine Gael to Labour
transfer rate in the June 1981 election was 87 per cent (Busteed, 1990, p. 61). This particular case will be discussed when the reanalysis of the transfer data for 1948–92 is
presented below. Before turning to this it is necessary to consider the other measurement problem – that of contamination.

Contamination occurs where some or all of the votes credited to a particular candidate whose votes are being redistributed originally belonged to a party other than the party of the candidate in question. For the purpose of making inferences about the behaviour of party supporters, contamination, or at least the more severe degrees of it, must be taken into account. We have already seen a particular case of contamination in the case of the Workers' Party origin of the parcel of votes examined in the distribution of Higgins' surplus in Galway West in 1989. The general problem of which this is an illustration is that, in the case of a surplus consisting of original votes *and* transferred votes, only the papers 'contained in the sub-parcel last received by [the elected] candidate' are examined (Electoral Act, 1992, section 121, subsection 3). The party of origin of this sub-parcel is not necessarily the same as the party of the elected candidate whose surplus is being redistributed. From a purely electoral point of view this makes no difference – votes are votes no matter what their origin. From the point of view of using this data to infer characteristics of parties or party voters, however, the discrepancy does make a difference because one would be using votes, most of which were originally cast for Party A, as a basis for drawing inferences about Party B.

The problem can be illustrated with a more dramatic example than that of Higgins' transfers in Galway West. In 1977, Richard Barry (Fine Gael) was elected on the sixth count in Cork North East with a surplus of 822 votes. This surplus was redistributed on the seventh count and produced a non-transferable vote of 411. Taking into account the point made above, we can calculate that 55.0 per cent of the votes examined (i.e. the last parcel received) became non-transferable, 12.1 per cent went to Fianna Fáil and only 32.8 per cent went to Barry's party colleague Hegarty of Fine Gael. Before inferring a lack of discipline among Fine Gael supporters in this instance, we should note that the party of origin of the last parcel received by Barry, and therefore the party of origin of the votes examined as Barry's and as Fine Gael votes, *was Sinn Féin The Workers' Party*. Though these votes can correctly be described as Fine Gael votes, especially since in this case they effected the election of two Fine Gael candidates, it is arguable that, for the purpose of inferring characteristics of the Fine Gael party supporters, the discrepant origin of these votes should be taken into account.

The problem of 'contamination' occurs in a less severe form on a much wider scale. In fact all sets of votes other than original votes are potentially 'contaminated' from the point of view of the party of origin by the addition at various stages of the count of transfer votes from candidates of other parties. Whether these votes become transferable as the last parcel received by candidates with a surplus (in this case assume the simple case – in which the last parcel and the surplus carry the same party label), or as the votes of an eliminated candidate, the degree of their 'contamination' can be calculated. For example in the constituency of Meath in 1977, 23.79 per cent of the votes of the eliminated Labour candidate were not originally cast for the Labour Party. It is arguable that, in inferring the characteristics of party supporters, discrepancies of this magnitude should be taken into account.

One approach to this problem is to acknowledge it and then set it aside, that is, to make inferences on the basis of 'the distribution of votes in the possession of the party' and to enter a qualification to this effect:

> it should be borne in mind that what is being measured is the distribution of votes in the possession of a party at some stage of the count, rather than the disposition of supporters of each party which cannot be precisely measured for a number of reasons. In many cases the votes transferred from a candidate to one party do not consist wholly of votes cast originally for that party, having become 'contaminated' by transfers from candidates of other parties.   (Gallagher, 1978, p. 2)

This is a practical but second-best solution, since what we are really interested in is precisely the 'disposition of supporters of each party'. Elimination of all instances of contamination would be a mammoth task and, it could be argued, would give rise to substantial loss of data. The reliability of the evidence can be significantly improved, however, by eliminating the cases of total contamination described above, i.e., the cases of last parcels of discrepant origin that arise from time to time in the distribution of surplus votes.[2]

Evidence of party loyalty, party distances and party proximities in transfer patterns, 1948–92

Party attachment and party identification at the individual level were considered at some length in chapter 6, and it was clear from the discussion that there were substantial methodological difficulties in measuring the phenomenon by means of survey or opinion poll data. Although, as is apparent from the discussion so far, there are also methodological difficulties involved in interpreting transfer patterns, the fact that the voting system produces such evidence is of considerable value in pursuing the question of the nature of the relationship between the voters and the parties they support. The individual level data in chapter 6 indicated a decline in attachment to Irish political parties that began in 1980. The transfer data provide evidence which can throw further light on this phenomenon. Party loyalty can be measured in two ways – first, in terms of the propensity of voters to transfer their votes within the party when candidates of the party are available and, secondly, a more extreme and perhaps somewhat perverse form of loyalty, in terms of the extent to which voters plump for the party when there are no other party candidates available to receive transfers. This latter phenomenon – plumping – can be thought of as an indication of the distance between the party in question and the other parties. Thinking of it in this way is useful because of the common use of spatial imagery in discussions of political parties that we have already encountered, and because it ties in with the discussion of inter-party differences in chapter 6. The other side of the distance coin – party proximities – can be assessed by considering the extent to which supporters of one party are willing to transfer their votes to another party that may be allied to it, or may just be considered compatible with it in ideological or policy terms. Consideration of this aspect of transfer behaviour also throws light on the first ques-

---

[2] The effect of contamination on the continuation of transfer patterns is currently the subject of a research project being carried out by the author and Brendan J. Whelan.

tion, that of party loyalty, because transfer behaviour that responds to the instructions or signals given by the party leadership can be thought of as an indirect measure of loyalty to the party.

Party loyalty

Party loyalty can be measured by observing the proportion of the transferred votes that stays within the party when votes from one of the party's candidates have been transferred and at least one other candidate of the same party is available to receive transfers.[3]

Fianna Fáil party loyalty, as measured in this way, is not quite as high as previously published estimates have put it. Taking the returns at face value, that is, including the reported zero non-transferable vote, which, it is argued above, should be *excluded* if we are to arrive at accurate estimates of transfer behaviour, gives an estimate of average Fianna Fáil loyalty of 82.2 per cent for the period 1948–77 and figures of 85 per cent for several individual elections (1951, 1965, 1973 and 1977) (Gallagher, 1978, p. 4). Revised estimates, which take account of the points regarding interpretation of the data made above, give an average for the period 1948–77 of 77.3 per cent and, as indicated in Figure 8.3, only put the figure above 80 per cent on one occasion (1951).

Although the loyalty of Fianna Fáil voters to their party is not quite as high as previously estimated, it is still very substantial.[4] It has shown remarkably little fluctuation over the period up to 1989. To the extent that there are fluctuations within this period, the low points occur in 1948, 1957, 1961 and 1977. A glance at these elections in Figure 4.2 in chapter 6 suggests, therefore, that party loyalty can decline significantly either when the party does very badly and when it does extremely well. This is presumably because, on the one hand, a fall in a party's popularity can be reflected not just in a fall in its first preference vote but a fall also in the loyalty of and reliability of transfers from those who do decide to give it a first preference vote. On the other hand, party loyalty may be reduced when the party's vote shows exceptional increases because the party attracts voters who have not previously voted for it and may not vote the full party ticket.

---

[3] Note that party loyalty is here operationally defined in terms of one-stage transfers of votes within a party, i.e., from one candidate of the party in question to one other candidate of the party. Obviously, intraparty transfers can be a multi-stage process – from candidate A to candidate B to candidate C and on to as many candidates of the party as have been nominated. Ideally, one would measure the loyalty of voters across all candidates of the party, a loyalty that could be thought of as voting the full party ticket and that will inevitably be lower than loyalty measured only over a one-stage transfer process. The problem is that the data rarely present themselves in a way in which this could be accurately measured. Measurement of it would require a sequence of (a) a transfer of votes from party A that elects a candidate of the same party, followed by (b) the distribution of the surplus of the elected candidate in a situation in which there is still another candidate of the party in contention and in which the distribution of the surplus is such as to lead to the reporting of a non-transferable vote. Such cases are quite rare (see footnotes 4 and 5) and therefore do not provide a very reliable base for making inferences about party loyalty. For this reason, the analysis reported here focuses on one-stage transfers as the operationalization of party loyalty.

[4] The loyalty of Fianna Fáil voters over two stages of intra-party transfers can be measured on only seven occasions in the fifteen elections since 1948. The figures are as follows: 1961–57 per cent; 1965–60 per cent; 1977–59 per cent; 1989–60 per cent (average over two cases); 1992–53 per cent (average over two cases).

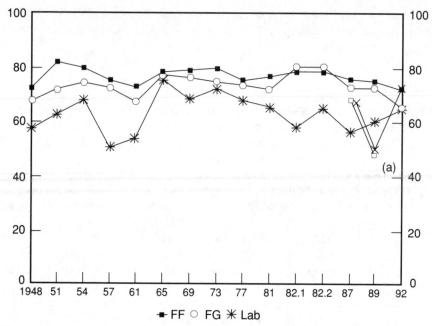

Note: (a) Labour loyalty could not be calculated for 1992

Figure 8.3 Transfer patterns 1948–92: party loyalty.

The impact of a decline in support for a party on internal party loyalty was certainly evident in the case of Fianna Fáil in 1992. In that election Fianna Fáil party loyalty fell from 77 per cent in 1989 to 69 per cent in 1992, the lowest loyalty figure in the more than forty years under consideration. The evidence in Figure 8.3 suggests that the decline in party attachment which occurred during the 1980s was not really reflected in disloyalty or lack of solidarity in the transfer process in the case of Fianna Fáil until 1992, but that then the drop was quite sharp.

Because the extent of the downward revision of estimates of party loyalty is some-what greater for Fianna Fáil than for Fine Gael, the gap in transfer loyalty between the two parties is not as great as has been previously assumed (see Figure 8.3). It is also noticeable that the fluctuations in Fine Gael loyalty, which are somewhat greater than those for Fianna Fáil, tend to coincide with the rise and fall of Fianna Fáil party loyalty. Thus, the low points for Fine Gael are also to be found in 1948 and 1961. In general, the gap between the two parties is greater in the 1950s than in the 1960s and 1970s, possibly reflecting the transition from a multi-party to a two-and-a-half party system, with, once the new system had become established, fewer temptations and opportuni-ties to defect from the party. In the two elections of 1982, Fine Gael loyalty reached exactly the same level as that of Fianna Fáil, a point that reinforces the impression gained in chapters 6 and 7 that these two elections witnessed a quite remarkable change in traditional Fine Gael voting patterns. As with the other aspects of the 1982 Fine Gael achievement, there was a significant falling off in Fine Gael loyalty in 1987 to 72 per cent, a level maintained in 1989. That 1992 marked a major upset in support for Fine Gael as well as for Fianna Fáil is confirmed by the decline in party loyalty among Fine Gael voters to 64 per cent.

The loyalty of Labour Party supporters seems on the face of it to fluctuate very considerably – see their two outstanding lows in 1957 and 1961. The February election of 1982 and the elections of 1987 and 1989 were also on the low side. In interpreting the Labour trend, however, it is essential to take into account the number of candidates fielded by the party, or more precisely the ratio of candidates to Dáil seats (see Figure 4.3 in chapter 4). In the elections of 1957, 1961 and 1982–89, the ratio of Labour candidates to Dáil seats was particularly low. In most constituencies there was only a single Labour candidate, thus reducing to a very few instances the opportunities for the expression and measurement of Labour-to-Labour transfers or Labour loyalty. In summary, the figures for 1957 and 1961, and for the 1982–89 period, should be treated with some caution. However, even discounting these cases, it is evident that, with just two exceptions, Labour loyalty is substantially less than that of the other two main parties. The most notable exception to the pattern of lower Labour Party loyalty occurred in 1965. It is quite remarkable that in this election the level of party loyalty of all the parties converges at a high level (76–78 per cent). The coincidence of this convergence with the introduction for the first time of the names of parties on the ballot paper suggests that this change in election procedure may well have contributed to a rise in party loyalty, particularly in the case of Fine Gael and Labour.

The high Labour loyalty of 1965 was not sustained in the next election. One might have expected that, in the ideologically more highly charged atmosphere of the 1969 election, party loyalty would actually increase for Labour, or at least be sustained at the previous level. As is evident from Figure 8.3, the loyalty of Labour Party voters declined significantly in 1969. The explanation may well be that, as noted in chapter 4, Labour nominated a very large number of candidates in that election, thereby greatly multiplying the opportunities for vote leakage. After 1973 the decline in Labour loyalty parallels the general decline in support for the party that was noted in chapter 4.

Unfortunately, for the methodological reasons discussed above, it is not possible to calculate Labour loyalty in the upswing in its vote in 1992.

Party distances

It has been suggested above that plumping is in a sense an extreme form of party loyalty. The true party loyalist or strong identifier would plump for the party rather than 'give a vote' to its opponents. Plumping occurs when a vote for a party becomes non-transferable in a situation in which all of the candidates of the party in question have been elected or eliminated, but in which the vote could transfer to other parties or candidates and thus, potentially at any rate, affect the destination of a further seat or seats. Plumping is a perverse form of loyalty. From the individual voter's point of view, and assuming the intention of maximising the effect of the vote on the outcome, plumping is irrational. From the point of view of the psychology of the individual voter, however, plumping may be, if not rational, then meaningful in that it may provide a way for voters to express the strength of their adherence to the party and their distance from opposing parties. Also, from a party point of view, it is possible to argue that any losses involved in failing to affect the outcome by not transferring beyond the party are more than compensated for by encouraging the party's supporters to think exclusively of the party, and not to contemplate the possibility of giving even lower order preferences to another party. The presumed effect of this would be to strengthen the voters' loyalty to the party and minimise leakage or defection in future elections. In this way the encouragement of plumping maintains the distinctiveness of the party and the distance between it and other parties.

Plumping must, of course, be interpreted in context and with some caution. It depends on the strategies of the parties and whether they are encouraging alliances and mutual transfer arrangements or not. It is also a crude measure, as it does not take account of the range of candidates that may be on offer when the votes for the last candidate of a particular party are being transferred; it merely records the proportion of the vote that becomes non-transferable when any candidates remain in contention.

Previous estimates of plumping in the case of Fianna Fáil have put the average for the period 1948 to 1977 at 49 per cent, and have suggested that plumping dropped as low as 32.4 per cent in 1977 (Gallagher, 1978, p. 9). These estimates would seem to indicate that Fianna Fáil has not been as exclusive a club as has some times been suggested, or to put the matter another way, that for almost half of Fianna Fáil voters, there has not been as a great distance between Fianna Fáil and the other parties. However, caution is indicated here in that the estimation of plumping is adversely affected by taking the occurrence of zero non-transferability in the transfer of the surplus votes at face value. Revised estimates based on the methodology outlined above suggest that the average for the 1948–77 period was 75 per cent, and that the lowest level that occurred between 1948 and 1977 was not 32 per cent but 64 per cent (in 1948). The revised estimate for 1973 is in fact 80 per cent. These revised estimates are much more in line with traditional conceptions of Fianna Fáil party loyalty and of the distance that has existed between Fianna Fáil and the other parties.

Looking at these revised estimates for Fianna Fáil over the period 1948–92 (Figure 8.4) indicates considerable stability up to 1977, followed by a sharp fall in the 1981 election. In the light of the absence of fluctuations between 1948 and 1977, the drop in Fianna Fáil party plumping in 1981 is all the more significant. Fianna Fáil loyalty as measured in this way weakened further in November 1982, recovered somewhat in 1987, and recovered almost to pre-1981 levels in 1992. The increase in the frequency of Fianna Fáil plumping in 1992 is presumably due to the substantial fall in the party's first preference vote with the attendant consequence that those who did vote for the party were those with a stronger sense of loyalty and therefore a greater probability of plumping. The decline in Fianna Fáil plumping in the early 1980s is consistent with the timing of the onset of a decline in party attachment as measured in the Eurobarometer study and discussed in chapter 6.

The data on Fine Gael and Labour plumping are more difficult to interpret. This is because plumping is measured by the level of non-transferability of terminal transfers from the party in question, without taking account of whether the remaining parties are allies or opponents of the party whose vote is being transferred (this issue will be addressed for Fine Gael and Labour in a moment). Given the on/off nature of the alliance between Fine Gael and Labour, the level of plumping in the case of both of these parties is very much subject to the context of particular elections, and to the context of the competitive situation in each constituency and at each count at which terminal votes for the party are being transferred. Even setting these factors aside for the moment, however, some significant trends in Fine Gael and Labour party plumping emerge (see Figure 8.4). The tendency of Fine Gael party supporters to plump increased on an almost continuous basis between 1948 and 1981, to a point at which it surpassed that of Fianna Fáil supporters. It declined sharply in February 1982 but rose again to a slightly higher level than Fianna Fáil in November of the same year. In 1987, with the drop in support for Fine Gael and with the emergence of the Progressive Democrats, it fell sharply to a level similar to that of the 1950s, a level which was repeated again in 1989 and 1992.

Labour Party plumping is at a much lower level than that of Fine Gael and shows no distinctive trends. The only movements of any significance have been a sharp rise in 1969, an even sharper fall in 1973. Plumping for Labour in 1969 may be due to the increased ideological intensity of that election and, or, to the narrowing of the opportunities for transfers to other parties that occurred because of the size of the Labour vote. The decline in 1973 was due to the negotiation of a coalition programme and a transfer pact with Fine Gael. The significance of such pacts and their abandonment is

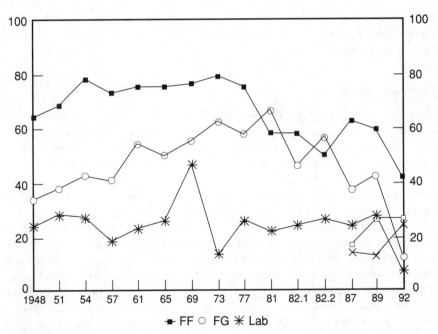

Figure 8.4 Transfer patterns 1948–92: party plumping.

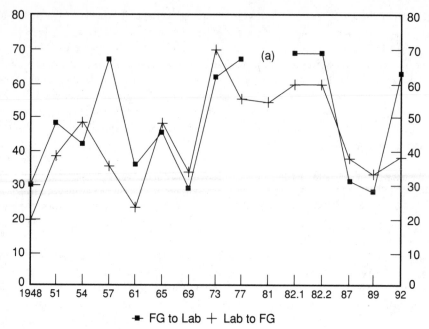

Note: (a) FG to Labour cannot be calculated for 1981. See text

Figure 8.5 Transfer patterns 1948–92: the Fine Gael/Labour alliance.

more readily apparent when we turn to examine the transfers between Fine Gael and Labour shown in Figure 8.5.

Party proximities

Inter-party alliances, in this case the alliance between Fine Gael and Labour, can be explored at the voter level by considering the terminal transfers of both parties in situations where at least one candidate of the other party in the alliance is available to receive transfers. As outlined briefly in chapter 2, an alliance between these two parties existed in elections between 1951 and 1957 and between 1973 and 1982. It must also be noted, however, that the enthusiasm and commitment behind these alliance arrangements varied from one period to the other and indeed from one election to another. The occurrence of these alliances is strongly reflected in the pattern of Fine Gael to Labour and Labour to Fine Gael terminal transfers over the period 1948 to 1992 (see Figure 8.5). In particular, the termination of the alliance in the 1961 election, its revival in 1973 and, finally, its abrupt termination in 1987 are all marked by very substantial changes in the behaviour of the supporters of each party. Clearly, party supporters' transfer behaviour responds quite effectively to the explicit signals or implicit cues emanating from the party leadership. The 1965 levels are an exception in that inter-party transferring was as high as in the elections of the early 50s. In the elections of

1951 and 1954 there was a formal alliance between the parties, whereas in the elections of the 1960s the Labour Party strategy was clearly on a 'go it alone' tack. The evidence of alliance behaviour by each party's supporters in 1965 may be a reflection of voters' perceptions of the impact of the Just Society document used as the Fine Gael manifesto in that election. It is worth noting also that with the exception of Fine Gael to Labour transfers in 1957, the level of inter-party transferring in the coalition arrangement of the 1950s was considerably below that of the level achieved in the coalitions of the 70s and early 80s.

Comparing the transfer behaviour of the two groups of voters, there is some tendency for Fine Gael supporters to be more enthusiastic about the relationship. In 1957 the enthusiasm of Fine Gael for a continuation of the inter-party arrangement was substantially ahead of that of Labour supporters, Fine Gael transfers to Labour increasing very significantly between 1954 and 1957 and Labour to Fine Gael transfers decreasing by a smaller but still substantial amount. In this sense it might be said that Labour Party voters anticipated and may have encouraged the parting of the ways that became apparent between 1957 and 1961. It is true that in 1973 Labour Party voters showed more support for the coalition arrangement. However, over the next decade Labour enthusiasm declined substantially (to 60 per cent or less), while that of Fine Gael supporters increased to and then remained at about the same level (70 per cent) as that witnessed in 1957. As noted above, estimates of Fine Gael to Labour transfers of 87 per cent have been published for the 1981 election. In fact, however, it is impossible to estimate Fine Gael to Labour transfers in 1981. The problem is that the figure of 87 per cent is based on two cases, both of which involved the transfer of surplus votes and in both of which the reported non-transferable vote was zero. Taking account of the methodological considerations outlined above, all that can be validly inferred from these cases is that the actual rate of non-transferability was between zero and 61 per cent in one case and between zero and 75 per cent in the other – clearly an extremely imprecise and not very useful inference. Accordingly, no reliance can be placed on estimates based on taking the published figures at face value and one has to accept that there is a gap in the data at this point (for details see Sinnott, 1987, pp. 92–3).

In 1987, following the break-up of the Fine Gael-Labour coalition, the voters for the two parties followed their leaders and went their separate ways. After five elections marked by high levels of transfers between the two parties, transfers plummeted to about the same level as in 1969, that is, just over 30 per cent each way. In 1989 transfers between the parties fell marginally again. In 1992, Fine Gael leader John Bruton had unilaterally put forward the idea of a three-party coalition (Fine Gael, Labour and the Progressive Democrats) early on in the campaign (Girvin, 1993, pp. 16–17). However, Labour threw cold water on the idea and only made use of it to raise the issue of sharing the office of Taoiseach. The Progressive Democrats expressed some interest but they too questioned the assumption that such a government would necessarily be led by John Bruton. The situation was further complicated by what seemed at the time a somewhat maverick call from Brian Lenihan of Fianna Fáil for transfers between Fianna Fáil and Labour 'so that the ethos of the next Dáil is one of social partnership' (quoted in Girvin, *ibid*.). In the event, Fine Gael to Labour transfers rose significantly relative to their 1989 level. However, this still left them radically short of the level achieved between 1973 and 1982 (see Figure 8.5). Labour to Fine Gael transfers rose slightly from their low point of 1989.

Conclusion

The analysis of transfer voting patterns broadly confirms the account of the relationship between the voters and the parties that emerges from the opinion poll data considered in chapter 6. This is evident in the loyal transfer of votes within parties – with Fianna Fáil showing the highest level of loyalty, closely followed by Fine Gael and, at some distance, by Labour. Party loyalty and party voting are also evident in the rate of plumping by Fianna Fáil and in the extent to which, at various times, Fine Gael and Labour voters have responded to the requests or signals or cues regarding transfer voting issued by or emanating from the party leadership. Finally, there is the evidence of change represented by the decline in party loyalty (either in terms of intra-party transferring or party plumping) beginning in the early- to mid-1980s and accelerating in 1992.

Because the concepts of party loyalty as measured by an opinion poll question and as measured by patterns of transfer voting are not identical, one cannot relate the distribution of one directly to the distribution of the other. This is particularly so given that the level of party loyalty as measured by each approach varies, depending in the one case on question wording (see the discussion in chapter 6) and in the other on whether one focuses on the evidence of single-stage intra-party transfers or on the much more rarely occuring evidence of multistage intra-party transfers. Accordingly, all of these various indicators of party loyalty must be treated as relative rather than absolute and must be interpreted with some caution. If this is done, though there are some signs of change, the evidence still points to the existence of a significant degree of party loyalty and party voting.[5] Alongside this loyal party voting, however, there are also complex patterns of cross-party and candidate voting, complexities that are facilitated by what is, on any reckoning, a subtle voting instrument. But, as emphasized in chapter 1, transfer voting is not the only additional means available to Irish voters to state their views, and parties and candidates are not the only objects of choice. On a much more specific front, and with some frequency, they have been asked to decide 'yes' or 'no' on a range of issues in a series of referendums examined in the next chapter.

[5] Some research on transfers has been carried out using opinion poll data but the conclusions drawn conflict with the evidence of actual transfer patterns in election results. See for example, Bowler and Farrell's conclusion that '. . . preferences could hardly be described as being significantly shaped by parties' (Bowler and Farrell, 1991a, p. 361; see also Bowler and Farrell, 1991b).

Chapter 9

Referendum voting: more evidence on stability and change

Constitutional background

The articles governing the referendum and initiative in the 1922 Constitution were a reflection of two factors – the spirit of democratic radicalism that influenced all constitution-making in the period, and the concern of the authors of the Constitution to emphasize popular sovereignty as a means of expressing Ireland's new national independence (Manning, 1978, pp. 193–7). Article 50 made a referendum obligatory in the case of constitutional amendment, after, that is, the passage of an eight-year period during which amendment was possible by ordinary vote of the Dáil. For any amendment put to referendum to be passed there was a constitutional requirement that a majority of voters on the register must have turned out to vote, and that the amendment must have been supported either by a majority of the voters on the register or by two-thirds of the votes recorded. In addition to this delayed requirement of a referendum for the purpose of amending the Constitution, Article 47 provided that a bill passed by the parliament could be submitted to referendum on the initiative of three-fifths of the members of the Senate or consequent on a petition signed by one-twentieth of the registered electorate (i.e., about 100,000 electors). Exempted from this provision were money bills and bills declared by both Houses to be necessary for the immediate preservation of the public peace, health or safety. Finally, Article 48 of the 1922 Constitution provided for the possibility of enacting a procedure of popular initiative on issues of law or constitutional amendment that had not come before the legislature. At this point, the constitution-makers were somewhat cautious. They did not actually insert a full popular initiative clause into the Constitution. Rather, they allowed for such a mechanism to come about, either as a result of a decision by the legislature or, failing that, as a result of a petition signed by at least 75,000 electors. In response to such a petition, the Oireachtas was obliged to either enact the required legislation or to submit the issue of implementing the initiative option to a referendum.

Despite these admittedly tentative pro–referendum provisions, there were no referendums in the period governed by the 1922 Constitution. The reason is simple. The referendum procedure itself became caught up in the pro-treaty versus anti-treaty conflict described in chapter 2. Having committed itself to full participation in constitutional politics in 1927, the newly-founded Fianna Fáil party was determined to use all available means to achieve its objective of undoing the Treaty settlement. The possibility of a popular initiative leading to a referendum on the most controversial aspect of that settlement – the oath of allegiance to the British monarch – presented one obvious means. In November 1927 the party began to organise a petition to implement the initiative mechanism and succeeded in securing the signatures of 96,000 electors. This action crystallised a view that had been held for some time by many in the pro-treaty government – that both the initiative and referendum provisions of Article 47 should be abolished – and a bill to do so was passed by the Dáil in June 1928. In the following year, again due to the intensity of the conflict between pro- and anti-treaty sides, the initial period of flexible amendment of the Constitution was extended by the pro-treaty majority for a further eight years. Since by the end of that eight-year period de Valera had introduced a new Constitution, the opportunity for a referendum on an amendment to the 1922 Constitution never arose.

Despite this rather inauspicious beginning for the referendum process in the new state, a requirement to hold a referendum on any proposed amendment to the new Constitution, and the possibility of referral of a bill to the people were both incorporated into the 1937 Constitution. Article 46.2 lays down the procedure for amending the Constitution:

> Every proposal for an amendment of this Constitution shall be initiated in Dáil Eireann as a Bill, and shall upon having been passed or deemed to have been passed by both Houses of the Oireachtas, be submitted by Referendum to the decision of the people . . .

Article 27 goes considerably further and raises the possibility of having a referendum on questions other than amendments to the Constitution, i.e., on a bill in regard to which the Seanad has been overruled by the Dáil:

> A majority of the members of Seanad Eireann and not less than one-third of the members of Dáil Eireann may by a joint petition addressed to the President by them under this Article request the President to decline to sign and promulgate as a law any Bill to which this Article applies on the ground that the Bill contains a proposal of such national importance that the will of the people thereon ought to be ascertained.   (Article 27.1)

This provision in Article 27 has never been acted upon and the conventional wisdom is that it is unlikely ever to be acted upon. There are several reasons for this view. First, the way in which the members of the Senate are elected or appointed is such that the likelihood of an anti-government majority has seemed up to now to be slight.[1] Secondly, the decision as to whether or not to submit the bill to the people is

---

[1] Forty-three of the sixty members are elected by an electoral college that consists of members of county and county borough councils, members of the Dáil and outgoing members of the Seanad. Eleven are appointed by the Taoiseach. The remaining six are elected by university graduates. The low expected probability of a government being without majority support in the Senate has been based on the implicit assumption that the formation of a government of a different party composition always follows an election and is therefore always followed by the appointment by the new Taoiseach of eleven senators. The formation of the Fine Gael – Labour – Democratic Left coalition in December 1994 invalidated this assumption by producing a government without a Senate majority.

entirely at the discretion of the President. Finally, the article specifies that the proposal in dispute can be approved either by way of a referendum or by means of a resolution passed by the Dáil after a new election. Thus, Article 27 goes on to say that if the President decides that the will of the people on a bill ought to be ascertained, he shall decline to sign and promulgate the bill as a law unless and until the proposal shall have been approved either

(i) by the people at a Referendum . . . within a period of eighteen months from the date of the President's decision, or
(ii) by a resolution of Dáil Eireann passed within the said period after a dissolution and reassembly of Dáil Eireann.   (Article 27.5.1)

The implication is that a general election, in which, presumably, the bill in question would be an issue, is equivalent to a referendum as a means of ascertaining 'the will of the people'. Moreover, the government of the day is given a substantial period within which to decide whether to resolve the issue by holding a referendum or by having a general election.

Although the formation at the end of 1994 of a government without a senate majority makes an article 27 referendum less improbable than it has previously been assumed to be, we are left with the process of constitutional amendment as the normal basis for the holding of referendums. This apparently narrow basis has in fact provided grounds for consulting the people on quite a large number of issues. This has been so because the Constitution incorporated such specific views about a range of fundamental issues (from basic nationalist principles, sovereignty, religion and moral issues to the details of the electoral system) that political events, and more especially the processes of change noted in chapter 1, have raised constitutional questions that, by definition, can only be resolved by resort to referendum. Also, the precedent of the specific nature of the Constitution in so many areas has encouraged conservatives to resort to constitutional change and therefore to referendum to deal with an issue not foreseen in the moral clauses of the 1937 Constitution – the issue of abortion.

Between 1937 and 1992 there have been seventeen referendums (this includes the 1937 plebiscite by which the new Constitution was enacted). Two of the seventeen can be set aside as involving merely technical constitutional adjustments.[2] However, the remaining fifteen referendums have dealt with issues of at least some importance. In fact, most of the referendums have dealt with issues of very considerable importance that have excited widespread debate, and on which the decisions taken by the people have had a fundamental impact on life and politics in Ireland. The fifteen issues can be subdivided into two categories: those dealing with regime-related issues and those dealing with religious–moral issues.

---

[2] These two issues – the Sixth Amendment of the Constitution (Adoption) Bill, 1978 and the Seventh Amendment of the Constitution (Election of Members of Seanad Eireann by Institutions of Higher Education) Bill, 1979 – were both put to the people on the same day (5 July 1979); the routine character of the issues was reflected in an extremely low poll (29 per cent) and in the very high support for the changes proposed by the Government (99.6 per cent in the first case and 92.4 per cent in the second).

Regime-related referendums

Regime-related issues have to do with the basic rules and principles of the political system. The plebiscite to enact a new constitution in 1937 was the most fundamental and encompassing regime-related referendum and, given some of the clauses in the new Constitution, could in fact be seen as spilling over into the religious–moral category. Strictly speaking, de Valera need not have put his new constitution to a referendum, since the extended period of legislative amendment of the 1922 Constitution was still operative in 1937. He could, therefore, have enacted the constitution by a simple Act of the Oireachtas. That this was not done was due to de Valera's opposition to the 1922 Constitution, to the way in which it had been enacted, and to the Treaty settlement that it embodied. Kelly has noted de Valera's desire to 'promote a fundamental break with the 1922 Constitution rather than merely to amend it':

> By securing the adoption of the draft Constitution at a popular plebiscite which was expressed to 'enact' it, while confining the Dáil to the role of merely 'approving' the draft before it was submitted to plebiscite, he by-passed the Constitution of 1922. . . . The whole proceeding amounted to a break in legal continuity; to a supplanting of one Grundnorm (albeit a disputed one) by another; and thus, legally speaking, to a revolution.   (Kelly, 1984, pp. 2–4)

Thus, the purpose of the 1937 referendum was to provide legitimacy for the new order. That new order involved relatively little change to political institutions. Two of those institutional change were, however, of considerable significance in terms of the structuring of opportunities for electoral behaviour. These were the specification of the single transferable vote as the form of proportional representation (see chapter 8) and the introduction of a directly elected presidency. In non-institutional areas, the 1937 Constitution was highly innovative. Among other things, it included a territorial claim to Northern Ireland (Articles 2 and 3), it gave a special position to the Catholic Church (Article 44.1.2) and it banned divorce (Article 41.3.2). The latter two provisions have been reconsidered in subsequent referendums (see under religious–moral referendums below), and it is generally acknowledged that in the context of any settlement of the Northern Ireland problem, changes to Articles 2 and 3 will have to be put to the same test.

The 1937 constitutional referendum was carried by a fairly comfortable margin (13 per cent – see Table 9.1). It was held on the same day as a general election and the high overall referendum turnout (75.8 per cent) is probably attributable to this coincidence. However, almost 10 per cent of the voting papers in the referendum were 'spoiled', i.e., either improperly completed or blank. The effective turnout in the referendum, therefore, was 68.3 per cent. This means that the 'yes' vote amounted to only 38.6 per cent of the registered electorate – hardly an overwhelming endorsement. Be that as it may, the new Constitution was now in place and twenty years were to pass before the voters were given another opportunity to express their views on any aspect of it; it was thirty-five years before they agreed to make any changes.

Five of the regime-related referendums dealt with one of the most basic aspects of the rules of the game – the rules governing voting. Two of the proposed changes in

Table 9.1: *Referendum results, 1937–92*

Date	Issue	% Yes	% No	Turnout	Spoilt or blank papers
Regime issues					
1.7.37	Approve Constitution	56.52	43.48	75.84	9.97
17.6.59	Replace PR by Straight Vote	48.21	51.79	58.36	4.00
16.10.68	Vary Ratio Deputy: Population	39.24	60.76	65.77	4.29
16.10.68	Replace PR by Straight Vote	39.16	60.84	65.77	4.27
10.5.72	Accession to EEC	83.10	16.90	70.88	0.83
7.12.72	Lower Voting Age to 18	84.64	15.36	50.65	5.21
14.6.84	Extend Voting Rights to Non-Citizens	75.40	24.60	47.47	3.53
26.5.87	Ratify Single European Act	69.92	30.08	44.09	0.45
18.6.92	Ratify Maastricht Treaty	69.10	30.90	57.30	0.50
Religious and moral issues					
7.12.72	Delete Art. 44 1.2 and 1.3	84.38	15.62	50.67	5.46
7.9.83	Insert anti-abortion clause	66.90	33.10	53.70	0.68
26.6.86	Delete ban on divorce	36.52	63.48	60.84	0.57
25.11.92	Amend anti-abortion clause	34.60	65.40	68.20	4.70
25.11.92	Travel	62.30	37.70	68.20	4.30
25.11.92	Information	60.00	40.00	68.10	4.30
Other issues					
5.7.79	Adoption	98.97	1.03	28.61	2.49
5.7.79	Permit alteration of University representation in Senate	92.40	7.60	28.57	3.94

these rules – the reduction of the voting age to eighteen years (7 December 1972) and the extension of voting rights to non-nationals (14 June 1984) – were relatively non-controversial and were passed by substantial majorities (84.6 per cent to 15.4 per cent and 75.4 per cent to 24.6 per cent, on turnouts of 51 per cent and 47 per cent respectively). The other proposed changes touched on the most fundamental aspect of voting – how votes are cast, counted, and translated into seats.

Proportional representation had been laid down as the method of election in the 1922 Constitution but no specific form of PR was stipulated. Despite having some doubts about PR-STV, doubts that related in particular to its ability to produce stable government (see O'Leary, 1979, pp. 30–3), de Valera accepted the prevailing system and inserted it, together with provisions governing the minimum number of seats per constituency and the ratio of Dáil deputies to population, into the new constitution. But then, in one of his last initiatives prior to his retirement as Taoiseach in 1959, he proposed the abolition of PR-STV and its replacement by the plurality system. Having been leader of Fianna Fáil for more than thirty years, having led the party in twelve general elections and been prime minister for nineteen years, he had well-formed views as to the effects of the electoral system on the possibility of forming governments with stable parliamentary majorities. In particular, he had reason to be sensitive to the variability and unpredictability of such effects. Prior to the 1957 election, he had, after all, only secured a majority of seats in the Dáil on the three occasions on which he resorted to the tactic of holding a snap election, taking advantage of the exhaustion of the smaller parties and playing on the desire for stability. Moreover, the exact same share of the popular vote had enabled him to form a government in 1943 and left him on the opposition benches in 1948. Most pertinently, he had seen his party's bonus in seats over votes reduced to 0.3 per cent in 1951 and to 1.1 per cent in 1954.[3] It could, perhaps, be argued that all of this would have been offset by the result of the 1957 election, in which Fianna Fáil received a bonus of 5.1 per cent and a substantial majority of seats. However, from bitter experience he knew that even a bonus of this size did not guarantee a majority of seats, nor was it something that could be relied on. Needless to say, the case for change was not articulated in terms of crude electoral calculations such as these but in terms of the dangers of party fragmentation and the need for stable government.

Fine Gael stilled whatever doubts it may have had about PR-STV and led the opposition to the change. Being a minority party, Labour had fewer doubts and immediately and wholeheartedly resisted the proposed move to plurality voting. The debate in the Dáil on the enabling legislation extended from mid-November 1958 to the end of January 1959 and ran to some 600,000 words in the official report (FitzGerald, 1959, p. 1). And that was not the end of it. The bill was then debated in the Senate, where the surprise outcome was a defeat for the government – the first defeat of a government bill in the Senate since the reconstitution of that body in 1937. This involved going back to the Dáil to override the veto by the Senate and, in O'Leary's words, a regurgitation of the arguments of the earlier debate (O'Leary, 1979, p. 55).

The government put forward two main arguments.[4] The first was that PR has a disintegrating effect, creating a multiplicity of parties and increasing the probability of governmental instability. The second was that whereas the plurality system enables the electorate to make a clear choice between two competing alternative governments, PR makes the formation of government a matter for post-election bargaining among parties, depriving the electorate of a direct say. The opposition counter-argument emphasized the issues of proportionality and fairness, particularly the question of the representation of minorities. Opposition speakers also attacked the proposal on the grounds that it would perpetuate Fianna Fáil rule indefinitely and undermine the parliamentary opposition. At the same time it would encourage unconstitutional opposition by effectively excluding the representation of groups such as Sinn Féin. Finally, the opposition called for a study of the problem by an impartial commission.

In addition to the parliamentary opponents of change, the government faced an array of opposition: all the national newspapers (except the Fianna Fáil-aligned *Irish Press*), the Workers' Union of Ireland, Dublin Corporation and, as the day of the referendum approached, the Irish Congress of Trades Unions. In addition, Enid Lakeman, who was then research secretary of the Proportional Representation Society of the United Kingdom and had already published substantially on the subject of PR,

---

[3] For a summary discussion of the political consequences of PR-STV see Sinnott, 1993.

[4] For a useful summary of the arguments in the Dáil see FitzGerald, 1959.

gave a series of lectures defending PR-STV and subsequently 'bombarded the Irish newspapers with letters on every aspect of the subject' (O'Leary, 1979, p. 52).[5] A civic-minded study group called Tuairim set out to produce an objective review of the arguments and evidence on both sides. Its conclusions, published in a pamphlet entitled *PR – For or against* (Tuairim, 1959) tended towards opposition to the proposed change, in so far as the report argued that if the system were to be changed it ought to be replaced by the best possible alternative and that an independent commission ought to be set up to decide what this might be.

A controversial aspect of the contest was de Valera's decision to run for election to the presidency and to hold the presidential election on the same day as the referendum. The defenders of PR argued that holding both contests on the same day was loading the dice in favour of the proposed change. In the event, whatever effect the coincidence may have had, it was not sufficient. De Valera was elected to the presidency, but his proposal to abolish PR was narrowly defeated. The voting was 48.2 per cent in favour; 51.8 per cent against, on a turnout of 58.4 per cent.

Obviously Fianna Fáil took some encouragement from the fact that it had lost by a narrow margin (33,667 votes). Otherwise it would be difficult to explain the party's decision to put the very same proposal to the people again within a decade. The underlying problem for Fianna Fáil – that of securing a single-party majority – remained. Séan Lemass had had to form a minority government in 1961 and only secured exactly half the seats in 1965 on the basis of 47.7 per cent of the popular vote. The party seemed to have toyed with the possibility of reforms other than a simple move to the first-past-the-post system. In the immediate aftermath of the 1965 result, Lemass argued that 'There are probably many methods of reducing the disadvantage of the present system of electing Dáil deputies other than those put forward in 1959, and there is an obligation on all of us to do some thinking about them' (quoted in O'Leary, 1979, p. 66). Lemass's call elicited at least one response. Garret FitzGerald, who was then campaigning as a Fine Gael candidate in the Senate election, published two newspaper articles arguing in favour of the alternative vote (*Irish Times*, 16 and 18 April 1965). However, Lemass retired as Taoiseach shortly thereafter, and an All-Party Committee of the Dáil established to review the Constitution failed to reach agreement on the question of the electoral system and simply set out the arguments for and against (Report of the Committee on the Constitution, 1967).

In the event the government opted for the same proposal as in 1959, i.e., to replace PR-STV by the plurality system. A second amendment proposed at the same time related to a requirement in the 1937 Constitution that the ratio of members of the Dáil to population in each constituency 'shall, so far as it is practicable, be the same throughout the country' (Article 16.2.3). The proposed change would allow a deviation of up to one-sixth from the national average. The purpose of the change was to enable rural areas with declining populations to maintain their level of parliamentary representation. It

[5] A brief biographical note on Ms Lakeman in a comparative book on electoral systems says 'She played a major part in the defeat by referendum of the Irish government's two attempts to introduce the British electoral system in 1959 and 1969' (Lijphart and Grofman, 1984, p. 272).

did not, however, go unnoticed that the areas that would benefit from such a change tended to be areas in which Fianna Fáil had widespread and stable support.

Essentially the same forces were ranged against the government on this occasion, the only difference being that the defenders of PR and of the status quo in regard to the ratio of deputies to population campaigned with more confidence and conviction.[6] The outcome was also more decisive. There was an increase in electoral participation – the overall turnout was 65.8 per cent. The result on the question of PR was 39.2 per cent in favour of abolition, 60.8 per cent in favour of retention. The voting on the other proposed amendment was virtually identical. The results reinforced the position of PR-STV in the Constitution and postponed any further debate on the issue of changes in the electoral system for at least two decades.

The remaining referendums in this regime category dealt with Ireland's participation in the European Economic Community. They are described here as regime-related referendums because they dealt with issues that were absolutely central to the question of how Ireland is governed. As noted in chapter 1, the moves towards a more open economy and towards a broader involvement in the international system had begun in the late 1950s and early 1960s. Such moves were, of course, initiated and pursued by the elite and had never been tested before public opinion. That test became constitutionally necessary when Ireland arrived at the point of actually joining the European Economic Communities in 1972; it has been repeated twice as the European Community took further steps towards integration with the Single European Act in 1987, and with the Maastricht Treaty in 1992. The problem in 1972 was that membership of the European Economic Communities would result in the application in Ireland of Community legislation. This was seen to be in conflict with Article 15 of the Constitution, which states that: 'The sole and exclusive power of making laws for the State is hereby vested in the Oireachtas (the National Parliament): no other legislative authority has power to make laws for the State' (Article 15.2.1). The proposed constitutional change consisted of adding a section to the article of the Constitution dealing with international relations (Article 29), which would enable the state to join the European Communities and would allow Community legislation to have the force of law in Ireland. Thus, the technical requirement of having to amend the Constitution had the beneficial effect of generating a major public debate on the merits and demerits of membership and of legitimising the decision to join by providing explicit endorsement by the public.

The forces ranged on either side of the issue were unevenly matched, at least in terms of numbers. On the pro-entry side were the two main political parties, the main farming and employer organisations, the Irish Council of the European Movement and all four national newspapers. The case against was put by the Labour Party, the Irish Congress of Trade Unions, representatives of some of the small farmers, the Common Market Defence Campaign and a number of nationalist cultural organisations (Manning, 1978, p. 207). Despite this imbalance, the debate was comprehensive and thorough and it succeeded in stimulating a very considerable degree of public interest,

---

[6] For a summary of the debate see O'Leary, 1979, pp. 66–70.

an interest that was reflected in the high turnout (70.9 per cent). Not only was the turnout high, the result was very decisive – 83.1 per cent voted in favour of the proposed constitutional change, in favour, in other words, of EEC entry.

The European Community question came up again for decision by referendum just fifteen years later. In late 1986, on the very eve of Ireland's ratification of the Single European Act, the economist and writer, Raymond Crotty, who had been a long-time critic of Ireland's membership of the Community, resorted to the Courts to seek a declaration and injunction restraining the Government from ratifying the Act. On appeal, the Supreme Court decided that, because of the content of Title III (the section dealing with European Political Cooperation), the Government could not proceed to ratify the Single European Act without an appropriate constitutional amendment. The majority (three to two) decision of the Court was greeted with surprise and, in some quarters, with disbelief. The Government, however, had no choice and moved quickly to reconvene the Dáil, which was in recess, to approve the legislation preparing the way for a referendum. Though some argued that the amendment should encompass the principle of the role of the executive in matters of foreign policy, the Government decided to play safe and confine the amendment to the immediate issue – ratification of the SEA. The line-up for and against the issue had been significantly modified since 1972. In the first place, the leadership (but not necessarily the rank and file) of the Labour Party and the bulk of the trade union movement were in favour of a 'yes' vote. Secondly, the 'no' side had become more complex (and fragmented), with the addition of various groups of Catholic activists concerned about what they saw as a threat to traditional religious and moral values, and of groups associated in general with the peace movement of the 1980s, who expressed concern about the erosion of Ireland's neutrality and the consequences of that erosion for world peace.

The debate did not match the high standard set in the 1972 EEC referendum and the issues were far from clear. This was partly because each side was fighting the battle on different ground. Those in favour argued that Ireland's very membership of the European Community was at stake, while the opponents denied that this was so and suggested the Single European Act could be re-negotiated to take account of Ireland's reservations on neutrality or other issues. The confusion in the campaign was reflected in the opinion polls, which showed that two-fifths of the voters were undecided with less than a week to go before polling day (*Irish Times*/MRBI Poll, 20 May 1987). The same confusion may well have affected the turnout which, at 44 per cent, was the lowest of all the referendums except the two described above as routine technical matters (see discussion of turnout in chapter 3). The result was 69.92 per cent in favour of the amendment, 30.08 per cent against. Perhaps inevitably, the proponents of the amendment claimed a resounding victory. It is, however, difficult to sustain this argument when so many did not vote. The effect of the low turnout was that the 'yes' vote amounted to only 30.7 per cent of the electorate. The aim of enabling the SEA to be ratified had been achieved, but the outcome fell short of the endorsement of participation in Europe that Euro-enthusiasts had hoped for.

Five years later the voters showed somewhat greater interest in the Maastricht Treaty. Turnout was 57 per cent and the result was virtually identical – 69.1 per cent in favour of ratification. Not surprisingly, the campaign was in many ways a re-run of 1987, the main difference being that the issues were somewhat clearer and the protagonists better prepared. Irish neutrality, the question of how much money Ireland would receive under the Community's structural funds, and even the question of conscription played a role in the debate. The campaign was notable for an all-party initiative encouraging a 'yes' vote. The outcome had a degree of European significance in that it came some two weeks after the narrow Danish 'no' to Maastricht.

Religious–moral issues

Most observers are agreed that the 1937 Constitution bears the imprint of the conservative Catholic social and political philosophy that was prevalent at the time it was written. The most important symbolic expression of that ethos was contained in Article 44.1.2, which stated: 'The State recognises the special position of the Holy Catholic Apostolic and Roman Church as the guardian of the Faith professed by the great majority of the citizens'. The next section of the same article went on to accord simple 'recognition' to the other main religious denominations (these were specifically named) and to a miscellaneous category of 'other religious denominations existing in Ireland at the date of the coming into operation of this Constitution' (Article 44.1.3). In this way, the Constitution created what became known as the 'special position' of the Roman Catholic Church. The article conferred no practical benefit on the Church but was of very considerable symbolic significance, especially in the context of the Northern Ireland problem and the state's claims and aspirations regarding Irish reunification that are expressed elsewhere in the Constitution.

In 1967, a parliamentary committee established to review the Constitution recommended that this article be deleted. The subject of the article – the Catholic Church – not only made no effort to resist the change, but gave it an unofficial 'nihil obstat' (see Chubb, 1978, pp. 67–70).[7] Even then the politicians were slow enough to move. The Committee on the Constitution had recommended the change in 1967; it was not until late 1972 that the referendum was held. When it did take place, there was little or no controversy; the change was supported by all the political parties, and was approved by the electorate by 84.4 per cent to 15.6 per cent (turnout was 50.7 per cent).

Some of the contributions to the Dáil debate which preceded the referendum on Article 44 envisaged it as the first instalment of a radical process of secularising the Constitution, or at least making it more pluralist (see Chubb, 1978, p. 69). From this perspective, the 1972 result might have been seen as a good omen. This emphasis on a continuing process of change was particularly to the fore among some opposition (Fine Gael and Labour) speakers. Though these two parties formed a government early the following year and held power until mid-1977, almost a decade was to pass before anything more was heard on the subject. By then both parties were under new leadership and had been back in government since June 1981. In September 1981, in a radio interview, Garret FitzGerald, Taoiseach and leader of Fine Gael, declared his intention of

---

[7] This was the view of the leadership of the Catholic Church. However, in the actual campaign there was some opposition at local level (see O'Loughlin and Parker, 1990).

embarking on a 'crusade' that would aim to alter both the nationalist and confessional aspects of the Constitution. For a number of reasons that crusade never really took off. FitzGerald was at the time leader of a minority coalition government that had other, more pressing preoccupations (see chapter 2). A further obstacle to his constitutional crusade was the deeply felt opposition of a minority within his own party.[8] The final factor, and the one which almost sank the constitutional crusade before it had even begun, was a commitment that FitzGerald had made to the Pro-Life Amendment Campaign in March 1981. PLAC, as it was known, was campaigning for the insertion into the Constitution of an amendment specifically outlawing abortion. With an election imminent, FitzGerald gave a commitment to this pressure group to hold a referendum on the issue and the commitment was formally underwritten in the Fine Gael manifesto for the election of June 1981 (O'Byrnes, 1986, p. 247).

The parliamentary instability and short-lived governments of the 1981–82 period meant that the abortion amendment issue continued to be caught up in electoral battles and in the manoeuvring for party advantage, and it fell to the victors in the November 1982 election – the Fine Gael/Labour coalition – to deliver on the commitment to hold a referendum on abortion that had been made by both Fianna Fáil and Fine Gael. After considerable contention concerning the wording of the proposed amendment, the issue was finally resolved by a Dáil vote at the end of April 1983. The proposed new clause, to be inserted in Article 44.3, reads as follows: 'The State acknowledges the right to life of the unborn and, with due regard to the equal right to life of the mother, guarantees in its laws to respect, and as far as practicable, by its laws to defend and vindicate that right'. Though the main political parties did not become formally involved in the ensuing campaign, it was quite clear where they stood. The wording of the amendment was the one that had been proposed by the Fianna Fáil government on the eve of the November 1982 election. It had been passed by the Dáil, in preference to the wording put forward by the Fine Gael-Labour government, by means of a combination of Fianna Fáil and eight Fine Gael and five Labour dissenting Deputies (Hesketh, 1990, p. 252). Thus, broadly speaking, Fianna Fáil and minorities from the Fine Gael and Labour parliamentary parties were in favour of the amendment as proposed. The bulk of Fine Gael was in favour of an anti-abortion amendment, but with a different, more 'moderate' wording. The Labour Party was more divided, some were in favour of the Fianna Fáil wording, some in favour of the 'moderate' wording, but a majority was against an amendment in any form. However, the parties as such did not get involved in the campaign, the three party leaders confining themselves to statements a few days before polling.

The fact that the parties stood back from the campaign may help to account for the relatively low turnout – 53.7 per cent. It did not, however, make the campaign any less divisive and the divisiveness took a denominational form, in the sense that the amendment was unequivocally and actively supported by the Catholic Church and opposed and roundly condemned by spokespersons for the various Protestant churches. When,

---

[8] Evidence of the existence of a confessional wing in Fine Gael in the mid-1970s was presented in Chapter 3. It was argued that this had virtually disappeared by 1987 but that it would still have exercised some influence in the early 1980s. See also Sinnott, 1989.

in the event, the proposal was passed by a substantial majority (66.9 per cent in favour, 33.1 per cent against), the result was inevitably seen as a severe blow to the kind of constitutional reform envisaged by the Fine Gael leader in 1981.

It was by no means, however, the end of the issue. The next round in the battle centred on the issue of divorce. Article 41 of the 1937 Constitution is quite unambiguous on the matter. It says simply: 'No law shall be enacted providing for the grant of a dissolution of marriage' (Article 41.3.2). The Divorce Action Group had been campaigning for several years for the removal of this prohibition, and, in the light of Garret FitzGerald's commitment to a pluralist constitution and the Labour Party's stated policy, they were assured of a sympathetic hearing in dealing with a Fine Gael/Labour coalition government. Government leaders, and in particular the Taoiseach, were at the same time listening to another voice – that of the opinion pollsters. Over a considerable period of time the polls had indicated that public opinion was very evenly divided on the issue of removing the constitutional ban on divorce. Given the outcome of the abortion referendum, this made Ireland's reforming politicans even more cautious than they might otherwise have been. They could, however, take some comfort from other findings in the opinion polls which, especially from mid-1985 on, suggested fairly widespread openness to the idea of divorce in limited circumstances. Then, in November 1985, the balance of opinion in the polls shifted in favour of removing the ban on divorce (for a discussion of the polling evidence, see Jones, 1986). In early 1986 a combination of what could be interpreted as somewhat favourable opinion-poll evidence and the pressure of political events induced the government to proceed. On 24 April 1986 it announced its intention of holding a referendum and a short time later the date was set for 26 June 1986. The issue to be put before the people was to remove the absolute prohibition on divorce noted above, and to replace it with a set of constitutional provisions allowing divorce in quite restricted circumstances.

On this occassion the two government parties, with the exception of some rebel Fine Gael backbenchers, campaigned in favour of the change. Fianna Fáil again officially took a neutral stance, but in the course of the campaign it became apparent that many Fianna Fáil politicians were opposed to the change on a personal basis. Furthermore, several Fianna Fáil politicians and many party members actively supported the anti-divorce side at local level during the campaign (Girvin, 1987, p. 95). The official line from the Catholic Church was that the decision was a matter for the voters, but this apparently neutral statement was accompanied by advice on the issues involved that left no doubt where the Church stood. As in the abortion referendum, the actual campaign was conducted by groups of conservative Catholics, with many individuals and organisations bringing to the anti-divorce campaign the experience gained in 1983.

The debate and the campaign were intense. Furthermore, they seem to have been exceptionally important in the sense that a major shift in public opinion occurred between the period immediately after the publication by the government of the proposed text of the new article, and the final stages of the campaign. The decline was progressive; in the period between the end of April and early June support for change dropped 9 percentage points, in the following ten days it dropped 22 points and fell a further 10 points between 20 June and the final pre-referendum poll three days before voting day. On voting day itself, the gap between 'yes' and 'no' was even greater – 63.5 per cent voting against the proposed change. Turnout, at 60 per cent, was up slightly compared to the abortion referendum. The problem of explaining this remarkable reversal will be considered in examining the determinants of referendum voting below.

With this second defeat for the liberal point of view, it might have been anticipated that the issue of constitutional change in this area would not arise again for some time. That might well have been so, were it not for a highly dramatic constitutional case that landed in the Supreme Court in early 1992. The case, which became known as the X case, arose from an injunction brought by the Attorney General preventing a fourteen-year-old alleged rape victim from going to Britain for an abortion. The injunction was brought on the basis of the anti-abortion article inserted in the Constitution in 1983. It was upheld by the High Court but overturned on appeal to the Supreme Court. The main basis of the Supreme Court decision was that there was a threat to the life of the individual involved in the form of demonstrable suicidal intent. Aspects of the Supreme Court's judgement raised, but did not resolve, two related constitutional issues – the right to travel to another country to avail of services legally available there and the right to information on such services. As a result, there was general agreement that the constitutional position on these latter two issues would have to be clarified by means of an amendment. However, opinion divided along conservative and liberal lines on the question of the response to the core of the Supreme Court judgement, which introduced for the first time the possibility of legal abortion in Ireland. The conservative preference was for a referendum that would alter the article inserted in 1983 so as to remove the grounds for the Supreme Court decision. The liberal preference was for legislation that would implement that decision. In the event, the government opted for an amendment to the Constitution that would restrict the scope of the Supreme Court decision, that is, would recognise 'a threat to the mother's life as distinct from her health' as grounds for abortion, but would specifically remove the threat of suicide as an allowable threat to life. In the event, this compromise proposal, which, in order to distinguish it from the travel and information amendments, became known as 'the substantive amendment', was opposed by both the conservative and liberal camps. The results of the three referendums are included in Table 9.1. The amendments confirming the right to travel and to information were passed by very similar majorities (62 and 60 per cent respectively). The substantive amendment was rejected by an equally decisive majority (65 per cent). The effect of this rejection was to uphold the existing Article 44.3 and, by implication, the Supreme Court judgement based on it.

Referendums and change

The relationship between demographic, economic and social change on the one hand and change in electoral behaviour on the other has been a recurring theme throughout this book. Trends in party support are in many ways rather unsatisfactory indicators of whether the Irish voter has been changing in response to social and demographic change. This is because an apparent lack of change in levels of party support may either mean that voting is impervious to social change, or it may reflect the adaptability of parties, so that a vote for the same party at two different times may not mean the same thing at all, and may not therefore indicate an absence of change among the voters. This problem can be dealt with to some extent by analysing what the parties stand for at different times, but a certain degree of ambiguity will always remain. In most instances, there is no such ambiguity about referendums. The whole point about them is that they give a clear majoritarian answer to a specific question. When, as in Ireland, major political issues have been covered in referendums, we are presented with a useful means of tackling, in a quite specific way, at least an aspect of the question of change in voting behaviour. There are, however, exceptions to the statement that referendums provide clear and unambiguously interpretable indicators of change, the referendum on the substantive aspect of the abortion issue in 1992 being one of the exceptions. The result in that case presents knotty problems of interpretation which are taken up below.

The test of change really begins in 1972. Prior to that voters had rejected three amendments to the Constitution, but it would be difficult to categorise these as pro- or anti-change in the broader sense. Since 1972, Irish voters have supported change on five out of five regime issues, ranging from voting age to joining the European Community, and in all cases have done so by substantial margins. There is a striking contrast between attitudes to change in these areas and attitudes to change in the religious–moral sphere. In the latter, change has been supported on three of the six issues, that is on deletion of Article 44 and on the right to travel and to information. However, these three could be seen to be changes of lesser significance in this area and, as we have seen, the Catholic Church had given explicit prior approval to the first change and had remained officially neutral on the other two.

In the case of the other three religious–moral referendums, the vote was against change. The divorce referendum in 1986 was clear-cut in this respect – a majority of the voters refused to delete the ban on divorce in the Constitution. In the case of the first abortion referendum (1983), technically the voters opted for a change in the Constitution, but this was essentially a conservative decision that reinforced the role of the Constitution in the moral sphere and was seen as a bulwark against change by its supporters. As noted above, the third amendment of November 1992, the rejected substantive amendment, is more difficult to categorise as an indicator of change or resistance to change. It was rejected by two-thirds of the voters, but it was quite clear both from the campaign and from the reaction of the various campaigners when the result was announced that this majority was made up of voters who opposed the amendment for very different reasons. In order to relate the outcome of the amendment on the substantive issue to the underlying question of whether and in what way Irish voters may be changing, it is essential to establish what proportion of those who opposed the amendment did so for conservative reasons and what proportion did so for liberal reasons. While there is no fully satisfactory way of doing this, the coincidence of three referendums on the abortion issue means that it is possible to make some approximate estimates.

With three referendums there are eight possible combinations of votes. Three of these combinations are substantially more probable than the others. The first of these three consists of those who voted 'no' on all three issues and they can be thought of as the 'ultra-conservatives'. Secondly, there are those who voted 'yes' on all three issues. This group can be thought of as adopting a pragmatic position. The pragmatists could be conservative pragmatists, that is, those who felt that a 'yes' vote on the substantive issue was the best way of limiting the effects of the Supreme Court decision, and that any other amendment that might be proposed would weaken rather than strengthen the 1993 amendment. Equally, the yes/yes/yes group could include liberal pragmatists who might have felt that the substantive amendment, though in their view too restrictive, was likely to be the best that would be offered. Acknowledging that the group may be internally differentiated in this way, it will be referred to from here on simply as the 'pragmatists'. The third combination consists of those who voted yes/yes/no. This group will be interpreted here as a mainly 'liberal' group, i.e., as made up for the most part of those who supported the right to travel and the right to information, but who opposed the substantive amendment on the grounds that it was too restrictive. It must be acknowledged, however, that this third combination may also have included voters who were willing to concede rights to travel and information but were opposed to the substantive amendment on the grounds that it went too far. Analysis of the socio-demographic correlates of the yes/yes/no vote to be presented below tends to support the view that it is made up mainly of liberals. Even given that, however, it must be borne in mind that it is a maximum estimate of the liberal vote.

Taking into account the fact that the various combinations of votes (the three just listed and the other possible, but less likely and less interpretable, combinations) must add up to the known results, it is possible to produce a system of equations from which, under certain assumptions and taking account of evidence from the opinion polls, the unknown proportions voting for each of the three combinations in which we are interested can be calculated (Sinnott, Walsh and Whelan, 1994). Application of this method suggests that the bulk of the voters (in the region of 85 per cent) were remarkably evenly divided between approximately 31 per cent ultra-conservatives (no/no/no), about 27 per cent pragmatists (yes/yes/yes) and about 29 per cent liberals (yes/yes/no). The remainder voted in very small proportions for the various less likely combinations of 'yes' and 'no' (Sinnott, Walsh and Whelan, 1994). Looking at the results another way, one can conclude that the majority who said 'no' to the substantive amendment appears to have been made up of equal proportions of conservatives and liberals (46 per cent conservatives, 43 per cent liberals and 12 per cent all other possible combinations). In relation to the more general question of change in voting behaviour, and taking into account that these are approximate estimates, one can think in round terms of Irish voters in 1992 being divided on a more or less 30-30-30 basis into conservative, pragmatic and liberal camps. The three referendums of November 1992 thus reveal a more complex picture of voter opinion in this area than would obtain if one simply focused on the two-thirds conservative majorities in the referendums of 1983 and 1986.

Determinants of referendum voting

These patterns of support for and opposition to change manifested in referendums lead directly and insistently to the question of the determinants of referendum voting. This question will be tackled here in terms of both regime and religious–moral referendums, that is, dealing first with the referendums of 1987 and 1992 on aspects of Ireland's membership of the European Community, and then with those on abortion and divorce in 1983, 1986 and 1992.

The Single European Act and the Maastricht Treaty

On the basis of straightforward self-interest, one might suppose that farming areas would vote 'yes' in EC constitutional referendums because of the benefits of the Common Agricultural Policy, and that working-class areas would tend to vote 'no' because of the particular impact on them of increased food prices consequent on that same policy. This rather obvious, though perhaps over-simplified, assumption accords with the line-up on the original 1972 referendum – farmers' (and employers') organisations in favour and the trade union movement against. However, by 1987, the trade union movement had reversed its position, arguing strongly in favour of ratification and maintaining this attitude in the Maastricht referendum of 1992. The position of the Labour Party is complicated. In 1972 it had opposed entry into the EEC; in 1987, the bulk of the leadership adopted a favourable position but there was some elite dissent and considerable dissent at lower levels of the party. In 1992 the party took a more uniformly favourable view and willingly combined with the other main parties in advocating a 'yes' vote.

In the case of the Single European Act referendum, the sources of the 'yes' vote conform to the expectations outlined above, with the qualification that the negative working-class effect was substantially greater than the positive farmer effect. The coefficients were 0.36 for farmers and –1.02 for the working class and the model accounts for a substantial 57 per cent of the variance (see Table 9.2). In 1992, however, the 'yes' vote was less predictable, the proportion of variance explained dropping to 45 per cent. More importantly, the farmer effect drops out of the equation and the only significant effect is the still substantial (–0.93) negative impact of the proportion in the working class. There are two possible explanations of the disappearance of the positive farmer effect on the 'yes' vote in 1992. One is that support for the Community in rural areas declined because of the onset of CAP reform. The other is that any falling off in support in rural areas was due to concerns about the implications of further European

Table 9.2: *Aggregate data analysis of voting on European Community treaty changes, 1987 and 1992*

	Constant	Proportion farmers	Proportion working–class	Adjusted R^2	N
Single European Act 1987: Yes	78.07	0.36 (5.18)	–1.02 (–4.00)	0.57	41
Maastricht Treaty 1992: Yes	79.21	0.10 (1.85)	–0.93 (–4.97)	0.45	41

Note: The main entry for each variable is the B coefficient, the figure beneath in brackets is the *t*-value. *T*-values in excess of 2.02 are significant at $p = 0.05$.

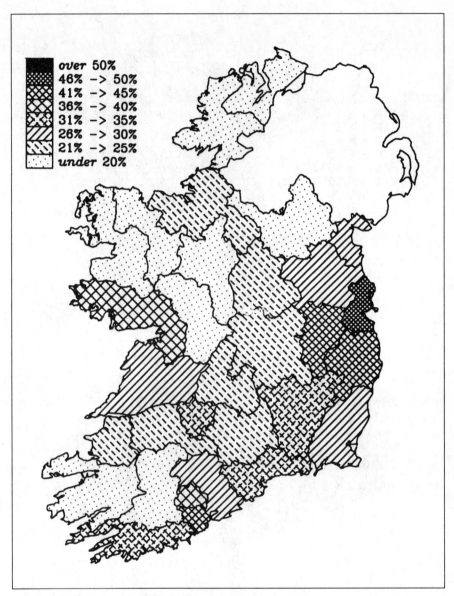

Figure 9.1 1983 abortion referendum – percentage 'no'.

integration for Ireland's conservative policy on such issues as abortion. In order to weigh up these conflicting interpretations of the sources of the Maastricht vote, it is necessary first to examine the determinants of voting in the divorce and abortion referendums themselves.

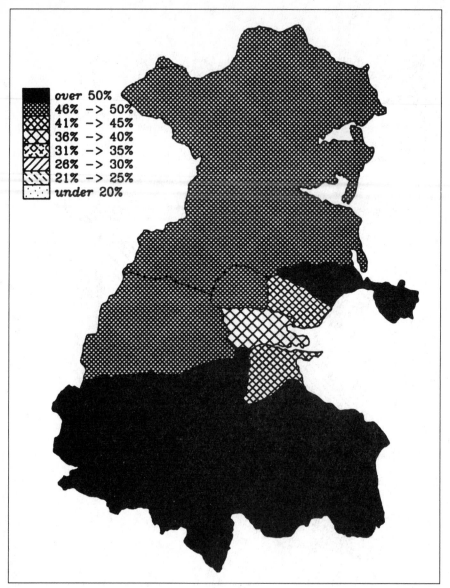

Figure 9.2 1983 abortion referendum, percentage 'no' – Dublin constituencies.

Abortion and divorce

The five referendums on religious–moral issues in the ten years from 1983–92 provide a means of investigating both the sources of conservative and liberal voting and the interaction between these kinds of voting and party support. As a baseline, it may be useful to follow the strategy used in chapter 5 and begin with some maps (see Figures 9.1 and 9.2). The areas of strength of the 1983 'no' vote were first of all the counties or consitutencies with total or substantial urban populations – Dublin, Wicklow, Kildare, Cork city and Galway West. After that there was a general contrast between most of the east, south-east and south, on the one hand, and the area north-west of a line that runs from Louth to South-west Cork. Beyond that line, the only pockets of greater support for the 'no' side were the already noted Galway West and, at a somewhat lower level of support, another constituency with a substantial urban population, Limerick East. The areas of relative weakness for the 'no' vote make up a rib running from Sligo through the middle of the country and around to Limerick West and North Kerry. Finally, the weakest areas were located in Ulster (Cavan-Monaghan and Donegal), much of Connacht (Galway East, Roscommon and Mayo) and in a pocket in the extreme south-west (i.e., the constituencies of North-West Cork and South Kerry).

Within Dublin there was a general north-south contrast. There are two exceptions to this neat geographical division – Dublin South-east being noticeably less opposed than other south-side constituencies and Dublin North-east being an exception in the other direction on the north-side. The map in Figure 9.2 also shows evidence of a contrast between the inner city and the suburbs.

Similar maps for the divorce referendum are presented in Figures 9.3 and 9.4. They need not be described in detail but it is evident that once allowance is made for the modest increase in support for the liberal position which puts most areas up a notch on the scale,[9] there are striking similarities in the geographical distribution of the liberal vote both across the country as a whole and within the Dublin area. This similarity is borne out by a statistical measure of the degree of association between the two votes – the simple correlation coefficient between the 'no' vote in 1983 and the 'yes' vote in 1986 is a remarkable 0.96. All of this suggests that similar structural factors probably underpin the pattern of liberal and conservative voting. The evidence of the maps suggests furthermore that these underlying factors should be sought in urban-rural contrasts and, within urban areas, in the contrast between more middle-class and more working-class areas.

Multivariate statistical analyses bear out these expectations. The votes in four of the five referendums (the 1983 anti-abortion amendment, the 1986 divorce amendment, and the 1992 right to information and the right to travel amendments) were highly structured. The extent of that structuring can be seen from the fact that in two of the four referendums (1983 and 1986), a simple two-variable model accounts for a remarkable 86 and 83 per cent of the variance and that the level of explanation in the travel and information referendums, while somewhat lower, is still very substantial (71 per cent in each). In each of the four referendums, conservative voting was positively related to high proportions of farmers and to high proportions in the working class, i.e., the higher the proportion of farmers or the higher the proportion of working-class voters in a constituency, the higher the conservative vote (Table 9.3). The coefficients attached to the variables give an idea of the size of the effect of each of the two variables. For the 1983 abortion referendum and the 1986 divorce referendum, the coeffi-

---

[9] Nationally the liberal vote went up from 33.1 per cent to 36.5. There were, however, some notable exceptions to the general trend, for example the Cork city and Cork South-west constituencies.

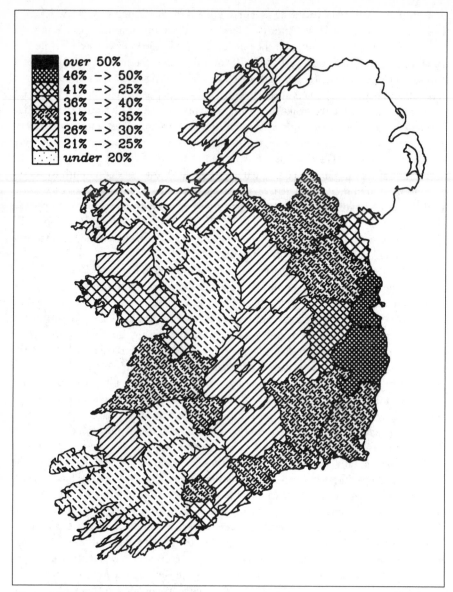

Figure 9.3 1986 divorce referendum – percentage 'yes'.

cients for farmers are 0.99 and 0.85; in the travel and information referendums, the farmer effect is somewhat lower (0.64 and 0.69) but is still substantial. The positive effect of the working-class variable on conservative voting is noticeably stronger than the farmer effect in the case of the three abortion amendments in question; it is also stronger in the case of the divorce amendment but in this case the difference between it and the farmer effect is less pronounced.

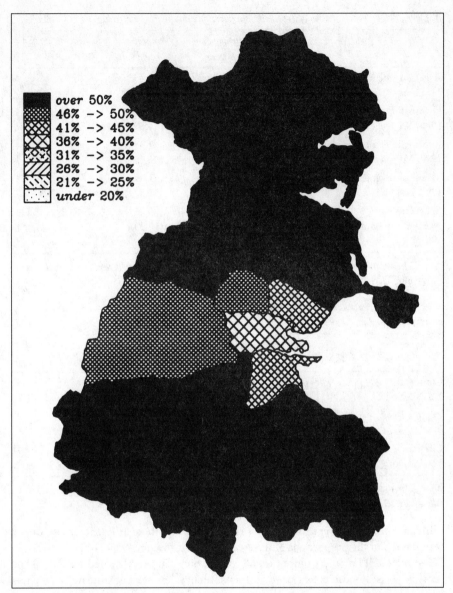

Figure 9.4 1986 divorce referendum, percentage 'yes' – Dublin constituencies.

In the case of the fifth abortion referendum, that on the substantive issue in November 1992, the predictability of the vote plummets. Only 2 per cent of the variance is explained by the model (see Table 9.3). In other words, the farmer and working-class variables tell us virtually nothing about the constituency-level sources of the 66 per cent 'no' majority on this issue. This confirms the interpretation outlined above that very different kinds of voters were voting 'no' to the substantive amendment and for very

Table 9.3: *Aggregate data analysis of voting in abortion and divorce referendums, 1983–92*

	Constant	Proportion farmers	Proportion working class	Adjusted R²	N
Abortion amendment 1983: Yes	34.76	0.99 (15.79)	1.42 (5.83)	0.86	41
Divorce amendment 1986: No	37.93	0.85 (13.41)	1.12 (4.69)	0.83	41
Information amendment 1992: No	14.97	0.64 (9.42)	1.38 (5.46)	0.71	41
Travel amendment 1992: No	9.29	0.69 (9.38)	1.59 (5.82)	0.71	41
Substantive abortion amendment 1992: No	67.35	–0.10 (–1.72)	–0.05 (–0.25)	0.02	41

Note: The main entry for each variable is the B coefficient, the figure beneath in brackets is the *t*-value. *T*-values in excess of 2.02 are significant at $p = 0.05$.

Table 9.4: *Aggregate data analysis of types of voting (conservative, pragmatist and liberal) in abortion referendums, 1992*

	Constant	Proportion farmers	Proportion working class	Adjusted R²	N
Conservatives No–No–No	1.75	0.66 (8.45)	1.58 (5.45)	0.67	41
Pragmatists Yes–Yes–Yes	25.38	0.09 (1.56)	0.03 (0.13)	0.01	41
Liberals Yes–Yes–No	3.63	–0.73 (–13.95)	–1.39 (–7.16)	0.84	41

Note: The main entry for each variable is the B coefficient, the figure beneath in brackets is the *t*-value. *T*-values in excess of 2.02 are significant at $p = 0.05$.

different reasons. However, we have also seen above that these different reasons can be teased out and the proportions of ultra-conservative, pragmatic and liberal voters can be estimated. The proportion of each type of voter can be calculated not just at the national level but also constituency by constituency, and the constituency character-istics associated with each of the three groups can therefore be analysed (Table 9.4).

In this analysis, the same model (farmers and working class) accounts for 67 per cent of the variance in the ultra-conservative (no/no/no) vote and 84 per cent of the vari-ance in the liberal (yes/yes/no) vote. Both variables have similar effects – both are pos-itively associated with ultra-conservative voting and negatively associated with liberal voting. The order of magnitude of the effects is also similar, the working-class variable having the more substantial effect in both cases. On the other hand, the model has no success at all in accounting for the pragmatic (yes/yes/yes) vote. Neither variable has a significant effect and the model explains only 1 per cent of the variance. This confirms the interpretation suggested above that the pragmatic (yes/yes/yes) vote consists of a combination of liberal pragmatists and conservative pragmatists, both voting 'yes' on travel and information and then 'yes' on the substantive issue, on the basis that it was the best that could be obtained for their respective positions. The high degree of predictability of the liberal (yes/yes/no) vote, and the fact that what determines that vote is the negative impact of the proportion of farmers and of the working class, also confirms the interpretation put forward above, i.e., that while notionally the yes/yes/no vote may have included some moderate conservatives, it was mainly a liberal vote. More generally, the analysis of these groups of ultra-conservative and liberal voters in 1992 confirms the account of the sources of voting on these issues that emerged from the analysis of the 1983 abortion and 1986 divorce votes.

Perhaps the most striking overall feature to emerge from all these analyses is that liberal and conservative voting appears to be much more rooted in the social structure of Irish society than party voting. It is as if there is a socially-structured cleavage in the society that is not expressed in the party system, but finds expression in these referendums. On the other hand, while such a socially-structured cleavage is certainly evident in referendums, it would be premature at this stage to conclude that it is unconnected with the party system. In other words, it is possible that this liberal–conservative cleavage among the voters does find at least partial expression in the pattern of party support. After all, we have seen that the farmer variable, which we now know is related to conservative voting, was also related to support for both Fianna Fáil and Fine Gael throughout the 1980s, and that in 1992 it had a marked effect on support for Fianna Fáil and Fine Gael, as against support for the parties on the left. Could it be that conservatism and liberalism are the real influences on party support and that this is the real source of the relationship between voting and the proportion of farmers in a constituency? Is this the explanation of the intensification of this relationship in 1992? This is precisely the 'crucial question' raised and postponed at the end of chapter 5.

The issue can be investigated by inserting a measure of liberalism-conservatism into the regression models used to explain party support in chapter 5. The test will be twofold: whether the inclusion of such a measure significantly improves the fit of the model, and how it affects the role of the farmer variable. For the elections of 1981 to 1989, the liberalism–conservatism measure is the proportion voting against the abortion amendment in 1983, and, for the 1992 election, it is the proportion voting yes/yes/no in the referendums held on the same day as that election. In addition, for 1992, we have a measure of ultra-conservatism, that is, the proportion voting no/no/no in the three abortion referendums of November 1992 (for the calculation of the yes/yes/no and no/no/no vote, see above). It should be emphasized that teasing out the separate effects of the proportion of farmers and the proportion of liberal or conservative voters is a complex process. This is because the two variables are themselves closely related and this imposes limitations on the ability of the statistical technique to sort out their respective influences. Despite this, however, some clarification of the relationships can be achieved.

The first point to note is that liberalism–conservatism did not have any effect on support for any of the parties in either the 1981 or February 1982 election. This is an important point, because it establishes that a farmer effect on party support existed independently of any liberal–conservative effect and regardless, therefore, of the connection between the proportion of farmers and conservative attitudes.[10] It would appear, however, that the liberal–conservative factor was activated to some extent in November 1982 and that it became a more general feature of the pattern of electoral support a decade later, that is, in the 1992 election. Because it did not affect all parties equally and at the same time, the impact of liberalism–conservatism on electoral support is best considered party-by-party.

At the outset of the November 1982 election, the issue of abortion had been defused at the level of the national campaign by Garret FitzGerald's acceptance of the text of an anti-abortion amendment published by the Fianna Fáil government just three days before the election was called (B. Farrell, 1987, p. 23). However, Farrell goes on to note that 'it surfaced in regard to some individual campaigns . . .' (*ibid.*, p. 24) and Hesketh, after a detailed consideration of the issue during the campaign, concludes that it was 'effectively neutralized . . . at national level. But . . ., it is equally clear that within some constituencies – particularly in the West – the amendment issue remained salient' (Hesketh, 1990, p. 188). In any event, elections are not just affected by what goes on within the campaign. In this respect what matters is that, because of dissension within both Fine Gael and Labour, the pro-amendment group had formed the view by the end of the summer of 1982 that their hopes of having a referendum rested with Fianna Fáil. This dependence was specifically noted in the Catholic religious press (Hesketh, 1990, pp. 136–7).

The aggregate data analysis of party support in November 1982 suggests that this dependence was also reflected in the general pattern of support for Fianna Fáil. When the liberal–conservative variable is introduced into the Fianna Fáil equation for November 1982 (in the form of the proportion of liberals, i.e., those opposing the amendment in 1983), the farmer and middle-class effects become insignificant and the main factor producing a significantly higher level of explanation of the variance in the Fianna Fáil vote is the negative impact of the proportion of liberals (or, the corollary of that, the positive impact of the proportion of conservatives). The proportion of the variance explained increases from 47 to 58 per cent (compare Tables 5.2 and 9.5). It would seem, however, that this mobilisation of conservative support behind Fianna Fáil was temporary and related to the particular circumstances of late 1982. In 1987, with the promised abortion referendum having been successfully implemented, from the conservatives' point of view, the

[10] It must be emphasized that the 1983 'no' vote is being used as a measure of an underlying characteristic of the constituencies, i.e., the extent of liberal or conservative opinion in them. This is assumed to exist independently of any referendum on such issues and could, in theory, account for the pattern of party support irrespective of whether a referendum had ever been held. On this assumption, the referendums merely reveal the underlying liberal or conservative syndrome. In fact, as the discussion in the text shows, liberalism, as measured in 1983, does help to account for party support in one of the elections prior to the referendum.

Table 9.5: *Aggregate data analysis of Fianna Fáil support, socio-demographic and liberal–conservative variables, Nov 1982 and 1992*

	Constant	Proportion farmers	Proportion middle class	Proportion liberals 1983 ('no' to abortion amendment)	Proportion liberals 1992 (Yes-Yes-No)	Donegal NE	Adjusted R^2	N
1982 Nov	57.05	0.10 (0.73)	-0.16 (-0.54)	-0.35 (-2.20)		-16.96 (-3.29)	0.58	41
1992	44.11	0.32 (2.52)	0.29 (0.83)		-0.42 (-1.97)	-8.18 (-1.57)	0.61	41

Note: The main entry for each variable is the B coefficient, the figure beneath in brackets is the *t*-value. *T*-values in excess of 2.02 are significant at $p = 0.05$.

best explanation of Fianna Fáil support reverted to the positive farmer, negative middle-class pattern established in February 1982. Then in 1989, as we have seen, the negative middle-class effect ceased and the predictability of the Fianna Fáil vote dropped substantially, and is not significantly improved by adding the liberal–conservative variable.[11] However, in the 1992 election liberalism–conservatism again played a role in the Fianna Fáil vote. Adding the proportion of liberals to the Fianna Fáil equation in 1992 produces a small but statistically significant improvement in the level of explanation (from 58 to 61 per cent).

In contrast to November 1982, however, the farmer effect does not disappear when the measure of liberalism–conservatism is added. In other words, in 1992 the Fianna Fáil vote is best accounted for in terms of the simultaneous and independent effect of the proportion of farmers (positive) and the proportion of liberals (negative) (see Table 9.5). It was noted above that the negative liberal effect in November 1982 could be interpreted also as a positive conservative effect, since the measure of the former is the proportion voting 'no' to the 1983 abortion amendment and the measure of the latter is the proportion voting 'yes'. In 1992, however, we have a more precise measure of conservatism in the form of the proportion voting 'no/no/no' in the three abortion amendments of that year, i.e., the ultra-conservatives. When this variable is inserted in the Fianna Fáil equation it has no significant effect and the overall equation does not improve on the R^2 by comparison with the equation in Table 5.2 in chapter 5. In summary, in 1992 liberal areas showed lower support for Fianna Fáil but ultra-conservative areas did not show higher support.

Turning to Fine Gael, the general measure of liberalism–conservatism (i.e., voting in the 1983 abortion referendum) does not appear to have had any significant effect on Fine Gael prior to the 1992 election. In 1992, however, when on the basis of purely socio-demographic variables, Fine Gael support is quite effectively predicted by the proportion of farmers in a constituency, entering the liberal–conservative variables into the equation does make a difference (see Table 9.6). When the 1992 measure of liberalism (i.e., voting yes/yes/no in the referendums) is added to the equation for Fine Gael, there is a significant increase in the R^2 (from 0.58 to 0.61). The farmer variable continues to play an important role, though its effect is reduced by comparison with the purely socio-demographic equation (see Table 5.3). The liberal effect itself is negative.[12] Of particular interest is the fact that the positive middle-class effect, which, as we have seen in chapter 5, dropped out of the Fine Gael equation in 1992, reappears as a substantial and significant effect. This arises because the proportion of middle class and the proportion of liberals are themselves positively related. As a consequence, the positive middle-class

[11] Only the regression equations showing significant effects are presented in Tables 9.5 to 9.8. The full set of regressions, i.e., for all the elections from 1981 to 1992 for each party is presented in Sinnott, Whelan and McBride (forthcoming), which also provides details of the statistical tests which were used to establish the significance of the effects. In the case of Fianna Fáil in the 1989 election, the liberal–conservative variable came fairly close to being significant ($p = 0.09$) but the expanded equation did not produce any significant improvement in the rather low R^2 for Fianna Fáil in that election, and the best explanation remains the proportion of farmers.

[12] The level of significance for the liberal effect on Fine Gael is 0.06, which is a fraction above the conventional cut-off point.

Table 9.6: *Aggregate data analysis of Fine Gael support, socio-demographic and liberal–conservative variables, 1992*

	Constant	Proportion farmers	Proportion middle class	Proportion liberals 1992 (Yes-Yes-No)	Proportion ultra-conservatives 1992 (No-No-No)	Adjusted R^2	N
1992	23.34	0.44 (3.21)	0.82 (2.08)	−0.44 (−1.92)		0.61	41
1992	3.97	0.53 (5.03)	0.55 (1.82)		0.29 (2.11)	0.61	41

Note: The main entry for each variable is the B coefficient, the figure beneath in brackets is the *t*-value. *T*-values in excess of 2.02 are significant at $p = 0.05$.

effect was being masked by the simultaneous negative impact of the proportion of liberals. Only when both variables are included in the model do their simulataneous and opposite effects appear. Table 9.6 presents two equations for Fine Gael in 1992. This is because, in contrast to the case of Fianna Fáil, the ultra-conservative variable does have an effect (positive) on the Fine Gael vote and, in combination with the proportion of farmers and the proportion of middle class,[13] produces the same level of variance explained as the equation that includes the negative liberal effect. In other words, the Fine Gael vote in 1992 was adversely affected by the proportion of liberals in a constituency and favourably affected by the proportion of ultra-conservatives.

Despite the foregoing indications that liberalism and conservatism were affecting support for Fianna Fáil in 1982 and 1992 and for Fine Gael in 1992, there is no evidence at the constituency level of a liberal effect on support for the Labour Party in either of these years or indeed in any of the other elections in the period examined.[14] There is evidence, however, of such an effect on support for the Workers' Party. Adding liberals to the Workers' Party/Democratic Left equations produces substantial increases in variance explained and shows significant liberal effects between November 1982 and 1989 but has no impact in 1992. In the latter election, as we have seen in chapter 5, the patterning of the Workers' Party/Democratic Left vote simply falls apart and is not reconstituted by adding the liberal–conservative variable. Apart from showing a substantial liberal effect on Workers' Party support between November 1982 and 1989, adding the liberal variable to the equations for those elections also brings out a substantially larger positive working-class effect on support for the Workers' Party than that estimated by the two variable equations used in chapter 5 (see Table 9.7).

Chapter 5 showed that support for the combined left was only very weakly structured between 1981 and 1989 but that a striking pattern emerged in 1992 when 56 per cent of the variation of the left vote can be explained in terms of the impact of a single variable – the proportion of farmers. Adding liberals to the equations alters this picture of the

[13] Note that the significance of the middle-class variable in the second equation (0.08) is above the conventional cut-off point.

[14] For details of the Labour equations see Sinnott, Whelan and McBride, forthcoming.

Table 9.7: *Aggregate data analysis of Workers' Party/Democratic Left support, socio-demographic and liberal–conservative variables, 1982–89*

	Constant	Proportion farmers	Proportion working class	Proportion liberals 1983 ('no' to abortion amendment)	Adjusted R^2	N
1982 Nov	−34.05	0.43 (1.93)	1.32 (3.70)	0.51 (2.70)	0.41	20
1987	−38.35	0.50 (2.34)	1.35 (4.57)	0.60 (3.56)	0.49	26
1989	−41.01	0.30 (0.88)	1.77 (4.35)	0.64 (2.54)	0.54	21

Note: The main entry for each variable is the B coefficient, the figure beneath in brackets is the *t*-value. *T*-values in excess of 2.02 are significant at $p = 0.05$.

combined left vote both for 1992 and for the preceding elections. The proportion of variance explained increases significantly in all four elections between November 1982 and 1992 (Table 9.8). The negative farmer effect evident in three of the four elections in the purely socio-demographic model disappears.[15] The working-class effect, which had appeared only in 1989, becomes significant for all elections and is very substantial for 1989. Finally, the liberal effect is significant and substantial throughout. Thus, when the impact of the farmer, working-class and liberal effects on the 1992 left vote are examined in combination, the degree of success in explaining the left vote is very considerable (67 per cent of variance explained), the apparent impact of the proportion of farmers is shown to be spurious and the best explanation lies in the combined positive liberal and positive working-class effects. Because the working-class and liberal variables are negatively related to each other, the positive impact of the working-class variable on the left vote is masked unless the liberal effect is included in the model.[16]

Before attempting to sum up the implications of these findings, there are two other aspects of the moral referendums of the 1980s and early 1990s that require attention. One is the vexed question of the effect of lower turnout in these referendums. The other is how to explain the dramatic reversal of opinion that occurred during the divorce referendum campaign in 1986.

An analysis of the pattern of turnout in the 1983 abortion referendum pointed out that 'other things being equal, the larger the fall in turnout in the Referendum relative

[15] In fact, in 1989 the farmer effect on left voting becomes positive when the impact of liberalism is taken into account.

[16] This aproach of adding the liberal–conservative variable to a socio-demographic equation can also be used to throw light on the issue raised at the end of the discussion of the determinants of voting in European Community referendums. The question is whether the disappearance of a pro-Europe farmer effect in the Maastricht referendum was likely to have been due to CAP reform, or to the rural conservative resistance to an alleged threat to traditional moral values. The fact that, when added to the equation, the liberal–conservative variable makes no difference to the level of explanation achieved and fails to show a significant coefficient suggests that the latter explanation can be rejected.

Table 9.8: *Aggregate data analysis of left-wing (Labour & WP/DL & Kemmy) support, socio-demographic and liberal–conservative variables, 1982–92*

	Constant	Proportion farmers	Proportion working class	Proportion liberals 1983 ('no' to abortion amendment)	Proportion liberals 1992 (Yes–Yes–No)	Adjusted R^2	N
1982 Nov	−24.81	0.32 (1.04)	1.27 (2.40)	0.56 (2.05)		0.26	36
1987	−23.93	0.30 (1.10)	0.99 (2.45)	0.58 (2.58)		0.32	34
1989	−57.55	1.16 (3.51)	2.13 (4.81)	1.10 (4.29)		0.46	29
1992	−23.11	−0.03 (−0.15)	0.97 (3.16)		0.82 (3.55)	0.67	39

Note: The main entry for each variable is the B coefficient, the figure beneath in brackets is the t-value. T-values in excess of 2.02 are significant at $p = 0.05$.

Table 9.9: *Aggregate data analysis of level of turn-out in referendums, 1983–92*

	Constant	Proportion farmers	Proportion working class	Proportion 20–29 yrs	Adjusted R^2	N
Abortion (1983)	86.99	−0.35 (−3.38)	−0.81 (−2.61)	−1.11 (−2.47)	0.23	41
Divorce (1986)	83.41	−0.22 (−3.25)	−0.39 (−1.96)	−0.95 (−3.30)	0.23	41
Single European Act (1987)	60.73	−0.24 (−3.39)	−0.67 (−3.71)	−0.34 (−1.31)	0.33	41
Maastricht (1992)	70.58	−0.20 (−2.76)	−0.47 (−2.55)	−0.31 (−1.21)	0.19	41

Note: The main entry for each variable is the B coefficient, the figure beneath in brackets is the t-value. T-values in excess of 2.02 are significant at $p = 0.05$.

to the General Election, the higher the 'yes' vote as a percentage of those voting'. Having considered various interpetations of this relationship, Walsh concluded: 'The most important general conclusion from the study is that the level of support for the amendment in the population seems to have been higher than that indicated in the referendum results' (Walsh, 1984a, p. 233). This analysis provoked a strenuous critical reaction, which began by questioning the validity of attempting to allocate a preference to those who did not vote and went on to argue that 'there is no basis in fact or logic' for the conclusion drawn (O'Donnell and Brannick, 1984, p. 68). The argument that one should not even inquire into the probable preferences of those who did not vote would seem to be unduly agnostic and can be set to one side. The argument that the evidence is inconclusive is more difficult to resolve on the basis of the evidence presented (but see Walsh, 1984b). The most useful approach, therefore, may be to bring some additional evidence to bear on the matter, such as the evidence of the socio-structural determinants of the pattern of turnout and abstention. Table 9.9 presents this evidence for the 1983 abortion referendum, the 1986 divorce referendum and two EC referendums (the SEA in 1987 and Maastricht in 1992). The pattern of turnout in these referendums is quite different from the pattern of turnout in general elections (compare Table 5.6). In the first place, the level of variance explained is much lower in the case of referendum turnout. Secondly, whereas the main determinant of turnout in general elections is the negative effect of high proportions of young people, with the proportion of farmers and the proportion of working class having only intermittent effects, all three factors (age, proportion of farmers and working class) affect referendum turnout. Thirdly, the proportion of farmers has a consistently opposite effect on referendum turnout compared to its occasional effect on turnout in general elections – in the 1981 and 1989 general elections it led to increases in turnout; in all four referendums considered it was associated with lower turnout.

Consideration of constituency rates of abstention in referendums (measured by the difference between referendum turnout and turnout in the previous general election) throws considerable light on the above contrasts (Table 9.10). High concentrations of young people, which tend to depress turnout in general elections, either have no effect on the rate of abstention in referendums relative to general elections or, in the case of the divorce and Single European Act referendums, actually reduce it. In contrast to this, in all four referendums, abstention was higher in areas with high proportions of farmers and, with the exception of the divorce referendum, in more working-class areas. From this it would appear that farming areas and working-class areas tend to show less inter-

Table 9.10: *Aggregate data analysis of abstention in referendums (i.e. change in turnout from previous election), 1983–92*

	Constant	Proportion farmers	Proportion working class	Proportion 20–29 yrs	Adjusted R^2	N
Abortion 1983 (decline compared with November 1982)	10.07	0.46 (5.04)	0.52 (1.93)	–0.32 (–0.82)	0.56	41
Divorce (decline compared with November 1982)	13.65	0.32 (7.51)	0.10 (0.80)	–0.48 (–2.60)	0.80	41
Single European Act (decline compared with 1987)	35.77	0.24 (4.49)	0.32 (2.37)	–0.87 (–4.53)	0.79	41
Maastricht (decline compared with 1989)	4.88	0.42 (8.75)	0.30 (2.52)	–0.18 (–1.04)	0.83	41

Note: The main entry for each variable is the B coefficient, the figure beneath in brackets is the *t*-value. *T*-values in excess of 2.02 are significant at $p = 0.05$.

est in referendums as compared with general elections, whether the referendum issue is a moral one or one related to the European Community. The relative lack of interest in the Single European Act and in the Maastricht referendums in farming areas is interesting, but the primary interest in the present context lies in the factors affecting the rate of abstention in referendums on moral issues. Walsh's argument was that abstention was likely to be associated with support for the amendment and that therefore, if the turnout had been higher, the 'yes' vote in 1983 would have been higher. Obviously, one cannot provide definitive proof and the foregoing analysis is subject to all of the qualifications attaching to ecological analysis. However, the results are at least compatible with Walsh's conclusion, in so far as they show that the determinants of abstention in the 1983 abortion referendum were quite similar to the determinants of the conservative vote. Of course, it is quite possible that this arose because non-conservatives in such areas abstained rather than voting against, and in this sense O'Donnell and Brannick's observation that abstention is a legitimate option in itself is relevant. However, the fact is that abstention also tends to be higher in other kinds of referendums in such areas, and hence cannot be put down to a specific impulse to abstain in the abortion referendum, such as might arise from a wish to protest against the holding of the referendum or from confusion regarding the specific issue. Perhaps the best way of putting the matter is to say that if the two opposing sides in the 1983 referendum had set out to increase their support by ensuring the highest possible turnout, the pro-amendment side would have been trawling in more congenial waters.

Turning to the problem of the reversal of opinion in the 1986 divorce referendum, the first point to be made is that such a reversal is not unique in referendums. Reversals of similar magnitude have occurred in referendums on water fluoridation and on the equal rights amendment in the United States, suggesting the existence of a 'pervasive referendum dynamic' (Darcy and Laver, 1990, p. 9). Clearly, if such a dynamic exists, it would have implications for our understanding of the determinants of the Irish vote on divorce. There is indeed some evidence of a tendency for conservative instincts to assert themselves in referendums (Butler and Ranney, 1978, *passim*). Faced with the uncertainties of change, voters opt for the status quo. This is particularly so if the opponents of change manage to raise doubts in the voters' minds about the consequences of the government's specific proposals.

Darcy and Laver argue that this was clearly the case in the Irish 1986 divorce referendum, and that the reversal of opinion was 'a shift away from the details of one specific proposal, not a shift away from support for divorce itself'. They argue, however, that this is not a sufficient explanation as it simply raises a new question – why do doubts about change become effective in some referendums and not in others? Their answer focuses on the phenomenon of elite withdrawal in the face of pervasive community conflict and a querulous campaign, run mainly by *ad hoc* groups and raising issues related to deeply-held ideological beliefs (Darcy and Laver, 1990, pp. 15–16). This description certainly fits the facts of the divorce campaign. In emphasizing the ideological dimension of the conflict, it also presents a more rounded and credible explanation than the one that was advanced with some frequency at the time – that the basis of the anti-divorce victory was concern about property rights and the purely economic issues raised by divorce. If that had been the basis of the change in the voters' attitudes, it would be difficult to account for the fact that the constituency configuration of opposition to divorce was so similar to the configuration of support for the clearly moral–ideological proposal to insert an anti-abortion clause into the Constitution in 1983. Finally, the identification of a 30-30-30 breakdown of opinion on the particular abortion issues in November 1992 may throw some retrospective light on the change of attitude in 1986. That change is more understandable if we see Irish society as being divided not into two monolithic camps (a two-thirds conservative majority and a one-third liberal minority), but three ways: ultra-conservatives, liberals and pragmatists. The existence of the latter group, which has the potential to be persuaded either way, would then help to account for the voters' change of mind in 1986. If this was a factor in 1986, then clearly the campaign in any future referendum on this or related issues will be crucial.[17]

Conclusion

Despite quite limited explicit grounds in the Irish Constitution for the holding of referendums, direct referral of issues to the voters has been quite frequent and the range of issues dealt with has been wide. The reason has been the combination of a highly specific constitution and a society undergoing rapid social, economic, and political change and existing in a changing international environment. In this process, major debates have occurred on the electoral system in the late 1950s and 1960s, on the European Community in 1972, 1987 and 1992, and on religious–moral issues in 1983, 1986 and 1992. Looked at in terms of stability and change, the outcomes at the end of these debates have varied depending on the nature of the change in question. The electoral system debate is difficult to categorise in terms of stability versus change, but the fact is that those seeking to defend the status quo (proportional representation) won through on both occasions. When the issue was Ireland's relationship to the international environment, change was at first resoundingly approved, and subsequently somewhat lethargically endorsed. On the six religious–moral issues, the picture has been mixed. The status quo has been affirmed or reaffirmed by clear majorities on two major issues – abortion (1983) and divorce (1986). Change has been endorsed by equally clear majorities on three other issues, though it could be argued that these are less crucial and testing ones (the 'special position' of the Catholic Church and the rights to travel and information). Finally, on the remaining issue (the substantive issue in 1992), a coalition of those opposed to change and those in favour of change decisively defeated a proposal that in the eyes of the former opened the floodgates, and in the eyes of the latter put the clock back to 1983 or beyond.

The fact that the voters were simultaneously faced with three issues in the referendums of November 1992 makes it possible to obtain a more nuanced picture of the range and distribution of opinion on these moral issues than the picture that would

[17] A necessary qualification to this argument is that the 30-30-30 breakdown of opinion in 1992 may be a function of the specific way in which the abortion-related issues were defined in the three referendums, and may, therefore, hold no implications for other moral–religious issues.

result if one simply focused on the large (two-thirds) conservative majorities in the 1983 and 1986 abortion and divorce referendums. Based on the results of the 1992 referendums, it appears that in this area, Irish voters are divided roughly three ways (virtually, 30-30-30) between ultra-conservatives, pragmatists and liberals, with the remaining one-tenth or slightly more expressing mixed preferences that cannot be categorised in these terms.

The determinants of conservative voting in the religious–moral sphere are remarkably clear and consistent. Between 1983 and 1992, areas with high levels of farmers and of the working class supported the conservative position in each of the individual votes or combinations of votes that can be categorised in liberal–conservative terms. It is notable indeed that referendum voting on such issues is much more highly structured than party voting. However, it would be wrong to conclude from this that referendum voting is something quite separate and distinct from the party system. In the first place, in two elections (November 1982 and 1992), liberalism–conservatism had clearly identifiable effects on the pattern of party support. In November 1982 it displaced the farmer effect in the cases of Fianna Fáil, the Workers' Party and the combined left. In 1992, its effect was more pervasive – liberal areas showing particularly low support for Fianna Fáil and Fine Gael, and high support for the combined left parties (but not influencing either of the main left parties considered separately). Ultra-conservative areas also showed high support for Fine Gael (but not for Fianna Fáil). The levels of explanation resulting from application of these models to the 1992 election are impressive. They are not, however, due solely to the influence of conservatism–liberalism. Firstly, in 1992 the proportion of farmers continues to affect Fianna Fáil and Fine Gael support, even when account is taken of liberalism and ultra-conservatism. Secondly, including liberalism and conservatism in the model and thus holding their effects constant clarifies the class effect on voting in that election, that is, the positive middle-class effect on Fine Gael, and the positive working-class effect on the combined left vote.

In the November 1982 election there is a fairly obvious explanation for the impact of liberalism–conservatism on party support, given the way in which the conflict about holding an abortion referendum was played out. Its impact in 1992 is less easily explained in terms of the explicit politics of the election campaign and of the accompanying referendums. In fact, in 1992 Fianna Fáil put forward a compromise position on the issues raised by the X case, a position that was explicitly rejected by the conservative campaigners. In theory, the proportion of liberals and ultra-conservatives ought to have had a negative effect on Fianna Fáil support and the proportion of pragmatists ought to have had a positive effect. In fact, only the first of these relationships was confirmed. Fine Gael put forward a liberal position, yet its vote was negatively affected by the proportion of liberals and positively affected by the proportion of ultra-conservatives. Apart from the X case and the referendums arising from it, the other potentially significant event since the previous general election was of course the 1990 presidential election. Could it have instigated at least a partial mobilisation of the liberal–conservative cleavage, which was then carried forward into the November 1992 general election? The next chapter explores voting in second-order elections and, in the context of discussing the 1990 presidential election, pays particular attention to this question.

Chapter 10

Second-order elections: contrasts and connections

Second-order elections

The key to understanding second-order elections derives from the simple observation that there is less at stake – such elections do not determine the distribution of power at the crucial national decision-making level. The concept of second-order elections has been used mainly in the study of European Parliament elections. However, it is clear that the concept has both wider origins and wider applicability, and is certainly worth bearing in mind when analysing local and regional elections and by-elections and, in the Irish case, presidential elections. According to this approach, the fact that power at the national level is not at stake leads to lower levels of participation, a higher percentage of invalid ballots, a tendency for government parties to lose and brighter prospects for new and small political parties (Reif and Schmitt, 1980, pp. 9–10). To say that there is less at stake is not to say that there is nothing at stake, and second-order elections will vary in the extent to which they simply reflect national issues, such as the popularity of the incumbent government, or are determined by issues specific to the particular area, be it local, European or presidential. Also, the issue of mid-term unpopularity must be distinguished from any longer-term trends that may be occurring in the main political arena. If real shifts in voting preferences are occurring between two first-order elections, these may affect voting in an intervening second-order election in a way that is not reducible to the mid-term dip in the popularity curve that characterises many governments' tenure of office.

Apart from the question of what is at stake, second-order elections can also differ in other respects. Thus, institutional-procedural differences may have an impact if, for example, different voting procedures are used in the first order and second-order arenas (Reif and Schmitt, 1980, pp. 12–13). In Ireland the same voting procedure is used for all elections, except in the case of the presidency, where because there is only one seat in contention, the system is not (despite what the Constitution says) 'the system of proportional representation by means of the single transferable vote' (Article 12.2.3) (it is actually the alternative vote system). The fact that there is only a single seat in contention may also have the effect of polarising the contest and of adding to its symbolic partisan value.

Differences in institutional context also have an effect on Irish local elections. First, those elected at local level constitute the electoral college for the majority of the seats in the Senate. Secondly, local office-holding is a major route of entry to national politics. For these reasons local elections in Ireland are much more competitive than one would expect if one simply focused on how much is at stake in terms of the immediate distribution of power.

A further factor that gives rise to variations in second-order elections and must therefore be taken into account is rooted in the strategy and tactics of political elites. An example in the Irish case is the way in which both the local and European elections of 1979 were consciously used by Fine Gael as a stage in the FitzGerald-led revitalisation of the party. Of course, despite the tendency for opposition parties to make use of second-order elections for party strategic purposes, it does not follow that poor performance by the governing party necessarily benefits the main opposition party or parties. As noted above, an alternative effect of second-order status is the boost that may be given to the fortunes of small or new parties. In the light of the strong tradition of independent representation in Ireland even in first-order elections, it is to be expected that, in a second-order election, the prospects for independents will also be better.

The study of second-order elections in Ireland is not sufficiently well advanced to permit a rigorous application of the above approach. Indeed, the approach itself may not be sufficiently well developed to support such an endeavour (see the cautionary remarks by Reif and Schmitt, 1980, p. 15). Nonetheless, it provides some useful ideas with which to approach a preliminary overview of voting behaviour in elections of this type.

By-elections

For the most part, by-elections are the ultimate second-order elections. They are intensely particular and local affairs and, at the same time, they are usually considered to be barometers of mid-term government popularity – a classic second-order election characteristic. On the other hand, in relatively rare circumstances, a great deal can be at stake. The fate of a government can hinge on a by-election. In other words, by-elections can reach or come close to first-order status. Such cases are, however, exceptional and the basic question is: does by-election voting behaviour in fact exhibit standard second-order election effects, for example, swings against the government or better than average performances by small parties?

By-election results pose tricky interpretative problems. In any given inter-election period, a particular party may appear to do very badly in by-elections in comparison to its national election performance, but this may simply reflect the fact that all or most of the by-elections in question have occurred in areas in which support for that party is weak. Some parties, and, as will be apparent in a moment, not just small ones, may not run candidates in all of the by-elections, thus greatly depressing their by-election total for that inter-election period.[1] Finally, there is the distortion of any

[1] For small-party and especially for independent candidates, the fact that the electoral system in a by-election is normally the alternative vote system with a quota of 50 per cent plus one (see chapter 1) is a distinct disincentive to putting themselves forward.

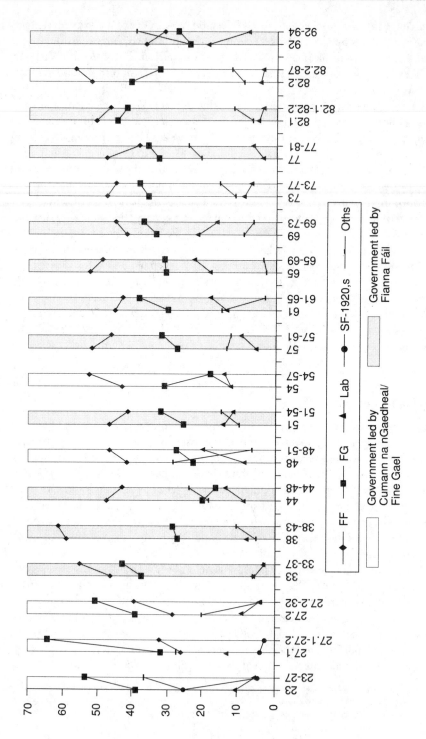

Figure 10.1 Party share of the vote in general and by-elections, 1923–94.

pro-government/anti-government swing in the not-infrequent situation of one of the candidates being a close relative of the deceased incumbent (for a discussion of the impact of this candidate selection strategy, see Gallagher, 1994).

It is possible to control for at least some of the effects of these special features of by-elections by comparing by-election results in any given period not to the overall result in the previous general election, but to the general election result in the constituencies in which contests occurred in the subsequent by-elections. This is done for by-elections since 1923 in Figure 10.1. Each bar in the graph presents a comparison between a party's performance in a given set of by-elections (the right-hand point of the line) with the party's performance in the same constituencies in the previous general election (the left-hand point). Since the purpose is to compare by-election performance to performance in the previous general election, general elections that were not followed by a by-election or by-elections are omitted from the graph.

Application of this approach to by-election performance since the 1920s indicates some general trends. The overall outline of by-election support for Fianna Fáil and Cumann na nGaedheal/Fine Gael is not dissimilar to that of the graph of each party's general election support. Thus Cumann na nGaedheal remains dominant up to and including the by-elections of the 1927–32 period, though the gap between it and Fianna Fáil is obviously closing. In the 1933–37 by-elections, Fianna Fáil established and subsequently maintained a predominant position. Fine Gael came close to Fianna Fáil in the by-elections of 1961–65 and 1982, but its low points of national support in 1948, 1957 and 1987 are also reflected in by-election performance in the preceding inter-election period.[2]

A striking feature of the trends in party support in by-elections is the contrasting pattern in the direction the lines take before and after 1943–44. In all the sets of by-elections between 1923 and 1943, the two main parties, Sinn Féin/Fianna Fáil and Cumann na nGaedheal/Fine Gael, increased their share of the vote in comparison to the vote they had won in the same constituencies in the previous election. This of course meant that the party in government increased its share of the vote in each of these sets of by-elections. This is certainly not the kind of pattern one would associate with second-order elections, in which, according to the model, governments are supposed to lose votes. The spell was broken in the 1944–48 period, and the timing points to the simple explanation for the contrast: in the early years the smaller parties and independents, very much in evidence in general elections, were much less likely to contest by-elections.

The post-1944 pattern fits in better with the second-order model. With just a few exceptions, the party in government lost votes, the gains made at its expense being divided between the second major party and the minor parties and independents, depending on the circumstances. Government losses were occasionally severe and delivered a real shock to the system. Thus Fianna Fáil emerged from the three by-elections of the 1977–81 period with an average of 37 per cent of the vote. They were only

---

[2] Part of the reason for Fine Gael's low overall by-election performance in 1944–48 and 1954–57 was the fact that the party did not contest all the by-elections that were held.

by-elections and in two of them Fianna Fáil was faced with strong 'other' candidates (representing Sinn Féin The Worker's Party in one case and Independent Fianna Fáil in the other). Nevertheless, coming after the disastrous European Parliament and local election performances of June 1979, they had considerable impact, the first two (in November 1979) precipitating the departure of Jack Lynch as Taoiseach. These two contests may have been second-order elections but they certainly had first-order effects.

By-elections between 1982 and 1987 also saw substantial losses by the Fine Gael-Labour coalition, mainly by Fine Gael. However, Fianna Fáil's 52.9 per cent of the first preference vote over these three by-elections was not a sign of impending return to single-party dominance. The remarkably high Fianna Fáil vote was partly a function of the fact that the three vacancies had been created by the deaths of three Fianna Fáil deputies and in two of these cases the Fianna Fáil candidate was a close relative of the deceased deputy. It was also, however, partly a swing against the incumbent government, which was confirmed in local elections in 1985 (see below) and from which Fine Gael in particular failed to recover in the 1987 general election.

Acknowledging the difficulties of disentangling the various factors that affect by-election outcomes, one can summarise the major trends in by-election results in three observations. First, the pattern tends to be in accord with long-run trends in overall party support. Secondly, the period since 1944 has seen a strong tendency for by-elections to act in classic second-order fashion, that is to reflect mid-term swings against the government, a pattern confirmed again in four by-elections in 1994, when the main beneficiary, in terms of first preference votes, was Democratic Left. In contrast, and this is the third observation, by-elections in the period up to 1943 were quite unlike second-order elections – government and the main opposition party both gained as minor parties and independents tended to stand on the sidelines, and by-elections reflected the underlying cleavage in the system and the shifting balance of support around it. However, it must again be emphasized that by-elections are peculiar because they are so particular – much depends on where and in what circumstances the vacancies occur.

Local elections

The structure of Irish local government is an inheritance from British local government reforms that were applied to Ireland in the late nineteenth century. The county is the most important unit of local government, the twenty-six county councils being augmented by the sub-division of one county (Tipperary) into two units (North Riding and South Riding) and the creation of separate administrations (borough counties) at a sub-county level in the four counties with large urban populations (Dublin, Cork, Waterford and Limerick). In addition to this tier of local government, there is a lower tier of representative authorities in smaller urban areas (borough corporations, urban district councils and town commissioners). There had originally been a set of rural district councils, but these were abolished and their powers transferred to the county councils in the 1920s.

The powers of local government, even of its most important tier, the county and county borough councils, are very limited. Its range of functions is highly restricted, the main area of local responsibility being the physical infrastructure, in the sense of public housing, roads, water supply, the sewerage system, and public recreation facilities. In addition, county councils have some secondary functions in the areas of education, health and welfare, but these are subordinate to the role of various specialised agencies in each of these areas. The establishment of single-function agencies at regional or national level and the transfer to them of functions formerly allocated to local authorities has been one, but only one, of the processes by which local autonomy has been diluted over the years (for a discussion of the functions of local government and the relationship between local government and various processes of regionalisation, see Coyle and Sinnott, 1992, pp. 73–82). Two other important elements in the general trend towards centralisation have been the establishment in the 1930s of a county managerial system, in which a centrally appointed chief executive for each county and county borough largely dominates the policy-making process, and secondly, the increasing dependence of local authorities on central government for funds. The latter trend was greatly reinforced in the late 1970s with the abolition of rates (a local property tax) on domestic dwellings and on land.

Despite the relative powerlessness of local government, local elections are, for the reasons suggested above, quite party-competitive. Turnout is relatively high, relative that is to the minimal amount of power actually exercised by the local councils (see chapter 3). The pattern of party support at local elections from 1960 to 1991 is remarkably clear. The first aspect of that pattern is that the Fianna Fáil vote fell well below its national average in five of the six local elections in the period (see Figure 10.2).[3] Since Fianna Fáil was in government for four of these five elections, the trend is in line with one of the expectations derived from the second-order elections approach, i.e., governments do badly. On the one occasion on which the Fianna Fáil vote rose (the 1985 local elections), the party was in opposition and the elections were clearly a mid-term test of government popularity. Admittedly, the party was also in opposition during the 1974 local elections and its vote fell. A possible explanation may be that the coalition government elected in February 1973 was still a new face after sixteen years of Fianna Fáil government and was still enjoying a honeymoon period, and that therefore the customary second-order election swing against the government did not occur. In fact, there was a slight swing against the government parties and the point about the main opposition party not benefiting from such a swing is consistent with the second-order model.

Also consistent with this feature is the slight tendency for Fine Gael local election support to be less than its support in the preceding general election, even when it is not in government. However, on one of the occasions when it was in government, the decline in its support (in the 1985 local election relative to the November 1982 general election) was dramatic and heralded the collapse of Fine Gael support nationally in 1987. In this case it seems that any mid-term swing against the government was

---

[3] Because of the lack of available data, this analysis of trends in local elections begins with 1960. For a discussion of the 1934 local elections, which despite the restricted franchise were of considerable partisan significance, see Manning, 1972, pp. 128–36.

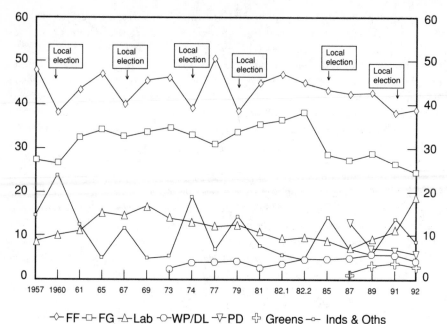

Figure 10.2 Party share of the vote in local and national elections, 1957–92.

compounded by the more long-term decline in support for Fine Gael between 1982 and 1987. In the case of Labour, local election performance since 1960 does not diverge markedly from previous general election performance; rather it seems for the most part to reflect the trend in Labour Party support in the surrounding general elections and to be part of an overall pattern.

The second feature of Irish local elections then is the swing to the category of 'independents and others' that has occurred in every local election in the period analysed.[4] A glance at Figure 10.2 shows the remarkable consistency of this swing – the vote for 'independents and others' rises by much the same amount at each local election and falls back by a more or less equal amount at the next general election, regardless of whether the period is one in which independents are doing badly in general elections (the late 1960s and early 1970s), or one in which they are doing moderately well (the late 1980s and early 1990s). The explanation for the consistent success of independents presumably relates both to the nature of the issues that are specific to this second-order electoral arena, and to the fact that the absolute number of votes required to be elected in a local election run on a PR-STV basis is quite low.

[4] For the most part this category consists of pure independents. It also includes minor parties other than those listed separately in Figure 10.2. Unfortunately, in the 1960 local election it is not possible, on the basis of available information, to separate support for the remnants of the minor parties of the 1940s and 1950s from support for independents. Accordingly, the figure of 25 per cent support for 'independents and others' in 1960 may not reflect the level of support for independent candidates as accurately as it does in later contests, when support for minor party candidates was minimal or can be separately identified.

European Parliament elections

As noted above, the second-order election concept has been developed and employed primarily in an attempt to understand European Parliament elections. European Parliament (EP) elections in Ireland certainly fit the bill. There is very little at stake in terms of the distribution of power. They lack the particular partisan significance of an Irish presidential election and the political recruitment and Senate electoral college functions associated with local government elections. One consequence has already been noted, viz., exceptionally low turnout in the two EP elections in which turnout was not boosted by a more competitive contest (1984 and 1994) (see chapter 3). An expected consequence is that voting in European Parliament elections would tend to reflect the trend in support for the parties domestically, and be particularly subject to mid-term anti-government swings.

On the other hand, there are reasons to expect that European Parliament elections will not be reducible to a mid-term government popularity test. A unique character-istic of European Parliament elections is the fact that they transcend national bound-aries. On the basis of this characteristic, Reif and Schmitt put forward the hypothesis that 'the legitimacy of parties playing a role in what traditionally has been the arena of diplomats thinking in terms of national, and not of partisan, interests, might be less' (Reif and Schmitt, 1980, p. 11). This could be expected to lead to a lower inclination to vote for parties as such, an inclination that might manifest itself in voting either for independents, or in deserting one's usual party to vote for a 'big name' candidate put forward by one of the other parties. The expectation that there may be what one might describe as an 'ambassadorial effect' is reinforced by qualitative research carried out for Fine Gael in the run-up to the first European Parliament elections in 1979, which showed that 'candidates ideally should be: well-known people with negotiating strength and ability, articulate and knowledgeable in European affairs, imbued with the culture and interests of Ireland, and not necessarily aligned with a political party'. The research report for Fine Gael goes on to note that the 'quality of person' criterion in regard to the selection of candidates was subsequently confirmed in a national sample survey conducted as part of the same campaign preparations (MRBI, 1979). Candidate selection in European Parliament elections generally has confirmed that the parties have absorbed this lesson. Indeed, the systematic and extensive application of the lesson in the run-up to the 1994 election led to considerable controversy about what became known as 'parachuting' (i.e. the inclusion of a prominent individual with little or no previous party experience on the party ticket, the inclusion usually being made at the behest of party headquarters).

Over and above this 'quality of candidate' issue, it is arguable that criticisms to the effect that European issues do not figure more prominently in European Parliament election campaigns may be based on unrealistic expectations. For European issues to figure prominently, voters would have to regard the issue in question as salient, the parties would have to hold different positions on the issue and the voters would have to form an accurate perception of the differences between the parties. In practice, European issues are relatively remote and are, for the most part, a matter of inter-party consensus. However, certain European issues have been raised in the European Parliament election campaigns to date. These have related mainly to the institutional development of the Community, to the question of Irish neutrality and to the Community policy that has the most obvious impact on Ireland – the Common Agricultural Policy. Institutional issues, in particular the role of the Parliament, and CAP issues figured in the first direct election (Carty, 1981). In 1984 the two main parties again differed on the question of the appropriate role of the European Parliament. On the other hand, both agreed on an extension of qualified majority voting in the Council of Ministers, a proposal that was opposed by Labour. Defence issues were only occasionally mentioned, and then only to reiterate Ireland's position of neutrality (Collins, 1984, pp. 32–3). In 1989, the neutrality issue was somewhat more prominent and environmental issues, the reform of the Common Agricultural Policy and the issue of Structural Funds were also raised (Holmes, 1990, p. 87). In 1994 there were complaints in the media that the election was the most issue-less so far. On the other hand, the success of the Greens in that election suggests that certain issues may have had a subterranean effect. Although some inter-party differences can be detected on the issues that have been raised, they have rarely if ever been such as to be likely to sway large numbers of voters. We are left then with two factors – underlying trends in party support based on national political issues, on the one hand, and European candidate-specific considerations (the ambassadorial effect), on the other – as the most likely determinants of voting behaviour in European Parliament elections.

Figure 10.3 shows the results of European Parliament elections between 1979 and 1994, together with the results of general elections since 1977. The expectations derived from the second-order concept are generally confirmed. The share of the vote of the parties in government has tended to be noticeably lower than in the previous – or, in the case of 1989, the concomitant – general election. Parties in government do badly but the main opposition parties do not necessarily gain. The exception to this is Fine Gael in 1979 – it was then clearly the main opposition party and its vote did increase by comparison with the previous general election. However, 1977 had been a low point for Fine Gael and the European election recovery still left it with a share of the national vote that was slightly below its share in the 1973 general election. In 1994 the Fine Gael vote held steady by comparison with its general election vote in 1992.

As a corollary of all of this, small parties and independents have done better in European Parliament elections. There are three clear peaks for the independents (1979, 1984, 1989), and 1994, though down somewhat, was higher for independents than any of the general elections in Figure 10.3. The small parties have also done well. The Labour Party increased its vote in 1979; in 1984, despite being in government, it suffered only a minor fall in comparison with its level of support in the previous general election. In 1989 its European vote was considerably better than its 1987 vote, and on a par with its concomitant general election recovery. Its substantial fall in 1994 may be in part a reflection of the size of its vote in 1992 and of its size or weight in government. The favourable small-party effect is more evident in the case of the Workers' Party, the Progressive Democrats prior to 1994 and the Greens. Thus, the Progressive Democrats did as well in the European election of 1989 as they had in their dramatic electoral debut

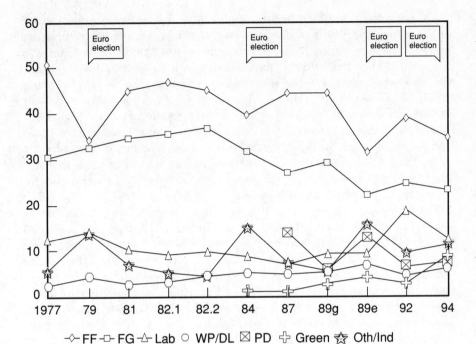

Figure 10.3 Party share of the vote in general and European Parliament elections, 1977–94.

in 1987; this of course meant that their 1989 Euro-vote was way ahead of their vote in the general election in 1989. And although they were generally regarded as having done badly in 1994, their actual vote was higher than in the 1992 general election. Similarly, the Workers' Party/Democratic Left has done better in each of the Euro-elections than in the preceding or following general election. This effect was particularly noticeable in 1989 *vis-à-vis* any of the three points of comparison one might choose – 1987, the 1989 general election, or 1992. Of course, what we are observing here in the case of Labour, the Progressive Democrats and the Workers' Party/Democratic Left is partly the fact that in European elections the parties in question have run candidates in all four constituencies; this has given them a country-wide coverage that they do not necessarily have in general elections. These general comments on the trends shown in Figure 10.3 must face the question: what should European election outcomes be compared with, general elections or European elections? They should be compared with both, with care being taken as to the inferences being drawn. Given the different levels of turnout, one has to be particularly careful about making sweeping generalisations about the decline in support for a given party on the basis of its Euro-election performance. Fianna Fáil and Labour did badly in the Euro-election of 1994, relative to the preceding general election. Given a 44 per cent turnout, this cannot be taken as evidence that support for either of them has collapsed. And there is a second qualification to be made – the national trends must be considered at a constituency, that is, at a regional level.

The favourable trends for this or that smaller party have been more pronounced in some constituencies than in others and have also varied somewhat over time (see Figure 10.4). Labour's moderately good performance nationally in the first European Parliament election was in fact limited to an outstanding performance in Dublin, which saw the election of two prominent Labour Party personalities – John O'Connell and Michael O'Leary. In 1989 also the improvement in left-wing prospects was mainly a Dublin phenomenon; the quite impressive Green performance was confined to Dublin and Leinster. Again in 1992, the Green break-through was in Dublin and Leinster (this time producing two seats for the party). The Progressive Democrat recovery in the European election of 1989 (relative, that is, to the considerable fall in its vote in the general election), was much more evident in Munster and in Connacht-Ulster than in the other two constituencies.

The strong showing of independents has been limited to two constituencies – Munster and Connacht-Ulster and to one case in one of the other constituencies – Dublin in 1984. Connacht-Ulster has had a long tradition of substantial support for independent candidates (see Figure 5.4 in chapter 5). On the other hand, Munster has been fairly barren territory for independents in general elections, yet it returned a very substantial independent vote in all four Euro-elections under consideration and caused a major upset in 1994 by returning incumbent MEP Pat Cox at the expense of his former party leader and colleague Des O'Malley. Cox had been elected for the Progressive Democrats in 1989, but in 1992 ran as an independent. The pattern suggests that whether independents thrive in European Parliament elections depends on who they are and what they stand for.

Independents are defined as 'non-party' but, in addition to their reputation and visibility based on some prior public role, they have tended also to be identified with a position on some issue or other. In this sense, the major independents in European Parliament elections can be classified as 'interest group' independents and 'political tendency' independents. The interest groups indirectly represented in this way can be a specific organised economic interest, as in the case of former Irish Farmers' Association president T. J. Maher, or a 'cause', such as in the case of Sean D. Dublin Bay Loftus in 1979 and 1984. Political tendency independents can be subdivided into 'nationalist' (Blaney in Connacht-Ulster in the three elections between 1979 and 1989 and Ryan in Munster in 1989) and 'Euro-critical' (Crotty in Dublin in 1989).[5] Maher and Blaney had sufficient stature on the national political scene and sufficient issue-identifiability to succeed in winning seats (Maher in 1979, 1984 and 1989 and Blaney in 1979 and 1989). Cox in Munster in 1994 might seem to be the exception and his election certainly had many exceptional features. However, given his Progressive Democrat background, the fact that he was a prominent incumbent MEP means that he conforms to the generalisation that success for independents depends on prior stature, position and visibility.

A second-order election that coincides with a general election is a special and

---

[5] Another prominent anti-EC activist, Noonan, ran in the Munster constituency in 1989 but won only 3.2 per cent of the vote. For details on candidates and campaigns in each constituency in 1989 and some background on the two previous elections see the various chapters in Hainsworth, 1992.

rather interesting case. It is interesting because the coincidence removes the mid-term election effect from the second-order contest and may therefore allow other issues to emerge. The outstanding feature of the 1989 European Parliament results is the extent of 'split ticket voting', that is voting for one party in the general election and for another in the European election. This is evident from the different performances of the parties in the two elections, and can be summarised by applying Pedersen's index of volatility. The index in this case is based on the sum of the absolute differences between each party's support in each election. The result for the two 1989 elections is 20. Comparing this with the general level of the index of volatility between successive general elections (see Figure 4.5) shows that voters departed from their regular voting pattern much more between the general and European election of 1989 than they tend to do between general elections. Moreover, if we apply the same index to the combined local and European elections in 1979, the result is 12.4. The greater concordance between the local and European elections in 1979, as compared to that between the national and European elections of 1989 lends support to the second-order election approach. That is, on the basis of the model, one would have predicted greater concordance in 1979 as both contests took on the character of mid-term elections. In 1989, however, the general election provided the ultimate and decisive opportunity for voters to vent their frustration on the government if they so wished. Thus, voters could split their ticket – voting on domestic issues in the general election and on some other criteria in the European Parliament election. Paradoxically, the European Parliament election of 1989, in which European concerns may appear to have been most swamped by the national first-order contest during the campaign, may have been the most European of the four European Parliament elections considered here. In regard to the other three elections, however, one should not underestimate the European dimension. The success of the Greens and the considerable evidence of 'personality voting' (better thought of perhaps as ambassadorial voting) may not reflect European issues as we conventionally think of them. On the other hand, they may point to some degree of European perspective in the minds of the voters.

Presidential elections

The main function of the President as specified in the Irish Constitution is to be a formal Head of State, who in most things acts on the advice of some other person or body, most often the Taoiseach or the government. However, in a number of areas the President has certain discretionary powers. All of them can be thought of as arising from the fact that the office of President is part of the legislative process – in the words of the Constitution: 'The Oireachtas [the National Parliament] shall consist of the President and two Houses [Dáil and Seanad]' (Article 15.1.2). Three of the powers relate to the protection of the rights of the Senate and to dealing with situations of conflict or potential conflict between the two houses. The most substantial of the three, the power to decide whether an issue should be referred to the people in a referendum, has already been discussed above, a discussion that underlined the reasons why the

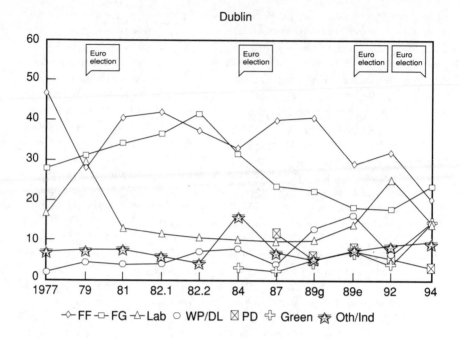

Dublin

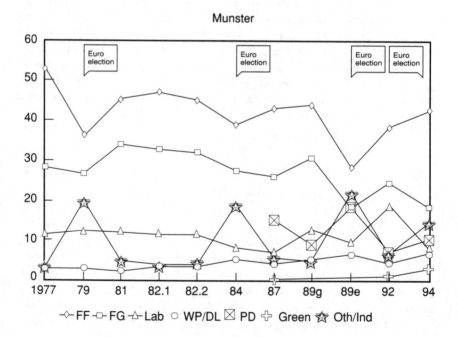

Munster

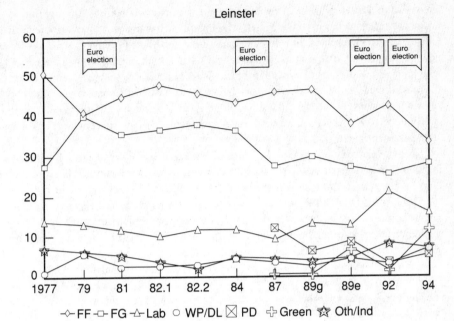

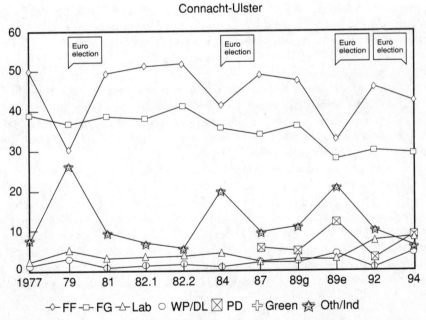

Figure 10.4 First preference results in European Parliament and general elections, by region, 1977–94.

likelihood of a referendum as a result of the provision is fairly remote. In addition to his or her role in relation to the Senate, the President has the power to convene both Houses of the Oireachtas, to refuse to sign a bill until the Supreme Court has pronounced on its constitutionality, and to refuse a dissolution of the Dáil to a Taoiseach who has lost the support of a majority of the Dáil. The last two powers mentioned are the most substantial. The first of the two has been exercised with some frequency. The second has never been exercised but the circumstances surrounding its possible exercise in February 1982 led, as we shall see in a moment, to dramatic controversy in the 1990 presidential election.

Though relatively powerless, the office of President has always been symbolically important in a partisan sense. It is like a mountain. It has to be climbed because it is there and, given a set of rules which create the possibility of a race to the top, the attitude has tended to be: it may as well be our flag rather than their flag that gets planted on the summit. On the other hand, if the prospective mountaineers have been busy scaling more rewarding heights, a dash for this particular summit will occasionally be passed up, provided this can be done with decorum.

The option of avoiding a contest and the grip of the political parties on this nominally non-partisan office is created by the closed nomination procedure. Former or retiring presidents may nominate themselves. Otherwise a candidate must be nominated, either by twenty members of the Dáil or Seanad or by 'the Councils of not less than four administrative Counties (including County Boroughs)' (Article 12.4.2). Given the hold that the parties have on both houses of the Oireachtas and on county councils this means that only parties can nominate candidates.[6] Thus they can decide to have or not to have a contest as the circumstances of their continuing quest for occupancy of the real locus of power dictate. They have decided on a contest on five occasions, and Figure 10.5 shows the outcome in terms of first preference votes in each case.

The first contested presidential election was in 1945, the previous incumbent, Douglas Hyde, having been selected in 1938 by agreement between the parties. In 1945 the contest was a three-cornered one, between two stalwarts of the main parties – Seán T. O'Kelly of Fianna Fáil and Seán MacEoin of Fine Gael – and an independent candidate – Patrick McCartan – supported by the Labour Party, Clann na Talmhain and some of the nationalist and radical elements that were subsequently to form Clann na Poblachta. Despite the fact that it was a three-cornered contest, Fianna Fáil came very close to winning on the first count with 49.5 per cent of the first preference votes, a share that left its candidate just 5,205 votes short of outright victory. O'Kelly emerged as the easy winner when he received 13 per cent (27,200 votes) of the votes of the eliminated independent candidate. For Fine Gael, the achievement of 31 per cent of the vote was a welcome boost after its catastrophic performance in the 1944 general election, though the gains did not translate into increased support in the arena that really

[6] Independents can run and have run but only with the agreement of a party or grouping of parties of a certain minimum size. The fate of the candidatures of Mary Robinson and Carmencita Hederman in 1990 illustrate the point (for details see O'Sullivan, 1991, p. 90).

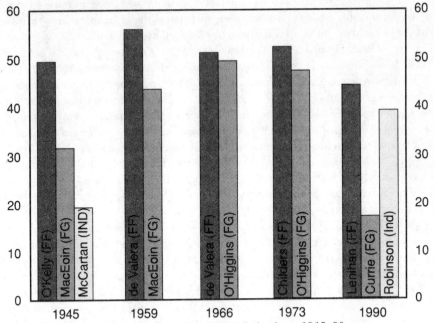

Figure 10.5 First preference vote in presidential elections, 1945–90.

matters. The party's vote in the next general election, 1948, was actually lower than that of 1944. Despite the successes of the minor parties and independents in the 1940s, the minor party/independent candidate succeeded in winning only 19.5 per cent of the vote. A study of the determinants of the first preference votes for the candidates of the two major parties in 1945 has identified a number of variables characteristic of traditional rural society as the best predictor of Fianna Fáil, producing levels of explanation of 50 per cent (Garvin, 1978, pp. 343–7).

In considering the 1959 referendum on PR in chapter 9, it was noted that de Valera's decision to hold the presidential election on the same day as the referendum was a matter of some controversy. De Valera was obviously on the point of retirement from active politics and it was a foregone conclusion that he would run for the office of President. Defending the decision to hold the two contests at the same time, de Valera said 'When two decisions have to be made, the public convenience is best met by having the two on the one day'. A deputy from the opposition benches put his finger on the contentious issue by interjecting 'And you will be in the scales'.[7] Seán MacEoin was again the Fine Gael candidate and this time it was a two-horse race. The focus of the campaign was very much on the referendum, which, as indicated in chapter 8, went narrowly against the Fianna Fáil government. However, De Valera won the presidency by a comfortable margin (56 to 44 per cent).

---

[7] Quoted in Longford and O'Neill, 1970, p. 448.

In 1966, at the end of his first seven-year term as President, de Valera celebrated his eighty-fourth birthday. There was some speculation that there might be agreement that he be asked to continue for a second term, as had happened in the case of Seán T. O'Kelly in 1952. However, Fine Gael had other ideas and announced that Thomas F. O'Higgins, a nephew of Kevin O'Higgins, would be the party's candidate. A reluctant de Valera was persuaded by Lemass to run but did not play any active role in the campaign (Longford and O'Neill, 1970, p. 461). O'Higgins was not much more than half de Valera's age and Fine Gael ran a vigorous campaign that argued for the need to, in the words of a participant in the campaign, move 'away from a traditional and inward looking nationalism to a more open and pluralist concept of Irish society' (FitzGerald, 1991, p. 76). In the event, it was an extremely close outcome with only 10,717 votes out of a total 1,107,005 giving victory to de Valera. Fianna Fáil had held on to the Presidency for the third time in succession, but the closeness of the result was a major boost for Fine Gael.

As we have seen, Fianna Fáil lost office in 1973 despite marginally increasing its share of the first preference vote. It was thus facing the difficulties of opposition after sixteen years in government, and in particular after the trauma of the Arms Crisis of 1970. A presidential election was due and, in the wake of unaccustomed electoral defeat, Fianna Fáil must have felt that it needed to win a fourth in a row. It put forward Erskine Childers, Tanaiste and Minister for Health in the defeated government, as its candidate. Fine Gael put Tom O'Higgins forward again, thus adding to the advantage of the honeymoon period of the new coalition government the further advantage of a candidate with presidential campaign experience who was a proven vote-winner. In the event, Childers' margin was slightly better than that in de Valera's second presidential contest – 52 per cent to 48 per cent. In the 1973 general election, Fianna Fáil had obtained 46 per cent of the vote in comparison to 48.8 for Fine Gael and Labour combined. It would seem, however, that the movement of votes between the two elections was much more than just a matter of Fianna Fáil adding on six percentage points. An analysis of the relationship between the presidential vote and that of the 1973 general election suggests that roughly one quarter of Fianna Fáil and Fine Gael supporters in 1973 voted for candidates of the opposite party and 35 per cent of Labour voters stayed at home (McCarthy and Ryan, 1976, p. 285).

Given the limited powers of the presidency, an election to the office is quintessentially a second-order election and therefore ought to be strongly subject to an anti-incumbent government effect. The first four presidential elections do not show such an effect. The government party won in three of the four (1945, 1959 and 1965) and, for the same reasons as outlined above in relation to the 1974 local elections, the remaining one (1973) cannot be considered to have been a typical mid-term election. One must presume that the normal effects of second-order election status are at least partly offset by the concentration of the contest on a single office, and the way in which this both heightens the partisan significance of the contest and, to an extent that depends on the candidates in question, personalises it.

On the face of it, and in contrast to the first four presidential elections, the 1990 presidential election conforms rather well to second-order election expectations. It was held well into the term of office of the government and was thus positioned in such a way that it could have functioned as a mid-term election. Typical of second-order elections, it was used and, as it turned out, very effectively used as part of a larger strategy by one of the party leaders. The outcome was also in line with second-order expectations in so far as the candidate of the party in government lost and the big gains were made by an independent candidate backed by some of the smaller parties. On the other hand, this was no run-of-the-mill second-order election. The campaign was intense. At a time when turnout in both general elections and local elections was falling, turnout in this contest was higher than in the previous presidential election. Most importantly, it was a second-order election with a difference, because there are indications that the wider political conflict that it reflected was not that of incumbent government versus opposition but rather the liberal–conservative conflict that had manifested itself in the abortion and divorce referendums of the 1980s. But this is to anticipate the argument. Before examining this crucial aspect of the contest, it is necessary to consider the origins and course of the campaign.

Brian Lenihan was an ideal Fianna Fáil candidate for the presidency – he had considerable cross-party appeal and a string of senior ministries behind him, and his already substantial personal popularity with the voters had been enhanced by his courageous struggle against a potentially fatal illness, a struggle that involved a last-minute liver transplant in the Mayo Clinic in the United States. Faced with such a formidable candidate, Fine Gael had difficulty finding a suitable nominee, a difficulty that was bound up with an on-going leadership struggle in the party and that was heightened by leader Alan Dukes' promise to field a 'candidate of substance'. Having apparently failed to persuade either of the party's two most prominent senior Dáil Deputies (Peter Barry and Garret FitzGerald) to stand, Dukes opted for Austin Currie. Currie had been a leading member of the Social Democratic and Labour Party in Northern Ireland since its inception, and had been a Minister in the power-sharing Executive in Northern Ireland in 1974. He had moved south and been elected as a TD for Dublin West in 1989.

Things would have been difficult for any Fine Gael candidate because the initiative on the anti-government, anti-Fianna Fáil side had been seized very early on by the Labour Party and the backers of the Robinson campaign. Labour Party leader Dick Spring was the first to insist that there should be a contest. In the face of suggestions within his own party in favour of one of two pronouncedly left-wing candidates, he hit upon the idea of nominating Mary Robinson, a former Labour Party Senator and a highly regarded Senior Counsel specialising in human rights and European law, and with a long and active association with liberal causes. Though nominated by the Labour Party and supported by the Workers' Party, Robinson insisted on running as an independent rather than as a Labour candidate. She also distanced herself from her publicly-known positions on divorce and abortion. It was not that she disavowed these positions. Rather she emphasized that, as President, her own views would be irrelevant as she would be bound by the decisions of the people in regard to such issues. Overtly then, the liberal agenda was not at issue in the campaign. On other hand there was no way of getting around the fact that, throughout her political career, Robinson had championed liberal positions on contraception, abortion and divorce (O'Reilly, 1991).

In the light of subsequent events, it is important to emphasize that as the 1990 presidential campaign got under way, the election was shaping up to be quite an even contest. Exclusion of the don't knows in the opinion polls from early October on (the complete figures are given in Table 10.1) shows Lenihan's clear majority of 52 per cent being whittled away to 49 per cent and then to 43 per cent by mid-October (poll of 10–20 October). Throughout this period, Robinson remained on one-third of the vote, rising to 38 per cent when Lenihan fell to 43. The most significant point, however, was that she was very substantially ahead of the Fine Gael candidate. On the poll figures of mid-October, Lenihan would have had either to recover significant ground in terms of first preference votes or obtain a substantial transfer from Currie. Of course either or both of these were entirely possible; they were not, however, certain. Thus a Robinson victory was a real possibility even before the extraordinary drama created by the Duffy tapes affair.

What was at issue in this controversy was whether or not the Fianna Fáil candidate, Brian Lenihan, had telephoned Áras an Uachtaráin (the President's residence) on the night of the defeat of the Fine Gael–Labour government's Budget and the dissolution of the twenty-second Dáil some eight years previously (27 January 1982). As noted above, the President has absolute discretion 'to refuse to dissolve Dáil Eireann on the advice of a Taoiseach who has ceased to retain the support of a majority in Dáil Eireann' (Article, 13.2.2). It must be emphasized that in the circumstances of a defeat for the government in the Dáil, there is nothing unconstitutional about senior members of the Opposition contacting the President to indicate their willingness to attempt to form a government. What was at issue, however, was the conflict between statements by Brian Lenihan during the 1990 election campaign, including one, on 22 October, on 'Questions and Answers' (a current affairs programme with high TAM ratings), that he had not telephoned Áras an Uachtaráin on the night in question, and a statement he had made five months previously in an interview given to a research student, Jim Duffy. As the controversy escalated in the wake of the 'Questions and Answers' programme, the *Irish Times*, which the previous month had published a series of articles by Duffy in which it was stated that Lenihan and others had attempted to ring the President on 27 January 1982, arranged a press conference at which a portion of the tape-recorded interview was played. The press conference took place on 25 October. In the excerpt Lenihan was heard to acknowledge that he had telephoned the President and to go on to say that he had actually spoken to him.

Lenihan took the position that what he had said to Duffy was 'rubbish' and that his 'mature recollection' was that he had not telephoned Áras an Uachtaráin on the night in question. Subsequent to the election he produced medical evidence to the effect that his state of health and the medication he was taking made his behaviour around the time of the research interview (May 1990) abnormal (Lenihan, 1991, p. 23). The immediate effect of the tapes incident during the campaign was a reversal in the levels of support for the two leading candidates. Excluding the don't knows, Lenihan's support dropped from 43 per cent to 32 per cent and that for Robinson rose from 38 per cent to 51 per cent. Currie's vote remained more or less as it was. The other change in the distribution of voting intentions was that the 'don't knows' dropped from 14 per cent to 6 per cent – a figure that is low even by general election standards.

Fine Gael and the Workers' Party tabled motions of no confidence in the government. The Progressive Democrats, Fianna Fáil's coalition partner, took the view that the credibility of the government was at stake and demanded that the Taoiseach, Charles Haughey, take appropriate action to rectify the situation. The action the Progressive Democrats had in mind was not publicly spelled out, but was assumed to be the dismissal of Lenihan as Tanaiste and Minister for Defence. The response of the Taoiseach was to seek Lenihan's resignation and, when he refused to resign, to dismiss him. There is evidence from the opinion polls that this sequence of events led to a considerable sympathy vote for Lenihan. This can be seen in the rise in support for Lenihan from 32 to 41 per cent between 29 October and 1 November, and to 42 per cent in a poll taken on the 2nd and 3rd of November. As a result, support for Robinson dropped from 51 to 46 per cent and then to 42 per cent. In the event, however, the Lenihan recovery was insufficient. Lenihan was ahead of Robinson on the first count (44.10 per cent to 38.88 per cent) but well short of the quota of 50 per cent plus one. He would have needed 35 per cent of Currie's transfers to win. In the event he got just 13.7 per cent. Robinson received 76.73 per cent of the transfers and was comfortably elected.

The determinants of voting in the 1990 presidential election

Interest in explaining the 1990 presidential vote is heightened by the novelty of the outcome. Mary Robinson was the first woman to gain the office, a breakthrough made all the more significant by fact that only 8 per cent of deputies in the contemporaneous Dáil were women. It was also the first victory by a non-Fianna Fáil candidate. It was seen by many as a reversal of the defeats suffered by campaigners for the liberalisation of Irish society in 1983 and 1986, and as a watershed election having an impact well beyond the narrow confines of presidential politics. However, the complexity of the task of explaining the outcome is also heightened, not least by the difficulty of pinning down the impact of the Duffy tapes affair. It is clear that the election outcome was not just a result of that controversy. There was a substantial challenge to the Fianna Fáil candidate well before that incident. On the other hand, the tapes affair cannot be lightly dismissed on the assumption that Robinson would have won anyway.

Sources of support
Table 10.1 shows voting intention by occupational class for the candidates for President between early October and early November 1990. Support for Lenihan in early October had shown some class bias, that is, it was significantly, though not overwhelmingly, stronger among working-class voters. The reverse was true of the Robinson candidacy, support for which among middle-class voters was about 34 per cent and among working-class voters 26 per cent. The effect of the tapes incident was felt right across the class spectrum and tended to diminish such class contrasts as had

Table 10.1: *Voting intention by occupational class, presidential election, 1990 (%)*

Candidate & date of poll	All classes	Upper- and middle class	Working classs	Farmers
Austin Currie				
1–9 October	13	16	14	18
5–6 October	17	17	13	25
10–20 October	15	16	13	17
27–29 October	16	16	11	28
1 November	13	13	10	19
2–3 November	13	11	11	21
Brian Lenihan				
1–9 October	43	36	45	45
5–6 October	42	33	48	44
10–20 October	34	29	35	39
27–29 October	30	24	31	35
1 November	37	30	41	38
2–3 November	39	36	42	38
Mary Robinson				
1–9 October	27	34	25	22
5–6 October	27	37	25	21
10–20 October	30	34	30	22
27–29 October	48	53	51	34
1 November	41	48	39	34
2–3 November	39	44	39	34
Don't know/refused /will not vote				
1–9 October	17	14	16	15
5–6 October	14	13	15	11
10–20 October	21	21	22	22
27–29 October	6	8	6	3
1 November	10	9	10	8
2–3 November	8	9	8	7

existed. In Lenihan's case a slight class contrast in support remained but, in the case of Robinson, support went up unequally and her candidacy was receiving almost equal support right across the urban class spectrum. The response to the tapes incident among those in farming occupations was out of line with the rest of the population – support for Robinson only moved from 21 to 34 per cent among farmers, whereas in the population as a whole it moved from 27 to 48 per cent. The net effect of the class-related shifts in voting intention in the urban sector, however, left only a modest difference in support for Robinson between the social classes, at least as measured on the weekend before polling.

Table 10.2: *Voting intention by gender, presidential election, 1990 (%)*

Candidate & date of poll	Male	Female
Austin Currie		
1–9 October	15	12
5–6 October	17	16
10–20 October	16	13
27–29 October	19	13
1 November	15	11
2–3 November	15	12
Brian Lenihan		
1–9 October	47	39
5–6 October	41	44
10–20 October	37	32
27–29 October	39	40
1 November	38	35
2–3 November	39	40
Mary Robinson		
1–9 October	21	33
5–6 October	24	30
10–20 October	23	36
27–29 October	43	54
1 November	37	45
2–3 November	37	41
Don't know/refused /will not vote		
1–9 October	17	16
5–6 October	18	10
10–20 October	25	19
27–29 October	6	6
1 November	11	9
2–3 November	9	7

In her victory speech, Robinson strongly emphasized that this was a victory for women. And indeed it was: to have a woman elected as the person who, in the words of the Constitution, 'shall take precedence over all other persons in the State' is of considerable significance in terms of the objective of ensuring gender equality. Looking at the gender factor in support for Robinson's candidacy (Table 10.2), it is evident that, in particular in comparison with the virtual absence of any gender effect in party support in general elections, gender played a considerable role at the outset of the campaign. Then there was a twelve percentage point difference between male and female support for Robinson. However, as the campaign went on, this gap narrowed. It reappeared (Robinson 43 per cent support among men, 54 per cent among women) in the wake of the tapes incident but narrowed again (37 per cent; 45 per cent) on 1 November and virtually disappeared in the final poll before the election (37 per cent; 41 per cent). In summary, taken at face value, this evidence suggests that at the end of the day the effect of 'the hand that rocks the cradle' may not have been as marked as the President-elect suggested in her remarks to 'mná na hÉireann' (women of Ireland) in the course of her victory speech.

In assessing the significance of the quite limited class and gender contrasts just discussed, it is necessary to bear in mind that the opinion–poll evidence may not be quite as useful as similar evidence in the case of general election voting. For one thing, the polls were not as accurate in predicting the outcome as they have tended to be in respect of general elections. On the basis of the last opinion poll, the Robinson vote was overestimated by 3 per cent and the Lenihan vote and Currie votes were under-estimated by 2 per cent and 3 per cent respectively. While these deviations are in line with normal sampling error, general election opinion polls in Ireland have tended to be more accurate. Moreover, it had been a very volatile campaign and the volatility may not have fully run its course at the time of interviewing for the final pre-election poll (Friday and Saturday, 2 and 3 November 1990). Many have argued that a personalised attack on Mary Robinson by a Fianna Fáil Minister, Padraig Flynn, and the stinging rebuke to him by Progressive Democrat Chairman Michael McDowell during the 'Saturday Live' radio programme on Saturday 3 November, both of which received widespread media coverage over the final weekend of the campaign, caused a swing to Robinson (see details in O'Sullivan, 1991, p. 94). If such a swing did occur, it only exac-erbates the problem of the overestimation of the Robinson vote in the opinion polls.

A more fundamental problem in analysing the social class and other determinants of presidential election voting arises from the pattern of turnout. We have seen that turnout in the presidential election was well below what is normal in a general elec-tion. Opinion polls interview a representative sample of the electorate as a whole and the lower the turnout, therefore, the greater the probability of error in predicting the outcome or identifying the characteristics of the voters. The problem is compounded by differential turnout. During the 1980s, there was a tendency for general election turnout to be substantially and negatively affected by the proportion of people aged 20 to 29, and to be only moderately and intermittently affected by the proportion of farmers and by the proportion in the working class (see chapter 5). Table 10.3 shows that the pattern of turnout in the 1990 presidential election was quite different. The farmer effect was insignificant, there was no negative youth effect and, most impor-tantly, there was a substantial negative working-class effect. If we take the decline in turnout (i.e., the difference between turnout in the presidential election and turnout in the previous general election) as the dependent variable, the proportion in the working class again appears to be the dominant factor. In this case there was also a slight but significant positive farmer effect – the higher the proportion of farmers the greater the decline in turnout. Again age appears to have no significant effect. The model accounts for over half the variance in the decline in turnout (see Table 10.3). These indications of differential turnout add to the argument that, in tracing the sources of party and candidate support in the 1990 presidential election, it will be nec-essary to pay particular attention to the actual election results themselves and to the

Table 10.3: *Aggregate analysis of turn-out in presidential election, 1990*

	Constant	Proportion farmers	Proportion working class	Proportion aged 20–29	Adjusted R^2	N
Turnout 1990	74.15	0.09 (1.15)	–0.66 (–3.24)	–0.21 (–0.14)	0.31	41
Abstention 1990 (turnout decline compared with 1989)	1.31	0.13 (2.72)	0.50 (4.23)	–0.28 (–1.68)	0.53	41

Note: The main entry for each variable is the B coefficient, the figure beneath in brackets is the *t*-value. *T*-values in excess of 2.02 are significant at $p = 0.05$.

inferences that ecological analysis, taking into account all the necessary qualifications, permits.

The spatial distribution of the first preference vote for Robinson is shown in Figure 10.6. The areas of Robinson's greatest strength were Dublin, Wicklow, Cork city, Limerick East, followed by Kildare and Galway West. These areas are either totally urban or have substantial urban concentrations. The Dublin-Wicklow-Kildare area support could also be seen as part of a band of support stretching from Dublin North-County along the east and south-east and into the south as far as Cork city. However, pockets of this level of support were also apparent in Mayo East and in North Kerry.[8] Her areas of weakness were in the north midlands, up into Cavan-Monaghan, in the north-west and in parts of the south-west. Within Dublin county, which was shown in Figure 10.6 just as a single unit, there is again an overall spatial contrast with some exceptions (see Figure 10.7). The overall contrast is between north and south of the river Liffey. Within south Dublin, there is some contrast between east and west; and in Dublin north of the Liffey there are two areas with a higher degree of support (i.e., Dublin North East and Dublin North West).

With the obvious exceptions of Mayo and Kerry, there are considerable similarities in the geographical structure of this vote to that of the liberal vote in the abortion and divorce referendums of 1983 and 1986 (see Figures 9.3 and 9.4). There is the same urban concentration, broadly similar contrasts between east and south-east versus areas in the west, north-west and south-west, and contrasts between north Dublin constituencies and south Dublin constituencies. Of course, as emphasized in Chapter 5, such cartographical comparisons remain very impressionistic. It is worth noting therefore that, in more precise statistical terms, the degree of association between these votes is indeed quite strong – the correlation between the 'yes' vote on divorce and the Robinson vote is a very substantial 0.86; that between the 'no' vote on the abortion amendment and the Robinson vote is 0.90. This suggests that in seeking an explanation of the Robinson vote at the aggregate level, we should look at

---

[8] The explanation in both cases would seem to be fairly obvious. Mary Robinson was born and brought up in Mayo. Kerry North is the constituency of Dick Spring, the leader of the Labour Party and the person widely perceived as the architect of the Robinson candidature.

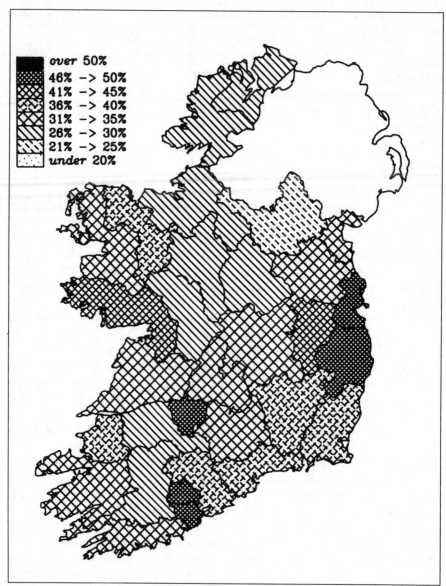

Figure 10.6 1990 presidential election – Robinson first preferences.

the factors that quite successfully account for the vote in the abortion and divorce
referendums (see chapter 9). This would lead to the hypothesis that the farmer and
working-class variables would both have negative effects on support for Robinson.
On the other hand, the fact that Robinson stood as the candidate nominated by the
Labour Party and supported by the Workers' Party might lead to the opposite
hypothesis in regard to the working-class effect, i.e., that there would be a positive

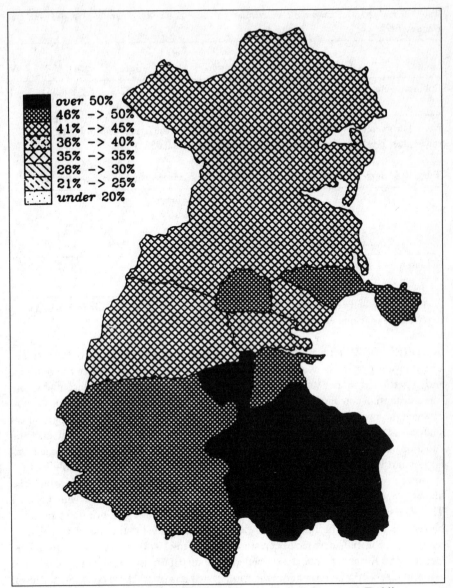

Figure 10.7 1990 presidential election – Robinson first preferences – Dublin.

association between the Robinson vote and the proportion in the working class.

Application of a simple two-variable model involving proportion of farmers and proportion in the working class shows that, at the aggregate level, the variables accounting for the Robinson vote were indeed very closely akin to those that account for liberal voting in the religious–moral referendums of the 1980s. Initial analysis shows that the variation in the Robinson vote is accounted for, to a very satisfactory

Table 10.4: *Aggregate analysis of Robinson support (socio-demographic variables), presidential election, 1990*

	Constant	Proportion farmers	Proportion working class	Mayo	Adjusted R^2	N
Robinson vote	56.93	−0.71	−0.74	7.83	0.82	41
		(−13.42)	(−4.00)	(2.90)		

Note: The main entry for each variable is the B coefficient, the figure beneath in brackets is the *t*-value. *T*-values in excess of 2.02 are significant at $p = 0.05$.

Table 10.5: *Aggregate analysis of Robinson support (socio-demographic and liberal variables)*

	Constant	Proportion farmers	Proportion working class	Proportion liberals 1983 ('no' to abortion amendment)	Mayo	Adjusted R^2	N
Robinson vote	31.49	−0.31	−0.21	0.40	8.35	0.87	41
		(−2.78)	(−1.04)	(4.00)	(3.66)		

Note: The main entry for each variable is the B coefficient, the figure beneath in brackets is the *t*-value. *T*-values in excess of 2.02 are significant at $p = 0.05$.

degree ($R^2 = 0.78$), in terms of the negative impact of a high proportion of farmers and a high proportion in the working class. However, whereas in the divorce referendum, and in particular in the 1983 abortion referendum, the working-class effect on the vote was substantially stronger than the farmer effect, in the presidential election the gap between the two effects was much smaller. In fact, if, in the light of the cartographical analysis above, pro-Robinson sentiment in County Mayo is incorporated into the equation, the overall negative effect of the proportion of farmers is strengthened and farmer and working-class effects are virtually identical in strength (see Table 10.4).

Since it was raised at the end of chapter 5, the question of the extent to which the liberal–conservative cleavage finds expression in party voting has been a recurring one. The analysis in chapter 9 showed that it manifested itself to a significant extent in the November 1982 and the 1992 general elections, and this led to the speculation that its reappearance in 1992 may have been stimulated by the 1990 presidential election. The fact that the Robinson vote closely reflects the distribution of the liberal vote in the divorce and abortion referendums and the fact that it is traceable, at constituency level, to the same social structural characteristics, strongly suggests that the liberal–conservative cleavage may indeed have been mobilised in the 1990 presidential election. The suggestion can be tested by inserting the liberal variable in the Robinson equation. The result is particularly interesting (Table 10.5). The R^2 increases from 82 to 87 per cent. The proportion of liberals has a substantial positive effect and the negative effect of the proportion of farmers, while it is reduced by comparison with the model in Table 10.4, remains significant. However, once we include the pro-Robinson liberal effect in the model (and, by implication, the anti-Robinson conservative effect), the negative

Table 10.6: *Aggregate analysis of Lenihan and Currie support (socio-demographic variables), presidential election, 1990*

	Constant	Proportion farmers	Proportion middle class	Adjusted R^2	N
Lenihan vote	51.30	0.19 (2.96)	−0.99 (−5.26)	0.61	41
Currie vote	9.54	0.33 (9.32)	0.33 (3.16)	0.68	41

Note: The main entry for each variable is the B coefficient, the figure beneath in brackets is the *t*-value. *T*-values in excess of 2.02 are significant at $p = 0.05$.

Table 10.7: *Aggregate analysis of Lenihan and Currie support (socio-demographic and liberal variables), presidential election, 1990*

	Constant	Proportion farmers	Proportion middle class	Proportion liberals 1983 ('no' to abortion amendment)	Adjusted R^2	N
Lenihan vote	65.11	−0.12 (−1.29)	−0.62 (−3.31)	−0.40 (−3.89)	0.72	41
Currie vote	9.06	0.34 (5.32)	0.32 (2.58)	0.01 (0.21)	0.68	41

Note: The main entry for each variable is the B coefficient, the figure beneath in brackets is the *t*-value. *T*-values in excess of 2.02 are significant at $p = 0.05$.

working-class effect becomes insignificant. In other words, controlling for the effect of liberalism–conservatism shows that the tendency for Robinson to do less well in working-class constituencies was more apparent than real, being an artefact of the tendency for her to do less well in conservative areas.

In general, the structuring of the vote for the other two candidates was the opposite to that of the vote for Robinson. But this does not mean that their vote had an identical structure, and the differences between the two are quite revealing. Analysing the votes for both Lenihan and Currie using a two-variable model (farmers and middle class), produces substantial explanation of the variance and indicates a positive farmer effect in both cases. The difference arises in regard to the middle-class effect and is quite pronounced. We have seen that the negative effect of the proportion of professional middle class on Fianna Fáil support evident from the general election of February 1982 through to that of 1987 had ceased to be statistically significant in 1989. In the 1990 presidential election, the Fianna Fáil deficit in middle-class areas was back with renewed vigour – the negative middle-class effect was a very substantial −0.99. In contrast there was a moderate pro-Currie effect in middle-class areas. The contrast between the structure of support for Lenihan and Currie widens further when the liberal variable is introduced into the equation (Table 10.7). In the case of support for Lenihan, there is a substantial rise in the level of variance explained and quite a considerable change in the pattern of effects – the farmer effect ceases to be significant and the variance in the Lenihan vote is seen to be traceable to the joint but independent negative effects of the proportion in the middle class and the proportion voting liberal in 1983. The structure of the Currie vote is unaffected by the introduction of the liberal variable, and the best explanation of the Currie vote remains the positive and equal impact of the proportion of farmers and the proportion in the middle class.

In summary, the line-up of first preference votes for and against Robinson reflected a dual cleavage. In the first instance it reflected a liberal–conservative cleavage and, secondly, even when this is taken into account, it reflected a further general urban–rural cleavage. Any apparent class effect on Robinson support seems to have been a function of the intertwining of liberal–conservative and class influences. The evidence of direct class effects on the structure of the vote in the presidential election is limited to the negative middle-class effect on Lenihan support and the positive middle-class effect on Currie support. Overall, the fact that this combination of liberal–conservative and urban–rural cleavages produces such a substantial level of predictability in the Robinson vote suggests that the 1990 presidential conflict did indeed touch a quite fundamental division in Irish society.

Conclusion

Ireland has had four kinds of second-order elections – by-election, local, European Parliament and presidential. There is some evidence that each electoral arena has its own agenda. For example, family connections may affect the outcome of many a by-election and local concerns undoubtedly help to account for the success of independent and minor party candidates in local elections; there is some evidence of an 'ambassadorial' effect in European Parliament elections and, obviously, candidate considerations play a substantial role in presidential elections. At the same time, all of these elections have on occasion displayed the characteristic mark of second-order elections, that is, their outcomes have been determined not by issues intrinsic to the arena in question but by the invasion of that arena by larger issues. The larger issue has most often been a mid-term swing against the incumbent government, though this seems to have had less of an impact in presidential elections. This does not mean that presidential elections are immune to the impact of larger issues. This was signally evident in 1990 when the liberal–conservative conflict concerning religious–moral issues, though not debated in the campaign and not germane to the role of the presidency as defined in the Constitution, impinged significantly on the outcome. This particular example of linkage between different electoral arenas has considerable implications for our understanding of contemporary voting behaviour and is considered more fully in the next and final chapter.

Chapter 11

Comparability, stability and change

In describing the severe political problems facing Lilliput, the Secretary to the Emperor said to Gulliver: 'As flourishing a Condition as we appear to be in to Foreigners, we labour under two mighty Evils . . .'. The first of these evils had to do with the Lilliputian party system. It was the problem of 'faction'. In the Secretary's words:

> As to the first, you are to understand, that for above seventy Moons past, there have been two struggling Parties in this Empire, under the Names of Tramecksan, and Slamecksan, from the high and low Heels on their Shoes, by which they distinguish themselves. It is alleged indeed, that the high Heels are most agreeable to our ancient Constitution; but however this may be, his Majesty hath determined to make use of only low Heels in the Administration of the Government, and all Offices in the Gift of the Crown. . . . The Animosities between these two Parties run so high, that they will neither eat nor drink, nor talk with each other.[1]

If we substitute Fianna Fáil and Fine Gael for Tramecksan and Slamecksan, seventy years for seventy moons and allow for a degree of hyperbole, this comment on the Lilliputian party system captures in a remarkably timeless way what many observers have been saying since the 1960s about party alignments in Ireland – they are peculiar, they are based on trivial differences, they are a problem and the sooner they are transformed, the better. Drawing on the evidence presented, the first section of this final chapter examines various interpretations of the Irish party system and electoral alignments in order to determine whether Irish parties and political cleavages can be incorporated into a comparative theory or whether the system really is unique, and what the implications are for our understanding of contemporary electoral politics. Consideration of these implications leads directly to the second theme of the chapter – stability and change, as manifested in both party choice and referendum voting.

A peculiar system?

The predominant view for many years seemed to be that, yes, the Irish party system is peculiar and that it is impossible to fit it into prevailing classifications of party systems

---

[1] Jonathan Swift, *Gulliver's Travels*, ed. Colin McKelvie (Belfast: The Appletree Press, 1976), pp. 50–1.

and theories of their development. Though it is no longer put forward with such categorical certainty as in the past, echoes of the view can be found, for example, in the argument that Irish politics are now, at long last, being 'Europeanised'. The interpretation of the system as being peculiar usually starts from an account of its historical origins. Such an account can be briefly summarised. Following the drama of the 1916 rebellion, the election of 1918, which was an election to the Westminster Parliament, was mainly about independence (secession). The new secessionist party won a large majority of the seats in the country as a whole, and almost a clean sweep in the part of the country that was to become an independent state. Pro-independence agitation and a guerrilla war led to partial secession. The compromise settlement split the independence movement and the split escalated into civil war. Following the defeat of the anti-treatyites, the two sides in the civil war set up opposing political parties and these became the two main parties in the new state.

One can regard this as a unique set of events that provides an historical, in the sense of a genetic, explanation of the party system. This is undoubtedly a valid level of explanation. It has the advantage of being contextual, of allowing adequate attention to be paid to the particularities of the historical circumstances. It would be possible to leave it at that and go on to describe how these unique parties fared, adapted and survived in this peculiar system, perhaps eventually becoming 'Europeanised'. A more challenging and more interesting perspective, however, is to see if an interpretation of these developments can be found which accounts for the conflict in more general terms and makes the development of the Irish party system comparable to the development of party systems elsewhere.

A commonly argued alternative to the above historical explanation is what we might call the covert class conflict interpretation. Taking account of the obvious fact that the small size of the Labour Party means that the system cannot be seen as a direct manifestation of class conflict, this approach argues that the conflict between pro- and anti-treaty and between Cumann na nGaedheal/Fine Gael and Fianna Fáil was really between haves and have-nots, between the wealthy farmers and the bourgeoisie, on the one hand, and an implicit alliance of the rural and urban poor on the other. Supporting arguments for such an interpretation have been noted in chapter 2. Perhaps the most impressive such argument, because it was almost contemporaneous, is that of Moss. The thesis has recently been forcefully re-stated by Lee – 'the division was one of socio-economic perceptions of status and self-interest'.[2]

It is certainly plausible that the pro- and anti-treaty positions appealed to the economic interests of sections of the electorate – an interest in stability and the status quo versus egalitarian expectations of economic betterment as an inherent part of the realisation of radical nationalist aspirations. In fact, the economic dimension of inter-party competition was not just implicit and an outgrowth of attitudes to the Treaty. Economic events and the Cumann na nGaedheal reaction to them meant that part of the image of that party was bound up with the protection of the interests of property

[2] See the full discussion and references in chapter 2. The references here are to Moss, 1933 and Lee, 1989.

and with conservative economic and financial policies. This image was fostered by Cumann na nGaedheal when it referred to the 'Bolshevist tendencies' of Fianna Fáil and to the attendant dangers of 'Materialism and Communism'. Fianna Fáil for its part set out quite consciously to appeal to the economic interests of the less well-off. This approach informed both its economic and its social policy. Moreover, nationalist issues and economic issues became intertwined through Fianna Fáil's promise to withhold the land annuities payable to the British government as a result of the settlement of the land issue in the late nineteenth century and in the early years of the twentieth century.

However, the evidence of electoral behaviour at the aggregate level (and this is the only evidence we have for the early decades) indicates that the best explanation of the pattern of the Fianna Fáil vote at constituency level up to and including 1938 is a general indicator of rural economy and society (the proportion of farmers), combined with two cultural variables (the proportion of Irish speakers and of non-Catholics). The more social–class-related variables, for example, the proportion of employers and managers and the rateable valuation of land per acre, are related to support for Fianna Fáil but, in a multi-variate analysis, are outweighed by the three variables mentioned. It is notable also that the level of unemployment was actually negatively related to Fianna Fáil support and the proportion of farm labourers quite unrelated to it. Areas with high proportions of farm labourers showed strong support for the Labour Party. On the other side of the class divide that, it is argued, underlay the pro-treaty, anti-treaty split, Cumann na nGaedheal/Fine Gael support across the constituencies only assumed a discernible class profile in 1932, and this lasted for an extremely brief period, i.e., for the elections of 1932 and 1933. Thus, the evidence from aggregate voting patterns indicates quite limited and transient class effects on the pattern of voting at constituency level. There is, in other words, some support for the view that the socio-economic policies of the parties appealed to different classes and for the view that the response to the nationalist issue had some class resonances. However, the evidence is insufficient to sustain the interpretation that the conflict between the parties was really a surrogate class conflict.

Another more general interpretation of the historical facts of the pro-treaty and anti-treaty division argues that the conflict was one between east and west, between a modernising and a traditional sector, or between the centre and the periphery. If this were indeed the case, it would provide a very clear comparative interpretation, as the Irish case would become another instance of a party system built on one of the four cleavages identified by Lipset and Rokkan – that between the modernising, state-building elite at the centre and the resistance of the periphery. An immediate problem with such an interpretation is that there is no clear evidence of an explicit appeal by the parties to the interests of the periphery versus the centre. There is certainly no evidence of regional identifications being articulated by the political leaders on either side, or of a co-ordinated and politicised campaign of resistance by the periphery to rule by the centre. Moreover, both sides stressed the traditionalist objective of reviving the Irish language; at the same time both were equally committed to economic modernisation. It is true that the apparent delayed electoral mobilisation of certain areas, mainly along the western seaboard, and the temporal coincidence between this mobilisation and the expansion of the Fianna Fáil vote seem to provide crucial supporting evidence for a centre-periphery interpretation. But we have seen that the late mobilisation of the periphery is more a matter of appearance than reality, the rising turnout in many western and north-western counties being largely a function of flaws in the electoral register in the early years. A further empirical difficulty with the internal centre-periphery theory is the rapidity of the Fianna Fáil nation-wide advance. This is particularly clear when Rumpf's pioneering cartographic analysis is redrawn to a constant rather than a variable scale. An internal centre-periphery interpretation fits in with one aspect of the Fianna Fáil vote – the persistent east-west contrast; it is, however, incompatible with the nationwide progress made by Fianna Fáil from as early as September 1927. The final difficulty for the internal centre-periphery interpretation is the fact that Cumann na nGaedheal was by no means exclusively a party of the centre.

If the conflict was not one of centre versus periphery, what would have appeared to have been the best possibility of incorporating the Irish case within the Lipset-Rokkan framework is a non-starter. The bleak implications for a comparative perspective on the Irish case have been drawn: 'The Irish party system deviates from the cleavage model which has so far provided a powerful accounting of the other causes of democratic political competition in Europe' (Carty, 1981, p. 6). Before concurring with this judgement, it is worth briefly spelling out the overall Lipset and Rokkan approach, examining the applicability of each aspect of it to the Irish case.

The approach has two main elements – a typology of cleavage and a generalisation linking the configuration of cleavage to the party system. The four types of cleavage are: centre versus periphery, church versus state, land versus industry and owner versus worker. The proposition or generalisation is that European party systems are best understood as the freezing of party alternatives and electoral alignments at the time when the mass of the population was mobilised for electoral participation (Lipset and Rokkan, 1967). The first point suggested by looking at the Irish case from this perspective is that the election of 1918 was a mobilising election (see chapter 2). Secondly, in the context of the United Kingdom, which was the context of the 1918 election, the dominant cleavage as far as Ireland was concerned was indeed a centre-periphery conflict, but one with the government in London as the centre and most, but not all, of Ireland as the periphery. Consequently, voters were mobilised in 1918 around the issue of centre-periphery relations. This conflict intensified with the outbreak of military conflict between centre and periphery in 1919. It was settled, as we have seen, by the partial breaking away of the periphery to constitute a more or less separate political system in 1922. Because electoral mobilisation had preceded secession, the majority of the voters in the new system were mobilised into a nationalist consensus based on the opposition of the periphery to rule by the centre. Because secession was incomplete, the issue of centre-periphery relations remained uppermost on the political agenda of the new state, leading to a deep and bitter division within the nationalist consensus that quickly escalated into civil war (1922–23). The civil war and the subsequent establishment of political parties embodying each side of the civil war conflict meant that voters underwent a further process of nationalist mobilisation, this time into strongly peripheralist and moderately peripheralist or strong nationalist and moderately nationalist camps. On this reading of the applicability of Lipset and Rokkan to the Irish system, a centre-periphery conflict was and remained at the heart of the emerging party system. It is understandable that this larger centre-periphery conflict would have been felt more deeply in parts of the western half of the country. However, for the reasons given above, this did not mean that the party system was built upon a conflict between an Irish centre and an Irish periphery.

This version of the applicability of the Lipset and Rokkan approach to the development of the Irish party system (i.e., in terms of a centre-periphery conflict between Britain and Ireland) can accommodate several specific features of the Irish case noted in preceding chapters: the combination of an early and rapid nationwide advance by Fianna Fáil with its persistent greater strength in western areas; the cultural and social profile of Fianna Fáil support in the first two decades after independence; and the lack of a distinct geographical and social base in the support for Cumann na nGaedheal and Fine Gael. In addition to helping to account for these specific aspects of the early development of the system, it throws considerable light on the nature, evolution and significance of the party system as a whole. This can be seen by considering the fate of the other three conflicts postulated by Lipset and Rokkan. Before turning to this, however, it is vital to clarify the role of the centre–periphery or nationalist conflict envisaged by the interpretation.

In particular, given the frequent use of the term 'civil war parties', as if the civil war were the only factor differentiating Fianna Fáil and Fine Gael, and given occasional arguments to the effect that the 'freezing hypothesis' implies that Irish politics remains untouched by contemporary events (Borooah and Borooah, 1990, p. 66 and p. 77), it is important to be clear on what the interpretation implies about the persistence of the original conflict. It does not mean anything as crude as the suggestions just noted. Firstly, it implies a certain degree of stability in voting patterns, a point which is taken up in detail below. Secondly, it implies that the parties are highly constrained in their response to nationalist and Anglo-Irish issues. Fianna Fáil can never be less nationalist than Fine Gael and is only likely to entertain compromise solutions on nationalist issues if it is the author of the compromise or if, at least, it is in government to implement the compromise. It therefore implies the persistence of differences between the parties, not in terms of nationalism and anti-nationalism but in terms of degrees of nationalism. Obviously, given the common origins of the parties in Sinn Féin and given the basis on which the original nationalist consensus was fractured, such differences may be quite subtle. We have seen that in the late 1980s and early 1990s experts postulated a Northern Ireland policy dimension as one of the main differentiating features of the party system. Similarly, nationalism figured prominently in the accounts of party differences given by party elites in the mid-1970s and in the way in which such elites discussed contemporary policy issues. In actual policy terms, clear nationalist differences manifested themselves in the New Ireland Forum and in the response to the 1985 Anglo-Irish agreement. Furthermore, despite the fact that the nationalist dimension does not appear, except to a very minor extent, in the manifestos of the parties in the period since 1948, voters do see such differences between the parties, specifically between Fianna Fáil and Fine Gael. The significance of this perception is heightened when it is recalled that voters seem to have considerable difficulty in differentiating the parties along a left–right dimension. It must be emphasized, however, that the theory of the freezing of an alignment around the issue of centre–periphery relations does not imply that every movement in party support is determined by such issues, or that other issues are entirely or largely irrelevant or that the party system is untouched by contemporary issues. On the contrary, the interpretation has quite specific implications for the role of other issues, implications that, as suggested above, can best be teased out by considering in turn each of the other three potential sources of conflict identified by Lipset and Rokkan.

The conflict of the periphery against the centre coincided with a long-standing church–state conflict (between the Irish Catholic Church and the British state) that had manifested itself on a range of issues throughout the nineteenth and into the twentieth century. The demands of the church and the demands of the periphery had in fact become intertwined and the Catholic Church was closely identified with the nationalist cause. Thus, when secession occurred and the periphery broke away, the result was a social and political system that was remarkably homogeneous in attitudes to church–state issues. Through most of the history of the state, all parties operated within a tacit conservative consensus on church–state relations and moral issues. However, the fact that the parties did not divide on these issues meant that they did not campaign on them, either during the period of the foundation of the party system or subsequently. Hence, they are not historically and institutionally committed to entrenched positions in this area and, when real pressures for change arise, they can, within certain limits, respond pragmatically or opportunistically, as circumstances dictate.

A similar process can be observed in regard to the third Lipset and Rokkan potential source of conflict – that between the agrarian sector and the industrial sector. The economy of the periphery was overwhelmingly agrarian and the result of secession was a political system in which the primacy of the agrarian sector was a matter of consensus. There were of course conflicts of interest within the agrarian sector but these received only variable and partial political expression, at different times giving rise to the Farmers' Party and to Clann na Talmhain and to more or less successful efforts by Fianna Fáil and Fine Gael to garner the bulk of the rural vote. The overriding fact, however, was that for a long period the interests of the agrarian economy were seen as the interests of the state, and that when economic circumstances required a shift from this approach to one which put equal emphasis on industrial development, this was done with remarkable ease and lack of controversy.

Not being territorially based, the fourth Lipset and Rokkan cleavage (owner versus worker) was not affected in such a radical way by secession. However, secession did create a society with a relatively weak industrial sector, with the land redistribution issue already substantially solved and with a religious consensus that inhibited the ideological expression of class conflict. In these circumstances, the conflict between owners and workers was unlikely to emerge as a prominent cleavage. On top of that, the course of events between 1918 and 1927, in particular the abstention of Labour in the 1918 election, institutionalised the marginalisation of the representatives of labour in the developing party system. The non-emergence of a left–right cleavage at the time of the foundation of the party system has meant that the pattern of programmatic flexibility characteristic of the church–state and agrarian–industrial cleavages has been evident also in the socio-economic realm. Of course, in all of these areas there are broad parameters. The main one in the socio-economic area is a shared commitment to private property (rather than private enterprise). However, within the context of basic agreement on this principle, the two major parties square up to each other largely unencumbered by long-standing or deeply-rooted commitments in regard to social and economic policies and programmes. Their identities are derived from a dimension that is largely irrelevant to the increasing responsibilities for welfare provision and economic management assumed by governments everywhere in the course of the twentieth century. We have seen that in the past, especially in the late 1920s and early 1930s, both parties had somewhat more clearly defined images in this respect – Fianna Fáil as the radical party, Cumann na nGaedheal/Fine Gael as the conservative party. Both have had very little difficulty, however, in shedding or at least shelving that side of their inheritance as circumstances indicated. Fianna Fáil's conversion from protectionism to free trade, and Fine Gael's partial conversion to the Just Society and to a moderate social democratic position, were manifestations of the search by the parties not just for new grounds for competition but for new solutions to changing economic and social problems. The key point is that in relation to a whole range of socio-economic issues, among them the basic question of the purpose and appropriate level of public expenditure, the two major parties move in an environment characterised by flexibility rather than constraint; in political science terms, they are non-programmatic.

As well as accounting for the changing nature of party appeals and coalition strategies over the years, this particular feature of the party system also helps to account for the crisis of party government in the 1980s. Lacking the twin buffers of a long-standing commitment to a social and economic programme *and* a constituency that could be relied upon to support that programme, the two main parties were severely exposed to the short-run demands and the clamour of the most vocal pressure group. As a result, policy in these areas, especially in time of recession, was more likely than it would otherwise have been to consist of *ad hoc* responses to the most immediate pressures. If instead of the virtual programmatic vacuum on this issue, the party system had had a more substantial and more salient left–right dimension, then debate and decision rather than drift might have characterised the growth of public expenditure in Ireland in the 1970s and early 1980s. In this sense it could be argued that the implications of the lack of a substantial left–right cleavage in the party system relate not just to the weakness of 'voice' from the left, but also to the virtual inaudibility of 'voice' from the other side of the political spectrum. One could also argue that the emergence of the Progressive Democrats was, to a substantial extent, a response to the dynamics of 'exit, voice and loyalty' in this particular policy realm.[3]

[3] On the notions of exit, voice and loyalty see Hirschmann, 1970.

The argument so far has suggested that the Irish party system conforms quite well to what is probably the standard theory of the development of party systems in Western Europe, and that this theory throws light on key aspects of Irish parties and electoral alignments.[4] In this sense, the Irish party system was 'Europeanised' from the outset and certainly does not deviate in any absolute way from the Lipset and Rokkan cleavage model. The argument concurs with Laver's view that the system is not peculiar (Laver, 1992, p. 380). However, the basis of the conclusion is different. Laver's view that the Irish party constellation 'most closely resembles the Mediterranean' (Laver, 1992, p. 375) involves analysing party differences in a two-dimensional space, the two dimensions being an economic left–right dimension and a 'social policy' (i.e., abortion and homosexuality dimension). Policy on abortion and homosexuality is used as the second dimension in preference to Northern Ireland policy on the grounds that it provides comparability with other systems and is so closely correlated with the Northern Ireland policy dimension as to be interchangeable with it. This has the advantage of producing a two-dimensional representation of the Irish party system that looks like some party systems elsewhere but it has the disadvantage of neglecting the dimension which is declared to be the most salient one by the experts whose judgments constitute the evidence on which the comparative analysis is based. The interpretation put forward here sets the present Irish party system in a historical and comparative perspective that accounts for the course taken by the four cleavage dimensions regarded as standard in much of the literature. The Northern Ireland issue is incorporated under the heading of nationalist or centre–periphery conflict and the interpretation emphasizes that the parties' positions have been more rigidly fixed on this dimension and more mobile and flexible on the other three.

It is against this background that the persistence of the electoral weakness of socialism must be seen. As suggested above, the persistent minority status of the left has roots in the cleavages and circumstances that prevailed during the phase of electoral mobilisation and party formation. It is not fully accounted for in these terms, however, and the notion that the present distribution of party support is to be explained simply by 'the inertia of tradition and the sheer force of history' is, as Mair rightly emphasizes, suspect (Mair, 1987a, pp. 43–60).[5] The weakness of the left over the years was not just due to the squeezing out of socialism by a preoccupation with nationalism or to the other factors listed above. It was also due to the freedom with which the two large parties could appropriate aspects of the socialist agenda, thus raising a significant barrier to entry to a party that espoused a moderate socialist position, by competing with that party in terms of the substance, though usually not the rhetoric, of its own ground.

This brings us directly to the question of change. The most distinctive aspect of the Lipset and Rokkan theory – the 'freezing' hypothesis – states that the effects of electoral mobilisation tend to last for a long time.[6] How long did the consequences atten-

---

[4] For a detailed review of the literature on the comparability-peculiarity issue up to the early 1980s, see Sinnott, 1984.

[5] In any event, it should be clear from the discussion in the text that the Lipset and Rokkan thesis is not reducible to the inertia of tradition and the force of history.

[6] For a recent survey of the comparative evidence on this issue see Bartolini and Mair, 1990.

dant on the formation of the Irish party system last? Early and substantial change in the electoral alignment established in the 1920s would lead either to a total rejection of the applicability of the approach in the Irish case, or at least to the conclusion that the Irish case, while not being an exception in terms of its genesis, is an exception in terms of the lack of longevity of the alignment. We are thus brought back to the general problem raised in chapter 1 – what is the relationship between change in the environment in which voting occurs – socio-demographic, economic, governmental, and international – and trends in voting behaviour? This is in turn related to other issues raised at various stages in the discussion – the extent and role of party identification; whether or not there is evidence of voting behaviour being increasingly determined by social class and/or by particular contemporary issues; the amount of stability or change manifested in the abortion and divorce referendums, and finally, how these latter contests and the presidential election of 1990 may have affected party alignments and party support.

Stability and change

Since electoral alignments are formed and reformed by the interaction between the strategy of the parties and the behaviour of the voters, the issue of stability and change must be examined at both levels. Focusing mainly on party strategy, one interpretation finds considerable potential for change, arguing that there have been three moments when the development of an alternative alignment was possible – 1927–33, the 1940s and 1973 (Mair, 1987, pp. 47–59). At each of these points, particularly in 1948 and 1973, opposition elites, especially the Labour Party, failed to grasp the opportunity to fashion a class-based realignment. The strategic failure in 1948 led to the development of a polarisation between Fianna Fáil on the one hand and all the remaining parties on the other, a polarisation defined not in policy terms but in terms of the ability to form a government. According to the argument, this in fact amounted to the replacement of one language of politics by another. 'The dominance of [the civil war] conflict had effectively ceased by the beginning of the post war period. Rather, and more crucially for Labour, it was a conflict between FF, on the one side, and virtually all other parties, including Labour, on the other'. In substantive terms, the new underlying issue was 'the ability to govern' (Mair, 1979, pp. 452–3; Mair, 1993, p. 168). If it is the case that the essence of the post-war system was the opposition between Fianna Fáil and the rest, an opposition maintained by the credibility of Fianna Fáil's insistence on no coalition, then the change brought about in 1989 and 1992 is very far-reaching indeed. In this view, in 1989 the Progressive Democrats 'effectively undermined the foundation on which the postwar party system had been based' (Mair, 1993, p. 172), and Labour's coalition with Fianna Fáil after the 1992 election 'may have destroyed that foundation in its entirety'. This leads to the conclusion that 'There is, in short, nothing which remains of the old order' (*ibid.*). But was the 'ability to govern' issue really the basis of the post-war party system? Could not that issue be equally well interpreted as just another of the issues that have been grafted onto the system? Could it not have imposed significant constraints on the strategies of the parties, in particular on that of the

Labour Party, without necessarily becoming the defining characteristic of the system? If one were to give positive answers to these questions, then the abandonment by Fianna Fáil of its 'core value' of single-party government, first tentatively in 1989 and then definitively in 1992, while of considerable importance, does not *ipso facto* transform the system or render it entirely unstructured. Similarly, the collapse of the Fianna Fáil – Labour coalition at the end of 1994 and the formation of a three-party coalition on the basis of the exclusion of Fianna Fáil from office does not necessarily return the system to a 'Fianna Fáil versus the rest' alignment. In order to assess the significance of the strategic decisions taken and of the moves made by the parties, it is essential to look also at the other side of the equation, in other words, at the evidence of voting behaviour. Does such evidence confirm that the system was on the verge of a fundamental realignment in 1927–33, or in the 1940s or in 1973? Was the alignment in the post-war period transformed into one based on the ability of govern? Was the existing alignment then undermined in 1989 and destroyed in 1992?

In June 1927, both party fragmentation and voter volatility were extremely high and seemed to indicate a very fluid electoral situation. What is crucial, however, is the location of that fragmentation and volatility. The fragmentation was mostly on the pro-treaty side and, while total volatility was remarkably high, block volatility was negligible. Voters moved but they did so within areas bounded by the main pro-treaty, anti-treaty cleavage line rather than across that line. With the ending of the policy of parliamentary abstentionism by Fianna Fáil and the moderation of its electoral appeal, significant numbers of voters did move across the line over the next three elections but, far from suggesting an alternative mobilisation, the process by which this came about illustrates the hold of the existing external centre–periphery cleavage. One should also bear in mind that the potential for the mobilisation of an alternative alignment in the late 1920s was more limited than might appear at first sight, because one apparent source of a new mobilisation (low recorded turnout in peripheral areas) was largely illusory, being an artefact of flaws in the electoral register in the early years.

In 1943, the number of parties jumped substantially again. Although the number declined in the context of a snap election in the following year, it increased still further in 1948. Inevitably, volatility jumped also, being particularly high in 1943. Unlike the 1920s, this time a substantial proportion of the volatility was block volatility that ate into the Fianna Fáil vote. We have seen the conflicting interpretations of electoral developments in the 1940s – in one view, Fianna Fáil was in an unassailable position; in the other, it was the object of a tripartite assault that contained the seeds of a potential realignment of the party system. The extent of block volatility in 1943 and 1948 suggests that Fianna Fáil was certainly not unassailable. Equally, however, the argument that there was real potential for a realignment of the system, if only opposition elites had made the right choices, must contend with considerable counter-evidence. The record emphasizes the transience of the challenge to Fianna Fáil. Unlike Fine Gael, Fianna Fáil recovered considerable ground in Connacht-Ulster, the heartland of Clann na Talmhan, in 1944. In 1944 also, the Labour challenge crumbled, partly because it was undermined by the split in the Labour ranks and partly because the strength of the 1943 Labour challenge had been exaggerated by the huge increase in the ratio of Labour candidates to Dáil seats in 1943. Then there was Clann na Poblachta, which, with its appeal to radical republicanism in both the socio-economic and political sense, might be thought to have constituted the most significant threat to Fianna Fáil. However, as we have seen, that threat too evaporated almost as suddenly as it had appeared. Given the fragility of the Labour and Clann na Poblachta challenges and the fact that they were sequential rather than concomitant, it is hard to see that, whatever strategies might have been pursued in the late 1940s, a left–right realignment was on the cards.

Over the next three decades (from the early 1950s to the early 1980s), aggregate volatility tended to decline. In other words, rather than accelerating as the social and economic changes identified in chapter 1 unfolded, change in voting behaviour slowed down. The 1969 and 1973 elections in fact showed levels of both total and block volatility that were among the lowest ever recorded in an Irish election. Labour's progress in 1965 and 1969 was really a Dublin phenomenon and, as in 1943, its 1969 peak was partly due to a large increase in the number of candidates it put forward. The counter-factual ('if Labour had pursued an independent strategy in 1973 . . .') is interesting and useful in bringing out the constraints on what parties can do. Because the issue is hypothetical, the voting behaviour evidence cannot be definitive. However, the evidence offers little support for the view that, by means of such a strategy, Labour could have initiated a realignment of the system and supplanted Fine Gael as the second party in the state.

In 1987, things did change, as the measure of aggregate volatility rose to the same level as in 1943. However, block volatility still remained low. It was not until 1992 that volatility once again significantly affected Fianna Fáil. Aggregate volatility is a crude measure. In this case, the aggregate volatility pattern is borne out by the individual level data, which confirms 1987 and 1992 as, in their different ways, the crucial moments of change in voting behaviour. This account of the timing of change must be qualified, however, by noting that the volatility of 1987 and 1992 was preceded by gradual change in the degree of attachment of voters to the political parties.

The available evidence suggests that the majority of Irish voters in the late 1970s and very early 1980s were party identifiers, at least in a minimal sense of the term. On the other hand, a more demanding measure of party attachment (i.e., 'feeling close to a particular party') began to decline in the early to mid-1980s and, in the early 1990s, was to be found among only two voters in five. The operation of the PR-STV electoral system also provides some evidence in this regard. Despite the fact that the system facilitates the emergence of minor party and independent candidates and perhaps even encourages an emphasis on candidate and local factors, the transfer data generated by the operation of the electoral system confirm that Irish voters tend to be party voters. Party loyalty, in the sense of voters assigning their preferences within their party, is high, though it declined in 1992 for both Fianna Fáil and Fine Gael. In the case of Fianna Fáil, there is further evidence of party voting in the remarkably high propensity to plump for the party, that is, to vote Fianna Fáil and only Fianna Fáil (making the vote non-transferable when all Fianna Fáil candidates have been elected or eliminated). Between 1954 and 1977 Fianna Fáil plumping was in the mid to high

70s[7]. It declined (to about 60 per cent) in 1981 and remained in that region through the five elections of the 1980s. However, when the Fianna Fáil vote dipped below 40 per cent in 1992 and the party was forced to rely more on its most committed supporters, Fianna Fáil plumping rose to almost the pre-1981 level. Consistent with the trends in party attachment, it declined (to about 60 per cent) in 1981. In the case of Fine Gael and Labour, there are also indications of party loyalty in the case of terminal transfer voting – in general, party supporters respond to the explicit requests or implicit positive or negative cues regarding inter-party transfers emanating from the leadership. In sum, the evidence of transfer patterns indicates a substantial and stable party orientation in preference voting prior to the 1980s, followed by some signs of change since then.

Evidence of an underlying process of change at the voter level, and at least some indication of a responsiveness on the part of the system to contemporary issues, can also be found in the variations in what was of concern to the voters since such concerns were first measured in 1969. Starting from a quite heterogeneous mix of preoccupations in 1969, there has been a tendency for a single issue – unemployment – to emerge as the dominant one. It can however be displaced, as shown by the 1989 election when it was pushed into second place by a concern with health cuts. Parties have on occasion enjoyed substantial leads on salient issues, suggesting, though not proving, that voters were at times being motivated by particular issue concerns. In the light of the discussion of the transformation of the basis of party competition above, it is also worth noting that when questions were asked about the salience of the issue of stable government in the early 1980s, the issue was of concern to very few voters and, on the one occasion when it was of any kind of widespread concern (to one voter in six in November 1982), it told against rather than in favour of Fianna Fáil. Concern with leadership as an issue increased in 1981 and again in 1982, but the evidence indicates that it has not had an impact on voting decisions commensurate with the divergences in preference that have occurred. Over and above the impact of particular issues or leaders or personalities at election time, there is substantial evidence to suggest that the fluctuations in support for political parties that occurred, not just at elections but in the intervals between elections, in the period 1975–87, were influenced by reactions to the performance of the economy.

There is also some evidence of class-related changes in party support in both the aggregate and individual-level data, particularly if the individual-level data is seen through the lens of a somewhat more refined set of class categories. However, these class-based gains and losses fall short of overthrowing the standard image of Irish electoral politics as 'politics without social bases'. That now famous phrase perhaps requires some qualification – it was indeed highly qualified in the original formulation (Whyte, 1974). If, however, it is taken to mean that Ireland does not have class politics in the sense of generally stable and contrasting class-based support for the main competing parties, it remains quite accurate. Such class-based voting as exists consists of some distinctive voting behaviour by some classes (primarily the middle

---

[7] This is substantially higher than previously published estimates; see the discussion in chapter 8.

class and farmers) at certain times. The key point is that these signs of class voting are limited and contingent. They are limited because, even taking all the qualifications into account, the main party in the system remains substantially a cross-class party. Their contingency can be seen in the shifting fortunes of Fianna Fáil among the middle class in the 1980s, and in the success of the Labour Party among this same class in 1992. What all of this suggests is that voting responds at particular times to particular issues, not that the system is undergoing a politicisation of class conflict.

Fluctuations also occur in the urban–rural support bases of the parties. These were quite significant in the 1920s and 1930s. They faded in the post-war period but became relatively pronounced again in the mid- to late 1960s. In the elections of the 1980s, especially in the two elections of 1982, they were reduced in significance, as Fine Gael put together its remarkable compendium of support from across various strata in the two elections of 1982, and as Fianna Fáil regained support in urban areas in 1987. Finally, in both the aggregate and individual-level data, urban–rural differences were quite a feature of party support in 1992.

Although an alignment, modified by the various accretions described above, may continue over a very long time, it is obviously possible, indeed it may be likely, that either a process of erosion will occur, leading to dealignment, or alternatively, that the indications of change and responsiveness will cohere into a particular pattern that spells a realignment of the system. Before considering this issue of realignment and dealignment, it is necessary to review what referendum voting and voting in the presidential election of 1990 tell us about the question of stability and change.

Given the nature of referendums, they can provide rather more clear-cut indications of stability or change than can be obtained from the results of general elections. Admittedly the evidence relates to particular issues but, given the kinds of issues covered in Irish referendums, the availability of referendums and the voting patterns exhibited in them have considerable implications for the question of stability and change in the party system and in electoral alignments.

In general, referendum voting has tended to endorse change in respect of regime-related issues (the referendums on the electoral system being notable exceptions), and endorse conservative positions on religious–moral issues (the deletion of Article 44 being an exception). Conservatism was particularly manifest in the abortion and divorce referendums of the 1980s. Then in 1992, two of the religious–moral referendums provided substantial majorities in favour of change, but the changes involved – the right to travel and the right to information – were quite limited. Even bearing the limited nature of those changes in mind, however, detailed analysis of the relationship between the votes in the three referendums of November 1992 points to the existence of three groups of voters, each constituting 30 per cent or close to 30 per cent of the active electorate. The three groups are the ultra-conservatives who voted 'no' on all three issues, the liberals who voted 'yes' on travel and information and 'no' on the substantive amendment and, finally, a group of pragmatic voters, both pragmatic liberals and pragmatic conservatives, who voted 'yes' on all three issues. This suggests that attitudes to change in the religious and moral sphere are quite complex, and that outright opposition to change in this area cannot be equated with the almost two-thirds majorities which supported the abortion amendment in 1983 and opposed the divorce amendment in 1986.

Analysis of the constituency-level determinants of liberal and conservative voting throws further light on the issue of stability and change. The pattern of liberal and conservative voting is highly structured in socio-demographic terms. In fact, it is much more highly structured than is party support. Over the eight votes or combinations of votes in the divorce and abortion referendums between 1983 and 1992, the proportion of farmers and the proportion of unskilled working class together explain between 67 and 88 per cent of the variance in all except the yes-yes-yes (i.e., the pragmatic) vote in the 1992 referendums. Both variables influence the outcome independently and in the same direction – the higher the proportion of farmers or the higher the proportion in the working class, the higher the resistance to change. Thus, analysis of the referendums of the 1980s not only provides evidence of the extent of the commitment to change and to the status quo but also provides considerable indications of the sources of support for and resistance to change.

Finally, as an element in the puzzle regarding stability and change, there is the presidential election of 1990. Was it indeed a cataclysmic, mould-breaking event that changed the face of Irish politics? Symbolically, it was certainly significant in that it provided a victory for the forces that had been twice defeated in the referendums of the 1980s. Note, however, that the actual first-preference voting figures in the presidential election did not reverse the voting pattern in the abortion and divorce referendums. At 38.9 per cent, the first-preference vote for Robinson was only 2.4 percentage points higher than the pro-divorce vote in 1986. Robinson won because, although five points behind Lenihan on the first count, she succeeded in winning 77 per cent of the votes of the eliminated Fine Gael candidate. In the circumstances, Currie's vote can be presumed to have come from a hard core of committed Fine Gael voters who had been voting and transferring votes against Fianna Fáil all their lives, and who would not have required much persuasion or incentive to transfer to Robinson. The significance of the presidential election, therefore, was not that it reversed the prevailing balance of opinion or that it was mould-breaking in the sense of radically altering the existing alignment. Its significance was that it gave distinctive representative political expression to a strand of opinion in Irish society which had not previously been represented in this way, and which, in the context of majoritarian decision rules in a referendum, had recently suffered two significant defeats. This interpretation is supported by the analysis of the pattern of the Robinson vote at constituency level.

The Robinson vote was highly correlated with the votes on abortion and divorce in 1983 and 1986. Furthermore, there is a very close parallel between the determinants of the first-preference vote for Robinson and the determinants of liberal voting in the divorce referendum and in the abortion referendums. The variation in the Robinson vote between constituencies is very well accounted for by the negative impact of high proportions of farmers and of high proportions in the working class. But further analysis suggests that the negative working-class effect is not a class effect as such. The Robinson vote is even better explained when one also introduces a measure of liberalism–conservatism into the equation and then the negative working-class effect disappears. All of this suggests that the liberal–conservative cleavage does have the

potential to affect voting behaviour beyond the immediate occasion of the relevant referendum. However, presidential elections are only second-order elections. Such elections are prone to being taken over or invaded by issues that are extraneous to the office
that is in contention, and voting patterns in them do not usually have mould-breaking
or realigning implications. On the other hand, there is some evidence that the
liberal–conservative cleavage underlying the presidential election did have an impact
on the general election of 1992. This then brings us to the final question – given the
balance of stability and change outlined above, what is the potential for realignment or
dealignment of the system? In addressing this issue, it is useful to examine two of the
cleavages that, for reasons outlined above, did not become embodied in the system
during the original process of mobilisation and alignment, but that now show some
potential for forming the basis of a realignment.

Class conflict was certainly sidelined in the formation and development of the party
system. Moreover, it is the cleavage that commentators most frequently have in mind
when they envisage the modernization of Irish party alignments. Volatility across the
left–right cleavage line was substantially higher in the 1992 election than in any
postwar Irish election (Mair, 1993, pp. 163–5). Despite this, however, social class
played only a very limited role in structuring the vote in 1992 and the Labour vote in
particular showed a remarkably cross-class character. Thus the evidence does not
suggest that the growth in support for the left in 1992 involves any real signs of the
mobilization of a class-based alignment. On the other hand, the evidence of voting
behaviour since the early 1980s does suggest that social class has played a significant
if variable role. What then of the potential for future realignment along class lines?

While it might be argued that the ideological climate and economic context of a
post-communist, post-industrial, and interdependent world are not very conducive to
a repolarization of domestic politics along class lines, the particular issues of redistribution, equity, and the role of the state in economic activity are not set to go away.
Though they are unlikely to fundamentally realign the party system, they may,
depending on party strategy and party fortunes, provide some degree of left–right
structuring. In this context, two events at the level of party strategy are crucial. The
first is the formation of a coalition between Fianna Fáil and Labour after the 1992 election. Though it had some historical roots and considerable policy justification, it was
a major reversal of long-standing coalition alignments and expectations. Part of its significance lies, as Mair has rightly argued, in freeing up the system by definitively doing
away with the ability-to-form-a-government constraint. Over and above this, its
potential significance may lie in creating the basis for a moderate, nuanced left–right
realignment of the party system (Fianna Fáil and Labour versus Fine Gael and the
Progressive Democrats) rather than for the thorough-going left–right realignment
envisaged in the more usual scenario of a coming together of Fianna Fáil and Fine
Gael and the expansion of the left wing parties in opposition to them. Given the
tenuous basis of the rupture between Fianna Fáil and Labour at the end of 1994 (as
evidenced in the several almost successful attempts to stitch the relationship together
again), it would seem that such an alliance will remain available. In fact, with the confirmation that Democratic Left is a willing and acceptable coalition partner, there may

be, depending on party performances in the next election, two potential versions of this kind of left-of-centre governing coalition. In sum, there are several scenarios in which the indications of class-based political behaviour documented in the foregoing chapters could develop and find expression in the party system. It is at this point that the second development in party strategy – the formation of the Fine Gael–Labour–Democratic Left coalition becomes relevant. One interpretation of the significance of this is that it inhibits the emergence of a class-based alignment by putting right and left together in a governing combination. However, it was clear from the discussions when that government was being formed (especially from the use of the term 'rainbow coalition') that this was envisaged as a coming together of left and right in which the identities of the parties would be sedulously maintained. Because of the more than residual importance of ideology on the left, one would have expected this in any event in the case of the left-wing parties. In the case of Fine Gael, the fact that the Progressive Democrats are outside the coalition, the fact indeed that they were consciously excluded from it, is likely to make Fine Gael more sensitive about its right of centre identity and more deliberate in projecting it. Accordingly, it would be premature to predict the permanent blocking of class-related alignment on the basis of party alliances in the Dáil at the end of 1994.

In the building of the party system, the sidelining of secular–confessional conflict was just as decisive as the marginalization of left–right conflict. However, even in a highly conservative society, change in the blanket consensus in this area was inevitable, though it may have been slower than modernization theorists would have predicted. And then there is the evidence of at least some degree of mobilization of the secular–confessional conflict in the election of November 1982, in the presidential election of 1990, and in the general election of 1992. Despite these developments, the likelihood of conflict along confessional–secular lines is considerably lessened by a number of factors. First of all there is the evidence, discussed in chapter 9, of a middle ground on confessional–secular issues that any party aspiring to major party status will want to cultivate. Secondly, the formation of the Fianna Fáil–Labour coalition after the 1992 election reduces the probability of a realignment of the party system along confessional–secular lines. This is a clear case of the impact of a strategic decision by the parties, an impact reflected in the carefully worded commitment in the Fianna Fáil–Labour programme for government to 'A major programme of family law reform, culminating in a referendum on divorce in 1994 . . .' and to 'legislation to regulate the position [in relation to abortion], recognising the sensitivity of the issue throughout the community' (Fianna Fáil and Labour, 1993)[8]. On the other hand, the fact that

[8] Court proceedings challenging the constitutionality of a number of aspects of family law that were seen to be an essential part of the preparation for divorce legislation led to the postponement, but not the abandonment, of the divorce referendum by the Fianna Fáil–Labour government. A commitment to hold such a referendum is contained in the Fine Gael–Labour–Democratic Left government programme. Towards the end of the period of the Fianna Fáil–Labour government, it also became evident that abortion legislation was on indefinite hold and that both parties accepted the necessity for such postponement. The incoming Fine Gael–Labour–Democratic Left government accepted this position, its programme simply saying that 'The Government will continue work on the complex ethical, legal and medical problems of the substantive issue raised by the "X" case' (*The Irish Times*, 15 December, 1994, p.7).

Fianna Fáil was back in opposition at the end of 1994 might suggest that the party would adopt an adversarial strategy on secular–confessional issues that would align it with the conservative position. It will certainly be under considerable pressure to do so. However, such a strategy is less likely in view of the need for Fianna Fáil to culti-vate the middle ground on these issues and in view of the need to keep the option of a post-election alliance with liberal political forces open. It would appear therefore that the only possibility of introducing a degree of realignment of the party system along secular–confessional lines lies in the possible emergence of a new party to represent the conservative point of view. The evidence of the existence of a substantial ultra-con-servative minority revealed by analysis of the outcomes of the 1992 abortion referen-dums suggests that such a development is possible. However, the performance of 'pro–life' candidates in recent general elections suggests that mobilizing the conserv-ative referendum vote to support a new political party would not be an easy task. This underlines the fact that referendum and general election voting are very different political acts. Indeed, it points to a third and particularly important factor inhibiting the takeover of the party system by secular confessional conflict, that is, the existence of an alternative channel for the resolution of the most contentious problems in this area. Despite the politicization of the secular–confessional conflict in the referendums of the 1980s and despite the evidence of the invasion of the 1990 presidential election by this conflict and some carry over from the presidential election to the 1992 general election, the overriding significance of the referendum process is that it insulates the party system from the full brunt of secular–confessional issues by providing an alter-native channel for the expression of this cleavage.

In summary, while not impossible, the prospects of a fundamental realignment of the party system look meagre. Turning to the alternative development, that is, dealign-ment, it is difficult to say precisely how far this process has gone. We have seen con-siderable evidence that the party system and voter alignments are still shaped by the way in which various cleavages were included or excluded when the foundations of the party system were laid. Moreover, until a durable solution to the problem of Northern Ireland is found, there will be, depending on the course of events, potential for the reactivation of the nationalist cleavage that was at the core of the party system at its foundation. In the light of this and the fact that many voters are still attached in some degree or other to the existing parties, the prevailing alignment cannot be written off. However, if demographic, social and economic changes have had any effect, it has been in making voters less inclined to adhere to a particular party and more concerned with particular issues. In a system for so long regarded as a peculiarity, it is interesting to note that this is in line with a general process of change in other countries in which cleavage structures have become increasingly irrelevant to partisanship. In assessing the implications of this loosening of the link between cleavage structures and the party system, Franklin argues that 'In those countries where cleavage politics no longer dominate, party choice depends on other factors. A natural concomitant of this liber-ation (where it has occurred) is that the fortunes of individual political parties have become much less certain, and are dependent more largely on variations in leadership skills and other contingencies' (Franklin, 1992. p. 403). The implications are summed up in the phrase 'the particularisation of voting choice' (van der Eijk, Franklin, Mackie and Valen, 1992, pp. 411–20) – voters are increasingly responding to a complex variety of issues and of diverse social structural characteristics and affiliations that cannot be subsumed into simple dichotomous classifications of left versus right, liberal versus conservative, working class versus middle class or whatever. This notion of the particularization of voting choice certainly fits with what we know of the role of issues, of leadership and of social class in the Irish general election of 1992. The parliamentary concomitant of the particularization of voter choice is an increase in the fluidity of parliamentary alliances, a further enhancement of the role of parliament in the formation of government and a weakening of the notion of electoral mandates for either policy platforms or alliances of parties. Reflection on the processes of government formation that took place after the 1992 election and at the end of 1994 suggests that, in Irish parliamentary government, these trends are already well under way.

Contrary to the usual aphorism about a week being a long time in politics, a year or several years can be a short time in the evolution, strengthening, weakening, dealignment or realignment of existing party systems and electoral alignments. In fact the relevant minimum timespan within which change in electoral alignment can be observed is the interval bounded by two elections. Accordingly, we shall not know the full implications of the 1992 election, or of the surprise formation of a Fianna Fáil–Labour government that resulted from it, or of the even greater surprise replacement of that government by a Fine Gael–Labour–Democratic Left government in the middle of the term of the 27th Dáil until at least after the next election. Inevitably, then, this discussion must close on a tentative note. In closing, it is worth emphasizing that the various realignment and dealignment scenarios in the preceding paragraphs are sketched and assessed without any prescriptive intent. Political scientists sometimes conclude inquiries of this sort by explicitly bemoaning the legacy of the past and by seeing light at the end of the tunnel. This usually involves at least an implicit model of what the party system ought to be like. But should political science get involved in redesigning the party system by backing this or that alignment? Should it applaud when signs of incipient class politics are found? Should it rejoice in the 'Europeanization' of the party system? Should it encourage the amalgamation of the 'civil war' parties and the opportunity for the expansion of the left that this would imply? Or should it rejoice in the formation of a cross–class alliance bringing together Fine Gael on the one side and Democratic Left on the other? Alternatively, should it regret the passing of the Fianna Fáil–Labour alliance, with its potential for the development of a moderate left–right polarization, and hope for its resurrection? Should it endorse one of these developments rather than another on the basis of how it affects the way in which the party system handles secular–confessional and nationalist issues? Or, finally, should it settle for dealignment, for the particularization of voter choice and for the increasing fluidity and unpredictability of alliances? The answer given here is that it should do none of these things. The fact is that, if the future shape of a party system undergoing change is difficult to predict, it is even more resistant to being designed, especially if the designing is being done from outside the system. Any such attempt might justifiably be regarded as presumptuous. The best course may be to follow Gulliver's example in his response to the Secretary's request for assistance in reforming the Lilliputian party system:

> I DESIRED the Secretary to present my humble Duty to the Emperor, and to let him know that it would not become me, who was a Foreigner, to interfere with Parties . . . .

Appendix 1

Glossary

Áras an Uachtaráin – (*aw*-rus un *ook*-ta-rawn) – residence of the President
ard-fheis – (ord-*esh*) – national convention of a political party
Bunreacht na hÉireann – (bunracht ne *hay*run) – Constitution of Ireland
Clann na Poblachta – (clown ne *pub*lakta) – 'party of the republic' (party name)
Clann na Talmhan – (clown ne ta*loon*) – 'party of the land' (party name)
Cumann na nGaedheal – (*kum*-man ne *ngale*) – 'party of the Irish' (party name)
Dáil Éireann – (dawl *ay*-run) – 'Assembly of Ireland' (lower house of the national parliament)
Fianna Fáil – (*fee*-an-a *fawl*) – 'soldiers of Ireland' (party name)
Fine Gael – (fin-a *gale*) – 'Irish race' (party name)
Oireachtas – (ih-*rock*-tus or *ih*-ruck-tus) – 'gathering' (the official title of the whole Parliament – President, Dáil and Seanad)
Seanad Éireann – (shanad *ay*-run) – Senate of Ireland (upper house of the national parliament)
Sinn Féin – (shin *fayn*) – 'ourselves' (party name)
Tánaiste – (*taw*-nish-deh) – deputy prime minister
Taoiseach – (*tee*-shuk) – prime minister
Teachta Dála – (*tak*-tuh *dawl*-uh) – Dáil deputy, TD
Uachtarán – (*ook*-ta-rawn) – president

Note: The above glossary is substantially based on the glossary in Coakley and Gallagher (1993, p. 279). There are considerable variations in the translation of the names of some of the Irish parties (compare the glossary in Coakley and Gallagher with that in Penniman and Farrell 1987, pp. 265–6 and see also Coakley, 1980, pp. 171–81). The pronunciation system indicated is approximate and follows that in Penniman and Farrell (*ibid.*). Italics indicate stressed syllables.

Appendix 2

Election and referendum results

I. First preference vote in general elections by region

Anti-Treaty Sinn Féin/ Fianna Fáil (FF)

Election	Ireland	Dublin	Leinster	Munster	Connacht–Ulster	Candidates	Seats
1922	21.3	11.7	15.6	28.4	31.4	58	36
1923	27.4	17.2	25.1	30.7	30.8	85	44
Jun. '27	26.2	24.3	26.2	24.4	29.6	87	44
Sept. '27	35.2	26.6	33.1	37.7	39.0	88	57
1932	44.5	34.1	44.0	46.1	48.9	104	72
1933	49.7	43.4	45.4	50.6	55.7	103	77
1937	45.2	41.3	44.5	42.8	51.7	101	69
1938	51.9	49.3	49.0	50.9	57.9	97	77
1943	41.8	45.1	39.8	40.9	42.5	106	67
1944	48.9	51.8	45.8	47.7	51.3	100	76
1948	41.9	38.9	41.3	42.3	44.1	119	68
1951	46.3	46.4	46.3	46.3	46.2	119	69
1954	43.4	39.3	43.6	45.0	44.5	112	65
1957	48.3	46.8	50.2	49.6	46.2	112	78
1961	43.8	44.6	41.8	43.9	45.0	107	70
1965	47.7	48.2	45.4	47.9	48.9	111	72
1969	44.6	39.5	43.7	49.0	49.8	122	75
1973	46.2	40.4	44.7	50.0	49.4	119	69
1977	50.6	46.8	50.7	54.0	50.2	132	84
1981	45.3	41.4	46.1	45.4	49.0	139	78
Feb. '82	47.3	42.6	48.4	47.7	51.5	131	81
Nov. '82	45.2	38.3	46.2	46.1	51.8	132	75
1987	44.2	40.5	45.7	42.7	49.7	122	81
1989	44.2	40.7	46.1	43.6	47.5	115	77
1992	39.1	32.9	40.9	38.6	46.5	122	68

Pro-Treaty Sinn Féin/Cumann na nGaedheal/Fine Gael (FG)

Election	Ireland	Dublin	Leinster	Munster	Connacht-Ulster	Candidates	Seats
1922	38.5	40.9	35.6	30.6	52.2	65	58
1923	39.0	50.3	33.0	33.9	43.7	107	63
Jun. '27	27.4	30.8	23.5	24.0	32.8	97	47
Sep. '27	38.6	47.8	36.3	34.8	39.7	89	62
1932	35.2	38.9	34.7	34.3	34.6	101	57
1933	30.4	40.4	26.4	28.9	29.6	85	48
1937	34.8	30.0	35.0	36.5	35.7	95	48
1938	33.3	33.9	33.0	33.8	32.7	76	45
1943	23.1	26.0	25.9	23.4	18.0	87	32
1944	20.5	26.4	23.3	18.5	16.0	55	30
1948	19.8	24.6	21.6	19.0	15.7	82	31
1951	25.8	26.2	26.3	27.0	23.3	77	40
1954	32.0	34.6	36.6	29.7	28.6	89	50
1957	26.6	26.5	29.6	25.2	26.0	82	40
1961	32.0	31.7	33.8	30.5	32.7	96	47
1965	34.1	29.5	33.3	30.9	43.8	102	47
1969	33.3	28.4	35.0	32.5	41.6	125	50
1973	35.1	32.2	35.4	33.2	40.8	111	54
1977	30.6	27.6	28.4	29.4	39.3	116	43
1981	36.5	36.2	35.8	35.2	39.3	126	65
Feb. '82	37.3	38.9	37.1	34.8	39.1	113	63
Nov. '82	39.2	41.1	38.8	36.2	41.7	115	70
1987	27.1	23.7	27.3	26.9	31.8	97	51
1989	29.3	23.0	30.9	30.4	34.6	86	55
1992	24.5	17.0	25.5	26.3	31.1	91	45

The Labour Party (Lab)

Election	Ireland	Dublin	Leinster	Munster	Connacht–Ulster	Candidates	Seats
1922	21.4	13.4	37.4	21.0	4.2	18	17
1923	10.6	4.6	19.0	12.5	4.8	44	14
Jun. '27	12.6	10.3	22.1	13.5	5.2	44	22
Sep. '27	9.1	5.2	15.4	11.2	3.8	28	13
1932	7.7	6.3	14.0	8.3	3.0	33	7
1933	5.7	3.6	12.5	6.2	1.1	19	8
1937	10.3	7.7	17.3	14.0	1.1	23	13
1938	10.0	6.7	16.3	12.6	3.2	30	9
1943	15.7	16.2	23.1	16.2	8.2	70	17
1944	8.7	11.6	11.7	10.4	1.2	31	8
1948	8.7	9.7	11.5	12.2	1.2	43	14
1951	11.4	10.8	17.3	15.4	1.7	37	16
1954	12.1	13.2	18.1	16.1	0.5	41	19
1957	9.1	8.1	14.3	12.6	0.8	31	12
1961	11.7	8.4	16.5	17.7	1.7	35	16
1965	15.4	18.5	19.2	18.5	4.3	44	22
1969	16.6	28.3	17.4	16.0	5.8	99	18
1973	13.7	22.3	14.4	14.0	2.5	55	19
1977	11.6	17.5	13.5	11.9	2.1	57	17
1981	9.9	12.2	11.7	12.0	2.0	60	15
Feb. '82	9.1	11.2	10.0	11.2	2.4	41	15
Nov. '82	9.4	10.5	11.8	11.3	2.3	40	16
1987	6.5	7.1	9.5	6.8	1.2	37	12
1989	9.5	9.5	13.5	10.9	2.4	33	15
1992	19.3	26.1	20.9	19.5	7.7	42	33

Sinn Féin (post–1926) (SF)

Election	Ireland	Dublin	Leinster	Munster	Connacht–Ulster	Candidates	Seats
Jun. '27	3.6	4.6	1.1	5.0	3.6	15	5
1954	0.2	0.0	0.3	0.2	0.0	2	0
1957	5.4	3.0	5.1	5.4	7.3	19	4
1961	3.1	1.1	2.5	3.8	4.6	21	0
1987	1.9	2.2	1.6	0.9	3.2	27	0
1989	1.2	1.9	0.9	0.2	2.3	14	0
1992	1.6	2.0	1.3	1.1	2.4	41	0

The Farmers' Party (FP)

Election	Ireland	Dublin	Leinster	Munster	Connacht–Ulster	Candidates	Seats
1922	7.9	2.7	10.3	11.2	4.9	13	7
1923	12.1	1.4	17.8	13.9	11.2	64	15
Jun. '27	8.9	0.0	12.4	12.6	6.7	39	11
Sep. '27	6.4	0.0	8.4	9.6	4.8	20	6
1932	1.9	0.0	0.6	5.4	0.0	7	3

National League (Nat Lg)

Election	Ireland	Dublin	Leinster	Munster	Connacht–Ulster	Candidates	Seats
Jun. '27	7.3	7.0	9.4	5.8	7.6	30	8
Sep. '27	1.6	0.2	3.6	2.4	0.0	6	2

Irish Workers' League

Election	Ireland	Dublin	Leinster	Munster	Connacht–Ulster	Candidates	Seats
Sept. '27	1.1	6.5	0.0	0.0	0.0	3	1

National Centre Party (NCP)

Election	Ireland	Dublin	Leinster	Munster	Connacht–Ulster	Candidates	Seats
1933	9.2	1.2	13.1	12.1	7.2	26	11

Clann na Talmhan (C-T)

Election	Ireland	Dublin	Leinster	Munster	Connacht–Ulster	Candidates	Seats
1943	9.0	0.6	5.9	12.1	13.7	40	11
1944	10.8	0.0	6.0	14.7	18.1	27	9
1948	5.5	0.0	0.4	7.9	11.1	25	7
1951	2.9	0.0	0.0	0.0	11.5	7	6
1954	3.1	0.0	0.0	1.8	10.1	10	5
1957	2.4	0.0	0.0	0.0	9.4	7	3
1961	1.5	0.0	0.0	0.0	6.3	6	2

National Labour (Nat Lab)

Election	Ireland	Dublin	Leinster	Munster	Connacht–Ulster	Candidates	Seats
1944	2.7	0.5	7.0	2.9	0.0	9	4
1948	2.6	0.8	5.4	2.7	1.5	14	5

Clann na Poblachta (C-P)

Election	Ireland	Dublin	Leinster	Munster	Connacht–Ulster	Candidates	Seats
1948	13.3	19.3	9.1	11.7	14.2	93	10
1951	4.1	3.8	1.8	4.0	6.4	26	2
1954	3.8	4.8	0.6	3.9	5.9	20	3
1957	1.7	3.7	0.4	1.2	1.8	12	1
1961	1.1	2.1	0.0	0.0	2.8	5	1
1965	0.8	1.1	0.0	0.0	2.1	4	1

National Progressive Democrats

Election	Ireland	Dublin	Leinster	Munster	Connacht-Ulster	Candidates	Seats
1965	1.0	1.9	0.6	0.0	1.9	3	2

Sinn Féin/Sinn Féin the Workers' Party/The Workers' Party (WP)

Election	Ireland	Dublin	Leinster	Munster	Connacht-Ulster	Candidates	Seats
1973	1.1	1.5	1.2	0.9	1.1	10	0
1977	1.7	1.5	1.1	2.5	1.2	16	0
1981	1.7	2.6	1.4	2.2	0.3	15	1
Feb. '82	2.2	3.1	1.4	2.9	0.8	14	3
Nov. '82	3.3	6.5	1.9	2.9	1.1	20	2
1987	3.8	7.5	2.2	3.2	1.4	29	4
1989	5.0	11.4	1.7	4.0	1.4	23	7
1992	0.7	1.3	0.1	0.9	0.1	18	0

Socialist Labour Party

Election	Ireland	Dublin	Leinster	Munster	Connacht-Ulster	Candidates	Seats
1981	0.4	1.5	0.1	0.0	0.0	7	1

Democratic Socialist Party

Election	Ireland	Dublin	Leinster	Munster	Connacht-Ulster	Candidates	Seats
Nov. '82	0.4	0.6	0.0	0.9	0.0	7	0
1987	0.4	0.3	0.0	1.1	0.0	4	1
1989	0.6	0.2	0.0	1.8	0.0	2	1

Progressive Democrats (PD)

Election	Ireland	Dublin	Leinster	Munster	Connacht-Ulster	Candidates	Seats
1987	11.9	13.6	11.0	15.0	5.6	51	14
1989	5.5	5.4	4.2	8.0	3.2	35	6
1992	4.7	5.5	2.5	6.7	3.1	20	10

Green Alliance/The Green Party (GP/Green)

Election	Ireland	Dublin	Leinster	Munster	Connacht–Ulster	Candidates	Seats
1987	0.4	1.1	0.2	0.2	0.0	9	0
1989	1.5	5.2	0.4	0.0	0.0	11	1
1992	1.4	3.5	0.8	0.7	0.2	19	1

Democratic Left (DL)

Election	Ireland	Dublin	Leinster	Munster	Connacht–Ulster	Candidates	Seats
1992	2.8	5.3	2.2	2.3	0.7	20	4

Independents and micro parties (Inds)

Election	Ireland	Dublin	Leinster	Munster	Connacht–Ulster	Candidates	Seats
1922	11.0	31.3	1.2	8.8	7.4	22	10
1923	10.9	26.5	5.1	9.0	9.5	76	17
Jun. '27	14.0	23.1	5.3	14.8	14.8	65	16
Sept. '27	7.9	13.3	3.3	4.5	12.7	31	12
1932	10.6	20.8	6.8	5.9	13.4	34	14
1933	5.0	11.4	2.6	2.2	6.4	13	9
1937	9.7	21.0	3.3	6.7	11.5	36	8
1938	4.7	10.1	1.8	2.7	6.2	11	7
1943	10.5	12.1	5.4	7.4	17.7	51	11
1944	8.5	9.7	6.2	5.8	13.4	30	11
1948	8.3	6.9	10.8	4.2	12.3	31	12
1951	9.6	12.8	8.3	7.4	10.9	31	14
1954	5.5	8.1	0.8	3.4	10.4	31	5
1957	6.6	11.8	0.5	6.0	8.5	26	9
1961	5.8	10.1	4.9	4.1	5.0	28	6
1965	2.1	2.6	2.1	2.7	0.9	20	2
1969	3.1	3.9	3.9	2.5	2.8	27	1
1973	3.9	3.6	4.4	1.9	6.3	40	2
1977	5.6	6.7	6.4	3.2	7.1	55	4
1981	6.7	7.7	5.0	5.2	9.4	57	6
Feb.'82	4.1	4.3	3.1	3.4	6.2	66	4
Nov.'82	3.0	3.6	1.4	3.5	3.1	57	3
1987	4.4	4.4	2.6	4.4	7.0	94	4
1989	3.9	2.9	2.5	3.0	8.7	53	5
1992	6.0	6.4	5.9	4.1	8.3	108	5

II. Presidential elections: first preference vote

	FF	*FG*	*Ind*
1945	49.5	30.9	19.6
1959	56.3	43.7	–
1966	50.5	49.6	–
1973	52.0	48.0	–
1990	44.1	17.0	38.9

III. 1990 Presidential election: first preference vote by constituency

	Currie *FG*	*Lenihan* *FF*	*Robinson* *Ind*
Carlow–Kilkenny	18.8	45.1	36.1
Cavan–Monaghan	21.2	53.6	25.2
Clare	18.3	50.0	31.7
Cork East	18.5	44.4	37.1
Cork North–Central	15.5	38.6	45.9
Cork North–West	27.7	45.5	26.8
Cork South–Central	17.3	33.9	48.9
Cork South–West	29.1	40.4	30.5
Donegal North–East	17.1	55.4	27.6
Donegal South–West	19.0	53.0	28.0
Dublin Central	12.3	46.7	41.0
Dublin North	11.4	43.1	45.5
Dublin North–Central	12.7	44.5	42.9
Dublin North–East	11.0	41.4	47.7
Dublin North–West	10.1	42.0	47.9
Dublin South	17.0	31.7	51.3
Dublin South–Central	13.0	39.3	47.6
Dublin South–East	16.6	31.7	51.7
Dublin South–West	9.9	41.7	48.4
Dublin West	13.4	45.6	41.0
Dun Laoghaire	17.0	28.4	54.6
Galway East	20.4	50.4	29.2
Galway West	17.6	41.1	41.3
Kerry North	17.2	46.0	36.9
Kerry South	17.2	50.0	32.8
Kildare	15.2	42.2	42.7
Laoighis–Offaly	17.1	50.4	32.6
Limerick East	17.6	34.2	48.2
Limerick West	19.4	52.2	28.5
Longford–Westmeath	18.7	52.9	28.4
Louth	14.1	50.8	35.1
Mayo East	18.7	44.2	37.1

Mayo West	18.3	47.1	34.6
Meath	16.7	49.0	34.4
Roscommon	23.0	51.3	25.7
Sligo–Leitrim	20.3	49.3	30.4
Tipperary North	20.0	49.4	30.7
Tipperary South	19.4	46.4	34.2
Waterford	15.9	44.5	39.6
Wexford	16.9	46.5	36.7
Wicklow	14.1	39.4	46.5

IV. Local elections 1960–1991

	FF	FG	Lab	Inds/Others
1960	38.4	26.5	10.2	24.9
1967	40.2	32.5	14.8	12.5
1974	40.1	33.7	12.8	13.4
1979	39.2	34.9	11.8	14.1
1985	45.5	29.8	7.7	17.0
1991	37.9	26.4	10.6	25.1

V. European Parliament elections

Fianna Fáil

Election	Ireland	Dublin	Leinster	Munster	Connacht-Ulster	Candidates	Seats
1979	34.7	28.4	41.5	37.5	30.0	15	5
1984	39.2	33.4	43.8	38.9	41.4	10	8
1989	31.5	29.1	36.9	28.8	32.7	9	6
1994	35.0	20.9	33.5	42.1	42.5	10	7

Fine Gael

Election	Ireland	Dublin	Leinster	Munster	Connacht-Ulster	Candidates	Seats
1979	33.1	30.4	40.7	26.9	37.0	13	4
1984	32.2	31.7	36.6	28.6	33.3	9	6
1989	21.6	17.2	26.9	17.6	28.0	9	4
1994	24.3	23.8	27.7	18.7	29.7	8	4

The Labour Party

Election	Ireland	Dublin	Leinster	Munster	Connacht–Ulster	Candidates	Seats
1979	14.5	29.5	13.1	12.5	4.3	6	4
1984	8.4	10.0	11.9	7.6	3.5	4	0
1989	9.5	12.8	13.2	8.9	1.6	5	1
1994	11.0	14.1	15.5	7.0	8.5	6	1

Sinn Féin the Workers' Party/ The Workers' Party

Election	Ireland	Dublin	Leinster	Munster	Connacht–Ulster	Candidates	Seats
1979	3.3	4.0	4.7	2.7	2.0	6	9
1984	4.3	6.9	3.4	5.1	1.1	4	0
1989	7.6	15.8	4.4	5.4	2.8	6	1
1994	1.9	5.7	0.0	1.7	0.0	2	0

Green Alliance/ The Green Party

Election	Ireland	Dublin	Leinster	Munster	Connacht–Ulster	Candidates	Seats
1984	0.5	1.9	0.0	0.0	0.0	1	0
1989	3.7	8.3	6.3	0.0	0.0	2	0
1994	7.9	14.5	11.8	2.8	3.7	4	2

Progressive Democrats

Election	Ireland	Dublin	Leinster	Munster	Connacht–Ulster	Candidates	Seats
1989	11.9	8.1	8.4	17.3	13.0	4	1
1994	6.5	3.0	4.8	8.7	9.1	4	0

Democratic Left

Election	Ireland	Dublin	Leinster	Munster	Connacht–Ulster	Candidates	Seats
1994	3.5	8.7	0.0	4.3	0.0	2	0

Independents/Others

Election	Ireland	Dublin	Leinster	Munster	Connacht–Ulster	Candidates	Seats
1979	14.4	7.7	0.0	20.6	26.8	6	2
1984	15.5	16.1	4.3	19.8	20.6	13	1
1989	14.1	8.6	4.0	22.0	21.9	18	2
1994	9.9	9.4	6.7	14.8	6.5	16	1

VI. By-elections: first preference vote in each inter-election period, and first preference vote in the same constituencies in the preceding general election

	FF	FG	Lab	SF	Inds/Others
1923 (by-election constituencies)	24.4	43.2	8.2		24.3
1923–27 (by-elections)	36.6	52.9	5.7		4.8
1927.1	25.4	31.5	12.3	3.4	27.5
1927	34.3	63.3	–	2.4	–
1927.2	29.1	42.7	7.5		20.8
1927–32	43.1	51.4	2.9		2.6
1933	46.4	39.0	7.3		7.3
1933–37	53.5	43.2	1.7		1.6
1938	60.2	27.6	7.7		4.6
1938–43	61.8	28.1	–		10.2
1944	50.1	21.2	8.9		19.9
1944–48	43.6	17.8	14.6		24.0
1948	41.8	23.2	6.8		28.2
1948–51	47.0	27.8	20.6		4.6
1951	47.5	27.9	14.6		10.1
1951–54	41.1	32.6	11.7		14.7
1954	42.5	34.6	11.8		11.3
1954–57	53.1	17.4	13.0		16.6
1957	51.1	27.9	5.9		15.1
1957–61	44.2	31.6	10.1		14.1
1961	43.7	30.2	12.2		13.8

1961–65	42.7	38.7	16.3	2.2
1965	51.6	30.8	16.0	1.6
1965–69	47.2	30.9	19.7	2.2
1969	40.6	32.7	18.9	7.8
1969–74	43.5	36.3	13.9	6.4
1973	46.8	35.1	7.9	10.2
1973–77	43.6	37.1	6.3	13.1
1977	47.1	31.8	4.0	17.2
1977–81	37.4	34.9	6.3	21.5
1982.1	47.3	42.2	4.6	5.9
1982	44.2	40.2	3.2	12.4
1982.2	48.5	39.4	4.1	8.0
1982–87	52.9	31.6	3.3	12.3
1992	34.9	23.2	18.8	23.2
1992–94	29.1	25.3	7.2	38.4

VII. Results of abortion (1983) and divorce (1986) referendums[1] by constituency[2]

	Insert anti-abortion amendent		Delete anti-divorce clause	
	Yes	No	Yes	No
Carlow-Kilkenny	68.8	31.2	31.9	68.2
Cavan-Monaghan	81.4	18.6	27.5	72.5
Clare	73.9	26.2	31.6	68.4
Cork East	71.9	28.1	29.5	70.6
Cork North-Central	64.7	35.3	30.5	69.5
Cork North-West	81.4	18.6	21.0	79.0
Cork South-Central	55.8	44.2	37.6	62.4
Cork South-West	77.0	23.0	26.9	73.1
Donegal North-East	82.9	17.1	26.6	73.4
Donegal South-West	82.2	17.8	30.2	69.8
Dublin Central	62.0	38.0	39.1	60.9
Dublin North	53.8	46.2	50.6	49.4
Dublin North-Central	57.3	42.7	44.0	64.0
Dublin North-East	49.2	50.8	51.1	49.0
Dublin North-West	52.5	47.6	47.6	52.4
Dublin South	45.4	54.6	54.4	45.6
Dublin South-Central	56.5	43.5	45.5	54.5

Dublin South-East	49.3	50.7	53.7	46.3
Dublin South-West	49.2	50.8	53.5	46.5
Dublin West	54.7	45.3	48.8	51.2
Dun Laoghaire	42.0	58.0	58.8	41.2
Galway East	80.3	19.7	23.2	76.8
Galway West	64.5	35.5	36.9	63.1
Kerry North	77.0	23.0	27.0	73.0
Kerry South	81.8	18.2	24.0	76.0
Kildare	59.4	40.6	45.0	55.0
Laoighis-Offaly	77.8	22.2	26.7	73.4
Limerick East	68.4	31.6	35.2	64.8
Limerick West	79.3	20.7	24.9	75.1
Longford-Westmeath	76.3	23.7	29.2	70.8
Louth	70.3	29.7	35.9	64.1
Mayo East	83.8	16.2	24.3	75.7
Mayo West	81.2	18.8	26.3	73.7
Meath	73.0	27.1	31.7	68.3
Roscommon	83.8	16.2	22.7	77.3
Sligo-Leitrim	77.1	22.9	29.5	70.5
Tipperary North	79.4	20.6	25.5	74.5
Tipperary South	76.1	23.9	27.2	72.8
Waterford	68.8	31.2	33.1	66.9
Wexford	72.9	27.2	30.8	69.2
Wicklow	57.2	42.8	46.9	53.1

Notes

[1] Results of all referendums, 1937–92, can be found in Table 9.1, in the text.

[2] 1983 and 1986 referendum question wordings were as follows:

1983 (abortion): 'The Eighth Amendment of the Constitution Bill, 1982, proposes to add the subsection here following to Article 40.3 of the Constitution.

> 3° The State acknowledges the right to life of the unborn and, with due regard to the equal right to life of the mother, guarantees in its laws to respect, and, as far as practicable, by its laws to defend and vindicate that right';

1986 (divorce): 'The Tenth Amendment of the Constitution Bill, 1985 proposes to delete subsection 2° of Article 41.3 of the Constitution, which states that no law shall be enacted providing for the grant of a dissolution of marriage, and to substitute the subsection here following:

> 2° Where, and only where, such court established under this Constitution as may be prescribed by law is satisfied that:-
>> (i) a marriage has failed,
>> (ii) the failure has continued for a period of, or periods amounting to, at least five years,
>> (iii) there is no reasonable possibility of reconciliation between the parties to the marriage, and
>> (iv) any other condition prescribed by law has been compiled with,

the court may in accordance with law grant a dissolution of the marriage provided that the court is satisfied that adequate and proper provision having regard to the circumstances will be made for any dependent spouse and for any child of or any child who is dependent on either spouse.'

VIII. Results of abortion referendums, 1992[3]

	Substantive issue		Right to travel		Right to information	
	Yes	No	Yes	No	Yes	No
Carlow-Kilkenny	38.0	62.0	61.6	38.4	59.2	40.8
Cavan-Monaghan	39.6	60.4	54.3	46.1	51.9	48.1
Clare	37.1	62.9	61.6	38.4	59.7	40.3
Cork East	32.6	70.0	53.1	46.9	52.3	47.7
Cork North-Central	31.6	68.4	58.0	42.0	55.2	44.8
Cork North-West	29.6	70.4	49.0	51.0	46.5	53.5
Cork South-Central	32.4	67.6	64.8	35.2	61.6	38.4
Cork South-West	32.5	67.5	53.1	46.9	50.6	49.4
Donegal North-East	27.9	72.1	41.1	58.9	41.4	58.6
Donegal South-West	29.2	69.5	38.6	61.4	41.8	58.2
Dublin Central	32.6	67.4	61.7	38.3	58.5	41.5
Dublin North	37.9	62.1	77.0	23.0	74.2	25.8
Dublin North-Central	31.7	68.3	68.3	31.7	64.9	35.1
Dublin North-East	36.2	63.8	74.9	25.1	72.2	27.8
Dublin North-West	34.0	66.0	69.3	30.7	66.2	33.8
Dublin South	27.4	72.6	78.0	22.0	74.4	25.6
Dublin South-Central	31.8	68.2	70.0	30.0	64.9	35.1
Dublin South-East	26.3	73.7	71.0	29.0	67.9	32.1
Dublin South-West	39.9	60.1	76.1	23.9	73.5	26.5
Dublin West	39.4	60.6	71.0	29.0	71.5	28.5
Dun Laoghaire	29.9	70.1	80.6	19.4	75.9	24.1
Galway East	38.1	61.9	56.6	43.4	54.4	45.6
Galway West	33.2	66.8	63.5	36.5	60.8	39.2
Kerry North	31.5	68.5	52.8	47.2	50.3	49.7
Kerry South	36.7	63.3	56.3	43.7	54.1	45.9
Kildare	39.1	60.9	71.9	28.1	67.7	32.3
Laoighis-Offaly	37.2	62.8	56.5	43.5	53.8	46.2
Limerick East	31.8	68.2	61.3	38.7	57.8	42.2
Limerick West	30.6	69.4	51.3	48.7	49.1	50.9
Longford-Roscommon	38.6	61.4	54.9	45.1	53.2	46.8
Louth	38.8	61.2	59.4	40.6	57.2	42.8
Mayo East	37.1	62.9	55.2	44.8	52.9	47.1
Mayo West	40.5	59.5	59.4	40.6	57.8	42.2
Meath	39.7	60.3	64.8	35.2	61.6	38.4
Sligo-Leitrim	37.3	62.7	56.6	43.4	54.4	45.6
Tipperary North	33.9	66.1	53.7	46.3	51.3	48.7
Tipperary South	33.8	66.2	52.7	47.3	53.0	47.0
Waterford	32.4	67.6	62.4	37.6	61.6	38.4
Westmeath	37.3	62.7	56.1	43.9	54.1	45.9
Wexford	37.0	63.0	61.3	38.7	56.9	43.1
Wicklow	36.6	63.9	68.9	31.1	66.1	33.9

[3] 1992 referendum question wordings were as follows:
Substantive issue: 'The Twelfth Amendment of the Constitution Bill, 1992 proposes to amend Article 40 of the Constitution by the addition of the text here following to subsection 3° of section 3 thereof:

"It shall be unlawful to terminate the life of an unborn unless such termination is necessary to save the life, as distinct from the health, of the mother where there is an illness or disorder of the mother giving rise to a real and substantial risk to her life, not being a risk of self-destruction"';

Right to travel: 'The Thirteenth Amendment of the Constitution Bill, 1992 proposes to amend Article 40 of the Constitution by the addition of the paragraph here following to subsection 3° of section 3 thereof:

"This subsection shall not limit freedom to travel between the State and another state"';

Right to information: 'The Fourteenth Amendment of the Constitution Bill, 1992 proposes to amend Article 40 of the Constitution by the addition of the paragraph here following to subsection 3° of section 3 thereof:

"This subsection shall not limit freedom to obtain or make available, in the State, subject to such conditions as may be laid down by law, information relating to services lawfully available in another state."'

IX. General election turnout by region

Election	Ireland	Dublin	Leinster	Munster	Connacht-Ulster
1922	60.6	65.2	62.2	62.0	52.3
1923	60.3	60.0	61.4	61.2	58.5
1927.1	66.2	65.5	68.5	67.9	62.9
1927.2	67.7	67.3	68.8	69.9	64.7
1932	73.9	70.3	75.8	73.3	75.2
1933	80.4	76.0	82.0	82.4	79.6
1937	74.6	69.6	77.3	77.8	72.2
1938	76.0	67.4	79.4	80.0	75.0
1943	73.5	68.4	74.8	76.9	72.0
1944	68.5	64.0	69.5	71.5	67.3
1948	73.6	69.8	74.6	75.9	72.9
1951	76.5	68.1	76.0	78.2	80.7
1954	75.7	68.2	77.9	79.8	75.9
1957	70.6	60.5	73.6	74.6	72.6
1961	70.1	60.4	72.9	74.6	71.6
1965	74.5	69.8	76.5	76.8	74.6
1969	76.9	72.4	79.1	79.6	76.8
1973	76.6	73.2	78.4	79.1	75.8
1977	76.3	70.2	78.8	79.4	77.9
1981	76.2	69.2	78.2	79.8	79.0
1982.1	73.8	68.3	75.6	76.8	75.5
1982.2	72.9	66.4	75.2	76.3	74.6
1987	73.3	69.4	74.7	76.0	73.9
1989	68.5	64.0	68.8	72.1	69.7
1992	68.5	66.2	68.1	70.8	68.9

X. Turnout in referendums, local, presidential and European elections

Year	Referendums	Local	Presidential	European
1937	75.8			
1945		63.0	63.0	
1950		62.0		
1955		65.0		
1959	58.4		58.4	
1960		60.0		
1966			65.3	
1967		69.0		
1968	65.8			
1972.1	70.9			
1972.2	50.7			
1973			62.2	
1974		67.0		
1979	28.6	66.0		63.6
1983	53.7			
1984	47.5			47.6
1985		63.0		
1986	60.8			
1987	44.1			
1989				68.3
1990			64.0	
1991		58.0		
1992.1	57.3			
1992.2	69.2			
1994				44.0

Appendix 3

Sources of opinion poll data used

Research company/ organization	Year	For	Fieldwork dates
ESRI	1971	Larsen, University of Bergen	June–August 1971
	1978	Davis and Sinnott, ESRI	July–September 1978
	1991	International Social Science Program (ISSP)	September–October 1991
Eurobarometer	1973–94	DG X, Commission of the EC	Various dates – usually biannual (Mar–Apr and Oct–Nov)
Gallup	1969	*Nusight*	April 1969
IMS	1973	*Irish Independent*	20–22 February 1973
	1976	RTE	30 August–8 September 1976
	1981a	*Irish Times*	22 May 1981
	1981b	*Irish Times*	7–8 June 1981
	1982a	*Irish Times*	2–3 February 1982
	1982b	*Irish Times*	13–14 February 1982
	1982c	*Sunday Independent*	9–10 November 1982
	1987a	*Irish Independent*	31 January–1 February 1987
	1987b	*Sunday Independent*	12 February 1987
	1989a	*Sunday Independent*	8 June 1989
	1989b	*Irish Independent*	11 June 1989
	1990a	*Sunday Independent*	1–9 October 1990
	1990b	*Irish Independent/ The Star*	27–29 October 1990
	1992a	*The Star*	7 November 1992
	1992b	*Sunday Independent*	13 November 1992
	1992c	*Irish Independent*	17 November 1992
Lansdowne	1989	*The Star*	26–27 May 1989

	1990a	*Sunday Press*	10–20 October 1990
	1990b	*Sunday Press*	1 November 1990
	1992	*Sunday Press*	19 November 1992
MRBI	1977	Fine Gael	
	1979	Fine Gael/Labour Party	July 1978–April 1979
	1982a	*Irish Independent*	11–13 February 1982
	1982b	*Sunday Independent*	3–4 February 1982
	1982c	*Irish Times*	19–20 November 1982
	1987a	*Irish Times*	22–23 January 1987
	1987b	*Irish Times*	2–3 February 1987
	1987c	*Irish Times*	11 February 1987
	1989	*Irish Times*	9 June 1989
	1990a	*Irish Times*	5–6 October 1990
	1990b	*Irish Times*	2–3 November 1990
	1992	*Irish Times*	17–18 November 1992
NOP	1977a	*Irish Times*	27–28 May 1977
	1977b	*Irish Times*	3 June 1977
	1977c	*Irish Times*	9 June 1977
RSI	1982	*Sunday Press*	10–11 November 1982

References

Allardt, E. (1969), 'Aggregate analysis: the problem of its informative value' in Dogan, M., and Rokkan, S. (eds.), *Quantitative Ecological Analysis in the Social Sciences*, The M.I.T. Press, Cambridge, Massachusetts.

Arnold, B. (1993), *Haughey: His Life and Unlucky Deeds*, HarperCollins Publishers, London.

Bartolini, S., and Mair, P. (1990), *Identity, Competition and Electoral Availability: The Stabilisation of European Electorates 1885–1985*, Cambridge University Press, Cambridge.

Beck, P. A. (1984), 'The dealignment era in America' in Dalton, R. J., Flanagan, S. C., and Beck, P. A., *Electoral Change in Advanced Industrial Democracies: Realignment or Dealignment?*, Princeton University Press, Princeton, pp. 240–66.

Beef Tribunal (1994), *Report of the Tribunal of Inquiry into the Beef Processing Industry* (Pn. 1007), The Stationery Office, Dublin.

Bew, P., and Patterson, H. (1982), *Seán Lemass and the Making of Modern Ireland 1945–66*, Gill and Macmillan, Dublin.

Bew, P., Hazelkorn, E., and Patterson, H. (1989), *The Dynamics of Irish Politics*, Lawrence and Wishart, London.

Blondel, J. (1969), *Introduction to Comparative Government*, Weidenfeld and Nicholson, London.

Blondel, J. (1990), *Comparative Government: An Introduction*, Philip Allan, New York.

Borooah, V. K., and Borooah, V. (1990), 'Economic performance and political popularity in the Republic of Ireland', *Public Choice*, LXVII, pp. 65–79.

Bowler, S., and Farrell, D. M. (1990), 'Irish voter rationality: the 1987 Irish general election revisited', *Economic and Social Review*, XXI, pp. 251–68.

Bowler, S., and Farrell, D. M. (1991a), 'Party loyalties in complex settings: STV and party identification', *Political Studies*, 39, 2, pp. 350–62.

Bowler, S., and Farrell, D. M. (1991b), 'Voter behavior under PR-STV: solving the puzzle of the Irish party system', *Political Behavior*, 13, 4, pp. 303–20.

Bowman, J. (1982), *De Valera and the Ulster Question 1917–1973*, Clarendon Press, Oxford.

Breen, R., and Whelan, C. T. (1994), 'Social class, class origins and political partisanship in the Republic of Ireland', *European Journal of Political Research*, 26, 2, pp. 117–34.

Breen, R., Hannan, D. G., Rottman, D. B., and Whelan, C. T. (1990), *Understanding Contemporary Ireland: State, Class and Development in the Republic of Ireland*, Macmillan, London.

Brennan, S., and Murphy, E. (1986), *Brennan's Key to Local Authorities*, Landscape Press, Dublin.

Browne, V. (ed.) (1981), *The Magill Book of Irish Politics*, Magill Publications, Dublin.

Browne, V. (ed.) (1982), *The Magill Book of Irish Politics 1982*, Magill Publications, Dublin.

Budge, I., and Farlie, D. (1976), 'A comparative analysis of factors correlated with turnout and voting choice', in Budge, I., Crewe, I., and Farlie, D. (eds.), *Party Identification and Beyond*, Wiley, London.

Budge, I., and Farlie, D. J. (1983), *Explaining and Predicting Elections: Issue Effects and Party Strategies in Twenty-three Democracies*, George Allen and Unwin, London.

Budge, I., Crewe, I., and Farlie, D. (eds.) (1976), *Party Identification and Beyond*, Wiley, London.

Budge, I., Robertson, D., and Hearl, D. (eds.) (1987), *Ideology, Strategy and Party Change: Spatial Analyses of Post-War Election Programmes in 19 Democracies*, Cambridge University Press, Cambridge.

Bunreacht Na hÉireann (Constitution of Ireland) (1937), Stationery Office, Dublin.

Busteed, M. A. (1990), *Voting Behaviour in the Republic of Ireland: A Geographical Perspective*, Clarendon Press, Oxford.

Butler, D., and Ranney, A. (eds.) (1978), *Referendums, A Comparative Study of Practice and Theory*, American Enterprise Institute for Public Policy Research, Washington DC.

Butler, D., and Stokes, D. (1974), *Political Change in Britain: The Evolution of Electoral Choice* (2nd edn.), Macmillan, London.

Butler, D., Penniman, H. R., and Ranney, A. (eds.) (1981), *Democracy at the Polls: A Comparative Study of Competitive National Elections*, Studies in Political and Social Processes, American Enterprise Institute for Public Policy Research, Washington DC.

Cain, B., Ferejohn, J., and Fiorina, M. (1987), *The Personal Vote: Constituency Service and Electoral Independence*, Harvard University Press, Cambridge, Mass.

Carty, R. K. (1976), 'Social cleavages and party systems: a reconsideration of the Irish case', *European Journal of Political Research*, IV, pp. 195–203.

Carty, R. K. (1980), 'Politicians and electoral laws: an anthropology of party competition in Ireland', *Political Studies*, 28, 4, pp. 550–66.

Carty, R. K. (1981a), *Party and Parish Pump: Electoral Politics in Ireland*, Wilfrid Laurier University Press, Waterloo, Ontario.

Carty, R. K. (1981b), 'Towards a European politics: the lessons of the European Parliament election in Ireland', *Revue d'intégration européenne/Journal of European Integration*, IV, 2, pp. 211–41.

Carty, R. K. (1993), 'From tradition to modernity and back again: party building in Ireland', in Hill, R. J. and Marsh, M. (eds.), *Modern Irish Democracy, Essays in Honour of Basil Chubb*, Irish Academic Press, Dublin.

Castles, F. G., and Mair, P. (1984), 'Left-right political scales: Some 'expert' judgments', *European Journal of Political Research*, 12, pp. 73–88.

Chubb, B. (1957), 'The Independent Member in Ireland', *Political Studies*, V, pp. 131–9.

Chubb, B. (1963), '"Going about persecuting civil servants": the role of the Irish parliamentary representative', *Political Studies*, XI, pp. 272–86.

Chubb, B. (1970), *The Government and Politics of Ireland*, Oxford University Press, London.

Chubb, B. (1978), *The Constitution and Constitutional Change in Ireland*, Institute of Public Administration, Dublin.

Chubb, B. (1982), *The Government and Politics of Ireland* (2nd edn.), Longman, London.

Chubb, B. (1987), 'Prospects for democratic politics in Ireland', in Penniman, H., and Farrell, B. (eds.), *Ireland at the Polls 1981, 1982, and 1987: A Study of Four General Elections*, Duke University, Durham NC, pp. 206–31.

Coakley, J. (1980), 'The significance of names: the evolution of Irish party labels', *Etudes Irlandaises*, 5, pp. 171–81.

Coakley, J. (1981), 'The referendum and popular participation in the Irish political system', paper presented at the workshop on Referendums at the Annual Meeting of the European Consortium for Political Research, University of Lancaster, 27 March to 4 April 1981.

Coakley, J. (1986), 'The evolution of Irish party politics', in Girvin, B. and Sturm, R. (eds.), *Politics and Society in Contemporary Ireland*, Gower, Dublin.

Coakley, J. (1987), 'Moral consensus in a secularising society: the Irish divorce referendum of 1986', *West European Politics*, X, pp. 291–6.

Coakley, J. (1990), 'Minor parties in Irish political life, 1922–1989', *Economic and Social Review*, XXI, pp. 269–97.

Coakley, J., and M. Gallagher (eds.) (1993), *Politics in the Republic of Ireland*, (2nd Edition), Dublin/Limerick, Folens/PSAI Press.

Coakley, J., and O'Neill, G. (1984), 'Chance in preferential voting systems: an unacceptable element in Irish electoral law?', *Economic and Social Review*, XVI, pp. 1–18.

Cohan, A. (1972), *The Irish Political Elite*, Studies in Irish Political Culture, 4, Gill and Macmillan, Dublin.

Cohan, A. S., McKinlay, R. D., and Mughan, A. (1975), 'The used vote and electoral outcomes: the Irish general election of 1973', *British Journal of Political Science*, V, pp. 363–83.

Collins, N. (1984), 'Perspectives on the 1984 European election in the Republic of Ireland' in Reif, K. (ed.), *European Elections 1979/1981 and 1984: Conclusions and Perspectives from Empirical Research*, Quorum, Berlin.

Collins, N. (1985), 'Ireland' in Reif, K. (ed.), *The European Elections*, Gower, Aldershot, pp. 105–117.

Collins, N. (1986), 'Ireland' in Lodge, J. (ed.), *Direct Elections to the European Parliament 1984*, Macmillan, London, pp. 138–54.

Collins, N. (1986), 'The 1985 local government elections in the Republic of Ireland, *Irish Political Studies*, I, pp. 97–102.

Collins, N. (1989), 'Ireland [European elections]', *Electoral Studies*, VIII, pp. 281–7.

Collins, N. (1991), 'The Irish presidential election of 1990', *Electoral Studies*, X, pp. 155–7.

Committee on the Constitution (1967), *Report of the Committee on the Constitution, December 1967*, Stationery Office, Dublin.

Coogan, T. P. (1987), *Disillusioned Decades: Ireland 1966–87*, Gill and Macmillan, Dublin.

Coyle, C., and Sinnott, R. (1992), 'Regional elites, regional "powerlessness" and European regional policy in Ireland', *Regional Politics & Policy*, II, pp. 71–108.

Crewe, I. (1981), 'Electoral participation' in Butler, D., Penniman, H. R., and Ranney, A. (eds.), *Democracy at the Polls: A Comparative Study of Competitive National Elections*, Studies in Political and Social Processes, American Enterprise Institute for Public Policy Research, Washington DC, pp. 216–23.

Crewe, I., and Denver, D. (eds.) (1985), *Electoral Change in Western Democracies: Patterns and Sources of Electoral Volatility*, Croom Helm, London.

Daalder, H., and Mair, P. (1983), *Western European Party Systems: Continuity and Change*, Sage Publications, London.

Darcy, R., and Laver, M. (1990), 'Referendum dynamics and the Irish divorce amendment', *Public Opinion Quarterly*, LIV, pp. 1–20.

Dittrich, K., and Johansen, L. N. (1983), 'Voting turnout in Europe, 1945–1978: myths and realities' in Daalder, H., and Mair, P., *Western European Party Systems: Continuity and Change*, Sage Publications, London, pp. 95–114.

Donnelly, S. (1993), *Partnership, The Story of the 1992 General Election*, Seán Donnelly, Dublin.

Downey, J. (1983), *Them & Us: Britain, Ireland and the Northern Question 1969–1982*, Ward River Press, Dublin.

Dunphy, R. (1992), 'The Workers' Party and Europe: trajectory of an idea', *Irish Political Studies*, 7, pp. 21–40.

Dwyer, T. R. (1987), *Charlie: The Political Biography of Charles J. Haughey*, Gill and Macmillan, Dublin.

Fahey, T. (1992), 'Catholicism and industrial society in Ireland', in J. H. Goldthorpe and C. T. Whelan (eds.), *The Development of Industrial Society in Ireland, Proceedings of the British Academy*, 79, pp. 241–63.

Fanning, R. (1978), *The Irish Department of Finance*, Institute of Public Administration, Dublin.

Fanning, R. (1983), *Independent Ireland*, Helicon History of Ireland, Helicon, Dublin.

Farrell, B. (1970), 'Labour and the Irish political party system: a suggested approach to analysis', *Economic and Social Review*, I, 477–502.

Farrell, B. (1971), *Chairman or Chief? The Role of Taoiseach in Irish Government*, Gill and Macmillan, Dublin.

Farrell, B. (1983), *Seán Lemass*, Gill and Macmillan, Dublin.

Farrell, B. (1985), 'Ireland: from friends and neighbours to clients and partisans' in Bogdanor, V. (ed.), *Representatives of the People?*, Gower, Aldershot, pp. 237–64.

Farrell, B. (1987), 'The context of three elections' in Penniman, H., and Farrell, B. (eds.), *Ireland at the Polls, 1981, 1982, and 1987: The Study of Four General Elections*, Duke University Press, Durham, North Carolina.

Farrell, B. (ed.) (1994), *The Creation of the Dáil*, Blackwater Press, Dublin.

Farrell, B., and Farrell, D. M. (1987), 'The General Election of 1987' in Penniman, H., and Farrell, B. (eds.), *Ireland at the Polls*.

Farrell, B., and Manning, M. (1978), 'The election', in Penniman, H. R. (ed.), *Ireland At The Polls: the Dáil Election of 1977*, American Enterprise Institute, Washington DC, pp. 133–64.

Farrell, D. M. (1984), 'Age, education and occupational backgrounds of TDs and "routes" to the Dáil: the effects of localism in the 1980s', *Administration*, 32, 3, pp. 323–41.

Farrell, D. M. (1986), 'The strategy to market Fine Gael in 1981', *Irish Political Studies*, I, pp. 1–14.

Farrell, D. M. (1987), 'The Irish general election of 1987', *Electoral Studies*, VI, pp. 160–3.

Farrell, D. M. (1989), 'Ireland: The "Green Alliance"', in Müller-Rommel, F. (ed.), *New Politics in Western Europe: The Rise and Success of Green Parties and Alternative Lists*, Westview Press, Boulder, Co, pp. 123–30.

Farrell, D. M. (1992), 'Ireland', in Katz, R. S. and Mair, P. (eds.), *Party Organizations: A Data Handbook on Party Organizations in Western Democracies, 1960–90*, Sage Publications, London.

Fianna Fáil and Labour (1993), 'Fianna Fáil and Labour Programme for a Partnership Government 1993–1997', in Gallagher, M. and Laver, M. (eds.), *How Ireland Voted 1992*, PSAI Press, Limerick.

Finlay, F. (1991), *Mary Robinson: A President with a Purpose*, O'Brien Press, Dublin.

Fisk, R. (1983), *In Time of War: Ireland, Ulster, and the Price of Neutrality, 1939–45*, Paladin, London.

FitzGerald, G. (1991), *All in a Life: An Autobiography*, Gill and Macmillan, Dublin.

FitzGerald, R. (1992), 'The 1991 local government elections in the Republic of Ireland', *Irish Political Studies*, 7, pp. 99–115.

Fitzpatrick, D. (1977), *Politics and Irish Life 1913–1921: Provincial Experience of War and Revolution*, Gill and Macmillan, Dublin.

Foster, R. F. (1988), *Modern Ireland 1600–1972*, Allen Lane, London.

Franklin, M. N. (1992), 'The decline of cleavage politics', in Franklin, M. N., Mackie, T. and

Valen, H. (eds.), *Electoral Change: Responses to Evolving and Attitudinal Structures in Western Countries*, Cambridge University Press, Cambridge, pp. 383–405.

Franklin, M. N., Mackie, T. T., and Valen, H. (1992), *Electoral Change: Responses to Evolving Social and Attitudinal Structures in Western Countries*, Cambridge University Press, Cambridge.

Gallagher, M. (1976), *Electoral Support for Irish Political Parties, 1927–1973*, Sage Publications, London and Beverly Hills.

Gallagher, M. (1978), 'Party solidarity, exclusivity and inter-party relationships in Ireland, 1922–1977: the evidence of transfers', *Economic and Social Review*, X, pp. 1–22.

Gallagher, M. (1979), 'The pact general election of 1922', *Irish Historical Studies*, XXI, pp. 404–21.

Gallagher, M. (1982), *The Irish Labour Party in Transition 1957–82*, Manchester University Press, Manchester.

Gallagher, M. (1983–4), '166 who rule: the Dáil deputies of November 1982', *Economic and Social Review*, XV, pp. 241–64.

Gallagher, M. (1985), *Political Parties in the Republic of Ireland*, Manchester University Press, Manchester.

Gallagher, M. (1986), 'The political consequences of the electoral system in the Republic of Ireland', *Electoral Studies*, 5, 3, pp. 253–75.

Gallagher, M. (1987), 'Ireland: the increasing role of the centre' in Gallagher, M., and Marsh, M. (eds.), *Candidate Selection in Comparative Perspective: The Secret Garden of Politics*, Sage Publications, London, pp. 119–44.

Gallagher, M. (1989), 'Subnational elections and electoral behaviour in the Republic of Ireland', *Irish Political Studies*, IV, pp. 21–42.

Gallagher, M. (1991), 'Proportionality, disproportionality and electoral systems', *Electoral Studies*, 10, 1, pp. 33–51.

Gallagher, M. (ed.) (1993), *Irish Elections 1922–44: Results and Analysis*, PSAI Press, Limerick.

Gallagher, M. (1994), 'By-elections to Dáil Eireann 1923–94', Typescript, Department of Political Science, Trinity College Dublin.

Gallagher, M., and Komito, L. (1992), 'Dáil deputies and their constituency work' in Coakley, J., and Gallagher, M. (eds.), *Politics in the Republic of Ireland*, PSAI Press, Galway.

Gallagher, M., and Laver, M. (eds.) (1993), *How Ireland Voted 1992*, Folens/PSAI Press, Dublin/Limerick.

Gallagher, M., and Marsh, M. (1991), 'Republic of Ireland presidential election: 7 November 1990', *West European Politics*, XIV, pp. 169–73.

Gallagher, M., and Sinnott, R. (eds.) (1990), *How Ireland Voted 1989*, Centre for the Study of Irish Elections, University College Galway, Galway.

Gallagher, M., and Unwin, A. R. (1986), 'Electoral distortion under STV sampling procedures', *British Journal of Political Science*, XVI, pp. 243–68.

Garvin, T. (1974), 'Political cleavages, party politics and urbanisation in Ireland: the case of the periphery-dominated centre', *European Journal of Political Research*, II, pp. 307–27.

Garvin, T. (1976), 'Comment on Dr Carty's Rejoinder', *European Journal of Political Research*, 4, p. 204.

Garvin, T. (1977), 'National elites, Irish voters and Irish political development: a comparative perspective', *Economic and Social Review*, VIII, pp. 161–86.

Garvin, T. (1978), 'The destiny of the soldiers: tradition and modernity in the politics of de Valera's Ireland', *Political Studies*, XXVI, pp. 328–47.

Garvin, T. (1981), *The Evolution of Irish Nationalist Politics*, Gill and Macmillan, Dublin.

Garvin, T., and Parker, A. (1972), 'Party loyalty and Irish voters: the EEC referendum as a case study', *Economic and Social Review*, 4, 1, pp. 35–9.

Gillmor, D. A. (1985), *Economic Activites in the Republic of Ireland: A Geographical Perspective*, Gill and Macmillan, Dublin.

Girvin, B. (1986), 'Social change and moral politics: the Irish constitutional referendum 1983', *Political Studies*, XXXIV, pp. 61–89.

Girvin, B. (1987), 'The divorce referendum in the Republic, June 1986', *Irish Political Studies*, II, pp. 93–9.

Girvin, B. (1993), 'The road to the election', in Gallagher, M. and Laver, M. (eds.), *How Ireland Voted 1992*, Folens/PSAI Press, Dublin/Limerick, pp. 1–20.

Girvin, B., and Sturm, R. (1986), *Politics and Society in Contemporary Ireland*, Gower, Hampshire.

Goldthorpe, J. H. (1980), *Social Mobility and Class Structure in Modern Britain*, Clarendon Press, London.

Hainsworth, P. (ed.) (1992), *Breaking and Preserving the Mould, The Third Direct Elections to the European Parliament (1989) – The Irish Republic and Northern Ireland*, Policy Research Institute, Coleraine.

Hardiman, N. (1988), *Pay, Politics, and Economic Performance in Ireland 1970–1987*, Clarendon Press, Oxford.

Hardiman, N. (1992), 'The state and economic interests: Ireland in comparative perspective', *Proceedings of the British Academy*, 79, pp. 329–58.

Hardiman, N., and Whelan, C. T. (1994), 'Values and political partnership', in Whelan, C. T. (ed.), *Values and Social Change in Ireland*, Gill and Macmillan, Dublin, pp. 136–86.

Hayes, B. C. (1987), 'Occupational classifications prevalent within Irish research materials: a review', *Social Studies*, IX, pp. 39–60.

Heath, A., Jowell, R., and Curtice, J. (1985), *How Britain Votes*, Pergamon Press, Oxford.

Hesketh, T. (1990), *The Second Partitioning of Ireland? The Abortion Referendum of 1983*, Brandsma Books Ltd, Dun Laoghaire.

Hirschman, A. O. (1945), *National Power and the Structure of Foreign Trade*, Studies in International Political Economy, University of California Press, Berkeley, California.

Hirschman, A. O. (1970), *Exit, Voice and Loyalty: Responses to Declines in Firms, Organisations and States*, Harvard University Press, Cambridge, Mass.

Hogan, J. (1945), *Election and Representation: An Enquiry into the Nature and Conditions of Representative Government*, Cork University Press, Cork.

Holmes, M. (1990), 'The 1989 election to the European Parliament in the Republic of Ireland', *Irish Political Studies*, V, pp. 85–92.

Hoppen, K. T. (1984), *Elections, Politics, and Society in Ireland, 1832–1885*, Clarendon Press, Oxford.

Hoppen, K. T. (1989), *Ireland since 1800: Conflict and Conformity*, Longman, London.

Horgan, J. (1986), *Labour: The Price of Power*, Gill and Macmillan, Dublin.

Inglehart, R., and Klingemann, H. D. (1976), 'Party identification, ideological preference and the left–right dimension among western mass publics', in Budge, I., Crewe, I., and Farlie, D. (eds.), *Party Identification and Beyond*, John Wiley, London, pp. 243–73.

Johnston, R. J., Shelley, F. M., and Taylor, P. J. (eds.) (1990), *Developments in Electoral Geography*, Routledge, London and New York.

Jones, J. (1986), *The Irish Constitutional Referendum 1986: The Role and Impact of Opinion Polls*, Market Research Bureau of Ireland Ltd., Dublin.

Jones, J. (1986), 'The development and problems of political polling in Ireland', *Irish Political Studies*, I, pp. 111–15.

Joyce, J., and Murtagh, P. (1983), *The Boss: Charles J. Haughey in Power*, Poolbeg Press, Dublin.

Kaase, M. (1976), 'Party identification and voting behaviour in the West German election of 1969', in Budge, I., Crewe, I., and Farlie, D. (eds.), *Party Identification and Beyond*, Wiley, London.

Katz, R. S. (1980), *A Theory of Parties and Electoral Systems*, The Johns Hopkins University Press, Baltimore, MD.

Katz, R. S. (1985), 'Measuring party identification with Eurobarometer data: a warning note', *West European Politics*, VIII, pp. 104–8.

Keatinge, P., and Marsh, M. (1990), 'The European Parliament election', in Gallagher, M. and Sinnott, R. (eds.), *How Ireland Voted 1989*, Centre for the Study of Irish Elections, University College Galway, Galway.

Kelly, J. M. (1984), *The Irish Constitution*, Jurist Publishing Co. Ltd., Dublin.

Kennedy, K. A., Giblin, T., and McHugh, D. (1988), *The Economic Development of Ireland in the Twentieth Century*, Routledge, London.

Kenny, S., and Keane, F. (1987), *Irish Politics Now, 'This Week' Guide to the 25th Dáil*, Brandon Book Publishers, Dingle.

Keogh, G., and Whelan, B. J. (1986), *A Statistical Analysis of the Irish Electoral Register and its Use for Population Estimation and Sample Surveys*, Economic and Social Research Institute, Dublin.

Komito, L. (1984), 'Irish clientelism: a reappraisal', *Economic and Social Review*, XV, pp. 173–94.

Komito, L. (1992), 'Brokerage or friendship? Politics and networks in Ireland', *The Economic and Social Review*, 23, 2, January, pp. 129–45.

Laakso, M., and Taagepera, R. (1979), '"Effective" number of parties: a measure with application to West Europe', *Comparative Political Studies*, 12, 1, April, pp. 3–27.

Labour Party (1986), *Report of the Commission on Electoral Strategy*, Labour Party, Dublin.

Laffan, M. (1971), 'The unification of Sinn Féin in 1917', *Irish Historical Studies*, XVII, pp. 353–79.

Laffan, M. (forthcoming), *The Sea of Politics: The Sinn Féin Party 1916–1923*.

Laver, M. (1986a), 'Ireland: Politics with some social bases: an interpretation based on aggregate data', *Economic and Social Review*, XVII, pp. 107–31.

Laver, M. (1986b), 'Ireland: politics with some social bases: an interpretation based on survey data', *Economic and Social Review*, XVII, pp. 193–213.

Laver, M. (1987), 'Measuring patterns of party support in Ireland', *Economic and Social Review*, XVIII, pp. 95–100.

Laver, M. (1992), 'Are Irish parties peculiar?' in Goldthorpe, J. H., and Whelan, C. T. (eds.), *The Development of Industrial Society in Ireland*, Proceedings of the British Academy, No. 79, Oxford University Press, Oxford.

Laver, M. (1994), 'Party policy and cabinet portfolios in Ireland 1992: results from an expert survey', *Irish Political Studies*, IX, pp. 157–64.

Laver, M., and Hunt, W. B. (1992), *Policy and Party Competition*, Routledge, London.

Laver, M., Mair, P., and Sinnott, R. (eds.) (1987), *How Ireland Voted: The Irish General Election 1987*, Poolbeg Press, Dublin.

Laver, M., Marsh, M., and Sinnott, R. (1987), 'Patterns of party support', in Laver, M., Mair, P., and Sinnott, R. (eds.), *How Ireland Voted: The Irish General Election, 1987*, Poolbeg Press, Dublin.

Lee, J. J. (1980), 'Irish nationalism and socialism: Rumpf reconsidered', *Soathar*, 6, pp. 59–64.

Lee, J. J. (1989), *Ireland 1912–1985: Politics and Society*, Cambridge University Press, Cambridge.

Lenihan, B. (1991), *For The Record*, Blackwater Press, Dublin.

Lijphart, A., and Grofman, B. (eds.) (1984), *Choosing an Electoral System, Issues and Alternatives*, Praeger, New York.

Linz, Juan J. (1969), 'Ecological analysis and survey research', in Dogan, M. and Rokkan, S. (eds.), *Quantitative Ecological Analysis in the Social Sciences*, MIT Press, Cambridge, pp. 91–133.

Lipset, S. M., and Rokkan, S. (1967), 'Cleavage structures, party systems and voter alignments: an introduction', in Lipset, S. M., and Rokkan, S. (eds.), *Party Systems and Voter Alignments*, Free Press, New York, pp. 1–64.

Longford, The Earl of, and O'Neill, T. P. (1970), *Eamon de Valera*, Gill and Macmillan, Dublin.

Lyne, T. (1987), 'The Progressive Democrats', *Irish Political Studies*, II, pp. 107–14.

Lyons, F. S. L. (1973), *Ireland Since the Famine* (2nd edn.), Fontana, UK.

Mair, P. (1977–78), 'Labour and the Irish party system revisited: party competition in the 1920s', *Economic and Social Review*, IX, pp. 59–70.

Mair, P. (1979), 'The autonomy of the political: the development of the Irish party sytem', *Comparative Politics*, XI, pp. 445–65.

Mair, P. (1983), 'Adaptation and control: towards an understanding of party and party system change', in Daalder, H. and Mair, P. (eds.) *Western European Party Systems: Continuity and Change*, European Consortium for Political Research, Sage Publications, London.

Mair, P. (1986a), 'Districting choices under the single transferable vote' in Grofman, B., and Lijphart, A. (eds.), *Electoral Laws and their Political Consequences*, Agathon Press, New York, pp. 289–307.

Mair, P. (1986b), 'Locating Irish political parties on a left–right scale: An empirical enquiry', *Political Studies*, XXXIV, pp. 456–65.

Mair, P. (1987a), *The Changing Irish Party System: Organisation, Ideology and Electoral Competition*, Frances Pinter, London.

Mair, P. (1987b), 'Policy competition', in Laver, M., Mair, P. and Sinnott, R. (eds.), *How Ireland Voted 1987*, Centre for the Study of Irish Elections, University College Galway, Galway.

Mair, P. (1989), 'Ireland: from predominance to moderate pluralism, and back again?', *West European Politics*, XII, pp. 129–42.

Mair, P. (1990), 'The Irish party system into the 1990s', in Gallagher, M., and Sinnott, R. (eds.), *How Ireland Voted 1989*, Centre for the Study of Irish Elections, University College Galway, Galway, pp. 208–20.

Mair, P. (1992a), 'Explaining the absence of class politics in Ireland' in Goldthorpe, J. H., and Whelan, C. T. (eds.), *The Development of Industrial Society in Ireland*, Proceedings of the British Academy, No. 79, Oxford University Press, Oxford.

Mair, P. (1992b), 'The party system' in Coakley, J., and Gallagher, M. (eds.), *Politics in the Republic of Ireland*, PSAI Press, Galway.

Mair, P. (1993), 'Fianna Fáil, Labour, and the Irish party system', in Gallagher, M. and Marsh, M. (eds.), *How Ireland Voted 1992*, PSAI Press/Folens, Limerick/Dublin.

Manning, M. (1972), *Irish Political Parties: An Introduction*, Studies in Irish Political Culture 3, Gill and Macmillan, Dublin.

Manning, M. (1978), 'Ireland', in Butler, D. and Ranney, A. (eds.), *Referendums, A Comparative Study of Practice and Theory*, American Enterprise Institute for Public Policy, Washington, DC, pp. 193–210.

Manning, M. (1987a), 'The Political Parties', in Penniman, H. R. (ed.), *Ireland at the Polls: the Dáil Elections of 1977*, American Enterprise Institute for Public Policy Research, Washington, DC, pp. 69–96.

Manning, M. (1987b), *The Blueshirts* (2nd edn.), Gill and Macmillan, Dublin.

Mansergh, N. (1966), 'Ireland and the British Commonwealth of Nations: The Dominion Settlement', in Williams, D. (ed.), *The Irish Struggle: 1916–1926*, Routledge and Kegan Paul, London, pp. 129–39.

Marsh, M. (1981a), 'Electoral preferences in Irish recruitment: the 1977 election', *European Journal of Political Research*, IX, pp. 61–74.

Marsh, M. (1981b), 'Localism, candidate selection and electoral preferences in Ireland: the general election of 1977', *Economic and Social Review*, XII, pp. 267–86.

Marsh, M. (1985), 'Ireland' in Crewe, I., and Denver, D. (eds.), *Electoral Change in Western Democracies: Patterns and Sources of Electoral Volatility*, Croom Helm, London, pp. 173–201.

Marsh, M. (1987a), 'Electoral evaluations of candidates in Irish general elections 1948–82, *Irish Political Studies*, II, pp. 65–76.

Marsh, M. (1989), 'Transformation with a small "t": candidates for the Dáil, 1948–82', *Irish Political Studies*, IV, pp. 59–82.

Marsh, M. (1991), 'Accident or design? Non-voting in Ireland', *Irish Political Studies*, VI, pp. 1–14.

Marsh, M. (1992), 'Ireland', in Franklin, M. N., Mackie, T. T., and Valen, H. (eds.), *Electoral Change: Responses to Evolving Social and Attitudinal Structures in Western Countries*, Cambridge University Press, Cambridge, pp. 219–37.

Marsh, M. (1995), 'Ireland: an electorate with its mind on lower things', in van der Eijk, C., and Franklin, M. (eds.), *The European Electorate on the Eve of Unification*, University of Michigan Press, Michigan.

Marsh, M., and Harrison, M. J. (1994), 'What can he do for us? The popularity of leaders and their parties in Ireland', *Electoral Studies*, 13, 4, pp. 289–312.

Marsh, M., and Sinnott, R. (1990), 'How the voters decided', in Gallagher, M., and Sinnott, R. (eds.), *How Ireland Voted 1989*, Centre for the Study of Irish Elections, University College Galway, Galway, pp. 68–93.

Marsh, M., and Sinnott, R. (1993), 'The voters: stability and change', in Gallagher, M., and Laver, M., *How Ireland Voted 1992*, PSAI Press/Folens, Dublin/Limerick.

Martin, H. (1921), *Ireland in Insurrection*, Daniel O'Connor, London.

McAllister, I., and O'Connell, D. (1984), 'The political sociology of party support in Ireland: a reassessment', *Comparative Politics*, 16, 2, pp. 191–204.

McCarthy, C., and Ryan, T. M. (1976), 'Party loyalty at referenda and general elections: evidence from recent Irish contests', *Economic and Social Review*, VII, pp. 279–88.

McCracken, J. L. (1958), *Representative Government in Ireland: A Study of Dáil Éireann 1919–48*, Oxford University Press, London.

McDowell, M. (1991), 'Public preferences for the level and structure of government expenditure and taxation: survey results and analysis', *Foundation for Fiscal Studies, Research Paper No. 3*, Dublin.

McKay, E. (1986), 'Changing with the tide: The Irish Labour Party, 1927–1933', *Saothar*, XI, pp. 27–38.

Meenan, J. (1970), *The Irish Economy Since 1992*, Liverpool University Press, Liverpool.

Mitchell, A. (1974), *Labour in Irish Politics, 1890–1930*, Irish University Press, Dublin.

Mjoset, L. (1992), *The Irish Economy in a Comparative Institutional Perspective*, National Economic and Social Council, Dublin.

Moss, W. (1933), *Political Parties in the Irish Free State*, Columbia University Press, New York.

Moynihan, M. (ed.) (1980), *Speeches and Statements by Éamon de Valera*, Gill and Macmillan, Dublin.

Munger, F. (1975), *The Legitimacy of Opposition: the change of government in Ireland in 1932*, Sage Professional Papers, Contemporary Political Sociology Series, London.

Murphy, J. A. (1979), '"Put them out!": parties and elections, 1948–69' in Lee, J. J. (ed.), *Ireland 1945–70*, Gill and Macmillan, Dublin, pp. 1–15.

Nealon, T. (1974), *Ireland, A Parliamentary Directory, 1973–74*, Institute of Public Administration, Dublin.

Nealon, T., and Brennan, S. (1981), *Nealon's Guide to the 22nd Dáil and Seanad*, Platform Press, Dublin.

Neary, J. P., and O Gráda, C. (1991), 'Protection, economic war and structural change: the 1930s in Ireland', *Irish Historical Studies*, XXVIII, pp. 250–66.

Neeson, E. (1969), *The Civil War in Ireland 1922–1923* (2nd edn.), The Mercier Press, Cork.

Niemi, R. G. and Weisberg, H. F. (1976), 'The study of voting and elections', in Niemi, R. G., and Weisberg, H. F., *Controversies in American Voting Behaviour*, W. H. Freeman, San Francisco, pp. 3–20.

O'Byrnes, S. (1986), *Hiding Behind A Face: Fine Gael Under FitzGerald*, Gill and Macmillan, Dublin.

O'Donnell, R., and Brannick, T. (1984), 'The influence of turnout on the results of the referendum to amend the constitution to include a clause on the "rights of the unborn": a review of Walsh's findings', *Economic and Social Review*, XVI, pp. 59–69.

O'Hare, A., Whelan, C. T., and Commins, P. (1991), 'The development of an Irish census-based social class scale', *Economic and Social Review*, XXII, pp. 135–56.

O'Leary, B. (1987), 'Towards Europeanisation and realignment? The Irish general election, February 1987', *West European Politics*, X, pp. 455–65.

O'Leary, B., and Peterson, J. (1990), 'Further Europeanisation? The Irish general election of June 1989', *West European Politics*, XIII, pp. 124–36.

O'Leary, C. (1979), *Irish Elections 1918–1977: Parties, Voters and Proportional Representation*, Gill and Macmillan, Dublin.

O'Leary, C. (1987), 'The Irish referendum on divorce (1986)', *Electoral Studies*, VI, pp. 69–74.

O'Loughlin, J., and Parker, A. J. (1990), 'Tradition contra change: the political geography of Irish referenda, 1937–87' in Johnston, R. J., Shelley, F. M., and Taylor, P. J. (eds.), *Developments in Electoral Geography*, Routledge, London and New York.

O'Malley, D. (1987), 'The development of the Irish Party system and its relationship to the establishment of the Progressive Democrats', *Etudes Irlandaises*, 12, December, pp. 193–99.

O'Reilly, E. (1991), *Candidate, the Truth Behind the Presidential Campaign*, Attic Press, Dublin.

Orridge, A. (1983), 'The blueshirts and the "economic war": a study of Ireland in the context of dependency theory', *Political Studies*, XXXI, pp. 351–69.

O'Sullivan, D. (1940), *The Irish Free State and Its Senate: A Study in Contemporary Politics*, Faber and Faber, London.

O'Sullivan, E. (1991), 'The 1990 presidential election in the Republic of Ireland', *Irish Political Studies*, VI, pp. 85–98.

Parker, A. J. (1982), 'The "friends and neighbours" voting effect in the Galway West constituency', *Political Geography Quarterly*, I, pp. 243–62.

Parker, A. J. (1983), 'Localism and bailiwicks: the Galway West constituency in the 1977 general election', *Proceedings of the Royal Irish Academy*, 83c, pp. 17–36.

Parker, A. J. (1984a), 'A note upon localism and party solidarity: the transfer of votes in the Udaras na Gaeltachta election of 1979', *Economic and Social Review*, XV, pp. 209–25.

Parker, A. J. (1984b), 'An ecological analysis of voting patterns in Galway West, 1977', *Irish Geography*, 17, pp. 42–64.

Parker, A. J. (1986), 'Geography and the Irish electoral system', *Irish Geography*, XIX, pp. 1–14.

Pedersen, M. N. (1979), 'The dynamics of European party systems: changing patterns of electoral volatility', *European Journal of Political Research*, VII, pp. 1–26.

Penniman, H. R. (ed.) (1978), *Ireland at the Polls: the Dáil Elections of 1977*, American Enterprise Institute for Public Policy Research, Washington, DC.

Penniman, H., and Farrell, B. (eds.) (1987), *Ireland at the Polls 1981, 1982, and 1987: A Study of Four General Elections*, Duke University Press for the American Enterprise Institute for Public Policy Research, Durham, NC.

Powell, G. B. (1980), 'Voting participation in thirty democracies: effects of socio-economic, legal and partisan environments', in Rose, R. (ed.), *Electoral Participation: A Comparative Analysis*, Sage Publications, Beverly Hills, CA.

Pringle, D. (1990), 'The 1990 presidential election', *Irish Geography*, XVIII, pp. 136–144?

Pyne, P. (1969–70), 'The Third Sinn Féin Party: 1923–1926', *Economic and Social Review*, I, pp. 29–50.

Pyne, P. (1970), 'The Third Sinn Féin Party: 1923–1926', *Economic and Social Review*, I, pp. 229–57.

Rae, D. W. (1967), *The Political Consequences of Electoral Laws*, Yale University Press, New Haven.

Raven, J., Whelan, C. T., Pfretzschner, P. A., and Borock, D. M. (1976), *Political Culture in Ireland: The Views of Two Generations*, Institute of Public Administration, Dublin.

Reif, K., and Schmitt, H. (1980), 'Nine second-order national elections – a conceptual framework for the analysis of European election results', *European Journal of Political Research* VIII, pp. 3–44.

Robertson, D. (1976), *A Theory of Party Competition*, Wiley, London.

Robertson, D. (1984), *Class and the British Electorate*, Basil Blackwell, Oxford.

Robinson, W. S. (1950), 'Ecological correlations and the behaviour of individuals', *American Sociological Review*, 15, pp. 351–57.

Roche, D. (1982), *Local Government in Ireland*, Institute of Public Administration, Dublin.

Rose, R. (ed.) (1974), *Electoral Behaviour: A Comparative Handbook*, The Free Press, New York.

Rose, R., and McAllister, I. (1986), *Voters Begin To Choose: From Closed-Class to Open Elections in Britain*, Sage Publications, London.

Rose, R., and Urwin, D. (1970), 'Persistence and change in western party sytems since 1945', *Political Studies*, XVIII, pp. 287–319.

Rottman, D., and O'Connell, P. (1982), 'The changing social structure of Ireland' in Litton, F. (ed.), *Unequal Achievement: the Irish Experience, 1957–1982*, Institute of Public Administration, Dublin, pp. 63–88.

Rottman, D. B., Hannan, D. F., Hardimann, N., and Wiley, M. M. (1982), *The Distribution of Income in the Republic of Ireland: A Study in Social Class and Family Cycle Inequalities*, Economic and Social Research Institute, Dublin.

Rumpf, E. (1959), *Nationalismus und Sozialismus in Irland: Historisch-soziologischer Versuch über die irische Revolution seit 1918*, Verlag Anton Hain K. G., Meisenheim am Glan.

Rumpf, E., and Hepburn, A. C. (1977), *Nationalism and Socialism in Twentieth Century Ireland*, Liverpool University Press, Liverpool.

Sacks, P. M. (1970), 'Bailiwicks, locality, and religion: three elements in an Irish Dáil constituency election', *Economic and Social Review*, pp. 531–54.

Sacks, P. M. (1976), *The Donegal Mafia*, Yale University Press, New Haven.

Sani, G., and Sartori, G. (1983), 'Polarization, fragmentation and competition in western democracies' in Daalder, H., and Mair, P. (eds.), _Western European Party Systems: Continuity and Change_, Sage Publications, London and Beverly Hills, pp. 307–40.

Särlvik, B., and Crewe, I. (1983), _Decade of Dealignment: The Conservative Victory of 1979 and Electoral Trends in the 1970s_, Cambridge University Press, Cambridge.

Sartori, G. (1976), _Parties and Party Systems: A Framework for Analysis_, vol. I, Cambridge University Press, Cambridge.

Schmitt, H. (1989), 'On party attachment in western Europe and the utility of Eurobarometer data', _West European Politics_, XII, pp. 122–39.

Schmitt, H., and Mannheimer, R. (1991), 'About voting and non-voting in the European elections of June 1989', _European Journal of Political Research_, XIX, pp. 31–54.

Sinnott, R. (1978), 'The electorate' in Penniman, H. R. (ed.), _Ireland At The Polls: The Dáil Election of 1977_, American Enterprise Institute, Washington DC, pp. 35–67.

Sinnott, R. (1983), _Inter-party differences in the Republic of Ireland_, PhD dissertation, Georgetown University, Washington DC.

Sinnott, R. (1984), 'Interpretations of the Irish party system', _European Journal of Political Research_, XII, pp. 289–307.

Sinnott, R. (1986a), 'Party differences and spatial representation: the Irish case', _British Journal of Political Science_, XVI, pp. 217–41.

Sinnott, R. (1986b), 'The North: Party images and party approaches in the Republic', _Irish Political Studies_, I, pp. 15–31.

Sinnott, R. (1987a), 'The general election in the republic, February 1987', _Irish Political Studies_, II, pp. 115–24.

Sinnott, R. (1987b), 'The voters, the issues, and the party system', in Pennimann, H., and Farrell, B. (eds.), _Ireland at the Polls 1981, 1982 and 1987: A Study of Four General Elections_, Duke University, Durham, NC, pp. 57–103.

Sinnott, R. (1988), 'Il referendum in Irlanda: disposizioni costituzionali e realta politica', _Revista trimestrale di diritto pubblico_, III, pp. 754–69.

Sinnott, R. (1989), 'Locating parties, factions and ministers in a policy space: a contribution to understanding the party-policy link', _European Journal of Political Research_, 17, pp. 689–705.

Sinnott, R. (1992), 'The electoral system' in Coakley, J., and Gallagher, M. (eds.), _Politics in the Republic of Ireland_, PSAI Press, Galway.

Sinnott, R. (1995), 'The Measurement of Party Attachment in Eurobarometer Surveys: a research note', _CEEPA Working Papers in European Economic and Public Affairs_, University College Dublin, Centre for European Economic and Public Affairs.

Sinnott, R., and Whelan, B. J. (1992), 'Turnout in second order elections: the case of EP elections in Dublin 1984 and 1989', _Economic and Social Review_, XXIII, pp. 147–66.

Sinnott, R., Walsh, B., and Whelan, B. J. (1995), 'Conservatives, liberals and pragmatists: disaggregating the results of the Irish abortion referendums of 1992', _Economic and Social Review_, 26, 2, pp. 207–19.

Sinnott, R., Whelan, B. J., and McBride, J. P. (forthcoming), 'Ecological correlates of party support, 1981–92'.

Swaddle, K., and Heath, A. (1989), 'Official and reported turnout in the British general election of 1987', _British Journal of Political Science_, 19, 537–51.

Taagepera, R., and Shugart, M. S. (1989), _Seats and Votes: The Effects and Determinants of Electoral Systems_, Yale University Press, New Haven.

Taylor, P. J., and Johnston, R. J. (1979), _Geography of Elections_, Penguin, Harmondsworth.

Trench, B., with Barry, G., Browne, V., O'Toole, F., and Whelan, S. (eds.) (1987), *Magill Book of Irish Politics: Election February 1987*, Magill Publications, Dublin.

Unwin, A., and Gallagher, M. (1989), 'The impact of random sampling on the counting of votes at elections in the Republic of Ireland', *Journal of the Statistical and Social Inquiry Society of Ireland*, XXV, pp. 195–219.

van der Eijk, C., Franklin, M. N., Mackie, T., and Valen, H. (1992), 'Cleavages, conflict resolution and democracy', in Franklin, M. N., Mackie, T. T., and Valen, H. (eds.), *Electoral Change: Responses to Evolving Social and Attitudinal Structures in Western Countries*, Cambridge University Press, Cambridge, pp. 406–31.

Walker, B. M. (ed.) (1978), *Parliamentary Election Results In Ireland 1801–1922*, A New History of Ireland Ancillary Publications IV, Royal Irish Academy, Dublin.

Walker, B. M. (ed.) (1992), *Parliamentary Election Results In Ireland, 1918–92: Irish elections to Parliaments and Parliamentary Assemblies at Westminster, Belfast, Dublin, Strasbourg*, A New History of Ireland Ancillary Publications V, Royal Irish Academy, Dublin.

Walsh, B. (1972), 'Post-war demographic developments in the Republic of Ireland', *Social Studies*, 1, 3, pp. 309–17.

Walsh, B. (1979), 'Economic growth and development, 1945–70', in Lee, J. J. (ed.), *Ireland 1945–70*, Gill and Macmillan, Dublin, pp. 27–37.

Walsh, B. (1980), 'Recent demographic changes in the Republic of Ireland', *Population Trends*, 21, Autumn, p. 4.

Walsh, B. (1984a), 'The influence of turnout on the results of the referendum to amend the constitution to include a clause on the rights of the unborn', *Economic and Social Review*, 15, pp. 227–34.

Walsh, B. (1984b), 'The influence of turnout on the results of the referendum to amend the constitution to include a clause on the rights of the unborn: a reply', *Economic and Social Review*, 16, 71–73.

Walsh, B. M., and Robson, C. (1975), *Alphabetical Voting: A Study of the 1973 General Election in the Republic of Ireland*, Economic and Social Research Institute, Dublin.

Walsh, D. (1986a), *Des O'Malley: A Political Profile*, Brandon, Kerry.

Walsh, D. (1986b), *The Party: Inside Fianna Fáil*, Gill and Macmillan, Dublin.

Whelan, C. T., Breen, R., and Whelan, B. J. (1992), 'Industrialisation, class formation and social mobility in Ireland' in Goldthorpe, J. H., and Whelan, C. T. (eds.), *The Development of Industrial Society in Ireland*, Proceedings of the British Academy, No. 79, Oxford University Press, Oxford.

Whiteman, D. (1990), 'The progress and potential of the Green Party in Ireland', *Irish Political Studies*, V, pp. 45–58.

Whyte, J. H. (1971), *Church and State in Modern Ireland 1923–1970*, Gill and Macmillan, Dublin.

Whyte, J. H. (1974), 'Ireland: politics without social bases' in Rose, R. (ed.), *Electoral Behaviour: A Comparative Handbook*, Free Press, New York, pp. 619–51.

Index

Note: 'n.' after a page reference indicates the number of a note on that page.

Internetworking With TCP/IP

Vol III:

Client-Server Programming
And Applications

BSD Socket Version

Internetworking With TCP/IP

Vol III:

Client-Server Programming
And Applications

BSD Socket Version

DOUGLAS E. COMER

and

DAVID L. STEVENS

Department of Computer Sciences
Purdue University
West Lafayette, IN 47907

Prentice-Hall International, Inc.

Library of Congress Cataloging-in-Publication Data
(Revised for vol. 3)

Comer, Douglas.
    Internetworking with TCP/IP.

    Includes bibliographical references and indexes.
    Contents: [v. 1] Principles, protocols, and
architecture -- v. 2. Design, implementation, and
internals -- v. 3. Client-server programming and
applications.
    1. Computer networks. 2. Computer network protocols.
3. Data transmission systems. I. Title.
TK5105.5.C59 1988   004.6   87-35201
ISBN 0-13-470154-2 (v. 1)

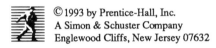 © 1993 by Prentice-Hall, Inc.
A Simon & Schuster Company
Englewood Cliffs, New Jersey 07632

UNIX is a registered trademark of AT&T Bell Laboratories; Sun is a trademark of Sun Microsystems, Incorporated;
DECNET is a trademark of Digital Equipment Corporation; SNA is a trademark of International Business Machines
Corporation.

Printed in the United States of America

10 9 8 7 6 5 4 3

ISBN   0-13-020272-X

Prentice-Hall International (UK) Limited, London
Prentice-Hall of Austria Pty. Limited, Sydney
Prentice-Hall Canada Inc., Toronto
Prentice-Hall Hispanoamericana, S.A., Mexico
Prentice-Hall of India Private Limited, New Delhi
Prentice-Hall of Japan, Inc., Tokyo
Simon & Schuster Asia Pte. Ltd., Singapore
Editora Prentice-Hall do Brasil, Ltda., Rio de Janeiro

To riding the wave

Contents

Chapter 8   Algorithms And Issues In Server Software Design   **95**

Chapter 9   Iterative, Connectionless Servers (UDP)   **115**

Chapter 14 Multiservice Servers (TCP, UDP)   155

Chapter 15 Uniform, Efficient Management Of Server Concurrency   171

Chapter 16 Concurrency In Clients   183

Chapter 20   Remote Procedure Call Concept (RPC)   233

Chapter 21   Distributed Program Generation (Rpcgen Concept)   255

Chapter 26   A TELNET Client (Implementation Details)   393

Chapter 27 Practical Hints And Techniques For UNIX Servers 425

Appendix 1 System Calls And Library Routines Used With Sockets 443

Appendix 2 Manipulation Of UNIX File And Socket Descriptors 473

Foreword

It is indeed a pleasure to introduce the reader to the third volume of Dr. Douglas E. Comer's remarkable series: Internetworking with TCP/IP. This series, which began so innocently back in 1987, is now the premiere source for learning about the suite of protocols that have made vendor-independent computer-communications possible – the Internet suite of protocols.

In Volume *1, Principles, Protocols, and Architectures*, we gained insight into the fundamental concepts which permeate the Internet suite. In Volume 2, *Design, Implementation, and Internals*, we gained an understanding as to how the Internet technological infrastructure is realized. To be sure, both of these works are essential to any understanding of internetworking, but it is this volume which I think has the potential for the greatest impact.

For it is in Volume *3, Client-Server Programming and Applications*, which Doug has authored with David L. Stevens, that a whole new world opens for us. This is the world of designing and implementing new applications for the Internet infrastructure. As the reader will soon discover, this volume is a worthy peer to its predecessors: in a surprisingly readable style, it describes not only the "how" but the "why." That is, not only will you learn how to architect and build client-server applications, but by reading this book you will also understand what trade-offs are involved with each design decision.

So, I invite you to sit back and enjoy reading the third volume in what I hope will be a never-ending series on the theory, design, and realization of internetworking technology.

Marshall T. Rose
Theorist, Implementor, and Agent Provocateur
Mountain View, California

Preface

The first two volumes of *Internetworking With TCP/IP* have enjoyed incredible popularity; we have received positive comments from around the world. Many readers have requested information on the design of application software that operates in an internet environment. This third volume extends the series and answers the requests.

Broadly speaking, Volume *1* of this series examines the question, "What is a TCP/IP internet?" Volume *2* examines the question, "How does TCP/IP software work?" It presents more details and explores greater depth than the first volume.

This volume examines the question, "How do applications use TCP/IP?" It focuses on the client-server paradigm, and examines algorithms for both the client and server components of a distributed program. It shows an implementation that illustrates each design, and discusses techniques like application-level gateways and tunneling. In addition, it reviews several standard application protocols, and uses them to illustrate the algorithms and implementation techniques.

Beginning chapters introduce basic ideas. They discuss the client-server paradigm, the socket interface that application programs use to access TCP/IP protocol software, and the operating system primitives that application programs call to invoke system services or perform I/O. The chapter on operating system services describes concurrent processes and the system functions used to create them.

Chapters that follow the introductory material discuss client and server algorithms or give a detailed example of a particular algorithm. We have tried to show that the myriad of possible designs are not random. Instead, they follow a pattern that can be understood by considering the choice of concurrency and transport. For example, one chapter discusses a nonconcurrent server design that uses connection-oriented transport (i.e., TCP), while another discusses a similar design that uses connectionless transport (i.e., UDP).

While we describe how each design fits into the space of possible implementations, we do not try to develop an abstract "theory" of client-server interactions. Instead, we emphasize design principles that underlie practical implementations; each implementation technique has advantages in some circumstances, and each has been used in working software. We believe that understanding the conceptual ties among the designs will help the reader appreciate the strengths and weaknesses of each approach and will make it easier to choose among them.

The text contains example programs that show how each design operates in practice. Most of the examples implement standard TCP/IP application protocols. In each case, we tried to select an application protocol that would convey a single design idea without being too complex to understand. Thus, while few of the example programs are exciting, they each illustrate one important concept. This version of Volume *3* uses the BSD UNIX socket mechanism in all programming examples; a companion edition contains the same examples using AT&T's TLI protocol interface.

Later chapters discuss the remote procedure call concept and describe how it can be used to construct distributed programs. They relate the remote procedure call technique to the client-server model, and show how software can be used to generate client and server programs from a remote procedure call description. Chapters on the Network File System illustrate how remote procedure call can be used to define an application protocol. The chapters on TELNET show how small details dominate a production program and how complex the code can become for even a simple character-oriented protocol.

Much of the text concentrates on concurrent processing. Many of the concepts described may seem familiar to students who have written concurrent programs because they apply to all concurrent programs, not only network applications. Students who have not written concurrent programs may find the concepts difficult.

The text is suitable for a single semester introductory networking course at the senior or graduate level. Because the text concentrates on how to use an internet rather than on how it works, students need little background in networking to understand the material. No particular concept is too difficult for lower level courses as long as the instructor proceeds at a suitable pace. A basic course in operating systems concepts or experience with concurrent programming may provide the best background.

Students will not appreciate the material until they use it first hand. Thus, any course should have programming exercises that force the students to apply the ideas to practical programs. Undergraduates can learn the basics by repeating the designs on other application protocols. Graduate students should build more complex distributed programs that emphasize some of the subtle techniques (e.g., the concurrency management techniques in Chapter *15* and the interconnection techniques in Chapter *17*).

Many people deserve credit for their help. Members of the Internet Research Group at Purdue contributed technical information and suggestions. Several of the members, including Bobby Minnear, John Lin, Longsong Lin, and Honghai Shen proofread early drafts of chapters. Bobby decoded the NFS file handle format.

Jeff Schwab, Chris Kantarjiev, and Craig Partridge provided valuable comments on the draft manuscript. Charlotte Tubis carefully proofread the text. Scott Ballew identified several subtle oversights in both the text and code.

The idea for the RPC dictionary example came from Thomas Narten who assigned a more complex version to students in his networking class.

Christine Comer provided invaluable help. She spotted many typos missed by others, made suggestions, and contributed to the wording throughout the text.

Douglas E. Comer
David L. Stevens

Internetworking With TCP/IP

Vol III:

Client-Server Programming
And Applications

BSD Socket Version

1

Introduction And Overview

1.1 Use Of TCP/IP

In 1982, the TCP/IP Internet included a few hundred computers at two dozen sites concentrated primarily in North America. By the Spring of 1992, over 700,000 computer systems attached to the Internet in *39* countries spread across *7* continents, and its size was doubling every ten months. Approximately one third of the *4500* networks that comprised the Internet in 1992 were located outside the US.

In addition, most large corporations have chosen TCP/IP protocols for their private corporate internets, many of which are now as large as the connected Internet was ten years ago. TCP/IP accounts for a significant fraction of networking throughout the world. Its use is growing rapidly in Europe, India, South America, and countries on the Pacific rim.

Besides quantitative growth, the past decade has witnessed an important change in the way sites use TCP/IP. Early use focused on a few basic services like electronic mail, file transfer, and remote login. Now, more users are designing application protocols and building their own application software. In fact, over one fifth of all traffic on the connected Internet arises from private applications. New applications rely on TCP/IP to provide basic transport services. They add rich functionality that has enhanced the Internet environment and has enabled new groups of users to benefit from connectivity.

The variety of applications using TCP/IP is staggering: it includes hotel reservation systems, applications that monitor and control offshore oil platforms, warehouse inventory control systems, applications that permit geographically distributed machines to share file access and display graphics, applications that transfer images and manage printing presses, as well as teleconferencing and multimedia systems. In addition to existing uses, the National Research and Education Network (*NREN*) initiative authorized by the United States Congress will provide improvements in the US national networking infrastructure, and will stimulate even more groups to develop applications.

As corporate internets mature, emphasis shifts from building internets to using them. As a result, more programmers need to know the fundamental principles and techniques used to design and implement distributed applications.

1.2 Designing Applications For A Distributed Environment

Programmers who build applications for a distributed computing environment follow a simple guideline: they try to make each distributed application behave as much as possible like the nondistributed version of the program. In essence, the goal of distributed computing is to provide an environment that hides the geographic location of computers and services and makes them appear to be local.

For example, a conventional database system stores information on the same machine as the application programs that access it. A distributed version of such a database system permits users to access data from computers other than the one on which the data resides. If the distributed database applications have been designed well, a user will not know whether the data being accessed is local or remote.

1.3 Standard And Nonstandard Application Protocols

The TCP/IP protocol suite includes many application protocols, and new application protocols appear daily. In fact, whenever a programmer devises a distributed program that uses TCP/IP to communicate, the programmer has invented a new application protocol. Of course, some application protocols have been documented in RFCs and adopted as part of the official TCP/IP protocol suite. We refer to such protocols as *standard application protocols*. Other protocols, invented by application programmers for private use, are referred to as *nonstandard application protocols*.

Most network managers choose to use standard application protocols whenever possible; one does not invent a new application protocol when an existing protocol suffices. For example, the TCP/IP suite contains standard application protocols for services like *file transfer*, *remote login*, and *electronic mail*. Thus, a programmer would use a standard protocol for such services.

1.4 An Example Of Standard Application Protocol Use

Remote login ranks among the most popular TCP/IP applications. Although a given remote login session only generates data at the speed a human can type and only receives data at the speed a human can read, remote login is the third highest source of packets on the connected Internet, exceeded only by file transfer and electronic mail. Many users rely on remote login as part of their working environment; they do not have a direct connection to the machines that they use for most computation.

The TCP/IP suite includes a standard application protocol for remote login known as *TELNET*. The TELNET protocol defines the format of data that an application program must send to a remote machine to log onto that system and the format of messages the remote machine sends back. It specifies how character data should be encoded for transmission and how one sends special messages to control the session or abort a remote operation.

For most users, the internal details of how the TELNET protocol encodes data are irrelevant; a user can invoke software that accesses a remote machine without knowing or caring about the implementation. In fact, using a remote service is usually as easy as using a local one. For example, computer systems that run TCP/IP protocols usually include a command that users invoke to run TELNET software. On Berkeley UNIX systems, the command is named *telnet*. To invoke it, a user types:

```
telnet machine
```

where the argument *machine* denotes the domain name of the machine to which remote login access is desired. Thus, to form a TELNET connection to machine *nic.ddn.mil* a user types:

```
telnet nic.ddn.mil
```

From the user's point of view, running *telnet* converts the user's terminal into a terminal that connects directly to the remote system. If the user is running in a windowing environment, the window in which the *telnet* command has been executed will be connected to the remote machine. Once the connection has been established, the *telnet* application sends each character the user types to the remote machine, and displays each character the remote machine emits on the user's screen.

After a user invokes *telnet* and connects to a remote system, the remote system displays a prompt that requests the user to type a login identifier and a password. The prompt a machine presents to a remote user is identical to the prompt it presents to users who login on local terminals. Thus, TELNET provides each remote user with the illusion of being on a directly-connected terminal.

1.5 An Example Connection

As an example, consider what happens when a user invokes *telnet* and connects to machine *nri.reston.va.us*:

```
telnet nri.reston.va.us
Trying...
Connected to nri.reston.va.us.
Escape character is '^]'.

SunOS UNIX (nri)

login:
```

The initial output message, *Trying...* appears while the *telnet* program converts the machine name to an IP address and tries to make a valid TCP connection to that address. As soon as the connection has been established, *telnet* prints the second and third lines, telling the user that the connection attempt has succeeded and identifying a special character that the user can type to escape from the *telnet* application temporarily if needed (e.g., if a failure occurs and the user needs to abort the connection). The notation ^] means that the user must hold the *CONTROL* key while striking the right bracket key.

The last few lines of output come from the remote machine. They identify the operating system as *SunOS*, and provide a standard login prompt. The cursor stops after the *login:* message, waiting for the user to type a valid login identifier. The user must have an account on the remote machine for the TELNET session to continue. After the user types a valid login identifier, the remote machine prompts for a password, and only permits access if the login identifier and password are valid.

1.6 Using TELNET To Access An Alternative Service

TCP/IP uses protocol port numbers to identify application services on a given machine. Software that implements a given service waits for requests at a predetermined (well-known) protocol port. For example, the remote login service accessed with the TELNET application protocol has been assigned port number *23*. Thus, when a user invokes the *telnet* program, the program connects to port *23* on the specified machine.

Interestingly, the TELNET protocol can be used to access services other than the standard remote login service. To do so, a user must specify the protocol port number of the desired service. The Berkeley UNIX *telnet* command uses an optional second argument to allow the user to specify an alternative protocol port. If the user does not supply a second argument, *telnet* uses port *23*. However, if the user supplies a port number, *telnet* connects to that port number. For example, if a user types:

```
telnet nri.reston.va.us 185
```

the *telnet* program will form a connection to protocol port number *185* at machine *nri.reston.va.us*. The machine is owned by the *Corporation For National Research Initiatives (CNRI)*.

Port *185* on the machine at *CNRI* does not supply remote login service. Instead, it offers a *Knowbot Information Service*. Thus, once a connection succeeds, the user receives information about the Knowbot service followed by a prompt for Knowbot commands:

```
Trying...
Connected to nri.reston.va.us.
Escape character is '^]'.
```

```
Knowbot Information Service (V1.0). Copyright CNRI 1990.
        All Rights Reserved.
Try ? or man for help.
>
```

The first three lines are the same as in the example above because they come from the *telnet* program and not the remote service. The remaining lines differ, and clearly show that the service available on port *185* is not a remote login service. The greater-than symbol on the last line serves as the prompt for Knowbot commands.

The Knowbot service searches well-known white pages directories to help a user find information about another user. For example, suppose one wanted to know the e-mail address for David Clark, a researcher at MIT. Typing *clark* in response to the Knowbot prompt retrieves 282 entries that each contain the name *Clark*. Most of the entries correspond to individuals with a first or last name of *Clark*, but some correspond to individuals with *Clark* in their affiliation (e.g., *Clark College*). Searching through the retrieved information reveals only one entry for a David Clark at MIT:

```
Name:          David D. Clark
Phone:         (617) 253-6003
E-Mail:        ddc@LCS.MIT.EDU
Source:        whois@nic.ddn.mil
Ident:         DDC1
Last updated:  (unknown)
```

1.7 Application Protocols And Software Flexibility

The example above shows how a single piece of software, in this instance the *telnet* program, can be used to access more than one service. The design of the TELNET protocol and its use to access the Knowbot service illustrate two important points. First, the goal of all protocol design is to find fundamental abstractions that can be reused in multiple applications. In practice, TELNET suffices for a wide variety of services because it provides a basic interactive communication facility. Conceptually, the protocol used to access a service remains separate from the service itself. Second, when architects specify application services, they use standard application protocols whenever possible. The Knowbot service described above can be accessed easily because it uses the standard TELNET protocol for communication. Furthermore, because most TCP/IP software includes an application program that users can invoke to run TELNET, no additional client software is needed to access the Knowbot service. Designers who invent new interactive applications can reuse software if they choose TELNET for their access protocol. The point can be summarized:

The TELNET protocol provides incredible flexibility because it only defines interactive communication and not the details of the service accessed. TELNET can be used as the communication mechanism for many interactive services besides remote login.

1.8 Viewing Services From The Provider's Perspective

The examples of application services given above show how a service appears from an individual user's point of view. The user runs a program that accesses a remote service, and expects to receive a reply with little or no delay.

From the perspective of a computer that supplies a service, the situation appears quite different. Users at multiple sites may choose to access a given service at the same time. When they do, each user expects to receive a response without delay.

To provide quick responses and handle many requests, a computer system that supplies an application service must use *concurrent processing*. That is, the provider cannot keep a new user waiting while it handles the previous user. Instead, the software must process more than one request at a time.

Because application programmers do not often write concurrent programs, concurrent processing can seem like magic. A single application program must manage multiple activities at the same time. In the case of TELNET, the program that provides remote login service must allow multiple users to login to a given machine and must manage multiple active login sessions. Communication for one login session must proceed without interference from others.

The need for concurrency complicates network software design, implementation, and maintenance. It mandates new algorithms and new programming techniques. Furthermore, because concurrency complicates debugging, programmers must be especially careful to document their designs and to follow good programming practices. Finally, programmers must choose a level of concurrency and consider whether their software will exhibit higher throughput if they increase or decrease the level of concurrency.

This text helps application programmers understand the design, construction, and optimization of network application software that uses concurrent processing. It describes the fundamental algorithms for both sequential and concurrent implementations of application protocols and provides an example of each. It considers the trade-offs and advantages of each design. Later chapters discuss the subtleties of concurrency management and review techniques that permit a programmer to optimize throughput automatically. To summarize:

Providing concurrent access to application services is important and difficult; many chapters of this text explain and discuss concurrent implementations of application protocol software.

1.9 The Remainder Of This Text

This text describes how to design and build distributed applications. Although it uses TCP/IP transport protocols to provide a concrete example, the discussion focuses on principles, algorithms, and general purpose techniques that apply to most network protocols. Early chapters introduce the client-server model and socket interface. Later chapters present specific algorithms and implementation techniques used in client and server software as well as interesting combinations of algorithms and techniques for managing concurrency.

In addition to its description of algorithms for client and server software, the text presents general techniques like tunneling, application-level gateways, and remote procedure calls. Finally, it examines a few standard application protocols like NFS and TELNET.

Most chapters contain example software that helps illustrate the principles discussed. The software should be considered part of the text. It shows clearly how all the details fit together and how the concepts appear in working programs.

1.10 Summary

Many programmers are building distributed applications that use TCP/IP as a transport mechanism. Before programmers can design and implement a distributed application, they need to understand the client-server model of computing, the operating system interface an application program uses to access protocol software, the fundamental algorithms used to implement client and server software, and alternatives to standard client-server interaction including the use of application gateways.

Most network services permit multiple users to access the service simultaneously. The technique of concurrent processing makes it possible to build an application program that can handle multiple requests at the same time. Much of this text focuses on techniques for the concurrent implementation of application protocols and on the problem of managing concurrency.

FOR FURTHER STUDY

The manuals that vendors supply with their operating systems contain information on how to invoke commands that access services like *TELNET*. Many sites augment the set of standard commands with locally-defined commands. Check with your site administrator to find out about locally-available commands.

EXERCISES

1.1   Use TELNET from your local machine to login to another machine. How much delay, if any, do you experience when the second machine connects to the same local area network? How much delay do you notice when connected to a remote machine?

1.2   Read the vendor's manual to find out whether your local version of the TELNET software permits connection to a port on the remote machine other than the standard port used for remote login.

1.3   Determine the set of TCP/IP services available on your local computer.

1.4   Use an FTP program to retrieve a file from a remote site. If the software does not provide statistics, estimate the transfer rate for a large file. Is the rate higher or lower than you expected?

1.5   Use the *finger* command to obtain information about users at a remote site.

2

The Client Server Model
And Software Design

2.1 Introduction

From the viewpoint of an application, TCP/IP, like most computer communication protocols, merely provides basic mechanisms used to transfer data. In particular, TCP/IP allows a programmer to establish communication between two application programs and to pass data back and forth. Thus, we say that TCP/IP provides *peer-to-peer* communication. The peer applications can execute on the same machine or on different machines.

Although TCP/IP specifies the details of how data passes between a pair of communicating applications, it does not dictate when or why peer applications interact, nor does it specify how programmers should organize such application programs in a distributed environment. In practice, one organizational method dominates the use of TCP/IP to such an extent that almost all applications use it. The method is known as the *client-server paradigm*. In fact, client-server interaction has become so fundamental in peer-to-peer networking systems that it forms the basis for most computer communication.

This text uses the client-server paradigm to describe all application programming. It considers the motivations behind the client-server model, describes the functions of the client and server components, and shows how to construct both client and server software.

Before considering how to construct software, it is important to define client-server concepts and terminology. The next sections define terminology that is used throughout the text.

9

2.2 Motivation

The fundamental motivation for the client-server paradigm arises from the problem of rendezvous. To understand the problem, imagine a human trying to start two programs on separate machines and have them communicate. Also remember that computers operate many orders of magnitude faster than humans. After the human initiates the first program, the program begins execution and sends a message to its peer. Within a few milliseconds, it determines that the peer does not yet exist, so it emits an error message and exits. Meanwhile, the human initiates the second program. Unfortunately, when the second program starts execution, it finds that the peer has already ceased execution. Even if the two programs retry to communicate continually, they can each execute so quickly that the probability of them sending messages to one another simultaneously is low.

The client-server model solves the rendezvous problem by asserting that in any pair of communicating applications, one side must start execution and wait (indefinitely) for the other side to contact it. The solution is important because TCP/IP does not respond to incoming communication requests on its own.

> *Because TCP/IP does not provide any mechanisms that automatically create running programs when a message arrives, a program must be waiting to accept communication before any requests arrive.*

Thus, to ensure that computers are ready to communicate, most system administrators arrange to have communication programs start automatically whenever the operating system boots. Each program runs forever, waiting for the next request to arrive for the service it offers.

2.3 Terminology And Concepts

The client-server paradigm divides communicating applications into two broad categories, depending on whether the application waits for communication or initiates it. This section provides a concise, comprehensive definition of the two categories, and relies on later chapters to illustrate them and explain many of the subtleties.

2.3.1 Clients And Servers

The client-server paradigm uses the direction of initiation to categorize whether a program is a client or server. In general, an application that initiates peer-to-peer communication is called a *client*. End users usually invoke client software when they use a network service. Most client software consists of conventional application programs. Each time a client application executes, it contacts a server, sends a request, and awaits a response. When the response arrives, the client continues processing. Clients are often easier to build than servers, and usually require no special system privileges to operate.

By comparison, a *server* is any program† that waits for incoming communication requests from a client. The server receives a client's request, performs the necessary computation, and returns the result to the client.

2.3.2 Privilege And Complexity

Because servers often need to access data, computations, or protocol ports that the operating system protects, server software usually requires special system privileges. Because a server executes with special system privilege, care must be taken to ensure that it does not inadvertently pass privileges on to the clients that use it. For example, a file server that operates as a privileged program must contain code to check whether a given file can be accessed by a given client. The server cannot rely on the usual operating system checks because its privileged status overrides them.

Servers must contain code that handles the issues of:

- *Authentication* – verifying the identity of the client
- *Authorization* – determining whether a given client is permitted to access the service the server supplies
- *Data security* – guaranteeing that data is not unintentionally revealed or compromised
- *Privacy* – keeping information about an individual from unauthorized access
- *Protection* – guaranteeing that network applications cannot abuse system resources.

As we will see in later chapters, servers that perform intense computation or handle large volumes of data operate more efficiently if they handle requests concurrently. The combination of special privileges and concurrent operation usually makes servers more difficult to design and implement than clients. Later chapters provide many examples that illustrate the differences between clients and servers.

2.3.3 Standard Vs. Nonstandard Client Software

Chapter *1* describes two broad classes of client application programs: those that invoke standard TCP/IP services (e.g., electronic mail) and those that invoke services defined by the site (e.g., an institution's private database system). *Standard application services* consist of those services defined by TCP/IP and assigned well-known, universally recognized protocol port identifiers; we consider all others to be *locally-defined application services* or *nonstandard application services*.

The distinction between standard services and others is only important when communicating outside the local environment. Within a given environment, system administrators usually arrange to define service names in such a way that users cannot distinguish between local and standard services. Programmers who build network applica-

---

†Technically, a *server* is a program and not a piece of hardware. However, computer users frequently (mis)apply the term to the computer responsible for running a particular server program. For example, they might say, ''That computer is our file server,'' when they mean, ''That computer runs our file server program.''

tions that will be used at other sites must understand the distinction, however, and must be careful to avoid depending on services that are only available locally.

Although TCP/IP defines many standard application protocols, most commercial computer vendors supply only a handful of standard application client programs with their TCP/IP software. For example, TCP/IP software usually includes a *remote terminal client* that uses the standard TELNET protocol for remote login, an *electronic mail client* that uses the standard SMTP protocol to transfer electronic mail to a remote system, and a *file transfer client* that uses the standard FTP protocol to transfer files between two machines.

Of course, many organizations build customized applications that use TCP/IP to communicate. Customized, nonstandard applications range from simple to complex, and include such diverse services as image transmission and video teleconferencing, voice transmission, remote real-time data collection, hotel and other on-line reservation systems, distributed database access, weather data distribution, and remote control of ocean-based drilling platforms.

2.3.4 Parameterization Of Clients

Some client software provides more generality than others. In particular, some client software allows the user to specify both the remote machine on which a server operates and the protocol port number at which the server is listening. For example, Chapter *1* shows how standard application client software can use the *TELNET* protocol to access services other than the conventional TELNET remote terminal service, as long as the program allows the user to specify a destination protocol port as well as a remote machine.

Conceptually, software that allows a user to specify a protocol port number has more input parameters than other software, so we use the term *fully parameterized client* to describe it. Many TELNET client implementations interpret an optional second argument as a port number. To specify only a remote machine, the user supplies the name of the remote machine:

> telnet *machine-name*

Given only a machine name, the *telnet* program uses the well-known port for the TEL-NET service. To specify both a remote machine and a port on that machine, the user specifies both the machine name and the port number:

> telnet *machine-name port*

Not all vendors provide full parameterization for their client application software. Therefore, on some systems, it may be difficult or impossible to use any port other than the official TELNET port. In fact, it may be necessary to modify the vendor's TEL-NET client software or to write new TELNET client software that accepts a port argument and uses that port. Of course, when building client software, full parameterization is recommended.

When designing client application software, include parameters that allow the user to fully specify the destination machine and destination protocol port number.

Full parameterization is especially useful when testing a new client or server because it allows testing to proceed independent of the existing software already in use. For example, a programmer can build a TELNET client and server pair, invoke them using nonstandard protocol ports, and proceed to test the software without disturbing standard services. Other users can continue to access the old TELNET service without interference during the testing.

2.3.5 Connectionless Vs. Connection-Oriented Servers

When programmers design client-server software, they must choose between two types of interaction: a *connectionless style* or a *connection-oriented style*. The two styles of interaction correspond directly to the two major transport protocols that the TCP/IP protocol suite supplies. If the client and server communicate using UDP, the interaction is connectionless; if they use TCP, the interaction is connection-oriented.

From the application programmer's point of view, the distinction between connectionless and connection-oriented interactions is critical because it determines the level of reliability that the underlying system provides. TCP provides all the reliability needed to communicate across an internet. It verifies that data arrives, and automatically retransmits segments that do not. It computes a checksum over the data to guarantee that it is not corrupted during transmission. It uses sequence numbers to ensure that the data arrives in order, and automatically eliminates duplicate packets. It provides flow control to ensure that the sender does not transmit data faster than the receiver can consume it. Finally, TCP informs both the client and server if the underlying network becomes inoperable for any reason.

By contrast, clients and servers that use UDP do not have any guarantees about reliable delivery. When a client sends a request, the request may be lost, duplicated, delayed, or delivered out of order. Similarly, a response the server sends back to a client may be lost, duplicated, delayed, or delivered out of order. The client and/or server application programs must take appropriate actions to detect and correct such errors.

UDP can be deceiving because it provides *best effort delivery*. UDP does not introduce errors – it merely depends on the underlying IP internet to deliver packets. IP, in turn, depends on the underlying hardware networks and intermediate gateways. From a programmer's point of view, the consequence of using UDP is that it works well if the underlying internet works well. For example, UDP works well in a local environment because reliability errors seldom occur in a local environment. Errors usually arise only when communication spans a wide area internet.

Programmers sometimes make the mistake of choosing connectionless transport (i.e., UDP), building an application that uses it, and then testing the application software only on a local area network. Because a local area network seldom or never delays packets, drops them, or delivers them out of order, the application software appears to work well. However, if the same software is used across a wide area internet, it may fail or produce incorrect results.

Beginners, as well as most experienced professionals, prefer to use the connection-oriented style of interaction. A connection-oriented protocol makes programming simpler, and relieves the programmer of the responsibility to detect and correct errors. In fact, adding reliability to a connectionless internet message protocol like UDP is a nontrivial undertaking that usually requires considerable experience with protocol design.

Usually, application programs only use UDP if: (1) the application protocol specifies that UDP must be used (presumably, the application protocol has been designed to handle reliability and delivery errors), (2) the application protocol relies on hardware broadcast or multicast, or (3) the application cannot tolerate the computational overhead or delay required for TCP virtual circuits. We can summarize:

> *When designing client-server applications, beginners are strongly advised to use TCP because it provides reliable, connection-oriented communication. Programs only use UDP if the application protocol handles reliability, the application requires hardware broadcast or multicast, or the application cannot tolerate virtual circuit overhead.*

2.3.6 Stateless Vs. Stateful Servers

Information that a server maintains about the status of ongoing interactions with clients is called *state information*. Servers that do not keep any state information are called *stateless servers*; others are called *stateful servers*.

The desire for efficiency motivates designers to keep state information in servers. Keeping a small amount of information in a server can reduce the size of messages that the client and server exchange, and can allow the server to respond to requests quickly. Essentially, state information allows a server to remember what the client requested previously and to compute an incremental response as each new request arrives. By contrast, the motivation for statelessness lies in protocol reliability: state information in a server can become incorrect if messages are lost, duplicated, or delivered out of order, or if the client computer crashes and reboots. If the server uses incorrect state information when computing a response, it may respond incorrectly.

2.3.7 A Stateful File Server Example

An example will help explain the distinction between stateless and stateful servers. Consider a file server that allows clients to remotely access information kept in the files on a local disk. The server operates as an application program. It waits for a client to contact it over the network. The client sends one of two request types. It either sends a request to extract data from a specified file or a request to store data in a specified file. The server performs the requested operation and replies to the client.

On one hand, if the file server is stateless, it maintains no information about the transactions. Each message from a client that requests the server to extract data from a file must specify the complete file name (the name could be quite lengthy), a position in the file from which the data should be extracted, and the number of bytes to extract. Similarly, each message that requests the server to store data in a file must specify the complete file name, a position in the file at which the data should be stored, and the data to store.

On the other hand, if the file server maintains state information for its clients, it can eliminate the need to pass file names in each message. The server maintains a table that holds state information about the file currently being accessed. Figure 2.1 shows one possible arrangement of the state information.

Handle	File Name	Current Position
1	test.program.c	0
2	tcp.book.doc	456
3	dept.budget.text	38
4	tetris.exe	128

Figure 2.1 Example table of state information for a stateful file server. To keep messages short, the server assigns a handle to each file. The handle appears in messages instead of a file name.

When a client first opens a file, the server adds an entry to its state table that contains the name of the file, a *handle* (a small integer used to identify the file), and a current position in the file (initially zero). The server then sends the handle back to the client for use in subsequent requests. Whenever the client wants to extract additional data from the file, it sends a small message that includes the handle. The server uses the handle to lookup the file name and current file position in its state table. The server increments the file position in the state table, so the next request from the client will extract new data. Thus, the client can send repeated requests to move through the entire file. When the client finishes using a file, it sends a message informing the server that the file will no longer be needed. In response, the server removes the stored state information. As long as all messages travel reliably between the client and server, a stateful design makes the interaction more efficient. The point is:

> In an ideal world, where networks deliver all messages reliably and computers never crash, having a server maintain a small amount of state information for each ongoing interaction can make messages smaller and processing simpler.

Although state information can improve efficiency, it can also be difficult or impossible to maintain correctly if the underlying network duplicates, delays, or delivers messages out of order (e.g., if the client and server use UDP to communicate). Consider what happens to our file server example if the network duplicates a *read* request. Recall that the server maintains a notion of file position in its state information. Assume that the server updates its notion of file position each time a client extracts data from a file. If the network duplicates a *read* request, the server will receive two copies. When the first copy arrives, the server extracts data from the file, updates the file position in its state information, and returns the result to the client. When the second copy arrives, the server extracts additional data, updates the file position again, and returns the new data to the client. The client may view the second response as a duplicate and discard it, or it may report an error because it received two different responses to a single request. In either case, the state information at the server can become incorrect because it disagrees with the client's notion of the true state.

When computers reboot, state information can also become incorrect. If a client crashes after performing an operation that creates additional state information, the server may never receive messages that allow it to discard the information. Eventually, the accumulated state information exhausts the server's memory. In our file server example, if a client opens *100* files and then crashes, the server will maintain *100* useless entries in its state table forever.

A stateful server may also become confused (or respond incorrectly) if a new client begins operation after a reboot using the same protocol port numbers as the previous client that was operating when the system crashed. It may seem that this problem can be overcome easily by having the server erase previous information from a client whenever a new request for interaction arrives. Remember, however, that the underlying internet may duplicate and delay messages, so any solution to the problem of new clients reusing protocol ports after a reboot must also handle the case where a client starts normally, but its first message to a server becomes duplicated and one copy is delayed.

In general, the problems of maintaining correct state can only be solved with complex protocols that accommodate the problems of unreliable delivery and computer system restart. To summarize:

> *In a real internet, where machines crash and reboot, and messages can be lost, delayed, duplicated, or delivered out of order, stateful designs lead to complex application protocols that are difficult to design, understand, and program correctly.*

2.3.8 Statelessness Is A Protocol Issue

Although we have discussed statelessness in the context of servers, the question of whether a server is stateless or stateful centers on the application protocol more than the implementation. If the application protocol specifies that the meaning of a particular message depends in some way on previous messages, it may be impossible to provide a stateless interaction.

In essence, the issue of statelessness focuses on whether the application protocol assumes the responsibility for reliable delivery. To avoid problems and make the interaction reliable, an application protocol designer must ensure that each message is completely unambiguous. That is, a message cannot depend on being delivered in order, nor can it depend on previous messages having been delivered. In essence, the protocol designer must build the interaction so the server gives the same response no matter when or how many times a request arrives. Mathematicians use the term *idempotent* to refer to a mathematical operation that always produces the same result. We use the term to refer to protocols that arrange for a server to give the same response to a given message no matter how many times it arrives.

> *In an internet where the underlying network can duplicate, delay or deliver messages out of order or where computers running client applications can crash unexpectedly, the server should be stateless. The server can only be stateless if the application protocol is designed to make operations idempotent.*

2.3.9 Servers As Clients

Programs do not always fit exactly into the definition of client or server. A server program may need to access network services that require it to act as a client. For example, suppose our file server program needs to obtain the time of day so it can stamp files with the time of access. Also suppose that the system on which it operates does not have a time-of-day clock. To obtain the time, the server acts as a client by sending a request to a time-of-day server as Figure 2.2 shows.

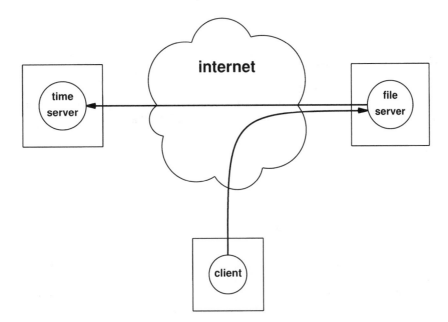

Figure 2.2 A file server program acting as a client to a time server. When the time server replies, the file server will finish its computation and return the result to the original client.

In a network environment that has many available servers, it is not unusual to find a server for one application acting as a client for another. Of course, designers must be careful to avoid circular dependencies among servers.

2.4 Summary

The client-server paradigm classifies a communicating application program as either a client or a server depending on whether it initiates communication. In addition to client and server software for standard applications, many TCP/IP users build client and server software for nonstandard applications that they define locally.

Beginners and most experienced programmers use TCP to transport messages between the client and server because it provides the reliability needed in an internet environment. Programmers only resort to UDP if TCP cannot solve the problem.

Keeping state information in the server can improve efficiency. However, if clients crash unexpectedly or the underlying transport system allows duplication, delay, or packet loss, state information can consume resources or become incorrect. Thus, most application protocol designers try to minimize state information. A stateless implementation may not be possible if the application protocol fails to make operations idempotent.

Programs cannot be divided easily into client and server categories because many programs perform both functions. A program that acts as a server for one service can act as a client to access other services.

FOR FURTHER STUDY

Stevens [1990] briefly describes the client-server model and gives UNIX examples. Other examples can be found by consulting applications that accompany various vendors' operating systems.

EXERCISES

2.1   Which of your local implementations of standard application clients are fully parameterized? Why is full parameterization needed?

2.2   Are standard application protocols like TELNET, FTP, SMTP, and NFS (Network File System) connectionless or connection-oriented?

2.3   What does TCP/IP specify should happen if no server exists when a client request arrives? (Hint: look at ICMP.) What happens on your local system?

2.4   Write down the data structures and message formats needed for a stateless file server. What happens if two or more clients access the same file? What happens if a client crashes before closing a file?

2.5   Write down the data structures and message formats needed for a stateful file server. Use the operations *open*, *read*, *write*, and *close* to access files. Arrange for *open* to return an integer used to access the file in *read* and *write* operations. How do you distinguish duplicate *open* requests from a client that sends an *open*, crashes, reboots, and sends an *open* again?

2.6   In the previous exercise, what happens in your design if two or more clients access the same file? What happens if a client crashes before closing a file?

2.7   Examine the NFS remote file access protocol carefully to identify which operations are idempotent. What errors can result if messages are lost, duplicated, or delayed?

3

Concurrent Processing In Client-Server Software

3.1 Introduction

The previous chapter defines the client-server paradigm. This chapter extends the notion of client-server interaction by discussing concurrency, a concept that provides much of the power behind client-server interactions but also makes the software difficult to design and build. The notion of concurrency also pervades later chapters, which explain in detail how servers provide concurrent access.

In addition to discussing the general concept of concurrency, this chapter also reviews the facilities that an operating system supplies to support concurrent process execution. It is important to understand the functions described in this chapter because they appear in many of the server implementations in later chapters.

3.2 Concurrency In Networks

The term *concurrency* refers to real or apparent simultaneous computing. For example, a multi-user computer system can achieve concurrency by *time-sharing*, a design that arranges to switch a single processor among multiple computations quickly enough to give the appearance of simultaneous progress; or by *multiprocessing*, a design in which multiple processors perform multiple computations simultaneously.

Concurrent processing is fundamental to distributed computing and occurs in many forms. Among machines on a single network, many pairs of application programs can communicate concurrently, sharing the network that interconnects them. For example, application A on one machine may communicate with application B on another machine, while application C on a third machine communicates with application D on a fourth. Although they all share a single network, the applications appear to proceed as if they operate independently. The network hardware enforces access rules that allow each pair of communicating machines to exchange messages. The access rules prevent a given pair of applications from excluding others by consuming all the network bandwidth.

Concurrency can also occur within a given computer system. For example, multiple users on a timesharing system can each invoke a client application that communicates with an application on another machine. One user can transfer a file while another user conducts a remote login session. From a user's point of view, it appears that all client programs proceed simultaneously.

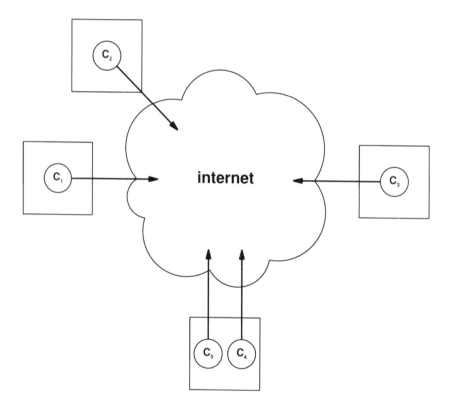

Figure 3.1 Concurrency among client programs occurs when users execute
them on multiple machines simultaneously or when a multitasking
operating system allows multiple copies to execute concurrently
on a single computer.

In addition to concurrency among clients on a single machine, the set of all clients on a set of machines can execute concurrently. Figure 3.1 illustrates concurrency among client programs running on several machines.

Client software does not usually require any special attention or effort on the part of the programmer to make it usable concurrently. The application programmer designs and constructs each client program without regard to concurrent execution; concurrency among multiple client programs occurs automatically because the operating system allows multiple users to each invoke a client concurrently. Thus, the individual clients operate much like any conventional program. To summarize:

> *Most client software achieves concurrent operation because the underlying operating system allows users to execute client programs concurrently or because users on many machines each execute client software simultaneously. An individual client program operates like any conventional program; it does not manage concurrency explicitly.*

3.3 Concurrency In Servers

In contrast to concurrent client software, concurrency within a server requires considerable effort. As figure 3.2 shows, a single server program must handle incoming requests concurrently.

To understand why concurrency is important, consider server operations that require substantial computation or communication. For example, think of a remote login server. If it operates with no concurrency, it can handle only one remote login at a time. Once a client contacts the server, the server must ignore or refuse subsequent requests until the first user finishes. Clearly, such a design limits the utility of the server, and prevents multiple remote users from accessing a given machine at the same time.

Chapter *8* discusses algorithms and design issues for concurrent servers, showing how they operate in principle. Chapters *9* through *13* each illustrate one of the algorithms, describing the design in more detail and showing code for a working server. The remainder of this chapter concentrates on terminology and basic concepts used throughout the text.

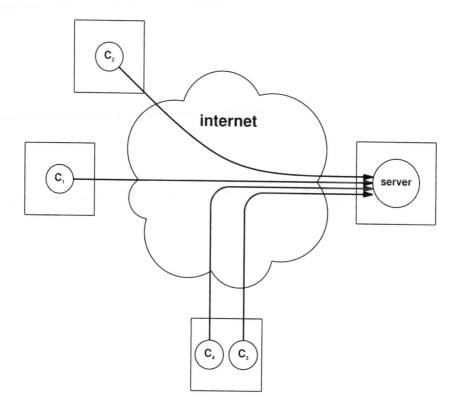

Figure 3.2 Server software must be explicitly programmed to handle concurrent requests because multiple clients contact a server using its
single, well-known protocol port.

3.4 Terminology And Concepts

Because few application programmers have experience with the design of concurrent programs, understanding concurrency in servers can be challenging. This section explains the basic concept of concurrent processing and shows how an operating
system supplies it. It gives examples that illustrate concurrency, and defines terminology used in later chapters.

3.4.1 The Process Concept

In concurrent processing systems, the *process* abstraction defines the fundamental unit of computation†. The most essential information associated with a process is an *instruction pointer* that specifies the address at which the process is executing. Other information associated with a process includes the identity of the user that owns it, the compiled program that it is executing, and the memory locations of the process' program text and data areas.

A process differs from a program because the process concept includes only the active execution of a computation, not the code. After the code has been loaded into a computer, the operating system allows one or more processes to execute it. In particular, a concurrent processing system allows multiple processes to execute the same piece of code ''at the same time.'' This means that multiple processes may each be executing at some point in the code. Each process proceeds at its own rate, and each may begin or finish at an arbitrary time. Because each has a separate instruction pointer that specifies which instruction it will execute next, there is never any confusion.

Of course, on a uniprocessor architecture, the single CPU can only execute one process at any instant in time. The operating system makes the computer appear to perform more than one computation at a time by switching the CPU among all executing processes rapidly. From a human observer's point of view, many processes appear to proceed simultaneously. In fact, one process proceeds for a short time, then another process proceeds for a short time, and so on. We use the term *concurrent execution* to capture the idea. It means ''apparently simultaneous execution.'' On a uniprocessor, the operating system handles concurrency, while on a multiprocessor, all CPUs can execute processes simultaneously.

The important concept is:

> *Application programmers build programs for a concurrent environment without knowing whether the underlying hardware consists of a uniprocessor or a multiprocessor.*

3.4.2 Programs vs. Processes

In a concurrent processing system, a conventional application program is merely a special case: it consists of a piece of code that is executed by exactly one process at a time. The notion of *process* differs from the conventional notion of *program* in other ways. For example, most application programmers think of the set of variables defined in the program as being associated with the code. However, if more than one process executes the code concurrently, it is essential that each process has its own copy of the variables. To understand why, consider the following segment of C code that prints the integers from *1* to *10*:

```
for ( i=0 ; i < 10 ; i++)
        printf("%d\n", i);
```

---

†Some systems use the terms *task*, *job*, or *thread* instead of *process*.

The iteration uses an index variable, i. In a conventional program, the programmer thinks of storage for variable i as being allocated with the code. However, if two or more processes execute the code segment concurrently, one of them may be on the sixth iteration when the other starts the first iteration. Each must have a different value for i. Thus, each process must have its own copy of variable i or confusion will result. To summarize:

> When multiple processes execute a piece of code concurrently, each process has its own, independent copy of the variables associated with the code.

3.4.3 Procedure Calls

In a procedure-oriented language, like Pascal or C, executed code can contain calls to subprograms (procedures or functions). Subprograms accept arguments, compute a result, and then return just after the point of the call. If multiple processes execute code concurrently, they can each be at a different point in the sequence of procedure calls. One process, A, can begin execution, call a procedure, and then call a second-level procedure before another process, B, begins. Process B may return from a first-level procedure call just as process A returns from a second-level call.

The run-time system for procedure-oriented programming languages uses a stack mechanism to handle procedure calls. The run-time system pushes a *procedure activation record* on the stack whenever it makes a procedure call. Among other things, the activation records stores information about the location in the code at which the procedure call occurs. When the procedure finishes execution, the run-time system pops the activation record from the top of the stack, and returns to the procedure from which the call occurred. Analogous to the rule for variables, concurrent programming systems provide separation between procedure calls in executing processes:

> When multiple processes execute a piece of code concurrently, each has its own run-time stack of procedure activation records.

3.5 An Example Of Concurrent Process Creation

3.5.1 A Sequential C Example

The following example illustrates concurrent processing in the UNIX operating system. As with most computational concepts, the programming language syntax is trivial; it occupies only a few lines of code. For example, the following code is a conventional C program that prints the integers from 1 to 5 along with their sum:

```
/* sum.c - A conventional C program that sums integers from 1 to 5  */
#include <stdio.h>
int     sum;                            /* sum is a global variable */

main() {
        int i;                          /* i is a local variable    */

        sum = 0;
        for (i=1 ; i <=5 ; i++) {       /* iterate i from 1 to 5     */
                printf("The value of i is %d\n", i);
                fflush(stdout);         /* flush the buffer          */
                sum += i;
        }
        printf("The sum is %d\n", sum);
        exit(0);                        /* terminate the program     */
}
```

When executed, the program emits six lines of output:

```
                        The value of i is 1
                        The value of i is 2
                        The value of i is 3
                        The value of i is 4
                        The value of i is 5
                        The sum is 15
```

3.5.2 A Concurrent Version

To create a new process in UNIX, a program calls the system function *fork*†. In essence, *fork* divides the running program into two (almost) identical processes, both executing at the same place in the same code. The two processes continue just as if two users had simultaneously started two copies of the application. For example, the following modified version of the above example calls *fork* to create a new process. (Note that although the introduction of concurrency changes the meaning of the program completely, the call to *fork* occupies only a single line of code.)

---

†To a programmer, the call to *fork* looks and acts like an ordinary function call in C. It is written `fork()`. At run-time, however, control passes to the operating system, which creates a new process.

```
#include <stdio.h>
int       sum;

main() {
        int i;

        sum = 0;
        fork();                               /* create a new process */
        for (i=0 ; i<=5 ; i++) {
                printf("The value of i is %d\n", i);
                fflush(stdout);
                sum += i;
        }
        printf("The sum is %d\n", sum);
        exit(0);
}
```

When a user executes the concurrent version of the program, the system begins
with a single process executing the code. However, when the process reaches the call
to *fork*, the system duplicates the process and allows both the original process and the
newly created process to execute. Of course, each process has its own copy of the variables that the program uses. In fact, the easiest way to envision what happens is to imagine that the system makes a second copy of the entire running program. Then imagine
that both copies run (just as if two users had both simultaneously executed the program). To summarize:

> To understand the fork function, imagine that fork *causes the operat-
> ing system to make a copy of the executing program and allows both
> copies to run at the same time.*

On one particular uniprocessor system, the execution of our example concurrent
program produces twelve lines of output:

```
                        The value of i is 1
                        The value of i is 2
                        The value of i is 3
                        The value of i is 4
                        The value of i is 5
                        The sum is 15
                        The value of i is 1
                        The value of i is 2
                        The value of i is 3
                        The value of i is 4
                        The value of i is 5
                        The sum is 15
```

On the hardware being used, the first process executed so rapidly that it was able to complete execution before the second process ran at all. Once the first process completed, the operating system switched the processor to the second process, which also ran to completion. The entire run took less than a second. The operating system overhead incurred in switching between processes and handling system calls, including the call to *fork* and the calls required to write the output, accounted for less than *20%* of the total time.

3.5.3 Timeslicing

In the example program, each process performed a trivial amount of computation as it iterated through a loop five times. Therefore, once a process gained control of the CPU, it quickly ran to completion. If we examine concurrent processes that perform substantially more computation, an interesting phenomenon occurs: the operating system allocates the available CPU power to each one for a short time before moving on to the next. We use the term *timeslicing* to describe systems that share the available CPU among several processes concurrently. For example, if a timeslicing system has only one CPU to allocate and a program divides into two processes, one of the processes will execute for a while, then the second will execute for a while, then the first will execute again, and so on. If the timeslicing system has many processes, it runs each for a short time before it runs the first one again.

A timeslicing mechanism attempts to allocate the available processing equally among all available processes. If only two processes are eligible to execute and the computer has a single processor, each receives approximately 50% of the CPU. If N processes are eligible on a computer with a single processor, each receives approximately $1/N$ of the CPU. Thus, all processes appear to proceed at an equal rate, no matter how many processes execute. With many processes executing, the rate is low; with few, the rate is high.

To see the effect of timeslicing, we need an example program in which each process executes longer than the allotted timeslice. Extending the concurrent program above to iterate 10000 times instead of *5* times produces:

```
#include <stdio.h>
int     sum;

main() {
        int i;

        sum = 0;
        fork();
        for (i=0 ; i <=10000 ; i++) {
                printf("The value of i is %d\n", i);
                fflush(stdout);
                sum += i;
        }
        printf("The total is %d\n", sum);
```

```
        exit(0);
}
```

When the resulting concurrent program is executed on the same system as before, it emits 20002 lines of output. However, instead of all output from the first process followed by all output from the second process, output from both processes is mixed together. In one run, the first process iterated *74* times before the second process executed at all. Then the second process iterated *63* times before the system switched back to the first process. On subsequent timeslices, the processes each received enough CPU service to iterate between *60* and *90* times. Of course, the two processes compete with all other processes executing on the computer, so the apparent rate of execution varies slightly depending on the mix of programs running.

3.5.4 Making Processes Diverge

So far, we have said that *fork* can be used to create a new process that executes exactly the same code as the original process. Creating a truly identical copy of a running program is neither interesting nor useful because it means that both copies perform exactly the same computation. In practice, the process created by *fork* is not absolutely identical to the original process: it differs in one small detail. *Fork* is a function that returns a value to its caller. When the function call returns, the value returned to the original process differs from the value returned to the newly created process. In the newly created process, the *fork* returns zero; in the original process, *fork* returns a small positive integer that identifies the newly created process. Technically, the value returned is called a *process identifier* or *process id*†.

Concurrent programs use the value returned by *fork* to decide how to proceed. In the most common case, the code contains a conditional statement that tests to see if the value returned is nonzero:

```
int      sum;

main() {
        int pid;

        sum = 0;
        pid = fork();
        if (pid != 0) {          /* original process       */

            printf("The original process prints this.\n");

        } else {                  /* newly created process */

            printf("The new process prints this.\n");

        }
        exit(0);
}
```

---

†Many programmers abbreviate *process id* as *pid*.

In the example code, variable *pid* records the value returned by the call to *fork*. Remember that each process has its own copy of all variables, and that *fork* will either return zero (in the newly created process) or nonzero (in the original process). Following the call to *fork*, the *if* statement checks variable *pid* to see whether the original or the newly created process is executing. The two processes each print an identifying message and exit. When the program runs, two messages appear: one from the original process and one from the newly created process. To summarize:

> *The value returned by* fork *differs in the original and newly created processes; concurrent programs use the difference to allow the new process to execute different code than the original process.*

3.6 Executing New Code

UNIX provides a mechanism that allows any process to execute an independent, separately-compiled program. The mechanism consists of a system call, *execve†*, that takes three arguments: the name of a file that contains an executable object program (i.e., a program that has been compiled), a pointer to a list of string arguments to pass to the program, and a pointer to a list of strings that comprise what UNIX calls the *environment*.

Execve replaces the code that the currently executing process runs with the code from the new program. The call does not affect any other processes. Thus, to create a new process that executes the object code from a file, a process must call *fork* and *execve*. For example, whenever the user types a command to one of the UNIX command interpreters, the command interpreter uses *fork* to create a new process for the command and *execve* to execute the code.

Execve is especially important for servers that handle diverse services. To keep the code for each service separate from the code for other services, a programmer can build, write, and compile each service as a separate program. When the server needs to handle a particular service, it can use *fork* and *execve* to create a process that runs one of the programs. Later chapters discuss the idea in more detail, and show examples of how servers use *execve*.

3.7 Context Switching And Protocol Software Design

Although the concurrent processing facilities that operating systems provide make programs more powerful and easier to understand, they do have computational cost. To make sure that all processes proceed concurrently, the operating system uses timeslicing, switching the CPU (or CPUs) among processes so fast that it appears to a human that the processes execute simultaneously.

When the operating system temporarily stops executing one process and switches to another, a *context switch* has occurred. Switching process context requires use of the CPU, and while the CPU is busy switching, none of the application processes receives

---

†Some versions of UNIX use the older name, *exec*.

any service. Thus, we view context switching as overhead needed to support concurrent processing.

To avoid unnecessary overhead, protocol software should be designed to minimize context switching. In particular, programmers must always be careful to ensure that the benefits of introducing concurrency into a server outweigh the cost of switching context among the concurrent processes. Later chapters discuss the use of concurrency in server software, present noncurrent designs as well as concurrent ones, and describe circumstances that justify the use of each.

3.8 Concurrency And Asynchronous I/O

In addition to providing support for concurrent use of the CPU, some operating systems allow a single application program to initiate and control concurrent input and output operations. In BSD UNIX, the *select* system call provides a fundamental operation around which programmers can build programs that manage concurrent I/O. In principle, *select* is easy to understand: it allows a program to ask the operating system which I/O devices are ready for use.

An an example, imagine an application program that reads characters from a TCP connection and writes them to the display screen. The program might also allow the user to type commands on the keyboard to control how the data is displayed. Because a user seldom (or never) types commands, the program cannot wait for input from the keyboard – it must continue to read and display text from the TCP connection. However, if the program attempts to read from the TCP connection and no data is available, the program will block. The user may type a command while the program is blocked waiting for input on the TCP connection. The problem is that the application cannot know whether input will arrive from the keyboard or the TCP connection first. To solve the dilemma, a UNIX program calls *select*. In doing so, it asks the operating system to let it know which source of input becomes available first. The call returns as soon as a source is ready, and the program reads from that source. For now, it is only important to understand the idea behind *select*; later chapters present the details and illustrate its use.

3.9 Summary

Concurrency is fundamental to TCP/IP applications because it allows users to access services without waiting for one another. Concurrency in clients arises easily because multiple users can execute client application software at the same time. Concurrency in servers is much more difficult to achieve because server software must be programmed explicitly to handle requests concurrently.

In UNIX, a program creates an additional process using the *fork* system call. We imagine that the call to *fork* causes the operating system to duplicate the program, causing two copies to execute instead of one. Technically, *fork* is a function call because it returns a value. The only difference between the original process and a process created by *fork* lies in the value that the call returns. In the newly created process, the call returns zero; in the original process, it returns the small, positive integer process id of the newly created process. Concurrent programs use the returned value to make new processes execute a different part of the program than the original process. A process can call *execve* at any time to have the process execute code from a separately-compiled program.

The *select* call permits a single process to manage concurrent I/O. A process uses *select* to find out which I/O device becomes ready first.

FOR FURTHER STUDY

Many texts on operating systems describe concurrent processing. Peterson and Silberschatz [1985] covers the general topic. Comer [1984] discusses the implementation of processes, message passing, and process coordination mechanisms. Leffler *et. al.* [1989] describes 4.3 BSD UNIX.

EXERCISES

3.1 Run the example programs on your local computer system. Approximately how many iterations of the output loop can a process make in a single timeslice?

3.2 Write a concurrent program that starts five processes. Arrange for each process to print a few lines of output and then halt.

3.3 Find out how systems other than UNIX create concurrent processes.

3.4 Read more about the UNIX *fork* function. What information does the newly created process share with the original process?

3.5 Write a program that uses *execve* to change the code a process executes.

3.6 Write a program that uses *select* to read from two terminals (serial lines), and displays the results on a screen with labels that identify the source.

3.7 Rewrite the program in the previous exercise so it does not use *select*. Which version is easier to understand? more efficient? easier to terminate cleanly?

4

Program Interface To Protocols

4.1 Introduction

Previous chapters describe the client-server model of interaction for communicating programs and discuss the relationship between concurrency and communication. This chapter considers general properties of the interface an application program uses to communicate in the client-server model. The following chapter illustrates these properties by giving details of a specific interface.

4.2 Loosely Specified Protocol Software Interface

In most implementations, TCP/IP protocol software resides in the computer's operating system. Thus, whenever an application program uses TCP/IP to communicate, it must interact with the operating system to request service. From a programmer's point of view, the routines the operating system supplies define the interface between the application and the protocol software, the *application interface*.

TCP/IP was designed to operate in a multi-vendor environment. To remain compatible with a wide variety of machines, TCP/IP designers carefully avoided choosing any vendor's internal data representation. In addition, the TCP/IP standards carefully avoid specifying the application interface in terms of features available only on a single vendor's operating system. Thus, the interface between TCP/IP and applications that use it has been *loosely specified*. In other words:

The TCP/IP standards do not specify the details of how application software interfaces with TCP/IP protocol software; they only suggest the required functionality, and allow system designers to choose the details.

4.2.1 Advantages And Disadvantages

Using a loose specification for the protocol interface has advantages and disadvantages. On the positive side, it provides flexibility and tolerance. It allows designers to implement TCP/IP using operating systems that range from the simplest systems available on personal computers to the sophisticated systems used on supercomputers. More important, it means designers can use either a procedural or message-passing interface style (whichever style the operating system supports).

On the negative side, a loose specification means that designers can make the interface details different for each operating system. As vendors add new interfaces that differ from existing interfaces, application programming becomes more difficult and applications become less portable across machines. Thus, while system designers favor a loose specification, application programmers desire a restricted specification because it means applications can be compiled for new machines without change.

In practice, only a few TCP/IP interfaces exist. The University of California at Berkeley defined an interface for the Berkeley UNIX operating system that has become known as the *socket interface*, or *sockets*. AT&T defined an interface for System V UNIX known by the acronym *TLI†*. A few other interfaces have been defined, but none has gained wide acceptance yet.

4.3 Interface Functionality

Although TCP/IP does not define an application program interface, the standards do suggest the functionality needed. An interface must support the following conceptual operations:

- Allocate local resources for communication
- Specify local and remote communication endpoints
- Initiate a connection (client side)
- Wait for an incoming connection (server side)
- Send or receive data
- Determine when data arrives
- Generate urgent data
- Handle incoming urgent data
- Terminate a connection gracefully
- Handle connection termination from the remote site
- Abort communication
- Handle error conditions or a connection abort
- Release local resources when communication finished

---

†TLI stands for *Transport Layer Interface.*

4.4 Conceptual Interface Specification

The TCP/IP standards do not leave implementors without any guidance. They specify a *conceptual interface* for TCP/IP that serves as an illustrative example. Because most operating systems use a procedural mechanism to transfer control from an application program into the system, the standard defines the conceptual interface as a set of procedures and functions. The standard suggests the parameters that each procedure or function requires as well as the semantics of the operation it performs. For example, the TCP standard discusses a *SEND* procedure, and lists the arguments an application needs to supply to send data on an existing TCP connection.

The point of defining conceptual operations is simple:

> *The conceptual interface defined by the TCP/IP standards does not specify data representations or programming details; it merely provides an example of one possible interface that an operating system can offer to application programs that use TCP/IP.*

Thus, the conceptual interface illustrates loosely how applications interact with TCP. Because it does not prescribe exact details, operating system designers are free to choose alternative procedure names or parameters as long as they offer equivalent functionality.

4.5 System Calls

Figure 4.1 illustrates the *system call* mechanism that most operating systems use to transfer control between an application program and the operating system procedures that supply services. To a programmer, system calls look and act like function calls.

As the figure shows, however, when an application invokes a system call, control passes from the application, through the system call interface, and into the operating system. The operating system directs the incoming call to an internal procedure that performs the requested operation. Once the internal procedure completes, control returns through the system call interface to the application, which then continues to execute. In essence, whenever an application program needs service from the operating system, the process executing the application climbs into the operating system, performs the necessary operation, and then climbs back out. As it passes through the system call interface, the process acquires privileges that allow it to read or modify data structures in the operating system. The operating system remains protected, however, because each system call branches to a procedure that the operating system designers have written.

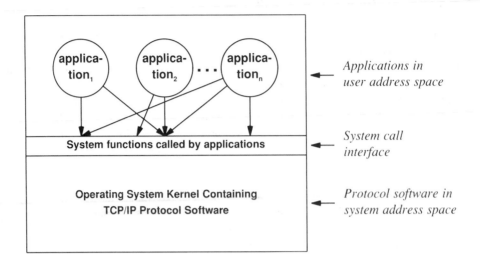

Figure 4.1 Applications interacting with TCP/IP protocol software through a
system call interface. System calls behave like other function
calls except that control transfers into the operating system.

4.6 Two Basic Approaches To Network Communication

Operating system designers must choose the exact set of procedures used to access
TCP/IP protocols when they install protocol software in an operating system. Implementations follow one of two approaches:

- The designer invents entirely new system calls that applications use to access TCP/IP.
- The designer attempts to use conventional I/O calls to access TCP/IP.

In the first approach, the designer makes a list of all conceptual operations, invents
names and parameters for each, and implements each as a system call. Because many
designers consider it unwise to create new system calls unless absolutely necessary, this
approach is seldom used. In the second approach, the designer uses conventional I/O
primitives but overloads them so they work with network protocols as well as conventional I/O devices. Of course, many designers choose a hybrid approach that uses basic
I/O functions whenever possible, but adds additional functions for those operations that
cannot be expressed conveniently.

4.7 The Basic I/O Functions Available In UNIX

To understand how conventional system calls can be extended to accommodate TCP/IP, consider the basic UNIX I/O functions. UNIX (and the many operating system variants derived from it) provides a basic set of six system functions used for input/output operations on devices or files. The table in Figure 4.2 lists the operations and their conventional meanings.

Operation	Meaning
open	Prepare a device or a file for input or output operations
close	Terminate use of a previously opened device or file
read	Obtain data from an input device or file, and place it in the application program's memory
write	Transmit data from the application program's memory to an output device or file
lseek	Move to a specific position in a file or device (this operation only applies to files or devices like disks)
ioctl†	Control a device or the software used to access it (e.g., specify the size of a buffer or change the character set mapping)

Figure 4.2 The basic I/O operations available in UNIX.

When an application program calls *open* to initiate input or output, the system returns a small integer called a *file descriptor* that the application uses in further I/O operations. The call to *open* takes three arguments: the name of a file or device to open, a set of bit flags that controls special cases such as whether to create the file if it does not exist, and an access mode that specifies read/write protections for newly created files. For example, the code segment:

```
int     desc;

desc = open("filename", O_RDWR, 0)
```

opens an existing file, *filename*, with a mode that allows both reading and writing. After obtaining the integer descriptor, *desc*, the application uses it in further I/O operations on the file. For example, the statement:

```
read(desc, buffer, 128);
```

reads *128* bytes of data from the file into array *buffer*.

---

†*ioctl* stands for Input Output ConTroL.

Finally, when an application finishes using a file, it calls *close* to deallocate the descriptor and release associated resources (e.g., internal buffers):

```
close(desc);
```

4.8 Using UNIX I/O With TCP/IP

When designers added TCP/IP protocols to UNIX, they extended the conventional UNIX I/O facilities. First, they extended the set of file descriptors and made it possible for applications to create descriptors used for network communication. Second, they extended the *read* and *write* system calls so they worked with the new network descriptors as well as with conventional file descriptors. Thus, when an application needs to send data across a TCP connection, it creates the appropriate descriptor, and then uses *write* to transfer data.

However, not all network communication fits easily into UNIX's *open-read-write-close* paradigm. An application must specify the local and remote protocol ports and the remote IP address it will use, whether it will use TCP or UDP, and whether it will initiate transfer or wait for an incoming connection (i.e., whether it wants to behave as a client or server). If it is a server, it must specify how many incoming connection requests the operating system should enqueue before rejecting them. Furthermore, if an application chooses to use UDP, it must be able to transfer UDP datagrams, not merely a stream of bytes. The designers of Berkeley UNIX added new system calls to UNIX to accommodate these special cases. The next chapter shows the details of the design.

4.9 Summary

Because TCP/IP is designed for a multi-vendor environment, the protocol standards loosely specify the interface that application programs use, allowing operating system designers freedom in choosing how to implement it. The standards do discuss a conceptual interface, but it is intended only as an illustrative example. Although the standards present the conceptual interface as a set of procedures, designers are free to choose different procedures or to use an entirely different style of interaction (e.g., message passing).

Operating systems often supply services through a mechanism known as the system call interface. When adding support for TCP/IP, designers attempt to minimize the number of new system calls by extending existing system calls where possible. However, because network communication requires operations that do not fit easily into conventional I/O procedures, most interfaces to TCP/IP require a few new system calls.

FOR FURTHER STUDY

Section *2* of the *UNIX Programmer's Manual* describes each of the socket calls in detail; section *4P* describes protocols and network device interfaces in more detail. [AT&T 1989] defines AT&T's TLI interface, an alternative to sockets used in System V UNIX.

EXERCISES

4.1   Examine a message-passing operating system. How would you extend the application program interface to accommodate network communication?

4.2   Compare the socket interface from Berkeley UNIX with AT&T's TLI. What are the major differences? How are the two similar? What reasons could designers have for choosing one design over the other?

4.3   Some hardware architectures limit the number of possible system calls to a small number (e.g., 64 or 128). How many system calls have already been assigned in your local operating system?

4.4   Think about the hardware limit on system calls discussed in the previous exercise. How can a system designer add additional system calls without changing the hardware?

4.5   Find out how recent versions of the Korn shell use */dev/tcp* to allow UNIX shell scripts to communicate with TCP. Write an example script.

5

The Socket Interface

5.1 Introduction

The previous chapter describes the interface between application programs and the TCP/IP software, and shows how most systems use the system call mechanism to transfer control to the TCP/IP software in an operating system. It also reviews the six basic I/O functions that UNIX supplies: *open*, *close*, *read*, *write*, *lseek*, and *ioctl*. This chapter describes the details of a specific set of UNIX system calls for TCP/IP and discusses how they use the UNIX I/O paradigm. It covers concepts in general, and gives the intended use of each call. Later chapters show how clients and servers use these calls, and provide examples that illustrate many of the details.

5.2 Berkeley Sockets

In the early 1980s, the Advanced Research Projects Agency (ARPA) funded a group at the University of California at Berkeley to transport TCP/IP software to the UNIX operating system and to make the resulting software available to other sites. As part of the project, the designers created an interface that applications use to communicate. They decided to use the existing UNIX system calls whenever possible and to add new system calls to support TCP/IP functions that did not fit easily into the existing set of functions. The result became known as the *socket interface*†, and the system is known as *Berkeley UNIX* or *BSD UNIX*. (TCP first appeared in release *4.1* of the Berkeley Software Distribution; the socket functions that this text describes are from release *4.3*.)

---

†The socket interface is sometimes called the *Berkeley socket interface*.

Because many computer vendors, especially workstation manufacturers like Sun Microsystems Incorporated, Tektronix Incorporated, and Digital Equipment Corporation, adopted Berkeley UNIX, the socket interface has become available on many machines. Consequently, the socket interface has become so widely accepted that it ranks as a *de facto* standard.

5.3 Specifying A Protocol Interface

When designers consider how to add functions to an operating system that provide application programs access to TCP/IP protocol software, they must choose names for the functions and must specify the parameters that each function accepts. In so doing, they decide the scope of services that the functions supply and the style in which applications use them. Designers must also consider whether to make the interface specific to the TCP/IP protocols or whether to plan for additional protocols. Thus, the designers must choose one of two broad approaches:

- Define functions specifically to support TCP/IP communication.
- Define functions that support network communication in general, and use parameters to make TCP/IP communication a special case.

Differences between the two approaches are easiest to understand by their impact on the names of system functions and the parameters that the functions require. For example, in the first approach, a designer might choose to have a system function named *maketcpconnection*, while in the second, a designer might choose to create a general function *makeconnection* and use a parameter to specify the TCP protocol.

Because the designers at Berkeley wanted to accommodate multiple sets of communication protocols, they used the second approach. In fact, throughout the design, they provided for generality far beyond TCP/IP. They allowed for multiple *families* of protocols, with all TCP/IP protocols represented as a single family (family *PF_INET*). They also decided to have applications specify operations using a *type of service* required instead of specifying the protocol name. Thus, instead of specifying that it wants a TCP connection, an application requests the *stream transfer* type of service using the Internet family of protocols. We can summarize:

> *The Berkeley socket interface provides generalized functions that support network communication using many possible protocols. Socket calls refer to all TCP/IP protocols as a single protocol family. The calls allow the programmer to specify the type of service required rather than the name of a specific protocol.*

The overall design of sockets and the generality they provide have been debated since their inception. Some computer scientists argue that generality is unnecessary and merely makes application programs difficult to read. Others argue that having programmers specify the type of service instead of the specific protocol makes it easier to program because it frees the programmer from understanding the details of each protocol family. Finally, some commercial vendors of TCP/IP software have argued in favor of alternative interfaces because sockets cannot be added to an operating system unless the customer has the source code, which usually requires a special license agreement and additional expense.

5.4 The Socket Abstraction

5.4.1 Socket Descriptors And File Descriptors

In UNIX, an application that needs to perform I/O calls the *open* function to create a file descriptor that it uses to access the file. As Figure 5.1 shows, the operating system implements file descriptors as an array of pointers to internal data structures. The system maintains a separate file descriptor table for each process. When a process opens a file, the system places a pointer to the internal data structures for that file in the process' file descriptor table and returns the table index to the caller. The application program only needs to remember the descriptor and to use it in subsequent calls that request operations on the file. The operating system uses the descriptor as an index into the process' descriptor table, and follows the pointer to the data structures that hold all information about the file.

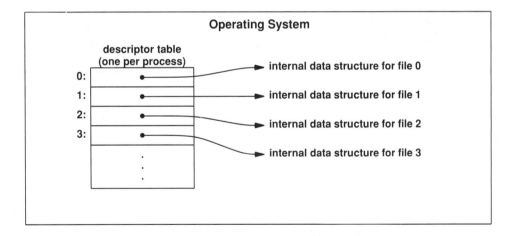

Figure 5.1 The per-process file descriptor table in UNIX. The operating system uses a process' descriptor table to store pointers to internal data structures for files that the process has opened. The process (application) uses the descriptor when referring to the file.

The socket interface adds a new abstraction for network communication, the *socket*. Like files, each active socket is identified by a small integer called its *socket descriptor*. UNIX allocates socket descriptors in the same descriptor table as file descriptors. Thus, an application cannot have both a file descriptor and a socket descriptor with the same value.

BSD UNIX contains a separate system function, *socket*, that applications call to create a socket; an application only uses *open* to create file descriptors.

The general idea underlying sockets is that a single system call is sufficient to create any socket. Once the socket has been created, an application must make additional system calls to specify the details of its exact use. The paradigm will become clear after we examine the data structures the system maintains.

5.4.2 System Data Structures For Sockets

The easiest way to understand the socket abstraction is to envision the data structures in the operating system. When an application calls *socket*, the operating system allocates a new data structure to hold the information needed for communication, and fills in a new descriptor table entry to contain a pointer to the data structure. For example, Figure 5.2 illustrates what happens to the descriptor table of Figure 5.1 after a call to *socket†*. In the example, arguments to the socket call have specified protocol family *PF_INET* and type of service *SOCK_STREAM*.

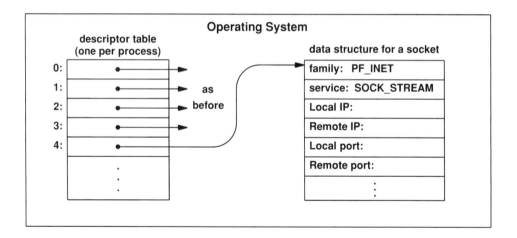

Figure 5.2 Conceptual operating system data structures after a call to *socket*. The system uses a single descriptor table for sockets and other I/O.

---

†UNIX data structures are more complex than shown in Figure 5.1; the diagram illustrates the concept, not the details.

Although the internal data structure for a socket contains many fields, the system leaves most of them unfilled when it creates the socket. As we will see, the application that created the socket must make additional system calls to fill in information in the socket data structure before the socket can be used.

5.4.3 Using Sockets

Once a socket has been created, it can be used to wait for an incoming connection or to initiate a connection. A socket used by a server to wait for an incoming connection is called a *passive socket*, while a socket used by a client to initiate a connection is called an *active socket*. The only difference between active and passive sockets lies in how applications use them; the sockets are created the same way initially.

5.5 Specifying An Endpoint Address

When a socket is created, it does not contain detailed information about how it will be used. In particular, the socket does not contain information about the protocol port numbers or IP addresses of either the local machine or the remote machine. Before an application uses a socket, it must specify one or both of these addresses.

TCP/IP protocols define a *communication endpoint* to consist of an IP address and a protocol port number. Other protocol families define their endpoint addresses in other ways. Because the socket abstraction accommodates multiple families of protocols, it does not specify how to define endpoint addresses nor does it define a particular protocol address format. Instead, it allows each protocol family to specify endpoints however it likes.

To allow protocol families the freedom to choose representations for their addresses the socket abstraction defines an *address family* for each type of address. A protocol family can use one or more address families to define address representations. The TCP/IP protocols all use a single address representation, with the address family denoted by the symbolic constant *AF_INET*.

In practice, much confusion arises between the TCP/IP protocol family, denoted *PF_INET*, and the address family it uses, denoted *AF_INET*. The chief problem is that both symbolic constants have the same numeric value (2), so programs that inadvertently use one in place of the other operate correctly. Even the Berkeley UNIX source code contains examples of misuse. Programmers should observe the distinction, however, because it helps clarify the meaning of variables and makes programs more portable.

5.6 A Generic Address Structure

Some software manipulates protocol addresses without knowing the details of how every protocol family defines its address representation. For example, it may be necessary to write a procedure that accepts an arbitrary protocol endpoint specification as an argument and chooses one of several possible actions depending on the address type. To accommodate such programs, the socket system defines a generalized format that all endpoint addresses use. The generalized format consists of a pair:

(address family, endpoint address in that family)

where the address family field contains a constant that denotes one of the preassigned address types, and the endpoint address field contains an endpoint address using the standard representation for the specified address type.

In practice, the socket software provides declarations of predefined C structures for address endpoints. Application programs use the predefined structures when they need to declare variables that store endpoint addresses or when they need to use an overlay to locate fields in a structure. The most general structure is known as a *sockaddr* structure. It contains a 2-byte address family identifier and a 14-byte array to hold an address†:

```
struct  sockaddr {           /* struct to hold an address */
    u_short sa_family;       /* type of address           */
    char    sa_data[14];     /* value of address          */
};
```

Unfortunately, not all address families define endpoints that fit into the *sockaddr* structure. For example, BSD UNIX defines the *AF_UNIX* address family to specify what UNIX programmers think of as a named *pipe*. Endpoint addresses in the *AF_UNIX* family consist of UNIX path names that can be much longer than 14 bytes. Therefore, application programs should not use *sockaddr* in variable declarations because a variable declared to be of type *sockaddr* is not large enough to hold all possible endpoint addresses.

Confusion often arises in practice because the *sockaddr* structure accommodates addresses in the *AF_INET* family. Thus, TCP/IP software works correctly even if the programmer declares variables to be of type *sockaddr*. However, to keep programs portable and maintainable, TCP/IP code should not use the *sockaddr* structure in declarations. Instead, *sockaddr* should be used only as an overlay, and code should reference only the *sa_family* field in it.

Each protocol family that uses sockets defines the exact representation of its endpoint addresses, and the socket software provides corresponding structure declarations. Each TCP/IP endpoint address consists of a 2-byte field that identifies the address type (it must contain *AF_INET*), a 2-byte port number field, a 4-byte IP address field, and an 8-byte field that remains unused. Predefined structure *sockaddr_in* specifies the format:

---

†Berkeley plans to add a length field to the sockaddr structure to accommodate more complex protocol families that will be included in release *4.4* of their software. This text describes the structure most widely used in 1992.

```
struct  sockaddr_in {     /* struct to hold an address          */
    u_short sin_family;   /* type of address                    */
    u_short sin_port;     /* protocol port number               */
    u_long  sin_addr;     /* IP address (declared to be type    */
                          /* 'struct in_addr' on some systems)  */
    char    sin_zero[8];  /* unused (set to zero)               */
};
```

An application that uses TCP/IP protocols exclusively can use structure *sockaddr_in* exclusively; it never needs to use the *sockaddr* structure‡. Thus,

> *When representing a TCP/IP communication endpoint, an application program uses structure* sockaddr_in, *which contains both an IP address and a protocol port number. Programmers must be careful when writing programs that use a mixture of protocols because some non-TCP/IP endpoint addresses require a larger structure.*

5.7 Major System Calls Used With Sockets

Socket calls can be separated into two groups: primary calls that provide access to the underlying functionality and utility routines that help the programmer. This section describes the calls that provide the primary functionality that clients and servers need.

The details of socket system calls, their parameters, and their semantics can seem overwhelming. Much of the complexity arises because sockets have parameters that allow programs to use them in many ways. A socket can be used by a client or by a server, for stream transfer (TCP) or datagram (UDP) communication, with a specific remote endpoint address (usually needed by a client) or with an unspecified remote endpoint address (usually needed by a server).

To help understand sockets, we will begin by examining the primary socket calls and describing how a straightforward client and server use them to communicate with TCP. Later chapters each discuss one way to use sockets, and illustrate many of the details and subtleties not covered here.

5.7.1 The Socket Call

An application calls *socket* to create a new socket that can be used for network communication. The call returns a descriptor for the newly created socket. Arguments to the call specify the protocol family that the application will use (e.g., *PF_INET* for TCP/IP) and the protocol or type of service it needs (i.e., stream or datagram). For a socket that uses the Internet protocol family, the protocol or type of service argument determines whether the socket will use TCP or UDP.

---

‡Structure *sockaddr* is used to cast (i.e., change the type of) pointers or the results of system functions to make programs pass the type checking in *lint*.

5.7.2 The Connect Call

After creating a socket, a client calls *connect* to establish an active connection to a remote server. An argument to *connect* allows the client to specify the remote endpoint, which includes the remote machine's IP address and protocol port number. Once a connection has been made, a client can transfer data across it.

5.7.3 The Write Call

Both clients and servers use *write* to send data across a TCP connection. Clients usually use *write* to send requests, while servers use it to send replies. A call to *write* requires three arguments. The application passes the descriptor of a socket to which the data should be sent, the address of the data to be sent, and the length of the data. Usually, *write* copies outgoing data into buffers in the operating system kernel, and allows the application to continue execution while it transmits the data across the network. If the system buffers become full, the call to *write* may block temporarily until TCP can send data across the network and make space in the buffer for new data.

5.7.4 The Read Call

Both clients and servers use *read* to receive data from a TCP connection. Usually, after a connection has been established, the server uses *read* to receive a request that the client sends by calling *write*. After sending its request, the client uses *read* to receive a reply.

To read from a connection, an application calls *read* with three arguments. The first specifies the socket descriptor to use, the second specifies the address of a buffer, and the third specifies the length of the buffer. *Read* extracts data bytes that have arrived at that socket, and copies them to the user's buffer area. If no data has arrived, the call to *read* blocks until it does. If more data has arrived than fits into the buffer, *read* only extracts enough to fill the buffer. If less data has arrived than fits into the buffer, *read* extracts all the data and returns the number of bytes it found.

Clients and servers can also use *read* to receive messages from sockets that use UDP. As with the connection-oriented case, the caller supplies three arguments that identify a socket descriptor, the address of a buffer into which the data should be placed, and the size of the buffer. Each call to *read* extracts one incoming UDP message (i.e., one user datagram). If the buffer cannot hold the entire message, *read* fills the buffer and discards the remainder.

5.7.5 The Close Call

Once a client or server finishes using a socket, it calls *close* to deallocate it. If only one process is using the socket, *close* immediately terminates the connection and deallocates the socket. If several processes share a socket, *close* decrements a reference count and deallocates the socket when the reference count reaches zero.

5.7.6 The Bind Call

When a socket is created, it does not have any notion of endpoint addresses (neither the local nor remote addresses are assigned). An application calls *bind* to specify the local endpoint address for a socket. The call takes arguments that specify a socket descriptor and an endpoint address. For TCP/IP protocols, the endpoint address uses the *sockaddr_in* structure, which includes both an IP address and a protocol port number. Primarily, servers use *bind* to specify the well-known port at which they will await connections.

5.7.7 The Listen Call

When a socket is created, the socket is neither *active* (i.e., ready for use by a client) nor *passive* (i.e., ready for use by a server) until the application takes further action. Connection-oriented servers call *listen* to place a socket in *passive mode* and make it ready to accept incoming connections.

Most servers consist of an infinite loop that accepts the next incoming connection, handles it, and then returns to accept the next connection. Even if handling a given connection takes only a few milliseconds, it may happen that a new connection request arrives during the time the server is busy handling an existing request. To ensure that no connection request is lost, a server must pass *listen* an argument that tells the operating system to enqueue connection requests for a socket. Thus, one argument to the *listen* call specifies a socket to be placed in passive mode, while the other specifies the size of the queue to be used for that socket.

5.7.8 The Accept Call

After a server calls *socket* to create a socket, *bind* to specify a local endpoint address, and *listen* to place it in passive mode, the server calls *accept* to extract the next incoming connection request. An argument to *accept* specifies the socket from which a connection should be accepted.

Accept creates a new socket for each new connection request, and returns the descriptor of the new socket to its caller. The server uses the new socket only for the new connection; it uses the original socket to accept additional connection requests. Once it has accepted a connection, the server can transfer data on the new socket. After it finishes using the new socket, the server closes it.

5.7.9 Summary Of Socket Calls Used With TCP

The table in Figure 5.3 provides a brief summary of the system functions related to sockets.

Function Name	Meaning
socket	Create a descriptor for use in network communication
connect	Connect to a remote peer (client)
write	Send outgoing data across a connection
read	Acquire incoming data from a connection
close	Terminate communication and deallocate a descriptor
bind	Bind a local IP address and protocol port to a socket
listen	Place the socket in passive mode and set the number of incoming TCP connections the system will enqueue (server)
accept	Accept the next incoming connection (server)
recv	Receive the next incoming datagram
recvmsg	Receive the next incoming datagram (variation of recv)
recvfrom	Receive the next incoming datagram and record its source endpoint address
send	Send an outgoing datagram
sendmsg	Send an outgoing datagram (variation of send)
sendto	Send an outgoing datagram, usually to a prerecorded endpoint address
shutdown	Terminate a TCP connection in one or both directions
getpeername	After a connection arrives, obtain the remote machine's endpoint address from a socket
getsockopt	Obtain the current options for a socket
setsockopt	Change the options for a socket

Figure 5.3 A summary of the socket functions and the meaning of each.

5.8 Utility Routines For Integer Conversion

TCP/IP specifies a standard representation for binary integers used in protocol headers. The representation, known as *network byte order*, represents integers with the most significant byte first.

Although the protocol software hides most values used in headers from application programs, a programmer must be aware of the standard because some socket routines require arguments to be stored in network byte order. For example, the protocol port field of a *sockaddr_in* structure uses network byte order.

The socket routines include several functions that convert between network byte order and the local host's byte order. Programs should always call the conversion routines even if the local machine's byte order is the same as the network byte order because doing so makes the source code portable to an arbitrary architecture.

The conversion routines are divided into *short* and *long* sets to operate on 16-bit integers and 32-bit integers. Functions *htons* and *ntohs* convert a short integer from the host's native byte order to the network byte order, and vice versa. Similarly, *htonl* and *ntohl* convert long integers from the host's native byte order to network byte order and vice versa. To summarize:

> *Software that uses TCP/IP calls functions* htons, ntohs, htonl *and* ntohl *to convert binary integers between the host's native byte order and network standard byte order. Doing so makes the source code portable to any machine, regardless of its native byte order.*

5.9 Using Socket Calls In A Program

Figure 5.4 illustrates a sequence of calls made by a client and a server using TCP.

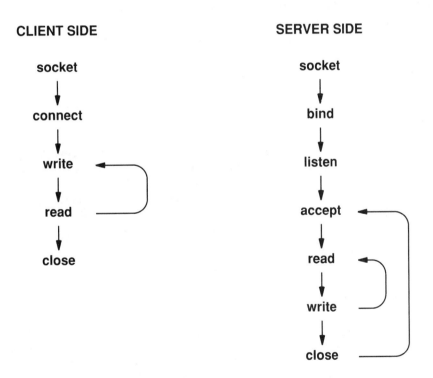

Figure 5.4 An example sequence of socket system calls made by a simple client and server using TCP. The server runs forever, waiting for new connections on the well-known port. It accepts each new connection, processes the request from the client, and then closes that connection.

The client creates a socket, calls *connect* to connect to the server, and then interacts using *write* to send requests and *read* to receive replies. When it finishes using the connection, it calls *close*. A server uses *bind* to specify the local (well-known) protocol port it will use, calls *listen* to set the length of the connection queue, and then enters a loop. Inside the loop, the server calls *accept* to wait until the next connection request arrives, uses *read* and *write* to interact with the client, and finally uses *close* to terminate the connection. The server then returns to the *accept* call, where it waits for the next connection.

5.10 Symbolic Constants For Socket Call Parameters

In addition to the system functions that implement sockets, BSD UNIX provides a set of predefined symbolic constants and data structure declarations that programs use to declare data and to specify arguments. For example, when specifying whether to use datagram service or stream service, an application program uses symbolic constants *SOCK_DGRAM* or *SOCK_STREAM*. To do so, the program must incorporate the appropriate definitions into each program with the C preprocessor *include* statement. Usually, *include* statements appear at the beginning of a source file; they must appear before any use of the constants they define. The *include* statements needed for sockets usually have the form:

```
#include <sys/types.h>
#include <sys/socket.h>
```

We will assume throughout the remainder of this text that programs always begin with these statements, even if they are not shown explicitly in the examples. To summarize:

> *UNIX supplies predefined symbolic constants and data structure declarations used with the socket system calls. Programs that reference these constants must begin with C preprocessor* include *statements that reference the files in which the definitions appear.*

5.11 Summary

BSD UNIX introduced the socket abstraction as a mechanism that allows application programs to interface with protocol software in the operating system. Because so many other vendors have adopted sockets, they have become a *de facto* standard.

A program calls *socket* to create a socket and obtain a descriptor for it. Arguments to the *socket* call specify the protocol family to be used and the type of service required. All TCP/IP protocols are part of the Internet family, specified with symbolic constant *PF_INET*. The system creates an internal data structure for the socket, fills in the protocol family, and uses the type of service argument to select a specific protocol (usually either UDP or TCP).

Additional system calls allow the application to specify a local endpoint address (*bind*), to force the socket into passive mode for use by a server (*listen*), or to force the socket into active mode for use by a client (*connect*). Servers can make further calls to obtain incoming connection requests (*accept*), and both clients and servers can send or receive information (*read* and *write*). Finally, both clients and servers can deallocate a socket once they have finished using it (*close*).

The socket structure allows each protocol family to define one or more address representations. All TCP/IP protocols use the Internet address family, *AF_INET*, which specifies that an endpoint address contains both an IP address and a protocol port number. When an application specifies a communication endpoint to a socket function, it uses predefined structure *sockaddr_in*. If a client specifies that it needs an arbitrary, unused local protocol port, the TCP/IP software will select one.

Before an application program written in C can use the predefined structures and symbolic constants associated with sockets, it must include several files that define them. In particular, we assume that all source programs begin with statements that include files *<sys/types.h>* and *<sys/socket.h>*.

FOR FURTHER STUDY

Leffler et. al. [1989] describes the Berkeley UNIX system in detail, and describes the internal data structures UNIX uses for sockets. Presotto and Ritchie [June 1990] describes an interface for TCP/IP protocols using the UNIX file system space. The *UNIX Programmer's Manual* contains specifications for the socket functions, including an exact description of arguments and return codes. The section entitled *The IPC Tutorial* is worth reading. Much of the information on socket calls can also be found in Appendix A.

EXERCISES

5.1 Look at the *include* file for sockets (usually */usr/include/sys/socket.h*). What socket types are allowed? Which socket types do not makes sense for TCP/IP protocols?

5.2 If your system has a clock with at least microsecond accuracy, measure how long it takes to execute each of the socket system calls. Why do some calls require orders of magnitude more time than others?

5.3 Read the BSD UNIX manual pages for *connect* carefully. What network traffic is generated if one calls *connect* on a socket of type *SOCK_DGRAM*?

5.4 Arrange to monitor your local network while an application executes *connect* for the first time on a socket of type *SOCK_STREAM*. How many packets do you see?

6

Algorithms And Issues In Client Software Design

6.1 Introduction

Previous chapters consider the socket abstraction that applications use to interface with TCP/IP software, and review the system calls associated with it. This chapter discusses the basic algorithms underlying client software. It shows how applications become clients by initiating communication, how they use TCP or UDP protocols to contact a server, and how they use socket calls to interact with those protocols. The next chapter continues the discussion, and shows complete client programs that implement the ideas discussed here.

6.2 Learning Algorithms Instead Of Details

Because TCP/IP provides rich functionality that allows programs to communicate in a variety of ways, an application that uses TCP/IP must specify many details about the desired communication. For example, the application must specify whether it wishes to act as a client or a server, the endpoint address (or addresses) it will use, whether it will communicate with a connectionless or connection-oriented protocol, how it will enforce authorization and protection rules, and details such as the size of the buffers it will need.

So far, we have examined the set of operations available to an application without discussing how applications should use them. Unfortunately, knowing the low-level details of all possible system calls and their exact parameters does not provide programmers with an understanding of how to build well-designed, distributed programs. In fact, while a general understanding of the system calls used for network communication is important, few programmers remember all the details. Instead, they learn and remember the possible ways in which programs can interact across a network, and they understand the tradeoffs of each possible design. In essence, programmers know enough about the algorithms underlying distributed computing to make design decisions and to choose among alternative algorithms quickly. They then consult a programming manual to find the details needed to write a program that implements a particular algorithm on a particular system. The point is that if the programmer knows *what* a program should do, finding out *how* to do it is straightforward.

> *Although programmers need to understand the conceptual capabilities of the protocol interface, they should concentrate on learning about ways to structure communicating programs instead of memorizing the details of a particular interface.*

6.3 Client Architecture

Applications that act as clients are conceptually simpler than applications that act as servers for several reasons. First, most client software does not explicitly handle concurrent interactions with multiple servers. Second, most client software executes as a conventional application program. Unlike server software, client software does not usually require special privilege because it does not usually access privileged protocol ports. Third, most client software does not need to enforce protections. Instead, client programs can rely on the operating system to enforce protections automatically. In fact, designing and implementing client software is so straightforward that experienced application programmers can learn to write basic client applications quickly. The next sections discuss client software in general; later sections will focus on the differences between clients that use TCP and those that use UDP.

6.4 Identifying The Location Of A Server

Client software can use one of several methods to find a server's IP address and protocol port number. A client can:

- have the server's domain name or IP address specified as a constant when the program is compiled,
- require the user to identify the server when invoking the program,
- obtain information about the server from stable storage (e.g., from a file on a local disk), or
- use a separate protocol to find a server (e.g., multicast or broadcast a message to which all servers respond).

Specifying the server's address as a constant makes the client software faster and less dependent on a particular local computing environment. However, it also means that the client must be recompiled if the server is moved. More important, it means that the client cannot be used with an alternative server, even temporarily for testing. As a compromise, some clients fix a machine name instead of an IP address. Fixing the name instead of an address delays the binding until run-time. It allows a site to choose a generic name for the server and add an alias to the domain name system for that name. Using aliases permits a site manager to change the location of a server without changing client software. To move the server, the manager needs to change only the alias. For example, it is possible to add an alias for *mailhost* in the local domain and to arrange for all clients to look up the string "mailhost" instead of a specific machine. Because all clients reference the generic name instead of a specific machine, the system manager can change the location of the mail host without recompiling client software.

Storing the server's address in a file makes the client more flexible, but it means that the client program cannot execute unless the file is available. Thus, the client software cannot be transported to another machine easily.

While using a broadcast protocol to find servers works in a small, local environment, it does not scale well to large internets. Furthermore, use of a dynamic search mechanism introduces additional complexity for both clients and servers, and adds additional broadcast traffic to the network.

To avoid unnecessary complexity and dependence on the computing environment, most clients solve the problem of server specification in a simple manner: they require the user to supply an argument that identifies the server when invoking the client program. Building client software to accept the server address as an argument makes the client software general and eliminates dependency on the computing environment.

> *Allowing the user to specify a server address when invoking client software makes the client program more general and makes it possible to change server locations.*

An important point to note is that using an argument to specify the server's address results in the most flexibility. A program that accepts an address argument can be combined with other programs that extract the server address from disk, find the address using a remote nameserver, or search for it with a broadcast protocol. Thus,

> *Building client software that accepts a server address as an argument makes it easy to build extended versions of the software that use other ways to find the server address (e.g., read the address from a file on disk).*

Some services require an explicit server, while others can use any available server. For example, when a user invokes a remote login client, the user has a specific target machine in mind; logging into another machine usually does not make sense. However, if the user merely wants to find the current time of day, the user does not care which server responds. To accommodate such services, the designer can modify any of the server lookup methods discussed above so they supply a set of server names instead of a single name. Clients must also be changed so they try each server in a set until they find one that responds.

6.5 Parsing An Address Argument

Usually, a user can specify arguments on the command line when invoking a client program. In most systems, each argument passed to a client program consists of a character string. The client uses an argument's syntax to interpret its meaning. For example, most client software allows the user to supply either the domain name of the machine on which the server operates:

merlin.cs.purdue.edu

or an IP address in dotted decimal notation:

128.10.2.3

To determine whether the user has specified a name or an address, the client scans the argument to see if it contains alphabetic characters. If so, it must be a name. If it contains only digits and decimal points, the client assumes it to be a dotted decimal address and parses it accordingly.

Of course, client programs sometimes need additional information beyond the server's machine name or IP address. In particular, fully parameterized client software allows a user to specify a protocol port as well as a machine. It is possible to use an additional argument or to encode such information in a single string. For example, to specify the protocol port associated with the *smtp* service on machine with name *merlin.cs.purdue.edu*, the client could accept two arguments:

merlin.cs.purdue.edu smtp

or could combine both the machine name and protocol port into a single argument:

merlin.cs.purdue.edu:smtp

Although each client can choose the details of its argument syntax independently, having many clients with their own syntax can be confusing. From the user's point of view, consistency is always important. Thus, programmers are advised to follow whatever conventions their local system uses for client software. For example, because most existing UNIX software uses separate arguments to specify the server's machine and protocol port, new client software written for UNIX should use two arguments instead of one.

6.6 Looking Up A Domain Name

A client must specify the address of a server using structure *sockaddr_in*. Doing so means converting an address in dotted decimal notation (or a domain name in text form) into a 32-bit IP address represented in binary. Converting from dotted decimal notation to binary is trivial. Converting from a domain name, however, requires considerably more effort. The socket interface in BSD UNIX includes library routines, *inet_addr* and *gethostbyname*, that perform the conversions. *Inet_addr* takes an ASCII string that contains a dotted decimal address and returns the equivalent IP address in binary. *Gethostbyname* takes an ASCII string that contains the domain name for a machine. It returns the address of a *hostent* structure that contains, among other things, the host's IP address in binary. The *hostent* structure is declared in include file *netdb.h*:

```
struct    hostent {
char      *h_name;       /* official host name   */
char      **h_aliases;   /* other aliases        */
int        h_addrtype;   /* address type         */
int        h_length;     /* address length       */
char      **h_addr_list; /* list of addresses    */
};
#define   h_addr  h_addr_list[0]
```

Fields that contain names and addresses must be lists because hosts that have multiple interfaces also have multiple names and addresses. For compatibility with earlier versions, the file also defines the identifier *h_addr* to refer to the first location in the host address list. Thus, a program can use *h_addr* as if it were a field of the structure.

Consider a simple example of name conversion. Suppose a client has been passed the domain name *merlin.cs.purdue.edu* in string form and needs to obtain the IP address. The client can call *gethostbyname* as in:

```
struct   hostent *hptr;
char     *examplenam = "merlin.cs.purdue.edu";

if ( hptr = gethostbyname( examplenam ) ) {
        /* IP address is now in  hptr->h_addr */
} else {
        /* error in name - handle it */
}
```

If the call is successful, *gethostbyname* returns a pointer to a valid *hostent* structure. If the name cannot be mapped into an IP address, the call returns zero. Thus, the client examines the value that *gethostbyname* returns to determine if an error occurred.

6.7 Looking Up A Well-Known Port By Name

Most client programs must look up the protocol port for the specific service they wish to invoke. For example, a client of an SMTP mail server needs to look up the well-known port assigned to SMTP. To do so, the client invokes library function *getservbyname*, which takes two arguments: a string that specifies the desired service and a string that specifies the protocol being used. It returns a pointer to a structure of type *servent*, also defined in include file *netdb.h*:

```
struct  servent {
        char  *s_name;       /* official service name */
        char **s_aliases;    /* other aliases         */
        int    s_port;       /* port for this service */
        char  *s_proto;      /* protocol to use       */
};
```

If a TCP client needs to look up the official protocol port number for SMTP, it calls *getservbyname*, as in the following example:

```
struct  servent *sptr;

if (sptr = getservbyname( "smtp", "tcp" )) {
        /* port number is now in sptr->s_port */
} else {
        /* error occurred - handle it */
}
```

6.8 Port Numbers And Network Byte Order

Function *getservbyname* returns the protocol port for the service in network byte order. Chapter 5 explains the concept of network byte order, and describes library routines that convert from network byte order to the byte order used on the local machine. It is sufficient to understand that *getservbyname* returns the port value in exactly the form needed for use in the *sockaddr_in* structure, but the representation may not agree with the local machine's usual representation. Thus, if a program prints out the value that *getservbyname* returns without converting to local byte order, it may appear to be incorrect.

6.9 Looking Up A Protocol By Name

The socket interface provides a mechanism that allows a client or server to map a protocol name to the integer constant assigned to that protocol. Library function *get-protobyname* performs the lookup. A call passes the protocol name in a string argument, and *getprotobyname* returns the address of a structure of type *protoent*. If *getpro-tobyname* cannot access the database or if the specified name does not exist, it returns zero. The database of protocol names allows a site to define aliases for each name. The *protoent* structure has a field for the official protocol name as well as a field that points to the list of aliases. The C include file *netdb.h* contains the structure declaration:

```
struct  protoent {
        char  *p_name;      /* official protocol name   */
        char **p_aliases;   /* list of aliases allowed  */
        int    p_proto;     /* official protocol number */
};
```

If a client needs to look up the official protocol number for UDP, it calls *getproto-byname*, as in the following example:

```
struct  protoent *pptr;

if (pptr = getprotobyname( "udp" )) {
        /* official protocol number is now in pptr->p_proto */
} else {
        /* error occurred - handle it */
}
```

6.10 The TCP Client Algorithm

Building client software is usually easier than building server software. Because TCP handles all reliability and flow control problems, building a client that uses TCP is the most straightforward of all network programming tasks. A TCP client follows Algorithm 6.1 to form a connection to a server and communicate with it. The sections following the algorithm discuss each of its steps in more detail.

Algorithm 6.1

1. Find the IP address and protocol port number of the server with which communication is desired.
2. Allocate a socket.
3. Specify that the connection needs an arbitrary, unused protocol port on the local machine, and allow TCP to choose one.
4. Connect the socket to the server.
5. Communicate with the server using the application-level protocol (this usually involves sending requests and awaiting replies).
6. Close the connection.

Algorithm 6.1 A connection-oriented client. The client application allocates a socket and connects it to a server. It then sends requests across the connection and receives replies back.

6.11 Allocating A Socket

Previous sections have already discussed the methods used to find the server's IP address and the *socket* function used to allocate a communication socket. Clients that use TCP must specify protocol family *PF_INET* and service *SOCK_STREAM*. A program begins with *include* statements that reference files which contain the definitions of symbolic constants used in the call and a declaration of the variable used to hold the socket descriptor. If more than one protocol in the family, specified by the first argument, offers the service requested by the second argument, the third argument to the *socket* call identifies a particular protocol. In the case of the Internet protocol family, only TCP offers the *SOCK_STREAM* service. Thus, the third argument is irrelevant; zero should be used.

```
#include <sys/types.h>
#include <sys/socket.h>

int     s;                    /* socket descriptor */

s = socket(PF_INET, SOCK_STREAM, 0);
```

6.12 Choosing A Local Protocol Port Number

An application needs to specify remote and local endpoint addresses for a socket before it can be used in communication. A server operates at a well-known protocol port address, which all clients must know. However, a TCP client does not operate on a preassigned port. Instead, it must select a local protocol port to use for its endpoint address. In general, the client does not care which port it uses as long as: (1) the port does not conflict with the ports that other processes on the machine are already using and (2) the port has not been assigned to a well-known service.

Of course, when a client needs a local protocol port, it could choose an arbitrary port at random until it finds one that meets the criteria given above. However, the socket interface makes choosing a client port much simpler because it provides a way that the client can allow TCP to choose a local port automatically. The choice of a local port that meets the criteria listed above happens as a side-effect of the *connect* call.

6.13 A Fundamental Problem In Choosing A Local IP Address

When forming a connection endpoint, a client must choose a local IP address as well as a local protocol port number. For a host that attaches to one network, the choice of a local IP address is trivial. However, because gateways or multi-homed hosts have multiple IP addresses, making the choice can be difficult.

In general, the difficulty in choosing an IP address arises because the correct choice depends on routing and applications seldom have access to routing information. To understand why, imagine a computer with multiple network interfaces and, therefore, multiple IP addresses. Before an application can use TCP, it must have an endpoint address for the connection. When TCP communicates with a foreign destination, it encapsulates each TCP segment in an IP datagram and passes the datagram to the IP software. IP uses the remote destination address and its routing table to select a next-hop address and a network interface that it can use to reach the next hop.

Herein lies the problem: the IP source address in an outgoing datagram should match the IP address of the network interface over which IP routes the datagram. However, if an application chooses one of the machine's IP addresses at random, it might select an address that does not match that of the interface over which IP routes the traffic.

In practice, a client may appear to work even if the programmer chooses an incorrect address because packets may travel back to the client by a different route than they travel to the server. However, using an incorrect address violates the specification, makes network management difficult and confusing, and makes the program less reliable.

To solve the problem, the socket calls make it possible for an application to leave the local IP address field unfilled and to allow TCP/IP software to choose a local IP address automatically at the time the client connects to a server.

Because choosing the correct local IP address requires the applica-
tion to interact with IP routing software, TCP client software usually
leaves the local endpoint address unfilled, and allows TCP/IP
software to select the correct local IP address and an unused local
protocol port number automatically.

6.14 Connecting A TCP Socket To A Server

The *connect* system call allows a TCP client to initiate a connection. In terms of
the underlying protocol, *connect* forces the initial TCP 3-way handshake. The call to
connect does not return until a TCP connection has been established or TCP reaches a
timeout threshold and gives up. The call returns *0* if the connection attempt succeeds or
-1 if it fails. *Connect* takes three arguments:

```
retcode = connect(s, remaddr, remaddrlen)
```

where *s* is the descriptor for a socket, *remaddr* is the address of a structure of type
sockaddr_in that specifies the remote endpoint to which a connection is desired, and
remaddrlen is the length (in bytes) of the second argument.

Connect performs four tasks. First, it tests to ensure that the specified socket is
valid and that it has not already been connected. Second, it fills in the remote endpoint
address in the socket from the second argument. Third, it chooses a local endpoint address for the connection (IP address and protocol port number) if the socket does not
have one. Fourth, it initiates a TCP connection and returns a value to tell the caller
whether the connection succeeded.

6.15 Communicating With The Server Using TCP

Assuming the *connect* call succeeds in establishing a connection, the client can use
the connection to communicate with the server. Usually, the application protocol specifies a *request-response interaction* in which the client sends a sequence of *requests* and
waits for a *response* to each.

Usually, a client calls *write* to transmit each request and *read* to await a response.
For the simplest application protocols, the client sends only a single request and receives only a single response. More complicated application protocols require the client
to iterate, sending a request and waiting for a response before sending the next request.
The following code illustrates the request-response interaction by showing how a program writes a simple request over a TCP connection and reads a response:

```
/* Example code segment */

#define BLEN 120     /* buffer length to use */
char    *req = "request of some sort";
char    buf[BLEN];   /* buffer for answer    */
char    *bptr;       /* pointer to buffer    */
int     n;           /* number of bytes read */
int     buflen;      /* space left in buffer */

bptr = buf;
buflen = BLEN;

/* send request */

write(s, req, strlen(req));

/* read response (may come in many pieces) */

while ((n = read(s, bptr, buflen) > 0) {
        bptr += n;
        buflen -= n;
}
```

6.16 Reading A Response From A TCP Connection

The code in the previous example shows a client that sends a small message to a server and expects a small response (less than *120* bytes). The code contains a single call to *write*, but makes repeated calls to *read*. As long as the call to *read* returns data, the code decrements the count of space available in the buffer and moves the buffer pointer forward past the data read. Iteration is necessary on input, even if the application at the other end of the connection sends only a small amount of data because TCP is not a block-oriented protocol. Instead, TCP is stream-oriented: it guarantees to deliver the sequence of bytes that the sender writes, but it does not guarantee to deliver them in the same grouping as they were written. TCP may choose to break a block of data into pieces and transmit each piece in a separate segment (e.g., it may choose to divide the data such that each piece fills the maximum sized segment, or it may need to send a small piece if the receiver does not have sufficient buffer space for a large one). Alternatively, TCP may choose to accumulate many bytes in its output buffer before sending a segment (e.g., to fill a datagram). As a result, the receiving application may receive data in small chunks, even if the sending application passes it to TCP in a single call to *write*. Or, the receiving application may receive data in a large chunk, even if the sending application passes it to TCP in a series of calls to *write*. The idea is fundamental to programming with TCP:

Because TCP does not preserve record boundaries, any program that reads from a TCP connection must be prepared to accept data a few bytes at a time. This rule holds even if the sending application writes data in large blocks.

6.17 Closing A TCP Connection

6.17.1 The Need For Partial Close

When an application finishes using a connection completely, it can call *close* to terminate the connection gracefully and deallocate the socket. However, closing a connection is seldom simple because TCP allows two-way communication. Thus, closing a connection usually requires coordination among the client and server.

To understand the problem, consider a client and server that use the request-response interaction described above. The client software repeatedly issues requests to which the server responds. On one hand, the server cannot terminate the connection because it cannot know whether the client will send additional requests. On the other hand, while the client knows when it has no more requests to send, it may not know whether all data has arrived from the server. The latter is especially important for application protocols that transfer arbitrary amounts of data in response to a request (e.g., the response to a database query).

6.17.2 A Partial Close Operation

To resolve the connection shutdown problem, most implementations of the socket interface include an additional primitive that permits applications to shutdown a TCP connection in one direction. The *shutdown* system call takes two arguments, a socket descriptor and a direction specification, and shuts down the socket in the specified direction:

```
errcode = shutdown(s, direction);
```

The *direction* argument is an integer. If it contains *0*, no further input is allowed. If it contains *1*, no further output is allowed. Finally, if the value is *2*, the connection is shutdown in both directions.

The advantage of a partial close should now be clear: when a client finishes sending requests, it can use *shutdown* to specify that it has no further data to send without deallocating the socket. The underlying protocol reports the shutdown to the remote machine, where the server application program receives an *end-of-file* signal. Once the server detects an end-of-file, it knows no more requests will arrive. After sending its last response, the server can close the connection. To summarize:

The partial close mechanism removes ambiguity for application proto-
cols that transmit arbitrary amounts of information in response to a
request. In such cases, the client issues a partial close after its last
request; the server then closes the connection after its last response.

6.18 Programming A UDP Client

At first glance, programming a UDP client seems like an easy task. Algorithm 6.2 shows that the basic UDP client algorithm is similar to the client algorithm for TCP (Algorithm 6.1).

Algorithm 6.2

1. Find the IP address and protocol port number of the server with which communication is desired.
2. Allocate a socket.
3. Specify that the communication needs an arbitrary, unused protocol port on the local machine, and allow UDP to choose one.
4. Specify the server to which messages must be sent.
5. Communicate with the server using the application-level protocol (this usually involves sending requests and awaiting replies).
6. Close the socket.

Algorithm 6.2 A connectionless client. The sending process creates a connected socket and uses it to send one or more requests iteratively. This algorithm ignores the issue of reliability.

The first few steps of the UDP client algorithm are much like the corresponding steps of the TCP client algorithm. A UDP client obtains the server address and protocol port number, and then allocates a socket for communication.

6.19 Connected And Unconnected UDP Sockets

Client applications can use UDP in one of two basic modes: *connected* and *unconnected*. In connected mode, the client uses the *connect* call to specify a remote endpoint address (i.e., the server's IP address and protocol port number). Once it has specified the remote endpoint, the client can send and receive messages much like a TCP client does. In unconnected mode, the client does not connect the socket to a specific remote endpoint. Instead, it specifies the remote destination each time it sends a message. The chief advantage of connected UDP sockets lies in their convenience for conventional client software that interacts with only one server at a time: the application only needs to specify the server once no matter how many datagrams it sends. The chief advantage of unconnected sockets lies in their flexibility; the client can wait to decide which server to contact until it has a request to send. Furthermore, the client can easily send each request to a different server.

> *UDP sockets can be* connected, *making it convenient to interact with a specific server, or they can be* unconnected, *making it necessary for the application to specify the server's address each time it sends a message.*

6.20 Using Connect With UDP

Although a client can connect a socket of type *SOCK_DGRAM*, the *connect* call does not initiate any packet exchange, nor does it test the validity of the remote end-point address. Instead, it merely records the remote endpoint information in the socket data structure for later use. Thus, when applied to *SOCK_DGRAM* sockets, *connect* only stores an address. Even if the *connect* call succeeds, it does not mean that the remote endpoint address is valid or that the server is reachable.

6.21 Communicating With A Server Using UDP

After a UDP client calls *connect*, it can use *write* to send a message or *read* to receive a response. Unlike TCP, UDP provides message transfer. Each time the client calls *write*, UDP sends a single message to the server. The message contains all the data passed to *write*. Similarly, each call to *read* returns one complete message. Assuming the client has specified a sufficiently large buffer, the *read* call returns all the data from the next message. Therefore, a UDP client does not need to make repeated calls to *read* to obtain a single message.

6.22 Closing A Socket That Uses UDP

A UDP client calls *close* to close a socket and release the resources associated with it. Once a socket has been closed, the UDP software will reject further messages that arrive addressed to the protocol port that the socket had allocated. However, the machine on which the *close* occurs does not inform the remote endpoint that the socket is closed. Therefore, an application that uses connectionless transport must be designed so the remote side knows how long to retain a socket before closing it.

6.23 Partial Close For UDP

Shutdown can be used with a connected UDP socket to stop further transmission in a given direction. Unfortunately, unlike the partial close on a TCP connection, when applied to a UDP socket, *shutdown* does not send any messages to the other side. Instead, it merely marks the local socket as unwilling to transfer data in the direction(s) specified. Thus, if a client shuts down further output on its socket, the server will not receive any indication that the communication has ceased.

6.24 A Warning About UDP Unreliability

Our simplistic UDP client algorithm ignores a fundamental aspect of UDP: namely, that it provides unreliable datagram delivery. While a simplistic UDP client can work well on local networks that exhibit low loss, low delay, and no packet reordering, clients that follow our algorithm will not work across a complex internet. To work in an internet environment, a client must implement reliability through timeout and retransmission. It must also handle the problems of duplicate or out-of-order packets. Adding reliability can be difficult, and requires expertise in protocol design.

> *Client software that uses UDP must implement reliability with techniques like packet sequencing, acknowledgements, timeouts, and retransmission. Designing protocols that are correct, reliable, and efficient for an internet environment requires considerable expertise.*

6.25 Summary

Client programs are among the most simple network programs. The client must obtain the server's IP address and protocol port number before it can communicate; to increase flexibility, client programs often require the user to identify the server when invoking the client. The client then converts the server's address from dotted decimal notation into binary, or uses the domain name system to convert from a textual machine name into an IP address.

The TCP client algorithm is straightforward: a TCP client allocates a socket and connects it to a server. The client uses *write* to send requests to the server and *read* to receive replies. Once it finishes using a connection, either the client or server invokes *close* to terminate it.

Although a client must explicitly specify the endpoint address of the server with which it wishes to communicate, it can allow TCP/IP software to choose an unused protocol port number and to fill in the correct local IP address. Doing so avoids the problem that can arise on a gateway or multi-homed host when a client inadvertently chooses an IP address that differs from the IP address of the interface over which IP routes the traffic.

The client uses *connect* to specify a remote endpoint address for a socket. When used with TCP, *connect* initiates a 3-way handshake and ensures that communication is possible. When used with UDP, *connect* merely records the server's endpoint address for later use.

Connection shutdown can be difficult if neither the client nor the server know exactly when communication has ended. To solve the problem, the socket interface supplies the *shutdown* primitive that causes a partial close and lets the other side know that no more data will arrive. A client uses *shutdown* to close the path leading to the server; the server receives an end-of-file signal on the connection that indicates the client has finished. After the server finishes sending its last response, it uses *close* to terminate the connection.

FOR FURTHER STUDY

Many RFCs that define protocols also suggest algorithms or implementation techniques for client code. Stevens [1990] also reviews client implementation.

EXERCISES

6.1   Read about the *sendto* and *recvfrom* socket calls. Do they work with sockets using TCP or sockets using UDP?

6.2   When the domain name system resolves a machine name, it returns a set of one or more IP addresses. Why?

6.3   Build client software that uses *gethostbyname* to look up machine names at your site and print all information returned. Which official names, if any, surprised you? Do you tend to use official machine names or aliases? Describe the circumstances, if any, when aliases may not work correctly.

6.4   Measure the time required to look up a machine name (*gethostbyname*) and a service entry (*getservent*). Repeat the test for both valid and invalid names. Does a lookup for an invalid name take substantially longer than for a valid one? Explain any differences you observe.

6.5   Use a network monitor to watch the network traffic your computer generates when you look up an IP address name using *gethostbyname*. Run the experiment more than one time for each machine name you resolve. Explain the differences in network traffic between lookups.

6.6   To test whether your machine's local byte order is the same as the network byte order, write a program that uses *getservbyname* to look up the *ECHO* service for UDP and then prints the resulting protocol port value. If the local byte order and network byte order agree, the value will be 7.

6.7 Write a program that allocates a local protocol port, closes the socket, delays a few seconds, and allocates another local port. Run the program on an idle machine and on a busy timesharing system. Which port values did your program receive on each system? If they are not the same, explain.

6.8 Under what circumstances can a client program use *close* instead of *shutdown*?

6.9 Should a client use the same protocol port number each time it begins? Why or why not?

7

Example Client Software

7.1 Introduction

The previous chapter discusses the basic algorithms underlying client applications as well as specific techniques used to implement those algorithms. This chapter gives examples of complete, working client programs that illustrate the concepts in more detail. The examples use UDP as well as TCP. Most important, the chapter shows how a programmer can build a library of procedures that hide the details of socket calls and make it easier to construct client software that is portable and maintainable.

7.2 The Importance Of Small Examples

TCP/IP defines a myriad of services and the standard application protocols for accessing them. The services range in complexity from the trivial (e.g., a character generator service used only for testing protocol software) to the complex (e.g., a file transfer service that provides authentication and protection). The examples in this chapter and the next few chapters concentrate on implementations of client-server software for simple services. Later chapters review client-server applications for several of the complex services.

While it may seem that the protocols used in the examples do not offer interesting or useful services, studying them is important. First, because the services themselves require little code, the client and server software that implements them is easy to understand. More important, the small program size highlights fundamental algorithms and illustrates clearly how client and server programs use system functions. Second, studying simple services provides the reader with an intuition about the relative size of services and the number of services available. Having an intuitive understanding of small services will be especially important for the chapters that discuss the need for multiprotocol and multiservice designs.

7.3 Hiding Details

Most programmers understand the advantage of dividing large, complex programs into a set of procedures: a modular program becomes easier to understand, debug, and modify than an equivalent monolithic program. If programmers design procedures carefully, they can reuse them in other programs. Finally, choosing procedures carefully can also make a program easier to port to new computer systems.

Conceptually, procedures raise the level of the language that programmers use by hiding details. Programmers working with the low-level facilities available in most programming languages find programming tedious and prone to error. They also find themselves repeating basic segments of code in each program they write. Using procedures helps avoid repetition by providing higher-level operations. Once a particular algorithm has been encoded in a procedure, the programmer can use it in many programs without having to consider the implementation details again.

A careful use of procedures is especially important when building client and server programs. First, because network software includes declarations for items like endpoint addresses, building programs that use network services involves a myriad of tedious details not found in conventional programs. Using procedures to hide those details reduces the chance for error. Second, much of the code needed to allocate a socket, bind addresses, and form a network connection is repeated in each client; placing it in procedures allows programmers to reuse the code instead of replicating it. Third, because TCP/IP was designed to interconnect heterogeneous machines, network applications often operate on many different machine architectures. Programmers can use procedures to isolate operating system dependencies, making it easier to port code to a new machine.

7.4 An Example Procedure Library For Client Programs

To understand how procedures can make the programming task easier, consider the problem of building client programs. To establish connectivity with a server, a client must choose a protocol (like TCP or UDP), look up the server's machine name, look up and map the desired service into a protocol port number, allocate a socket, and connect it. Writing the code for each of these steps from scratch for each application wastes time. Furthermore, if programmers ever need to change any of the details, they have to modify each application. To minimize programming time, a programmer can write the code once, place it in a procedure, and simply call the procedure from each client program.

The first step of designing a procedure library is abstraction: a programmer must imagine high-level operations that would make writing programs simpler. For example, an application programmer might imagine two procedures that handle the work of allocating and connecting a socket:

$$socket = connectTCP(\ machine,\ service\ );$$

and

$$socket = connectUDP(\ machine,\ service\ );$$

It is important to understand that this is not a prescription for the ''right'' set of abstractions, it merely gives one possible way to form such a set. The important idea is:

> *The procedural abstraction allows programmers to define high-level operations, share code among applications, and reduce the chances of making mistakes with small details. Our example procedures used throughout this text merely illustrate one possible approach; programmers should feel free to choose their own abstractions.*

7.5 Implementation Of ConnectTCP

Because both of the proposed procedures, *connectTCP* and *connectUDP*, need to allocate a socket and fill in basic information, we chose to place all the low-level code in a third procedure, *connectsock*, and to implement both higher-level operations as simple calls. File *connectTCP.c* illustrates the concept:

```
/* connectTCP.c - connectTCP */

/*------------------------------------------------------------------------
 * connectTCP - connect to a specified TCP service on a specified host
 *------------------------------------------------------------------------
 */
int
connectTCP( host, service )
char    *host;          /* name of host to which connection is desired */
char    *service;       /* service associated with the desired port    */
{
        return connectsock( host, service, "tcp");
}
```

7.6 Implementation Of ConnectUDP

File *connectUDP.c* shows how *connectsock* can be used to establish a connected socket that uses UDP.

```
/* connectUDP.c - connectUDP */

/*------------------------------------------------------------------------
 * connectUDP - connect to a specified UDP service on a specified host
 *------------------------------------------------------------------------
 */
int
connectUDP( host, service )
char    *host;          /* name of host to which connection is desired  */
char    *service;       /* service associated with the desired port     */
{
        return connectsock(host, service, "udp");
}
```

7.7 A Procedure That Forms Connections

Procedure *connectsock* contains all the code needed to allocate a socket and connect it. The caller specifies whether to create a UDP socket or a TCP socket.

```
/* connectsock.c - connectsock */

#include <sys/types.h>
#include <sys/socket.h>

#include <netinet/in.h>

#include <netdb.h>

#ifndef INADDR_NONE
#define INADDR_NONE     0xffffffff
#endif  /* INADDR_NONE */

extern int      errno;
extern char     *sys_errlist[];

u_short htons();
u_long  inet_addr();
```

```
/*------------------------------------------------------------------------
 * connectsock - allocate & connect a socket using TCP or UDP
 *------------------------------------------------------------------------
 */
int
connectsock( host, service, protocol )
char    *host;          /* name of host to which connection is desired */
char    *service;       /* service associated with the desired port    */
char    *protocol;      /* name of protocol to use ("tcp" or "udp")    */
{
        struct hostent  *phe;   /* pointer to host information entry    */
        struct servent  *pse;   /* pointer to service information entry */
        struct protoent *ppe;   /* pointer to protocol information entry*/
        struct sockaddr_in sin; /* an Internet endpoint address         */
        int     s, type;        /* socket descriptor and socket type    */


        bzero((char *)&sin, sizeof(sin));
        sin.sin_family = AF_INET;

    /* Map service name to port number */
        if ( pse = getservbyname(service, protocol) )
                sin.sin_port = pse->s_port;
        else if ( (sin.sin_port = htons((u_short)atoi(service))) == 0 )
                errexit("can't get \"%s\" service entry\n", service);

    /* Map host name to IP address, allowing for dotted decimal */
        if ( phe = gethostbyname(host) )
                bcopy(phe->h_addr, (char *)&sin.sin_addr, phe->h_length);
        else if ( (sin.sin_addr.s_addr = inet_addr(host)) == INADDR_NONE )
                errexit("can't get \"%s\" host entry\n", host);

    /* Map protocol name to protocol number */
        if ( (ppe = getprotobyname(protocol)) == 0)
                errexit("can't get \"%s\" protocol entry\n", protocol);

    /* Use protocol to choose a socket type */
        if (strcmp(protocol, "udp") == 0)
                type = SOCK_DGRAM;
        else
                type = SOCK_STREAM;

    /* Allocate a socket */
```

```
        s = socket(PF_INET, type, ppe->p_proto);
        if (s < 0)
                errexit("can't create socket: %s\n", sys_errlist[errno]);

    /* Connect the socket */
        if (connect(s, (struct sockaddr *)&sin, sizeof(sin)) < 0)
                errexit("can't connect to %s.%s: %s\n", host, service,
                        sys_errlist[errno]);
        return s;
}
```

Although most steps are straightforward, a few details make the code seem complicated. First, the C language permits complex expressions. As a result, the expressions
in many of the condition statements contain a function call, an assignment, and a comparison, all on one line. For example, the call to *getprotobyname* appears in an expression that assigns the result to variable *ppe*, and then compares the result to *0*. If the
value returned is zero (i.e., an error occurred), the *if* statement executes a call to *errexit*.
Otherwise, the procedure continues execution. Second, the code uses two library procedures available in BSD UNIX, *bzero* and *bcopy*. Procedure *bzero* places bytes containing zero in a block of memory; it is the fastest way to zero a large structure or array.
Procedure *bcopy* copies a block of bytes from one memory location to another, regardless of the contents†. *Connectsock* uses *bzero* to fill the entire *sockaddr_in* structure
with zeroes, and then uses *bcopy* to copy the bytes of the server's IP address into field
sin_addr. Finally, *connectsock* calls procedure *connect* to connect the socket. If an error occurs, it calls *errexit*.

```
/* errexit.c - errexit */

#include <varargs.h>
#include <stdio.h>

/*------------------------------------------------------------------------
 * errexit - print an error message and exit
 *------------------------------------------------------------------------
 */
/*VARARGS1*/
int
errexit(format, va_alist)
char    *format;
va_dcl
{
        va_list args;
```

---

†Programs that copy IP addresses cannot use the UNIX library routine *strcpy* because IP addresses may
contain bytes with the value zero, which *strcpy* interprets as *end of string*.

```
        va_start(args);
        _doprnt(format, args, stderr);
        va_end(args);
        exit(1);
}
```

Errexit takes a variable number of arguments, which it passes on to *_doprnt* for output. *Errexit* follows the *printf* conventions for formatted output. The first argument specifies how the output should be formatted; remaining arguments specify values to be printed according to the given format.

7.8 Using The Example Library

Once programmers have selected abstractions and built a library of procedures, they can construct client applications. If the abstractions have been selected well, they make application programming simple and hide many of the details. To illustrate how our example library works, we will use it to construct example client applications. Because the clients each access one of the standard TCP/IP services, they also serve to illustrate several of the simpler application protocols.

7.9 The DAYTIME Service

The TCP/IP standards define an application protocol that allows a user to obtain the date and time of day in a format fit for human consumption. The service is officially named the *DAYTIME service*.

To access the DAYTIME service, the user invokes a client application. The client contacts a server to obtain the information, and then prints it. Although the standard does not specify the exact syntax, it suggests several possible formats. For example, DAYTIME could supply a date in the form:

weekday, month day, year time-timezone

like

Tuesday, February 22, 1982 17:37:43-PST

The standard specifies that DAYTIME is available for both TCP and UDP. In both cases, it operates at protocol port *13*.

The TCP version of DAYTIME uses the presence of a TCP connection to trigger output: as soon as a new connection arrives, the server forms a text string that contains the current date and time, sends the string, and then closes the connection. Thus, the client need not send any request at all. In fact, the standard specifies that the server must discard any data sent by the client.

The UDP version of DAYTIME requires the client to send a request. A request consists of an arbitrary UDP datagram. Whenever a server receives a datagram, it formats the current date and time, places the resulting string in an outgoing datagram, and sends it back to the client. Once it has sent a reply, the server discards the datagram that triggered the response.

7.10 Implementation Of A TCP Client For DAYTIME

File *TCPdaytime.c* contains code for a TCP client that accesses the DAYTIME service.

```
/* TCPdaytime.c - TCPdaytime, main */

#include <stdio.h>

extern int      errno;
extern char     *sys_errlist[];

#define LINELEN         128

/*------------------------------------------------------------------------
 * main - TCP client for DAYTIME service
 *------------------------------------------------------------------------
 */
int
main(argc, argv)
int     argc;
char    *argv[];
{
        char    *host = "localhost";    /* host to use if none supplied */
        char    *service = "daytime";   /* default service port         */

        switch (argc) {
        case 1:
                host = "localhost";
                break;
        case 3:
                service = argv[2];
                /* FALL THROUGH */
        case 2:
                host = argv[1];
                break;
        default:
```

```
                        fprintf(stderr, "usage: TCPdaytime [host [port]]\n");
                        exit(1);
                }
                TCPdaytime(host, service);
                exit(0);
        }
```

```
/*------------------------------------------------------------------------
 * TCPdaytime - invoke Daytime on specified host and print results
 *------------------------------------------------------------------------
 */
TCPdaytime(host, service)
char    *host;
char    *service;
{
        char    buf[LINELEN+1];          /* buffer for one line of text  */
        int     s, n;                    /* socket, read count           */

        s = connectTCP(host, service);

        while( (n = read(s, buf, LINELEN)) > 0) {
                buf[n] = '\0';           /* insure null-terminated       */
                (void) fputs( buf, stdout );
        }
}
```

Notice how using *connectTCP* simplifies the code. Once a connection has been established, DAYTIME merely reads input from the connection and prints it, iterating until it detects an end of file condition.

7.11 Reading From A TCP Connection

The DAYTIME example illustrates an important idea: TCP offers a stream service that does not guarantee to preserve record boundaries. In practice, the stream paradigm means that TCP decouples the sending and receiving applications. For example, suppose the sending application transfers *64* bytes of data in a single call to *write*, followed by *64* bytes in a second call. The receiving application may receive all *128* bytes in a single call to *read*, or it may receive *10* bytes in the first call, *100* bytes in the second call, and *18* bytes in a third call. The number of bytes returned in a call depends on the size of datagrams in the underlying internet, the buffer space available, and the delays encountered when crossing the internet.

Because the TCP stream service does not guarantee to deliver data in the same blocks that it was written, an application receiving data from a TCP connection cannot depend on all data being delivered in a single transfer; it must repeatedly call read *until all data has been obtained.*

7.12 The TIME Service

TCP/IP defines a service that allows one machine to obtain the current date and time of day from another. Officially named *TIME*, the service is quite simple: a client program executing on one machine sends a request to a server executing on another. Whenever the server receives a request, it obtains the current date and time of day from the local operating system, encodes the information in a standard format, and sends it back to the client in a response.

To avoid the problems that occur if the client and server reside in different timezones, the TIME protocol specifies that all time and date information must be represented in *Universal Coordinated Time†*, abbreviated *UCT* or *UT*. Thus, a server converts from its local time to universal time before sending a reply, and a client converts from universal time to its local time when the reply arrives.

Unlike the DAYTIME service, which is intended for human users, the TIME service is intended for use by programs that store or manipulate times. The TIME protocol always specifies time in a 32-bit integer, representing the number of seconds since an *epoch date*. The TIME protocol uses midnight, January 1, 1900, as its epoch.

Using an integer representation allows computers to transfer time from one machine to another quickly, without waiting to convert it into a text string and back into an integer. Thus, the TIME service makes it possible for one computer to set its time-of-day clock from the clock on another system.

7.13 Accessing The TIME Service

Clients can use either TCP or UDP to access the TIME service at protocol port *37* (technically, the standards define two separate services, one for UDP and one for TCP). A TIME server built for TCP uses the presence of a connection to trigger output, much like the DAYTIME service discussed above. The client forms a TCP connection to a TIME server and waits to read output. When the server detects a new connection, it sends the current time encoded as an integer, and then closes the connection. The client does not send any data because the server never reads from the connection.

Clients can also access a TIME service with UDP. To do so, a client sends a request, which consists of a single datagram. The server does not process the incoming

---

†Universal Coordinated Time was formerly known as *Greenwich Mean Time*.

datagram, except to extract the sender's address and protocol port number for use in a reply. The server encodes the current time as an integer, places it in a datagram, and sends the datagram back to the client.

7.14 Accurate Times And Network Delays

Although the TIME service accommodates differences in timezones, it does not handle the problem of network latency. If it takes *3* seconds for a message to travel from the server to the client, the client will receive a time that is *3* seconds behind that of the server. Other, more complex protocols handle clock synchronization. However, the TIME service remains popular for three reasons. First, TIME is extremely simple compared to clock synchronization protocols. Second, most clients contact servers on a local area network, where network latency accounts for only a few milliseconds. Third, except when using programs that use timestamps to control processing, humans do not care if the clocks on their computers differ by small amounts.

In cases where more accuracy is required, it is possible to improve TIME or use an alternative protocol. The easiest way to improve the accuracy of TIME is to compute an approximation of network delay between the server and client, and then add that approximation to the time value that the server reports. For example, one way to approximate latency requires the client to compute the time that elapses during the round trip from client to server and back. The client assumes equal delay in both directions, and obtains an approximation for the trip back by dividing the round trip time in half. It adds the delay approximation to the time of day that the server returns.

7.15 A UDP Client For The TIME Service

File *UDPtime.c* contains code that implements a UDP client for the TIME service.

```c
/* UDPtime.c - main */

#include <sys/types.h>

#include <stdio.h>

#define BUFSIZE 64

#define UNIXEPOCH       2208988800      /* UNIX epoch, in UCT secs      */
#define MSG             "what time is it?\n"

extern int      errno;
extern char     *sys_errlist[];

char    *ctime();
u_long  ntohl();

/*------------------------------------------------------------------------
 * main - UDP client for TIME service that prints the resulting time
 *------------------------------------------------------------------------
 */
int
main(argc, argv)
int     argc;
char    *argv[];
{
        char    *host = "localhost";    /* host to use if none supplied */
        char    *service = "time";      /* default service name         */
        time_t  now;                    /* 32-bit integer to hold time  */
        int     s, n;                   /* socket descriptor, read count*/

        switch (argc) {
        case 1:
                host = "localhost";
                break;
        case 3:
                service = argv[2];
                /* FALL THROUGH */
        case 2:
                host = argv[1];
                break;
        default:
                fprintf(stderr, "usage: UDPtime [host [port]]\n");
                exit(1);
        }
```

```
        s = connectUDP(host, service);

        (void) write(s, MSG, strlen(MSG));

        /* Read the time */

        n = read(s, (char *)&now, sizeof(now));
        if (n < 0)
                errexit("read failed: %s\n", sys_errlist[errno]);
        now = ntohl((u_long)now);       /* put in host byte order      */
        now -= UNIXEPOCH;               /* convert UCT to UNIX epoch    */
        printf("%s", ctime(&now));
        exit(0);
}
```

The example code contacts the TIME service by sending a datagram. It then calls *read* to wait for a reply and extract the time value from it. Once *UDPtime* has obtained the time, it must convert the time into a form suitable for the local machine. First, it uses *ntohl* to convert the 32-bit value (a *long* in C) from network standard byte order into the local host byte order. Second, *UDPtime* must convert to the machine's local representation. The example code is designed for UNIX. Like the Internet protocols, UNIX represents time in a 32-bit integer and interprets the integer to be a count of seconds. Unlike the Internet, however, UNIX assumes an epoch date of January 1, 1970. Thus, to convert from the TIME protocol epoch to the UNIX epoch, the client must subtract the number of seconds between January 1, 1900 and January 1, 1970. The example code uses the conversion value *2208988800*. Once the time has been converted to a representation compatible with that of the local machine, *UDPtime* can invoke the library procedure *ctime*, which converts the value into a human readable form for output.

7.16 The ECHO Service

TCP/IP standards specify an *ECHO service* for both UDP and TCP protocols. At first glance, ECHO services seem almost useless because an ECHO server merely returns all the data it receives from a client. Despite their simplicity, ECHO services are important tools that network managers use to test reachability, debug protocol software, and identify routing problems.

The TCP ECHO service specifies that a server must accept incoming connection requests, read data from the connection, and write the data back over the connection until the client terminates the transfer. Meanwhile, the client sends input and then reads it back.

7.17 A TCP Client For The ECHO Service

File *TCPecho.c* contains a simple client for the ECHO service.

```
/* TCPecho.c - main, TCPecho */

#include <stdio.h>

extern int      errno;
extern char     *sys_errlist[];

#define LINELEN         128

/*------------------------------------------------------------------
 * main - TCP client for ECHO service
 *------------------------------------------------------------------
 */
int
main(argc, argv)
int     argc;
char    *argv[];
{
        char    *host = "localhost";    /* host to use if none supplied */
        char    *service = "echo";      /* default service name         */

        switch (argc) {
        case 1:
                host = "localhost";
                break;
        case 3:
                service = argv[2];
                /* FALL THROUGH */
        case 2:
                host = argv[1];
                break;
        default:
                fprintf(stderr, "usage: TCPecho [host [port]]\n");
                exit(1);
        }
        TCPecho(host, service);
        exit(0);
}
```

```
/*-------------------------------------------------------------------
 * TCPecho - send input to ECHO service on specified host and print reply
 *-------------------------------------------------------------------
 */
int
TCPecho(host, service)
char    *host;
char    *service;
{
        char    buf[LINELEN+1];         /* buffer for one line of text  */
        int     s, n;                   /* socket descriptor, read count*/
        int     outchars, inchars;      /* characters sent and received */

        s = connectTCP(host, service);

        while (fgets(buf, sizeof(buf), stdin)) {
                buf[LINELEN] = '\0';    /* insure line null-terminated  */
                outchars = strlen(buf);
                (void) write(s, buf, outchars);

                /* read it back */
                for (inchars = 0; inchars < outchars; inchars+=n ) {
                        n = read(s, &buf[inchars], outchars - inchars);
                        if (n < 0)
                                errexit("socket read failed: %s\n",
                                        sys_errlist[errno]);
                }
                fputs(buf, stdout);
        }
}
```

After opening a connection, *TCPecho* enters a loop that repeatedly reads one line of input, sends the line across the TCP connection to the ECHO server, reads it back again, and prints it. After all input lines have been sent to the server, received back, and printed successfully, the client exits.

7.18 A UDP Client For The ECHO Service

File *UDPecho.c* shows how a client uses UDP to access an ECHO service.

```
/* UDPecho.c - main, UDPecho */

#include <stdio.h>

extern int      errno;
extern char     *sys_errlist[];

#define LINELEN         128

/*------------------------------------------------------------------------
 * main - UDP client for ECHO service
 *------------------------------------------------------------------------
 */
int
main(argc, argv)
int     argc;
char    *argv[];
{
        char    *host = "localhost";
        char    *service = "echo";

        switch (argc) {
        case 1:
                host = "localhost";
                break;
        case 3:
                service = argv[2];
                /* FALL THROUGH */
        case 2:
                host = argv[1];
                break;
        default:
                fprintf(stderr, "usage: UDPecho [host [port]]\n");
                exit(1);
        }
        UDPecho(host, service);
        exit(0);
}

/*------------------------------------------------------------------------
 * UDPecho - send input to ECHO service on specified host and print reply
 *------------------------------------------------------------------------
 */
int
```

```
UDPecho(host, service)
char    *host;
char    *service;
{
        char    buf[LINELEN+1];          /* buffer for one line of text  */
        int     s, nchars;               /* socket descriptor, read count*/

        s = connectUDP(host, service);

        while (fgets(buf, sizeof(buf), stdin)) {
                buf[LINELEN] = '\0';     /* insure null-terminated */
                nchars = strlen(buf);
                (void) write(s, buf, nchars);

                if (read(s, buf, nchars) < 0)
                        errexit("socket read failed: %s\n",
                                        sys_errlist[errno]);
                fputs(buf, stdout);
        }
}
```

The example UDP ECHO client follows the same general algorithm as the TCP version. It repeatedly reads a line of input, sends it to the server, reads it back from the server, and prints it. The biggest difference between the UDP and TCP versions lies in how they treat data received from the server. Because UDP is datagram-oriented, the client treats an input line as a unit and places each in a single datagram. Similarly, the ECHO server receives and returns complete datagrams. Thus, while the TCP client reads incoming data as a stream of bytes, the UDP client either receives an entire line back from the server or receives none of it; each call to *read* returns the entire line unless an error has occurred.

7.19 Summary

Programmers use the procedural abstraction to keep programs flexible and easy to maintain, to hide details, and to make it easy to port programs to new computers. Once a programmer writes and debugs a procedure, he or she places it in a library where it can be reused in many programs easily. A library of procedures is especially important for programs that use TCP/IP because they often operate on multiple computers.

This chapter presents an example library of procedures used to create client software. The primary procedures in our library, *connectTCP* and *connectUDP*, make it easy to allocate and connect a socket to a specified service on a specified host.

The chapter presents examples of a few client applications. Each example contains the code for a complete C program that implements a standard application protocol: DAYTIME (used to obtain and print the time of day in a human-readable format), TIME (used to obtain the time in 32-bit integer form), and ECHO (used to test network connectivity). The example code shows how a library of procedures hides many of the details associated with socket allocation and makes it easier to write client software.

FOR FURTHER STUDY

The application protocols described here are each part of the TCP/IP standard. Postel [RFC 867] contains the standard for the DAYTIME protocol, Postel and Harrenstien [RFC 868] contains the standard for the TIME protocol, and Postel [RFC 862] contains the standard for the ECHO protocol. Mills [RFC 1119] specifies the Network Time Protocol, NTP.

EXERCISES

7.1   Use program *TCPdaytime* to contact servers on several machines. How does each format the time and date?

7.2   The Internet standard represents time in a 32-bit integer that gives seconds past the epoch, midnight January 1, 1900. UNIX systems also represent time in a 32-bit integer that measures seconds, but UNIX uses January 1, 1970 as its epoch. What is the maximum date and time that can be represented in each system?

7.3   Improve the TIME client so it checks the date received to verify that it is greater than January 1, 1992 (or some other date you know to be in the recent past).

7.4   Modify the TIME client so it computes E, the time that elapses between when it sends the request and when it receives a response. Add one-half E to the time the server sends.

7.5   Build a TIME client that contacts two TIME servers, and reports the differences between the times they return.

7.6   Explain how deadlock can occur if a programmer changes the line size in the TCP ECHO client to be arbitrarily large (e.g., 20,000).

7.7   The ECHO clients presented in this chapter do not verify that the text they receive back from the server matches the text they sent. Modify them to verify the data received.

7.8   The ECHO clients presented in this chapter do not count the characters sent or received. What happens if a server incorrectly sends one additional character back that the client did not send?

7.9   The example ECHO clients in this chapter do not use *shutdown*. Explain how the use of *shutdown* can improve client performance.

7.10 Rewrite the code in *UDPecho.c* so it tests reachability by generating a message, sending it, and timing the reply. If the reply does not arrive in 5 seconds, declare the destination host to be unreachable. Be sure to retransmit the request at least once in case the internet happens to lose a datagram.

7.11 Rewrite the code in *UDPecho.c* so it creates and sends a new message once per second, checks replies to be sure they match transmissions, and reports only the round trip time for each reply without printing the contents of the message itself.

7.12 Explain what happens to *UDPecho* when the underlying network: duplicates a request sent from the client to the server, duplicates a response sent from the server to the client, loses a request sent from the client to the server, or loses a response sent from the server to the client. Modify the code to handle each of these problems.

8

Algorithms And Issues In Server Software Design

8.1 Introduction

This chapter considers the design of server software. It discusses fundamental issues, including: connectionless vs. connection-oriented server access, stateless vs. stateful applications, and iterative vs. concurrent server implementations. It describes the advantages of each approach, and gives examples of situations in which the approach is valid. Later chapters illustrate the concepts by showing complete server programs that each implement one of the basic design ideas.

8.2 The Conceptual Server Algorithm

Conceptually, each server follows a simple algorithm: it creates a socket and binds the socket to the well-known port at which it desires to receive requests. It then enters an infinite loop in which it accepts the next request that arrives from a client, processes the request, formulates a reply, and sends the reply back to the client.

Unfortunately, this unsophisticated, conceptual algorithm suffices only for the most trivial services. To understand why, consider a service like file transfer that requires substantial time to handle each request. Suppose the first client to contact the server requests the transfer of a giant file (e.g., 200 megabytes), while the second client to contact the server requests the transfer of a trivially small file (e.g., 20 bytes). If the server waits until the first transfer completes before starting the second transfer, the second client may wait an unreasonable amount of time for a small transfer. The second user would expect a small request to be handled immediately. Most practical servers do handle small requests quickly, because they handle more than one request at a time.

8.3 Concurrent Vs. Iterative Servers

We use the term *iterative server* to describe a server implementation that processes one request at a time, and the term *concurrent server* to describe a server that handles multiple requests at one time. Although most concurrent servers achieve apparent concurrency, we will see that a concurrent implementation may not be required – it depends on the application protocol. In particular, if a server performs small amounts of processing relative to the amount of I/O it performs, it may be possible to implement the server as a single process that uses asynchronous I/O to allow simultaneous use of multiple communication channels. From a client's perspective, the server appears to communicate with multiple clients concurrently. The point is:

> *The term* concurrent server *refers to whether the server handles multiple requests concurrently, not to whether the underlying implementation uses multiple concurrent processes.*

In general, concurrent servers are more difficult to design and build, and the resulting code is more complex and difficult to modify. Most programmers choose concurrent server implementations, however, because iterative servers cause unnecessary delays in distributed applications and can become a performance bottleneck that affects many client applications. We can summarize:

> *Iterative server implementations, which are easier to build and understand, may result in poor performance because they make clients wait for service. In contrast, concurrent server implementations, which are more difficult to design and build, yield better performance.*

8.4 Connection-Oriented Vs. Connectionless Access

The issue of connectivity centers around the transport protocol that a client uses to access a server. In the TCP/IP protocol suite, TCP provides a *connection-oriented* transport service, while UDP provides a *connectionless* service. Thus, servers that use TCP are, by definition, *connection-oriented servers*, while those that use UDP are *connectionless servers*†.

Although we apply the terminology to servers, it would be more accurate if we restricted it to application protocols, because the choice between connectionless and connection-oriented implementations depends on the application protocol. An application protocol designed to use a connection-oriented transport service may perform incorrectly or inefficiently when using a connectionless transport protocol. To summarize:

---

†The socket interface does permit an application to *connect* a UDP socket to a remote endpoint, but practical servers do not do so, and UDP is not a connection-oriented protocol.

When considering the advantages and disadvantages of various server implementation strategies, the designer must remember that the application protocol used may restrict some or all of the choices.

8.5 Connection-Oriented Servers

The chief advantage of a connection-oriented approach lies in ease of programming. In particular, because the transport protocol handles packet loss and out-of-order delivery problems automatically, the server need not worry about them. Instead, a connection-oriented server manages and uses *connections*. It accepts an incoming connection from a client, and then sends all communication across the connection. It receives requests from the client and sends replies. Finally, the server closes the connection after it completes the interaction.

While a connection remains open, TCP provides all the needed reliability. It retransmits lost data, verifies that data arrives without transmission errors, and reorders incoming packets as necessary. When a client sends a request, TCP either delivers it reliably or informs the client that the connection has been broken. Similarly, the server can depend on TCP to deliver responses or inform it that the connection has broken.

Connection-oriented servers also have disadvantages. Connection-oriented designs require a separate socket for each connection, while connectionless designs permit communication with multiple hosts from a single socket. Socket allocation and the resulting connection management can be especially important inside an operating system that must run forever without exhausting resources. For trivial applications, the overhead of the 3-way handshake used to establish and terminate a connection makes TCP expensive compared to UDP. The most important disadvantage arises because TCP does not send any packets across an idle connection. Suppose a client establishes a connection to a server, exchanges a request and a response, and then crashes. Because the client has crashed, it will never send further requests. However, because the server has already responded to all requests received so far, it will never send more data to the client. The problem with such a situation lies in resource use: the server has data structures (including buffer space) allocated for the connection and these resources cannot be reclaimed. Remember that a server must be designed to run forever. If clients crash repeatedly, the server will run out of resources (e.g., sockets, buffer space, TCP connections) and cease to operate.

8.6 Connectionless Servers

Connectionless servers also have advantages and disadvantages. While connectionless servers do not suffer from the problem of resource depletion, they cannot depend on the underlying transport for reliable delivery. One side or the other must take responsibility for reliable delivery. Usually, clients take responsibility for retransmitting requests if no response arrives. If the server needs to divide its response into multiple data packets, it may need to implement a retransmission mechanism as well.

Achieving reliability through timeout and retransmission can be extremely difficult. In fact, it requires considerable expertise in protocol design. Because TCP/IP operates in an internet environment where end-to-end delays change quickly, using fixed values for timeout does not work. Many programmers learn this lesson the hard way when they move their applications from local area networks (which have small delays with little variation) to wider area internets (which have large delays with greater variation). To accommodate an internet environment, the retransmission strategy must be adaptive. Thus, applications must implement a retransmission scheme as complex as the one used in TCP. As a result, novice programmers are encouraged to use connection-oriented transport.

> *Because UDP does not supply reliable delivery, connectionless tran-sport requires the application protocol to provide reliability, if need-ed, through a complex, sophisticated technique known as adaptive re-transmission. Adding adaptive retransmission to an existing applica-tion is difficult and requires considerable expertise.*

Another consideration in choosing connectionless vs. connection-oriented design focuses on whether the service requires broadcast or multicast communication. Because TCP offers point-to-point communication, it cannot supply broadcast or multicast communication; such services require UDP. Thus, any server that accepts or responds to multicast communication must be connectionless. In practice, most sites try to avoid broadcasting whenever possible; none of the standard TCP/IP application protocols currently require multicast. However, future applications could depend more on multicast.

8.7 Failure, Reliability, And Statelessness

As Chapter 2 states, information that a server maintains about the status of ongoing interactions with clients is called *state information*. Servers that do not keep any state information are called *stateless servers*, while those that maintain state information are called *stateful servers*.

The issue of statelessness arises from a need to ensure reliability, especially when using connectionless transport. Remember that in an internet, messages can be duplicat-ed, delayed, lost, or delivered out of order. If the transport protocol does not guarantee reliable delivery, and UDP does not, the application protocol must be designed to en-sure it. Furthermore, the server implementation must be done carefully so it does not introduce state dependencies (and inefficiencies) unintentionally.

8.8 Optimizing Stateless Servers

To understand the subtleties involved in optimization, consider a connectionless server that allows clients to read information from files stored on the server's computer. To keep the protocol stateless, the designer requires each client request to specify a file name, a position in the file, and the number of bytes to read. The most straightforward server implementation handles each request independently: it opens the specified file, seeks to the specified position, reads the specified number of bytes, sends the information back to the client, and then closes the file.

A clever programmer assigned to write a server observes that: (1) the overhead of opening and closing files is high, (2) the clients using this server may read only a dozen bytes in each request, and (3) clients tend to read files sequentially. Furthermore, the programmer knows from experience that the server can extract data from a buffer in memory several orders of magnitude faster than it can read data from a disk. So, to optimize server performance, the programmer decides to maintain a small table of file information as Figure 8.1 shows.

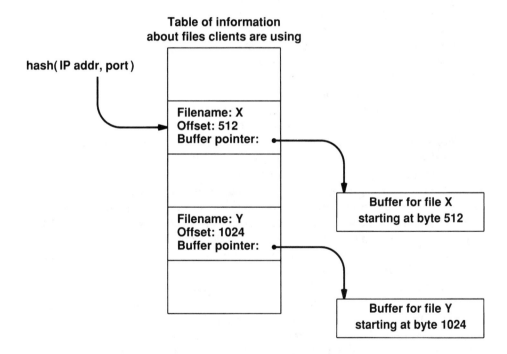

Figure 8.1 A table of information kept to improve server performance. The server uses the client's IP address and protocol port number to find an entry. This optimization introduces state information.

The programmer uses the client's IP address and protocol port number as an index into the table, and arranges for each table entry to contain a pointer to a large buffer of data from the file being read. When a client issues its first request, the server searches the table and finds that it has no record of the client. It allocates a large buffer to hold data from the file, allocates a new table entry to point to the buffer, opens the specified file, and reads data into the buffer. It then copies information out of the buffer when forming a reply. The next time a request arrives from the same client, the server finds the matching entry in the table, follows the pointer to the buffer, and extracts data from it without opening the file. Once the client has read the entire file, the server deallocates the buffer and the table entry, making the resources available for use by another client.

Of course, our clever programmer builds the software carefully so that it checks to make sure the requested data resides in the buffer and reads new data into the buffer from the file if necessary. The server also compares the file specified in a request with the file name in the table entry to verify that the client is still using the same file as the previous request.

If the clients follow the assumptions listed above and the programmer is careful, adding large file buffers and a simple table to the server can improve its performance dramatically. Furthermore, under the assumptions given, the optimized version of the server will perform at least as fast as the original version because the server spends little time maintaining the data structures compared to the time required to read from a disk. Thus, the optimization seems to improve performance without any penalty.

Adding the proposed table changes the server in a subtle way, however, because it introduces state information. Of course, state information chosen carelessly could introduce errors in the way the server responds. For example, if the server used the client's IP address and protocol port number to find the buffer without checking the file name or file offset in the request, duplicate or out-of-order requests could cause the server to return incorrect data. But remember we said that the programmer who designed the optimized version was clever and programmed the server to check the file name and offset in each request, just in case the network duplicates or drops a request or the client decides to read from a new file instead of reading sequentially from the old file. Thus, it may seem that the addition of state information does not change the way the server replies. In fact, if the programmer is careful, the protocol will remain correct. If so, what harm can the state information do?

Unfortunately, even a small amount of state information can cause a server to perform badly when machines, client programs, or networks fail. To understand why, consider what happens if one of the client programs fails (i.e., crashes) and must be restarted. Chances are high that the client will ask for an arbitrary protocol port number and UDP will assign a new protocol port number different from the one assigned for earlier requests. When the server receives a request from the client, it cannot know that the client has crashed and restarted, so it allocates a new buffer for the file and a new slot in the table. Consequently, it cannot know that the old table entry the client was using should be removed. If the server does not remove old entries, it will eventually run out of table slots.

It may seem that leaving an idle table entry around does not cause any problem as long as the server chooses an entry to delete when it needs a new one. For example, the server might choose to delete the *least recently used* (LRU) entry, much like the LRU page replacement strategy used in many virtual memory systems. However, in a network where multiple clients access a single server, frequent crashes can cause one client to dominate the table by filling it with entries that will never be reused. In the worst case, each request that arrives causes the server to delete an entry and reuse it. If one client crashes and reboots frequently enough, it can cause the server to remove entries for legitimate clients. Thus, the server expends more effort managing the table and buffers than it does answering requests†.

The important point here is that:

> *A programmer must be extremely careful when optimizing a stateless server because managing small amounts of state information can consume resources if clients crash and reboot frequently or if the underlying network duplicates or delays messages.*

8.9 Four Basic Types Of Servers

Servers can be iterative or concurrent, and can use connection-oriented transport or connectionless transport. Figure 8.2 shows that these properties group servers into four general categories.

iterative connectionless	**iterative connection-oriented**
concurrent connectionless	**concurrent connection-oriented**

Figure 8.2 The four general server categories defined by whether they offer concurrency and whether they use connection-oriented transport.

---

†Virtual memory systems describe this phenomenon as *thrashing*.

8.10 Request Processing Time

In general, iterative servers suffice only for the most trivial application protocols because they make each client wait in turn. The test of whether an iterative implementation will suffice focuses on the response time needed, which can be measured locally or globally.

We define the server's *request processing time* to be the total time the server takes to handle a single isolated request, and we define the client's *observed response time* as the total delay between the time it sends a request and the time the server responds. Obviously, the response time observed by a client can never be less than the server's request processing time. However, if the server has a queue of requests to handle, the observed response time can be much greater than the request processing time.

Iterative servers handle one request at a time. If another request arrives while the server is busy handling an existing request, the system enqueues the new request. Once the server finishes processing a request, it looks at the queue to see if it has a new request to handle. If N denotes the average length of the request queue, the observed response time for an arriving request will be approximately $N/2 + 1$ times the server's request processing time. Because the observed response time increases in proportion to N, most implementations restrict N to a small value (e.g., 5) and expect programmers to use concurrent servers in cases where a small queue does not suffice.

Another way of looking at the question of whether an iterative server suffices focuses on the overall load the server must handle. A server designed to handle K clients, each sending R requests per second must have a request processing time of less than $1/KR$ seconds per request. If the server cannot handle requests at the required rate, its queue of waiting requests will eventually overflow. To avoid overflow in servers that may have large request processing times, a designer should consider concurrent implementations.

8.11 Iterative Server Algorithms

An iterative server is the easiest to design, program, debug, and modify. Thus, most programmers choose an iterative design whenever iterative execution provides sufficiently fast response for the expected load. Usually, iterative servers work best with simple services accessed by a connectionless access protocol. As the next sections show, however, it is possible to use iterative implementations with both connectionless and connection-oriented transport.

8.12 An Iterative, Connection-Oriented Server Algorithm

Algorithm 8.1 presents the algorithm for an iterative server accessed via the TCP connection-oriented transport. The sections following the algorithm describe each of the steps in more detail.

Algorithm 8.1

1. Create a socket and bind to the well-known address for the service being offered.
2. Place the socket in passive mode, making it ready for use by a server.
3. Accept the next connection request from the socket, and obtain a new socket for the connection.
4. Repeatedly read a request from the client, formulate a response, and send a reply back to the client according to the application protocol.
5. When finished with a particular client, close the connection and return to step *3* to accept a new connection.

Algorithm 8.1 An iterative, connection-oriented server. A single process handles connections from clients one at a time.

8.13 Binding To A Well-Known Address Using INADDR_ANY

A server needs to create a socket and bind it to the well-known port for the service it offers. Like clients, servers use procedure *getportbyname* to map a service name into the corresponding well-known port number. For example, TCP/IP defines an *ECHO* service. A server that implements ECHO uses *getportbyname* to map the string ''echo'' to the assigned port, 7.

Remember that when *bind* specifies a connection endpoint for a socket, it uses structure *sockaddr_in*, which contains both an IP address and a protocol port number. Thus, *bind* cannot specify a protocol port number for a socket without also specifying an IP address. Unfortunately, selecting a specific IP address at which a server will accept connections can cause difficulty. For hosts that have a single network connection, the choice is obvious because the host has only one IP address. However, gateways and multi-homed hosts have multiple IP addresses. If the server specifies one particular IP address when binding a socket to a protocol port number, the socket will not accept communications that clients send to the machine's other IP addresses.

To solve the problem, the socket interface defines a special constant, *INADDR_ANY*, that can be used in place of an IP address. *INADDR_ANY* specifies a *wildcard address* that matches any of the host's IP addresses. Using *INADDR_ANY* makes it possible to have a single server on a gateway accept incoming communication addressed to any of the gateway's IP addresses. To summarize:

> *When specifying a local endpoint for a socket, servers use* INADDR_ANY, *instead of a specific IP address, to allow the socket to receive datagrams sent to any of the machine's IP addresses.*

8.14 Placing The Socket In Passive Mode

A TCP server calls *listen* to place a socket in passive mode. *Listen* also takes an argument that specifies the length of an internal request queue for the socket. The request queue holds the set of incoming TCP connection requests from clients that have each requested a connection with the server.

8.15 Accepting Connections And Using Them

A TCP server calls *accept* to obtain the next incoming connection request (i.e., extract it from the request queue). The call returns the descriptor of a socket to be used for the new connection. Once it has accepted a new connection, the server uses *read* to obtain application protocol requests from the client, and *write* to send replies back. Finally, once the server finishes with the connection, it calls *close* to release the socket.

8.16 An Iterative, Connectionless Server Algorithm

Recall that iterative servers work best for services that have a low request processing time. Because connection-oriented transport protocols like TCP have higher overhead than connectionless transport protocols like UDP, most iterative servers use connectionless transport. Algorithm 8.2 gives the general algorithm for an iterative server that uses UDP.

Creation of a socket for an iterative, connectionless server proceeds in the same way as for a connection-oriented server. The server's socket remains unconnected and can accept incoming datagrams from any client.

Algorithm 8.2

1. Create a socket and bind to the well-known address for the service being offered.
2. Repeatedly read the next request from a client, formulate a response, and send a reply back to the client according to the application protocol.

Algorithm 8.2 An iterative, connectionless server. A single process handles requests (datagrams) from clients one at a time.

8.17 Forming A Reply Address In A Connectionless Server

The socket interface provides two ways of specifying a remote endpoint. Chapters 6 and 7 discuss how clients use *connect* to specify a server's address. After a client calls *connect*, it can use *write* to send data because the internal socket data structure contains the remote endpoint address as well as the local endpoint address. A connectionless server cannot use *connect*, however, because doing so restricts the socket to communication with one specific remote host and port; the server cannot use the socket again to receive datagrams from arbitrary clients. Thus, a connectionless server uses an unconnected socket. It generates reply addresses explicitly, and uses the *sendto* socket call to specify both a datagram to be sent and an address to which it should go. *Sendto* has the form:

```
retcode = sendto(s, message, len, flags, toaddr, toaddrlen);
```

where *s* is an unconnected socket, *message* is the address of a buffer that contains the data to be sent, *len* specifies the number of bytes in the buffer, *flags* specifies debugging or control options, *toaddr* is a pointer to a *sockaddr_in* structure that contains the endpoint address to which the message should be sent, and *toaddrlen* is an integer that specifies the length of the address structure.

The socket calls provide an easy way for connectionless servers to obtain the address of a client: the server obtains the address for a reply from the source address found in the request. In fact, the socket interface provides a call that servers can use to receive the sender's address along with the next datagram that arrives. The call, *recvfrom*, takes two arguments that specify two buffers. The system places the arriving datagram in one buffer and the sender's address in the second buffer. A call to *recvfrom* has the form:

```
retcode = recvfrom(s, buf, len, flags, from, fromlen);
```

where argument *s* specifies a socket to use, *buf* specifies a buffer into which the system will place the next datagram, *len* specifies the space available in the buffer, *from* specifies a second buffer into which the system will place the source address, and *fromlen* specifies the address of an integer. Initially, *fromlen* specifies the length of the *from* buffer. When the call returns, *fromlen* will contain the length of the source address the system placed in the buffer. To generate a reply, the server uses the address that *recvfrom* stored in the *from* buffer when the request arrived.

8.18 Concurrent Server Algorithms

The primary reason for introducing concurrency into a server arises from a need to provide faster response times to multiple clients. Concurrency improves response time if:

- forming a response requires significant I/O,
- the processing time required varies dramatically among requests, or
- the server executes on a computer with multiple processors.

In the first case, allowing the server to compute responses concurrently means that it can overlap use of the processor and peripheral devices, even if the machine has only one CPU. While the processor works to compute one response, the I/O devices can be transferring data into memory that will be needed for other responses. In the second case, timeslicing permits a single processor to handle requests that only require small amounts of processing without waiting for requests that take longer. In the third case, concurrent execution on a computer with multiple processors allows one processor to compute a response to one request while another processor computes a response to another. In fact, most concurrent servers adapt to the underlying hardware automatically – given more hardware resources (e.g., more processors) they perform better.

> *Concurrent servers achieve high performance by overlapping processing and I/O. They are usually designed so performance improves automatically if the server is run on hardware that offers more resources.*

8.19 Master And Slave Processes

Although it is possible for a server to achieve some concurrency using a single process, most concurrent servers use multiple processes. They can be divided into two types: a single *master server process* begins execution initially. The master process opens a socket at the well-known port, waits for the next request, and creates a *slave server process* to handle each request. The master server never communicates directly with a client – it passes that responsibility to a slave. Each slave process handles communication with one client. After the slave forms a response and sends it to the client, it exits. The next sections will explain the concept of master and slave in more detail, and will show how it applies to both connectionless and connection-oriented concurrent servers.

8.20 A Concurrent, Connectionless Server Algorithm

The most straightforward version of a concurrent, connectionless server follows Algorithm 8.3.

Algorithm 8.3

Master 1. Create a socket and bind to the well-known address for the service being offered. Leave the socket unconnected.

Master 2. Repeatedly call *recvfrom* to receive the next request from a client, and create a new slave process to handle the response.

Slave 1. Receive a specific request upon creation as well as access to the socket.

Slave 2. Form a reply according to the application protocol and send it back to the client using *sendto*.

Slave 3. Exit (i.e., a slave process terminates after handling one request).

Algorithm 8.3 A concurrent, connectionless server. The master server process accepts incoming requests (datagrams) and creates a slave process to handle each.

Programmers should remember that although the exact cost of creating a process depends on the operating system and underlying architecture, the operation can be expensive. In the case of a connectionless protocol, one must consider carefully whether the cost of concurrency will be greater than the gain in speed. In fact:

> *Because process creation is expensive, few connectionless servers have concurrent implementations.*

8.21 A Concurrent, Connection-Oriented Server Algorithm

Connection-oriented application protocols use a connection as the basic paradigm for communication. They allow a client to establish a connection to a server, communicate over that connection, and then discard it. In most cases, the connection between client and server handles more than a single request: the protocol allows a client to repeatedly send requests and receive responses without terminating the connection or creating a new one. Thus,

Connection-oriented servers implement concurrency among connections rather than among individual requests.

Algorithm 8.4 specifies the steps that a concurrent server uses for a connection-oriented protocol.

Algorithm 8.4

Master 1. Create a socket and bind to the well-known address for the service being offered. Leave the socket unconnected.

Master 2. Place the socket in passive mode, making it ready for use by a server.

Master 3. Repeatedly call *accept* to receive the next request from a client, and create a new slave process to handle the response.

Slave 1. Receive a connection request (i.e., socket for the connection) upon creation.

Slave 2. Interact with the client using the connection: read request(s) and send back response(s).

Slave 3. Close the connection and exit. The slave process exits after handling all requests from one client.

Algorithm 8.4 A concurrent, connection-oriented server. The master server process accepts incoming connections and creates a slave process to handle each. Once the slave finishes, it closes the connection.

As in the connectionless case, the master server process never communicates with the client directly. As soon as a new connection arrives, the master creates a slave to handle that connection. While the slave interacts with the client, the master waits for other connections.

8.22 Using Separate Programs As Slaves

Algorithm 8.4 shows how a concurrent server creates a new process for each connection. In UNIX, the master server does so by calling the *fork* system call. For simple application protocols, a single server program can contain all the code needed for both the master and slave processes. After the call to *fork*, the original process loops back to accept the next incoming connection, while the new process becomes the slave and handles the connection. In some cases, however, it may be more convenient to have the slave process execute code from a program that has been written and compiled independently. UNIX can handle such cases easily because it allows the slave process to call *execve* after the call to *fork*. The general idea is:

> *For many services, a single program can contain code for both the master and server processes. In cases where an independent program makes the slave process easier to program or understand, the master program contains a call to* execve *after the call to* fork.

8.23 Apparent Concurrency Using A Single Process

Previous sections discuss concurrent servers implemented with concurrent processes. In some cases, however, it makes sense to use a single process to handle client requests concurrently. In particular, some operating systems make process creation so expensive that a server cannot afford to create a new process for each request or each connection. More important, many applications require the server to share information among all connections.

To understand the motivation for a server that provides *apparent concurrency* with a single process, consider the X window system. X allows multiple clients to paint text and graphics in windows that appear on a bit-mapped display. Each client controls one window, sending requests that update the contents. Each client operates independently, and may wait many hours before changing the display or may update the display frequently. For example, an application that displays the time by drawing a picture of a clock might update its display every minute. Meanwhile, an application that displays the status of a user's electronic mail waits until new mail arrives before it changes the display.

A server for the X window system integrates information it obtains from clients into a single, contiguous section of memory called the *display buffer*. Because data arriving from all clients contributes to a single, shared data structure and because BSD UNIX does not allow independent processes to share memory, the server cannot execute as separate UNIX processes. Thus, a conflict arises between a desire for concurrency among processes that share memory and a lack of support for such concurrency in UNIX.

Although it may not be possible to achieve *real concurrency* among processes that share memory, it may be possible to achieve *apparent concurrency* if the total load of requests presented to the server does not exceed its capacity to handle them. To do so, the server operates as a single UNIX process that uses the *select* system call for asynchronous I/O. Algorithm 8.5 describes the steps a single-process server takes to handle multiple connections.

Algorithm 8.5

1. Create a socket and bind to the well-known port for the service. Add socket to the list of those on which I/O is possible.
2. Use *select* to wait for I/O on existing sockets.
3. If original socket is ready, use *accept* to obtain the next connection, and add the new socket to the list of those on which I/O is possible.
4. If some socket other than the original is ready, use *read* to obtain the next request, form a response, and use *write* to send the response back to the client.
5. Continue processing with step 2 above.

Algorithm 8.5 A concurrent, connection-oriented server implemented by a single process. The server process waits for the next descriptor that is ready, which could mean a new connection has arrived or that a client has sent a request on an existing connection.

8.24 When To Use Each Server Type

Iterative vs. Concurrent: Iterative servers are easier to design, implement, and maintain, but concurrent servers can provide quicker response to requests. Use an iterative implementation if request processing time is short and an iterative solution produces response times that are sufficiently fast for the application.

Real vs. Apparent Concurrency: A single-process server must manage multiple connections and use asynchronous I/O; a multi-process server allows the operating system to provide concurrency automatically. Use a single-process solution if the server must share or exchange data among connections. Use a multi-process solution if each slave can operate in isolation or to achieve maximal concurrency (e.g., on a multiprocessor).

Connection-Oriented vs. Connectionless: Because connection-oriented access means using TCP, it implies reliable delivery. Because connectionless transport means using UDP, it implies unreliable delivery. Only use connectionless transport if the application protocol handles reliability (almost none do) or each client accesses its server on a local area network that exhibits extremely low loss and no packet reordering. Use connection-oriented transport whenever a wide area network separates the client and server. Never move a connectionless client and server to a wide area environment without checking to see if the application protocol handles the reliability problems.

8.25 A Summary of Server Types

Iterative, Connectionless Server

The most common form of connectionless server, used especially for services that require a trivial amount of processing for each request. Iterative servers are often stateless, making them easier to understand and less susceptible to failures.

Iterative, Connection-Oriented Server

A less common server type used for services that require a trivial amount of processing for each request, but for which reliable transport is necessary. Because the overhead associated with establishing and terminating connections can be high, the average response time can be non-trivial.

Concurrent, Connectionless Server

An uncommon type in which the server creates a new process to handle each request. On many systems, the added cost of process creation dominates the added efficiency gained from concurrency. To justify concurrency, either the time required to create a new process must be significantly less than the time required to compute a response or concurrent requests must be able to use many I/O devices simultaneously.

Concurrent, Connection-Oriented Server

The most general type of server because it offers reliable transport (i.e., it can be used across a wide area internet) as well as the ability to handle multiple requests concurrently. Two basic implementations exist: the most common implementation uses concurrent processes to handle connections; a far less common implementation relies on a single process and asynchronous I/O to handle multiple connections.

In a concurrent process implementation, the master server process creates a slave process to handle each connection. Using multiple processes makes it easy to execute a separately compiled program for each connection instead of writing all the code in a single, large server program.

In the single-process implementation, the server process manages multiple connections. It achieves apparent concurrency by using asynchronous I/O. The process repeatedly waits for I/O on any of the connections it has open and handles that request. Because a single process handles all connections, it can share data among them. However, because the server has only one process, it cannot handle requests faster than an iterative server, even on a computer that has multiple processors. The application must need data sharing or the processing time for each request must be short to justify this server implementation.

8.26 The Important Problem Of Server Deadlock

Many server implementations share an important flaw: namely, the server can be subject to deadlock†. To understand how deadlock can happen, consider an iterative, connection-oriented server. Suppose some client application, *C*, misbehaves. In the simplest case, assume *C* makes a connection to a server, but never sends a request. The server will accept the new connection, and call *read* to extract the next request. The server process blocks in the call to *read* waiting for a request that will never arrive.

Server deadlock can arise in a much more subtle way if clients misbehave by not consuming responses. For example, assume that a client *C* makes a connection to a server, sends it a sequence of requests, but never reads the responses. The server keeps accepting requests, generating responses, and sending them back to the client. At the server, TCP protocol software transmits the first few bytes over the connection to the client. Eventually, TCP will fill the client's receive window and will stop transmitting data. If the server application program continues to generate responses, the local buffer TCP uses to store outgoing data for the connection will become full and the server process will block.

Deadlock arises because processes block when the operating system cannot satisfy a system call. In particular, a call to *write* will block the calling process if TCP has no local buffer space for the data being sent; a call to *read* will block the calling process until TCP receives data. For concurrent servers, only the single slave process associated with a particular client blocks if the client fails to send requests or read responses. For a single-process implementation, however, the central server process will block. If the central server process blocks, it cannot handle other connections. The important point is that any server using only one process can be subject to deadlock.

> *A misbehaving client can cause deadlock in a single-process server if the server uses system functions that can block when communicating with the client. Deadlock is a serious liability in servers because it means the behavior of one client can prevent the server from handling other clients.*

8.27 Alternative Implementations

Chapters *9* through *12* provide examples of the server algorithms described in this chapter. Chapters *13* and *14* extend the ideas by discussing two important practical implementation techniques not described here: multiprotocol and multiservice servers. While both techniques provide interesting advantages for some applications, they have not been included here because they are best understood as simple generalizations of the single-process server algorithm illustrated in Chapter *12*.

---

†The term *deadlock* refers to a condition in which a program or set of programs cannot proceed because they are blocked waiting for an event that will never happen. In the case of servers, deadlock means that the server ceases to answer requests.

8.28 Summary

Conceptually, a server consists of a simple algorithm that iterates forever, waiting for the next request from a client, handling the request, and sending a reply. In practice, however, servers use a variety of implementations to achieve reliability, flexibility, and efficiency.

Iterative implementations work well for services that require little computation. When using a connection-oriented transport, an iterative server handles one connection at a time; for connectionless transport, an iterative server handles one request at a time.

To achieve efficiency, servers often provide concurrent service by handling multiple requests at the same time. A connection-oriented server provides for concurrency among connections by creating a process to handle each new connection. A connectionless server provides concurrency by creating a new process to handle each new request.

Any server implemented with a single process that uses synchronous system functions like *read* or *write* can be subject to deadlock. Deadlock can arise in iterative servers as well as in concurrent servers that use a single-process implementation. Server deadlock is especially serious because it means a single misbehaving client can prevent the server from handling requests for other clients.

FOR FURTHER STUDY

Stevens [1990] describes some of the server algorithms covered in this chapter and shows implementation details. BSD UNIX contains examples of many server algorithms; programmers often consult the UNIX source code for programming techniques.

EXERCISES

8.1 Calculate how long an iterative server takes to transfer a 200 megabyte file if the internet has a throughput of 2.3 Kbytes per second.

8.2 If 20 clients each send 2 requests per second to an iterative server, what is the maximum time that the server can spend on each request?

8.3 How long does it take a concurrent, connection-oriented server to accept a new connection and create a new process to handle it on the computers to which you have access?

8.4 Write an algorithm for a concurrent, connectionless server that creates one new process for each request.

8.5 Modify the algorithm in the previous problem so the server creates one new process per client instead of one new process per request. How does your algorithm handle process termination?

8.6 Connection-oriented servers provide concurrency among connections. Does it make sense for a concurrent, connection-oriented server to increase concurrency even further by having the slave processes create additional processes for each request? Explain.

8.7 Rewrite the TCP echo client so it uses a single process to concurrently handle input from the keyboard, input from its TCP connection, and output to its TCP connection.

8.8 Can clients cause deadlock or disrupt service in concurrent servers? Why or why not?

8.9 Look carefully at the *select* system call. How can a single-process server use *select* to avoid deadlock?

8.10 The *select* call takes an argument that specifies how many I/O descriptors it should check. Explain how the argument makes a single-process server program portable across many UNIX systems.

9

Iterative, Connectionless Servers (UDP)

9.1 Introduction

The previous chapter discusses many possible server designs, comparing the advantages and disadvantages of each. This chapter gives an example of an iterative server implementation that uses connectionless transport. The example server follows Algorithm 8.2†. Later chapters continue the discussion by providing example implementations of other server algorithms.

9.2 Creating A Passive Socket

The steps required to create a passive socket are similar to those required to create an active socket. They involve many details, and require the program to lookup a service name to obtain a well-known protocol port number.

To help simplify server code, programmers should use procedures to hide the details of socket allocation. As in the client examples, our example implementations use two high-level procedures, *passiveUDP* and *passiveTCP*, that allocate a passive socket and bind it to the server's well-known port. Each server invokes one of these procedures, with the choice dependent on whether the server uses connectionless or connection-oriented transport. This chapter considers *passiveUDP*; the next chapter shows the code for *passiveTCP*. Because the two procedures have many details in common, they both call the low-level procedure, *passivesock* to perform the work.

---

†See page 105 for a description of Algorithm 8.2.

A connectionless server calls function *passiveUDP* to create a socket for the service that it offers. If the server needs to use one of the ports reserved for well-known services (i.e., a port numbered below *1024*), the server process must have special privilege†. An arbitrary application program can use *passiveUDP* to create a socket for nonprivileged services. *PassiveUDP* calls *passivesock* to create a connectionless socket, and then returns the socket descriptor to its caller.

To make it easy to test client and server software, *passivesock* relocates all port values by adding the contents of global integer *portbase*. The importance of using *portbase* will become clearer in later chapters. However, the basic idea is fairly easy to understand:

> *If a new version of a client-server application uses the same protocol*
> *port numbers as an existing, production version, the new software*
> *cannot be tested while the production version continues to execute.*

Using *portbase* allows a programmer to compile a modified version of a server, and then to have the server look up the standard protocol port and compute a final port number as a function of the standard port and the value of *portbase*. If the programmer selects a unique value of *portbase* for each particular version of a client-server pair, the ports used by the new version will not conflict with the ports used by the production version. In fact, using *portbase* makes it possible to test multiple versions of a client-server pair at the same time without interference because each pair communicates independently of other pairs.

```
/* passiveUDP.c - passiveUDP */


/*------------------------------------------------------------------------
 * passiveUDP - create a passive socket for use in a UDP server
 *------------------------------------------------------------------------
 */
int
passiveUDP( service )
char    *service;         /* service associated with the desired port    */
{
        return passivesock(service, "udp", 0);
}
```

Procedure *passivesock* contains the socket allocation details, including the use of *portbase*. It takes three arguments. The first argument specifies the name of a service, the second specifies the name of the protocol, and the third (used only for TCP sockets) specifies the desired length of the connection request queue. *Passivesock* allocates either a datagram or stream socket, binds the socket to the well-known port for the service, and returns the socket descriptor to its caller.

---

†In UNIX, an application must execute as root (i.e., be the superuser) to have sufficient privilege to bind to a reserved port.

Recall that when a server binds a socket to a well-known port, it must specify the address using structure *sockaddr_in*, which includes an IP address as well as a protocol port number. *Passivesock* uses the constant *INADDR_ANY* instead of a specific local IP address, enabling it to work either on hosts that have a single IP address or on gateways and multi-homed hosts that have multiple IP addresses. Using *INADDR_ANY* means that the server will receive communication addressed to its well-known port at any of the machine's IP addresses.

```
/* passivesock.c - passivesock */

#include <sys/types.h>
#include <sys/socket.h>

#include <netinet/in.h>

#include <netdb.h>

extern int      errno;
extern char     *sys_errlist[];

u_short htons(), ntohs();

u_short portbase = 0;               /* port base, for non-root servers      */

/*------------------------------------------------------------------------
 * passivesock - allocate & bind a server socket using TCP or UDP
 *------------------------------------------------------------------------
 */
int
passivesock( service, protocol, qlen )
char    *service;       /* service associated with the desired port     */
char    *protocol;      /* name of protocol to use ("tcp" or "udp")     */
int     qlen;           /* maximum length of the server request queue   */
{
        struct servent  *pse;   /* pointer to service information entry */
        struct protoent *ppe;   /* pointer to protocol information entry*/
        struct sockaddr_in sin; /* an Internet endpoint address         */
        int     s, type;        /* socket descriptor and socket type    */

        bzero((char *)&sin, sizeof(sin));
        sin.sin_family = AF_INET;
        sin.sin_addr.s_addr = INADDR_ANY;
```

```
    /* Map service name to port number */
        if ( pse = getservbyname(service, protocol) )
                sin.sin_port = htons(ntohs((u_short)pse->s_port)
                        + portbase);
        else if ( (sin.sin_port = htons((u_short)atoi(service))) == 0 )
                errexit("can't get \"%s\" service entry\n", service);

    /* Map protocol name to protocol number */
        if ( (ppe = getprotobyname(protocol)) == 0)
                errexit("can't get \"%s\" protocol entry\n", protocol);

    /* Use protocol to choose a socket type */
        if (strcmp(protocol, "udp") == 0)
                type = SOCK_DGRAM;
        else
                type = SOCK_STREAM;

    /* Allocate a socket */
        s = socket(PF_INET, type, ppe->p_proto);
        if (s < 0)
                errexit("can't create socket: %s\n", sys_errlist[errno]);

    /* Bind the socket */
        if (bind(s, (struct sockaddr *)&sin, sizeof(sin)) < 0)
                errexit("can't bind to %s port: %s\n", service,
                        sys_errlist[errno]);
        if (type == SOCK_STREAM && listen(s, qlen) < 0)
                errexit("can't listen on %s port: %s\n", service,
                        sys_errlist[errno]);
        return s;
}
```

9.3 Process Structure

Figure 9.1 illustrates the simple process structure used for an iterative, connection-less server.

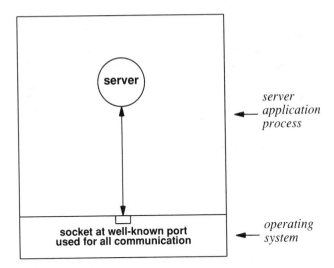

Figure 9.1 The process structure for an iterative, connectionless server. A
single server process communicates with many clients using one
socket.

The single server process executes forever. It uses a single passive socket that has been
bound to the well-known protocol port for the service it offers. The server obtains a request from the socket, computes a response, and sends a reply back to the client using
the same socket. The server uses the source address in the request as the destination address in the reply.

9.4 An Example TIME Server

An example will illustrate how a connectionless server process uses the socket allocation procedures described above. Recall from Chapter 7 that clients use the TIME
service to obtain the current time of day from a server on another system. Because
TIME requires little computation, an iterative server implementation works well. File
UDPtimed.c contains the code for an iterative, connectionless TIME server.

```
/* UDPtimed.c - main */

#include <sys/types.h>
#include <sys/socket.h>
#include <netinet/in.h>

#include <stdio.h>

extern int      errno;
extern char     *sys_errlist[];

time_t  time();
u_long  htonl();

#define UNIXEPOCH       2208988800      /* UNIX epoch, in UCT secs      */

/*------------------------------------------------------------------------
 * main - Iterative UDP server for TIME service
 *------------------------------------------------------------------------
 */
int
main(argc, argv)
int     argc;
char    *argv[];
{
        struct sockaddr_in fsin;        /* the from address of a client */
        char    *service = "time";      /* service name or port number  */
        char    buf[1];                 /* "input" buffer; any size > 0 */
        int     sock;                   /* server socket                */
        time_t  now;                    /* current time                 */
        int     alen;                   /* from-address length          */

        switch (argc) {
        case    1:
                break;
        case    2:
                service = argv[1];
                break;
        default:
                errexit("usage: UDPtimed [port]\n");
        }

        sock = passiveUDP(service);
```

```
        while (1) {
                alen = sizeof(fsin);
                if (recvfrom(sock, buf, sizeof(buf), 0,
                                (struct sockaddr *)&fsin, &alen) < 0)
                        errexit("recvfrom: %s\n", sys_errlist[errno]);
                (void) time(&now);
                now = htonl((u_long)(now + UNIXEPOCH));
                (void) sendto(sock, (char *)&now, sizeof(now), 0,
                                (struct sockaddr *)&fsin, sizeof(fsin));
        }
}
```

Like any server, the *UDPtimed* process must execute forever. Thus, the main body of code consists of an infinite loop that accepts a request, computes the current time, and sends a reply back to the client that sent the request.

The code contains several details. After parsing its arguments, *UDPtimed* calls *passiveUDP* to create a passive socket for the TIME service. It then enters the infinite loop. The TIME protocol specifies that a client can send an arbitrary datagram to trigger a reply. The datagram can be of any length and can contain any values because the server does not interpret its contents. The example implementation uses *recvfrom* to read the next datagram. *Recvfrom* places the incoming datagram in buffer *buf*, and places the endpoint address of the client that sent the datagram in structure *fsin*. Because it does not need to examine the data, the implementation uses a single-character buffer. If the datagram contains more than one byte of data, *recvfrom* discards all remaining bytes.

UDPtimed uses the UNIX system routine *time* to obtain the current time. Recall from Chapter 7 that UNIX uses a 32-bit integer to represent time, measuring from the epoch of midnight, January 1, 1970. After obtaining the time from UNIX, *UDPtimed* must convert it to a value measured from the Internet epoch and place the result in network byte order. To perform the conversion, it adds constant *UNIXEPOCH*, which is defined to have the value *2208988800*, the difference in seconds between the Internet epoch and the UNIX epoch. It then calls function *htonl* to convert the result to network byte order. Finally, *UDPtimed* calls *sendto* to transmit the result back to the client. *Sendto* uses the endpoint address in structure *fsin* as the destination address (i.e., it uses the address of the client that sent the datagram).

9.5 Summary

For simple services, where a server does little computation for each request, an iterative implementation works well. This chapter presented an example of an iterative server for the TIME service that uses UDP for connectionless access. The example illustrates how procedures hide the details of socket allocation and make the server code simpler and easier to understand.

FOR FURTHER STUDY

Harrenstien [RFC 738] specifies the TIME protocol. Mills [RFC 1119] describes the Network Time Protocol (NTP); Mills [September 1991] summarizes issues related to using NTP in practical networks. Marzullo and Owicki [July 1985] also discusses how to maintain clocks in a distributed environment.

EXERCISES

9.1 Instrument *UDPtimed* to determine how much time it expends processing each request. If you have access to a network analyzer, also measure the time that elapses between the request and response packets.

9.2 Suppose *UDPtimed* inadvertently clobbered the client's address between the time it received a request and sent a response (i.e., the server accidentally assigned *fsin* a random value before using it in the call to *sendto*). What would happen? Why?

9.3 Conduct an experiment to determine what happens if N clients all send requests to *UDPtimed* simultaneously. Vary both N, the number of senders, and the size of the datagram they send. Explain why the server fails to respond to all requests. (Hint: look at the manual page for *listen*.)

9.4 The example code in *UDPtimed.c* specifies a buffer size of *1* when it calls *recvfrom*. What happens if it specifies a buffer size of *0*?

9.5 Compute the difference between the UNIX time epoch and the Internet time epoch. Remember to account for leap years. Does the value you compute agree with the constant *UNIXEPOCH* defined in *UDPtimed*? If not, explain. (Hint: read about leap seconds.)

9.6 As a security check, the system manager asks you to modify *UDPtimed* so it keeps a written log of all clients who access the service. Modify the code to print a line on the console whenever a request arrives. Explain how logging can affect the service.

9.7 If you have access to a pair of machines connected by a wide-area internet, use the *UDPtime* client in Chapter 7 and the *UDPtimed* server in this chapter to see if your internet drops or duplicates packets.

10

Iterative, Connection-
Oriented Servers (TCP)

10.1 Introduction

The previous chapter provides an example of an iterative server that uses UDP for connectionless transport. This chapter shows how an interactive server can use TCP for connection-oriented transport. The example server follows Algorithm 8.1†.

10.2 Allocating A Passive TCP Socket

Chapter 9 mentions that a connection-oriented server uses function *passiveTCP* to allocate a stream socket and bind it to the well-known port for the service being offered. *PassiveTCP* takes two arguments. The first argument, a character string, specifies the name or number of a service, and the second specifies the desired length of the incoming connection request queue. If the first argument contains a name, it must match one of the entries in the service database accessed by library function *getservbyname*. If the first argument specifies a port number, it must represent the number as a text string (e.g., "79").

---

†See page 103 for a description of Algorithm 8.1.

```
/* passiveTCP.c - passiveTCP */

/*------------------------------------------------------------------
 * passiveTCP - create a passive socket for use in a TCP server
 *------------------------------------------------------------------
 */
int
passiveTCP( service, qlen )
char    *service;       /* service associated with the desired port    */
int     qlen;           /* maximum server request queue length         */
{
        return passivesock(service, "tcp", qlen);
}
```

10.3 A Server For The DAYTIME Service

Recall from Chapter 7 that the DAYTIME service allows a user on one machine to obtain the current date and time of day from another machine. Because the DAYTIME service is intended for humans, it specifies that the server must format the date in an easily readable string of ASCII text when it sends a reply. Thus, the client can display the response for a user exactly as it is received.

Chapter 7 shows how a client uses TCP to contact a DAYTIME server and to display the text that the server sends back. Because obtaining and formatting a date requires little processing and one expects little demand for the service, a DAYTIME server need not be optimized for speed. If additional clients attempt to make connection requests while the server is busy handling a request, the protocol software enqueues the additional requests. Thus, an iterative implementation suffices.

10.4 Process Structure

As Figure 10.1 shows, an iterative, connection-oriented server consists of a single process. The process iterates forever, using one socket to handle incoming requests and a second, temporary socket to handle communication with a client.

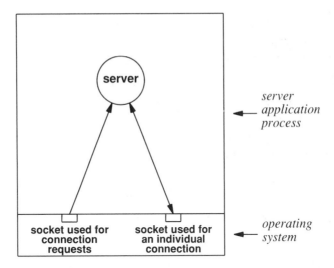

Figure 10.1 The process structure of an iterative, connection-oriented server.
The server waits at the well-known port for a connection, and
then communicates with the client over that connection.

A server that uses connection-oriented transport iterates on connections: it waits at the
well-known port for the next connection to arrive from a client, accepts the connection,
handles it, closes the connection, and then waits again. The DAYTIME service makes
the implementation especially simple because the server does not need to receive an explicit request from the client – it uses the presence of an incoming connection to trigger
a response. Because the client does not send an explicit request, the server does not
read data from the connection.

10.5 An Example DAYTIME Server

File *TCPdaytimed.c* contains example code for an iterative, connection-oriented
DAYTIME server.

```
/* TCPdaytimed.c - main */

#include <sys/types.h>
#include <sys/socket.h>
#include <netinet/in.h>

#include <stdio.h>

extern int      errno;
extern char     *sys_errlist[];


long    time();


#define QLEN    5


/*------------------------------------------------------------------------
 * main - Iterative TCP server for DAYTIME service
 *------------------------------------------------------------------------
 */
int
main(argc, argv)
int     argc;
char    *argv[];
{
        struct  sockaddr_in fsin;       /* the from address of a client */
        char    *service = "daytime";   /* service name or port number  */
        int     msock, ssock;           /* master & slave sockets       */
        int     alen;                   /* from-address length          */

        switch (argc) {
        case    1:
                break;
        case    2:
                service = argv[1];
                break;
        default:
                errexit("usage: TCPdaytimed [port]\n");
        }

        msock = passiveTCP(service, QLEN);

        while (1) {
                ssock = accept(msock, (struct sockaddr *)&fsin, &alen);
                if (ssock < 0)
```

```
                        errexit("accept failed: %s\n",sys_errlist[errno]);
                (void) TCPdaytimed(ssock);
                (void) close(ssock);
        }
}


/*------------------------------------------------------------------------
 * TCPdaytimed - do TCP DAYTIME protocol
 *------------------------------------------------------------------------
 */
int
TCPdaytimed(fd)
int     fd;
{
        char    *pts;                    /* pointer to time string      */
        time_t  now;                     /* current time                */
        char    *ctime();

        (void) time(&now);
        pts = ctime(&now);
        (void) write(fd, pts, strlen(pts));
        return 0;
}
```

Like the iterative, connectionless server described in the previous chapter, an iterative, connection-oriented server must run forever. After creating a socket that listens at the well-known port, the server enters an infinite loop in which it accepts and handles connections.

The code for the server is fairly short because the call to *passiveTCP* hides the details of socket allocation and binding. The call to *passiveTCP* creates a master socket associated with the well-known port for the DAYTIME service. The second argument specifies that the master socket will have a request queue length of *QLEN*, allowing the system to enqueue connection requests that arrive from *QLEN* additional clients while the server is busy replying to a request from a given client.

After creating the master socket, the server's main program enters an infinite loop. During each iteration of the loop, the server calls *accept* to obtain the next connection request from the master socket. To prevent the server from consuming resources while waiting for a connection from a client, the call to *accept* blocks the server process until a connection arrives. When a connection request arrives, the TCP protocol software engages in a 3-way handshake to establish a connection. Once the handshake completes and the system allocates a new socket for the incoming connection, the call to *accept* returns the descriptor of the new socket, allowing the server to continue execution. If no connection arrives, the server process remains blocked forever in the *accept* call.

Each time a new connection arrives, the server calls procedure *TCPdaytimed* to handle it. The code in *TCPdaytimed* centers around calls to the UNIX functions *time* and *ctime*. Procedure *time* returns a 32-bit integer that gives the current time in seconds since the UNIX epoch. The UNIX library function *ctime* takes an integer argument that specifies a time in seconds since the UNIX epoch, and returns the address of an ASCII string that contains the time and date formatted so a human can understand it. Once the server obtains the time and date in an ASCII string, it calls *write* to send the string back to the client over the TCP connection.

Once the call to *TCPdaytimed* returns, the main program continues executing the loop, and encounters the *accept* call again. The *accept* call blocks the server until another request arrives.

10.6 Closing Connections

After it has written the response, the call to procedure *TCPdaytimed* returns. Once the call returns, the main program explicitly closes the socket on which the connection arrived.

Calling *close* requests a graceful shutdown. In particular, TCP guarantees that all data will be reliably delivered to the client and acknowledged before it terminates the connection. Thus, when calling *close*, a programmer does not need to worry about data being delivered.

Of course, TCP's definition of graceful shutdown means that the call to *close* may not return instantly – the call will block until TCP on the server receives a reply from TCP on the client. Once the client acknowledges both the receipt of all data and the request to terminate the connection, the *close* call returns.

10.7 Connection Termination And Server Vulnerability

The application protocol determines how a server manages TCP connections. In particular, the application protocol usually dictates the choice of the termination strategy. For example, arranging for the server to close connections works well for the DAYTIME protocol because the server knows when it has finished sending data. Applications that have more complex client-server interactions cannot choose to have the server close a connection immediately after processing one request because they must wait to see if the client chooses to send additional request messages. For example, consider an ECHO server. The client controls server processing because it determines the amount of data to be echoed. Because the server must process arbitrary amounts of data, it cannot close the connection after reading and writing once. Thus, the client must signal completion so the server knows when to terminate the connection.

Allowing a client to control connection duration can be dangerous because it allows clients to control resource use. In particular, misbehaving clients can cause the server to consume resources like sockets and TCP connections. It may seem that our example server will never run out of resources because it explicitly closes connections. Even our simple connection termination strategy can be vulnerable to misbehaving clients. To understand why, recall that TCP defines a connection timeout period of *2* times the maximum segment lifetime (2*MSL) after a connection closes. During the timeout, TCP keeps a record of the connection so it can correctly reject any old packets that may have been delayed. Thus, if clients make repeated requests rapidly, they can use up resources at the server. Although programmers may have little control over protocols, they should understand how protocols can make distributed software vulnerable to network failures and try to avoid such vulnerabilities when designing servers.

10.8 Summary

An iterative, connection-oriented server iterates once per connection. Until a connection request arrives from a client, the server remains blocked in a call to *accept*. Once the underlying protocol software establishes the new connection and creates a new socket, the call to *accept* returns the socket descriptor and allows the server to continue execution.

Recall from Chapter *7* that the DAYTIME protocol uses the presence of a connection to trigger a response from the server. The client does not need to send a request because the server responds as soon as it detects a new connection. To form a response, the server obtains the current time from the operating system, formats the information into a string suitable for humans to read, and then sends the response back to the client. The example server closes the socket that corresponds to an individual connection after sending a response. The strategy of closing the connection immediately works because the DAYTIME service only allows one response per connection. Servers that allow multiple requests to arrive over a single connection must wait for the client to close the connection.

FOR FURTHER STUDY

Postel [RFC 867] describes the DAYTIME protocol used in this chapter.

EXERCISES

10.1   Does a process need special privilege to run a DAYTIME server on your local system? Does it need special privilege to run a DAYTIME client?

10.2   What is the chief advantage of using the presence of a connection to trigger a response from a server? The chief disadvantage?

10.3   Some DAYTIME servers terminate the line of text by a combination of two characters: *carriage return (CR)* and *linefeed (LF)*. Modify the example server to send *CR-LF* at the end of the line instead of sending only *LF*. How does the standard specify lines should be terminated?

10.4   TCP software usually allocates a fixed-size queue for additional connection requests that arrive while a server is busy, and allows the server to change the queue size using *listen*. How large is the queue that your local TCP software provides? How large can the server make the queue with *listen*?

10.5   Modify the example server code in *TCPdaytimed.c* so it does not explicitly close the connection after writing a response. Does it still work correctly? Why or why not?

10.6   Compare a connection-oriented server that explicitly closes each connection after sending a response to one that allows the client to hold a connection arbitrarily long before closing the connection. What are the advantages and disadvantages of each approach?

10.7   Assume that TCP uses a connection timeout of *4* minutes (i.e., keeps information for *4* minutes after a connection closes). If a DAYTIME server runs on a system that has 100 slots for TCP connection information, what is the maximum rate at which the server can handle requests without running out of slots?

11

Concurrent, Connection-Oriented Servers (TCP)

11.1 Introduction

The previous chapter illustrates how an iterative server uses a connection-oriented transport protocol. This chapter gives an example of a concurrent server that uses a connection-oriented transport. The example server follows Algorithm 8.4†, the design that programmers use most often when they build concurrent TCP servers. The server relies on the operating system's support for concurrent processing to achieve concurrency when computing responses. The system manager arranges to have the master server process start automatically when the system boots. The master server runs forever waiting for new connection requests to arrive from clients. The master creates a new slave process to handle each new connection, and allows each slave to handle all communication with its client.

Later chapters consider alternative implementations of concurrent servers, and show how to extend the basic ideas presented here.

11.2 Concurrent ECHO

Consider the ECHO service described in Chapter 7. A client opens a connection to a server, and then repeatedly sends data across the connection and reads the "echo" the server returns. The ECHO server responds to each client. It accepts a connection, reads from the connection, and then sends back the same data it receives.

---

†See page 108 for a description of Algorithm 8.4.

To allow a client to send arbitrary amounts of data, the server does not read the entire input before it sends a response. Instead, it alternates between reading and writing. When a new connection arrives, the server enters a loop. On each iteration of the loop, the server first reads from the connection and then writes the data back to the connection. The server continues iterating until it encounters an end-of-file condition, at which time it closes the connection.

11.3 Iterative Vs. Concurrent Implementations

An iterative implementation of an ECHO server can perform poorly because it requires a given client to wait while it handles all prior connection requests. If a client chooses to send large amounts of data (e.g., many megabytes), an iterative server will delay all other clients until it can satisfy the request.

A concurrent implementation of an ECHO server avoids long delays because it does not allow a single client to hold all resources. Instead, a concurrent server allows its communication with many clients to proceed simultaneously. Thus, from a client's point of view, a concurrent server offers better observed response time than an iterative server.

11.4 Process Structure

Figure 11.1 illustrates the process structure of a concurrent, connection-oriented server. As the figure shows, the master server process does not communicate with clients directly. Instead, it merely waits at the well-known port for the next connection request. Once a request has arrived, the system returns the socket descriptor of the new socket to use for that connection. The master server process creates a slave process to handle the connection, and allows the slave to operate concurrently. At any time, the server consists of one master process and zero or more slave processes.

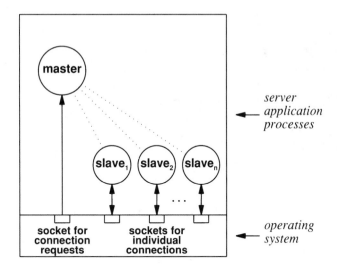

Figure 11.1 The process structure of a concurrent, connection-oriented server.
A master server process accepts each incoming connection, and
creates a slave process to handle it.

To avoid using CPU resources while it waits for connections, the master server
uses a blocking call of *accept* to obtain the next connection from the well-known port.
Thus, like the iterative server process in Chapter *10*, the master server process in a concurrent server spends most of its time blocked in a call to *accept*. When a connection
request arrives, the call to *accept* returns, allowing the master process to execute. The
master creates a slave to handle the request, and reissues the call to *accept*. The call
blocks the server again until another connection request arrives.

11.5 An Example Concurrent ECHO Server

File *TCPechod.c* contains the code for an ECHO server that uses concurrent
processes to provide concurrent service to multiple clients.

```
/* TCPechod.c - main, TCPechod */

#include <sys/types.h>
#include <sys/signal.h>
#include <sys/socket.h>
#include <sys/time.h>
#include <sys/resource.h>
#include <sys/wait.h>
#include <sys/errno.h>
#include <netinet/in.h>

#include <stdio.h>

#define QLEN                 5      /* maximum connection queue length      */
#define BUFSIZE           4096

extern int       errno;
extern char      *sys_errlist[];

int       reaper();

/*------------------------------------------------------------------------
 * main - Concurrent TCP server for ECHO service
 *------------------------------------------------------------------------
 */
int
main(argc, argv)
int       argc;
char      *argv[];
{
        char    *service = "echo";      /* service name or port number */
        struct  sockaddr_in fsin;       /* the address of a client     */
        int     alen;                   /* length of client's address  */
        int     msock;                  /* master server socket        */
        int     ssock;                  /* slave server socket         */

        switch (argc) {
        case    1:
                break;
        case    2:
                service = argv[1];
                break;
        default:
                errexit("usage: TCPechod [port]\n");
        }
```

```
        msock = passiveTCP(service, QLEN);

        (void) signal(SIGCHLD, reaper);

        while (1) {
                alen = sizeof(fsin);
                ssock = accept(msock, (struct sockaddr *)&fsin, &alen);
                if (ssock < 0) {
                        if (errno == EINTR)
                                continue;
                        errexit("accept: %s\n", sys_errlist[errno]);
                }
                switch (fork()) {
                case 0:         /* child */
                        (void) close(msock);
                        exit(TCPechod(ssock));
                default:        /* parent */
                        (void) close(ssock);
                        break;
                case -1:
                        errexit("fork: %s\n", sys_errlist[errno]);
                }
        }
}


/*------------------------------------------------------------------------
 * TCPechod - echo data until end of file
 *------------------------------------------------------------------------
 */
int
TCPechod(fd)
int     fd;
{
        char    buf[BUFSIZ];
        int     cc;

        while (cc = read(fd, buf, sizeof buf)) {
                if (cc < 0)
                        errexit("echo read: %s\n", sys_errlist[errno]);
                if (write(fd, buf, cc) < 0)
                        errexit("echo write: %s\n", sys_errlist[errno]);
        }
        return 0;
}
```

```
/*------------------------------------------------------------------------
 * reaper - clean up zombie children
 *------------------------------------------------------------------------
 */
int
reaper()
{
        union wait      status;

        while (wait3(&status, WNOHANG, (struct rusage *)0) >= 0)
                /* empty */;
}
```

As the example shows, the calls that control concurrency occupy only a small portion of the code. A master server process begins executing at *main*. After it checks its arguments, the master server calls *passiveTCP* to create a passive socket for the well-known protocol port. It then enters an infinite loop.

During each iteration of the loop, the master server calls *accept* to wait for a connection request from a client. As in the iterative server, the call blocks until a request arrives. After the underlying TCP protocol software receives a connection request, the system creates a socket for the new connection, and the call to *accept* returns the socket descriptor.

After *accept* returns, the master server creates a slave process to handle the connection. To do so, the master process calls *fork* to divide itself into two processes†. The newly created child process first closes the master socket, and then calls procedure *TCPechod* to handle the connection. The parent process closes the socket that was created to handle the new connection, and continues executing the infinite loop. The next iteration of the loop will wait at the *accept* call for another new connection to arrive. Note that both the original and new processes have access to open sockets after the call to *fork()*, and that they both must close a socket before the system deallocates it. Thus, when the master process calls *close* for the new connection, the socket for that connection only disappears from the master process. Similarly, when the slave process calls *close* for the master socket, the socket only disappears from the slave process. The slave process continues to retain access to the socket for the new connection until the slave exits; the master server continues to retain access to the socket that corresponds to the well-known port.

After the slave closes the master socket, it calls procedure *TCPechod*, which provides the ECHO service for one connection. Procedure *TCPechod* consists of a loop that repeatedly calls *read* to obtain data from the connection and then calls *write* to send the same data back over the connection. Normally, *read* returns the (positive) count of bytes read. It returns a value less than zero if an error occurs (e.g., the network connec-

---

†Recall from Chapter *3* that *fork* creates two processes, both executing the same code. The return value distinguishes between the original parent process and the newly created child.

tion between the client and server breaks) or zero if it encounters an *end-of-file* condition (i.e., no more data can be extracted from the socket). Similarly, *write* normally returns the count of characters written, but returns a value less than zero if an error occurs. The slave checks the return codes, and uses *errexit* to print a message if an error occurs.

TCPechod returns zero if it can echo all data without error. When *TCPechod* returns, the main program uses the returned value as the argument in a call to *exit*. UNIX interprets the *exit* call as a request to terminate the process, and uses the argument as a process exit code. By convention, a process uses exit code zero to denote normal termination. Thus, the slave process exits normally after performing the ECHO service. When the slave exits, the system automatically closes all open descriptors, including the descriptor for the TCP connection.

11.6 Cleaning Up Errant Processes

Because concurrent servers generate processes dynamically, they introduce a potential problem of incompletely terminated processes. UNIX solves the problem by sending a *signal* to the parent whenever a child process exits. The exiting process remains in a *zombie* state until the parent executes a *wait3* system call. To terminate a child completely (i.e., to eliminate a zombie process), our example ECHO server catches the child termination signal and executes a signal handling function. The call

```
signal(SIGCHLD, reaper);
```

informs the operating system that the master server process should execute function *reaper* whenever it receives a signal that a child process has exited (signal *SIGCHLD*). After the call to *signal*, the system automatically invokes *reaper* each time the server process receives a *SIGCHLD* signal.

Function *reaper* calls system function *wait3* to complete termination for a child that exits. *Wait3* blocks until one or more children exit (for any reason). It returns a value in the status structure that can be examined to find out about the process that exited. Because the program calls *wait3* when a *SIGCHLD* signal arrives, it will always be called after a child has exited. To ensure that an erroneous call does not deadlock the server, the program uses argument *WNOHANG* to specify that *wait3* should not block waiting for a process to exit, but should return immediately, even if no process has exited.

11.7 Summary

Connection-oriented servers achieve concurrency by allowing multiple clients to communicate with the server. The straightforward implementation in this chapter uses the *fork* function to create a new slave process each time a connection arrives. The master process never interacts with any clients; it merely accepts connections and creates a slave to handle each of them.

Each slave process begins execution in the main program immediately following the call to *fork*. The master process closes its copy of the descriptor for the new connection, and the slave closes its copy of the master descriptor. A connection to a client terminates after the slave exits because the operating system closes the slave's copy of the socket.

FOR FURTHER STUDY

Postel [RFC 862] defines the ECHO protocol used in the example TCP server.

EXERCISES

11.1   Instrument the server so it keeps a log of the time at which it creates each slave process and the time at which the slave terminates. How many clients must you start before you can find any overlap between the slave processes?

11.2   How many clients can access the example concurrent server simultaneously before any client must be denied service? How many can access the iterative server in Chapter *10* before any is denied service?

11.3   Build an iterative implementation of an ECHO server. Conduct an experiment to determine if a human can sense the difference in response time between the concurrent and iterative versions.

11.4   Modify the example server so procedure *TCPechod* explicitly closes the connection before it returns. Explain why an explicit call to *close* might make the code easier to maintain.

12

Single-Process, Concurrent Servers (TCP)

12.1 Introduction

The previous chapter illustrates how most concurrent, connection-oriented servers operate. They use operating system facilities to create a separate process for each connection, and allow the operating system to timeslice the processor among the processes. This chapter illustrates a design idea that is interesting, but not obvious: it shows how a server can offer apparent concurrency to clients while using only a single process. First, it examines the general idea. It discusses why such an approach is feasible and when it may be superior to an implementation using multiple processes. Second, it considers how a single-process server uses the UNIX system calls to handle multiple connections concurrently. The example server follows Algorithm 8.5†.

12.2 Data-driven Processing In A Server

For applications where I/O dominates the cost of preparing a response to a request, a server can use asynchronous I/O to provide apparent concurrency among clients. The idea is simple: arrange for a single server process to keep TCP connections open to multiple clients, and have the server handle a given connection when data arrives. Thus, the server uses the arrival of data to trigger processing.

To understand why the approach works, consider the concurrent ECHO server described in the previous chapter. To achieve concurrent execution, the server creates a separate slave process to handle each new connection. In theory, the server depends on

---

†See page 110 for a description of Algorithm 8.5.

the operating system's timeslicing mechanism to share the CPU among the processes, and hence, among the connections.

In practice, however, an ECHO server seldom depends on timeslicing. If one were able to watch the execution of a concurrent ECHO server closely, one would find that the arrival of data often controls processing. The reason relates to data flow across an internet. Data arrives at the server in bursts, not in a steady stream, because the underlying internet delivers data in discrete packets. Clients add to the bursty behavior if they choose to send blocks of data so that the resulting TCP segments each fit into a single IP datagram. At the server, each slave process spends most of its time blocked in a call to *read* waiting for the next burst to arrive. Once the data arrives, the *read* call returns and the slave process executes. The slave calls *write* to send the data back to the client, and then calls *read* again to wait for more data. A CPU that can handle the load of many clients without slowing down must execute sufficiently fast to complete the cycle of reading and writing before data arrives for another slave.

Of course, if the load becomes so great that the CPU cannot process one request before another arrives, timesharing takes over. The operating system switches the processor among all slaves that have data to process. For simple services that require little processing for each request, chances are high that execution will be driven by the arrival of data. To summarize:

> *Concurrent servers that require little processing time per request often behave in a sequential manner where the arrival of data triggers execution. Timesharing only takes over if the load becomes so high that the CPU cannot handle it sequentially.*

12.3 Data-Driven Processing With A Single Process

Understanding the sequential nature of a concurrent server's behavior allows us to understand how a single process can perform the same task. Imagine a single server process that has TCP connections open to many clients. The process blocks waiting for data to arrive. As soon as data arrives on any connection, the process awakens, handles the request, and sends a reply. It then blocks again, waiting for more data to arrive from another connection. As long as the CPU is fast enough to satisfy the load presented to the server, the single process version handles requests as well as a version with multiple processes. In fact, because a single-process implementation requires less switching between process contexts, it may be able to handle a slightly higher load than an implementation that uses multiple processes.

The key to programming a single-process concurrent server lies in the use of asynchronous I/O through the operating system primitive *select*. A server creates a socket for each of the connections it must manage, and then calls *select* to wait for data to arrive on any of them. In fact, because *select* can wait for I/O on all possible sockets, it can also wait for new connections at the same time. Algorithm 8.5 lists the detailed steps a single-process server uses.

12.4 Process Structure Of A Single-Process Server

Figure 12.1 illustrates the process and socket structure of a single-process concurrent server. One process manages all sockets.

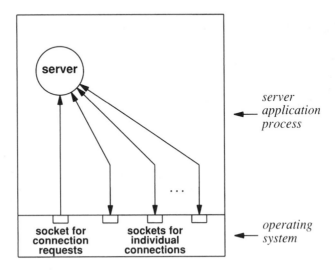

Figure 12.1 The process structure of a connection-oriented server that
achieves concurrency with a single process. The process
manages multiple sockets.

In essence, a single process server must perform the duties of both the master and
slave processes. It maintains a set of sockets, with one socket in the set bound to the
well-known port at which the master would accept connections. The other sockets in
the set each correspond to a connection over which a slave would handle requests. The
server passes the set of socket descriptors as an argument to *select*, and waits for activity on any of them. When *select* returns, it passes back a bit mask that specifies which
of the descriptors in the set is ready. The server uses the order in which descriptors become ready to decide how to proceed.

To distinguish between master and slave operations, a single-process server uses
the descriptor. If the descriptor that corresponds to the master socket becomes ready,
the server performs the same operation the master would perform: it calls *accept* on the
socket to obtain a new connection. If a descriptor that corresponds to a slave socket becomes ready, the server performs the operation a slave would perform: it calls *read* to
obtain a request, and then answers it.

12.5 An Example Single-Process ECHO Server

An example will help clarify the ideas and explain how a single-process, concurrent server works. Consider file *TCPmechod.c*, which contains the code for a single-process server that implements the ECHO service.

```c
/* TCPmechod.c - main, echo */

#include <sys/types.h>
#include <sys/socket.h>
#include <sys/time.h>
#include <netinet/in.h>

#include <stdio.h>

#define QLEN              5      /* maximum connection queue length    */
#define BUFSIZE        4096

extern int      errno;
extern char     *sys_errlist[];

/*------------------------------------------------------------------------
 * main - Concurrent TCP server for ECHO service
 *------------------------------------------------------------------------
 */
int
main(argc, argv)
int     argc;
char    *argv[];
{
        char    *service = "echo";      /* service name or port number  */
        struct sockaddr_in fsin;        /* the from address of a client */
        int     msock;                  /* master server socket         */
        fd_set  rfds;                   /* read file descriptor set     */
        fd_set  afds;                   /* active file descriptor set   */
        int     alen;                   /* from-address length          */
        int     fd, nfds;

        switch (argc) {
        case    1:
                break;
        case    2:
                service = argv[1];
                break;
```

```
            default:
                    errexit("usage: TCPmechod [port]\n");
            }

            msock = passiveTCP(service, QLEN);

            nfds = getdtablesize();
            FD_ZERO(&afds);
            FD_SET(msock, &afds);

            while (1) {
                    bcopy((char *)&afds, (char *)&rfds, sizeof(rfds));

                    if (select(nfds, &rfds, (fd_set *)0, (fd_set *)0,
                                    (struct timeval *)0) < 0)
                            errexit("select: %s\n", sys_errlist[errno]);
                    if (FD_ISSET(msock, &rfds)) {
                            int     ssock;

                            alen = sizeof(fsin);
                            ssock = accept(msock, (struct sockaddr *)&fsin,
                                    &alen);
                            if (ssock < 0)
                                    errexit("accept: %s\n",
                                            sys_errlist[errno]);
                            FD_SET(ssock, &afds);
                    }
                    for (fd=0; fd<nfds; ++fd)
                            if (fd != msock && FD_ISSET(fd, &rfds))
                                    if (echo(fd) == 0) {
                                            (void) close(fd);
                                            FD_CLR(fd, &afds);
                                    }
            }
    }

    /*------------------------------------------------------------------------
     * echo - echo one buffer of data, returning byte count
     *------------------------------------------------------------------------
     */
    int
    echo(fd)
    int     fd;
    {
```

```
char     buf[BUFSIZ];
int      cc;

cc = read(fd, buf, sizeof buf);
if (cc < 0)
        errexit("echo read: %s\n", sys_errlist[errno]);
if (cc && write(fd, buf, cc) < 0)
        errexit("echo write: %s\n", sys_errlist[errno]);
return cc;
}
```

The single-process server begins, like the master server in a multiple-process implementation, by opening a passive socket at the well-known port. It uses *FD_ZERO*
and *FD_SET* to create a bit vector that corresponds to the socket descriptors that it
wishes to test. The server then enters an infinite loop in which it calls *select* to wait for
one or more of the descriptors to become ready.

If the master descriptor becomes ready, the server calls *accept* to obtain a new connection. It adds the descriptor for the new connection to the set it manages, and continues to wait for more activity. If a slave descriptor becomes ready, the server calls procedure *echo* which calls *read* to obtain data from the connection and *write* to send it
back to the client. If one of the slave descriptors reports an end-of-file condition, the
server closes the descriptor and uses macro *FD_CLR* to remove it from the set of
descriptors *select* uses.

12.6 Summary

Execution in concurrent servers is often driven by the arrival of data and not by the
timeslicing mechanism in the underlying operating system. In cases where the service
requires little processing, a single-process implementation can use asynchronous I/O to
manage connections to multiple clients as effectively as an implementation that uses
multiple processes.

The single-process implementation performs the duties of the master and slave
processes. When the master socket becomes ready, it accepts a new connection. When
any other socket becomes ready, it reads a request and sends a reply. An example
single-process server for the ECHO service illustrates the ideas and shows the programming details.

FOR FURTHER STUDY

A good protocol specification does not constrain the implementation. For example, the single-process server described in this chapter implements the ECHO protocol defined by Postel [RFC 862]. Chapter *11* shows an example of a multiple-process, concurrent server built from the same protocol specification.

EXERCISES

12.1   Conduct an experiment that proves the example ECHO server can handle connections concurrently.

12.2   Does it make sense to use the implementation discussed in this chapter for the DAYTIME service? Why or why not?

12.3   Read the *UNIX Programmer's Manual* to find out the exact representation of descriptors in the list passed to *select*. Write the *FD_SET* and *FD_CLR* macros.

12.4   Compare the performance of single-process and multiple-process server implementations on a computer with multiple processors. Under what circumstances will a single-process version perform better than (or equal to) a multiple-process version?

12.5   Suppose a large number of clients (e.g., *100*) access the example server in this chapter at the same time. Explain what each client might observe.

12.6   Can a single-process server ever deprive one client of service while it repeatedly honors requests from another? Can a multiple-process implementation ever exhibit the same behavior? Explain.

13

Multiprotocol Servers (TCP, UDP)

13.1 Introduction

The previous chapter describes how to construct a single-process server that uses asynchronous I/O to provide apparent concurrency among multiple connections. This chapter expands the concept. It shows how a single-process server can accommodate multiple transport protocols. It illustrates the idea by showing a single process server that provides the DAYTIME service through both UDP and TCP. While the example server handles requests iteratively, the basic idea generalizes directly to servers that handle requests concurrently.

13.2 The Motivation For Reducing The Number Of Servers

In most cases, a given server handles requests for one particular service accessed through one particular transport protocol. For example, a computer system that offers the DAYTIME service often runs two servers – one server handles requests that arrive via UDP, while the other handles requests that arrive via TCP.

The chief advantage of using a separate server for each protocol lies in control: a system manager can easily control which protocols a computer offers by controlling which of the servers the system runs. The chief disadvantage of using one server per protocol lies in replication. Because many services can be accessed through either UDP or TCP, each service can require two servers. Furthermore, because both UDP and TCP servers use the same basic algorithm to compute a response, they both contain the code needed to perform the computation. If two programs both contain code to perform a given service, software management and debugging can become tedious. The programmer must ensure that both server programs remain the same when correcting bugs or when changing servers to accommodate new releases of system software. Furthermore, the system manager must coordinate execution carefully to ensure that the TCP and UDP servers executing at any time both supply exactly the same version of the service. Another disadvantage of running separate servers for each protocol arises from the use of resources: multiple server processes unnecessarily consume process table entries and other system resources. The magnitude of the problem becomes clear when one remembers that the TCP/IP standards define dozens of services.

13.3 Multiprotocol Server Design

A multiprotocol server consists of a single process that uses asynchronous I/O to handle communication over either UDP or TCP. The server initially opens two sockets: one that uses a connectionless transport (UDP) and one that uses a connection-oriented transport (TCP). The server then uses asynchronous I/O to wait for one of the sockets to become ready. If the TCP socket becomes ready, a client has requested a TCP connection. The server uses *accept* to obtain the new connection, and then communicates with the client over that connection. If the UDP socket becomes ready, a client has sent a request in the form of a UDP datagram. The server uses *recvfrom* to read the request and record the sender's endpoint address. Once it has computed a response, the server sends the response back to the client using *sendto*.

13.4 Process Structure

Figure 13.1 illustrates the process structure of an iterative, multiprotocol server.

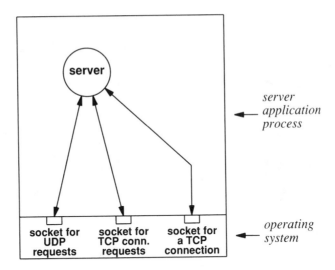

Figure 13.1 The process structure of an iterative, multiprotocol server. At any time, the server has at most three sockets open: one for UDP requests, one for TCP connection requests, and a temporary one for an individual TCP connection.

An iterative, multiprotocol server has at most three sockets open at any given time. Initially, it opens one socket to accept incoming UDP datagrams and a second socket to accept incoming TCP connection requests. When a datagram arrives on the UDP socket, the server computes a response and sends it back to the client using the same socket. When a connection request arrives on the TCP socket, the server uses *accept* to obtain the new connection. *Accept* creates a third socket for the connection, and the server uses the new socket to communicate with the client. Once it finishes interacting, the server closes the third socket and waits for activity on the other two.

13.5 An Example Multiprotocol DAYTIME Server

Program *daytimed* illustrates how a multiprotocol server operates. It consists of a single process that provides the DAYTIME service for both UDP and TCP.

```c
/* daytimed.c - main */

#include <sys/types.h>
#include <sys/socket.h>
#include <sys/time.h>
#include <netinet/in.h>

#include <stdio.h>

extern int      errno;
extern char     *sys_errlist[];

#define MAX(x, y)        ((x) > (y) ? (x) : (y))

#define QLEN             5

#define LINELEN          128

/*------------------------------------------------------------------------
 * main - Iterative server for DAYTIME service
 *------------------------------------------------------------------------
 */
int
main(argc, argv)
int     argc;
char    *argv[];
{
        char    *service = "daytime";   /* service name or port number  */
        char    buf[LINELEN+1];         /* buffer for one line of text  */
        struct sockaddr_in fsin;        /* the request from address     */
        int     alen;                   /* from-address length          */
        int     tsock;                  /* TCP master socket            */
        int     usock;                  /* UDP socket                   */
        int     nfds;
        fd_set  rfds;                   /* readable file descriptors    */

        switch (argc) {
        case    1:
                break;
        case    2:
                service = argv[1];
                break;
        default:
                errexit("usage: daytimed [port]\n");
        }
```

```
        tsock = passiveTCP(service, QLEN);
        usock = passiveUDP(service);
        nfds = MAX(tsock, usock) + 1;    /* bit number of max fd */


        FD_ZERO(&rfds);


        while (1) {
                FD_SET(tsock, &rfds);
                FD_SET(usock, &rfds);

                if (select(nfds, &rfds, (fd_set *)0, (fd_set *)0,
                                (struct timeval *)0) < 0)
                        errexit("select error: %s\n", sys_errlist[errno]);
                if (FD_ISSET(tsock, &rfds)) {
                        int     ssock;              /* TCP slave socket      */

                        alen = sizeof(fsin);
                        ssock = accept(tsock, (struct sockaddr *)&fsin,
                                &alen);
                        if (ssock < 0)
                                errexit("accept failed: %s\n",
                                                sys_errlist[errno]);
                        daytime(buf);
                        (void) write(ssock, buf, strlen(buf));
                        (void) close(ssock);
                }
                if (FD_ISSET(usock, &rfds)) {
                        alen = sizeof(fsin);
                        if (recvfrom(usock, buf, sizeof(buf), 0,
                                (struct sockaddr *)&fsin, &alen) < 0)
                                errexit("recvfrom: %s\n",
                                        sys_errlist[errno]);
                        daytime(buf);
                        (void) sendto(usock, buf, strlen(buf), 0,
                                (struct sockaddr *)&fsin, sizeof(fsin));
                }
        }
}

/*------------------------------------------------------------------------
 * daytime - fill the given buffer with the time of day
 *------------------------------------------------------------------------
 */
int
daytime(buf)
char    buf[];
```

```
{
        char    *ctime();
        time_t  time(), now;

        (void) time(&now);
        sprintf(buf, "%s", ctime(&now));
}
```

Daytimed takes an optional argument that allows the user to specify a service name or protocol port number. If the user does not supply an argument, *daytimed* uses the port for service *daytime*.

After parsing its arguments, *daytimed* calls *passiveTCP* and *passiveUDP* to create two passive sockets for use with TCP and UDP. Both sockets use the same service and, for most services, both will use the same protocol port number. Think of these as the master sockets – the server keeps them open forever, and all initial contact from a client arrives through one of them. The call to *passiveTCP* specifies that the system must enqueue up to *QLEN* connection requests.

After the server creates the master sockets, it prepares to use *select* to wait for one or both to be ready for I/O. First, it sets variable *nfds* to the index in the descriptor bitmask of the larger of the two sockets and clears the bitmask (variable *rfds*). The server then enters an infinite loop. In each iteration of the loop, it uses macro *FD_SET* to build a bitmask with bits set for the descriptors that correspond to the two master sockets. It then uses *select* to wait for input activity on either of them.

When the *select* call returns, one or both of the master sockets is ready. The server uses macro *FD_ISSET* to check the TCP socket and again to check the UDP socket. The server must check both because if a UDP datagram happened to arrive at exactly the same time as a TCP connection request, both sockets would be ready.

If the TCP socket becomes ready, it means that a client initiated a connection request. The server uses *accept* to establish the connection. *Accept* returns the descriptor of a new, temporary socket used only for the new connection. The server calls procedure *daytime* to compute the response, *write* to send the response across the new connection, and *close* to terminate the connection and release resources.

If the UDP socket becomes ready, it means that a client sent a datagram to prompt for a DAYTIME response. The server calls *recvfrom* to read the incoming datagram and record the client's endpoint address. It uses procedure *daytime* to compute the response, and then calls *sendto* to send the response back to the client. Because it uses the master UDP socket for all communication, the server does not issue a *close* after sending the UDP response.

13.6 The Concept Of Shared Code

Our example server illustrates an important idea:

A multiprotocol server design permits the designer to create a single procedure that responds to requests for a given service and to call that procedure regardless of whether requests arrive via UDP or TCP.

In the DAYTIME example, of course, the shared code occupies only a few lines. It has been placed in a single procedure, *daytime*. In most practical servers, however, the code needed to compute a response can span hundreds or thousands of lines and usually involves many procedures. It should be obvious that keeping the code in a single place where it can be shared makes maintenance easier and guarantees that the service offered by both transport protocols will be identical.

13.7 Concurrent Multiprotocol Servers

Like the single-protocol DAYTIME servers shown earlier, the example multiprotocol DAYTIME server uses an iterative method to handle requests. The reason for using an iterative solution is the same as for the earlier servers that supply the DAYTIME service: an iterative server suffices because the DAYTIME service performs minimal computation for each request.

An iterative implementation may not suffice for other services that require more computation per request. In such cases, the multiprotocol design can be extended to handle the requests concurrently. In the simplest case, a multiprotocol server can create a new process to handle each TCP connection concurrently, while it handles UDP requests iteratively. The multiprotocol design can also be extended to use the single-process implementation described in Chapter *12*. Such an implementation provides apparent concurrency among requests that arrive over multiple TCP connections or via UDP.

13.8 Summary

A multiprotocol server allows the designer to encapsulate all the code for a given service in a single program, eliminating replication and making it easier to coordinate changes. The multiprotocol server consists of a single process. The process opens master sockets for both UDP and TCP, and uses *select* to wait for either or both of them to become ready. If the TCP socket becomes ready, the server accepts the new connection and handles requests using it. If the UDP socket becomes ready, the server reads the request and responds.

The multiprotocol server design illustrated in this chapter can be extended to allow concurrent TCP connections or to use a single-process implementation that handles requests concurrently regardless of whether they arrive via TCP or UDP.

Multiprotocol servers eliminate replication of code by using a single procedure to compute the response for the service. They also eliminate unnecessary use of system resources, especially processes.

FOR FURTHER STUDY

Reynolds and Postel [RFC 1060] specifies a list of application protocols along with the UDP and TCP protocol ports assigned to each.

EXERCISES

13.1   Extend the example server in this chapter to handle requests concurrently.

13.2   Study some of the most common services defined for TCP/IP. Can you find examples where a multiprotocol server cannot use shared code to compute the responses? Explain.

13.3   The example code allows the user to specify a service name or protocol port number as an argument, and uses the argument when creating passive sockets for the service. Is there an example of a service that uses a different protocol port number for UDP than for TCP? Change the code to allow the user to specify a separate protocol port number for each protocol.

13.4   The example server does not allow the system manager to control which protocols it uses. Modify the server to include arguments that allow a manager to specify whether to offer the service for TCP, UDP, or both.

13.5   Consider a site that decides to implement security through an authorization scheme. The site provides each server with a list of authorized client machines, and makes the rule that the server must disallow requests that originate from machines other than those on the list. Implement the authorization scheme for the example multiprotocol server. (Hint: look carefully at the socket functions to see how to do it for TCP.)

14

Multiservice Servers (TCP, UDP)

14.1 Introduction

Chapter *12* describes how to construct a single-process server that uses asynchronous I/O to provide apparent concurrency among multiple connections, and Chapter *13* shows how a multiprotocol server supplies a service over both the TCP and UDP transport protocols. This chapter expands the concepts and combines them with some of the iterative and concurrent server designs discussed in earlier chapters. It shows how a single server can supply multiple services, and illustrates the idea using a single process server that handles a set of services.

14.2 Consolidating Servers

In most cases, programmers design an individual server to handle each service. The example servers in previous chapters illustrate the single-service approach – each waits at a well-known port and answers requests for the service associated with that port. Thus, a computer usually runs one server for the DAYTIME service, another for the ECHO service, and so on. The previous chapter discusses how a server that uses multiple protocols helps conserve system resources and makes maintenance easier. The same advantages that motivate multiprotocol servers motivate consolidating multiple services into a single, multiservice server.

To appreciate the cost of creating one server per service, one needs to examine the set of standardized services. TCP/IP defines a large set of *simple services* that are intended to help test, debug, and maintain a network of computers. Earlier chapters discuss a few examples like DAYTIME, ECHO, and TIME, but many other services exist. A system that runs one server for every standardized service can have dozens of server processes even though most of them will never receive a request. Thus, consolidating many services into a single server process can reduce the number of executing processes dramatically†. Furthermore, because many of the small services can be handled with a trivial computation, most of the code in a server handles the details of accepting requests and sending replies. Consolidating many services into a single server reduces the total code required.

14.3 A Connectionless, Multiservice Server Design

Multiservice servers can use either connectionless or connection-oriented transport protocols. Figure 14.1 illustrates one possible process structure for a connectionless, multiservice server.

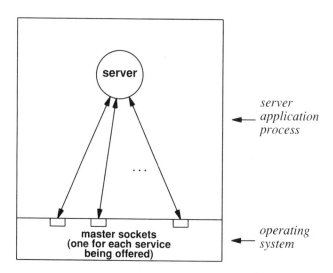

Figure 14.1 An iterative, connectionless, multiservice server. The server waits for a datagram on any of several sockets, where each socket corresponds to an individual service.

As Figure 14.1 shows, an iterative, connectionless, multiservice server usually consists of a single process that contains all the code needed for the services it supplies. The server opens a set of UDP sockets, and binds each to a well-known port for one of

---

†Because UNIX implementations limit the maximum number of sockets a single process can open, it may not be possible for a single server to offer all services. However, if a process can open *N* sockets, using multiservice servers can reduce the number of processes required by a factor of *N*.

the services being offered. It uses a small table to map sockets to services. For each socket descriptor, the table records the address of a procedure that handles the service offered on that socket. The server uses the *select* system call to wait for a datagram to arrive on any of the sockets.

When a datagram arrives, the server calls the appropriate procedure to compute a response and send a reply. Because the mapping table records the service offered by each socket, the server can easily map the socket descriptor to the procedure that handles the service.

14.4 A Connection-Oriented, Multiservice Server Design

A connection-oriented, multiservice server can also follow an iterative algorithm. In principle, such a server performs the same tasks as a set of iterative, connection-oriented servers. To be more precise, the single process in a multiservice server replaces the master server processes in a set of connection-oriented servers. At the top level, the multiservice server uses asynchronous I/O to handle its duties. Figure 14.2 shows the process structure.

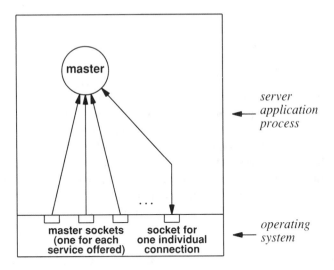

Figure 14.2 The process structure of an iterative, connection-oriented, multiservice server. At any time, the server has one socket open for each service and at most one additional socket open to handle a particular connection.

When it begins execution, the multiservice server creates one socket for each service it offers, binds each socket to the well-known port for the service, and uses *select* to wait for an incoming connection request on any of them. When one of the sockets becomes ready, the server calls *accept* to obtain the new connection that has arrived. *Accept* creates a new socket for the incoming connection. The server uses the new socket to interact with a client, and then closes it. Thus, besides one master socket for each service, the server has at most one additional socket open at any time.

As in the connectionless case, the server keeps a table of mappings so it can decide how to handle each incoming connection. When the server begins, it allocates master sockets. For each master socket, the server adds an entry to the mapping table that specifies the socket number and a procedure that implements the service offered by that socket. After it has allocated a master socket for each service, the server calls *select* to wait for a connection. Once a connection arrives, the server uses the mapping table to decide which of many internal procedures to call to handle the service that the client requested.

14.5 A Concurrent, Connection-Oriented, Multiservice Server

The procedure called by a multiservice server when a connection request arrives can accept and handle the new connection directly (making the server iterative), or it can create a slave process to handle it (making the server concurrent). In fact, a multiservice server can choose to handle some services iteratively and other services concurrently; the programmer does not need to choose a single style for all services. Figure 14.3 shows the process structure for a multiservice server that uses a concurrent, connection-oriented implementation.

In an iterative implementation, once the procedure finishes communicating with the client, it closes the new connection. In the concurrent case, the master server process closes the connection as soon as it has created a slave process; the connection remains open in the slave process. The slave process works exactly like a slave in a conventional, concurrent, connection-oriented server. It communicates with the client over the connection, honoring requests and sending replies. When it finishes the interaction, the slave closes the socket, breaks the communication with the client, and exits.

14.6 A Single-Process, Multiservice Server Implementation

It is possible, although uncommon, to manage all activity in a multiservice server with a single process, using a design exactly like the single-process server discussed in Chapter *12*. Instead of creating a slave process for each incoming connection, a single-process server adds the socket for each new connection to the set it uses with *select*. If one of the master sockets becomes ready, the single-process server calls *accept*; if one of the slave sockets becomes ready, the single-process server calls *read* to obtain an incoming request from the client, forms a response, and calls *write* to send the response back to the client.

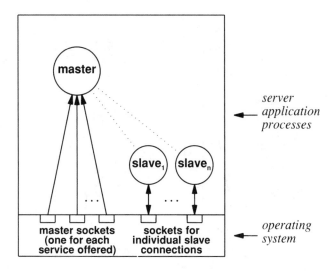

Figure 14.3 The process structure for a concurrent, connection-oriented, multiservice server. The master process handles incoming connection requests, while a slave process handles each connection.

14.7 Invoking Separate Programs From A Multiservice Server

One of the chief disadvantages of most of the designs discussed so far is their inflexibility: changing the code for any single service requires recompilation of the entire multiservice server. The disadvantage does not become important until one considers a server that handles many services. Any small change requires the programmer to recompile the server, terminate the executing server process, and restart the server process using the newly compiled code.

If a multiservice server offers many services, the chances are higher that at least one client will be communicating with it at any given time. Thus, terminating the server process may cause a problem for some clients. In addition, the more services a given server offers, the higher the probability that it will need to be modified.

Designers often choose to break a large, monolithic multiservice server into independent components by using independently compiled programs to handle each service. The idea is easiest to understand when applied to a concurrent, connection-oriented design.

Consider the concurrent, connection-oriented server illustrated in Figure 14.3. The master server process waits for a connection request from a set of master sockets. Once a connection request arrives, the master process calls *fork* to create a slave process that will handle the connection. The server must have the code for all services compiled into the master program. Figure 14.4 illustrates how the design can be modified to break the large server into separate pieces.

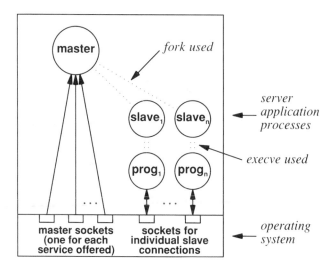

Figure 14.4 The process structure of a connection-oriented, multiservice
server that uses *execve* to execute a separate program to handle
each connection.

As the figure shows, the master server uses *fork* to create a new process to handle
each connection. Unlike the earlier design, however, the slave process calls *execve* to
replace the original code with a new program that handles all client communication.

Because *execve* retrieves the new program from a file, the design described above
allows a system manager to replace the file without recompiling the multiservice server,
terminating the server process, or restarting it. Conceptually, using *execve* separates the
programs that handle each service from the master server code that sets up connections.

> *In a multiservice server, the UNIX* execve *call makes it possible to
> separate the code that handles an individual service from the code
> that manages initial requests from clients.*

14.8 Multiservice, Multiprotocol Designs

Although it may seem natural to think of a multiservice server as either connectionless or connection-oriented, a multiprotocol design is also possible. As described in
Chapter *13*, a multiprotocol design allows a single server process to manage both a
UDP socket and a TCP socket for the same service. In the case of a multiservice
server, the server can manage UDP and TCP sockets for some or all of the services it
offers.

Many networking experts use the term *super server* to refer to a multiservice, multiprotocol server. In principle, a super server operates much the same as a conventional multiservice server. Initially, the server opens one or two master sockets for each service it offers. The master sockets for a given service correspond to connectionless transport (UDP) or connection-oriented transport (TCP). The server uses *select* to wait for any socket to become ready. If a UDP socket becomes ready, the server calls a procedure that reads the next request (datagram) from the socket, computes a response, and sends a reply. If a TCP socket becomes ready, the server calls a procedure that accepts the next connection from the socket and handles it. The server can handle the connection directly, making it iterative, or it can create a new process to handle the connection, making it concurrent.

14.9 An Example Multiservice Server

The multiservice server in file *superd.c* extends the single-process server implementation in Chapter *12*. After initializing data structures and opening sockets for each of the services it offers, the main program enters an infinite loop. Each iteration of the loop calls *select* to wait for one of the sockets to become ready. The *select* call returns when a request arrives.

When *select* returns, the server iterates through each possible socket descriptor and used macro *FD_ISSET* to test whether the descriptor is ready. If it finds a ready descriptor, the server invokes a function to handle the request. To do so, it first uses array *fd2sv* to map from the descriptor number to an entry in array *svent*.

Each entry in *svent* contains a structure of type *service* that maps a socket descriptor to a service. Field *sv_func* contains the address of a function to handle the service. After mapping the descriptor to an entry in *svent*, the program calls the selected function. For a UDP socket, the server calls the service handler directly; for a TCP socket, the server calls the service handler indirectly through procedure *doTCP*.

TCP services require the additional procedure because a TCP socket corresponds to the master socket in a connection-oriented server. When such a socket becomes ready, it means that a connection request has arrived at the socket. The server needs to create a new process to manage the connection. Thus, procedure *doTCP* calls *accept* to accept the new connection. It then calls *fork* to create a new slave process. After closing extraneous file descriptors, *doTCP* invokes the service handler function (*sv_func*). When the service function returns, the slave process exits.

```
/* superd.c - main */

#include <sys/types.h>
#include <sys/param.h>
#include <sys/socket.h>
#include <sys/time.h>
#include <sys/resource.h>
#include <sys/errno.h>
#include <sys/signal.h>
#include <sys/wait.h>
#include <netinet/in.h>

#include <stdio.h>

extern int      errno;
extern char     *sys_errlist[];

#define UDP_SERV        0
#define TCP_SERV        1

#define NOSOCK          -1      /* an invalid socket descriptor */

int     TCPechod(), TCPchargend(), TCPdaytimed(), TCPtimed(), reaper();

struct service {
        char    *sv_name;
        char    sv_useTCP;
        int     sv_sock;
        int     (*sv_func)();
} svent[] = {   { "echo", TCP_SERV, NOSOCK, TCPechod },
                { "chargen", TCP_SERV, NOSOCK, TCPchargend },
                { "daytime", TCP_SERV, NOSOCK, TCPdaytimed },
                { "time", TCP_SERV, NOSOCK, TCPtimed },
                { 0, 0, 0, 0 },
        };

#ifndef MAX
#define MAX(x, y)       ((x) > (y) ? (x) : (y))
#endif  /* MAX */

#define QLEN            5

#define LINELEN         128
```

```
extern  u_short portbase;          /* from passivesock()    */

/*------------------------------------------------------------------------
 * main - Super-server main program
 *------------------------------------------------------------------------
 */
int
main(argc, argv)
int     argc;
char    *argv[];
{
        struct service  *psv,          /* service table pointer     */
                *fd2sv[NOFILE];        /* map fd to service pointer  */
        int     fd, nfds;
        fd_set  afds, rfds;            /* readable file descriptors  */

        switch (argc) {
        case 1:
                break;
        case 2:
                portbase = (u_short) atoi(argv[1]);
                break;
        default:
                errexit("usage: superd [portbase]\n");
        }

        nfds = 0;
        FD_ZERO(&afds);
        for (psv = &svent[0]; psv->sv_name; ++psv) {
                if (psv->sv_useTCP)
                        psv->sv_sock = passiveTCP(psv->sv_name, QLEN);
                else
                        psv->sv_sock = passiveUDP(psv->sv_name);
                fd2sv[psv->sv_sock] = psv;
                nfds = MAX(psv->sv_sock+1, nfds);
                FD_SET(psv->sv_sock, &afds);
        }
        (void) signal(SIGCHLD, reaper);

        while (1) {
                bcopy((char *)&afds, (char *)&rfds, sizeof(rfds));
                if (select(nfds, &rfds, (fd_set *)0, (fd_set *)0,
                                (struct timeval *)0) < 0) {
                        if (errno == EINTR)
```

```
                                continue;
                        errexit("select error: %s\n", sys_errlist[errno]);
                }
                for (fd=0; fd<nfds; ++fd)
                        if (FD_ISSET(fd, &rfds)) {
                                psv = fd2sv[fd];
                                if (psv->sv_useTCP)
                                        doTCP(psv);
                                else
                                        psv->sv_func(psv->sv_sock);
                        }
        }
}


/*------------------------------------------------------------------------
 * doTCP - handle a TCP service connection request
 *------------------------------------------------------------------------
 */
int
doTCP(psv)
struct service  *psv;
{
        struct sockaddr_in fsin;        /* the request from address      */
        int     alen;                   /* from-address length           */
        int     fd, ssock;

        alen = sizeof(fsin);
        ssock = accept(psv->sv_sock, (struct sockaddr *)&fsin, &alen);
        if (ssock < 0)
                errexit("accept: %s\n", sys_errlist[errno]);
        switch (fork()) {
        case 0:
                break;
        case -1:
                errexit("fork: %s\n", sys_errlist[errno]);
        default:
                (void) close(ssock);
                return;         /* parent */
        }
        /* child */

        for (fd = NOFILE; fd >= 0; --fd)
                if (fd != ssock)
                        (void) close(fd);
```

```
            exit(psv->sv_func(ssock));
}


/*-------------------------------------------------------------------------
 * reaper - clean up zombie children
 *-------------------------------------------------------------------------
 */
int
reaper()
{
        union wait      status;

        while (wait3(&status, WNOHANG, (struct rusage *)0) >= 0)
                /* empty */;
}
```

The example super server supplies four services: ECHO, CHARGEN, DAYTIME, and TIME. The services other than CHARGEN appear in examples in earlier chapters. Programmers use the CHARGEN service to test client software. Once a client forms a connection to a CHARGEN server, the server generates an infinite sequence of characters and sends it to the client.

File *sv_funcs.c* contains the code for the functions that handle each of the individual services.

```
/* sv_funcs.c - TCPechod, TCPchargend, TCPdaytimed, TCPtimed */

#include <sys/types.h>

#define BUFSIZ   4096              /* max read buffer size */

extern  int     errno;
extern  char    *sys_errlist[];

/*------------------------------------------------------------------------
 * TCPecho - do TCP ECHO on the given socket
 *------------------------------------------------------------------------
 */
int
TCPechod(fd)
int     fd;
{
        char    buf[BUFSIZ];
        int     cc;

        while (cc = read(fd, buf, sizeof buf)) {
                if (cc < 0)
                        errexit("echo read: %s\n", sys_errlist[errno]);
                if (write(fd, buf, cc) < 0)
                        errexit("echo write: %s\n", sys_errlist[errno]);
        }
        return 0;
}

#define LINELEN          72

/*------------------------------------------------------------------------
 * TCPchargend - do TCP CHARGEN on the given socket
 *------------------------------------------------------------------------
 */
int
TCPchargend(fd)
{
        char    c, buf[LINELEN+2];        /* print LINELEN chars + \r\n */

        c = ' ';
        buf[LINELEN] = '\r';
        buf[LINELEN+1] = '\n';
        while (1) {
```

```
                        int      i;

                        for (i=0; i<LINELEN; ++i) {
                                buf[i] = c++;
                                if (c > '~')
                                        c = ' ';
                        }
                        if (write(fd, buf, LINELEN+2) < 0)
                                break;
                }
        return 0;
}


/*------------------------------------------------------------------------
 * TCPdaytimed - do TCP DAYTIME protocol
 *------------------------------------------------------------------------
 */
int
TCPdaytimed(fd)
int     fd;
{
        char    buf[LINELEN], *ctime();
        time_t  time(), now;

        (void) time(&now);
        sprintf(buf, "%s", ctime(&now));
        (void) write(fd, buf, strlen(buf));
        return 0;
}

#define UNIXEPOCH       2208988800      /* UNIX epoch, in UCT secs      */

/*------------------------------------------------------------------------
 * TCPtimed - do TCP TIME protocol
 *------------------------------------------------------------------------
 */
int
TCPtimed(fd)
int     fd;
{
        time_t  now, time();
        u_long  htonl();

        (void) time(&now);
```

```
        now = htonl((u_long)(now + UNIXEPOCH));
        (void) write(fd, (char *)&now, sizeof(now));
        return 0;
}
```

Code for most of the individual functions should seem familiar; it has been derived from the example servers in earlier chapters. The code for the CHARGEN service can be found in procedure *TCPchargend*; it is straightforward. The procedure consists of a loop that repeatedly creates a buffer filled with ASCII characters and calls *write* to send the contents of the buffer to the client.

14.10 The BSD UNIX Super Server, Inetd

In practice, many implementations of TCP/IP supply the skeleton of a super server to which system administrators can add additional services. In fact, the system may already have a super server process running. Thus, it may be possible for a manager to add new services to an existing multiservice server without creating a new process.

The BSD UNIX program *inetd* is perhaps the most well-known super server. It supplies many of the small TCP/IP services that network managers use for testing. *Inetd* uses a configuration file to make the addition of new services easier.

14.11 Summary

When designing a server, a programmer can choose among a myriad of possible implementations. While most servers offer only a single service, the programmer can choose a multiservice implementation to reduce the number of server processes. Among multiservice servers, most use a single transport protocol. However, multiple transport protocols can be used to combine connectionless and connection-oriented services into a single server. Finally, the programmer can choose to implement a concurrent, multiservice server with concurrent processes or with a single process that uses asynchronous I/O to provide apparent concurrency.

The example server presented in this chapter illustrates how a multiservice server uses asynchronous I/O to replace a set of master servers.

FOR FURTHER STUDY

Section 8 of the *UNIX Programmer's Manual* describes the *inetd* super server. It also describes the syntax of entries in the *inetd* configuration file, */etc/inetd.conf.*

EXERCISES

14.1   If a connection-oriented, concurrent, multiservice server handles K services, what is the maximum number of sockets it will use?

14.2   How many sockets can a single process create on your local computer system?

14.3   Consider a single-process implementation of a multiservice server. Write an algorithm that shows how the server manages connections.

14.4   Add a UDP service to the example multiservice server described in this chapter.

14.5   Read RFC 1288 to find out about the FINGER service. Add FINGER to the example multiservice server described in this chapter.

14.6   Design a super server that allows new services to be added without recompiling or restarting processes.

14.7   For each of the iterative and concurrent multiservice server designs discussed in this chapter, write an expression for the maximum number of sockets the server allocates. Express your answer as a function of the number of services offered and the number of requests handled concurrently.

14.8   What is the chief disadvantage of a super server that forks a process to handle each connection and then uses *execve* to run a program that supplies the service?

14.9   Consult the *UNIX Programmer's Manual* and find out how to add a new service to *inetd*. How much effort is involved? Which programs must be recompiled? Does one need to restart the server?

14.10 Look at the configuration file on a BSD UNIX machine to find out which services *inetd* offers.

14.11 Read the manual page that describes the *inetd* program and its configuration. Explain the relationship between its use of the *wait* option and concurrency in servers.

15

Uniform, Efficient Management Of Server Concurrency

15.1 Introduction

Earlier chapters present specific server designs, and show how each design uses iterative or concurrent processing. The previous chapter considers how some of the designs can be combined to create a multiservice server.

This chapter considers concurrent servers in a broader sense. It examines the issues underlying server design and several techniques for managing concurrency that can apply to many of the previous designs. The techniques increase design flexibility and allow a designer to optimize server performance. Although the two main approaches presented here may seem contradictory, they can each improve server performance in some circumstances. Furthermore, we will see that both techniques arise from a single concept.

15.2 Choosing Between An Iterative And A Concurrent Design

The server designs discussed so far have been partitioned into two categories: those that handle requests iteratively and those that handle them concurrently. The discussions in previous chapters imply that the designer must make a clear choice between the two basic approaches before the server is constructed.

The choice between iterative and concurrent implementations is fundamental because it influences the entire program structure, the perceived response time, and the ability of a server to handle multiple requests. If the designer makes an incorrect decision early in the design process, the cost to change can be high; much of the program may need to be rewritten.

How can a programmer know whether concurrency is warranted? How can a programmer know which server design is optimal? More important, how can a programmer estimate demand or service times? These questions are not easy to answer because networks change: experience shows that networks tend to grow rapidly and unexpectedly. Once users hear about the available services, they want access. As the set of connected users increases, the demand on individual servers increases. At the same time, new technologies and products continually improve communication and processing speeds. However, increases in communication and processing capabilities do not usually occur at the same rate. First one, then the other, becomes faster.

One might wonder exactly how a designer can make a fundamental design choice in a world that is constantly changing. The answer usually comes from experience and intuition: a designer makes the best estimate possible by looking at recent trends. In essence, the designer extrapolates from recent history to formulate an estimate for the near future. Of course, designers can only provide an approximation: as technologies and user demands change, the designer must reevaluate the decisions and, possibly, change the design. The point is:

> *Choosing between iterative and concurrent server designs can be difficult because user demands, processing speeds, and communication capabilities change rapidly. Most designers extrapolate from recent trends when making a choice.*

15.3 Level Of Concurrency

Consider one of the details of concurrent server implementation: the level of concurrency permitted. We define the *level of concurrency* for a server to be the total number of processes the server has running at a given time. The level of concurrency varies over time as the server creates a process to handle an incoming request or as a slave completes a request and exits. Programmers and system administrators are not concerned with tracking the level of concurrency at any given instant, but they do care about the maximum level of concurrency a server exhibits over its lifetime.

Only a few of the designs presented so far require the designer to specify the maximum level of concurrency for a server. Most of the designs permit the master server process to create as many concurrent slave processes as needed to handle incoming requests.

Usually, a concurrent, connection-oriented server creates one process for each connection it receives from a client. Of course, a practical server cannot handle arbitrarily many connections. Each implementation of TCP places a bound on the number of active connections possible, and each operating system places a bound on the number of processes available (the system must restrict either the number of processes available per user or the total number available). When the server reaches one of these limits, the system will deny its requests for more processes.

To increase server flexibility, many programmers avoid placing a fixed upper bound on the maximum level of concurrency in the program. If the server code does not have a predefined maximum level of concurrency, the single implementation can operate either in an environment that does not demand much concurrency or in an environment that has much demand. The programmer does not need to change the code or recompile when moving a server from the former type of environment to the latter. However, servers that do not bound concurrency are a risk in an environment that presents a heavy load. Concurrency can increase until the server's operating system becomes swamped with processes.

15.4 Demand-Driven Concurrency

To achieve flexibility, most of the concurrent server designs presented in earlier chapters use incoming requests to trigger an increase in concurrency. We call such schemes *demand-driven*, and say that the level of concurrency increases *on demand*.

Servers that increase concurrency on demand may seem optimal because they do not use system resources (e.g., process table slots or buffers) unless needed. Thus, demand-driven servers do not use resources unnecessarily. However, demand-driven servers provide low observed response times because they can handle multiple requests without waiting for processing to complete on an existing request.

15.5 The Cost Of Concurrency

While the general motivation for demand-driven concurrency is laudable, the implementations presented in earlier chapters may not produce optimal results. To understand why, we must consider the subtleties of process creation and scheduling as well as the details of server operation. The central issue is one of how to measure the costs and benefits. In particular, one must consider the cost of concurrency as well as its benefits.

15.6 Overhead And Delay

The server designs presented in earlier chapters all use incoming requests as a measure of demand and as a trigger for increased concurrency. The master server waits for a request, and creates a new slave process to handle it immediately after the request arrives. Thus, the level of concurrency at any instant reflects the number of requests the server has received, but has not finished processing.

Despite the apparent simplicity of the request-driven scheme, creating a new process for each request can be expensive. Whether the server uses connectionless or connection-oriented transport, the operating system must inform the master server that a message or a connection has arrived. The master must then ask the system to create a slave process.

Receiving a request from a network and creating a new process can take considerable time. In addition to delaying request processing, creating a process consumes system resources. Thus, on a conventional uniprocessor, the server will not execute while the operating system creates a new process and switches process context.

15.7 Small Delays Can Matter

Does the short delay incurred while creating new processes matter? Figure 15.1 shows how it can.

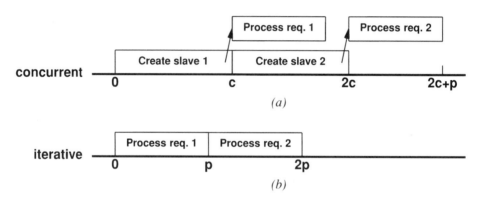

Figure 15.1 (a) The time required to process two requests in a concurrent server and (b) in an iterative version of the server. The iterative version has lower delay because the time required to process a request, p, is less than the time required to create a process, c.

The figure shows an example in which the time required to process a request is less than the time required to create a new process. Let p denote the processing time, and let c denote the time required to create a process. Assume that two requests arrive in a burst at time 0. The concurrent version completes processing the first request after $c + p$ time units, and it finishes processing the second after $2c + p$ time units. Thus, it requires an average of $3c/2 + p$ time units per request. An iterative server completes processing the first request at time p and the second at time $2p$, yielding an average of only $3p/2$ time units per request. Thus, the iterative server design exhibits lower average delay than the concurrent version.

The small additional delay may seem unimportant when considering only a few requests. However, the delay can be significant if one considers the continuous operation of a server under heavy load. If many requests arrive close to the same time, they must wait while the server creates processes to handle them. If additional requests arrive faster than the server can process them, the delays accumulate.

In the short term, small delays in the server affect the observed response time but not the overall throughput. If a burst of requests arrives at or near the same time, protocol software in the operating system will place them in a queue until the server can extract and process them. For example, if the server uses a connection-oriented transport, TCP will enqueue connection requests. If the server uses a connectionless transport, UDP will enqueue incoming datagrams.

In the long term, extra delays can cause requests to be lost. To see how, imagine a server that takes c time units to create a process, but only p time units ($p < c$) to process a request. A concurrent implementation of the server can handle an average of $1/c$ requests per unit time, while an iterative version can handle $1/p$ requests per unit time.

A problem arises when the rate at which requests arrive exceeds $1/c$, but remains less than $1/p$. An iterative implementation can handle the load, but a concurrent implementation spends too much time creating processes. In the concurrent version, queues in the protocol software eventually become full and the software begins rejecting further requests.

In practice, few servers operate close to their maximum throughput. Furthermore, few designers use concurrent servers when the cost of creating a process exceeds the cost of processing. Thus, request delay or loss does not occur in many applications. However, servers designed to provide optimum response under heavy load must consider alternatives to on-demand concurrency.

15.8 Process Preallocation

A straightforward technique can be used to control delay, limit the maximum level of concurrency, and maintain high throughput in concurrent servers when process creation time is significant. The technique consists of preallocating concurrent processes to avoid the cost of creating them.

To use the preallocation technique, a designer programs the master server to create N slave processes when it begins execution. Each process uses facilities available in the operating system to wait for a request to arrive. When a request arrives, one of the waiting slave processes begins execution and handles the request. When it finishes handling a request, the slave does not exit. Instead, it returns to the code that waits for another request.

The chief advantage of preallocation arises from lower operating system overhead. Because the server does not need to create a process when a request arrives, it can handle requests faster. The technique is especially important when request processing involves more I/O than computation. Preallocation allows the server system to switch to another process and begin to handle the next request while waiting for I/O activity associated with the previous request. To summarize:

> *When using preallocation, a server creates concurrent slave processes at startup. Preallocation can lower server delay because it avoids the cost of creating a process each time a request arrives and allows processing of one request to overlap I/O activity associated with another.*

15.8.1 Preallocation In UNIX

Some operating systems make the interaction between the master and preallocated slave processes easy because the system offers shared memory or message passing facilities. In UNIX, processes do not share memory. However, process preallocation is still possible. Coordination relies on shared sockets:

> *When a UNIX process calls* fork, *the newly created child process receives a copy of all open descriptors, including descriptors that correspond to sockets.*

To take advantage of socket sharing, a master server process opens the necessary socket before it preallocates slave processes. In particular, when it starts, the master server process opens a socket for the well-known port at which it will receive requests. The master then calls *fork* to create as many slave processes as desired. Because each process inherits copies of socket descriptors from the parent, all slaves have access to the socket for the well-known port. The next sections discuss the details of how UNIX handles preallocation for connection-oriented and connectionless servers.

15.8.2 Preallocation In A Connection-Oriented Server

If a concurrent server uses TCP for communication, the level of concurrency depends on the number of active connections. Each incoming connection request must be handled by an independent process. Fortunately, the UNIX implementation provides mutual exclusion for multiple processes that all attempt to accept a connection from the same socket. Each slave calls *accept*, which blocks awaiting receipt of an incoming connection request to the well-known port. When a connection request arrives, the system unblocks exactly one of the slave processes. In an individual slave process, when the call to *accept* returns, it provides a new file descriptor used for the incoming connection. The slave handles the connection, closes the new socket, and then calls *accept* to wait for the next request. Figure 15.2 shows the process structure.

As the figure shows, all slaves inherit access to the socket for the well-known port. An individual slave receives a new socket used for an individual connection when its call to *accept* returns. Although the master creates the socket that corresponds to the well-known port, it does not use the socket for other operations. The dashed line in the diagram denotes the difference between the master's use of the socket and the slaves' use.

Although Figure 15.2 shows a master process running at the same time as the slaves, the distinction between master and slave is somewhat blurred. In practice, the master has no role after it preallocates the slave processes. Thus, the master process can simply exit once the slaves have been started†. A clever programmer can even arrange for the master process to create all except the last slave process. The master process then becomes the last slave, thereby saving the cost of one extra process creation. In UNIX, the code required to do so is trivial.

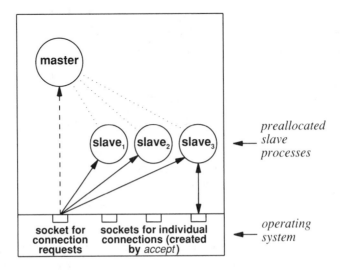

Figure 15.2 The process structure in a concurrent, connection-oriented server that preallocates slave processes. The example shows three preallocated slaves with one of them actively handling a connection. The master opens the socket for the well-known port, but does not use it.

15.8.3 Preallocation In A Connectionless Server

If a concurrent server uses connectionless transport, the level of concurrency depends on the number of requests that arrive. Each incoming request arrives in a separate UDP datagram, and each must be given to a separate process. Concurrent, connectionless designs usually arrange for a master server to create a separate slave process when a request arrives.

UNIX permits a connectionless server to preallocate slave processes using the same preallocation strategy as is used in connection-oriented servers. Figure 15.3 shows the process structure.

---

†In practice, if the master exits, the slaves will be owned by the UNIX *init* process. The master can eliminate *zombie processes* if it enters a loop that repeatedly calls the system function *wait3*.

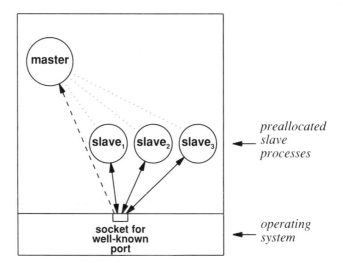

Figure 15.3 The process structure for a concurrent, connectionless server that
preallocates slave processes. The diagram shows three slaves
that all read from the socket for the well-known port. Only one
slave receives each incoming request.

As the figure shows, each slave process inherits the socket for the well-known port.
Because communication is connectionless, the slaves can use a single socket to send
responses as well as to receive incoming requests. A slave calls *recvfrom* to obtain the
sender's address as well as a datagram from that sender; it calls *sendto* to transmit a reply.

As in a connection-oriented server that uses preallocation, the master process for
the connectionless case has little to do after it opens the socket for the well-known port
and preallocates the slaves. Thus, it can either exit or choose to transform itself into the
last slave to avoid the overhead of creating the last process.

15.8.4 Preallocation, Bursty Traffic, And NFS

Experience has shown that because most implementations of UDP do not provide
large queues for arriving datagrams, bursts of incoming requests can easily overrun a
queue. UDP merely discards datagrams that arrive after the receiver's queue has filled,
so bursts of traffic can cause loss.

The problem of overrun is especially difficult because UDP software often resides
in the operating system. Thus, application programmers cannot always modify it easily.
However, application programmers can preallocate slave processes. The preallocation is
usually sufficient to eliminate loss.

Many implementations of NFS use preallocation to avoid datagram loss. If one examines a system running NFS, one often finds a set of preallocated server processes all reading from the same UDP socket. In fact, preallocation can mean the difference between a usable and an unusable implementation of NFS.

15.8.5 Process Preallocation On A Multiprocessor

Preallocation on a multiprocessor has a special purpose. It permits the designer to relate the level of concurrency in a server to the hardware's capability. If the machine has K processors, the designer can preallocate K slave processes. Because multiprocessor operating systems give each process to a separate processor, a preallocation ensures that the level of concurrency matches the hardware. When a request arrives, the operating system passes it to one of the preallocated processes and assigns that process to a processor. Because the process has been preallocated, little time is required to start it running. Thus, the system will distribute requests quickly. If a burst of requests arrives, each processor will handle one request, giving the maximum possible speed.

15.9 Delayed Process Allocation

Although preallocation can improve efficiency, it does not solve all problems. Surprisingly, in some circumstances efficiency can be improved by using the opposite approach: namely, delaying slave process allocation.

To understand how delay can help, recall that process creation requires time and resources. Creating additional processes can only be justified if doing so will somehow increase the system throughput or lower delay. Creating a process not only takes time, it also adds overhead to the operating system component that must manage processes. In addition, preallocating processes that all attempt to receive incoming requests may add overhead to the networking code.

We said that concurrency will lower delay if the cost of creating a process is smaller than the cost of processing a request. An iterative solution works best if the cost of processing a request is smaller. However, a programmer cannot always know how the costs will compare because the time required may depend on the request (e.g., the time required to search a database may depend on the query).

In addition, the programmer may not know whether an error will be found quickly. To understand why, consider how most server software works. When a request arrives, the server software checks the message to verify that the fields contain appropriate values and that the client is authorized to make a request. Verification can take a few microseconds, or it may involve further network communication that can take several orders of magnitude longer. On one hand, if the server detects an error in the message, it will reject the request quickly, making the total time required to process the message negligible. On the other hand, if the server receives a valid request, it may take considerable processing time. In cases where processing time is short, concurrent processing is unwarranted; an iterative server exhibits lower delay and higher throughput.

How can designers optimize delay and throughput when they do not know whether concurrent processing is justified? The answer lies in a technique for *delayed process allocation*. The idea is straightforward: instead of choosing an iterative or concurrent design, allow a server to measure processing cost and choose between iterative handling or concurrent handling dynamically. The choice is dynamic because it can vary from one request to the next.

To implement dynamic, delayed allocation, servers usually estimate processing cost by measuring elapsed time. The master server receives a request, sets a timer, and begins processing the request (iteratively). If the server finishes processing the request before the timer expires, the server cancels the timer. If the timer expires before the server finishes processing the request, the server creates a slave process and allows the slave to handle the request. To summarize:

> When using delayed process allocation, a server begins processing each request iteratively. The server creates a concurrent process to handle the request only if processing takes substantial time. Doing so allows the master to check for errors and handle short requests before it creates a process or switches context.

In UNIX, delayed allocation is easy. Because UNIX includes an *alarm* mechanism, the master process can set a timer and arrange to execute a procedure when the timer expires. Because the UNIX *fork* function permits a newly created process to inherit open sockets as well as a copy of the executing program and data from its parent, the master can create a slave that continues processing exactly at the point where the master was executing when the timer expired.

15.10 The Uniform Basis For Both Techniques

It may seem that the techniques of slave preallocation and delayed slave allocation have nothing in common. In fact, they seem to be exact opposites. However, they share much in common because they both arise from the same conceptual principle: it is possible to improve the performance of some concurrent servers by relaxing the interval between request arrival and slave process creation. Preallocation increases the level of server concurrency before requests arrive; delayed allocation increases server concurrency after requests arrive. The idea can be summarized:

> Preallocation and delayed allocation arise from a single principle: by detaching the level of server concurrency from the number of currently active requests, the designer can gain flexibility and improve server efficiency.

15.11 Combining Techniques

The techniques of delayed allocation and preallocation can be combined. A server can begin with no preallocated processes and can use delayed allocation. It waits for a request to arrive, and only creates a slave if processing takes a long time (i.e., if its timer expires). Once a slave has been created, however, the slave need not exit immediately; it can consider itself permanently allocated and persist. After processing one request, the slave can wait for the next incoming request to arrive.

The biggest problem with a combined system arises from the need to control concurrency. It is easy to know when to create additional slave processes, but more difficult to know when a slave should exit instead of persisting. One possible solution arranges for the master to specify a maximum propagation value, M, when creating a slave. The slave can create up to M additional slaves, each of which can create zero more. Thus, the system begins with only a master process, but eventually reaches a fixed maximum level of concurrency. Another technique for controlling concurrency involves arranging for a slave to exit after a period of inactivity. The slave starts a timer before it waits for the next request. If the timer expires before a request arrives, the slave exits.

In some systems, the slaves can use facilities like shared memory to coordinate their activities. They can store a shared integer that records the level of concurrency at any instant, and can use that value to determine whether to persist or exit after handling a request. In systems that permit an application to find out the number of requests enqueued at a socket, a slave can also use the queue length to help it decide the level of concurrency.

15.12 Summary

Two main techniques permit a designer to improve concurrent server performance: preallocation and delayed allocation of slave processes.

Preallocation optimizes delay by arranging to create slave processes before they are needed. The master server opens a socket for the well-known port it will use and then preallocates all slave processes. Because the slaves inherit access to the socket, they can all wait for a request to arrive. The system hands each incoming request to one process. Preallocation is important for concurrent, connectionless servers because the time required to process a request is usually small, making the overhead of process creation significant. Preallocation also makes concurrent, connectionless designs efficient on multiprocessor systems.

Delayed allocation uses a lazy approach to process allocation. A master server begins processing each request iteratively, but sets a timer. It creates a concurrent process to handle the request if the timer expires before the master finishes. Delayed allocation works well in cases where processing times vary among requests or when a server must check a request for correctness (i.e., to verify that the client is authorized). Delayed allocation eliminates process creation overhead for short requests or requests that contain errors.

Although they appear to be opposite, both optimization techniques arise from the same basic principle: they relax the strict coordination between the level of concurrency in the server and the number of pending requests. Doing so can improve server performance.

FOR FURTHER STUDY

Chapters *23* and *24* describe the *Network File System* (NFS). Many implementations of NFS use preallocation to help avoid loss of requests.

EXERCISES

15.1   Modify one of the example servers in previous chapters to use preallocation. How does the performance change?

15.2   Modify one of the example servers in previous chapters to use delayed allocation. How does the performance change?

15.3   Test a connectionless server that uses preallocation on a multiprocessor. Be sure to arrange for clients that transmit bursts of requests. How does the useful level of concurrency relate to the number of processors? If the two are not the same, explain why.

15.4   Write a server algorithm that combines delayed allocation with preallocation. How can you limit the maximum level of concurrency?

15.5   In the previous question, if your operating system offered a message passing facility, how could you use it to control the level of concurrency?

15.6   What advantages can one obtain by combining the techniques discussed in this chapter with a concurrent, single-process server?

15.7   How can a designer use the techniques discussed in this chapter with a multiservice server?

16

Concurrency In Clients

16.1 Introduction

The previous chapters show how servers can handle requests concurrently. This chapter considers the issue of concurrency in client software. It discusses how a client can benefit from concurrency and how a concurrent client operates. Finally, it shows an example client that illustrates concurrent operation.

16.2 The Advantages Of Concurrency

Servers use concurrency for two main reasons:

- Concurrency can improve the observed response time (and therefore the overall throughput to all clients).
- Concurrency can eliminate potential deadlocks.

In addition, a concurrent implementation permits the designer to create multiprotocol or multiservice servers easily. Finally, concurrent implementations that use multiple processes are extremely flexible because they operate well on a variety of hardware platforms. When ported to a computer that has a single CPU, they work correctly. When ported to a computer that has multiple processors, they operate more efficiently because they take advantage of the additional processing power without any changes to the code.

It may seem that clients could not benefit from concurrency, primarily because a client usually performs only one activity at a time. Once it sends a request to a server, the client cannot proceed until it receives a response. Furthermore, the issue of client efficiency and deadlock are not as serious as the issue of server deadlock because if a client slows or ceases to execute, it stops only itself – other clients continue to operate.

Despite appearances, concurrency does have advantages in clients. First, concurrent implementations can be easier to program because they separate functionality into conceptually separate components. Second, concurrent implementations can be easier to maintain and extend because they make the code modular. Third, concurrent clients can contact several servers at the same time either to compare response times or to merge the results the servers return. Fourth, concurrency can allow the user to change parameters, inquire about the client status, or control processing dynamically. This chapter will focus on the idea of interacting with multiple servers at the same time.

The key advantage of using concurrency in clients lies in asynchrony. It allows a client to handle multiple tasks simultaneously without imposing a strict execution order on them.

16.3 The Motivation For Exercising Control

One possible use of asynchrony arises from the need to separate control functions from normal processing. For example, consider a client used to query a large demographic database. Assume a user can generate queries like:

Find all people who live on Elm Street.

If the database contains information for a single town, the response could include fewer than *100* names. If the database contains information about all people in the United States, however, the response could contain hundreds of thousands of names. Furthermore, if the database system consists of many servers distributed across a wide geographic area, the lookup could take many minutes.

The database example illustrates an important idea underlying many client-server interactions: a user who invokes a client may have little or no idea how long it will take to receive a response or how large that response will be.

Most client software merely waits until a response arrives. Of course, if the server malfunctions, deadlock occurs and the client will block attempting to read a response that will never arrive. Unfortunately, the user cannot know if a true deadlock has occurred or if processing is merely slow because network delays are high or the server is overloaded. Furthermore, the user cannot know whether the client has received any messages from the server.

If a user becomes impatient or decides that a particular response requires too much time, the user has only one option: abort the client program and try again later. In such situations, concurrency can help because an appropriately designed concurrent client can permit the user to continue to interact with the client while the client waits for a response. The user can find out whether any data has been received, choose to send a different request, or terminate the communication gracefully.

As an example, consider the hypothetical database client described above. A concurrent implementation can read and process commands from the user's keyboard concurrently with database lookup. Thus, a user can type a command like *status* to determine whether the client has successfully opened a connection to the server and whether the client has sent a request. The user can type *abort* to stop communication, or the user can type *newserver* to instruct the client to terminate the existing communication and attempt to communicate with another server.

Separating client control from normal processing allows a user to interact with a client even if the normal input for the client comes from a file. Thus, even after the user starts a client handling a large input file, he or she can interact with the running client program to find out how processing has progressed. Similarly, a concurrent client can proceed to place responses in an output file while keeping its interaction with the user separate.

16.4 Concurrent Contact With Multiple Servers

Concurrency can allow a single client to contact several servers at the same time and to report to the user as soon as it receives a response from any of them. For example, a concurrent client for the TIME service can send to multiple servers and either accept the first response that arrives or take the average of several responses.

Consider a client that uses the ECHO service to measure the throughput to a given destination. Assume the client forms a TCP connection to an ECHO server, sends a large volume of data, reads the echo back, computes the total time required for the task, and reports the throughput in bytes per second. A user can invoke such a client to determine the current network throughput.

Now consider how concurrency can enhance a client that uses ECHO to measure throughput. Instead of measuring one connection at a time, a concurrent client can access multiple destinations at the same time. It can send to any of them and read from any of them concurrently. Because it performs all measurements concurrently, it executes faster than a non-concurrent client. Furthermore, because it makes all measurements at the same time, they are all affected equally by the loads on the CPU and the local network.

16.5 Implementing Concurrent Clients

Like concurrent servers, most concurrent client implementations follow one of two basic approaches:

- The client divides into two or more processes that each handle one function, or

- The client consists of a single process that uses *select* to handle multiple input and output events asynchronously.

Some operating systems support interprocess memory sharing and interprocess communications. Figure 16.1 illustrates how the multiple process approach can be used in such systems to support a connection-oriented application protocol.

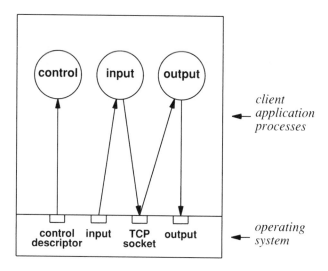

Figure 16.1 One possible process structure for a connection-oriented client that uses multiple processes to achieve concurrent processing. One process handles input and sends requests to the server, while another retrieves responses and handles output.

As Figure 16.1 illustrates, multiple processes allow the client to separate input and output processing. The figure shows how the processes interact with file descriptors and a socket descriptor. An *input process* reads from standard input, formulates requests, and sends them to the server over the TCP connection, while a separate *output process* receives responses from the server and writes them to standard output. Meanwhile, a third *control process* accepts commands from the user that control processing.

16.6 Single-Process Implementations

Unfortunately, most UNIX implementations do not allow separate processes to share memory. Thus, the multiple process implementation does not work well under UNIX. Instead, concurrent clients built for UNIX usually implement concurrency with a single-process algorithm similar to Algorithm 8.5† and the examples in Chapters *12* through *14*. Figure 16.2 illustrates the process structure.

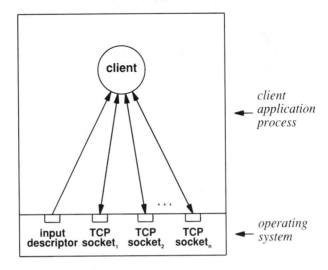

Figure 16.2 The process structure most often used with UNIX to provide apparent concurrency in a single-process, connection-oriented client. The client uses *select* to handle multiple connections concurrently.

A single-process client uses asynchronous I/O like a single-process server. The client creates socket descriptors for its TCP connections to multiple servers. It may also have a descriptor from which it obtains input. The body of a client program consists of a loop that uses *select* to wait for one of its descriptors to become ready. If the input descriptor becomes ready, the client reads the input and either stores it for later use or acts on it immediately. If a TCP connection becomes ready for output, the client prepares and sends a request across the TCP connection. If a TCP connection becomes ready for input, the client reads the response that the server has sent and handles it.

Of course, a single-process concurrent client shares many advantages and disadvantages with a single-process server implementation. The client reads input or responses from the server at whatever rate they are generated. Local processing will continue even if the server delays for a short time. Thus, the client will continue to read and honor control commands even if the server fails to respond.

---

†See page 110 for a description of Algorithm 8.5.

A single-process client can become deadlocked if it invokes a system function that blocks. Thus, the programmer must be careful to ensure that the client process does not block indefinitely waiting for an event that will not occur. Of course, the programmer may choose to ignore some cases and to allow the user to detect that deadlock problems have occurred. It is important for the programmer to understand the subtleties and to make conscious decisions about each case.

16.7 An Example Concurrent Client That Uses ECHO

An example client that achieves concurrency with a single process will clarify the ideas presented above. The example concurrent client shown below in file *TCPtecho.c* uses the ECHO service described in Chapter 7 to measure network throughput to a set of machines.

```
/* TCPtecho.c - main, TCPtecho, reader, writer, mstime */

#include <sys/types.h>
#include <sys/param.h>
#include <sys/ioctl.h>
#include <sys/time.h>

#include <stdio.h>

extern int      errno;
extern char     *sys_errlist[];

#define BUFSIZE         4096            /* write buffer size        */
#define CCOUNT          64*1024         /* default character count  */

#define USAGE   "usage: TCPtecho [ -c count ] host1 host2...\n"

char    *hname[NOFILE];                 /* fd to host name mapping      */
int     rc[NOFILE], wc[NOFILE];         /* read/write character counts  */
char    buf[BUFSIZE];                   /* read/write data buffer       */
long    mstime();


/*------------------------------------------------------------------------
 * main - concurrent TCP client for ECHO service timing
 *------------------------------------------------------------------------
 */
int
main(argc, argv)
```

```
int     argc;
char    *argv[];
{
        int     ccount = CCOUNT;
        int     i, hcount, maxfd, fd;
        int     one = 1;
        fd_set  afds;

        hcount = 0;
        maxfd = -1;
        for (i=1; i<argc; ++i) {
                if (strcmp(argv[i], "-c") == 0) {
                        if (++i < argc && (ccount = atoi(argv[i])))
                                continue;
                        errexit(USAGE);
                }
                /* else, a host */

                fd = connectTCP(argv[i], "echo");
                if (ioctl(fd, FIONBIO, (char *)&one))
                        errexit("can't mark socket nonblocking: %s\n",
                                sys_errlist[errno]);
                if (fd > maxfd)
                        maxfd = fd;
                hname[fd] = argv[i];
                ++hcount;
                FD_SET(fd, &afds);
        }
        TCPtecho(&afds, maxfd+1, ccount, hcount);
        exit(0);
}


/*------------------------------------------------------------------------
 * TCPtecho - time TCP ECHO requests to multiple servers
 *------------------------------------------------------------------------
 */
int
TCPtecho(pafds, nfds, ccount, hcount)
fd_set  *pafds;
int     nfds, ccount, hcount;
{
        fd_set  rfds, wfds;             /* read/write fd sets         */
        fd_set  rcfds, wcfds;           /* read/write fd sets (copy)  */
        int     fd, i;
```

```
        for (i=0; i<BUFSIZE; ++i)            /* echo data    */
                buf[i] = 'D';
        bcopy((char *)pafds, (char *)&rcfds, sizeof(rcfds));
        bcopy((char *)pafds, (char *)&wcfds, sizeof(wcfds));
        for (fd=0; fd<nfds; ++fd)
                rc[fd] = wc[fd] = ccount;

        (void) mstime((long *)0);            /* set the epoch */

        while (hcount) {
                bcopy((char *)&rcfds, (char *)&rfds, sizeof(rfds));
                bcopy((char *)&wcfds, (char *)&wfds, sizeof(wfds));

                if (select(nfds, &rfds, &wfds, (fd_set *)0,
                                (struct timeval *)0) < 0)
                        errexit("select failed: %s\n",sys_errlist[errno]);
                for (fd=0; fd<nfds; ++fd) {
                        if (FD_ISSET(fd, &rfds))
                                if (reader(fd, &rcfds) == 0)
                                        hcount--;
                        if (FD_ISSET(fd, &wfds))
                                writer(fd, &wcfds);
                }
        }
}


/*------------------------------------------------------------------------
 * reader - handle ECHO reads
 *------------------------------------------------------------------------
 */
int
reader(fd, pfdset)
int     fd;
fd_set  *pfdset;
{
        long    now;
        int     cc;

        cc = read(fd, buf, sizeof(buf));
        if (cc < 0)
                errexit("read: %s\n", sys_errlist[errno]);
        if (cc == 0)
                errexit("read: premature end of file\n");
```

```
            rc[fd] -= cc;
            if (rc[fd])
                    return 1;
            (void) mstime(&now);
            printf("%s: %d ms\n", hname[fd], now);
            (void) close(fd);
            FD_CLR(fd, pfdset);
            return 0;
}


/*-------------------------------------------------------------------------
 * writer - handle ECHO writes
 *-------------------------------------------------------------------------
 */
int
writer(fd, pfdset)
int     fd;
fd_set  *pfdset;
{
            int     cc;

            cc = write(fd, buf, MIN(sizeof(buf), wc[fd]));
            if (cc < 0)
                    errexit("read: %s\n", sys_errlist[errno]);
            wc[fd] -= cc;
            if (wc[fd] == 0) {
                    (void) shutdown(fd, 1);
                    FD_CLR(fd, pfdset);
            }
}


/*-------------------------------------------------------------------------
 * mstime - report the number of milliseconds since Jan 1, 1970
 *-------------------------------------------------------------------------
 */
long
mstime(pms)
long    *pms;
{
            static struct timeval   epoch;
            struct timeval          now;

            if (gettimeofday(&now, (struct timezone *)0))
                    errexit("gettimeofday: %s\n", sys_errlist[errno]);
```

```
        if (!pms) {
                epoch = now;
                return 0;
        }
        *pms = (now.tv_sec - epoch.tv_sec) * 1000;
        *pms += (now.tv_usec - epoch.tv_usec + 500)/ 1000;
        return *pms;
}
```

16.8 Execution Of The Concurrent Client

TCPtecho accepts multiple machine names as arguments. For each machine, it opens a TCP connection to the ECHO server on that machine, sends *ccount* characters (bytes) across the connection, reads the bytes it receives back from each server, and prints the total time required to complete the task. Thus, *TCPtecho* can be used to measure the current throughput to a set of machines.

TCPtecho begins by initializing the character count variable to the default value, *CCOUNT*. It then parses its arguments to see if the user typed the -*c* option. If so, *TCPtecho* converts the specified count to an integer and stores it in variable *ccount* to replace the default.

TCPtecho assumes all arguments other than the -*c* flag specify the name of a machine. For each such argument, it calls *connectTCP* to form a TCP connection to the ECHO server on the named machine. *TCPtecho* records the machine name in array *hname*, and calls macro *FD_SET* to set the bit in the file descriptor mask that corresponds to the socket. It also records the maximum descriptor number in *maxfd* (needed for the call to *select*).

Once it has established a TCP connection for each machine specified in the arguments, the main program calls procedure *TCPtecho* to handle the transmission and reception of data. *TCPtecho* handles all connections concurrently. It fills buffer *buf* with data to be sent (the letter *D*), and then calls *select* to wait for any TCP connection to become ready for input or for output. When the *select* call returns, *TCPtecho* iterates through all descriptors to see which are ready.

When a connection becomes ready for output, *TCPtecho* calls procedure *writer*, which sends as much data from the buffer as TCP will accept in a single call to *write*. If *write* finds that the entire buffer has been sent, it calls *shutdown* to close the descriptor for output and removes the descriptor from the output set used by *select*.

When a descriptor becomes ready for input, *TCPtecho* calls procedure *reader*, which accepts as much data from the connection as TCP can deliver and place in the buffer. Procedure *reader* reads data into the buffer and decrements the count of characters remaining. If the count reaches zero (i.e., the server has received as many characters as it sent), procedure *reader* computes how much time has elapsed since data transmission started, prints a message, and closes the connection. It also removes the descriptor from the input set used by *select*. Thus, a message that reports the total time required to echo data appears on the output each time a connection completes.

After performing a single input or output operation on a connection, procedures *reader* and *writer* each return and the loop in *TCPtecho* continues to iterate, calling *select* again. *Reader* returns a value of *0* if it detected an end of file condition and closed a connection, and a value of *1*, otherwise. *TCPtecho* uses *reader*'s return code to determine whether it should decrement the count of active connections. When the count of connections reaches zero, the loop in *TCPtecho* terminates, *TCPtecho* returns to the main program, and the client process exits.

Figure 16.3 shows sample output from three separate executions of *TCPtecho*. The first invocation shows that *TCPtecho* only requires *311* milliseconds to send data to the ECHO server on the local machine. The command line has a single argument, *localhost*. Because the second invocation has three arguments (*ector*, *arthur*, and *merlin*), it causes *TCPtecho* to interact with all three machines concurrently. The third invocation measures the time required to reach machine *sage*, but the command line specifies that *TCPtecho* should only send *1000* characters instead of the default (64K).

```
% TCPtecho localhost
localhost: 311 ms

% TCPtecho ector arthur merlin
arthur:   601 ms
merlin: 4921 ms
ector: 11791 ms

% TCPtecho -c 1000 sage
sage: 80 ms
```

Figure 16.3 An example of the output from three separate executions of *TCPtecho* for machines at Purdue University. A machine requires more time if it is further away from the client or has a slower processor.

16.9 Concurrency In The Example Code

A concurrent implementation of *TCPtecho* improves the program in two ways. First, a concurrent implementation obtains a more accurate measure of the time required for each connection because it measures the throughput on all connections during the same time interval. Thus, congestion affects all connections equally. Second, a concurrent implementation makes *TCPtecho* more appealing to users. To understand why, look again at the times reported in the sample output for the second trial. The output message for machine *arthur* appears in a little over one half of a second, the message for machine *merlin* appears after about five seconds, and the final message, for *ector*, appears after about twelve seconds. If the user had to wait for all tests to run sequentially, the total execution would require approximately eighteen seconds. When measuring machines further away on the Internet, individual times can be substantially longer, making the concurrent version much faster. In many circumstances, using a sequential client implementation to measure *N* machines can take approximately *N* times longer than a concurrent version.

16.10 Summary

Concurrent execution provides a powerful tool that can be used in clients as well as servers. Concurrent client implementations can offer faster response time and can avoid deadlock problems. Finally, concurrency can help designers separate control and status processing from normal input and output.

We studied an example connection-oriented client that measures the time required to access the ECHO server on one or more machines. Because the client executes concurrently, it can avoid the differences in throughput caused by network congestion by making all measurements during the same time interval. The concurrent implementation also appeals to users because it overlaps the measurements instead of making the user wait to perform them sequentially.

EXERCISES

16.1   Notice that the example server checks ready file descriptors sequentially. If many descriptors become ready simultaneously, the server will handle the descriptors with lowest numbers first, and then iterate through the others. After handling all ready descriptors, it again calls *select* to wait until another descriptor becomes ready. Consider the time that elapses between handling a ready descriptor and calling *select*. Less time elapses after operations on descriptors with higher numbers than elapses after operations on descriptors with low numbers. Can the difference lead to starvation? Explain.

16.2   Modify the example server to avoid the unfairness discussed in the previous exercise.

16.3   For each of the iterative and concurrent client designs discussed in this chapter, write an expression that gives the maximum number of sockets used.

17

Tunneling At The Transport And Application Levels

17.1 Introduction

Previous chapters describe the design of client and server software for cases where a TCP/IP internet interconnects all communicating machines. Many of the designs presented assume that clients and servers will run on reasonably powerful computers that have operating system support for concurrent processes as well as full support for TCP/IP protocols.

This chapter begins to explore the techniques system managers and programmers use to exploit alternative topologies. In particular, it examines techniques that allow computers to use a high-level protocol service to carry IP traffic and designs that use IP to carry traffic for other protocol systems.

17.2 Multiprotocol Environments

In an ideal world, programmers using TCP/IP only need to build client and server software for computers that connect directly to a TCP/IP internet and provide full support for TCP/IP protocols. In reality, however, not all machines provide complete TCP/IP support, and not all organizations use TCP/IP exclusively to interconnect computers. For example, an organization may have small personal computers with insufficient capacity to run server software, or it may have groups of machines connected to networks that use protocols like *DECNET*, *SNA*, or *X.25*. In fact, networking in most organizations has grown over time as the organization has added new networks to interconnect existing groups of computers. Usually, network managers choose a hardware technology and a protocol suite for each group of computers independently. They use factors such as cost, distance, desired speed, and vendor availability when making a choice. Organizations that installed networks before TCP/IP protocols were available may have selected a vendor-specific protocol suite. As a result of such network evolution, most large organizations have several groups of machines, with each group using its own protocol suite. The point is:

> *Because networking has evolved slowly over many years, because vendors promoted proprietary network systems, and because TCP/IP was not always available, large organizations often have groups of computers using alternative protocol systems to communicate. Furthermore, to minimize expense, organizations often continue to use older network systems until they can phase in new technologies.*

For example, Figure 17.1 illustrates an organization that uses three networks at its two sites. Each site has its own Ethernet. A single wide area network that uses X.25 protocols interconnects hosts at the two sites. As the figure shows, a subset of machines connect to each network.

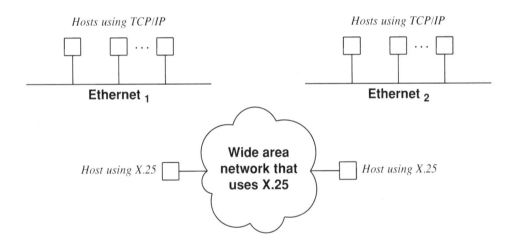

Figure 17.1 An example organization with three networks. All computers connected to the wide area network use the X.25 protocol while all computers connected to the local area networks use TCP/IP.

The chief disadvantages of having multiple network systems arise from duplication of effort and limitations on interoperability. Hosts that connect to an X.25 wide area network must use X.25 protocols instead of TCP/IP protocols. Thus, if a client and server run on hosts connected to the X.25 network shown in Figure 17.1, they must use an X.25 virtual circuit for communication. Meanwhile, clients and servers running on an Ethernet use TCP virtual circuits.

17.3 Mixing Network Technologies

Usually, a TCP/IP internet consists of a set of hosts on physical networks interconnected by gateways (routers). All hosts and gateways in the internet must use TCP/IP protocols. Similarly, a network running the DECNET protocols consists of physical links and computers that use DECNET exclusively, while a network running SNA protocols usually consists of physical links and computers that use SNA exclusively. However, because a transport-level service can deliver packets from one point to another as easily as packet-switching hardware can, it should be possible to substitute any transport-level switching service in place of a single physical link in another packet switching system.

Many internets have been built that use transport-level switching services instead of physical networks. For example, consider the networks shown in Figure 17.1 again. Assume the organization decides to interconnect its two Ethernets to form a single TCP/IP internet that will allow all the hosts attached to the Ethernets to communicate. The most obvious strategy involves installing two gateways between them. However, if a large geographic distance separates the two Ethernets, the cost of adding a dedicated leased line to interconnect the two networks may be prohibitive. The additional cost may be especially difficult to justify because the organization already has an X.25 network connecting the two sites.

Figure 17.2 illustrates how the organization shown in Figure 17.1 can use existing X.25 network connectivity to provide a TCP/IP internet connection between its two sites.

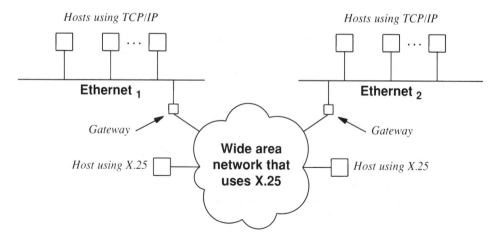

Figure 17.2 IP gateways using an X.25 transport-level service in place of a physical network.

The organization installs a new gateway at each site. Each of the new gateways connects to the X.25 network and to the local Ethernet at its site. When the gateways boot, they use X.25 to form a conventional, transport-level virtual circuit to one another across the X.25 wide area network. Each gateway arranges its routing table so it routes nonlocal traffic across the X.25 circuit. The gateways use the X.25 protocol to send IP datagrams to one another. From the viewpoint of the gateways, X.25 merely provides a link over which datagrams can be sent. From the viewpoint of the X.25 network, IP software on the two gateways acts exactly like application software on other hosts. The X.25 service does not know that the data being sent across the virtual circuit consists of IP datagrams.

With the two gateways in place, a user on any host can invoke standard TCP/IP client software that contacts a server on any other host. Client-server interactions may cross a single Ethernet or may traverse the X.25 network to reach the other site. Neither the user nor the client-server applications needs to know that datagrams pass across an X.25 network when they travel from the Ethernet at one site to the Ethernet at the other. The two Ethernets merely form part of a TCP/IP internet. Furthermore, hosts using X.25 protocols on the wide area network do not need to change. They can continue to communicate without interference from the TCP/IP traffic because the virtual circuits they use will remain independent of the new connection between the gateways.

17.4 Dynamic Circuit Allocation

In the example topology that Figure 17.2 illustrates, the TCP/IP internet traffic needs only one X.25 virtual circuit through the X.25 network because the organization only has two sites. If the organization expands by adding additional sites, it can extend the topology by placing a gateway at each new site and creating additional circuits through the X.25 network to interconnect each new gateway to the gateways at existing sites.

The static scheme for circuits described above cannot expand to an arbitrary number of sites because most X.25 networks limit the number of circuits that a single computer can allocate simultaneously. Typically, the hardware limits a machine to *16* or *32* virtual circuits. An organization with N sites needs $(N*(N-1))/2$ circuits to interconnect all of them. Thus, a gateway needs *15* connections for *6* sites, and exceeds *32* connections when the organization reaches *9* sites.

Of course, it is possible to add additional gateways so that each individual gateway does not need a circuit to all destinations. However, to limit costs, most sites that use X.25 to transport datagrams take a different approach – they allocate circuits on demand and close circuits that are not being used. When a datagram arrives at a gateway, the gateway looks up the destination address to determine the route the datagram will follow. The routing lookup produces a *next-hop address*, the address of the next gateway to which the datagram should be sent. If the next hop address specifies a remote site, the gateway consults its table of active X.25 virtual circuits. If a circuit exists to the next-hop, the gateway forwards the datagram across the circuit. If no circuit exists, the gateway opens a new circuit to the desired destination dynamically.

If the gateway does not have an unused circuit when it needs to open a new circuit, the gateway must close an existing circuit to make one available. The problem becomes one of choosing which circuit to close. Usually, a gateway follows the same policy that a demand paging system uses: it closes the *least recently used* (LRU) circuit. After sending its datagram across the new circuit, the gateway leaves the circuit open. Often the outgoing datagrams will cause the receiver to reply, so keeping the circuit open helps minimize delay and cost.

By dynamically opening and closing virtual circuits, a gateway can limit the number of simultaneous connections it needs without losing the ability to communicate with all sites. The gateway only needs to have one circuit open for each site with which communication is currently in progress.

17.5 Encapsulation And Tunneling

The term *encapsulation* describes the process of placing an IP datagram inside a network packet or frame so that it can be sent across an underlying network. Encapsulation refers to how the network interface uses packet switching hardware. For example, two hosts that communicate across an Ethernet using IP encapsulate each datagram in a single Ethernet packet for transmission. The encapsulation standard for TCP/IP specifies that an IP datagram occupies the data portion of the Ethernet packet and that the Ethernet packet type must be set to a value that specifies IP.

By contrast, the term *tunneling* refers to the use of a high-level transport network service to carry packets or messages from another service. The example in Figure 17.2 shows that gateways can tunnel through an X.25 service to send IP datagrams to one another. The key difference between tunneling and encapsulation lies in whether IP transmits datagrams in hardware packets or uses a high-level transport service to deliver them.

> *IP encapsulates each datagram in a packet when it uses the hardware directly. It creates a tunnel when it uses a high-level transport delivery service to send datagrams from one point to another.*

17.6 Tunneling Through An IP Internet

After TCP/IP was first defined, researchers experimented to see how they could make IP software tunnel through existing networks (like X.25) to deliver datagrams. The motivation should be clear: many organizations had existing networks in place. Surprisingly, the trend has turned around. Most tunneling now occurs because vendors use IP protocols to deliver packets from non-TCP/IP protocols.

Understanding the change in tunneling requires us to understand a change in networking. As TCP/IP became popular, the TCP/IP internet became the universal packet delivery mechanism for many groups. In fact, IP now provides the widest connectivity among the computers at most organizations.

To see how the availability of IP affects other protocols, suppose two computers in an organization need to communicate using a vendor-specific protocol. Instead of adding additional physical network connections between the two computers, a manager can think of the organization's IP internet as a large network, and can allow the protocol software on the two computers to exchange messages by sending them in IP datagrams. Software is currently available that uses IP to carry IPX traffic (Novell), SNA traffic (IBM), and traffic from other high-level protocols. In addition, researchers have devised ways to allow IP networks to carry OSI traffic, allowing vendors to build and debug high-level OSI protocols before they have working implementations of lower layers.

17.7 Application-Level Tunneling Between Clients And Servers

Although the general notion of tunneling refers to the use of one transport-level protocol suite by another, programmers can extend the idea to client-server interactions. The programmer can use *application-level tunneling* to provide a communication path between a client and a server.

To understand how application-level tunneling works, think of two computers that attach to an X.25 network. Suppose a programmer wishes to run a UDP client application on one and a UDP server application on the other. Often, application programmers cannot make changes to the operating system software because they are only permitted to build application programs. Therefore, if the operating systems on the two computers do not support TCP/IP protocols and transport-level tunneling, a programmer may find it inconvenient or impossible to use UDP or to make IP datagrams tunnel through the X.25 network.

In such cases, application-level tunneling makes it possible for clients and servers to communicate across an X.25 network. To do so, the programmer must build a library of procedures that simulates the socket interface. The simulation library must allow an application to create an active or passive UDP socket and to send or receive UDP datagrams. Procedures in the socket simulation library translate calls to the standard socket routines (e.g., *socket*, *send*, and *receive*) into operations that allocate and manipulate local data structures and transmit the message across the X.25 network. When the client calls *socket* to create a socket, the *socket* library routine creates an X.25 connection to the server. When the client or server calls *send* to transmit a message, the *send* library routine transfers the UDP datagram across the X.25 connection.

Once a socket simulation library has been created, programmers can compile any UDP client or server program, link the compiled program using the simulation library, and then run the resulting application. Figure 17.3 illustrates the resulting software structure.

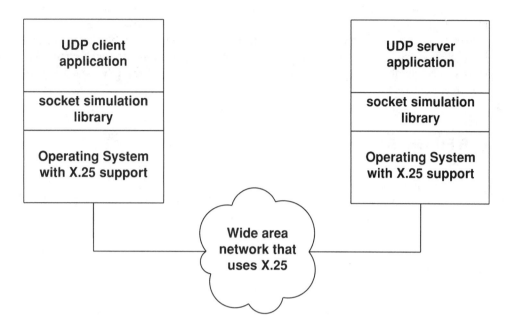

Figure 17.3 Conceptual organization of software in a client and server using application-level tunneling through an X.25 network. The socket simulation library allows the client and server to exchange UDP datagrams across a non-TCP/IP transport service.

17.8 Summary

Tunneling consists of sending packets between computers using a transport-level packet delivery system instead of sending them directly across physical networks. Early work on tunneling IP through existing network systems was motivated by organizations that already had large wide area networks in place. These organizations wanted to avoid the cost of adding new physical connections to run IP. Researchers devised ways to allow IP to use the existing networks to transfer packets without changing the networks. IP treats the transport service as a single hardware link; the transport service treats IP traffic the same as traffic sent by any application.

IP has become the delivery system that provides the most interoperability. Consequently, current work on tunneling concentrates on finding ways to use IP as a packet delivery system that carries packets for other network protocols. Many vendors have announced software that enables their proprietary networking systems to communicate across an underlying IP internet.

Programmers can apply the idea of tunneling to application software by building a library that simulates a socket interface but uses a non-TCP/IP transport service to deliver messages. In particular, it is easy to build a socket simulation library that allows clients and servers to communicate using UDP, even if the only connection between the client and server computers consists of a transport-level switching system like an X.25 network.

FOR FURTHER STUDY

Comer and Korb [1983] describes how to tunnel IP through an X.25 network, including how to manage X.25 virtual circuits when the hardware imposes a fixed limit on simultaneous connections. RFC 877 gives the technical encoding details.

EXERCISES

17.1   Read RFC 877. How does a gateway that tunnels through an X.25 network map a destination IP address to an equivalent X.25 address?

17.2   Many transport-level services use their own retransmission scheme to provide reliable delivery. What can happen if both TCP and the underlying network protocols retransmit messages?

17.3   We said that a gateway uses dynamic virtual circuit allocation to tunnel through X.25, and that it usually applies an LRU heuristic when it needs to close an existing circuit to make one available. Explain what happens in a gateway if its X.25 interface allows K simultaneous circuits and the gateway attempts to communicate with $K+1$ other sites simultaneously.

17.4   Build a socket simulation library that allows client and server applications to exchange UDP datagrams over a non-TCP/IP transport-level protocol. Test it by arranging for a UDP ECHO client to communicate with a UDP ECHO server.

18

Application Level Gateways

18.1 Introduction

The previous chapter examines tunneling, a technique that allows one protocol suite to use the transport-level delivery service from another protocol suite in place of a physical network. From an application programmer's viewpoint, tunneling makes it possible for a client and server to communicate using TCP/IP even if the only path between them includes a non-TCP/IP network.

This chapter continues the exploration of techniques that clients and servers use to communicate across environments that do not provide full TCP/IP connectivity. It shows how clients operating on systems with limited protocol support can use an application program on an intermediate machine to forward requests, and how the use of such intermediaries can expand the range of available services.

18.2 Clients And Servers In Constrained Environments

18.2.1 The Reality Of Multiple Technologies

Not all computer systems have direct access to a TCP/IP internet. Furthermore, access limitations can complicate client and server software because they arise for economic and political reasons as well as technical ones. Chapter *17* points out that networking has evolved slowly in many organizations. As a result, subgroups may each have their own network and the networks may each use a different protocol suite. More important, a group of users may become accustomed to the application software available from a particular vendor or a particular computer. If the application software only operates with one set of protocols, the users may want to keep the network in place.

Network technologies can also gain inertia as managers gain expertise. As a technology becomes entrenched, an organization invests in training for personnel who install, manage, or operate the network. In addition to people who plan and manage the physical network, programmers invest time learning how to write software that uses the network. Once a manager learns the details and subtleties of a given technology, it becomes easier to expand the existing network than to replace it with a new technology. Thus, organizations that have multiple groups, each managing an independent network, often find that the initial cost of consolidation can be high because many groups must retrain their personnel.

For programmers, multiple network technologies often result in incompatible systems that do not provide interoperability. Unless the organization provides tunneling, programmers cannot depend on end-to-end transport-level connectivity. Thus, they cannot use a single transport protocol, nor can they easily communicate between clients and servers on arbitrary machines. Finally, programmers often build and maintain programs that duplicate functionality for each network technology. For example, programmers must maintain multiple electronic mail systems.

18.2.2 Computers With Limited Functionality

In addition to contending with multiple networks, programmers must sometimes create software for computers that offer limited network functionality. For example, many organizations have groups of small personal computers that lack operating system facilities for concurrent processing or asynchronous I/O. Such computers cannot support the concurrent server algorithms discussed in Chapter 8 or the concurrent client algorithms discussed in Chapter 15.

18.2.3 Connectivity Constraints That Arise From Security

Organizations may institute security policies that also constrain how clients and servers communicate. Some organizations partition computers into *secure* and *unsecure* subsets. To prevent client and server programs from compromising security, the network manager places policy constraints on connectivity. The manager restrains computers in the secure partition so they can communicate among themselves, but they can neither initiate contact to servers nor accept requests from clients on computers in the unsecure partition. Although such policies ensure security, they can make it difficult for programmers to design applications that use client-server interactions. In particular, computers in one partition cannot directly access services available on computers in the other partition.

18.3 Using Application Gateways

Programmers who need to design client-server interactions in restricted environments usually rely on a single, powerful technique to overcome connectivity constraints.
The technique consists of adding application programs that run on intermediate
machines, and enabling the applications to relay information between a client and the
desired server. An intermediate program that provides such service is known as an *application gateway*†. If the intermediate machine has been dedicated to running one particular application gateway program, programmers or network managers sometimes
refer to the machine as a *gateway machine*. For example, a computer dedicated to running a program that passes electronic mail between two groups may be called a *mail
gateway*. Technically, of course, the term *application gateway* refers to the running
program – programmers stretch the terminology when they refer to a machine as an application gateway.

Figure 18.1 illustrates a common use of an application gateway as an intermediary
between two electronic mail systems.

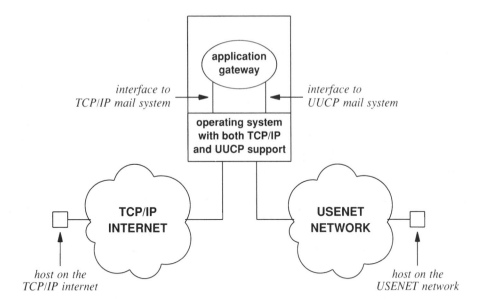

Figure 18.1 An application program used to pass electronic mail between two
network systems. The application gateway understands the syn-
tax and semantics of both mail systems, and translates messages
between them.

---

†Use of the term *gateway* is unfortunate because IP uses the term to refer to computers that route datagrams. To avoid confusion, one should always distinguish the two carefully.

The organization depicted in Figure 18.1 has access to two main network systems: the USENET network and a TCP/IP internet. Each network system has its own electronic mail system. In a broad conceptual sense, the two mail systems provide the same services. Each system allows a user to compose and transmit an outgoing message or to receive and read an incoming message. However, the two systems cannot interoperate directly because each has its own destination address syntax and its own mail transport protocol.

To allow users on one network system to send mail to users on the other, the organization has installed an application program that serves as a mail gateway. In the example, the mail gateway program runs on a computer that attaches to both networks. The mail gateway must be designed carefully so it can communicate with any host in the organization. It must understand how to send messages using either of the two mail systems, and it must have logical connections to both networks.

18.4 Interoperability Through A Mail Gateway

For the organization shown in Figure 18.1, a single mail gateway program can provide all the facilities the organization needs to establish interoperability for electronic mail. As usual, each host throughout the organization checks the destination address of outgoing mail, and chooses a next-hop machine. If an outgoing memo is destined for a machine on the same network as the sending machine, the sending machine uses the electronic mail system available on its local network to deliver the message. However, if a host encounters outgoing mail destined for a machine that attaches to a nonlocal network, the sending machine cannot deliver the message directly. Instead, the sender transmits the message to the mail gateway program. All machines can reach the mail gateway directly because it runs on a computer that attaches to both networks and communicates using either of the two mail delivery protocols.

Once a memo arrives at the mail gateway, it must be routed again. The mail gateway examines the destination mail address to determine how to proceed. It may also consult a database of destinations to help make the decision. Once it knows the intended destination and the network over which it must deliver the message, the mail gateway selects the appropriate network and mail transport protocols.

The gateway may need to reformat a mail message or change the message header when forwarding it from one network to another. In particular, a mail gateway usually modifies the reply field in the mail header so the receiver's mail interface can correctly construct a reply address. The reply address modification may be trivial (e.g., adding a suffix that identifies the sender's network), or it may be complicated (e.g., adding information that identifies the mail gateway as an intermediate machine that will lead back to the source).

18.5 Implementation Of A Mail Gateway

In theory, a single process suffices to implement a mail gateway. In practice, however, most implementations divide the functionality into two processes. One process handles incoming mail messages, while the other manages outgoing mail. The process that handles incoming mail never sends a message. It computes a reply address, routes the mail to its destination, and then deposits the outgoing message in a queue to await transmission. The process that handles outgoing messages does not accept incoming messages directly. Instead, it scans the output queue periodically. For each message it finds in the output queue, the output process makes a network connection to the destination, and sends the message. If it cannot make a connection to the destination (e.g., because the destination machine has crashed), the output process leaves the message in the output queue and continues processing with the next message in the queue. Later, when it rescans the queue, the output process will try again to contact the destination and deliver the message. If a message remains in the output queue for an extended time (e.g., three days), the output process reports a delivery error to the user who originally sent the message.

Separating the mail gateway into input and output components allows each component to proceed independently. The output process can try to deliver a message, wait to see if the connection attempt succeeds, and then go on to the next message without coordinating its activities with those of the input process. If the connection attempt succeeds, the output process can send a message without regard to its length. It does not need to interrupt transmission to accept incoming messages because the input process handles them. Meanwhile, the input process can continue to accept incoming messages, route them, and store them for later transmission. Because the components operate independently, a long output message does not block input processing, nor does a long input message interfere with output processing.

18.6 A Comparison Of Application Gateways And Tunneling

The previous chapter showed that designers could choose tunneling to provide interoperability in a heterogeneous environment. It may be difficult to choose between tunneling and application gateways because neither technique solves all problems well and each technique provides advantages in some situations.

The chief advantage of using an application gateway instead of tunneling arises because programmers can create application gateways without modifying the computer's operating system. In many circumstances, programmers cannot modify the system either because they do not have access to the source code or because they do not have the expertise required. An application gateway can be built using conventional programming tools; the gateway does not require any change to the underlying protocol software. Furthermore, once an application gateway is in place, the site can use standard client and server programs.

Using application gateways has a secondary advantage: it allows all existing network systems to continue operation undisturbed. Managers do not need to learn about new network technologies, nor do they need to change any physical network connections. Similarly, users do not need to learn a new interface for services; each user continues to use existing client software associated with the networks to which they are accustomed.

Application gateways do have some disadvantages. The application gateway technique requires programmers to construct a separate application gateway program for each service. A mail gateway interconnects the mail services of two separate systems, but does not supply remote file access or remote login capabilities. Each time the organization adds a new service to its network systems, programmers must construct a new application gateway that interconnects the new service between multiple networks.

Application gateways may also require additional hardware resources. The organization may need to purchase new computers, or it may need to add network connections to existing computers. Adding new network connections may mean acquiring additional software as well as additional hardware. Because the translation required when forwarding a message or data can be complex, application gateways can use large amounts of CPU or memory. Thus, it may be necessary for an organization to purchase additional computers or upgrade existing machines to handle the load as it adds new services. The demand for CPU resources also introduces computational delay, which adds to the delay between the client and server. If the delay becomes too long, clients may timeout and resend a message.

In contrast to the application gateway approach, tunneling does not require any changes when new services appear. Once in place, a transport-level tunnel becomes part of the underlying network structure. Because applications remain unaware of the tunnel, it can be used for any application service. Tunneling also provides uniformity because it means the organization can use a single transport protocol.

Tunneling does have some disadvantages when compared to the application gateway solution. To install a transport-level tunnel that provides full functionality, the site must modify the operating system that runs on the gateway connecting the two network systems. Surprisingly, the organization may also need to modify software on hosts that use the tunnel. To understand how the need for modifications arises, imagine an X.25 network configured to serve as a tunnel for IP traffic. Consider a host connected to the network. Before an application can use the IP tunnel, it must have access to TCP/IP protocol software, and the IP software must know how to tunnel datagrams through the X.25 network. Thus, the host operating system must supply an IP interface (i.e., a socket-level interface) for application programs and must route traffic across the tunnel. If the operating system does not contain TCP/IP protocol software, it must be added. If existing IP protocol software does not know how to route through a tunnel, it must be changed.

Tunneling can also have a dramatic impact on users. Organizations adopt tunneling as a way to provide uniform transport services over heterogeneous networks. Once the organization establishes a tunnel, all hosts can begin using a single transport protocol for client-server interactions. For example, if an organization chooses to use IP and creates a tunnel through an X.25 network to provide connectivity, computers throughout the organization can use TCP/IP for transport connections. As an immediate consequence, all computers can support client-server interactions that use TCP/IP.

Unfortunately, a change in the underlying network protocols usually results in changes to client software with which users interact. Most organizations purchase commercially available client software for standard applications like electronic mail. Thus, the organization must use whatever software is available for a given transport protocol. If the organization adopts a universal transport protocol, it must purchase new client software that uses the new protocol suite. From the user's point of view, changing to the new software means learning a new interface. Unless the new interface offers all the functionality of the existing interface, users may be dissatisfied.

To avoid changing the users' environment, many organizations choose the application gateway solution. Programmers construct the application gateway carefully so it does not require changes to the user interface on any network. For example, after an organization adds an application gateway for electronic mail, users can use the old client software to send and receive mail. The mail system can use the destination address syntax to distinguish between messages sent to local destinations and those sent to foreign networks. Doing so allows users to use old addresses for local destinations, and only requires them to learn new addresses for new destinations.

18.7 Application Gateways And Limited Functionality Systems

Application gateways can increase the range of services accessible from small computers. For example, consider the network of personal computers shown in Figure 18.2.

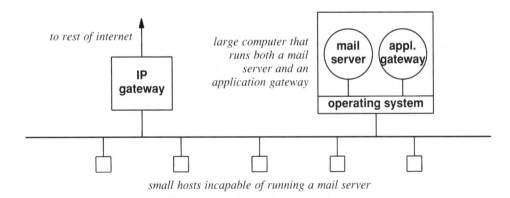

Figure 18.2 A network of personal computers incapable of running a concurrent mail server and the application gateway that they use to receive electronic mail.

The operating systems on small personal computers often provide limited facilities that do not include support for concurrent processing. The lack of concurrent processing limits client-server interactions because the computer must be dedicated to a single task at any time. In particular, it is often impossible for a user to run a server in the background while using the computer for other processing.

To understand how the lack of background processing limits client-server interaction, consider electronic mail. A personal computer can support mail client software because it can wait until the user decides to send a message before executing client software. Furthermore, once the user composes a message, the client program can make the user wait while it transmits the message to its destination. However, a computer system that does not support concurrent processing cannot run server software in the background. Thus, it cannot have a server ready to accept incoming mail until the user decides to run the server. Unfortunately, users cannot run any other application while the mail server operates because the machine must stop receiving mail while performing any other task. As a result, users seldom use such computers to run electronic mail servers.

An organization that has many personal computers can use an application gateway to solve the server problem. Consider the computers in Figure 18.2 again. The organization has purchased one large, powerful computer on which it runs a standard server that accepts incoming electronic mail. The server, which runs in the background, remains available to accept mail at all times. When a message arrives, the server places it in a file on disk. Files that store mail are often called *mailbox files* or *mailboxes*. The system may have one mailbox file for each user, or may place each message in a separate file. Usually, implementations that use a separate file for each message collect the files together into directories, where each directory corresponds to a single user.

In addition to the standard mail server, the computer must also run a specialized application gateway that allows users on personal computers to access their mailboxes. To read mail, a user on one of the personal computers invokes a client that contacts the special application gateway. The gateway retrieves each message from the user's mailbox, and sends it to the personal computer for the user to read.

Using a powerful machine to run a conventional server that accepts incoming mail solves the server problem because it means that small personal computers do not need to run a mail server continuously. Using a mail gateway program to provide users with access to their mailboxes eliminates the need for users to log into the mail server machine.

18.8 Application Gateways Used For Security

Many organizations choose application gateways to solve the problem of security. For example, suppose an organization needs to restrict remote login. Imagine that the organization classifies its employees as either authorized or unauthorized for remote login. Figure 18.3 illustrates how the organization can use an application gateway to implement its security policy.

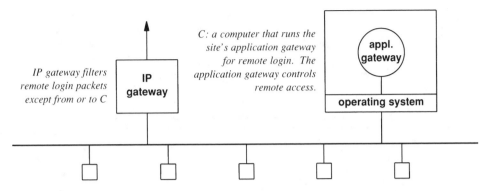

conventional hosts prohibited from sending remote login packets except through application gateway

Figure 18.3 An application gateway used to implement a remote login security policy. A user must communicate with remote machines
through the application gateway which enforces authorization
controls.

The organization depicted in the figure uses a conventional IP gateway filter to block all
datagrams that contain remote login connection requests unless they originate from the
host that runs the application gateway. To form a remote login connection, a user on
any host in the organization invokes a client that first connects to the application gateway. After the user obtains authorization, the application gateway connects the user to
the desired destination.

18.9 Application Gateways And The Extra Hop Problem

The *extra hop problem* refers to a situation in which datagrams pass across the
same network twice on their way to a final destination. The problem is usually caused
by incorrect routing tables.

Introduction of an application gateway into an existing network can also create a
form of the extra hop problem. To understand why, consider the network topology that
Figure 18.4a illustrates. The figure shows the path a message would travel from a host
to a remote server if the host supported the same transport protocol as the server. Now
assume that the existing host wishes to access a service that is only available through
some protocol other than the one the host uses. Interoperability can be achieved by introducing an application gateway as Figure 18.4b shows. The application gateway accepts requests using one protocol system and sends them to the remote server using
another. Unfortunately, each message traverses the network twice. The figure is realistic: network managers often acquire a new physical computer for each application gateway program because they want to avoid overloading existing machines.

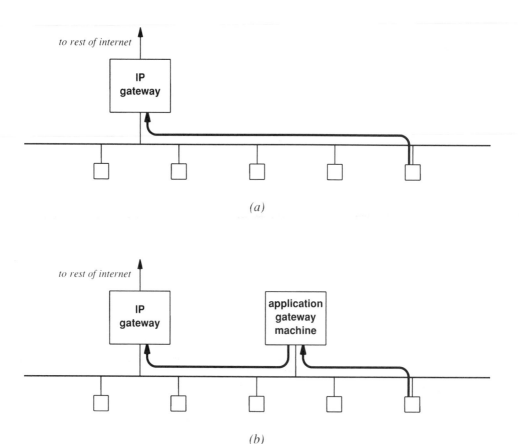

Figure 18.4 (a) A set of hosts and a gateway. The darkened arrow shows the
path a message takes from a host to a remote server and (b) the
path of a message after an application gateway is introduced.
The new gateway causes each message to traverse the network
twice.

Once the application gateway has been introduced, clients executing on existing
hosts use the application gateway to access the service it offers. A client sends its request to the application gateway using one protocol, which forwards the request on to
the remote server using another protocol. When the server returns its result to the application gateway, the gateway sends a response back to the client. The system appears to
work well. Existing protocol software on the hosts need not be changed. After the application gateway has been installed, a client executing on an arbitrary host will be able
to access the desired service through the gateway.

Unfortunately, close examination of the underlying network reveals that the configuration in Figure 18.4b does not make good use of network resources. It creates the extra hop problem. Each request must pass across the local area network twice: once when it travels from the original host to the application gateway machine, and once when it travels from the application gateway machine on toward the ultimate server. If the server lies in the TCP/IP internet beyond the IP gateway, the second transmission occurs when the message passes from the application gateway machine to the IP gateway. If the server lies on the local net, the second transmission occurs when the message passes from the application gateway machine to the machine running the server.

For services that do not require much network traffic, the extra hop may be unimportant. Indeed, several vendors build products that use the topology Figure 18.4b illustrates. If the network is heavily loaded, however, or if the service requires significant network traffic, the extra hop may make such a solution too expensive. Thus, designers need to calculate expected load carefully before they adopt the application gateway approach.

18.10 An Example Application Gateway

An application gateway can extend services by providing access to client machines that do not run all protocols. For example, consider a user on a host that has access to electronic mail but has no access to file transfer protocols like FTP. Such restrictions may arise from economic considerations (i.e., the cost of FTP software is too high), commercial realities (i.e., no one sells FTP client software for the computer in question), or security reasons (e.g., the site decides to reduce its security risk by prohibiting high-speed data transfer).

Suppose users on a restricted machine need access to the *Request For Comments* documents (RFCs). The application gateway technique can solve the access problem by allowing the organization to interconnect electronic mail and FTP services, while controlling access and ensuring authorization.

To provide RFC access from electronic mail, an application gateway must connect to both services. To use the gateway, a user must send the gateway an e-mail message that specifies the desired RFC. The application gateway verifies that the user is authorized to access RFCs, makes an FTP connection, obtains a copy of the RFC, and sends the RFC document back to the user in an e-mail message.

For example, imagine an application gateway located at e-mail address *rfc* on machine *somewhere.com*. Imagine that the application gateway accepts a mail message that mentions an RFC number on the subject line, uses FTP to retrieve that RFC, and mails the results back to the sender.

To use such a gateway, a user would create a mail message addressed to *rfc@somewhere.com*:

```
To: rfc@somewhere.com
From: user@elsewhere.edu
Subject: 791

Body of message (possibly empty).
```

This mail message requests RFC 791 from the application gateway. Because the gateway only looks at the number on the *Subject:* line, the text in the message body is irrelevant; it can be empty.

18.11 Implementation Of An Application Gateway

To implement the example application gateway described above, a programmer needs three facilities: a machine that has access to both electronic mail and FTP, a program that will act as the application gateway, and a mechanism that passes each incoming electronic mail message for a specified destination to the gateway program.

UNIX systems permit a system administrator to establish the necessary components easily. The administrator can create a special mail destination, *rfc*, by adding it to the e-mail alias file, or the administrator can create an account for a fictitious user named *rfc* and arrange to forward all mail for that user to a program. In fact, most UNIX systems allow an individual user to redirect their incoming e-mail to a program, so it is possible for a nonprivileged user to build and test an e-mail application gateway.

Among other tasks, the application gateway needs to retrieve an RFC. Our example implementation uses a separate program to retrieve an RFC document. The program, shown in file *rfc* below, is a UNIX shell script.

```
#! /bin/sh
#
# rfc:          retrieve an RFC document given its number
#
# operation:    check the local cache for a copy of the requested
#               document and use FTP to obtain a copy from the NIC if
#               none present.  Store a copy in the local cache when
#               retrieving from the NIC.
#
# method:       keep the local cache in directory /usr/tmp/RFC; use in-line
#               commands to invoke the ftp command.  Assume any file name that
#               ends in .Z contains a compressed file and run zcat to
#               decompress it.
#
HOST=nic.ddn.mil
PATH=/bin:/usr/bin:/usr/ucb
PUB=/usr/tmp/RFC
```

```
umask 022

if test  ! -d $PUB
then
        mkdir $PUB
        chmod 777 $PUB
fi
for i
do
        if test $i = "index"
        then
                i="-index"
        fi
        if test ! -r $PUB/$i -a ! -r $PUB/$i".Z" -o $i = "-index"
        then
            trap "rm -f $PUB/$i;
                echo int - $PUB/$i removed;exit 1" 1 2 3 13 15 24 25
                ftp -n ${HOST}  >/dev/null <<!
user anonymous guest
binary
get rfc/rfc$i.txt $PUB/$i
quit
!
                trap 1 2 3 13 15 24 25
        fi

        if test -r $PUB/$i
        then
                cat $PUB/$i
        elif test -r $PUB/$i".Z"
        then
                zcat $PUB/$i
        else
                echo Could not retrieve RFC $i
        fi
done
chmod 666 $PUB/-index >/dev/null 2>&1
```

The *rfc* script takes an argument that specifies either an RFC number or the word *index* (to denote the RFC index). It creates the needed FTP commands and then invokes the *ftp* program. The commands instruct *ftp* to open a connection to the Network Information Center and retrieve a copy of the specified RFC.

The *rfc* script is more complex than necessary because it contains an optimization. The code caches a copy of each RFC it retrieves in directory */usr/tmp/RFC*. Before it retrieves an RFC, *rfc* checks to see if a copy currently resides in the cache. If it does, the script retrieves the copy from the cache, avoiding unnecessary network traffic.

18.12 Code For The Application Gateway

Once the *rfc* script has been installed in a system, building an application gateway that accesses RFCs is straightforward. File *rfcd* contains the code. Like the *rfc* program above, it is a shell script. *Rfcd* uses the *rfc* program to retrieve an RFC document; it uses a conventional e-mail program (*/usr/ucb/mail*) to send the results back to the user who requested it.

```
#!/bin/sh
#
# rfcd:          an application gateway between e-mail and FTP
#
# operation:     receive an e-mail message, extract an RFC number from the
#                subject line, invoke a program that obtains a copy of the
#                RFC, and send it back to the user that sent the e-mail
#
# method:        use awk to parse the input, extract information, and form
#                a shell program; pipe the program directly into the shell
#                to execute it.
#
PATH=/bin:/usr/bin
RFCPROG=/usr/local/bin/rfc
awk "
    BEGIN       { fnd = 0 }

    /^From:/    { retaddr = substr(\$0, 6) ; next }

    /^Subject:/{ rfcnum = substr(\$0, 9) ; fnd++ ; next }

    /^ *\$/     { if (fnd==0 || rfcnum!~/^[0-9 ]*$/) exit
                cmd = \"\$RFCPROG \"rfcnum
                cmd = cmd \" | /usr/ucb/mail -s 'RFC \"rfcnum\" '\"
                cmd = cmd \" '\"retaddr\" '\"
                print cmd ; exit
                }" | /bin/sh
```

Although the details may seem complex to readers unfamiliar with shell scripts and the UNIX *awk* utility, it should be apparent that little programming effort was required to create the script.

In essence, the *rfcd* script reads a mail message and extracts the contents of the *From:* and *Subject:* lines. It uses an *awk* program to do most of the work. The *awk* program scans each line of the incoming mail message. It assumes the *Subject:* line contains an RFC number and the *From:* line contains the e-mail address of the sender. The sender's address becomes the destination when *rfcd* generates a reply.

Once the *awk* program in *rfcd* detects an empty line, it knows that it has reached the end of the mail headers. It stops processing and forms and prints a shell program. Because *rfcd* feeds the output of the *awk* program directly into the command interpreter (*sh*), the generated·program will be executed immediately.

If the incoming message contains a valid *Subject:* line in its headers, the generated program calls */usr/local/bin/rfc* to obtain the specified RFC and */usr/ucb/mail* to mail it back to whoever sent the request. If the mail message contains no subject or if the subject line contains anything other than digits or blanks, the *awk* program exits without generating any output. When the *awk* program exits early, *rfcd* does not attempt to obtain an RFC and does not send any mail (i.e., this version does not even send back an error message).

18.13 An Example Gateway Exchange

An example will clarify the steps. Suppose user *comer* decides to request RFC *1094*. *Comer* sends mail to the application gateway address, *rfc@somewhere.com*, specifying a *Subject:* line of *1094*. The message contains:

```
To: rfc@somewhere.com
From: comer
Subject: 1094

Body of message (possibly empty).
```

The mail system on *somewhere.com* has been configured to pass the incoming message to the *rfcd* script.

When *rfcd* runs, the *awk* code extracts *1094* from the *Subject:* line in the mail message and stores it in variable *rfcnum*. It extracts *comer* from the *From:* line and stores it in variable *retaddr*. When *rfcd* encounters the empty line that separates the header from the body of the message, it generates the following command line:

```
/usr/local/bin/rfc 1094 | /usr/ucb/mail -s 'RFC 1094' 'comer'
```

UNIX users will recognize this line as valid input to the UNIX command interpreter, *sh*. It specifies that the command interpreter should run the program in file
/usr/local/bin/rfc with argument *1094*, and then connect the output to the program in
file */usr/ucb/mail* using the UNIX *pipe* mechanism. The mail program has three arguments: *-s*, *RFC 1094*, and *comer*. The first two specify that the subject consists of the
string *RFC 1094*. The third argument specifies that the recipient is *comer*. The body of
the message consists of the RFC document retrieved by the *rfc* script.

Because *rfcd* sends the output of the *awk* program directly to the command interpreter, the command interpreter will execute the command line shown above. It will
run the *rfc* program, and then mail the results to user *comer*.

18.14 Using Rfcd With UNIX's .forward

An individual user can use his or her own e-mail account to test *rfcd*. To do so,
the user creates a file named *.forward* in his or her home directory. Each time the mail
system receives a message, it extracts the recipient's name from the *To:* field and examines that user's home directory for a *.forward* file. If it finds one, the mail system
reads the *.forward* file and honors the specification in it. For example, suppose a user
wishes the mailer to send each of his or her incoming messages to a program with the
full path name */usr/XXX/Q*. The user places a single line in his or her *.forward* file:

                              | "/usr/XXX/Q"

The mail system interprets this line to mean: *invoke program /usr/XXX/Q with the incoming mail message as standard input*. Thus, to invoke the e-mail application gateway shown above, a user must place the *rfcd* script in a file, make the file executable,
and make the *.forward* entry reference it. Of course, a user should not install a *.for-
ward* entry without testing the program it specifies or mail could be lost.

18.15 Summary

Although tunneling allows one protocol system to use another high-level protocol
as a transport device, tunneling is restricted to cases where the designer has access to
the operating system code. The application gateway technique, an alternative to tunneling, permits application programmers to interconnect heterogeneous systems without
changing the operating system.

An application gateway is a program that accepts requests using one high-level
protocol and fulfills requests using another high-level protocol. In essence, each application gateway is a server for one service and a client of another.

We examined an application gateway that accepts a request for an RFC from an
electronic mail message, uses FTP to obtain the specified RFC, and returns the RFC to
the original requester using electronic mail. The example shows that application gate-

ways need not be complex nor written in a low-level language. Our example code consists of a UNIX shell script and an *awk* program.

Many sites use application gateways to implement authorization and security checks. Because the gateway operates as a conventional application program, little effort is required to program the gateway to filter unwanted access or to keep a record of all requests.

FOR FURTHER STUDY

More information on the UNIX shell and the *awk* programming language can be found in the documentation that accompanies the operating system. Aho, Kernighan, and Weinberger [1988] describes *awk* programming in detail. Bolsky and Korn [1989] describes a more advanced UNIX shell and shows examples of shell programs.

The BSD UNIX program *sendmail* handles e-mail transfers over a variety of transport protocols; it can be configured to act as an application gateway. Information on *sendmail* can be found in the *UNIX Programmer's Manual*.

EXERCISES

18.1   Add authorization checks to the example application gateway in this chapter that permit a system administrator to limit access.

18.2   Add a logging mechanism to the example application gateway in this chapter that accumulates a list of all users who request RFCs.

18.3   How can a sender request a copy of the RFC index through the application gateway in this chapter?

18.4   Observe that if a user invokes the *rfc* script to request an RFC at exactly the same time the application gateway is using it to request the same RFC, the user may obtain an empty or partial file. Modify the script to correct this weakness.

18.5   How does the *sendmail* system permit a system administrator to establish an application gateway?

19

External Data Representation (XDR)

19.1 Introduction

Previous chapters describe algorithms, mechanisms, and implementation techniques for client and server programs. This chapter begins a discussion of the concepts and techniques that help programmers use the client-server paradigm and the mechanisms that provide programming support for these concepts. In particular, it examines a *de facto* standard for external data representation and presentation as well as a set of library procedures used to perform data conversion.

This chapter describes the general motivations for using an external data representation and the details of one particular implementation. The next chapter shows how an external data representation standard helps simplify client and server communication, and illustrates how a standard makes it possible to use a single, uniform remote access mechanism for client-server communication.

19.2 Representations For Data In Computers

Each computer architecture provides its own definition for the representation of data. Some computers store the least significant byte of an integer at the lowest memory address, others store the most significant byte at the lowest address, and others do not store bytes contiguously in memory. For example, Figure 19.1 shows the two most popular representations for 32-bit integers.

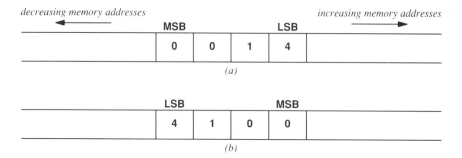

Figure 19.1 Two representations for the value *260* stored as a 32-bit binary
integer: (a) "big endian" order with the most significant byte at
the lowest memory address and (b) "little endian" order with
the least significant byte at the lowest memory address.
Numbers give the decimal value of each 8-bit byte.

Programmers who write programs for a single computer do not need to think about
data representation because a given computer usually only permits one representation.
When a programmer declares a variable to be an integer (e.g., by using Pascal's *integer*
declaration or C's *int* declaration), the compiler uses the computer's *native data
representation* when it allocates storage for the integer or when it generates code to
fetch, store, or compare values.

Programmers who create client and server software must contend with data
representation, however, because both endpoints must agree on the exact representation
for all data sent across the communication channel between them. If the native data
representations on two machines differ, data sent from a program on one machine to a
program on the other must be converted.

19.3 The N-Squared Conversion Problem

The central issue underlying data representation is software portability. At one extreme, a programmer could choose to embed knowledge of the computers' architecture
in each client-server pair so the client and server agree on which side will convert the
data. Designs that convert directly from the client's representation to the server's
representation use *asymmetric data conversion* because one side or the other performs
conversion. Unfortunately, using asymmetric data conversion means that the programmer must write a different version of the client-server pair for each pair of architectures
on which they will be used.

To understand why building separate client-server pairs for each architecture combination can be costly, consider a set of *N* computers. If each computer uses a different
data representation to store floating point numbers, a programmer must construct a total
of

$$(N^2 - N) / 2$$

versions of any client-server program that exchanges floating point values. We call this the *n-squared conversion problem†* to emphasize that the programming effort is proportional to the square of the number of different data representations.

Another way to view the n-squared conversion problem is to imagine the effort required to add a new architecture to an existing set of N machines. Each time a new computer arrives, the programmer must build N new versions of each client-server pair before the new computer can interoperate with each of the existing computers.

Even if the programmer uses conditional compilation (e.g., the C preprocessor's *ifdef* construct), creating, testing, maintaining, and managing N^2 versions of a program can be difficult. Furthermore, users may need to distinguish among versions when they invoke a client. To summarize:

> *If client-server software is designed to convert from the client's native data representation directly to the server's native data representation asymmetrically, the number of versions of the software grows as the square of the number of architectures.*

To avoid the problems inherent in maintaining N-squared versions of a client-server program, programmers try to avoid asymmetric data conversion. Instead, they write client and server software in such a way that each source program can be compiled and executed on a variety of machines without change. Doing so makes programming easier because it results in a highly portable program. It also makes accessing a service easier because users only need to remember how to invoke one version of the client.

19.4 Network Standard Byte Order

How can a single source program compile and execute correctly on a variety of architectures if the architectures use multiple representations for data? More important, how can a client or server program send data to a program on another machine if the two machines use a different data representation? Chapter 5 describes how TCP/IP solves the representation problem for simple integer data by using functions that convert from the computer's native byte order to a network standard byte order and vice versa.

Conceptually, the use of a standard representation for data sent across a network in protocol headers means the TCP/IP protocol software employs *symmetric data conversion*. Both ends perform the required conversion. As a result, only one version of the protocol software is needed because all protocol headers represent data in a standard, machine-independent form.

Most programmers adopt the same symmetric data conversion technique when they build client-server application software. Instead of converting directly from one machine's representation to the other's, both client and server perform a data conver-

---

†Some literature refers to the problem as the $n * m$ problem to emphasize that clients can operate on n architectures while servers can operate on m architectures.

sion. Before sending across the network, they convert data from the sending computer's native representation into a standard, machine-independent representation. Likewise, they convert from the machine-independent representation to the receiving computer's native representation after receiving data from the network. The standard representation used for data traversing the network is known as the *external data representation.*

Using a standard external data representation has both advantages and disadvantages. The chief advantage lies in flexibility: neither the client nor the server needs to understand the architecture of the other. A single client can contact a server on an arbitrary machine without knowing the machine architecture. The total programming effort required will be proportional to the number of machine architectures instead of the square of that number.

The chief disadvantage of symmetric conversion is computational overhead. In cases where the client and server both operate on computers that have the same architecture, the cost seems unwarranted. One end converts all data from the native architecture's representation to the external representation before sending it, and the other end converts from the external representation back to the original representation after receiving it.

Even if the client and server machines do not share a common architecture, using an intermediate form introduces additional computation. Instead of converting directly from the sender's representation to the receiver's, the client and server must each spend CPU time converting between their local representations and the external representation. Furthermore, because the external representation may add information to the data or align it on word boundaries, the conversion may result in a larger stream of bytes than necessary.

Despite the additional overhead and network bandwidth required, most programmers agree that using symmetric conversion is worthwhile. It simplifies programming, reduces errors, and increases interoperability among programs. It also makes network management and debugging easier because the network manager can interpret the contents of packets without knowing the architectures of the sending and receiving machines.

19.5 A De Facto Standard External Data Representation

Sun Microsystems, Incorporated devised an external data representation that specifies how to represent common forms of data when transferring data across a network. Known by the initials *XDR*, Sun's *eXternal Data Representation* has become a *de facto* standard for most client-server applications.

XDR specifies data formats for most of the data types that clients and servers exchange. For example, XDR specifies that 32-bit binary integers should be represented in "big endian" order (i.e., with the most significant byte in the lowest memory address).

19.6 XDR Data Types

The table in Figure 19.2 lists the data types for which XDR defines a standard representation.

Data Type	Size	Description
int	32 bits	32-bit signed binary integer
unsigned int	32-bits	32-bit unsigned binary integer
bool	32 bits	Boolean value (*false* or *true*) represented by *0* or *1*
enum	arb.	Enumeration type with values defined by integers (e.g., *RED=1, WHITE=2, BLUE=3*)
hyper	64 bits	64-bit signed binary integer
unsigned hyper	64-bits	64-bit unsigned binary integer
float	32 bits	Single precision floating point number
double	64 bits	Double precision floating point number
opaque	arb.	Unconverted data (i.e., data in the sender's native representation)
string	arb.	String of ASCII characters
fixed array	arb.	A fixed-size array of any other data type
counted array	arb.	Array in which the type has a fixed upper limit, but individual arrays may vary up to that size
structure	arb.	A data aggregate, like C's *struct*
discriminated union	arb.	A data structure that allows one of several alternative forms, like C's *union* or Pascal's variant record
void	0	Used if no data is present where a data item is optional (e.g., in a structure)
symbolic constant	arb.	A symbolic constant and associated value
optional data	arb.	Allows zero or one occurrences of an item

Figure 19.2 The types for which XDR defines an external representation. The standard specifies how data items for each type should be encoded when sent across a network.

The types in Figure 19.2 cover most of the data structures found in application programs because they allow the programmer to compose aggregate types from other types. For example, in addition to allowing an array of integers, XDR allows an array of structures, each of which can have multiple fields that can each be an array, structure, or union. Thus, XDR provides representations for most of the structures that a C programmer can specify.

19.7 Implicit Types

The XDR standard specifies how a data object should be encoded for each of the data types listed in Figure 19.2. However, the encodings contain only the data items and not information about their types. For example, XDR specifies using "big-endian" order for 32-bit binary integers (the same encoding used in TCP/IP protocol headers). If an application program uses XDR representation to encode a 32-bit integer, the result occupies exactly 32 bits; the encoding does not contain additional bits to identify it as an integer or to specify its length. Thus, clients and servers using XDR must agree on the exact format of messages they will exchange. A program cannot interpret an XDR-encoded message unless it knows the exact format and the types of all data fields.

19.8 Software Support For Using XDR

Programmers who choose to use the XDR representation for symmetric data conversion must be careful to place each data item in external form before sending it across a network. Similarly, a receiving program must be careful to convert each incoming item to native representation. Chapter 5 shows one method programmers can use to perform the conversion: insert a function call in the code to convert each data item in a message to external form before sending the message, and insert a function call to convert each data item to internal form when a message arrives.

Most programmers could write the required XDR conversion functions with little effort. However, some conversions require considerable expertise (e.g., converting from a computer's native floating point representation to the XDR standard without losing precision may require an understanding of basic numerical analysis). To eliminate potential conversion errors, an implementation of XDR includes library routines that perform the necessary conversions.

19.9 XDR Library Routines

XDR library routines for a given machine can convert data items from the computer's native representation to the XDR standard representation and vice versa. Most implementations of XDR use a *buffer paradigm* that allows a programmer to create a complete message in XDR form.

19.10 Building A Message One Piece At A Time

The buffer paradigm XDR uses requires a program to allocate a buffer large enough to hold the external representation of a message and to add items (i.e., fields) one at a time. For example, the version of XDR available under the SunOS operating system provides conversion routines that each append an external representation to the end of a buffer in memory. A program first invokes procedure *xdrmem_create* to allocate a buffer in memory and inform XDR that it intends to compose an external representation in it. *Xdrmem_create* initializes the memory so it represents an *XDR stream* that can be used to encode (convert to standard representation) or decode (convert to native representation) data. The call initializes the XDR stream to be empty by assigning the address of the beginning of the buffer to an internal pointer. *Xdrmem_create* returns a pointer to the stream, which must then be used in successive calls to XDR routines. The declarations and calls needed to create an XDR stream using C are:

```
#include <rpc/xdr.h>
#define BUFSIZE 4000              /* size of memory for encoding  */

    XDR    *xdrs;                 /* pointer to an XDR "stream"    */
    char   buf[BUFSIZE];          /* memory area to hold XDR data */

    xdrmem_create(xdrs, buf, BUFSIZE, XDR_ENCODE);
```

Once a program has created an XDR stream, it can call individual XDR conversion routines to convert native data objects into external form. Each call encodes one data object and appends the encoded information on the end of the stream (i.e., places the encoded data in the next available locations in the buffer and then updates the internal stream pointer). For example, procedure *xdr_int* converts a 32-bit binary integer from the native representation to the standard XDR representation and appends it to an XDR stream. A program invokes *xdr_int* by passing it a pointer to an XDR stream and a pointer to an integer:

```
    int    i;              /* integer in native representation       */
    . . .                  /* assume stream initialized for ENCODE */
    i = 260;               /* assign integer value to be converted */
    xdr_int(xdrs, &i);     /* convert integer and append to stream */
```

Figure 19.3 illustrates how the call to *xdr_int* shown in the sample code adds four bytes of data to the XDR stream.

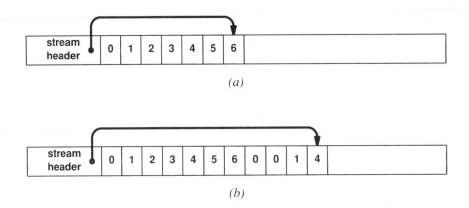

Figure 19.3 (a) An XDR stream that has been initialized for *ENCODE* and already contains *7* bytes of data, and (b) the same XDR stream after a call to *xdr_int* appends a 32-bit integer with value *260*.

19.11 Conversion Routines In The XDR Library

The table in Figure 19.4 lists the XDR conversion routines.

Procedure	arguments	Data Type Converted
xdr_bool	xdrs, ptrbool	Boolean (*int* in C)
xdr_bytes	xdrs, ptrstr, strsize, maxsize	Counted byte string
xdr_char	xdrs, ptrchar	Character
xdr_double	xdrs, ptrdouble	Double precision floating point
xdr_enum	xdrs, ptrint	Variable of enumerated data type (an *int* in C)
xdr_float	xdrs, ptrfloat	Single precision floating point
xdr_int	xdrs, ip	32-bit integer
xdr_long	xdrs, ptrlong	64-bit integer
xdr_opaque	xdrs, ptrchar, count	Bytes sent without conversion
xdr_pointer	xdrs, ptrobj, objsize, xdrobj	A pointer (used in linked data structures like lists or trees)
xdr_short	xdrs, ptrshort	16-bit integer
xdr_string	xdrs, ptrstr, maxsize	A C string
xdr_u_char	xdrs, ptruchar	Unsigned 8-bit integer
xdr_u_int	xdrs, ptrint	Unsigned 32-bit integer
xdr_u_long	xdrs, ptrulong	Unsigned 64-bit integer
xdr_u_short	xdrs, ptrushort	Unsigned 16-bit integer
xdr_union	xdrs, ptrdiscrim, ptrunion, choicefcn, default	Discriminated union
xdr_vector	xdrs, ptrarray, size, elemsize, elemproc	Fixed length array
xdr_void	-none-	Not a conversion (used to denote empty part of a data structure)

Figure 19.4 The XDR data conversion routines found in an XDR library. The routines can convert in either direction because most arguments are pointers to data objects and not data values.

To form a message, the application calls XDR conversion routines for each data item in the message. After encoding each data item and placing it in an XDR stream, the application can send the message by sending the resulting stream. The receiving application must reverse the entire process. It calls *xdrmem_create* to create a memory buffer that will hold an XDR stream, and places the incoming message in a buffer area. XDR records the direction of conversion in the stream itself where the conversion routines can access it. The receiver specifies *XDR_DECODE* as the third argument of *xdrmem_create* when creating an XDR stream that will be used for input. As a result, whenever the receiver calls an individual conversion routine on an input stream, the routine extracts an item from the stream and converts it to native mode. For example, if the receiver has established an XDR stream used for input (i.e., the call specified

XDR_DECODE), it can extract a 32-bit integer and convert it to the native representation by calling *xdr_int*:

```
int     i;           /* integer using native representation  */
. . .                /* assume stream initialized for DECODE */

xdr_int(xdrs, &i);   /* extract integer from stream          */
```

Thus, unlike the conversion routines *htons* and *ntohs* found in BSD UNIX, individual XDR conversion routines do not specify the direction of conversion. Instead, they require the program to specify the direction when creating the XDR stream. To summarize:

> *Individual XDR conversion routines do not specify the direction of conversion. Instead, a single routine that can convert in either direction determines the direction of the conversion by examining the XDR stream being used.*

19.12 XDR Streams, I/O, and TCP

The code fragments above create an XDR stream associated with a buffer in memory. Using memory to buffer data can make a program efficient because it allows the application to convert large amounts of data to external form before sending it across a network. After items have been converted to external form and placed in the buffer, the application must call an I/O function like *write* to send it across a TCP connection.

It is possible to arrange to have XDR conversion routines send data across a TCP connection automatically each time they convert a data item to external form. To do so, an application program first creates a TCP socket, and then calls *fdopen* to attach a UNIX *standard I/O stream* to the socket. Instead of calling *xdrmem_create*, the application calls *xdrstdio_create* to create an XDR stream and connect it to the existing I/O descriptor. XDR streams attached to a TCP socket do not require explicit calls to *write* or *read*. Each time the application calls an XDR conversion routine, the conversion routine automatically performs a buffered *read* or *write* operation using the underlying descriptor. A *write* causes TCP to transmit outgoing data to the socket; a *read* causes TCP to read incoming data from the socket. The application can also call conventional functions from the UNIX standard I/O library to act on the I/O stream. For example, if output is desired, the application can use *fflush* to flush the output buffer after only a few bytes of data have been converted.

19.13 Records, Record Boundaries, And Datagram I/O

As described, the XDR mechanism works well when connected to a TCP socket because both XDR and TCP implementations use the stream abstraction. To make XDR work with UDP as easily as it works with TCP, the designers added a second interface. The alternative design provides an application with a *record-oriented interface*.

To use the record-oriented interface, a program calls function *xdrrec_create* when creating an XDR stream. The call includes two arguments, *inproc* and *outproc*, that specify an input procedure and an output procedure. When converting to external form, each conversion routine checks the buffer. If the buffer becomes full, the conversion routine calls *outproc* to send the existing buffer contents and make space for the new data. Similarly, each time the application calls a conversion routine to convert from external form to the native representation, the routine checks the buffer to see if it contains data. If the buffer is empty, the conversion routine calls *inproc* to obtain more data.

To use XDR with UDP, an application creates a record-oriented XDR stream. It arranges for the input and output procedures associated with the stream to call *read* and *write* (or *recv* and *send*). When the application fills a buffer, the conversion routines call *write* to transmit the buffer in a single UDP datagram. Similarly, when an application calls a conversion routine to extract data, the conversion routine calls *read* to obtain the next incoming datagram and place it in the buffer.

XDR streams created by *xdrrec_create* differ from other XDR streams in several ways. Record-oriented streams allow an application to mark record boundaries. Furthermore, the sender can specify whether to send the record immediately or to wait for the buffer to fill before sending it. The receiver can detect record boundaries, skip a fixed number of records in the input, or find out whether additional records have been received.

19.14 Summary

Because computers do not use a common data representation, client and server programs must contend with representation issues. To solve the problem, client-server interaction can be *asymmetric* or *symmetric*. Asymmetric conversion requires either the client or the server to convert between its own representation and the other machine's native representation. Symmetric conversion uses a standard network representation, and requires both the client and server to convert between the network standard and the local representation.

The chief problem with asymmetric interaction arises because multiple versions of each program are required. If the network supports N architectures, asymmetric interaction requires programming effort proportional to N^2. While symmetric designs may require slightly more computational overhead, they provide interoperability with one program per architecture. Thus, most designers choose symmetric solutions because they require programming effort proportional to N.

Sun Microsystems, Incorporated has defined an external data representation that has become, *de facto*, a standard. Known as XDR, the Sun standard provides definitions for data aggregates (e.g., arrays and structures) as well as for basic data types (e.g., integers and character strings). XDR library routines provide conversion from a computer's native data representation to the external standard and vice versa. Client and server programs can use XDR routines to convert data to external form before sending it and to internal form after receiving it. The conversion routines can be associated with input and output using TCP or UDP.

FOR FURTHER STUDY

Sun Microsystems, Incorporated [RFC 1014] defines the XDR encoding and the standard XDR conversion routines. Additional information can be found in the *Network Programming Guide* that accompanies the SunOS operating system.

International Organization for Standardization [1987a and 1987b] defines an alternative external data representation known as *Abstract Syntax Notation One (ASN.1)*. Although some protocols in the TCP/IP suite use the ASN.1 representation, most application programmers use XDR. Partridge and Rose [1989] shows that XDR and ASN.1 have equivalent expressive power.

Padlipsky [1983] discusses the problem of asymmetric conversion and points out that it requires $n * m$ possible conversions.

EXERCISES

19.1   Construct a version of *ntohs* and conduct an experiment that compares the execution time of your version to the execution time of the version in your system's library or *include* files. Explain the results.

19.2   How does XDR's use of the buffer paradigm make programming easier?

19.3   Design an external data representation that includes a type field before each data item. What is the chief advantage of such a solution? What is the chief disadvantage?

19.4   Read the *UNIX Programmer's Manual* to find out more about the format of an XDR stream. What information is kept in the header?

19.5   Argue that programs would be easier to read if the designers of XDR had chosen to use separate conversion routines for encoding and decoding instead of recording the conversion direction in the stream header. What is the disadvantage of keeping separate conversion routines?

19.6   Under what circumstances might a programmer need to pass *opaque* data objects between a client and a server?

20

Remote Procedure Call Concept (RPC)

20.1 Introduction

The previous chapter begins a discussion of techniques and mechanisms that help programmers use the client-server paradigm. It considers the advantages of using symmetric data conversion, and describes how the XDR external data representation standard and associated library routines provide symmetric conversion.

This chapter continues the discussion. It introduces the remote procedure call concept in general, and describes a particular implementation of a remote procedure call that uses the XDR standard for data representation. It shows how the remote procedure concept simplifies the design of client-server software and makes the resulting programs easier to understand. The next two chapters complete the discussion of remote procedure call by describing a tool that generates much of the C code needed to implement a program that uses remote calls. They contain a complete working example that shows how the tool can generate a client and a server that use remote procedure calls.

20.2 Remote Procedure Call Model

So far, we have described client-server programs by examining the structure of the client and server components separately. However, when programmers build a client-server application, they cannot focus exclusively on one component at a time. Instead, they must consider how the entire system will function and how the two components will interact.

To help programmers design and understand client-server interaction, researchers have devised a conceptual framework for building distributed programs. Known as the *remote procedure call model* or *RPC model*, the framework uses familiar concepts from conventional programs as the basis for the design of distributed applications.

20.3 Two Paradigms For Building Distributed Programs

A programmer can use one of two approaches when designing a distributed application:

- **Communication-Oriented Design**
  Begin with the communication protocol. Design a message format and syntax. Design the client and server components by specifying how each reacts to incoming messages and how each generates outgoing messages.

- **Application-Oriented Design**
  Begin with the application. Design a conventional application program to solve the problem. Build and test a working version of the conventional program that operates on a single machine. Divide the program into two or more pieces, and add communication protocols that allow each piece to execute on a separate computer.

A communication-oriented design sometimes leads to problems. First, by focusing on the communication protocol, the programmer may miss important subtleties in the application and may find that the protocol does not provide all the needed functionality. Second, because few programmers have experience and expertise with protocol design, they often produce awkward, incorrect, or inefficient protocols. Small oversights in protocol design can lead to fundamental errors that remain hidden until the programs run under stress (e.g., the possibility of deadlock). Third, because the programmer concentrates on communication, it usually becomes the centerpiece of the resulting programs, making them difficult to understand or modify. In particular, because the server is specified by giving a list of messages and the actions required when each message arrives, it may be difficult to understand the intended interaction or the underlying motivations.

The remote procedure call model uses the application-oriented approach, which emphasizes the problem to be solved instead of the communication needed. Using the remote procedure call model, a programmer first designs a conventional program to solve the problem, and then divides the program into pieces that run on two or more computers. The programmer can follow good design principles that make the code modular and maintainable.

In an ideal situation, the remote procedure call model provides more than an abstract concept. It allows a programmer to build, compile, and test a conventional version of the program to ensure that it solves the problem correctly before dividing the program into pieces that operate on separate machines. Furthermore, because RPC divides programs at procedure boundaries, the split into local and remote parts can be made without major modifications to the program structure. In fact, it may be possible to move some of the procedures from a program to remote machines without changing or even recompiling the main program itself. Thus, RPC separates the solution of a problem from the task of making the solution operate in a distributed environment.

> *The remote procedure call paradigm for programming focuses on the application. It allows a programmer to concentrate on devising a conventional program that solves the problem before attempting to divide the program into pieces that operate on multiple computers.*

20.4 A Conceptual Model For Conventional Procedure Calls

The remote procedure call model draws heavily from the procedure call mechanism found in conventional programming languages. Procedures offer a powerful abstraction that allows programmers to divide programs into small, manageable, easily-understood pieces. Procedures are especially useful because they have a straightforward implementation that provides a conceptual model of program execution. Figure 20.1 illustrates the concept.

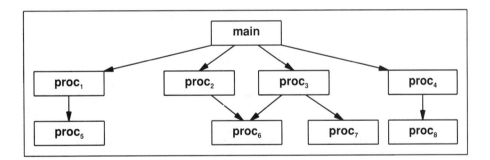

Figure 20.1 The procedure concept. A conventional program consists of one or more procedures, usually arranged in a hierarchy of calls. An arrow from procedure n to procedure m denotes a call from n to m.

20.5 An Extension Of the Procedural Model

The remote procedure call model uses the same procedural abstraction as a conventional program, but allows a procedure call to span the boundary between two computers. Figure 20.2 illustrates how the remote procedure call paradigm can be used to divide a program into two pieces that each execute on a separate computer. Of course, a conventional procedure call cannot pass from one computer to another. Before a program can use remote procedure calls, it must be augmented with protocol software that allows it to communicate with the remote procedure.

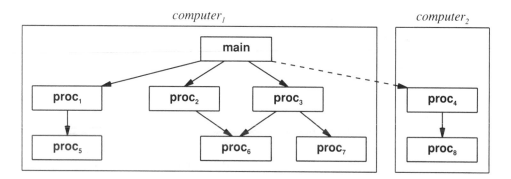

Figure 20.2 A distributed program that shows how the program from Figure 20.1 can be extended to use the remote procedure call paradigm. The division occurs between the main program and procedure *4*. A communication protocol is required to implement the remote call.

20.6 Execution Of Conventional Procedure Call And Return

The procedural model for programs provides a conceptual explanation of program execution that extends directly to remote procedure calls. The concept can be understood best by considering the relationship of control flow to compiled program code in memory. For example, Figure 20.3 illustrates how control flows from a main program through two procedures and back.

According to the procedural execution model, a single *thread of control* or *thread of execution* flows through all procedures. The computer begins execution in a *main* program and continues until it encounters a *procedure call*. The call causes execution to branch to code in the specified procedure and continue. If it encounters another call, the computer branches to a second procedure.

Execution continues in the called procedure until the computer encounters a *return* statement. The return statement causes execution to resume at a point just after the last call. For example, in Figure 20.3, executing the return in procedure *B* causes control to pass back to procedure *A* at a point just after the call to *B*.

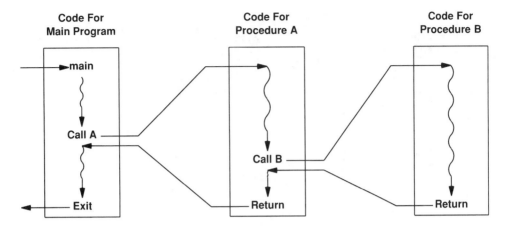

Figure 20.3 A conceptual model of execution that explains flow of control
during procedure call and return. A single thread of control begins in the main program, passes through procedures *A* and *B*,
and eventually returns to the main program.

In the conceptual model, only one thread of execution continues at any time.
Therefore, the execution of one procedure must ''stop'' temporarily while the computer
executes the call to another procedure. The computer suspends the calling procedure,
leaving the values in all variables frozen during the call. Later, when execution returns
from the procedure call, the computer resumes execution in the caller with the values in
all variables available again. A called procedure may make further procedure calls because the computer remembers the sequence of calls and always returns to the most recently executing caller.

20.7 The Procedural Model In Distributed Systems

The execution model of procedure calls that programmers use when thinking about
conventional computer programs can help us to understand how execution proceeds in a
distributed program. Instead of thinking about a client program and a server program
exchanging messages, imagine that each server implements a (remote) procedure and
that the interactions between a client and a server correspond to a procedure call and return. A request sent from a client to a server corresponds to a call of a remote procedure, and a response sent from a server back to a client corresponds to the execution
of a return instruction. Figure 20.4 illustrates the analogy.

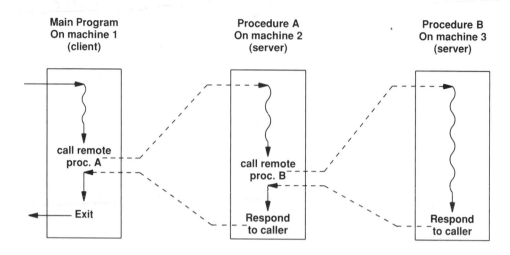

Figure 20.4 The model of execution used with remote procedure calls. A single thread of control executes in a distributed environment. Dashed lines show how control passes from a client to a server during a remote procedure call, and how it passes back when the server responds.

20.8 Analogy Between Client-Server And RPC

The remote procedure call concept provides a strong analogy that allows programmers to think about client-server interactions in a familiar context. Like a conventional procedure call, a remote procedure call transfers control to the called procedure. Also like a conventional procedure call, the system suspends execution of the calling procedure during the call and only allows the called procedure to execute.

When a remote program issues a response, it corresponds to the execution of a *return* in a conventional procedure call. Control flows back to the caller, and the called procedure ceases to execute. The notion of nested procedure calls also applies to remote procedure calls. One remote procedure may call another remote procedure. As Figure 20.4 illustrates, nested remote procedure calls correspond to a server that becomes a client of another service.

Of course, the analogy between remote procedure call and client-server interaction does not explain all the details. For example, we know that a conventional procedure remains completely inactive until the flow of control passes to it (i.e., until it is called). In contrast, a server process must exist in the remote system and be waiting to compute a response before it receives the first request from a client. Further differences arise in the way data flows to a remote procedure. Conventional procedures usually accept a few arguments and return only a few results. However, a server can accept or return ar-

bitrary amounts of data (i.e., it can accept or return an arbitrary stream over a TCP connection).

Although it would be ideal if local and remote procedure calls behaved identically, several practical constraints prevent it. First, network delays can make a remote procedure call several orders of magnitude more expensive than a conventional procedure call. Second, because the called procedure operates in the same address space as the calling procedure, conventional programs can pass pointers as arguments. A remote procedure call cannot have pointers as arguments because the remote procedure operates in a completely different address space than the caller. Third, because a remote procedure does not share the caller's environment, it does not have direct access to the caller's I/O descriptors or operating system functions. For example, a remote procedure cannot write error messages directly to the caller's standard error file.

20.9 Distributed Computation As A Program

The key to appreciating remote procedure call is to understand that, despite its practical limitations, the paradigm helps programmers design distributed programs easily. To see how, imagine that each distributed computation consists of an individual program that runs in a distributed environment. Instead of thinking about the client and server software that implements communication, imagine how easy it would be to build distributed programs if a program simply invoked a procedure when it needed access to a remote service. Imagine that the program's thread of execution could pass across the network to the remote machine, execute the remote procedure on that machine, and then return back to the caller. From the programmer's point of view, remote services would be as easy to access as local procedures or local operating system services. In short, distributed programs would become as easy to construct as conventional programs because they could draw on the programmer's intuition and experience with conventional procedure calls. Furthermore, programmers familiar with the procedure parameter mechanism could define client-server communication precisely without any need for a special notation or language. To summarize:

> *Thinking of a distributed computation as a single program in which control passes across the network to a remote procedure and back helps programmers specify client-server interactions; it relates the interaction of distributed computations to the familiar notions of procedure call and return.*

20.10 Sun Microsystems' Remote Procedure Call Definition

Sun Microsystems, Incorporated has defined a specific form of remote procedure call. Known as *Sun RPC*, or simply *RPC†*, Sun's remote procedure call definition has received wide acceptance in the industry. It has been used as an implementation mechanism for many applications, including Sun's Network File System (NFS‡).

Sun RPC defines the format of messages that the caller (client) sends to invoke a remote procedure on a server, the format of arguments, and the format of results that the called procedure returns to the caller. It permits the calling program to use either UDP or TCP to carry messages, and uses XDR to represent procedure arguments as well as other items in an RPC message header. Finally, in addition to the protocol specification, Sun RPC includes a compiler system that helps programmers build distributed programs automatically.

20.11 Remote Programs And Procedures

Sun RPC extends the remote procedure call model by defining a remote execution environment. It defines a *remote program* as the basic unit of software that executes on a remote machine. Each remote program corresponds to what we think of as a server, and contains a set of one or more remote procedures plus global data. The procedures inside a remote program all share access to its global data. Thus, a set of cooperative remote procedures can share state information. For example, one can implement a simple remote database by constructing a single remote program that includes data structures to hold shared information and three remote procedures to manipulate it: *insert*, *delete*, and *lookup*. As Figure 20.5 illustrates, all remote procedures inside the remote program can share access to the single database.

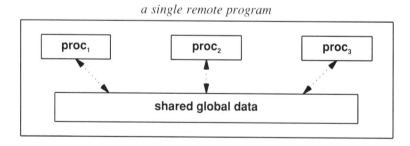

Figure 20.5 Conceptual organization of three remote procedures in a single remote program that implements a database. All three procedures share access to global data in the program, just as conventional procedures share access to global data in a conventional program.

---

†We will use the term *RPC* throughout the remainder of this text to refer to Sun RPC unless otherwise noted.

‡Chapter *23* discusses NFS in detail.

20.12 Reducing The Number Of Arguments

Because most programming languages use positional notation to represent arguments, a procedure call that contains more than a handful of arguments can be difficult to read. Programmers can reduce the problem by collecting many arguments into a single data aggregate (e.g., a C *struct*) and passing the resulting aggregate as a single argument. The caller assigns each field in the structure a value before passing the structure to the called procedure; the caller extracts return values from the structure after the call returns. To summarize:

> *Using a structure instead of multiple arguments makes the program*
> *more readable because the structure field names serve as keywords*
> *that tell the reader how each argument will be used.*

Because we will assume throughout the remainder of this discussion that all programs using RPC collect their arguments into a structure, each remote procedure will need only a single argument.

20.13 Identifying Remote Programs And Procedures

The Sun RPC standard specifies that each remote program executing on a computer must be assigned a unique 32-bit integer that the caller uses to identify it. Furthermore, Sun RPC assigns an integer identifier to each remote procedure inside a given remote program. The procedures are numbered sequentially: *1, 2, ..., N*†. Conceptually, a specific remote procedure on a given remote computer can be identified by a pair:

$$(prog, proc)$$

where *prog* identifies the remote program and *proc* identifies a remote procedure within the program. To help ensure that program numbers defined by separate organizations do not conflict, Sun RPC has divided the set of program numbers into eight groups as Figure 20.6 shows.

---

†By convention, the number *0* is always reserved for an echo procedure that can be used to test whether the remote program can be reached.

From		To	Values Assigned By
0x00000000	-	0x1fffffff	Sun Microsystems, Inc.
0x20000000	-	0x3fffffff	The system manager at a user's site
0x40000000	-	0x5fffffff	Transient (temporary)
0x60000000	-	0x7fffffff	Reserved
0x80000000	-	0x9fffffff	Reserved
0xa0000000	-	0xbfffffff	Reserved
0xc0000000	-	0xdfffffff	Reserved
0xe0000000	-	0xffffffff	Reserved

Figure 20.6 The division into eight groups of 32-bit numbers that Sun RPC uses to identify remote programs. Each remote program is assigned a unique number.

Sun Microsystems, Incorporated administers the first group of identifiers, allowing anyone to apply for a standard RPC program number. Because Sun publishes the assignments, all computers that run RPC use the standard values. Of the 2^{29} program numbers available in the first group, Sun has only assigned a handful of numbers. Figure 20.7 summarizes some of the assignments.

20.14 Accommodating Multiple Versions Of A Remote Program

In addition to a program number, Sun RPC includes an integer *version number* for each remote program. Usually, the first version of a program is assigned version *1*. Later versions each receive a unique version number.

Version numbers provide the ability to change the details of a remote procedure call without obtaining a new program number. In practice, each RPC message identifies the intended recipient on a given computer by a triple:

$$(prog, vers, proc)$$

where *prog* identifies the remote program, *vers* specifies the version of the program to which the message has been sent, and *proc* identifies a remote procedure within that remote program. The RPC specification permits a computer to run multiple versions of a remote program simultaneously, allowing for graceful migration during changes. The idea can be summarized:

> *Because all Sun RPC messages identify a remote program, the version of that program, and a remote procedure in the program, it is possible to migrate from one version of a remote procedure to another gracefully and to test a new version of the server while an old version continues to operate.*

Name	assigned number	Description
portmap	100000	port mapper
rstatd	100001	rstat, rup, and perfmeter
rusersd	100002	remote users
nfs	100003	network file system
ypserv	100004	yp (now called NIS)
mountd	100005	mount, showmount
dbxd	100006	DBXprog (debugger)
ypbind	100007	NIS binder
walld	100008	rwall, shutdown
yppasswdd	100009	yppasswd
etherstatd	100010	ethernet statistics
rquotad	100011	rquotaprog, quota, rquota
sprayd	100012	spray
selection_svc	100015	selection service
dbsessionmgr	100016	unify, netdbms, dbms
rexd	100017	rex, remote_exec
office_auto	100018	alice
lockd	100020	klmprog
lockd	100021	nlmprog
statd	100024	status monitor
bootparamd	100026	bootstrap
pcnfsd	150001	NFS for PC

Figure 20.7 Example RPC program numbers currently assigned by Sun Microsystems, Inc.

20.15 Mutual Exclusion For Procedures In A Remote Program

The Sun RPC mechanism specifies that at most one remote procedure in a remote program can be invoked at a given time. Thus, RPC provides automatic mutual exclusion among procedures within a given remote program. Such exclusion can be important for remote programs that maintain shared data accessed by several procedures. For example, if a remote database program includes remote procedures for *insert* and *delete* operations, the programmer does not need to worry about two remote procedure calls interfering with one another because the mechanism only permits one call to execute at a time. The system blocks other calls until the current call finishes. To summarize:

Sun RPC provides mutual exclusion among remote procedures within a single remote program; at most one remote procedure call can execute in a remote program at one time.

20.16 Communication Semantics

When choosing the semantics for Sun RPC, the designers had to choose between two possibilities. On one hand, to make a remote procedure call behave as much like a local procedure call as possible, RPC should use a reliable transport like TCP and should guarantee reliability to the programmer. The remote procedure call mechanism should either transfer the call to the remote procedure and receive a reply, or it should report that communication is impossible. On the other hand, to allow programmers to use efficient, connectionless transport protocols, the remote procedure call mechanism should support communication through a datagram protocol like UDP.

Sun RPC does not enforce reliable semantics. It allows each application to choose TCP or UDP as a transport protocol. Furthermore, the standard does not specify additional protocols or mechanisms to achieve reliable delivery. Instead, it defines RPC semantics as a function of the semantics of the underlying transport protocol. For example, because UDP permits datagrams to be lost or duplicated, Sun RPC specifies that remote procedure calls using UDP may experience loss or duplication.

20.17 At Least Once Semantics

Sun RPC defines the semantics of a remote procedure call in the simplest way by specifying that a program should only draw the weakest possible conclusion from any interaction. For example, when using UDP, a request or reply message (call to a remote procedure or return from one) can be lost or duplicated. If a remote procedure call does not return, the caller cannot conclude that the remote procedure has not been called because the reply could have been lost, even if the request was not. If a remote procedure call does return, the caller can conclude that the remote procedure was called *at least once*. However, the calling procedure cannot conclude that the remote procedure was called exactly once because the request could have been duplicated or a reply message could have been lost.

The Sun RPC standard uses the term *at least once semantics* to describe RPC execution when the caller receives a reply, and *zero or more semantics* to describe the behavior of a remote procedure call when the caller does not receive a reply.

RPC's zero-or-more semantics imposes an important responsibility on the programmer:

> *Programmers who choose to use UDP as the transport protocol for a*
> *Sun RPC application must build the application to tolerate zero-or-*
> *more execution semantics.*

In practice, zero-or-more semantics usually means that a programmer makes each remote procedure call *idempotent*†. For example, consider a remote file access application. A remote procedure that appends data to a file is not idempotent because repeated executions of the procedure will append data repeatedly. On the other hand, a remote procedure that writes data to a specified position in a file is idempotent because repeated executions will always write data to the same position.

20.18 RPC Retransmission

The library software supplied with Sun's RPC implementation includes a simple timeout and retransmission strategy, but does not guarantee reliability in the strict sense. The default timeout mechanism implements a fixed (nonadaptive) timeout with a fixed number of retries. When the RPC library software sends a message that corresponds to a remote procedure call, it starts a timer. The software retransmits the request if the timer expires before a response arrives. Programmers can adjust the timeout and retry limits for a given application, but the software does not adapt automatically to long network delays or to changes in delay over time.

Of course, a simple retransmission strategy does not guarantee reliability, nor does it guarantee that the calling application can draw a correct conclusion about execution of the remote procedure. For example, if the network loses all responses, the caller may retransmit the request several times and each request may result in an execution of the remote procedure. Ultimately, however, library software on the caller's machine will reach its retry limit and declare that the remote procedure cannot be executed. Most important, an application cannot interpret failure as a guarantee that the remote procedure was never executed (in fact, it may have executed several times).

20.19 Mapping A Remote Program To A Protocol Port

UDP and TCP transport protocols use 16-bit protocol port numbers to identify communication endpoints. Earlier chapters describe how a server creates a passive socket, binds the socket to a well-known protocol port, and waits for client programs to contact it. To make it possible for clients and servers to rendezvous, we assume that each service is assigned a unique protocol port number and that the assignments are well-known. Thus, both the server and client agree on the protocol port at which the server accepts requests because they both consult a published list of port assignments.

---

†The term is taken from mathematics, where an operation is said to be idempotent if repeated applications of the operation produce the same result.

Sun RPC introduces an interesting problem: because it uses 32-bit numbers to identify remote programs, RPC programs can outnumber protocol ports. Thus, it is impossible to map RPC program numbers onto protocol ports directly. More important, because RPC programs cannot all be assigned a unique protocol port, programmers cannot use a scheme that depends on well-known protocol port assignments.

Although the potential number of RPC programs rules out well-known port assignments, RPC does not differ dramatically from other services. At any given time, a single computer executes only a small number of remote programs. Thus, as long as the port assignments are temporary, each RPC program can obtain a protocol port number and use it for communication.

If an RPC program does not use a reserved, well-known protocol port, clients cannot contact it directly. To see why, think of the server and client components. When the server (remote program) begins execution, it asks the operating system to allocate an unused protocol port number. The server uses the newly allocated protocol port for all communication. The system may choose a different protocol port number each time the server begins (i.e., the server may have a different port assigned each time the system boots).

The client (the program that issues the remote procedure call) knows the machine address and RPC program number for the remote program it wishes to contact. However, because the RPC program (server) only obtains a protocol port after it begins execution, the client cannot know which protocol port the server obtained. Thus, the client cannot contact the remote program directly.

20.20 Dynamic Port Mapping

To solve the port identification problem, a client must be able to map from an RPC program number and a machine address to the protocol port that the server obtained on the destination machine when it started. The mapping must be dynamic because it can change if the machine reboots or if the RPC program starts execution again.

To allow clients to contact remote programs, the Sun RPC mechanism includes a dynamic mapping service. Each machine that offers an RPC program (i.e., that runs a server) maintains a database of port mappings and provides a mechanism that allows a caller to map RPC program numbers to protocol ports. Called the *RPC port mapper* or sometimes simply the *port mapper*, the RPC port mapping mechanism uses a server to maintain a small database on each machine. Figure 20.8 illustrates that the port mapper operates as a separate server process.

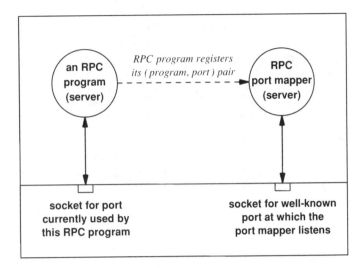

Figure 20.8 The Sun RPC port mapper. Each RPC program registers its program number and protocol port number with the port mapper on its local machine. A caller always contacts the port mapper on a machine to find the protocol port to use for a given RPC program on that machine.

20.21 RPC Port Mapper Algorithm

One port mapper operates on each machine using Algorithm 20.1. The port mapper allows clients to reach remote programs even though the remote programs dynamically allocate protocol ports. Whenever a remote program (i.e., a server) begins execution, it allocates a local protocol port that it will use for communication. The remote program then contacts the port mapper on its local machine and adds a pair of integers to the database:

$$(RPC\ prog\ number,\ protocol\ port\ number)$$

Once an RPC program has registered itself, callers on other machines can find its protocol port by sending a request to the port mapper.

Algorithm 20.1

1. Create a passive socket bound to the well-known port assigned to the Sun RPC port mapper service (*111*).

2. Repeatedly accept requests to register an RPC program number or to lookup a protocol port given an RPC program number.

    Registration requests come from RPC programs on the same machine as the port mapper. Each registration request specifies a pair consisting of the RPC program number and the protocol port currently used to reach that program. When a registration request arrives, the port mapper adds the pair to its database of mappings.

    Lookup requests come from arbitrary machines. They each specify a remote program number, and request the number of a protocol port that can be used to reach the remote program. The port mapper looks up the remote program in its database, and responds by returning the corresponding protocol port for that program.

Algorithm 20.1 The Sun RPC port mapper algorithm. One port mapper server runs on each machine that implements the server side of an RPC program.

The port mapper on a given machine works like directory assistance in the U.S. telephone system: a caller can ask the port mapper how to reach a particular RPC program on that machine. To contact a remote program, a caller must know the address of the machine on which the remote program executes as well as the RPC program number assigned to the program. The caller first contacts the RPC port mapper on the target machine, and then sends the port mapper an RPC program number. The port mapper returns the protocol port number that the specified program is currently using. A caller can always reach the port mapper because the port mapper communicates using the well-known protocol port, *111*. Once a caller knows the protocol port number the target program is using, it can contact the remote program directly.

20.22 Sun RPC Message Format

Unlike many TCP/IP protocols, Sun RPC does not use a fixed format for messages. The protocol standard defines the general format of RPC messages as well as the data items in each field using a language known as the *XDR Language*. Because XDR language resembles data structure declarations in C, programmers familiar with C can usually read and understand the language without much explanation. In general, the language specifies how to assemble a sequence of data items that comprise a message. Each item is encoded using the XDR representation standard.

A message type field in the RPC message header distinguishes between messages that a client uses to initiate a remote procedure call and messages that a remote procedure uses to reply. Constants used in the message type field can be defined using XDR language. For example, the declarations:

```
enum msg_type {              /* RPC message type constants */
    CALL  = 0;
    REPLY = 1;
};
```

declare the symbolic constants *CALL* and *REPLY* to be the values of an enumerated type, *msg_type*.

Data structures in XDR language can be considered a sequence of XDR types, and can be interpreted as instructions for assembling a message by composing data using XDR. For example, once values have been declared for symbolic constants, the XDR language can define the format of an RPC message:

```
struct rpc_msg {             /* Format of an RPC message     */
    unsigned int mesgid;     /* used to match reply to call  */
    union switch (msg_type mesgt) {
        case CALL:
            call_body cbody;
        case REPLY:
            rply_body rbody;
    } body;
```

The declaration specifies that an RPC message, *rpc_msg* consists of an integer message identifier, *mesgid*, followed by the XDR representation of a discriminated union. Using the XDR representation, each union begins with an integer, *mesgt* in this case. *Mesgt* determines the format of the remainder of the RPC message; it contains a value that defines the message to be either a *CALL* or a *REPLY*. A CALL message contains further information in the form of a *call_body*; a REPLY contains information in the form of a *rply_body*. The declarations for *call_body* and *rply_body* must be given elsewhere. For example, RPC defines a *call_body* to have the form:

```
struct call_body {            /* format of RPC CALL            */
    unsigned int rpcvers;     /* which version of RPC?         */
    unsigned int rprog;       /* number of remote program      */
    unsigned int rprogvers;   /* version number of remote prog*/
    unsigned int rproc;       /* number of remote procedure    */
    opaque_auth cred;         /* credentials for called auth.  */
    opaque_auth verf;         /* authentication verifier       */
    /* ARGS */                /* arguments for remote proc.    */
};
```

The first few items in the body of a remote procedure call present no surprises. The caller must supply the RPC protocol version number in field *rpcvers* to ensure that both client and server are using the same message format. Integer fields *rprog*, *rprogvers*, and *rproc* identify the remote program being called, the desired version of that program, and the remote procedure within that program. Fields *cred* and *verf* contain information that the called program can use to authenticate the caller's identity.

20.23 Marshaling Arguments For A Remote Procedure

Fields in an RPC message following the authentication information contain arguments for the remote procedure. The number of arguments and the type of each depend on the remote procedure being called.

RPC must represent all arguments in an external form that allows them to be transferred between computers. In particular, if any of the arguments passed to the remote procedure consists of a complex data structure like a linked list, it must be encoded into a compact representation that can be sent across the network. We use the terms *marshal*, *linearize*, or *serialize* to denote the task of encoding arguments. We say that the client side of RPC marshals arguments into the message and the server side unmarshals them. A programmer must remember that although RPC allows an RPC call to contain complex data objects, marshaling and unmarshaling large data structures can require significant CPU time and network bandwidth. Thus, most programmers avoid passing linked structures as arguments.

20.24 Authentication

RPC defines several possible forms of authentication, including a simple authentication scheme that relies on UNIX and a more complex scheme that uses the *Data Encryption Standard* (*DES*) originally published by The National Bureau Of Standards†. Authentication information can have one of the four types shown in the following declaration:

---

†NBS has changed its name to the National Institute For Standards and Technology (NIST).

```
enum auth_type  {          /* possible forms of auth.      */
    AUTH_NULL  = 0;         /* no authentication           */
    AUTH_UNIX  = 1;         /* UNIX machine name authentic. */
    AUTH_SHORT = 2;         /* Used for short form auth. in */
                           /*   messages after the first  */
    AUTH_DES   = 3;         /* NIST's (NBS's) DES standard  */
};
```

In each case, RPC leaves the format and interpretation of the authentication information up to the authentication subsystem. Therefore, the declaration of the authentication structure in an RPC message uses the keyword *opaque* to indicate that it appears in the message without any interpretation:

```
struct opaque_auth {       /* structure for authent. info. */
    auth_type atype;       /* which type of authentication */
    opaque body<400>;      /* data for the type specified  */
};
```

Of course, each authentication method uses a specific format for encoding data. For example, most sites that send RPC messages use the UNIX operating system. UNIX authentication defines the structure of its authentication information to contain several fields:

```
struct auth_unix {         /* format of UNIX authentication*/
    unsigned int timestamp;    /* integer timestamp            */
    string smachine<255>;      /* name of sender's machine    */
    unsigned int userid;       /* user id of user making req.  */
    unsigned int grpid;        /* group id of user making req. */
    unsigned int grpids<10>;   /* other group ids for the user */
};
```

UNIX authentication relies on the client machine to supply its name in field *smachine* and the numeric identifier of the user making the request in field *userid*. The client also specifies its local time in field *timestamp*, which can be used to sequence requests. Finally, the client sends the main numeric group identifier and secondary group identifiers of the sending user in fields *grpid* and *grpids*.

20.25 An Example Of RPC Message Representation

XDR defines the size and external format of each field in an RPC message. For example, XDR specifies that an integer (either signed or unsigned) occupies 32 bits and is stored in big-endian byte order.

Figure 20.9 shows the size of fields in an example RPC *CALL* message.

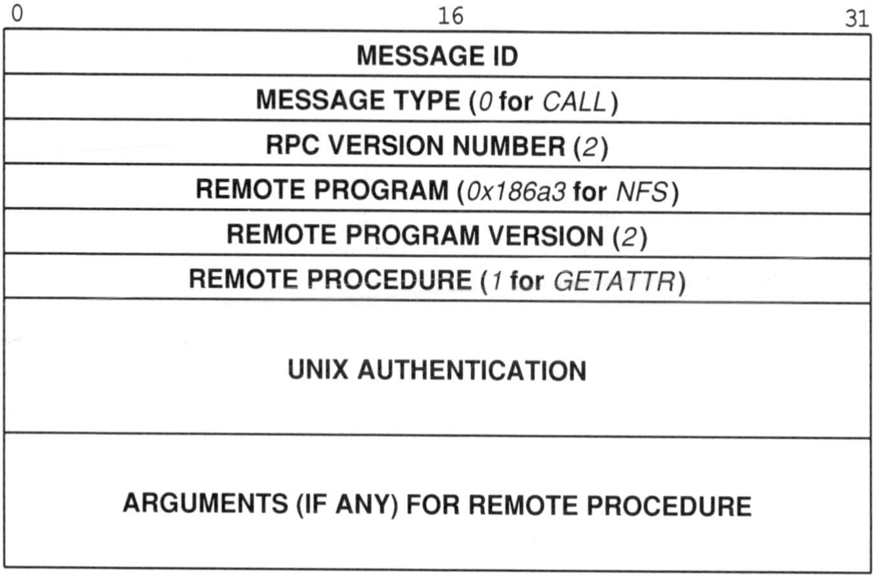

0	16	31

MESSAGE ID
MESSAGE TYPE (*0* for *CALL*)
RPC VERSION NUMBER (*2*)
REMOTE PROGRAM (*0x186a3* for *NFS*)
REMOTE PROGRAM VERSION (*2*)
REMOTE PROCEDURE (*1* for *GETATTR*)
UNIX AUTHENTICATION
ARGUMENTS (IF ANY) FOR REMOTE PROCEDURE

Figure 20.9 An example of the external format used for an RPC *CALL* message. The first fields of the message have a fixed size, but the sizes of later fields vary with their content.

20.26 An Example Of The UNIX Authentication Field

The size of the authentication field in an RPC message depends on its contents. For example the second field in a UNIX authentication structure is a machine name in a variable-length format. XDR represents a variable-length string as a 4-byte integer length followed by the bytes of the string itself. Figure 20.10 shows an example of the representation for a UNIX authentication field. In the example, the computer's name, *merlin.cs.purdue.edu*, contains *20* characters.

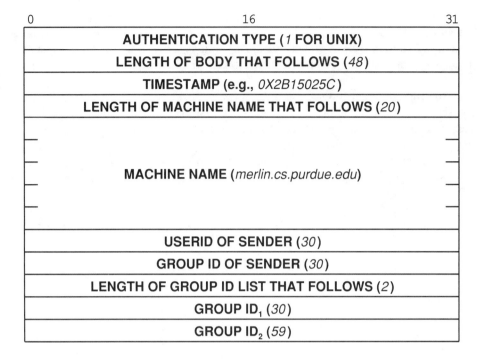

Figure 20.10 Example representation for UNIX authentication within a Sun RPC message. The example values are taken from a message sent by a user with numeric login identifier *30* on machine *merlin.cs.purdue.edu.*

20.27 Summary

The remote procedure model helps make distributed programs easy to design and understand because it relates client-server communication to conventional procedure calls. The remote procedure call model views each server as implementing one or more procedures. A message sent from a client to a server corresponds to a "call" of a remote procedure, and a response from the server to the client corresponds to a "return" from a procedure call.

Like conventional procedures, remote procedures accept arguments and return one or more results. The arguments and results passed between the caller and the called procedure provide a precise definition of the communication between the client and the server.

Using the remote procedure call model helps programmers focus on the application instead of the communication protocol. The programmer can build and test a conventional program that solves a particular problem, and then can divide the program into parts that execute on two or more computers.

Sun Microsystems, Incorporated defined a particular form of remote procedure call that has become a *de facto* standard. Sun RPC specifies a scheme for identifying remote procedures as well as a standard for the format of RPC messages. The standard uses the external data representation, XDR, to keep message representations machine independent.

Sun RPC programs do not use well-known protocol ports like conventional clients and servers. Instead, they use a dynamic binding mechanism that allows each RPC program to choose an arbitrary, unused protocol port when it begins. Called the RPC port mapper, the binding mechanism requires each computer that offers RPC programs to also run a port mapper server at a well-known protocol port. Each RPC program registers with the port mapper on its local machine after it obtains a protocol port. When an RPC client wants to contact an RPC program, it first contacts the port mapper on the target machine. The port mapper responds by telling the client which port the target RPC program is using. Once a client obtains the correct protocol port for a target RPC program, it contacts the target RPC program directly using that port.

FOR FURTHER STUDY

Sun Microsystems, Incorporated [RFC 1057] defines the standard for Sun RPC and describes most of the ideas presented in this chapter. Additional information can be found in the *Network Programming Guide* that accompanies the SunOS operating system.

EXERCISES

20.1   Read the Sun RPC specification and create a diagram that shows the size of the fields in a typical return message.

20.2   Conduct an experiment to measure the overhead that using a port mapper introduces.

20.3   A client can avoid needless overhead by caching protocol port bindings. That is, after a client contacts the port mapper to obtain a protocol port for the target RPC program, it can store the binding in a cache to avoid looking it up again. How long will a binding remain valid?

20.4   Can the port mapper concept be extended to services other than RPC? Explain your answer.

20.5   What are the major advantages and disadvantages of using a port mapper instead of well-known ports?

20.6   When an RPC client contacts a port mapper, it must either specify or learn whether the target program has opened a UDP port or a TCP port. Read the specification carefully to find out how an RPC client distinguishes between the two.

21

Distributed Program Generation (Rpcgen Concept)

21.1 Introduction

The previous chapter presents the principles underlying the remote procedure call model. It describes the remote procedure call concept, and explains how programmers can use remote procedure calls to build programs that operate in the client-server paradigm. Finally, it describes the Sun RPC mechanism.

This chapter continues the discussion. It focuses on the structure of programs that use RPC, and shows how programs can be divided along procedural boundaries. It introduces the stub procedure concept and a program generator tool that automates much of the code generation associated with Sun RPC. It also discusses a library of procedures that makes it easy to build servers that offer remote procedures and clients that call them.

The next chapter completes the discussion of the generator. It shows the sequence of steps a programmer takes to create a conventional program and then to divide the program into local and remote components. It presents a simple example application, and then uses the example to follow through the process of constructing a distributed program. The example in the next chapter complements the conceptual description in this chapter by illustrating many of the details and showing the code that the generator produces.

21.2 Using Remote Procedure Calls

The remote procedure call model is general. A programmer can choose to use the remote procedure paradigm in any of the following ways:

- As a program specification technique only. To do so, the programmer follows the RPC model and specifies all interaction between a client and server as either a remote procedure call or a return. Procedure arguments specify the data passed between the client and server. The programmer can ignore the procedural structure when designing the client and server, but use the procedural specification to verify the correctness of the resulting system.

- For both program specification and as an abstraction during program design. To implement this approach, think about remote procedure calls when designing the application programs and the communication protocol. Design a communication protocol in which each message corresponds closely to one of the remote procedure calls.

- For the conceptual design and explicitly in the implementation. To include RPC in the implementation, the programmer designs a generalized RPC message format and a protocol for passing control to a remote procedure. The programmer follows the procedural specification precisely when passing data between the client and server. The program uses a standard external data representation to encode arguments, and follows the exact data type specifications given in the design. It calls standard library routines to convert between the computer's native representation and the external representation used when crossing a network.

- For design and implementation, constructing all software from scratch. The programmer builds a conventional application that solves the problem, and then divides it into pieces along procedural boundaries, moving the pieces to separate machines. The program uses the Sun RPC message format (including the XDR data representation) and the Sun RPC program numbering scheme when calling a remote procedure. The programmer builds the implementation from the RPC specifications alone, using the Sun RPC port mapper to bind a remote program number to the corresponding protocol port.

- For design and implementation, using standard libraries. The programmer builds an application and divides it into pieces using the Sun RPC specification, but relies on existing RPC library routines whenever possible. For example, the programmer uses library routines to register with the port mapper, to compose and send a remote procedure call message, and to compose a reply.

- For an automated implementation. The programmer follows the Sun RPC specification completely, and uses an automatic program generator tool to help automate construction of the necessary pieces of client and server code and the calls to RPC library routines that perform tasks like registering a program with the port mapper, constructing a message, and dispatching a call to the appropriate remote procedure in a remote program.

21.3 Programming Mechanisms To Support RPC

Sun RPC specifications are both extensive and complicated. Building an application that implements RPC without using any existing software can be tedious and time consuming. Most programmers prefer to avoid duplicating the effort for each application. Instead, they rely on library routines and programming tools to handle much of the work.

Implementations of Sun RPC provide significant help for those who wish to avoid unnecessary programming. Assistance comes in four forms:

1. XDR library routines that convert individual data items from internal form to the XDR standard external representation
2. XDR library routines that format the complex data aggregates (e.g., arrays and structures) used to define RPC messages
3. RPC run-time library routines that allow a program to call a remote procedure, register a service with the port mapper, or dispatch an incoming call to the correct remote procedure inside a remote program
4. A program generator† tool that produces many of the C source files needed to build a distributed program that uses RPC

The RPC run-time library has procedures that supply most of the functionality needed for RPC. For example, procedure *callrpc* sends an RPC message to a server. It has the form:

```
callrpc(host, prog, progver, procnum, inproc, in, outproc, out);
```

Argument *host* points to a character string that contains the name of a machine on which the remote procedure executes. Arguments *prog*, *progver*, and *procnum* identify the remote program number, the version of the program to use, and the remote procedure number. Argument *inproc* gives the address of a local procedure that can be called to marshal arguments into an RPC message, and argument *in* gives the address of the arguments for the remote procedure. Argument *outproc* gives the address of a local procedure that can be called to decode the results, and *out* gives the address in memory where the results should go.

While *callrpc* handles many of the chores required to send an RPC message, the Sun RPC library contains many other procedures. For example, a client calls function:

```
handle = clnt_create(host, prog, vers, proto);
```

to create an integer identifier that can be used to send RPC messages. RPC calls the integer identifier a *handle*; several RPC library procedures take a handle as one of their arguments. Arguments to *clnt_create* specify the name of a remote host, a remote program on that host, the version of that program, and a protocol (TCP or UDP).

---

†Programmers often refer to the program generator as a *stub generator*. The reason that such terminology has become popular will become apparent when we review how the generator works.

The library also contains routines that create, store, and manipulate authentication information. For example, procedure:

```
authunix_create(host, uid, gid, len, aup_gids);
```

creates an authentication handle for a given user on a given host computer. Arguments specify a remote host, the user's login and primary group identifiers, and a set of groups to which the user belongs, *aup_gids*. Argument *len* specifies the number of items in the set.

Although programmers can write applications that call the RPC library routines directly, few programmers do. Most rely on the program generator tool discussed later in this chapter. The code it generates contains many calls to the library procedures.

21.4 Dividing A Program Into Local And Remote Procedures

To understand how the RPC programming tools work, it is necessary to understand how a program can be divided into local and remote procedures. Think of the procedure calls in a conventional application. Figure 21.1 illustrates one such call.

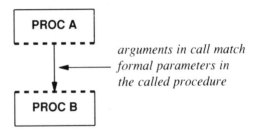

Figure 21.1 An example procedure call that illustrates the procedural interface used by a calling procedure and a called procedure. The dashed lines denote a match between arguments in the procedure call and parameters in the called procedure.

Each procedure has a set of formal parameters, and each procedure call specifies a set of arguments. The total number of arguments in the caller must equal the total number of formal parameters in the called procedure, and the type of each argument must match the declared type of the corresponding formal parameter. In other words, the parameters define the interface between a calling procedure and a called procedure.

21.5 Adding Code For RPC

Moving one or more procedures to a remote machine requires a programmer to add code between the procedure call and the remote procedure. On the client side, the new code must marshal arguments and translate them to a machine-independent representation, create an RPC *CALL* message, send the message to the remote program, wait for the results, and translate the resulting values back to the client's native representation. On the server side, the new code must accept an incoming RPC request, translate arguments to the server's native data representation, dispatch the message to the appropriate procedure, form a reply message by translating values to the machine-independent data representation, and send the result back to the client.

To keep the program structure intact and to isolate the code that handles RPC from the code that handles the application, the additional code required for RPC can be added in the form of two extra procedures that completely hide the communication details. The new procedures can add the required functionality without changing the interface between the original calling and called procedures. Preserving the original interface helps reduce the chance for errors because it keeps the communication details separate from the original application.

21.6 Stub Procedures

The additional procedures added to a program to implement RPC are called *stub procedures*. The easiest way to understand stub procedures is to imagine a conventional program being divided into two programs with an existing procedure being moved to a remote machine. On the caller's (client) side, a stub procedure replaces the called procedure. On the remote procedure's (server) side, a stub procedure replaces the caller. The two stubs implement all the communication required for the remote procedure call, leaving the original calling and called procedures unchanged. Figure 21.2 illustrates the stub concept, showing how stub procedures allow the procedure call shown in Figure 21.1 to be separated into local and remote parts.

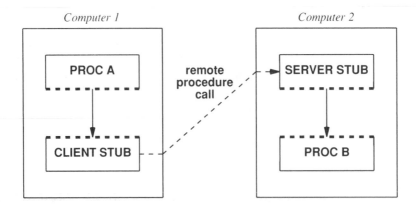

Figure 21.2 Stub procedures added to a program implement a remote procedure call. Because stubs use the same interface as the original
call, adding them does not require a change to either the original
calling procedure or the called procedure.

21.7 Multiple Remote Procedures And Dispatching

Figure 21.2 presents a simplified view of RPC because it only shows a single remote procedure call. In practice, a given server process usually includes several remote
procedures in a single remote program. Each RPC call consists of a message that identifies a specific remote procedure. When an RPC message arrives, the server uses the
remote procedure number in the message to *dispatch* the call to the correct procedure.
Figure 21.3 illustrates the concept.

The figure shows how RPC relates to a conventional client-server implementation.
The remote program consists of a single server process that must be running before any
messages arrive. A remote procedure call, which can originate from any client, must
specify the address of the machine on which the server operates as well as the number
of the remote procedure to call on that machine. The server program consists of a
dispatcher routine plus the remote procedures and server-side stub procedures. The
dispatcher understands how the remote procedure numbers correspond to the server-side
stubs, and uses the correspondence to forward each incoming remote procedure call to
an appropriate stub.

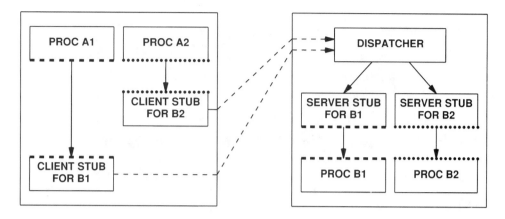

Figure 21.3 Message dispatch in an RPC server. Clients send RPC requests
to a single server program. The server uses the remote procedure number in a message to decide which procedure should
receive the call. In the example, procedure *A1* calls procedure
B1, and *A2* calls *B2*. Dashed and dotted lines show which interface each procedure uses.

21.8 Name Of The Client-Side Stub Procedure

The transition from a conventional application to a distributed program can be
trivial if the programmer chooses to name the client stub the same as the called procedure. To see why, consider again the stub procedures shown in Figure 21.3. The original caller, procedure *A1*, contains a call to procedure *B1*. After the program has been
divided, *A1* becomes part of the client and must call a stub to communicate with the remote procedure. If the programmer names the client-side stub *B1* and builds it to have
exactly the same interface as the original procedure *B1*, the calling procedure (*A1*) does
not need to change. In fact, it may even be possible to make the change without recompiling procedure *A1*. The original compiled binary for *A1* can be linked with the new
client-side stub for *B1* to produce a valid client. Adding a client-side stub without
changing the original caller isolates the RPC code from the original application program
code, making programming easier and reducing the chance of introducing errors.

Of course, naming the client stub *B1* makes source code management more difficult because it means that the distributed version of the program will have two procedures named *B1*: the client-side stub and the original procedure that becomes part of
the server. The two versions of *B1* are never part of the same linked program. In most
cases, they will not execute on the same computer. Thus, as long as the programmer
exercises caution when building object programs, the stub approach works well. To
summarize:

> *To build a distributed version of an application program, a program-*
> *mer must move one or more procedures to a remote machine. When*
> *doing so, the addition of stub procedures allows the original calling*
> *and called procedures to remain unchanged as long as the client-side*
> *stub has the same name as the original called procedure.*

21.9 Using Rpcgen To Generate Distributed Programs

It should be obvious that much of the code needed to implement an RPC server does not change. For example, if the mapping between remote procedure numbers and server-side stubs is kept in a data structure, all servers can use the same dispatcher routine. Similarly, all servers can use the same code to register their services with the port mapper.

To avoid unnecessary programming, implementations of Sun RPC include a tool that generates much of the code needed to implement a distributed program automatically. Called *rpcgen*, the tool reads a specification file as input and generates files of C source code as output. The specification file contains the declarations for constants, global data types, global data, and remote procedures (including the procedure argument and result types). The files that rpcgen produces contain most of the source code needed to implement the client and server programs that provide the specified remote procedure calls. In particular, rpcgen generates code for the client-side and server-side stub procedures, including the code to marshal arguments, to send an RPC message, to dispatch an incoming call to the correct procedure, to send a reply, and to translate arguments and results between the external representation and native data representation. When combined with an application program and a few files that the programmer writes, the rpcgen output produces complete client and server programs.

Because rpcgen produces source code as output, the programmer can choose to edit the code (e.g., to hand-optimize the code to improve performance) or to combine it with other files. In most cases, programmers use rpcgen to handle as many of the details as possible. They try to avoid changing the output by hand to keep the entire process of generating a client and server automated. If the program specifications change or new remote procedure calls are needed, the programmer can modify the specifications and use rpcgen again to produce a new client and server without manual intervention.

21.10 Rpcgen Output And Interface Procedures

To maintain flexibility and to allow automatic generation of significant portions of the stub code, rpcgen separates each stub procedure into two parts. One part, common to almost all applications that use RPC, provides basic client-server communication; the other part provides an interface to the application program. Rpcgen produces the communication portion of the stub automatically from a description of the remote procedure and its arguments. Because rpcgen produces code for the communication stub, it specifies the arguments required on the client side and the calling sequence on the server side. The programmer must accept rpcgen calling conventions when using the communication stubs that rpcgen generates.

The idea behind separating the stub into communication and interface routines is simple: it allows rpcgen to choose the calling conventions the communication stubs use, while it allows the programmer to choose the calling conventions the remote procedures use. The programmer creates interface stubs to map between the remote procedure calling conventions and the conventions provided by the communication stub procedures that rpcgen generates. Figure 21.4 illustrates how all the routines interact.

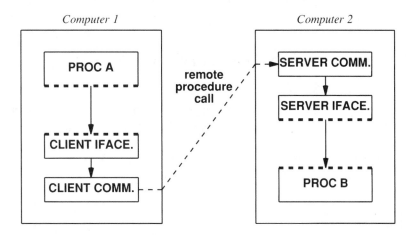

Figure 21.4 The form of a distributed program created using rpcgen. Rpcgen generates the basic communication stubs automatically; the programmer supplies the two interface procedures.

As Figure 21.4 illustrates, the two parts of a stub each consist of two separate procedures. On the client side, the interface procedure calls the communication procedure. On the server side, the communication procedure calls the interface procedure. If the stub interface procedures are defined carefully, the original caller and the original called procedure can remain unchanged.

21.11 Rpcgen Input And Output

Rpcgen reads an input file that contains a specification of a remote program. It produces four output files, each of which contains source code. Rpcgen derives names for the output files from the name of the input file. If the specification file has name *Q*.x, all output files will begin with *Q*. The table in Figure 21.5 lists the output files and describes their contents.

File Name	Contents
Q.h	Declarations of constants and types used in the code generated for both the client and server
*Q*_xdr.c	XDR procedure calls used in the client and server to marshal arguments
*Q*_clnt.c	Client-side communication stub procedure
*Q*_svc.c	Server-side communication stub procedure

Figure 21.5 The output files produced by rpcgen for an input file named *Q*.x. As their names imply, the output files contain the C source code for both programs and data declarations.

21.12 Using Rpcgen To Build A Client And Server

Figure 21.6 illustrates the files that a programmer must write to build a client and server using rpcgen. In essence, rpcgen requires the programmer to write an application, the procedures it calls, and the interface portions of the client-side and server-side stubs. The programmer divides the application into a driver program (the client) and a set of procedures that comprise the remote program (the server). The programmer then writes a specification for the remote program and uses rpcgen to generate the remaining pieces.

When rpcgen runs, it reads the specification and generates C source code that must be compiled and linked to produce running programs. After rpcgen runs, two separate compile-and-link steps occur. One produces the executable client program and the other produces an executable server.

Figure 21.6 only provides an overview of rpcgen input and output. The next chapter provides additional details on its use. The chapter presents a simple example application, and shows the steps a programmer takes to transform it into a distributed program. The chapter describes the specification file rpcgen takes as input as well as the code rpcgen produces.

21.13 Summary

RPC is a broad concept that can help programmers design client-server software. A programmer can use RPC to help specify or implement a distributed program. When using Sun RPC, the programmer can choose to follow the specification while building code from scratch, to use procedures found in the RPC library, or to use an automatic program generation tool called *rpcgen*.

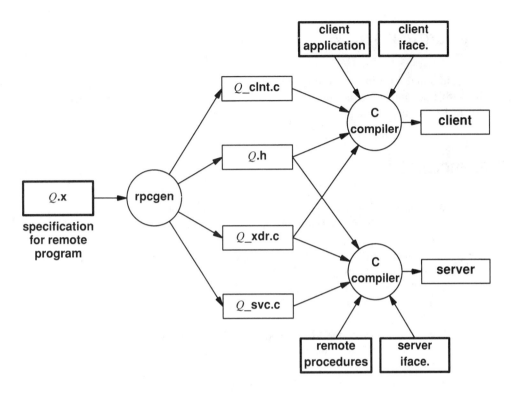

Figure 21.6 The files required to build a client and server from the output of rpcgen, and the compilation steps required to process them. Darkened boxes show the input that the programmer supplies.

RPC allows a programmer to construct a conventional program and then to transform it into a distributed program by moving some procedures to a remote machine. When doing so, the programmer can minimize changes and reduce the chance of introducing errors by adding stub procedures to the program. The stub procedures implement the necessary communication. Using stubs allows the original calling and called procedures to remain unchanged.

Because most distributed programs using RPC follow the same general architecture, rpcgen can generate much of the required code automatically. In addition to creating a specification file, the programmer only needs to supply a pair of interface procedures and the procedures associated with the application. Rpcgen generates the rest of the client and server programs, including procedures that register the server with the port mapper, provide communication between client and server, and dispatch incoming calls to the correct remote procedure.

FOR FURTHER STUDY

Additional information on *rpcgen* can be found in the *Network Programming Guide* that accompanies the SunOS operating system. Stevens [1990] describes the details of RPC exception handling.

EXERCISES

21.1   Write down the sequence of steps a server takes when an RPC CALL message arrives. Be sure to specify when data values are converted from the external representation to native representation.

21.2   Read about the RPC library routines in the UNIX documentation. What are the arguments for function *svc_sendreply*? Why is each needed?

21.3   The RPC library includes routines that allow a server to register with the port mapper. Read the documentation to find out what procedure *pmap_unset* does. Why is it necessary?

21.4   If you have access to the source code for RPC library routines, find out how many lines of code they occupy. Compare the library size to the size of the source code for the rpcgen program. Why is rpcgen as large as it is?

21.5   Rpcgen produces C source code instead of object code. The documentation that accompanies rpcgen suggests that having source code allows a programmer to modify the generated code. Why might a programmer make such modifications?

21.6   Refer to the previous question. What are the disadvantages of modifying the rpcgen output?

21.7   It is possible to design a remote procedure call mechanism that combines all procedures from a remote program into a single procedure by using an additional argument to decide which procedure to call (e.g., the remote procedure consists of a C *switch* statement that uses the new argument to make a choice among alternative actions). What are the chief advantages of such an approach compared to the Sun RPC approach? What are the chief disadvantages?

21.8   If the server side of a Sun RPC program uses sockets, what are the possible methods it can use to implement mutual exclusion (i.e., how can it guarantee that only one remote procedure will be called at any time)? What are the advantages and disadvantages of each method? Hint: consider the socket options and the creation of a file.

22

Distributed Program Generation (Rpcgen Example)

22.1 Introduction

The previous chapters present the principles underlying the remote procedure call model and the Sun RPC mechanism. They discuss the remote procedure call concept and explain how programs can be divided along procedure call boundaries. They also describe how the rpcgen tool and associated library routines automate much of the code generation for programs that use Sun RPC.

This chapter completes the discussion of rpcgen. It presents the sequence of steps a programmer takes to first create a conventional program and then divide the program into local and remote components. It uses an example application to follow through each step of the process. It shows the output from rpcgen and the additional code required to create the client and server components of a distributed program that uses RPC.

22.2 An Example To Illustrate Rpcgen

An example will clarify how rpcgen works and will illustrate most of the details. Because the point of the example is to explain how rpcgen works, we have selected an extremely simple application. In practice, of course, few RPC programs are as trivial or easy to follow as our example. Thus, one should think of the example as a tutorial and not question whether the application warrants a distributed solution.

22.3 Dictionary Lookup

As an example of using rpcgen, consider an application that implements a simple database. The database offers four basic operations: *initialize* to initialize the database (i.e., erase all previously stored values), *insert* to insert a new item, *delete* to remove an item, and *lookup* to search for an item. We will assume that items in the database are individual words. Thus, the database will function as a dictionary. The application inserts a set of valid words, and then uses the database to check new words to see if each is in the dictionary.

To keep the example simple, we will assume that input to the application is a text file, where each line contains a one-letter command followed by a word. The table in Figure 22.1 lists the commands, and gives the meaning of each:

one-letter command	Argument	Meaning
I	-none-	Initialize the database by removing all words
i	word	insert *word* into the database
d	word	delete *word* from the database
l	word	lookup *word* in the database
q	-none-	quit

Figure 22.1 Input commands for the example database application and their meanings. Some commands must be followed by a word that can be thought of as an argument to the command.

For example, the following input contains a sequence of data commands. The commands initialize the dictionary, insert names of computer vendors, delete some of the names, and look up three names:

```
          I
          i  Navy
          i  IBM
          i  RCA
          i  Encore
```

```
i  Digital
d  RCA
d  Navy
l  IBM
d  Encore
l  CDC
l  Encore
q
```

When this file of commands is presented as input, the dictionary application should find *IBM* in the dictionary, but it should not find *Encore* or *CDC*.

22.4 Eight Steps To A Distributed Application

Figure 21.6† shows the input required for rpcgen and the output files it generates. To create the required files and combine them into a client and server, a programmer takes the following eight steps:

1. Build and test a conventional application that solves the problem.

2. Divide the program by choosing a set of procedures to move to a remote machine. Place the selected procedures in a separate file.

3. Write an rpcgen specification for the remote program, including names and numbers for the remote procedures and the declarations of their arguments. Choose a remote program number and a version number (usually *1*).

4. Run rpcgen to check the specification and, if valid, generate the four source code files that will be used in the client and server.

5. Write stub interface routines for the client side and server side.

6. Compile and link together the client program. It consists of four main files: the original application program (with the remote procedures removed), the client-side stub (generated by rpcgen), the client-side interface stub, and the XDR procedures (generated by rpcgen). When all these files have been compiled and linked together, the resulting executable program becomes the client.

7. Compile and link together the server program. It consists of four main files: the procedures taken from the original application that now comprise the remote program, the server-side stub (generated by rpcgen), the server-side interface stub, and the XDR procedures (generated by rpcgen). When all these files have been compiled and linked together, the resulting executable program becomes the server.

8. Start the server on the remote machine, and then invoke the client on the local machine.

---

†Figure 21.6 can be found on page 265.

The next sections examine each step in more detail and use the dictionary application to illustrate the subtleties.

22.5 Step 1: Build A Conventional Application Program

The first step in building a distributed version of the example dictionary application requires the programmer to construct a conventional program that solves the problem. File *dict.c* contains an application program for the dictionary problem written in the C language.

```
/* dict.c - main, initw, nextin, insertw, deletew, lookupw */

#include <stdio.h>
#include <ctype.h>

#define MAXWORD 50              /* maximum length of a command or word  */
#define DICTSIZ 100             /* maximum number of entries in diction.*/
char    dict[DICTSIZ][MAXWORD+1];/* storage for a dictionary of words   */
int     nwords = 0;            /* number of words in the dictionary    */

/*----------------------------------------------------------------------
 * main - insert, delete, or lookup words in a dictionary as specified
 *----------------------------------------------------------------------
 */
int
main(argc, argv)
int     argc;
char    *argv[];
{
        char    word[MAXWORD+1]; /* space to hold word from input line  */
        char    cmd;
        int     wrdlen;          /* length of input word                */

        while (1) {
                wrdlen = nextin(&cmd, word);
                if (wrdlen < 0)
                        exit(0);
                switch (cmd) {
                case 'I':        /* "initialize" */
                        initw();
                        printf("Dictionary initialized to empty.\n");
                        break;
                case 'i':        /* "insert" */
```

```
                                insertw(word);
                                printf("%s inserted.\n",word);
                                break;
                        case 'd':          /* "delete" */
                                if (deletew(word))
                                        printf("%s deleted.\n",word);
                                else
                                        printf("%s not found.\n",word);
                                break;
                        case 'l':          /* "lookup" */
                                if (lookupw(word))
                                        printf("%s was found.\n",word);
                                else
                                        printf("%s was not found.\n",word);
                                break;
                        case 'q':          /* quit */
                                printf("program quits.\n");
                                exit(0);
                        default:           /* illegal input */
                                printf("command %c invalid.\n", cmd);
                                break;
                }
        }
}


/*-------------------------------------------------------------------------
 * nextin - read a command and (possibly) a word from the next input line
 *-------------------------------------------------------------------------
 */
int
nextin(cmd, word)
char    *cmd, *word;
{
        int     i, ch;

        ch = getc(stdin);
        while (ch == ' ')
                ch = getc(stdin);
        if (ch == EOF)
                return -1;
        *cmd = (char) ch;
        ch = getc(stdin);
        while (ch == ' ')
                ch = getc(stdin);
```

```
        if (ch == EOF)
                return -1;
        if (ch == '\n')
                return 0;
        i = 0;
        while ((ch != ' ') && (ch != '\n')) {
                if (++i > MAXWORD) {
                        printf("error: word too long.\n");
                        exit(1);
                }
                *word++ = ch;
                ch = getc(stdin);
        }
        return i;
}


/*-------------------------------------------------------------------
 * initw - initialize the dictionary to contain no words at all
 *-------------------------------------------------------------------
 */
int
initw()
{
        nwords = 0;
        return 1;
}


/*-------------------------------------------------------------------
 * insertw - insert  a word in the dictionary
 *-------------------------------------------------------------------
 */
int
insertw(word)
char    *word;
{
        strcpy(dict[nwords], word);
        nwords++;
        return nwords;
}

/*-------------------------------------------------------------------
 * deletew - delete  a word from the dictionary
 *-------------------------------------------------------------------
 */
```

```
int
deletew(word)
char    *word;
{
        int     i;

        for (i=0 ; i<nwords ; i++)
                if (strcmp(word, dict[i]) == 0) {
                        nwords--;
                        strcpy(dict[i], dict[nwords]);
                        return 1;

                }
        return 0;

}


/*-----------------------------------------------------------------------
 * lookupw - look up a word in the dictionary
 *-----------------------------------------------------------------------
 */
int
lookupw(word)
char    *word;
{
        int     i;

        for (i=0 ; i<nwords ; i++)
                if (strcmp(word, dict[i]) == 0)
                        return 1;
        return 0;

}
```

To keep the application simple and easy to understand, the conventional program in file *dict.c* uses a two-dimensional array to store words. A global variable, *nwords*, counts the number of words in the dictionary at any time. The main program contains a loop that reads and processes one line of input on each iteration. It calls procedure *nextin* to read a command (and possibly a word) from the next input line, and then uses a C *switch* statement to select one of six possible cases. The cases correspond to the five valid commands plus a default case that handles illegal input.

Each case in the main program calls a procedure to handle the details. For example, the case that corresponds to an insertion command, *i*, calls procedure *insertw*. Procedure *insertw* inserts a new word at the end of the array and increments *nwords*.

The other procedures operate as expected. Procedure *deletew* searches for the word to be deleted. If it finds the word, *deletew* replaces it with the last word in the dictionary and decrements *nwords*. Finally, *lookupw* searches the array sequentially to determine if the specified word is present. It returns *1* if the word is present in the dictionary and *0* otherwise.

To produce an executable binary for the application, the programmer invokes the C compiler. Most UNIX systems use the command:

```
cc -o dict dict.c
```

to produce an executable binary file named *dict* from the source program in file *dict.c*.

22.6 Step 2: Divide The Program Into Two Parts

Once a conventional application has been built and tested, it can be partitioned into local and remote components. Programmers must have a conceptual model of a program's procedure call graph before they can partition the program. For example, Figure 22.2 shows the procedural organization of the original dictionary application.

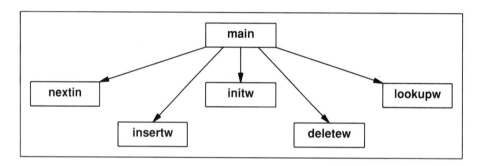

Figure 22.2 The procedure call graph for the original, conventional program that solves the dictionary problem. A call graph represents a program's procedural organization.

When considering which procedures can be moved to a remote machine, the programmer must consider the facilities that each procedure needs. For example, procedure *nextin* reads and parses the next input line each time it is called. Because it needs access to the program's standard input file, *nextin* must be kept with the main program. To summarize:

Procedures that perform I/O or otherwise access file descriptors cannot be moved to a remote machine easily.

The programmer must also consider the location of data that each procedure accesses. For example, procedure *lookupw* needs to access the entire database of words. If *lookupw* executes on a machine other than the machine where the dictionary resides, the RPC call to *lookupw* must pass the entire dictionary as an argument.

Passing large data structures as arguments to remote procedures is extremely inefficient because the RPC mechanism must read and encode the entire data structure for each remote procedure call. In general:

> *Procedures should execute on the same machine as the data they access. Passing large data structures as arguments to remote procedures is inefficient.*

After considering the original dictionary program and the data each procedure accesses, it should be obvious that procedures *insertw*, *deletew*, *initw*, and *lookupw* belong on the same machine as the dictionary itself.

Assume that the programmer decides to move the dictionary storage and associated procedures to a remote machine. To help understand the consequences of moving some procedures to a remote machine, programmers usually create a mental image, or even a sketch, of the distributed program and data structures. Figure 22.3 illustrates the new structure of the dictionary application with the data and access procedures moved to a remote machine.

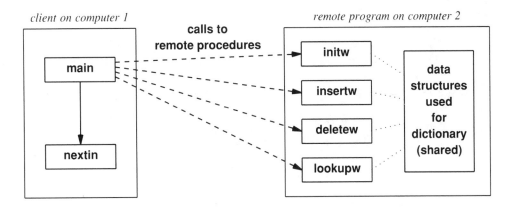

Figure 22.3 The conceptual division of the dictionary program into local and
remote components. The remote component contains the data
for the dictionary and the procedures that access and search it.

A simple drawing like the one in Figure 22.3 can help a programmer think about the division of a program into local and remote components. The programmer must consider whether each procedure has access to the data and services it needs, and must consider the arguments that each remote procedure will require along with the cost of passing that information across a network. Finally, the diagram helps the programmer assess how network delays will affect program performance.

Assuming the programmer chooses a conceptual division and decides to proceed, the next step is to divide the source program into two components. The programmer identifies the constants and data structures used by each component, and places each component in a separate file. In the dictionary example, the division is straightforward because the original source file can be divided between procedure *nextin* and procedure *initw*. File *dict1.c* contains the main program and procedure *nextin*:

```c
/* dict1.c - main, nextin */

#include <stdio.h>
#include <ctype.h>

#define MAXWORD 50              /* maximum length of a command or word  */

/*--------------------------------------------------------------------------
 * main - insert, delete, or lookup words in a dictionary as specified
 *--------------------------------------------------------------------------
 */
int
main(argc, argv)
int     argc;
char    *argv[];
{
        char    word[MAXWORD+1]; /* space to hold word from input line  */
        char    cmd;
        int     wrdlen;          /* length of input word                */

        while (1) {
                wrdlen = nextin(&cmd, word);
                if (wrdlen < 0)
                        exit(0);
                switch (cmd) {
                case 'I':       /* "initialize" */
                        initw();
                        printf("Dictionary initialized to empty.\n");
                        break;
                case 'i':       /* "insert" */
                        insertw(word);
                        printf("%s inserted.\n",word);
                        break;
                case 'd':       /* "delete" */
                        if (deletew(word))
```

```
                                    printf("%s deleted.\n",word);
                        else
                                    printf("%s not found.\n",word);
                        break;
                case 'l':        /* "lookup" */
                        if (lookupw(word))
                                    printf("%s was found.\n",word);
                        else
                                    printf("%s was not found.\n",word);
                        break;
                case 'q':        /* quit */
                        printf("program quits.\n");
                        exit(0);
                default:          /* illegal input */
                        printf("command %c invalid.\n", cmd);
                        break;
                }
        }
}


/*----------------------------------------------------------------------
 * nextin - read a command and (possibly) a word from the next input line
 *----------------------------------------------------------------------
 */
int
nextin(cmd, word)
char    *cmd, *word;
{
        int     i, ch;

        ch = getc(stdin);
        while (ch == ' ')
                ch = getc(stdin);
        if (ch == EOF)
                return -1;
        *cmd = (char) ch;
        ch = getc(stdin);
        while (ch == ' ')
                ch = getc(stdin);
        if (ch == EOF)
                return -1;
        if (ch == '\n')
                return 0;
        i = 0;
```

```
        while ((ch != ' ') && (ch != '\n')) {
                if (++i > MAXWORD) {
                        printf("error: word too long.\n");
                        exit(1);
                }
                *word++ = ch;
                ch = getc(stdin);
        }
        return i;
}
```

File *dict2.c* contains the procedures from the original application that will become part of the remote program. In addition, it contains declarations for the global data that the procedures will share. At this point, the file does not contain a complete program – the remaining code will be added later.

```
/* dict2.c - initw, insertw, deletew, lookupw */

#define MAXWORD 50              /* maximum length of a command or word  */
#define DICTSIZ 100             /* maximum number of entries in diction.*/
char    dict[DICTSIZ][MAXWORD+1];/* storage for a dictionary of words   */
int     nwords = 0;             /* number of words in the dictionary    */

/*-------------------------------------------------------------------
 * initw - initialize the dictionary to contain no words at all
 *-------------------------------------------------------------------
 */
int
initw()
{
        nwords = 0;
        return 1;
}


/*-------------------------------------------------------------------
 * insertw - insert  a word in the dictionary
 *-------------------------------------------------------------------
 */
int
insertw(word)
char    *word;
{
        strcpy(dict[nwords], word);
```

```
            nwords++;
            return nwords;
}


/*-------------------------------------------------------------------------
 * deletew - delete  a word from the dictionary
 *-------------------------------------------------------------------------
 */
int
deletew(word)
char    *word;
{
        int     i;

        for (i=0 ; i<nwords ; i++)
                if (strcmp(word, dict[i]) == 0) {
                        nwords--;
                        strcpy(dict[i], dict[nwords]);
                        return 1;
                }
        return 0;
}


/*-------------------------------------------------------------------------
 * lookupw - look up a word in the dictionary
 *-------------------------------------------------------------------------
 */
int
lookupw(word)
char    *word;
{
        int     i;

        for (i=0 ; i<nwords ; i++)
                if (strcmp(word, dict[i]) == 0)
                        return 1;
        return 0;
}
```

Note that the definition of symbolic constant *MAXWORD* appears in both components because they both declare variables used to store words. Only file *dict2.c* contains the declarations for data structures used to store the dictionary, however, because only the remote program will include the dictionary data structures.

From a practical point of view, separating the application into two files makes it possible to compile the client and server pieces separately. The compiler checks for problems like symbolic constants referenced by both parts, and the linker checks to see that all data structures have been collected together with the procedures that reference them. On a UNIX system, the commands:

```
cc -c dict1.c
cc -c dict2.c
```

produce object files (not complete programs) for the two components. The components must be linked together to produce an executable program, but that is not the immediate reason to compile them: the compiler checks that both files are syntactically correct.

When thinking about the utility of having a compiler check the code, remember that most distributed programs are much more complex than our trivial example. A compilation may find problems in a large program that escape the programmer's attention. Catching such problems before additional code has been inserted makes them easier to repair.

22.7 Step 3: Create An Rpcgen Specification

Once the programmer selects a structure for the distributed program, he or she can prepare an rpcgen specification. In essence, an rpcgen specification file contains a declaration of a remote program, including the data structures it uses.

The specification file contains constants, type definitions, and declarations for the client and server programs. More precisely, the specification file contains:

- declarations for constants used in the client or, more often, in the server (remote program),
- declarations of data types used (especially in arguments to remote procedures), and
- declarations of remote programs, the procedures contained in each program, and the types of their parameters.

Recall that RPC uses numbers to identify remote programs and the remote procedures within them. The program declaration in a specification file defines such details as a program's RPC number, its version number, and the numbers assigned to each procedure within the program.

All specifications must be given in the RPC programming language, not C. While the differences are minor, they can be frustrating. For example, RPC language uses the keyword *string* to denote null-terminated character strings, while C uses *char* *. Even experienced programmers may require multiple iterations to produce a correct specification.

File *rdict.x* illustrates an rpcgen specification. It contains example declarations for the RPC version of the dictionary program.

```
/* rdict.x */

/* RPC declarations for dictionary program */

const   MAXWORD = 50;          /* maximum length of a command or word */
const   DICTSIZ = 100;         /* number of entries in dictionary      */


struct example {               /* unused structure declared here to    */
        int     exfield1;      /* illustrate how rpcgen builds XDR      */
        char    exfield2;      /* routines to convert structures.       */
};


/*---------------------------------------------------------------------
 * RDICTPROG - remote program that provides insert, delete, and lookup
 *---------------------------------------------------------------------
 */
program RDICTPROG {               /* name of remote program (not used)   */
    version RDICTVERS {           /* declaration of version (see below)  */
        int INITW(void)    = 1;/* first procedure in this program      */
        int INSERTW(string) = 2;/* second procedure in this program     */
        int DELETEW(string) = 3;/* third procedure in this program      */
        int LOOKUPW(string) = 4;/* fourth procedure in this program     */
    } = 1;                        /* definition of the program version   */
} = 0x30090949;                   /* remote program number (must be      */
                                  /*   unique)                           */
```

An rpcgen specification file does not contain entries for all declarations found in the original program. Instead, it only defines those constants and types shared across the client and server or needed to specify arguments.

The example specification file begins by defining constants *MAXWORD* and *DICTSIZE*. In the original application, both were defined to be symbolic constants using a C preprocessor *define* statement. RPC language does not use C symbolic constant declarations. Instead it requires symbolic constants to be declared with the *const* keyword and assigned a value using the equal symbol (=).

Following suggested conventions, the specification file uses upper case names to define procedures and programs. As we will see later, the names become symbolic constants that can be used in C programs. Using upper case is not absolutely required, but it helps avoid name conflicts.

22.8 Step 4: Run Rpcgen

After the specification has been completed, the programmer runs rpcgen to check for syntax errors and generate four† files of code as Figure 21.6 shows‡. On most UNIX systems, the command syntax is:

```
rpcgen rdict.x
```

Rpcgen uses the name of the input file when generating the names of the four output files. For example, because the input file began with *rdict*, the output files will be named: *rdict.h*, *rdict_clnt.c*, *rdict_svc.c*, and *rdict_xdr.c*.

22.9 The .h File Produced By Rpcgen

Figure 22.4 shows the contents of file *rdict.h*, which contains valid C declarations for any constants and data types declared in the specification file. In addition, rpcgen adds definitions for the remote procedures. In the example code, rpcgen defines upper case *INSERTW* to be 2 because the specification declared procedure *INSERTW* to be the second procedure in the remote program.

The external procedure declarations in *rdict.h* require an explanation. The declared procedures comprise the interface portion of the server-side stub. Procedure names have been generated by taking the declared procedure names, mapping them to lower case, and appending an underscore followed by the program version number. For example, the sample specification file declares that the remote program contains procedure *DELETEW*, so *dict.h* contains an *extern* declaration for procedure *deletew_1*. To understand why rpcgen declares these interface routines, recall the purpose of the interface portion of the stub: it allows rpcgen to choose its own calling conventions, while allowing the original called procedure to remain unchanged.

As an example of interface stub naming, consider procedure *insertw*. The original procedure will become part of the server and will remain unchanged. Thus, the server will have a procedure named *insertw* that has the same arguments as in the original application. To avoid a naming conflict, the server must use a different name for the interface stub procedure. Rpcgen arranges for the server-side communication stub to call an interface stub procedure named *insertw_1*. The call uses rpcgen's choice of arguments, and allows the programmer to design *insertw_1* so that it calls *insertw* using the correct arguments.

---

†If a particular output file would be empty, rpcgen will not create it. Therefore, some specifications produce fewer than four files.

‡Figure 21.6 can be found on page 265.

```
#define MAXWORD 50
#define DICTSIZ 100

struct example {
        int exfield1;
        char exfield2;
};
typedef struct example example;
bool_t xdr_example();


#define RDICTPROG ((u_long)0x30090949)
#define RDICTVERS ((u_long)1)
#define INITW ((u_long)1)
extern int *initw_1();
#define INSERTW ((u_long)2)
extern int *insertw_1();
#define DELETEW ((u_long)3)
extern int *deletew_1();
#define LOOKUPW ((u_long)4)
extern int *lookupw_1();
```

Figure 22.4 File *rdict.h* – an example *.h* file that rpcgen produces.

22.10 The XDR Conversion File Produced By Rpcgen

Rpcgen produces a file that contains calls to routines that perform XDR conversions for all data types declared in the remote program. For example, file *rdict_xdr.c* contains calls to conversion routines for the data types declared in the dictionary program.

```
#include <rpc/rpc.h>
#include "rdict.h"


bool_t
xdr_example(xdrs, objp)
        XDR *xdrs;
        example *objp;
{
        if (!xdr_int(xdrs, &objp->exfield1)) {
                return (FALSE);
        }
        if (!xdr_char(xdrs, &objp->exfield2)) {
                return (FALSE);
        }
        return (TRUE);
}
```

Figure 22.5 File *rdict_xdr.c* – an example file of XDR conversion routines
that rpcgen produces.

In our example, the only type declaration that appears in the specification file has
the name *example*. It defines a structure that has one integer field and one character
field. File *rdict_xdr.c* contains the code needed to convert a structure of type *example*
between the native data representation and the external data representation. The code,
which has been generated automatically by rpcgen, calls routines from the XDR library
for each field of the structure. Once a declaration has been given, the declared type can
be used for arguments to remote procedures. If one of the remote procedures did use an
example structure as an argument, rpcgen would generate code in both the client and
server to call procedure *xdr_example* to convert the representation.

22.11 The Client Code Produced By Rpcgen

For the example dictionary application, rpcgen produces file *rdict_clnt.c*, a source
program that will become the client-side communication stub in the distributed version
of the program.

```c
#include <rpc/rpc.h>
#include <sys/time.h>
#include "rdict.h"

/* Default timeout can be changed using clnt_control() */
static struct timeval TIMEOUT = { 25, 0 };

int *
initw_1(argp, clnt)
        void *argp;
        CLIENT *clnt;
{
        static int res;

        bzero((char *)&res, sizeof(res));
        if (clnt_call(clnt, INITW, xdr_void, argp, xdr_int, &res, TIMEOUT)
                != RPC_SUCCESS) {
                return (NULL);
        }
        return (&res);
}


int *
insertw_1(argp, clnt)
        char **argp;
        CLIENT *clnt;
{
        static int res;

        bzero((char *)&res, sizeof(res));
        if (clnt_call(clnt, INSERTW, xdr_wrapstring, argp, xdr_int, &res,
                TIMEOUT) != RPC_SUCCESS) {
                return (NULL);
        }
        return (&res);
}


int *
deletew_1(argp, clnt)
        char **argp;
        CLIENT *clnt;
{
```

```
        static int res;

        bzero((char *)&res, sizeof(res));
        if (clnt_call(clnt, DELETEW, xdr_wrapstring, argp, xdr_int, &res,
                TIMEOUT) != RPC_SUCCESS) {
                return (NULL);
        }
        return (&res);
}


int *
lookupw_1(argp, clnt)
        char **argp;
        CLIENT *clnt;
{

        static int res;

        bzero((char *)&res, sizeof(res));
        if (clnt_call(clnt, LOOKUPW, xdr_wrapstring, argp, xdr_int, &res,
                TIMEOUT) != RPC_SUCCESS) {
                return (NULL);
        }
        return (&res);
}
```

Figure 22.6 File *rdict_clnt.c* – an example of the client stub that rpcgen produces.

The file contains a communication stub procedure for each of the procedures in the remote program. As with the server, names have been chosen to avoid conflicts.

22.12 The Server Code Produced By Rpcgen

For the dictionary example, rpcgen produces a fourth file, *rdict_svc.c*, that contains the code needed for a server. The file contains a main program that executes when the server begins. It obtains a protocol port, registers the RPC program with the port mapper, and then waits to receive RPC calls. It dispatches each call to the appropriate server-side stub interface routine. When the called procedure responds, the server creates an RPC reply and sends it back to the client.

```
#include <stdio.h>
#include <rpc/rpc.h>
#include "rdict.h"

static void rdictprog_1();

main()
{
        SVCXPRT *transp;

        (void)pmap_unset(RDICTPROG, RDICTVERS);

        transp = svcudp_create(RPC_ANYSOCK);
        if (transp == NULL) {
                (void)fprintf(stderr, "cannot create udp service.\n");
                exit(1);
        }
        if (!svc_register(transp, RDICTPROG, RDICTVERS, rdictprog_1,
                        IPPROTO_UDP)) {
                (void)fprintf(stderr,
                    "unable to register (RDICTPROG,RDICTVERS, udp).\n");
                exit(1);
        }

        transp = svctcp_create(RPC_ANYSOCK, 0, 0);
        if (transp == NULL) {
                (void)fprintf(stderr, "cannot create tcp service.\n");
                exit(1);
        }
        if (!svc_register(transp, RDICTPROG, RDICTVERS, rdictprog_1,
                        IPPROTO_TCP)) {
                (void)fprintf(stderr,
                    "unable to register (RDICTPROG, RDICTVERS, tcp).\n");
                exit(1);
        }
        svc_run();
        (void)fprintf(stderr, "svc_run returned\n");
        exit(1);
}

static void
rdictprog_1(rqstp, transp)
        struct svc_req *rqstp;
        SVCXPRT *transp;
```

```
{
        union {
                char *insertw_1_arg;
                char *deletew_1_arg;
                char *lookupw_1_arg;
        } argument;
        char *result;
        bool_t (*xdr_argument)(), (*xdr_result)();
        char *(*local)();

        switch (rqstp->rq_proc) {
        case NULLPROC:
                (void)svc_sendreply(transp, xdr_void, (char *)NULL);
                return;

        case INITW:
                xdr_argument = xdr_void;
                xdr_result = xdr_int;
                local = (char *(*)()) initw_1;
                break;

        case INSERTW:
                xdr_argument = xdr_wrapstring;
                xdr_result = xdr_int;
                local = (char *(*)()) insertw_1;
                break;

        case DELETEW:
                xdr_argument = xdr_wrapstring;
                xdr_result = xdr_int;
                local = (char *(*)()) deletew_1;
                break;

        case LOOKUPW:
                xdr_argument = xdr_wrapstring;
                xdr_result = xdr_int;
                local = (char *(*)()) lookupw_1;
                break;

        default:
                svcerr_noproc(transp);
                return;
        }
        bzero((char *)&argument, sizeof(argument));
```

```
        if (!svc_getargs(transp, xdr_argument, &argument)) {
                svcerr_decode(transp);
                return;
        }
        result = (*local)(&argument, rqstp);
        if (result != NULL && !svc_sendreply(transp, xdr_result, result)) {
                svcerr_systemerr(transp);
        }
        if (!svc_freeargs(transp, xdr_argument, &argument)) {
                (void)fprintf(stderr, "unable to free arguments\n");
                exit(1);
        }
}
```

Figure 22.7 File *rdict_svc.c* – an example server stub that rpcgen produces.

Once the files have been generated, they can be compiled and kept in object form. In UNIX, the commands to compile all three files that contain generated code are:

```
                        cc -c dict_clnt.c
                        cc -c dict_svc.c
                        cc -c dict_xdr.c
```

Each command takes a C source file and produces a corresponding object file. Object file names have ".o" in place of the ".c" suffix†. For example, the compiled version of *rdict_clnt.c* will be placed in file *rdict_clnt.o*.

22.13 Step 5: Write Stub Interface Procedures

22.13.1 Client-Side Interface Routines

The files that rpcgen produces do not form complete programs. They require client-side and server-side interface routines that the programmer must write. One interface procedure must exist for each remote procedure in the remote program.

On the client side, the original application program controls processing. It calls interface procedures using the same procedure names and argument types as it originally used to call those procedures which have become remote in the distributed version. Each interface procedure must convert its arguments to the form used by rpcgen, and must then call the corresponding client-side communication procedure. For example, because the original program contained a procedure named *insertw* that takes a pointer to a character string as an argument, the client-side interface must contain such a pro-

---

†UNIX programmers sometimes refer to object files as "dot oh" files.

cedure. The interface procedure calls *insertw_1*, the client-side communication stub
generated by rpcgen.

The chief difference between conventional procedure parameters and the parameters used by the communication stubs is that the arguments for all procedures produced
by rpcgen use indirection. For example, if the original procedure had an integer argument, the corresponding argument in the communication stub for that procedure must be
a pointer to an integer. In the dictionary program, most procedures require a character
string argument, declared in C to be a character pointer (*char* *). The corresponding
communication stubs all require that their arguments be a pointer to a character pointer
(*char* **).

File *rdict_cif.c* illustrates how interface routines convert arguments to the form expected by the code produced by rpcgen. The file contains one client-side interface procedure for each of the remote procedures in the program.

```
/* rdict_cif.c - initw, insertw, deletew, lookupw */

#include <rpc/rpc.h>

#include <stdio.h>

#include "rdict.h"

/* Client-side stub interface routines written by programmer */

extern  CLIENT  *handle;                    /* handle for remote procedure  */

/*------------------------------------------------------------------------
 * initw - client interface routine that calls initw_1
 *------------------------------------------------------------------------
 */
int
initw()
{
        return *initw_1(handle);
}

/*------------------------------------------------------------------------
 * insertw - client interface routine that calls insertw_1
 *------------------------------------------------------------------------
 */
int
insertw(word)
char    *word;
{
```

```
        char    **arg;                      /* pointer to argument */
        arg = &word;
        return *insertw_1(arg, handle);
}


/*------------------------------------------------------------------------
 * deletew - client interface routine that calls deletew_1
 *------------------------------------------------------------------------
 */
int
deletew(word)
char    *word;
{
        char    **arg;                      /* pointer to argument */

        arg = &word;
        return *deletew_1(arg, handle);
}


/*------------------------------------------------------------------------
 * lookupw - client interface routine that calls lookupw_1
 *------------------------------------------------------------------------
 */
int
lookupw(word)
char    *word;
{
        char    **arg;                      /* pointer to argument */

        arg = &word;
        return *lookupw_1(arg, handle);
}
```

22.13.2 Server-Side Interface Routines

On the server side, the interface routines accept calls from the communication stubs that rpcgen produces, and pass control to the procedure that implements the specified call. As with the client side, server-side interface routines must translate from argument types chosen by rpcgen to the argument types that the called procedures use. In most cases, the difference lies in an extra indirection – rpcgen passes a pointer to an object instead of the object itself. To convert an argument, an interface procedure only needs to apply the C indirection operator (*). File *rdict_sif.c* illustrates the concept. It contains the server-side interface routines for the dictionary program.

```
/* rdict_sif.c - init_1, insert_1, delete_1, lookup_1 */

#include <rpc/rpc.h>

#include "rdict.h"

/* Server-side stub inteface routines written by programmer */

static  int retcode;

/*-----------------------------------------------------------------------
 * insertw_1 -  server side interface to remote procedure insertw
 *-----------------------------------------------------------------------
 */
int     *
insertw_1(w)
char    **w;
{
        retcode = insertw(*w);
        return &retcode;
}


/*-----------------------------------------------------------------------
 * initw_1 -  server side interface to remote procedure initw
 *-----------------------------------------------------------------------
 */
int     *
initw_1()
{
        retcode = initw();
        return &retcode;
}


/*-----------------------------------------------------------------------
 * deletew_1 -  server side interface to remote procedure deletew
 *-----------------------------------------------------------------------
 */
int     *
deletew_1(w)
char    **w;
{
        retcode = deletew(*w);
        return &retcode;
}
```

```
/*-------------------------------------------------------------------
 * lookupw_1 -   server side interface to remote procedure lookupw
 *-------------------------------------------------------------------
 */
int      *
lookupw_1(w)
char     **w;
{
        retcode = lookupw(*w);
        return &retcode;
}
```

22.14 Step 6: Compile And Link The Client Program

Once the client interface routines have been written and placed in a source file, they can be compiled. For example, file *rdict_cif.c* contains all the interface routines for the dictionary example. On UNIX systems, the command needed to compile the result is:

`cc -c rdict_cif.c`

The compiler produces output file *rdict_cif.o*. To complete the client, the programmer needs to add a few details to the original main program. Because the new version uses RPC, it needs the C *include* file for RPC declarations. It also needs to include file *rdict.h* because that file contains definitions for constants used by both the client and server.

The client program also needs to declare and initialize a *handle* that the RPC communication routines can use to communicate with the server. Most clients declare the handle using the defined type *CLIENT*, and initialize the handle by calling the RPC library routine, *clnt_create*. File *rdict.c* shows an example of the necessary code:

```
/* rdict.c - main, nextin */

#include <rpc/rpc.h>

#include <stdio.h>
#include <ctype.h>

#include "rdict.h"

#define RMACHINE        "localhost"     /* name of remote machine      */
CLIENT  *handle;                        /* handle for remote procedure */

/*------------------------------------------------------------------------
 * main - insert, delete, or lookup words in a dictionary as specified
 *------------------------------------------------------------------------
 */
int
main(argc, argv)
int     argc;
char    *argv[];
{
        char    word[MAXWORD+1]; /* space to hold word from input line */
        char    cmd;
        int     wrdlen;          /* length of input word               */

     /* set up connection for remote procedure call  */

       handle = clnt_create(RMACHINE, RDICTPROG, RDICTVERS, "tcp");
       if (handle == 0) {
               printf("Could not contact remote program.\n");
               exit(1);
       }

       while (1) {
               wrdlen = nextin(&cmd, word);
               if (wrdlen < 0)
                       exit(0);
               switch (cmd) {
               case 'I':       /* "initialize" */
                       initw();
                       printf("Dictionary initialized to empty.\n");
                       break;
               case 'i':       /* "insert" */
                       insertw(word);
```

```
                                  printf("%s inserted.\n",word);
                                  break;
                     case 'd':          /* "delete" */
                          if (deletew(word))
                                  printf("%s deleted.\n",word);
                          else
                                  printf("%s not found.\n",word);
                          break;
                     case 'l':          /* "lookup" */
                          if (lookupw(word))
                                  printf("%s was found.\n",word);
                          else
                                  printf("%s was not found.\n",word);
                          break;
                     case 'q':          /* quit */
                          printf("program quits.\n");
                          exit(0);
                     default:           /* illegal input */
                          printf("command %c invalid.\n", cmd);
                          break;
                }
        }
}


/*-----------------------------------------------------------------------
 * nextin - read a command and (possibly) a word from the next input line
 *-----------------------------------------------------------------------
 */
int
nextin(cmd, word)
char    *cmd, *word;
{
        int     i, ch;

        ch = getc(stdin);
        while (ch == ' ')
                ch = getc(stdin);
        if (ch == EOF)
                return -1;
        *cmd = (char) ch;
        ch = getc(stdin);
        while (ch == ' ')
                ch = getc(stdin);
        if (ch == EOF)
```

```
                    return -1;
        if (ch == '\n')
                    return 0;
        i = 0;
        while ((ch != ' ') && (ch != '\n')) {
                    if (++i > MAXWORD) {
                                printf("error: word too long.\n");
                                exit(1);
                    }
                    *word++ = ch;
                    ch = getc(stdin);
        }
        return i;
}
```

Compare *rdict.c* with *dict1.c*† from which it was derived to see how little code has been added. The sample code uses symbolic constant *RMACHINE* to specify the domain name of the remote machine. To make testing easy *RMACHINE* has been de-fined to be *localhost*, which means the client and server will operate on the same machine. Of course, once testing has been completed on a distributed program, the pro-grammer will change the definition to specify the permanent location of the server.

Clnt_create attempts to make a connection to a specified remote machine. If the connection attempt fails, *clnt_create* returns the value *NULL*, allowing the application to report an error to the user. Our sample code exits if *clnt_create* reports an error. In practice, a client may choose to try repeatedly, or may maintain a list of machines and try each of them.

Like other C source files, *rdict.c* can be compiled with a single command:

```
cc -c rdict.c
```

Once the object program for *rdict.c* has been compiled, all files that comprise the client can be linked together into an executable program. The UNIX *cc* command invokes the linker for .o files. It can be invoked with the *-o* option to put the output in a named file. For example, the command line below links the .o files together and places the resulting executable client program in file *rdict*:

```
cc -o rdict rdict.o rdict_clnt.o rdict_xdr.o rdict_cif.o
```

---

†File *dict1.c* can be found on page 276.

22.15 Step 7: Compile And Link The Server Program

The output generated by rpcgen includes most of the code needed for a server. The programmer supplies two additional files: the server interface routines (which we have chosen to place in file *rdict_sif.c*) and the remote procedures themselves. For the dictionary example, the final version of the remote procedures appears in file *rdict_srp.c*. The code for the procedures has been derived from the code in the original application.

```c
/* rdict_srp.c - initw, insertw, deletew, lookupw */

#include <rpc/rpc.h>

#include "rdict.h"

/* Server-side remote procedures and the global data they use */

char    dict[DICTSIZ][MAXWORD+1];/* storage for a dictionary of words   */
int     nwords = 0;              /* number of words in the dictionary   */

/*-------------------------------------------------------------------
 * initw - initialize the dictionary to contain no words at all
 *-------------------------------------------------------------------
 */
int
initw()
{
        nwords = 0;
        return 1;
}


/*-------------------------------------------------------------------
 * insertw - insert  a word in the dictionary
 *-------------------------------------------------------------------
 */
int
insertw(word)
char    *word;
{
        strcpy(dict[nwords], word);
        nwords++;
        return nwords;
}
```

```
/*-----------------------------------------------------------------------
 * deletew - delete  a word from the dictionary
 *-----------------------------------------------------------------------
 */
int
deletew(word)
char    *word;
{
        int     i;

        for (i=0 ; i<nwords ; i++)
                if (strcmp(word, dict[i]) == 0) {
                        nwords--;
                        strcpy(dict[i], dict[nwords]);
                        return 1;
                }
        return 0;
}


/*-----------------------------------------------------------------------
 * lookupw - look up a word in the dictionary
 *-----------------------------------------------------------------------
 */
int
lookupw(word)
char    *word;
{
        int     i;

        for (i=0 ; i<nwords ; i++)
                if (strcmp(word, dict[i]) == 0)
                        return 1;
        return 0;
}
```

Once the file containing remote procedures has been compiled using command:

cc -c rdict_srp.c

the object programs that comprise the server can be linked together into an executable file with the command:

```
cc -o rdictd rdict_svc.o rdict_xdr.o rdict_sif.o rdict_srp.o
```

When the command runs, it leaves the executable code in file *rdictd*†.

22.16 Step 8: Start The Server And Execute The Client

The first serious test of the entire system occurs when both the client and server components operate together on the same machine. The server must begin execution before the client attempts to contact it or the client will print the message:

Could not contact remote program.

and halt. On a UNIX system, the command:

```
./rdictd &
```

starts the server running in the background and leaves the user's terminal free to accept other commands. One can invoke the client interactively by typing its name and then typing the input. Alternatively, one can redirect the input from a file when invoking the client.

22.17 Using The UNIX Make Utility

Managing all the files associated with a distributed program can become tiresome. The UNIX utility program *make* helps because it automates the task of determining which programs should be recompiled after a change has been made. *Make* reads a specification file that lists dependencies among files and gives commands to run to rebuild complicated programs automatically. While the details of *make* are beyond the scope of this book, it is instructive to see how a simple input to *make* can specify all the files and commands needed to build the original or distributed versions of the dictionary program. File *Makefile* contains the specifications:

---

†UNIX systems often name servers with a trailing ''*d*'' to stand for *daemon*, the technical term UNIX applies to programs that run in the background.

```
#
#  Makefile for example dictionary application (conventional and RPC)
#
all:            dict dict1.o dict2.o rdict rdictd

install:        all
                @echo nothing to install.

clean:
                rm *.o dict rdict rdictd

#
# Original (conventional) application
#
dict:           dict.c
                cc -o dict dict.c

#
# Test division into two parts to see if they compile
#
dict1.o:        dict1.c
                cc -c dict1.c

dict2.o:        dict2.c
                cc -c dict2.c

#
# Dependencies for files generated by rpcgen
#
rdict_clnt.c:   rdict.h rdict.x

rdict_svc.c:    rdict.h rdict.x

rdict_xdr.c:    rdict.h rdict.x

rdict.h:        rdict.x
                rpcgen rdict.x

#
# Link client-side files for RPC version
#
rdict:          rdict_clnt.o rdict_cif.o rdict.o rdict_xdr.o
                cc -o rdict rdict_clnt.o rdict_cif.o rdict.o \
                    rdict_xdr.o
```

```
                chmod 755 rdict

#
# Link server-side files for RPC version
#
rdictd:         rdict_svc.o rdict_sif.o rdict_srp.o rdict_xdr.o
                cc -o rdictd rdict_svc.o rdict_sif.o rdict_srp.o \
                        rdict_xdr.o
                chmod 755 rdictd

#
# Individual object file dependencies
#
rdict.o:        rdict.c rdict.h rdict.x
                cc -c rdict.c

rdict_clnt.o:   rdict_clnt.c rdict.h rdict.x
                cc -c rdict_clnt.c

rdict_svc.o:    rdict_svc.c rdict.h rdict.x
                cc -c rdict_svc.c

rdict_xdr.o:    rdict_xdr.c rdict.h rdict.x
                cc -c rdict_xdr.c

rdict_cif.o:    rdict_cif.c rdict.h rdict.x
                cc -c rdict_cif.c

rdict_sif.o:    rdict_sif.c rdict.h rdict.x
                cc -c rdict_sif.c

rdict_srp.o:    rdict_srp.c rdict.h rdict.x
                cc -c rdict_srp.c
```

Once the *Makefile* has been established, recompilation of the client and server are completely automatic. For example, if one starts in a directory that contains the rpcgen specification file, the *Makefile*, and all the source files described in this chapter, invoking *make* in that directory executes the following sequence of commands:

```
        cc -o dict dict.c
        cc -c dict1.c
        cc -c dict2.c
        rpcgen rdict.x
        cc -c rdict_clnt.c
```

```
cc -c rdict_cif.c
cc  -c rdict.c
cc  -c rdict_xdr.c
cc -o rdict rdict_clnt.o rdict_cif.o rdict.o  rdict_xdr.o
chmod 755 rdict
cc -c rdict_svc.c
cc  -c rdict_sif.c
cc -c rdict_srp.c
cc -o rdictd rdict_svc.o rdict_sif.o rdict_srp.o  rdict_xdr.o
chmod 755 rdictd
```

Thus, running *make* produces an executable client, *rdict*, and an executable server, *rdictd*.

22.18 Summary

Constructing a distributed program using rpcgen consists of eight steps. The programmer begins with a conventional application program to solve the problem, decides how to partition the program into components that execute locally and remotely, divides the application into two physical parts, creates a specification file that describes the remote program, and runs rpcgen to produce needed files. The programmer then writes client-side and server-side interface routines and combines them with the code produced by rpcgen. Finally, the programmer compiles and links the client-side files and the server-side files to produce executable client and server programs.

Although rpcgen eliminates much of the coding required for RPC, building a distributed program requires careful thought. When considering how to partition a program into local and remote components, the programmer must examine the data accessed by each piece to minimize data movement. The programmer must also consider the delay that each remote procedure call will introduce as well as how each piece will access I/O facilities.

The example dictionary application in this chapter shows how much effort is required to transform a trivial application into a distributed program. More complicated applications require substantially more complex specifications and interface procedures. In particular, applications that pass structured data to remote procedures or that check client authorizations can require substantially more code.

FOR FURTHER STUDY

Information about rpcgen can be found in the *Network Programming Guide* that accompanies the SunOS operating system. The *UNIX Programmer's Manual* describes the details of the *make* utility.

EXERCISES

22.1   Modify the example program from this chapter so the client interface routine keeps a cache of recently referenced words and searches the cache before making a remote procedure call. How much additional computational overhead does the cache require? How much time does the cache save when an entry can be found locally?

22.2   Build a distributed application that provides access to files on the remote machine. Include remote procedures that permit the client to *read* or *write* data to a specified location in a specified file.

22.3   Build a distributed program that passes a linked list as an argument to a remote procedure. Hint: use relative pointers instead of absolute memory addresses.

22.4   Try to modify the example dictionary program so the remote procedures can write error messages on the client's standard error file. What problems did you encounter? How did you solve them?

22.5   Rpcgen could have been designed so it automatically assigns each remote procedure a unique number, 1, 2, and so on. What are the advantages of having the programmer assign remote procedure numbers manually in the specification file instead of assigning them automatically? What are the disadvantages?

22.6   What limitations does rpcgen have? Hint: consider trying to build a server that is also a client for another service.

22.7   Look carefully at the code in *rdict_clnt.c*. What steps does the client take when it begins execution?

22.8   Try building and testing two versions of the distributed dictionary program simultaneously. Would it be possible to test new versions if the server side used well-known port numbers? Explain.

22.9   The example dictionary program recognizes blanks as separator characters in the input. Revise procedure *nextin* to allow tabs as well as blanks.

23

Network File System
Concepts (NFS)

23.1 Introduction

The previous chapters describe the Sun RPC facility, explain the relationship between RPC and client-server interaction, and show how RPC can be used to create a distributed version of an application program. This chapter and the next focus on an application and a protocol that is specified, designed, and implemented using RPC. This chapter describes the general concept of remote file access, and reviews the concepts underlying a particular remote file access mechanism. Because the mechanism derives many ideas and details from UNIX, this chapter reviews the UNIX file system and the semantics of file operations. It discusses hierarchical directory structures and path names, and shows how a remote file access mechanism implements operations on hierarchies. The next chapter provides additional details about the protocol, and shows how the protocol specification uses RPC to define remote file operations.

23.2 Remote File Access Vs. Transfer

Many early network systems provided *file transfer* services that permitted users to move a copy of a file from one machine to another. More recent network systems provide *file access* services that permit an application program to access a file from a remote machine. A remote file access mechanism keeps one copy of each file, and allows one or more application programs to access the copy on demand.

Applications that use a remote file mechanism to access a file can execute on the machine where the file resides, or they can execute on remote machines. When an application accesses a file that resides on a remote machine, the program's operating system invokes client software that contacts a server on the remote machine and performs the requested operations on the file. Unlike a file transfer service, the application's system does not retrieve or store an entire file at once. Instead, it requests transfers of one small block of data at a time.

To provide remote access to some or all of the files that reside on a computer, the system manager must arrange for the computer to run a server that responds to access requests. The server checks each request to verify that the client is authorized to access the specified file, performs the specified operation, and returns a result to the client.

Sun Microsystems, Incorporated defined a remote file access mechanism that has become widely accepted throughout the computer industry. Known as Sun's *Network File System*, or simply *NFS*, the mechanism allows a computer to run a server that makes some or all of its files available for remote access, and allows applications on other computers to access those files.

23.3 Operations On Remote Files

NFS provides the same operations on remote files that one expects to use on local files. An application can *open* a remote file to obtain access, *read* data from the file, *write* data to the file, *seek* to a specified position in the file (either at the beginning, the end, or elsewhere), and *close* the file when finished using it.

23.4 File Access Among Heterogeneous Computers

Providing remote file access can be nontrivial. In addition to the basic mechanisms for reading and writing files, a file access service must provide ways to create and destroy files, peruse directories, authenticate requests, honor file protections, and translate information between the representations used on various computers. Because a remote file access service connects two machines, it must handle differences in the way the client and server systems name files, denote paths through directories, and store information about files. More important, the file access software must accommodate differences in the semantic interpretation of file operations.

NFS was designed to accommodate heterogeneous computer systems. From the beginning, the NFS protocol, operations, and semantics were chosen to allow a variety of systems to interact. Of course, NFS cannot provide all the file system subtleties available in all possible operating systems. Instead, it tries to define file operations that accommodate as many systems as possible without becoming inefficient or hopelessly complex. In practice, most of the choices work well.

23.5 Stateless Servers

The NFS design stores state information at the client site, allowing servers to remain stateless. Because the server is stateless, disruptions in service will not affect client operation. In theory, for example, a client will be able to continue file access after a stateless server crashes and reboots; the application program, which runs on the client system, can remain unaware of the server reboot. Furthermore, because a stateless server does not need to allocate resources for each client, a stateless design can scale to handle many more clients than a stateful design.

NFS's stateless server design affects both the protocol and its implementation. Most important, a server cannot keep any notion of *position*, whether in a file or directory. We will see how NFS achieves a stateless design after examining the operations that NFS provides.

23.6 NFS And UNIX File Semantics

Although NFS was designed to accommodate heterogeneous file systems, the UNIX file system strongly influenced its overall design, the terminology used, and many of the protocol details. The NFS designers adopted UNIX file system semantics when defining the meaning of individual operations. Thus, to understand NFS, one must begin with the UNIX file system.

Chapter *3* contains a brief description of UNIX I/O; the next section expands that description. It discusses file storage and access under UNIX, concentrating on those concepts and details that are most pertinent to NFS. Later sections show how NFS borrowed many ideas from the UNIX file system directly and adopted many of the details with only slight modifications. To summarize:

> *Understanding the UNIX file system is essential to understanding NFS because NFS uses the UNIX file system terminology and semantics.*

23.7 Review Of The UNIX File System

23.7.1 Basic Definitions

From the user's point of view, UNIX defines a *file* to consist of a sequence of bytes. In theory, a UNIX file can grow arbitrarily large; in practice, a file is limited by the space available on the physical storage device. UNIX files can grow dynamically. The file system does not require predeclaration of the expected size or preallocation of space. Instead, a file grows automatically to accommodate whatever data an application writes into it.

Conceptually, UNIX numbers the bytes in a file starting at zero. At any time, the *size* of a file is defined to be the number of bytes in it. The UNIX file system permits random access to any file, using the byte numbers as a reference. It allows an application to move to any byte position in a file and to access data at that position.

23.7.2 A Byte Sequence Without Record Boundaries

Each UNIX file is a sequence of bytes; the system does not provide any additional structure for a file beyond the data itself. In particular, UNIX does not have notions of *record boundaries*, *record blocking*, *indexed files*, or *typed files* found in other systems. Of course, it is possible for an application to create a file of records and to access them later. The point is that the file system itself does not understand the file contents: applications that use a file must agree on the format.

23.7.3 A File's Owner And Group Identifiers

UNIX systems provide accounts for multiple users, and assign each user a numeric user identifier used for accounting and authentication throughout the system. Each UNIX file has a single *owner*, represented by the numeric identifier of the user who created the file. Ownership information is stored with the file (i.e., as opposed to the directory system).

In addition to user identifiers, UNIX provides for file sharing among groups of users by allowing the system manager to assign a subset of users a numeric *group identifier*. At any time, a given user can belong to one or more UNIX groups. When a user runs an application program (e.g., a spreadsheet program or a text editor), the running program inherits the user's owner and group identifiers. Each UNIX file belongs to one group and has its numeric group identifier stored with it. The system compares the owner and group identifiers stored with a file to the user and group identifiers of a particular application process to determine what operations that program can perform on the file.

23.7.4 Protection And Access

The UNIX access protection mechanism allows a file's owner to control file access separately for the owner, members of the file's group, and all other users. For each of the three sets, the protection mechanism allows the owner to specify whether the users in that set have permission to *read*, *write*, or *execute* the file. Figure 23.1 shows that the UNIX file access permissions can be viewed as a matrix of protection bits.

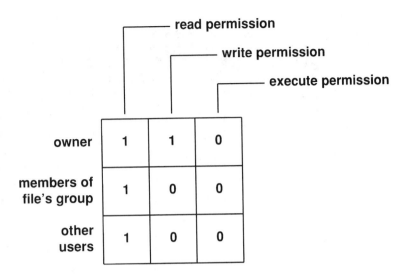

Figure 23.1 UNIX file access permissions viewed as a matrix of protection
bits.

UNIX encodes the file access protection matrix in the low-order bits of a single
binary integer, and uses the terms *file mode* or *file access mode* when referring to the
integer that encodes the protection bits. Figure 23.2 illustrates how UNIX encodes file
protection bits into the 9 low-order bits of a file mode integer. In addition to the protection bits illustrated in Figure 23.2, UNIX defines additional bits of the mode integer
to specify other properties of the file (e.g., mode bits specify whether the file is a regular file or a directory).

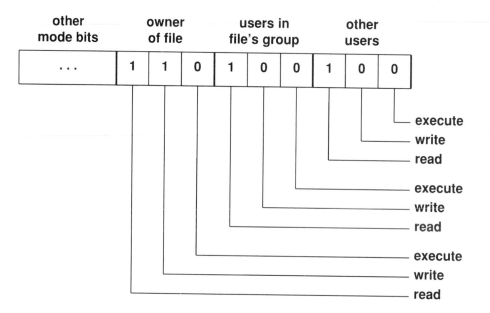

Figure 23.2 UNIX file access permissions stored in the low-order nine bits of the mode integer. A value of *1* grants permission; a value of *0* denies it. When written in octal, the protections illustrated have the value *0644*.

When the value of the protection integer is written in octal, the rightmost three digits give the protections for the owner, members of the file's group, and other users. Thus, a protection value of *0700* specifies that the owner can read, write, or execute the file, but no other users can have access. A protection mode value of *0644* specifies that all users can read the file, but only the owner can write to it.

23.7.5 The Open-Read-Write-Close Paradigm

Under UNIX, applications use the *open-read-write-close* to access files. To establish access to a file, an application must call function *open*, passing it the name of the file and an argument that describes the desired access. *Open* returns an integer file descriptor that the application uses for all further operations on the file. For example, the code:

```
fdesc = open("filename", O_CREAT | O_RDWR, 0644);
```

opens a file with name *filename*. The value *O_CREAT* in the second argument specifies that the file should be created if it does not already exist, and the value *O_RDWR* specifies that the file should be created for both reading and writing. The octal value *0644* specifies protection mode bits to assign to the file if it is created. Other values for the second argument can be used to specify whether the file should be truncated and whether it should be opened for reading, writing, or both.

23.7.6 Data Transfer

An application uses *read* to transfer data from a file into memory, and uses *write* to transfer data from memory to a file. The *read* function takes three arguments: the descriptor for an open file, a buffer address, and the number of bytes to read. For example, the following code requests that the system read *24* bytes of data from the file with descriptor *fdesc*:

```
n = read(fdesc, buff, 24);
```

Both *read* and *write* begin transfer at the current file position, and both operations update the file position when they finish. For example, if an application opens a file, moves to position *0*, and reads *10* bytes from the file, the file position will be *10* after the *read* operation completes. Thus, a program can extract all data from a file sequentially by starting at position zero and calling *read* repeatedly.

If an application attempts to *read* more bytes than the file contains, the *read* function extracts as many bytes as the file contains and returns the number read as its result. If the file is positioned at the end of a file when an application calls *read*, the *read* call returns zero to indicate an *end-of-file* condition.

23.7.7 Permission To Search A Directory

UNIX organizes files into a *hierarchy* using *directories*† to hold files and other directories. The system uses the same *9*-bit protection mode scheme for directories as it uses for regular data files. The *read* permission bits determine whether an application can obtain a list of the files in a directory, and the *write* permission bits determine whether an application can insert or delete files in the directory. Each individual file has a separate set of permission bits that determine which operations are allowed on the contents of the file. The directory permissions only specify which operations are allowed on the directory itself.

Directories can contain application programs, but they do not consist of compiled code themselves. Thus, they cannot be executed like an application program, so *execute* permission is meaningless for a directory. UNIX interprets the *execute* permission bits for directories to mean *search permission*. If an application has search permission, it can reference a file that lies in a directory; otherwise, the system will not permit any references to the file. Search permission can be used to hide or uncover an entire subtree of the file hierarchy without modifying the permissions on individual files in the subtree.

23.7.8 Random Access

When a file is opened, the position can be set to the beginning of the file (e.g., to access the file sequentially) or to the end of the file (e.g., to append data to an existing file). After a file has been opened, the position can be changed by calling function

---

†Other systems sometimes use the term *folder* to denote what UNIX calls a *directory*.

lseek. *Lseek* takes three arguments that specify a file descriptor, an offset, and a measure for the offset. The third argument allows an application to specify whether the offset gives an absolute location in the file (e.g., byte *512*), a new location relative to the current position (e.g., a byte that is *64* beyond the current position), or a position relative to the end of the file (e.g., *2* bytes before the end of the file). For example, the constant *L_SET* specifies that the system should interpret the offset as an absolute value. Thus, the call:

```
lseek(fdesc, 100L, L_SET);
```

specifies that the current position of the file with descriptor *fdesc* should be moved to byte number *100*.

23.7.9 Seeking Beyond The End Of File

The UNIX file system permits an application to move to any position in a file, even if the specified position lies beyond the current end of the file. If the application seeks to an existing byte position and writes new data, the new data replaces the old data at that position. If the application seeks beyond the end of the file and writes new data, the file system extends the file size. From the user's point of view, the system appears to fill any gap between existing data and new data with null bytes (bytes with value zero). Later, if an application attempts to read from the byte positions that comprise the gap, the file system will return bytes with zeros in them. Figure 23.3 illustrates the concept:

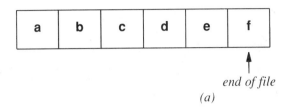

end of file
(a)

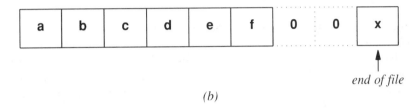

end of file
(b)

Figure 23.3 (a) a UNIX file that contains 6 bytes consisting of the characters
a through *f* and (b) the file after an application seeks to position
8 and writes a byte containing the character *x*. Unwritten bytes
appear to contain zeroes.

Although the file system appears to fill gaps with null bytes, the storage structure makes
it possible to simulate null bytes without representing them on the physical medium.
Thus, the file size records the highest byte position into which data has been written,
not the total number of bytes written.

23.7.10 File Position And Concurrent Access

The UNIX file system permits multiple application programs to access a file concurrently. The descriptor for each open file references a data structure that records a
current position in the file. When a process calls *fork* to create a new process, the child
inherits copies of all file descriptors the parent had open at the time of the fork. The
descriptors point to a common underlying data structure used to access the file. Thus, if
one of the two processes changes the file position, the position changes for the other
process as well.

Each call to *open* generates a new descriptor with a file position that is independent of that obtained by previous calls to *open*. Thus, if two applications both call *open*
on the same file, they can each maintain an independent position in the file. One application can move to the end of the file, while the other remains at the beginning. Programmers must decide when designing an application whether it needs to share the file
position with another process or have a separate position.

Understanding the separation between file position and files will become important when we examine operations on remote files. The concept can be summarized:

> *Each call to* open *produces a new file access point that stores a file offset. Separating the current file position from the file itself permits multiple applications to access a file concurrently without interference. It also allows an* lseek *operation to modify an application's position in a file without changing the file itself.*

23.7.11 Semantics Of Write During Concurrent Access

When two programs write a file concurrently, they may introduce conflicts. For example, suppose two concurrent programs each read the first two bytes of a file, exchange the bytes, and write them back into the file. If the scheduler chooses to run one program and then the other, the first program will swap the two bytes and write them back to the file. The second program will read the bytes in reversed order, swap them back to their original positions, and write them back to the file. However, if the scheduler starts both programs running, and allows them each to read from the file before either writes to it, they will both read the bytes in original order and then both write the bytes in reverse order. As a consequence, the byte order in the file depends on how the system scheduler chooses to delegate the CPU to the two programs.

UNIX does not provide mutual exclusion or define the semantics of concurrent access except to specify that a file always contains the data written most recently. Responsibility for correctness falls to the programmer†. A programmer must be careful to construct concurrent programs in such a way that they always produce the same results.

23.7.12 File Names And Paths

UNIX provides a hierarchical file namespace. Each file and directory in a UNIX file system has an individual name that can be represented by an ASCII string. In addition, each directory or file has a *full path name* that denotes the position of the file within the hierarchy. Figure 23.4 illustrates the names of files and directories for a small example of a UNIX hierarchy.

---

†Some versions of UNIX offer an advisory lock mechanism such as *flock* or *lockf*; others offer exclusive access with argument *O_EXCL* in the *open* call.

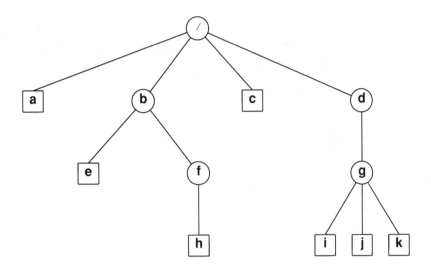

Figure 23.4 An example hierarchical file system. Circles denote directories and squares denote files. In this example, the top level directory contains two files (*a* and *c*) and two directories (*b* and *d*). In practice, UNIX files seldom have single-character names.

As the figure shows, the top directory of the file system, called the *root*, has full path name / (usually pronounced ''slash''). The full path name of a file can be thought of as the concatenation of labels on the path in the hierarchy from the root to the file, using / as a separator character. For example, the file with name *a* that appears in the root directory has full path name */a*. The file with name *e* that appears in directory *b* has full path name */b/e*, and the file with name *k* has full path name */d/g/k*.

23.7.13 Inode: Information Stored With A File

In addition to the data itself, UNIX stores information about each file on stable storage. The information is kept in a structure known as the file's *inode*†. The inode contains many fields, including: the owner and group identifiers, the mode integer (described in Section 23.7.4), the time of last access, the time of last modification, the file size, the disk device and file system on which the file resides, the number of directory entries for the file, the number of disk blocks currently used by the file, and the basic type (e.g., regular file or directory).

The inode concept helps explain several features of the UNIX file system that are also used in NFS. First, UNIX separates information such as ownership and file protection bits from the directory entry for a file. Doing so makes it possible to have two directory entries that point to the same file. UNIX uses the term *link* or *hard link* to refer to a directory entry for a file. As Figure 23.5 illustrates, when a file has more than one hard link, it appears in more than one directory.

---

†*Inode*, usually pronounced ''eye-node,'' is an abbreviation for *index node*.

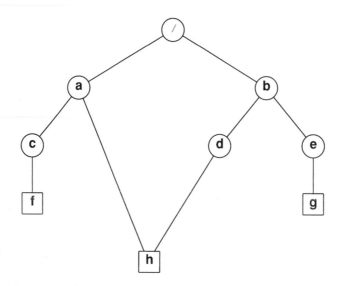

Figure 23.5 An illustration of hard links. File *h* has two links, one from
directory *a* and one from directory *d*. File *h* can be accessed by
path name */a/h* or path name */b/d/h*.

Files with multiple hard links can be accessed by more than one full path name.
For example, in Figure *23.5*, file *h* can be accessed by full path name */a/h* because it appears in directory *a*. It can also be accessed by full path name */b/d/h* because it appears
in directory *d*. As the example shows, the path names for a file with multiple links can
differ in length.

Because UNIX stores information about a file in its inode and not in the directory,
ownership and protection information for file *h* remain consistent no matter which name
an application uses to access the file. If the owner changes the protection mode of file
/a/h, the protection mode will also change on file */b/d/h*.

23.7.14 Stat Operation

The UNIX system function *stat* extracts information about a file from its inode and
returns the information to the caller. The call takes two arguments: the path name of a
file and the address of a structure into which it places the results:

```
stat( pathname, &result_struct );
```

The second argument must be the address of an area in memory large enough to hold the following structure:

```
struct stat {                       /* structure returned by stat   */
        dev_t   st_dev;             /* device on which inode resides*/
        ino_t   st_ino;             /* file's inode number          */
        u_short st_mode;            /* protection bits              */
        short   st_nlink;           /* total hard links to the file */
        short   st_uid;             /* user id of file's owner      */
        short   st_gid;             /* group id assigned to file    */
        dev_t   st_rdev;            /* used for devices, not files  */
        long    st_size;            /* total size of file in bytes  */
        time_t  st_atime;           /* time of last file access     */
        int     st_unused1;         /* not used                     */
        time_t  st_mtime;           /* time of last modification    */
        int     st_unused2;         /* not used                     */
        time_t  st_ctime;           /* time of last inode change    */
};
```

Any user can call *stat* to obtain information about a file, even if the file itself is not readable. However, the caller must have permission to search all the directories along the path to the specified file or *stat* will return an error.

23.7.15 The File Naming Mechanism

Although users imagine all files and directories to be part of a single hierarchy, the hierarchy is achieved through a file naming mechanism. The naming mechanism allows a system manager to piece together a single, conceptual hierarchy out of several smaller hierarchies. Users seldom understand the underlying file system structure or how the various components form the UNIX hierarchy because the naming mechanism hides the structure completely. We will see that when NFS runs under UNIX, it takes advantage of the UNIX naming mechanism to integrate remote files with local ones.

The original motivation for the UNIX naming mechanism arose because computer systems have multiple physical storage devices (i.e., multiple hard disks). Instead of forcing users to identify a disk as well as a file, the UNIX designers invented the idea of allowing the system manager to attach the hierarchy on one disk to the hierarchy on another. The result is a single, unified file namespace that permits the user to work without knowing the location of files. The naming mechanism operates as follows:

- The manager designates the hierarchy on one of the disks to be the root.
- The manager creates an empty directory in the root hierarchy. Let the full path name of the empty directory be given by a string $/\alpha$.
- The manager instructs the naming mechanism to overlay a new hierarchy (usually one from some other disk) over directory $/\alpha$.

Once the manager has attached the new hierarchy, the naming mechanism automatically maps names of the form $/\alpha/\beta$ to the file or subdirectory with path β in the attached hierarchy. The important concept is:

> *The UNIX naming mechanism provides users and application programs with a single, uniform file hierarchy even though the underlying files span multiple physical disks.*

In fact, the UNIX system is more general than a system that attaches entire disks as part of the hierarchy. It allows a system manager to partition a single physical disk into one or more *file systems*. Each file system is an independent hierarchy; it includes both files and directories. A file system can be attached to the unified hierarchy at any point. The example in the next section will clarify the naming mechanism.

23.7.16 File System Mounts

The UNIX naming mechanism relies on the *mount* system call to construct the unified hierarchy. The system manager uses *mount* to specify how a file system on one disk should be attached in the hierarchy. Usually, the manager arranges to perform necessary mounts automatically at system startup. Figure 23.6 illustrates three file systems that have been mounted to form a single hierarchy.

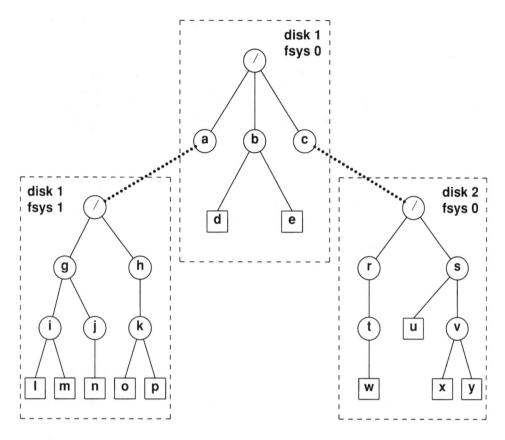

Figure 23.6 Three UNIX file systems mounted to form a single, uniform hierarchy. After the mounts, the boundaries between disks become invisible. For example, file system *0* on disk *2* appears to be directory */c*.

In the figure, file system *0* on disk *1* has been mounted on the root of the hierarchy. File system *1* on the same disk has been mounted on directory */a*, and file system *0* on disk *2* has been mounted on directory */c*. A mount completely overlays an original directory with a new file system. Usually, the system administrator creates a directory to be used for mounting. However, if the directory on which a file system is mounted contains any files before the mount occurs, they will be completely hidden (i.e., inaccessible, even to system administrators) until the file system is unmounted again.

From the user's point of view, the mounts are completely invisible†. If the user lists the contents of directory */*, the system reports three subdirectories: *a*, *b*, and *c*. If the user lists the contents of directory */a*, the system reports two directories: *g* and *h*. If the user lists the contents of directory */c/s*, the system reports a file, *u*, and a directory, *v*.

---

†Users cannot create hard links that cross file system boundaries.

Path names do not denote the boundaries between file systems; users do not know where files reside. For example, the file named *n* (located in file system *1* on disk *1*) can be accessed using the full path name */a/g/j/n*.

> *Once a UNIX file system hierarchy has been constructed using the* mount *system function, attachments between individual file systems become transparent. Some files and directories can reside on one disk, while other files and directories reside on another disk. The user cannot distinguish among them because mounting hides all the boundaries under a uniform naming scheme.*

In practice, users can find out how the file systems have been mounted if they are interested. The system includes an executable application named *mount* that queries the system, and then displays the list of mounted file systems. A manager can also use the *mount* command to create new mounts. For example, running the *mount* command on one computer produced the following output:

```
/dev/ra0a on /          type ufs (rw,noquota)
/dev/ra1h on /usr       type ufs (rw,noquota)
/dev/ra0b on /usr/src   type ufs (rw,noquota)
```

The first line of output shows that file system *ra0a* (the first file system on disk *0*) has been mounted on */* and forms the root of the hierarchy. The words *type ufs* indicate that the mount refers to a *UNIX File System*, and the items in parentheses mean that the file system has been mounted for both reading and writing and that it does not have accounting quotas. File system *ra1h* (the main file system on disk *1*) has been mounted on */usr*. Thus, files that appear in directory */usr* reside on a different disk than those in */*. Finally, file system *ra0b* (the second file system on disk *0*) has been mounted on */usr/src*. The third mount provides an interesting twist because it means that although most files in */usr* reside on disk *1*, files in the subtree */usr/src* reside on disk *0*. The point is that the *mount* mechanism permits a manager to combine many file systems on many disks into a single, uniform directory hierarchy; a user or an application program uses the uniform hierarchy without knowing the location of files.

The concept of mounting file systems to form a single hierarchy provides incredible flexibility. It allows managers to choose an allocation of files to disks for economy, to reduce access contention, or to keep directories isolated in case of accidental loss. As we will see, it also provides a convenient way to introduce remote files into a UNIX hierarchy.

23.7.17 UNIX File Name Resolution

When presented with a full path name, the UNIX file system mechanism traces through the conceptual hierarchy to *resolve* the name. In UNIX, name resolution means finding the inode that identifies a file. To resolve a full path name, the file system begins at the root of the hierarchy and traces through directories one at a time. For example, given a name like */a/b/c/d*, the file system opens the root directory and searches in it for a subdirectory named *a*. Once it finds */a*, it opens that directory and searches it for a subdirectory named *b*. Similarly, it searches in *b* for a directory named *c*, and searches in *c* for a file or subdirectory named *d*. The name resolution software can extract one component of the full path name at each step because the slash character always separates individual components.

While the details of UNIX file name resolution are unimportant, the concept is essential:

> *UNIX resolves a path name one component at a time. It begins at the root of the hierarchy and at the beginning of the path. It repeatedly extracts the next component from the path and finds a file or subdirectory with that name.*

We will see that NFS takes the same approach as UNIX when resolving a name.

23.7.18 Symbolic Links

Later versions of the UNIX file system permit a special file type known as a *symbolic link*. A symbolic link is a special text file that contains the name of another file. For example, one can create a file named */a/b/c* that contains a symbolic link with value */a/q*. If a program opens file */a/b/c*, the system finds that it contains a symbolic link and automatically switches to file */a/q*.

The chief advantage of symbolic links lies in their generality: because a symbolic link can contain an arbitrary string, it can name any file or directory. For example, although the file system forbids making a hard link to a directory, it permits a user to create a symbolic link to a directory. Furthermore, because a symbolic link can refer to an arbitrary path, it can be used to abbreviate a long path name or to make a directory in a distant part of the hierarchy appear to be much closer.

The chief disadvantage of symbolic links arises from their lack of consistency and reliability. One can create a symbolic link to a file and then remove the file, leaving the symbolic link naming a nonexistent object. In fact, one can create a symbolic link to a nonexistent file because the system does not check the contents of a symbolic link when creating it. One can also create a set of symbolic links that forms a cycle or two symbolic links that point to one another. Calling *open* on such a link results in a run-time error.

23.8 Files Under NFS

NFS uses many of the UNIX file system definitions. It views a file as a sequence of bytes, permits files to grow arbitrarily large, and allows random access using byte positions in the file as a reference. It honors the same open-read-write-close paradigm as UNIX, and offers most of the same services.

Like UNIX, NFS assumes a hierarchical naming system. The NFS hierarchy uses
UNIX terminology; it considers the file hierarchy to be composed of *directories* and
files. A directory can contain files and other directories.

NFS has also adopted many of the UNIX file system details, leaving some unchanged, and making minor modifications to others. The next sections describe several
features of NFS and show how they relate to the UNIX file system described earlier.

23.9 NFS File Types

NFS uses the same basic file types as UNIX. It defines enumerated values that a
server can use when specifying a file type:

```
enum ftype {
        NFNON = 0,              /* Specified name is not a file */
        NFREG = 1,              /* Regular data file            */
        NFDIR = 2,              /* Directory                    */
        NFBLK = 3,              /* Block-oriented device        */
        NFCHR = 4,              /* Character-oriented device    */
        NFLNK = 5               /* Symbolic link                */
};
```

The set of types, including *NFBLK* and *NFCHR*, come directly from UNIX. In particular, UNIX permits system managers to configure I/O devices in the file system
namespace, making it possible for application programs to open an I/O device and
transfer data to or from it using the conventional open-read-write-close paradigm. NFS
has adopted UNIX's terminology that divides I/O devices into block-oriented (e.g., a
disk that always transfers data in 512-byte blocks) and character-oriented (e.g., an
ASCII terminal device that transfers data one character at a time) devices. NFS literature sometimes uses the UNIX term *special file* to denote device names. A file name
that corresponds to a block-oriented device has type *block-special*, while a name that
corresponds to a character-oriented device has type *character-special*.

23.10 NFS File Modes

Like UNIX, NFS assumes that each file or directory has a *mode* that specifies its
type and access protection. Figure 23.7 lists individual bits of the NFS mode integer
and gives their meanings. The table uses octal values to represent bits; the definitions
correspond directly to those returned by the UNIX *stat* function.

Mode Bit	Meaning
0040000	This is a directory; the "type" should be *NFDIR*.
0020000	This is a character-special file; the "type" should be *NFCHR*.
0060000	This is a block-special file; the type should be *NFBLK*
0100000	This is a regular file; the type should be *NFREG*
0120000	This is a symbolic link; the type should be *NFLNK*
0140000	This is a named socket; the type should be *NFNON*
0004000	Set user id on execution
0002000	Set group id on execution
0001000	Save swapped text after use
0000400	Read permission for owner
0000200	Write permission for owner
0000100	Execute or directory search permission for owner
0000040	Read permission for group
0000020	Write permission for group
0000010	Execute or directory search permission for group
0000004	Read permission for others
0000002	Write permission for others
0000001	Execute or directory search permission for others

Figure 23.7 The meaning of bits in the NFS *mode* integer. The definitions have been taken directly from UNIX.

Although NFS defines file types for devices, it does not permit remote device access (e.g., a client may not *read* or *write* a remote device). Thus, while it is possible for a client to obtain information about a file name, it is not possible for a client to manipulate devices, even if the protection modes permit it.

Although NFS defines file protection bits that determine whether a client can read or write a particular file, NFS denies a remote machine access to all devices, even if the protection bits specify that access is allowed.

23.11 NFS File Attributes

Similar to UNIX, NFS assumes that it is possible to obtain information about a file. NFS uses the term *file attributes* when referring to file information. Structure *fattr* describes the file attributes that NFS provides:

```
struct fattr {                    /* NFS file attributes        */
        ftype        type;        /* type: file, directory, etc */
        unsigned int mode;        /* file's protection bits     */
        unsigned int nlink;       /* total hard links to the file */
```

```
        unsigned int userid;    /* user id of file's owner      */
        unsigned int groupid;   /* group id assigned to file    */
        unsigned int size;      /* total size of file in bytes  */
        unsigned int blocksize; /* block size used to store file*/
        unsigned int devnum;    /* dev. num. if file is device  */
        unsigned int blocks;    /* number of blocks file uses   */
        unsigned int fsid;      /* file system id for file      */
        unsigned int fileid;    /* unique id for file           */
        timeval      atime;     /* time of last file access     */
        timeval      mtime;     /* time of last modification    */
        timeval      ctime;     /* time of last inode change    */
    };
```

As the structure shows, the concept and most of the details have been derived from the information that the UNIX *stat* function returns.

23.12 NFS Client And Server

An *NFS server* runs on a machine that has a local file system. The server makes some of the local files available to remote machines. An *NFS client* runs on an arbitrary machine, and accesses the files on machines that run NFS servers. Often, an organization will choose to dedicate a computer that has large disks to the server function. Such a machine is often called a *file server*. Forbidding users from running application programs on an NFS file server machine helps keep the load low and guarantees faster response to access requests. Dedicating a computer to the file server function also guarantees that remote file access traffic will not reduce the CPU time available for application programs.

Most NFS client implementations integrate NFS files with the computer's native file system, hiding file locations from application programs and users. For example, consider an *MS-DOS* environment. MS-DOS files have names of the form: $X{:}\alpha$, where X is a single-character disk identifier and α denotes a path name on that disk. MS-DOS uses the backslash character (\) to separate components in the path. Thus, the MS-DOS name $C{:}\backslash D\backslash E\backslash F$ denotes file F in subdirectory E in directory D on the system's hard disk. If an NFS client is added to the system and configured to access files on a remote server, it can use the MS-DOS naming scheme. For example, the manager might choose names of the form $R{:}\beta$ for all remote files, where β denotes a path on the remote file system.

When an application program calls *open* to obtain access to a file, the operating system uses the syntax of the path name to choose between local and remote file access procedures. If the path refers to a remote file, the system uses NFS client software to access the remote file. If the path refers to a local file, the system uses the computer's standard file system software to access the file. Figure 23.8 illustrates how the modules in an operating system interact when making the choice.

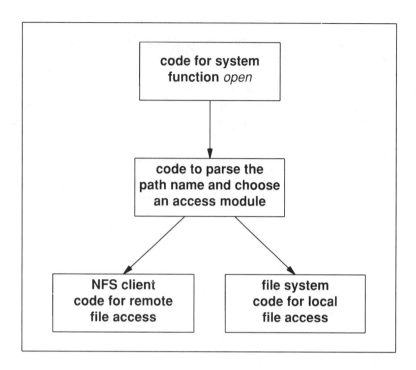

Figure 23.8 Procedures in an operating system that are called when an application opens a file. The system uses the path name syntax to choose between NFS, which will open a remote file, or the standard file system, which will open a local one.

23.13 NFS Client Operation

Recall that NFS was designed to accommodate heterogeneous computer systems. When system managers install NFS client code in an operating system, they try to integrate it into the system's file naming scheme. However, the path name syntax used by the remote file system may differ from that of the client machine. For example, when NFS client code running on a machine that uses MS-DOS connects to an NFS server running on a machine that uses UNIX, the client's system uses backslash (\) as a separator character, while the server's file system uses slash (/).

To accommodate potential differences between the client and server path name syntax, NFS follows a simple rule: only the client side interprets full path names. To trace a full path name through the server's hierarchical directory system, the client sends each individual path name component one at a time. For example, if a client that uses slash as a separator needs to look up path name /a/b/c on a server, it begins by obtaining information about the server's root directory. It then asks the server to look up name *a* in that directory. The server sends back information about *a*. Presumably, the information will show that *a* is a directory. The client then asks the server to look up name *b* in that directory. When the server replies, the client verifies that *b* is a directory, and if it is, asks the server to look up name *c* in it. Finally, the server will respond by sending information about *c*.

The chief disadvantage of requiring the client to parse path names should be obvious: it requires an exchange across the network for each component in the path. The chief advantage should also be obvious: applications on a given computer can access remote files using the same path name syntax they use for local files. More important, both the applications and the client code can be written to access remote files without knowing where files will be located or the naming conventions used by the file systems on the servers. Thus, none of the client applications needs to change when the system manager upgrades one of the server machines, even if the new computer uses a different operating system or a different file naming scheme than the original. To summarize:

> *To keep applications on client machines independent of file locations and server computer systems, NFS requires that only clients interpret full path names. A client traces a path through the server's hierarchy by sending the server one component at a time and receiving information about the file or directory it names.*

23.14 NFS Client And UNIX

Recall that UNIX uses the *mount* mechanism to construct a single, unified naming hierarchy from individual file systems on multiple disks. UNIX implementations of NFS client code use an extended version of the *mount* mechanism to integrate remote file systems into the naming hierarchy along with local file systems. From the application program's perspective, the chief advantage of using the *mount* mechanism is consistency: all file names have the same form. An application program cannot tell whether a file is local or remote from the name syntax alone. When an application opens a remote file, it receives an integer descriptor for the file exactly as it would for a local file. Internal information associated with the descriptor specifies that the file is a remote file accessible through NFS.

Whenever an application performs an operation on a file descriptor (e.g., *read*), the system checks to see whether the descriptor refers to a local file or a remote file. If the file is local, the operating system handles the operation as usual. If the file is remote, the operating system calls NFS client code that translates the operation into an equivalent NFS operation and places a remote procedure call to the server.

23.15 NFS Mounts

When managers add NFS mount entries to a UNIX mount table, they must specify a remote machine that operates an NFS server, a hierarchy on that server, a local directory onto which the mount will be added, and information that specifies details about the mount. For example, the following output from the UNIX *mount* command shows some of the NFS mounts used on a UNIX system at Purdue (non-NFS mounts have been deleted):

```
arthur:/p1 on /p1    type nfs (rw,grpid,intr,bg,noquota)
arthur:/p4 on /p4    type nfs (rw,grpid,intr,bg,noquota)
ector:/u4  on /u4    type nfs (rw,grpid,soft,bg,noquota)
gwen:/     on /gwen type nfs (rw,grpid,soft,bg,noquota)
gwen:/u5   on /u5    type nfs (rw,grpid,soft,bg,noquota)
```

In this output, each line corresponds to a single NFS file system mount. The first field of each line specifies a machine that runs an NFS server and a hierarchy on that server, while the third field specifies a local directory on which the remote file system has been mounted. For example, *arthur:/p1* specifies the */p1* hierarchy on machine *arthur*. It has been mounted on the local directory named */p1*. The system manager chose to mount arthur's */p1* file system on a local directory with the same name so users on both machines could access the files using identical names.

All mounts shown in the example above have type *nfs*, which means they refer to remote file systems available via NFS. In addition, the parenthesized parameters on each line specify further details about the mount. Like mounts for local file systems, the remote file system mounts can specify whether to allow *reading* and *writing* (*rw*) or reading only (*r*).

NFS defines two basic paradigms for remote mounts in UNIX. Using a *soft mount* specifies that an NFS client should implement a timeout mechanism and consider the server offline if the timeout expires. Using a *hard mount* specifies that an NFS client should not use a timeout mechanism.

UNIX administrators usually arrange to have all mounts created automatically at system startup. Once an NFS mount has been created, application programs and users cannot distinguish between local and remote files. The user can use a conventional application program to manipulate a remote file as easily as the program can manipulate a local file. For example, a user can run a standard text editor to edit a remote file; the editor operates on the file the same way it operates on a local file. Furthermore, the user can change to a remote directory or back to a local directory simply by giving a path name that crosses one of the mount points.

23.16 File Handle

Once a client has identified and opened a file, it needs a way to identify that file for subsequent operations (e.g., *read* and *write*). Furthermore, a client needs a way to identify an individual directory or file as it traces through the server's hierarchy. To solve these problems, NFS arranges for a server to assign each file a unique *file handle* that it uses as an identifier. The server makes up a handle and sends it to the client when the client first *open*s the file. The client sends the handle back to the server when it requests operations on the file.

From the client's point of view, the file handle consists of a 32-byte string that the server uses to identify a file. From the server's point of view, a file handle can be chosen to be any convenient set of bytes that uniquely identify an individual file. For example, a file handle can encode information that allows the server to decode a handle and locate a file quickly.

In NFS terminology, a file handle is *opaque* to the client, meaning that a client cannot decode the handle or fabricate a handle itself. Only servers create file handles, and servers only recognize handles that they create. Furthermore, secure implementations of NFS servers use a sophisticated encoding to prevent a client from guessing the handle for a file. In particular, servers choose some of the bits in a handle at random to help ensure that clients cannot fabricate a valid handle.

To improve security, servers can also limit the time a handle can be used. Doing so makes it impossible for a client to keep a handle forever. To limit a handle's lifetime, the server encodes a *timestamp* in the handle. If the handle expires, the server refuses to perform further operations on a file using it. The client must obtain a fresh handle before it can continue access. In practice, NFS timestamps are usually long enough to permit any reasonable access. Applications that have legitimate use of a file can always obtain a fresh handle (the transactions required can be hidden from the application completely).

23.17 Handles Replace Path Names

To understand why handles are needed, consider naming files in a remote directory hierarchy. Recall that to isolate clients from the server's path name syntax and to allow heterogeneous machines to access hierarchical files, NFS requires that the client perform all path name interpretation. As a consequence, a client cannot use a full path name to specify a file when requesting an operation on that file. Instead, the client must obtain a handle that it can use to reference the file.

Having the server provide handles for directories as well as files permits a client to trace a path through the server's hierarchy. To see how, consider Figure 23.9, which illustrates the exchange between a client and server as the client looks up a file with path /a/b/c in the server's hierarchy.

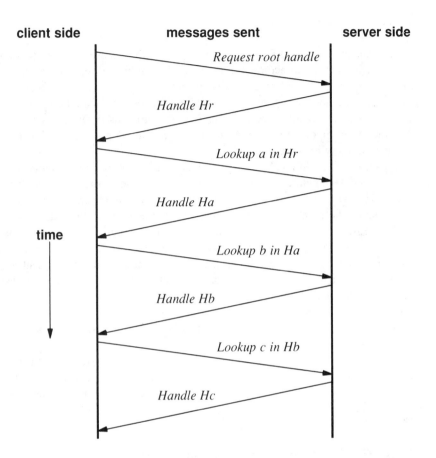

Figure 23.9 The messages a client and a server exchange as the client looks
up a file that has full path name /a/b/c, where "/" denotes the
client's component separator. The handle for a file or directory
named x is denoted Hx. In practice, a separate protocol provides
the root handle.

The figure shows that the server returns a handle for each directory along the path.
The client uses each handle in the next remote procedure call. For example, once the
client obtains a handle for directory a, it sends that handle back to the server and requests that the server search for b in directory a. The client cannot reference the file as
/a/b nor can it reference the directory as /a because the client does not know the
server's path name syntax.

23.18 An NFS Client In UNIX

When managers install NFS client code in UNIX, they use the file system mount
facility to integrate remote directories into UNIX's hierarchical directory system. A remote file system mount works much like a standard UNIX file system mount. The
manager creates an empty directory in the existing system, and then mounts an NFS remote file system on it. Whenever an application program calls *open*, the system parses
the path name one component at a time. It looks up each component in a directory and
finds the next directory to search.

If the path specified in a call to *open* includes an NFS-mounted directory, the system will eventually encounter the remote mount point and pass control to the NFS
client code. The NFS client finishes opening the file by continuing to parse and look
up components of the path. Because the remaining directories in the path reside on a
remote machine, the NFS client code cannot search them directly. Instead, to lookup a
component, it must contact the appropriate NFS server and obtain a handle. It then uses
the handle to ask the server to search the directory. Eventually, the NFS client reaches
the end of the path name and returns information about the remote file. The system
creates a descriptor for the remote file, and the application uses that descriptor for subsequent *read* or *write* operations.

Whenever an application performs an operation on a file descriptor, the operating
system checks to see if the descriptor refers to a local or a remote file. If the descriptor
refers to a local file, the system passes control to the local file system, which performs
the operation as usual. If the descriptor refers to a remote file, the system passes control to the NFS client code, which uses the file handle when it communicates with the
server.

23.19 File Positioning With A Stateless Server

Because NFS uses a stateless server design, the server cannot store a file position
for each application that is using a file. Instead, the client stores all file position information, and each request sent to the server must specify the file position to use. Storing
position information at the client also helps optimize operations that change the file position. For example, in a UNIX implementation, NFS uses the local file table to store
the position for a remote file just as UNIX uses it to store the position in a local file. If
the client calls *lseek*, the system records the new file position in the table without sending a message to the server. Any subsequent access operation extracts the file position
from the table and sends it to the server along with the access request. Because *lseek*
does not send any messages across the network, seeking in a remote file is as efficient
as seeking in a local one.

23.20 Operations On Directories

Conceptually, NFS defines a directory to consist of a set of pairs, where each pair contains a file name and a pointer to the named file. A directory can be arbitrarily large; there is no preset limit on its size.

NFS provides operations that permit a client to: *insert* a file in a directory, *delete* a file from a directory, *search* a directory for a name, and *read* the contents of a directory.

23.21 Reading A Directory Statelessly

Because directories can be arbitrarily large and communication networks impose a fixed limit on the size of a single message, reading the contents of a directory may require multiple requests. Because NFS servers are stateless, the server cannot keep a record of each client's position in the directory.

The NFS designers chose to overcome the limitations of stateless servers by arranging for an NFS server to return a *position identifier* when it answers a request for an entry from a directory. The client uses the position identifier in the next request to specify which entries it has already received and which it still needs. Thus, when a client wishes to read entries from a remote directory, it steps through the directory by making repeated requests that each specify the position identifier returned in the previous request.

Using informal terminology popular among systems programmers, NFS calls its directory position identifier a *magic cookie*. The term is meant to imply that the client does not interpret the identifier, nor can it fabricate an identifier itself. Only a server can create a magic cookie (hence the term *magic*); a client can only use a magic cookie that has been supplied by a server.

A magic cookie does not guarantee atomicity, nor does it lock the directory. Thus, two applications that perform operations on a directory may interfere with one another. For example, imagine a server that is handling requests from two or more clients concurrently. Suppose that after reading three directory entries from some directory, *D*, the first client receives a magic cookie that refers to a position before the fourth entry. Then suppose another client performs a series of operations that *insert* and *delete* files in directory *D*. If the first client attempts to read remaining entries from *D* using the old magic cookie, it may not receive all the changes.

In practice, the potential problems of concurrent directory access seldom affect users because they do not depend on instantaneous insertion or deletion of files. In fact, many conventional operating systems exhibit the same behavior as NFS; users seldom understand the details of how the system interprets concurrent directory operations because they rarely need to know.

23.22 Multiple Hierarchies In An NFS Server

Recall that to make NFS interoperate across heterogeneous machines, the designers chose to have the client parse all path names. Doing so allows both the client and server to each use the file naming scheme native to its operating system without requiring either of them to understand the other's environment.

Restricting the use of full path names has little effect on most file operations. However, it does introduce a serious problem because it means that a client cannot use a full path name to identify a remote file system or directory.

Early versions of the NFS protocol assumed that each server only provided access to a single remote hierarchy. The original protocol included a function named *NFSPROC_ROOT* that a client could call to obtain the handle for the root directory in the server's hierarchy. Once the client had a handle for the root, it could read directory entries and follow an arbitrary path through the hierarchy.

Later versions of NFS allow a single server to provide remote access to files located in several hierarchies. In such cases, a procedure that returns the handle of a single root directory does not suffice. To enable a single server to handle multiple hierarchies, NFS requires an additional mechanism. The additional mechanism allows a client to specify one of the possible hierarchies and obtain a handle for its root.

23.23 The Mount Protocol

The current version of NFS uses a separate protocol to handle the problem of finding a root directory. Called the *mount protocol*, it is defined using RPC. However, the mount protocol is not part of the NFS remote program. Although it is required for an NFS server, the mount protocol operates as a separate remote program.

The mount protocol provides four basic services that clients need before they can use NFS. First, it allows the client to obtain a list of the directory hierarchies (i.e., file systems) that the client can access through NFS. Second, it accepts full path names that allow the client to identify a particular directory hierarchy. Third, it authenticates each client's request and validates the client's permission to access the requested hierarchy. Fourth, it returns a file handle for the root directory of the hierarchy a client specifies. The client uses the root handle obtained from the mount protocol when making NFS calls.

The name and idea for the mount protocol come from UNIX: a UNIX system uses the mount protocol when it creates a remote file system mount in its namespace. A client system uses the mount protocol to contact a server and verify access to the remote file system before adding the remote mount to its local hierarchical namespace. If the mount protocol denies access, the client code reports an error to the system manager. If the mount protocol approves access, the client code stores the handle for the root of the remote file system so it can use the handle later when an application tries to open a file on that file system.

23.24 Summary

Sun Microsystems, Incorporated defined a remote file access mechanism called *NFS* that has become an industry standard. To allow many clients to access a server and to keep the servers isolated from client crashes, NFS uses stateless servers.

Because NFS is designed for a heterogeneous environment, a client cannot know the path name syntax on all servers. To accommodate heterogeneity, NFS requires the client to parse path names and look up each component individually. When a client looks up a particular component name, the server returns a 32-byte file handle that the client uses as a reference to the file or directory in subsequent operations.

Most of the NFS definitions and file system semantics have been derived from UNIX. NFS supports a hierarchical directory system, views a file as a sequence of bytes, allows files to grow dynamically, provides sequential or random access, and provides information about files almost identical to the information provided by the UNIX *stat* function.

Many of the conceptual file operations used in NFS have been derived from operations provided by the UNIX file system. NFS adopted the open-read-write-close access paradigm used in UNIX, along with basic file types and file protection modes.

A companion to NFS, the mount protocol makes it possible for a single NFS server to provide access to multiple directory hierarchies. The mount protocol implements access authentication, and allows a client to obtain the handle for the root of a particular directory hierarchy. Once the client obtains a handle for the root, it can use NFS procedures to access directories and files in that hierarchy. UNIX systems use the mount protocol when the system manager installs remote mounts in the UNIX hierarchical namespace.

FOR FURTHER STUDY

Ritchie and Thompson [1974] explains the original UNIX file system, and discusses the implementation of files using inodes and descriptors. Bach [1986] covers Unix file system semantics. McKusick *et. al.* [August 1984] describes the fast file system used in later releases of BSD UNIX. Sun Microsystems, Incorporated [RFC 1094] specifies the details of both NFS and the mount protocol. It mentions most of the concepts presented here.

EXERCISES

23.1   Build a program that obtains a magic cookie from an NFS server. Use the program to obtain magic cookies for several directories on several servers and print their contents in hexadecimal. Try to guess what information the cookie contains and how the server encodes it.

23.2   Use a network analyzer to watch messages exchanged between an NFS client and a
            server. How many packets are exchanged for each of the following operations: *open* a
            file not in the top level directory, *read 10* bytes from the file, and *close* the file?

23.3   Suppose the network that connects an NFS client and an NFS server delivers packets out
            of order. What errors can result from reordering NFS operations?

23.4   Suppose the network that connects an NFS client and an NFS server can duplicate pack-
            ets as well as deliver packets out of order. What errors can result from duplicating and
            reordering NFS operations? Compare your answer to your response for the previous ex-
            ercise. Does packet duplication introduce any additional error conditions? Why or why
            not?

24

Network File System Protocol (NFS, Mount)

24.1 Introduction

The previous chapter describes the concepts underlying Sun's Network File System (NFS), and shows that much of the terminology and many of the details were derived from the UNIX file system. This chapter continues the discussion of NFS by describing the protocol. It shows how NFS is defined to be a remote program using Sun RPC and how each operation on a file corresponds to a remote procedure call.

24.2 Using RPC To Define A Protocol

Chapters *20* through *22* show how RPC can be used to divide a program into components that execute on separate machines. Most programmers use RPC in the exact way described in those chapters: they first write a conventional program, and then use RPC to form a distributed version. This chapter takes another approach. It shows how RPC can be used to define a protocol without tying it to any particular program.

The chief difference between using RPC to construct a distributed version of a program and a general-purpose protocol arises in the way the designer thinks about the issues. When building a distributed version of a program, the programmer starts from an existing program that includes both procedures and data structures. When devising a protocol, the programmer starts from a set of desired services and devises abstract procedures that support them.

Designing a protocol requires thought about how services will be used as well as thought about how programmers will implement programs that supply those services. The designer must choose a protocol definition that strikes a balance between precision and freedom. The protocol must be precise enough to guarantee interoperability among programs that adhere to it, but it must be general enough to permit a wide variety of implementations.

Thinking about protocol design in a vacuum is seldom sufficient. Successful protocol specification requires the designer to be proficient with the technical details of communication and to have good intuition about the design. The intuition required usually arises from extensive experience with computer systems, application programs, and other communication protocols. Thus, protocol design can be more difficult than it appears. In particular, one should not confuse the apparent simplicity of a protocol like NFS with the notion that the design did not take much thought. The point is:

> *Although RPC provides a convenient way to specify a protocol, it does not make protocol design easier nor does it guarantee efficiency.*

24.3 Defining A Protocol With Data Structures And Procedures

To specify a protocol using RPC, one must:

- provide declarations for the constants, types, and data structures used as procedure arguments or function results,
- provide a declaration for each remote procedure that specifies the arguments, results, and semantics of the action it performs, and
- define the semantics for each remote procedure by specifying how it processes its arguments and computes a return value.

Conceptually, a protocol specified using RPC defines a server to be a single remote program. An operation sent from the client to the server corresponds to a remote procedure call, and a message returned from the server to the client corresponds to a procedure return. Thus, in any RPC-defined protocol, the client must initiate all operations; a server can only respond to individual client requests.

For NFS, requiring the client to initiate each operation makes sense because a file access protocol can be designed to be driven from the client. A server offers procedures that permit a client to: *create* or *delete* files, directories, and symbolic links; *read* or *write* data; *search* a directory for a named file; and obtain *status* information about an entire remote file system or about an individual file or directory. Although other application protocols may not lend themselves to RPC specification as directly as NFS, experience shows that most client-server interactions can be cast into the remote procedure call paradigm with modest effort.

NFS provides an interesting example of RPC specification because the protocol is sufficiently complex to require several remote procedures and data types, yet it is intuitive and conceptually simple enough to understand. The next section describes examples of the basic constant and type declarations used in the NFS protocol. Later sections show how the procedure declarations use the constants and types to specify arguments and results.

24.4 NFS Constant, Type, And Data Declarations

The NFS protocol standard defines constants, type names, and data structures that are used throughout the procedural declarations. All declarations are given using RPC declaration syntax.

24.4.1 NFS Constants

NFS defines six basic constants that specify the sizes of arrays used by the protocol. The declarations are given using the RPC language:

```
const MAXDATA    = 8192; /* Maximum bytes in a data transfer   */
const MAXPATHLEN = 1024; /* Maximum characters in a path name  */
const MAXNAMLEN  =  255; /* Maximum characters in a name       */
const COOKIESIZE =    4; /* Octets in a NFS magic cookie       */
const FHSIZE     =   32; /* Octets in an NFS file handle       */
```

In addition to the basic constants, the protocol also defines an enumerated set of constants used to report error status. Each remote procedure call returns one of these status values. The set is named *stat*, and is declared as:

```
enum stat {
    NFS_OK             = 0   /* Successful call                     */
    NFSERR_PERM        = 1,  /* Ownership mismatch or error         */
    NFSERR_NOENT       = 2,  /* File does not exist                 */
    NFSERR_IO          = 5,  /* I/O device error occurred           */
    NFSERR_NXIO        = 6,  /* Device or address does not exist    */
    NFSERR_ACCES       = 13, /* Permission to access was denied     */
    NFSERR_EXIST       = 17, /* Specified file already exists       */
    NFSERR_NODEV       = 19, /* Specified device does not exist     */
    NFSERR_NOTDIR      = 20, /* Specified item not a directory      */
    NFSERR_ISDIR       = 21, /* Specified item is a directory       */
    NFSERR_FBIG        = 27, /* File is too large for server        */
    NFSERR_NOSPC       = 28, /* No space left on device (disk)      */
    NFSERR_ROFS        = 30, /* Write to read-only file system      */
    NFSERR_NAMETOOLONG = 63, /* File name was too long              */
    NFSERR_NOTEMPTY    = 66, /* Directory not empty                 */
    NFSERR_DQUOT       = 69, /* Disk quota exceeded                 */
    NFSERR_STALE       = 70, /* File handle is stale                */
    NFSERR_WFLUSH      = 99  /* Write cache was flushed to disk     */
    };
```

Each of these error values makes sense in the context of some call. For example, if a client attempts to perform a directory operation on a regular file, the server returns error code *NFSERR_NOTDIR*. If the client attempts to perform a regular file operation on a directory, the server returns error code *NFSERR_ISDIR*.

24.4.2 NFS Typedef Declarations

To make its structure declarations clearer, the NFS protocol standard defines names for types used in multiple structures. For example, the type *filename* is defined to be an array of characters large enough to contain a component name. In RPC syntax, the keyword *string* must be used to declare an array of characters. Thus, the declaration is:

```
typedef string filename<MAXNAMLEN>;
```

Similarly, the standard defines *fhandle* to be the type of a *32*-byte array that contains a file handle. The type is declared to be *opaque* because the client does not know the internal structure:

```
typedef opaque fhandle[FHSIZE];
```

24.4.3 NFS Data Structures

With constant and type definitions in place, a protocol designer can specify the types of all data structures used. NFS follows the convention of combining all the arguments for a remote procedure call into a single structure. Thus, the standard defines an argument structure for each remote procedure and a separate structure for each procedure result. In addition, the standard defines a few structures shared by several procedures. For example, Chapter *22* describes the *fattr* structure that NFS uses to specify file attributes. *Fattr* was derived from the data returned by the UNIX *stat* structure.

Some fields in the *fattr* structure record the time at which a file was last modified or accessed. Such fields are declared to be of type *timeval*, a structure:

```
struct timeval {            /* date and time used by NFS     */
    unsigned int seconds;   /* seconds past epoch (1/1/70)   */
    unsigned int useconds;  /* additional microseconds       */
};
```

The declaration specifies that NFS stores a time value in two *32*-bit integers. The first integer records the number of seconds past an epoch date, and the second integer records additional microseconds (allowing for more precision). NFS uses the epoch date of January 1, 1970† to measure time values.

Most of the remaining declarations define the type of arguments passed to a remote procedure or the result the procedure returns. For example, when calling a procedure that performs an operation on a directory (e.g., *delete* a file), the client must pass the name of a file. NFS declares the argument type to be a structure, *diropargs* (*directory operation arguments*):

---

†The designers chose the NFS time epoch to be the same as that used by UNIX.

```
struct diropargs {          /* directory operation arguments   */
      fhandle  dir;         /* handle for directory file is in */
      filename name;        /* name of file in that directory  */
};
```

The structure shows that the argument consists of a file handle for the directory and the name of a file in that directory. To understand why *diropargs* is needed, recall that the NFS client parses all path names. Thus, a client cannot use a full path name to identify a file. Instead, NFS requires all operations on files to be specified by giving the handle for the directory in which the file resides and the name of the file in that directory.

In addition to declarations for argument types, the standard defines the types returned by remote procedures. For example, a directory operation returns a union type named *diropres*:

```
union diropres switch (stat status) { /* result of dir. op  */
case NFS_OK:                 /* If operation was successful      */
    struct {                 /*    structure for success results */
        fhandle file;        /*    file handle for new file      */
        fattr  attributes;/* status of the file               */
    } diropok;               /* end of structure for success     */
default:                     /* If operation failed              */
    void;                    /*    get nothing back              */
};
```

The union allows two possible forms of a return value, with the choice depending on the status. If the operation succeeds, the status will have value *NFS_OK*, and the return value will consist of a file handle for the newly created file (or the file that changed) and a structure that contains the file's attributes. If the operation fails, the call will not return anything.

The arguments for other remote procedures sometimes include one or more file specifications. For example, the remote procedure used to rename a file requires two file names: the name of an existing file and the new name for that file. The arguments for the *rename* procedure are declared to be of type *renameargs*, a structure:

```
struct renameargs {         /* arguments to RENAME               */
      diropargs from;       /* an existing file                  */
      diropargs to;         /* new location/name for file        */
};
```

Individual fields that give the old and new file names are declared to be of type *diropargs*.

Most other NFS argument types correspond to remote procedures. For example, NFS defines structure *writeargs* to specify arguments used in a call to *write* data to a file:

```
struct writeargs {                   /* arguments to WRITE       */
        fhandle  file;               /* file to be written       */
        unsigned beginoffset;        /* obsolete (ignore)        */
        unsigned offset;             /* where to write data      */
        unsigned totalcount;         /* obsolete (ignore)        */
        nfsdata  data;               /* data to put into file    */
};
```

Similarly, structure *readargs* specifies the arguments for the *read* operation:

```
struct readargs {                    /* arguments to READ        */
        fhandle  file;               /* file to be read          */
        unsigned offset;             /* where to read data       */
        unsigned count;              /* num. of bytes requested */
        unsigned totalcount;         /* obsolete (ignore)        */
};
```

Procedure *readlink* allows the client to read the contents of a symbolic link. Its results are defined by the union *readlinkres*:

```
union readlinkres {      /* result of READLINK                   */
case NFS_OK:             /* result if successful                 */
case NFS_OK:             /* If operation was successful          */
    path data;           /*       path name found in link        */
default:                 /* If operation failed                  */
    void;                /*       nothing                        */
};
```

24.5 NFS Procedures

Once constants and data types have been declared, one only needs to specify the remote procedures that implement the protocol. An NFS server provides a remote program that implements *18* procedures. Using RPC language, the program can be declared:

```
program NFS_PROGRAM {
      version NFS_VERSION {
          void           NFSPROC_NULL(void)          = 0;

          attrstat       NFSPROC_GETATTR(fhandle)    = 1;

          attrstat       NFSPROC_SETATTR(sattrargs)  = 2;

          void           NFSPROC_ROOT(void)          = 3;

          diropres       NFSPROC_LOOKUP(diropargs)   = 4;

          readlinkres    NFSPROC_READLINK(fhandle)   = 5;

          readres        NFSPROC_READ(readargs)      = 6;

          void           NFSPROC_WRITECACHE(void)    = 7;

          attrstat       NFSPROC_WRITE(writeargs)    = 8;

          diropres       NFSPROC_CREATE(createargs)  = 9;

          stat           NFSPROC_REMOVE(diropargs)   = 10;

          stat           NFSPROC_RENAME(renameargs)  = 11;

          stat           NFSPROC_LINK(linkargs)      = 12;

          stat           NFSPROC_SYMLINK(symlinkargs)= 13;

          diropres       NFSPROC_MKDIR(createargs)   = 14;

          stat           NFSPROC_RMDIR(diropargs)    = 15;

          readdirres     NFSPROC_READDIR(readdirargs)= 16;

          statfsres      NFSPROC_STATFS(fhandle)     = 17;

      } = 2;           /* current version of NFS protocol   */
} = 100003;          /* RPC program number assigned to NFS */
```

24.6 Semantics Of NFS Operations

The semantics for most NFS operations follow the semantics of file operations in
UNIX. The following sections each describe how one of the NFS remote procedures
operates.

24.6.1 NFSPROC_NULL (Procedure 0)

By convention, procedure *0* in any RPC program is termed *null* because it does not perform any action. An application can call it to test whether a given server is responding.

24.6.2 NFSPROC_GETATTR (Procedure 1)

A client calls procedure *1* to obtain the attributes of a file, which include such items as the protection mode, owner, size, and time of last access.

24.6.3 NFSPROC_SETATTR (Procedure 2)

Procedure *2* permits a client to set some of the attributes of a file. The client cannot set all attributes (e.g., it cannot change the recorded file size except by adding bytes to the file or truncating it). If the call succeeds, the result returned contains the file's attributes after the changes have been applied.

24.6.4 NFSPROC_ROOT (Procedure 3)

Procedure *3* was defined for earlier versions of NFS, but is now obsolete. It has been replaced by the mount protocol.

24.6.5 NFSPROC_LOOKUP (Procedure 4)

Clients call procedure *4* to search for a file in a directory. If successful, the returned value consists of a file handle and the attributes for the specified file.

24.6.6 NFSPROC_READLINK (Procedure 5)

Procedure *5* permits the client to read the value from a symbolic link.

24.6.7 NFSPROC_READ (Procedure 6)

Procedure *6* provides one of the most important functions because it permits a client to read data from a file. The result returned by the server is a union, *readres*. If the operation succeeds, the result contains attributes for the file as well as the data requested. If the operation fails, the status value contains an error code.

24.6.8 NFSPROC_WRITECACHE (Procedure 7)

Procedure *7* is not used in the current protocol; it is intended for the next version of the protocol.

24.6.9 NFSPROC_WRITE (Procedure 8)

Procedure *8* provides another of the basic functions: it permits a client to write data into a remote file. The call returns a union, *attrstat*, that either contains an error code, if the operation fails, or the attributes of the file, if the operation succeeds.

24.6.10 NFSPROC_CREATE (Procedure 9)

A client calls procedure *9* to create a file in a specified directory. The file must not exist or the call will return an error. The call returns a union of type *diropres* that either contains an error status or a handle for the new file along with its attributes.

24.6.11 NFSPROC_REMOVE (Procedure 10)

A client invokes procedure *10* to delete an existing file. The call returns a status value. The status either indicates that the operation succeeded or provides an error code that tells why it failed.

24.6.12 NFSPROC_RENAME (Procedure 11)

Procedure *11* permits a client to rename a file. Because the arguments allow the client to specify a new directory for the file as well as a new name, the *rename* operation corresponds to the UNIX *mv* (*move*) command. NFS guarantees that *rename* will be atomic on the server (i.e., it cannot be interrupted). The guarantee of atomicity is important because it means the old name for the file will not be removed until the new name has been installed. Thus, the file will not appear to be missing during a *rename* operation.

24.6.13 NFSPROC_LINK (Procedure 12)

Clients call procedure *12* to form a hard link to an existing file. NFS guarantees that if a file has multiple hard links, the attributes visible for the file will be identical no matter which link is used to access it.

24.6.14 NFSPROC_SYMLINK (Procedure 13)

Procedure *13* creates a symbolic link. The arguments specify a directory handle and the name of a file to be created as well as a string that will become the contents of the symbolic link. The server creates the symbolic link, and then returns a status value that either indicates success or gives a reason for the failure.

24.6.15 NFSPROC_MKDIR (Procedure 14)

A client calls procedure *14* to create a directory. If the call succeeds, the server returns a handle for the new directory along with a list of its attributes. If the call fails, the returned status value indicates the reason for the failure.

24.6.16 NFSPROC_RMDIR (Procedure 15)

A client can use procedure *15* to remove a directory. As in UNIX, a directory must be empty before it can be removed. Thus, to remove an entire subtree, a client must traverse the subtree removing all files, and then remove the empty directories that remain. Usually, the removal of files and empty directories is accomplished in a single pass by using a post-order traversal of the directory tree.

24.6.17 NFSPROC_READDIR (Procedure 16)

A client calls procedure *16* to read entries from a directory. The argument structure, *readdirargs*, specifies a handle for the directory to be read, a magic cookie, and a maximum count of characters to read. On the initial call, the client specifies a magic cookie containing zero, which causes the server to read entries from the beginning of the directory. The value returned, of type *readdirres*, contains a linked list of zero or more directory entries and a Boolean value to indicate whether the last entry returned lies at the end of the directory.

After a successful return, each directory entry on the linked list contains the name of a file, a unique identifier for the file, a magic cookie that gives the file's position in the directory, and a pointer to the next entry on the list.

To read the sequence of entries in a directory, the client begins by calling *NFSPROC_READDIR* with a magic cookie value of zero and a character count equal to its internal buffer size. The server returns as many directory entries as fit into the buffer. The client iterates through the list of entries and processes each file name. If the returned value shows that the client has reached the end of the directory, it stops processing. Otherwise, the client uses the magic cookie in the last entry to make another call to the server and obtain more entries. The client continues reading groups of entries until it reaches the end of the directory.

24.6.18 NFSPROC_STATFS (Procedure 17)

Procedure *17* permits a client to obtain information about the remote file system on which a file resides. The returned result, a structure of type *statfsres*, contains fields that specify the optimum transfer size (i.e., the size of data in *read* or *write* requests that produces optimal transfer rates), the size of data blocks on the storage device, the number of blocks on the device, the number of blocks currently unused, and the number of unused blocks available to nonprivileged users.

A sophisticated client program can use *NFSPROC_STATFS* to optimize transfers or to estimate whether sufficient space remains on a disk to accommodate a *write* request.

24.7 The Mount Protocol

The mount protocol described in Chapter *22* is also defined using RPC. Although an NFS server must have a companion mount server, the two have been defined as separate remote programs. Thus, the protocol standard for mount specifies constants, types, and a set of remote procedures that comprise the server.

24.7.1 Mount Constant Definitions

Although the two protocols are defined separately, the values for many of the constants and types defined for the mount protocol have been derived from corresponding constants used in the NFS protocol. Indeed, the two protocols could not work together well unless they both used a common representation for objects like file handles. For example, mount defines the sizes of a file name, a path name, and a file handle as follows:

```
const MNTNAMLEN = 255;

const MNTPATHLEN = 1024;

const FHSIZE = 32;
```

The declarations use RPC syntax; they each express the lengths as a number of bytes.

24.7.2 Mount Type Definitions

The mount protocol also specifies type definitions that agree with their counterparts found in the NFS protocol. For example, mount specifies the type of a file handle:

```
typedef opaque fhandle[FHSIZE];
```

Similarly, the mount protocol specifies that a path name consists of an array of characters:

```
typedef string dirpath<MNTPATHLEN>;
```

24.7.3 Mount Data Structures

Because the mount protocol has been defined using RPC, it follows the convention of declaring a structure for the argument and result of each remote procedure. For example, one of the basic procedures in the protocol returns a file handle for the root directory in a named hierarchy. The value returned consists of a union, *fhstatus*, declared to be:

```
union fhstatus switch (unsigned status) {
case 0:                        /* If successful                      */
    fhandle directory;         /*    handle for specified root       */
default:                       /* Otherwise                          */
    void;                      /*    nothing                         */
};
```

As in the NFS protocol, each remote procedure in the mount protocol returns a status value along with other information. If the operation fails, the status value indicates the reason.

In addition to a procedure that returns a file handle, the mount protocol provides a procedure that allows a client to determine which file systems are available for access. The procedure returns the results in a linked list called an *export list*†. The type of a node on the export list is declared with structure *exportlist*:

```
struct *exportlist {           /* list of available hierarchies      */
    dirpath filesys;           /* path name for this hierarchy       */
    groups groups;             /* groups allowed to access it        */
    exportlist next;           /* pointer to next item in list       */
};
```

Field *groups* in an *exportlist* node contains a pointer to a linked list that specifies which protection groups are allowed to access the named hierarchy. Nodes on the list are defined to be a structure of type *groups*:

```
struct *groups {               /* list of group names                */
    name grname;               /* name of one group                  */
    groups grnext;             /* pointer to next item on list       */
};
```

The mount protocol also allows a client to determine which remote file systems a given machine is accessing. Thus, it is possible to construct an NFS cross-reference list for a set of machines. To do so, one asks each of the machines in the set for a list of the remote file systems that the machine is accessing. Note that the set of remote file systems a given machine is accessing will be disjoint from the set of local file systems that the machine has exported for others to access.

---

†The term *export* refers to the idea that a server *exports* some of its files to other machines.

A reply from the mount protocol that lists remote accesses is a linked list where each node has type *mountlist*:

```
struct *mountlist {            /* list of remote mounts          */
        name     hostname; /* machine on which files resides */
        dirpath  directory;/* path name of hierarchy         */
        mountlist nextentry;/* pointer to next item on the list*/
};
```

24.8 Procedures In The Mount Protocol

Like NFS, the mount protocol defines all operations as procedures in a remote program. The RPC declaration of the mount program is:

```
program MOUNTPROG {
        version MOUNTVERS {

        void       MOUNTPROC_NULL(void)      = 0;

        fhstatus   MOUNTPROC_MNT(dirpath)    = 1;

        mountlist  MOUNTPROC_DUMP(void)      = 2;

        void       MOUNTPROC_UMNT(dirpath)   = 3;

        void       MOUNTPROC_UMNTALL(void)   = 4;

        exportlist MOUNTPROC_EXPORT(void)    = 5;
        } = 1;         /* mount version 1 matches NFS vers. 2 */
} = 100005;            /* RPC program number assigned to mount*/
```

24.9 Semantics of Mount Operations

The mount protocol defines the semantics of each of the operations listed above. The following sections give a brief summary of each.

24.9.1 MNTPROC_NULL (Procedure 0)

Following the RPC convention, procedure *0* does not perform any action.

24.9.2 MNTPROC_MNT (Procedure 1)

A client calls procedure *1* to obtain the handle for a particular hierarchy. The argument contains a path name that the server uses to distinguish among the hierarchies it exports for access; the result has type *fhstatus*. Names for the hierarchies available on a given server can be obtained by calling *MNTPROC_EXPORT* (see below).

24.9.3 MNTPROC_DUMP (Procedure 2)

Procedure *2* permits a client to obtain a list of the remote file systems that a particular machine is using. The information provided by *MNTPROC_DUMP* has little value to conventional applications; it is intended for system administrators.

24.9.4 MNTPROC_UMNT (Procedure 3)

A client can use procedure *3* to inform another machine that it will be out of service. For example, if machine *A* has mounted one or more file systems from the server on machine *B*, machine *B* can use *MNTPROC_UMNT* to inform *A* that a particular file system will be out of service (e.g., for disk maintenance). Doing so keeps *A* from sending additional requests to *B* while the files are offline.

24.9.5 MNTPROC_UMNTALL (Procedure 4)

Procedure *4* allows one machine to tell another that all of its NFS file systems will be unavailable. For example, a server can tell clients to unmount all its file systems before it reboots.

24.9.6 MNTPROC_EXPORT (Procedure 5)

Procedure *5* provides an important service: it allows a client to obtain the names of all the hierarchies accessible on a given server. The call returns a linked list that contains a single node of type *exportlist* for each available file system. The client must use one of the directory path names found in the export list when calling *MNTPROC_MNT* (procedure *1*).

24.10 NFS And Mount Authentication

NFS relies on the mount protocol to provide authentication. The mount protocol authenticates a client's request for the handle of a root directory, but NFS does not authenticate each individual client request.

Surprisingly, the mount protocol does not offer much protection. It uses RPC's *AUTH_UNIX* or *AUTH_NONE* to authenticate the client. Once a client has obtained a handle for a root directory, protections on individual files mean little. For example, if programmers obtain privilege on their private workstations, they may be able to access arbitrary files on NFS servers as well as on their local machines. Furthermore, if a programmer can guess the contents of an opaque file handle, the programmer can manufacture handles for arbitrary directories.

Early versions of NFS created handles by combining information about a file or directory in fixed ways. For example, Figure 24.1 shows how one UNIX implementation divides the *32*-byte handle into ten fields:

Field	Size	Contents
Fileid	4	UNIX's major and minor device numbers for the file
one	1	Always *1*
length$_1$	2	Total length of next three fields
zero$_1$	2	Always *0*
inode	4	UNIX's inode number for the file
igener	4	Generation number for file inode (randomized for security)
length$_2$	2	Total length of next three fields
zero$_2$	2	Always *0*
rinode	4	Unix's inode number for root of file system
rigener	4	Generation number for root inode (randomized for security)

Figure 24.1 The contents of the fields in an NFS file handle. This particular format comes from an NFS server that runs under the UNIX operating system; not all servers construct file handles the same way.

The chief danger in using a fixed format for file handles arises because NFS offers little protection against unauthorized access. A client wishing to access files can circumvent the mount protocol by manufacturing a handle for an arbitrary UNIX file. It can then obtain attribute information for the file, including the file ownership and protection bits. Thus, it will be able to access world-readable files even if the mount protocol does not authorize access. Furthermore, if the client has root privilege on the local machine, it will be able to send requests to a server that contain arbitrary user identifiers. Thus, a client that has root privilege can first find out who owns a particular file, and then send a request claiming to be that user.

To make it more difficult to guess file handles, many UNIX administrators use a utility that randomizes inode generation numbers. The utility goes through all the inodes on a disk and stores a random number in the inode's generation field. The mount protocol uses the generation number when passing out a file handle, and NFS checks that the value in the handle matches the generation number found in the inode.

Randomizing generation numbers increases security, but it does not increase the computational overhead required to form a handle because randomization is performed before the mount protocol runs. However, randomization makes file handles difficult to guess. A client attempting to obtain unauthorized access must choose among 2^{32} possible values for the generation number. Because the probability of guessing a valid handle is low, the probability of obtaining unauthorized access to a file is also low.

24.11 Summary

When using RPC to define a protocol, one must provide definitions for the constants and data types used in the specification, the definitions of the procedures that a server offers, the types of all procedure arguments and results, and the semantics of each procedure. Protocol definition differs from the use of RPC to form a distributed version of a program because it requires the designer to deal with abstract concepts instead of an existing program.

NFS has been defined using RPC. The protocol standard specifies *18* procedures that comprise a server. In addition to operations that allow a client to *read* or *write* a file, the protocol defines data structures and operations that permit a client to read entries from a directory, create a file, remove a file, rename a file, or obtain information about a file.

A companion to NFS, the mount protocol provides client authentication and allows a client to find the handle for the root of a hierarchy. The mount protocol permits a given server to export multiple hierarchies, and allows the client to specify a particular hierarchy using a full path name.

NFS relies on the mount protocol for security. It assumes that any client can send access requests once the client obtains the handle for a root directory. Most NFS implementations construct a handle for a file by encoding information about the file. Among other items, NFS servers running on a UNIX system often encode the file's inode generation number in the handle. To prevent clients from guessing a file handle and then using it to obtain unauthorized access, many UNIX administrators use a tool that randomizes inode generation numbers. The randomization makes it difficult for clients to guess a valid file handle.

FOR FURTHER STUDY

Sun Microsystems, Incorporated [RFC 1094] defines both the NFS and mount protocols using RPC. It provides declarations for the constants, types, and procedures that comprise each protocol as well as a description of the intended semantics and implementation hints. Another version of the document can be found in the *Network Programmer's Guide* that accompanies the SunOS operating system.

EXERCISES

24.1   Write a program that uses the mount protocol to obtain file handles. Does your system use UNIX authentication?

24.2   Using the program described in the previous exercise, check several files on a given UNIX server to see if the administrator has randomized inode generation numbers on that server's file systems.

24.3 Consult the protocol standard to find out about the *NFSPROC_WRITECACHE* operation that will become part of later versions of NFS. What is its purpose?

24.4 NFS uses UDP for transport. Several companies now market software that uses TCP instead. How can the protocol be optimized to take advantage of a reliable stream transport?

24.5 The NFS protocol specification mentions that several operations are potentially not idempotent. Find the operations and explain how each could be non-idempotent.

24.6 NFS semantics guarantee that a *write* request will not complete until the data has been stored on a stable storage device (e.g., a disk). Estimate how much faster a *write* operation would execute on your local server if the protocol permitted the server to copy the data into an output buffer and allowed the procedure call to return without waiting for the buffer to be written to the disk.

24.7 NFS is designed to permit clients and servers to operate in a heterogeneous environment. Explain how symbolic links cause problems. (Hint: consider the protocol carefully to determine whether the client or server interprets a symbolic link).

24.8 Read the protocol specification and find out which file attributes can be set by a client.

24.9 Because RPC uses UDP, a remote procedure call can be duplicated, delayed, and delivered out of order. Explain how a valid set of NFS calls can appear from the client's perspective to create a file and write data into it, and yet result in a zero-length file.

24.10 Suppose a client calls *NFSPROC_STATFS* to find the preferred data transfer size. What constraints may make transfers of that size suboptimal?

24.11 Read the protocol specification to find out about stale file handles. Why might a server declare that a handle has become stale? How can making a handle stale improve security?

24.12 Write a program that calls *MOUNTPROC_UMNTALL* on some server, *S*. Does the call have any effect on subsequent calls to *S*? Why or why not?

24.13 Write a program that calls *MOUNTPROC_EXPORT*. Run the program and print the list of exported file system names.

25

A TELNET Client (Program Structure)

25.1 Introduction

Previous chapters use simple examples to illustrate the concepts and techniques used in client-server software. This chapter and the next explore how the client-server paradigm applies to a complex application protocol. The example protocol is *TELNET*, one of the most widely used application protocols in the TCP/IP suite.

This chapter focuses on the overall program structure. It assumes the reader is familiar with the basics of the TELNET protocol, and concentrates on explaining an implementation. It discusses the design of the client software, the process structure, and the use of finite state machines to control processing. It also reviews UNIX terminal I/O and shows how a client maps TELNET communication to a UNIX terminal.

The next chapter completes the description. It focuses on the details of routines invoked to perform semantic actions associated with transitions of the finite state machines. The example code throughout both chapters illustrates clearly how the programming details dominate the code and how they complicate the implementation.

25.2 Overview

25.2.1 The User's Terminal

The TELNET protocol defines an interactive communication facility that permits users to communicate with a service on a remote machine. In most cases, users use TELNET to communicate with a remote login service. As the example in Chapter *1* shows, a well-designed TELNET client also permits a user to contact other services.

The TELNET protocol defines interactive, character-oriented communication. It specifies a *network virtual terminal* (*NVT*) that consists of a keyboard and display screen. The protocol defines the character set for the virtual terminal. Several of the keys correspond to conceptual operations instead of data values. For example, one key causes an *interrupt* or *abort*. The chief advantage of using a network virtual terminal is that it permits clients from a variety of computers to connect to a service. Like the XDR standard described in Chapter *19*, TELNET uses a symmetric data representation. Each client maps from its local terminal's character representation to the NVT character representation when it sends data, and from the NVT representation to the local character set when it receives data. To summarize:

> *TELNET is a character-oriented protocol that uses a standard encoding when it transfers data.*

25.2.2 Command And Control Information

In addition to character data, TELNET permits the client and server to exchange *command* or *control* information. Because all communication between the client and server passes across a single TCP connection, the protocol arranges to encode command or control information so the receiver can distinguish it from normal data. Thus, much of the protocol focuses on the definition of how the sender encodes a command and how the receiver recognizes it.

25.2.3 Terminals, Windows, and Files

TELNET defines communication between a user's *terminal* and a remote service. The protocol specification assumes that the terminal consists of a keyboard on which the user can enter characters and a display screen that can display multiple lines of text.

In practice, a user can decide to invoke a client with an input file in place of a keyboard or an output file in place of a display. Alternatively, the user can invoke the client from within a window on a bitmapped display. Although such alternatives introduce small additions to the code, it will be easiest to understand both the protocol and the implementation if we imagine that users who invoke the client each have a conventional terminal. To summarize:

> *TELNET client software is designed to handle interactive communication with a user's terminal.*

25.2.4 The Need For Concurrency

Conceptually, a TELNET client transfers characters between the user's terminal and a remote service. On one side, it uses the local operating system functions when it interacts with the user's terminal. On the other side, it uses a TCP connection when it communicates with the remote service. Figure 25.1 illustrates the concept:

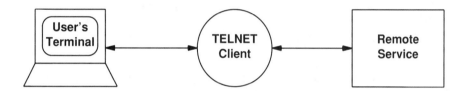

Figure 25.1 Conceptual role of a TELNET client. The client must transfer characters from the user's keyboard to a remote service, and it must transfer characters from the remote service to the user's display.

To provide a full-duplex connection between the user's terminal and a remote service, a TELNET client must perform two tasks simultaneously:

- The client must read characters that the user types on the keyboard and send them across a TCP connection to the remote service.
- The client must read characters that arrive from the TCP connection and display them on the user's terminal screen.

Because the remote service can emit output at any time or the user can type at any time, the client cannot know which source of data will become available first. Thus, it cannot block indefinitely waiting for input from one of the two sources without also checking for input from the other. In short, the client must transfer data in both directions concurrently.

25.2.5 A Process Model For A TELNET Client

To accommodate concurrent data transfer, a client must either consist of multiple processes that execute concurrently or it must implement concurrent I/O in a single process. Our example code uses the latter strategy: the client consists of a single process that blocks until one of the sources is ready. Figure 25.2 illustrates the process structure we have chosen:

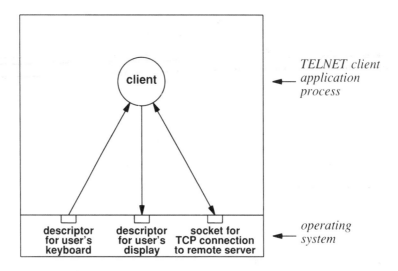

Figure 25.2 The process structure of the example TELNET client. A single process reads characters from the user's keyboard and sends them to the remote service across a TCP connection. The process also reads characters from the remote service and sends them to the user's display.

25.3 A TELNET Client Algorithm

Algorithm 25.1 specifies how a single-process TELNET client operates. Like the single-process, concurrent server design described in Chapter *12*, a UNIX implementation of a single-process, concurrent client uses the *select* system function to implement Step *3* of Algorithm *25.1*. When the client calls *select*, it specifies that the process should block until input arrives on the descriptor that corresponds to the user's keyboard or on the socket descriptor that corresponds to the TCP connection. When either descriptor becomes ready, the call to *select* returns and the client reads from whichever descriptor became ready.

Algorithm 25.1

1. Parse arguments and initialize data structures.
2. Open a TCP connection to the specified port on the specified remote host.
3. Block until the user types input or data arrives over the TCP connection.
4. If data arrived from the keyboard, read it, process it, translate it to NVT representation, and send it over the TCP connection. Otherwise, read data from the TCP connection, process it, translate it to the local character representation, and send it to the user's display.
5. Return to step *3* above.

Algorithm 25.1 A TELNET client. The single process relays characters in both directions; it blocks until data is available from the keyboard or socket.

25.4 Terminal I/O In UNIX

Algorithm 25.1 may seem extremely simple. However, the details of the TELNET protocol and the terminal I/O complicate the code. To understand how TELNET client software interacts with a user's terminal, one must understand in detail how the client operating system handles terminal I/O. This section describes how UNIX handles terminal I/O, and shows examples of code that controls the user's terminal.

In UNIX, I/O to a terminal device follows the same *open-read-write-close* paradigm used for I/O to files or sockets. An application program calls *open* to obtain an *I/O descriptor* for a terminal's keyboard or screen, *read* to receive data that the user types on the keyboard, and *write* to transfer data to the terminal's screen.

In practice, most applications do not call *open* to create a descriptor for the user's terminal because the command interpreter provides open descriptors automatically. The command interpreter usually leaves the keyboard connected to descriptor *0* (standard input) and the terminal screen connected to descriptor *1* (standard output).

Although terminal I/O follows the same basic paradigm as file I/O, a myriad of details complicate it. Many of the details arise because terminal hardware is primitive. For example, although most users think of the keyboard and display as a single unit, the hardware separates keyboard input from display output and treats them as two separate devices. Thus, the hardware does not automatically display each character that the user types. Instead, the hardware merely delivers characters as keyboard input and requires the computer to write a copy of each character to the display.

Most applications expect that users will see a copy of each character on the display as they type, but some applications need to suppress printing of input. In particular, to keep passwords from being observed, an application that requests a password usually stops displaying input characters while the user types the password.

Rather than have each application handle all the details associated with terminal I/O and character display, the UNIX operating system provides software to handle them automatically. Known as a *terminal device driver*, the software resides in the operating system kernel as Figure 25.3 illustrates.

The device driver associates keyboard input with the corresponding terminal display. It can be instructed to *echo* input characters (i.e., display each character the user types) or to suppress the echo (i.e., turn off display of input characters). It can allow the user to edit mistakes using a *backspace* or *delete* key, or it can pass all characters, including *backspace* and *delete*, directly to the application. The driver can also generate the special sequence of characters that position the cursor at the beginning of a new line when the application sends an end-of-line character†. Finally, the device driver can recognize a special character (or characters) that causes the system to *interrupt* or *abort* the current process. When the user types the special character, the device driver translates it into a UNIX *signal* that aborts the application program.

25.4.1 Controlling A Device Driver

Application programs use the system function *ioctl* (*I/O control*) to control the device driver. *Ioctl* permits the application to obtain or set parameter values that control the operation of the driver. Most important, a TELNET client can use *ioctl* to obtain a copy of all device driver parameters when it begins, then to change the parameters to make the terminal behave differently, and finally to restore the original parameter values before it exits. Thus, from the user's point of view, although terminal parameters change while the client operates, they return to their original value when the client exits or suspends.

---

†Most terminals require the operating system to send a *linefeed* character as well as a *carriage return* character to move the cursor to the beginning of the next line. The *linefeed* moves down the screen vertically, and the *carriage return* moves to the beginning of the current line.

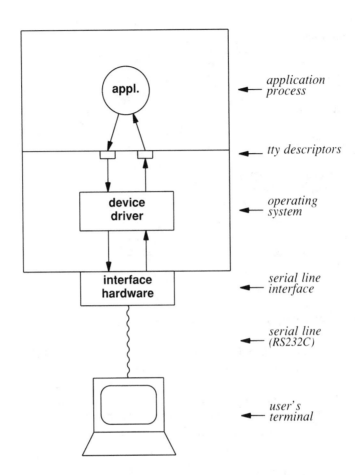

Figure 25.3 A terminal device driver in UNIX and the paths data follows when it flows into the system from a keyboard or out of the system to a terminal display. All terminal I/O passes through the device driver.

File *ttymode.c* contains code that uses the *ioctl* system function to manipulate terminal information.

```
/* ttymode.c - ttysave, ttyrestore */

#include <stdio.h>

#include "local.h"

extern int      errno;
extern char     *sys_errlist[];

/*------------------------------------------------------------------------
 * ttysave - get and save tty parameters and special characters
 *------------------------------------------------------------------------
 */
int
ttysave(pts)
struct ttystate *pts;
{
        if (ioctl(0, TIOCGETP, (char *)&pts->ts_sgttyb))
                errexit("can't get tty modes: %s\n", sys_errlist[errno]);
        if (ioctl(0, TIOCGETC, (char *)&pts->ts_tchars))
                errexit("can't get tty chars: %s\n", sys_errlist[errno]);
        if (ioctl(0, TIOCGLTC, (char *)&pts->ts_ltchars))
                errexit("can't get tty chars: %s\n", sys_errlist[errno]);
}


/*------------------------------------------------------------------------
 * ttyrestore - set tty characters and special characters
 *------------------------------------------------------------------------
 */
int
ttyrestore(pts)
struct ttystate *pts;
{
        if (ioctl(0, TIOCSETP, (char *)&pts->ts_sgttyb))
                errexit("can't set tty modes: %s\n", sys_errlist[errno]);
        if (ioctl(0, TIOCSETC, (char *)&pts->ts_tchars))
                errexit("can't set tty chars: %s\n", sys_errlist[errno]);
        if (ioctl(0, TIOCSLTC, (char *)&pts->ts_ltchars))
                errexit("can't set tty chars: %s\n", sys_errlist[errno]);
}
```

Procedure *ttysave* extracts the current parameters from the device driver associated with the keyboard (device *0*) and saves them in a structure of type *ttystate*. Procedure *ttyrestore* takes parameters previously saved in a *ttystate* structure and passes them to the device driver. Each procedure takes a single argument that gives the address of the structure to use.

25.5 Establishing Terminal Modes

When the client begins, it calls procedure *ttysetup* to establish parameters for the terminal device driver. File *ttysetup.c* contains the code.

```
/* ttysetup.c - ttysetup */

#include <stdio.h>

#include "local.h"

/*------------------------------------------------------------------------
 * ttysetup - set up tty
 *------------------------------------------------------------------------
 */
int
ttysetup()
{
        extern struct ttystate  tntty;

        ttysave(&oldtty);          /* save original tty state      */

        sg_erase = oldtty.ts_sgttyb.sg_erase;
        sg_kill = oldtty.ts_sgttyb.sg_kill;
        t_intrc = oldtty.ts_tchars.t_intrc;
        t_quitc = oldtty.ts_tchars.t_quitc;
        t_flushc = oldtty.ts_ltchars.t_flushc;

        tntty = oldtty;

        /* disable some special characters */
        tntty.ts_tchars.t_intrc = -1;
        tntty.ts_tchars.t_quitc = -1;
        tntty.ts_ltchars.t_suspc = -1;
        tntty.ts_ltchars.t_dsuspc = -1;

        ttyrestore(&tntty);
}
```

Ttysetup calls *ttysave* to record the initial terminal modes in global variable *oldtty*. Because *ioctl* only permits a program to extract or load all parameters at once, the client cannot set each parameter separately. To change one or more parameters, the client must make a copy of the initial parameters in local variable *tntty*, modify the copy to change one or more parameters, and then call *ttyrestore* to store the new parameters in the terminal device driver. The changes in *ttysetup* disable characters that cause *interrupt*, *quit*, *suspend*, and *delayed suspend*. In essence, setting the specified values to *-1* prevents the local device driver from interrupting or suspending the client program. Because *ttysetup* applies the changes to a copy of the initial terminal parameters, it leaves other terminal characteristics unchanged. For example, if the user has defined *control-C* to mean *abort the running program*, disabling it in the device driver means the client will be able to read *control-C* just like any other character. However, because *ttysetup* begins with a copy of the parameters, disabling interpretation of *control-C* does not affect other terminal characteristics (e.g., *echo*). We will see that the client uses the saved terminal mode to determine which character the user has defined for the interrupt signal. It sends the server side an interrupt command when the user types that character.

25.6 Global Variable Used For Stored State

File *local.h* contains the declaration of global variable *oldtty* along with other global variables that refer to the local terminal. It also defines structure *ttystate*, which contains all the important terminal characteristics.

```
/* local.h */

#include <sys/ioctl.h>

struct ttystate {
        struct sgttyb    ts_sgttyb;
        struct tchars    ts_tchars;
        struct ltchars   ts_ltchars;
};

extern FILE        *scrfp;
extern char        scrname[];
extern struct ttystate  oldtty;

extern char        t_flushc, t_intrc, t_quitc, sg_erase, sg_kill;
```

25.7 Restoring Terminal Modes Before Exit

When the client begins, it saves the original terminal modes in variable *oldtty*. When it exits, the client process calls *ttyrestore* to restore the saved terminal modes. For example, procedure *dcon* disconnects the TCP connection to a server; the client calls *dcon* when the user requests connection termination. *Dcon* prints a message, restores the terminal modes, and exits normally (i.e., it uses exit code *0*). File *dcon.c* contains the code:

```
/* dcon.c - dcon */

#include <sys/ioctl.h>

#include <stdio.h>

#include "local.h"

/*-------------------------------------------------------------------
 * dcon - disconnect from remote
 *-------------------------------------------------------------------
 */
/*ARGSUSED*/
int
dcon(sfp, tfp, c)
FILE    *sfp, *tfp;
int     c;
{
        fprintf(tfp, "disconnecting.\n");
        ttyrestore(&oldtty);
        exit(0);
}
```

If an error occurs, the client calls procedure *cerrexit* found in file *cerrexit.c*:

```
/* cerrexit.c - cerrexit */

#include <stdio.h>
#include <varargs.h>

#include "local.h"

/*------------------------------------------------------------------
 * cerrexit - cleanup and exit with an error message
 *------------------------------------------------------------------
 */
/*VARARGS1*/
int
cerrexit(format, va_alist)
char    *format;
va_dcl
{
        va_list args;

        va_start(args);
        _doprnt(format, args, stderr);
        ttyrestore(&oldtty);
        va_end(args);
        exit(1);
}
```

Like procedure *dcon*, *cerrexit* prints a message and restores the terminal modes before it exits. Unlike *dcon*, however, *cerrexit* uses exit code *1* to indicate an abnormal exit.

25.8 Client Suspension And Resumption

UNIX allows the user to suspend a running program temporarily. During suspension, control of the user's terminal reverts to another process, usually a command interpreter. When a TELNET client receives a signal that causes process suspension, it must restore the original terminal parameters before suspending and must reset the parameters to the values the client uses when the process resumes. File *suspend.c* contains the code for function *suspend* that restores the original terminal modes before it suspends the client process. When the client resumes execution, *suspend* regains control, resets the terminal modes, and returns to its caller.

```
/* suspend.c - */

#include <sys/types.h>
#include <sys/signal.h>

#include <stdio.h>

#include "local.h"

extern struct ttystate  tntty;

/*------------------------------------------------------------------------
 * suspend - suspend execution temporarily
 *------------------------------------------------------------------------
 */
/*ARGSUSED*/
int
suspend(sfp, tfp, c)
FILE    *sfp, *tfp;
int     c;
{
        ttysave(&tntty);         /* save current tty state       */
        ttyrestore(&oldtty);     /* restore old tty state        */

        (void) kill(0, SIGTSTP);

        ttysave(&oldtty);        /* may have changed             */
        ttyrestore(&tntty);      /* restore telnet modes         */
        return 0;
}
```

25.9 Finite State Machine Specification

The TELNET protocol specifies how a client passes characters to a remote service and how the client displays data that the remote service returns. Most of the traffic that passes across the connection consists of individual data characters. Data characters originate at the client when the user types on the keyboard; they originate from the server when the remote session generates output. In addition to data characters, TELNET also permits the client and server to exchange control information. In particular, the client can send a sequence of characters that comprise a *command* to the server that controls execution of the remote service. For example, a client can send a command sequence that *interrupt*s the remote application program.

Most implementations of TELNET use a *finite state machine* (*FSM*) to specify the exact syntax and interpretation of command sequences. As a specification tool, a finite state machine provides a precise description of the protocol. It shows exactly how the sender embeds command sequences in the stream of data, and specifies exactly how the receiver interprets such sequences. More important, the finite state machine can be converted directly into a program that follows the protocol. Thus, it is possible to verify that the resulting program obeys the protocol specification. To summarize:

> *Because TELNET is a character-oriented protocol that embeds command sequences in the data stream between the client and server, most implementations use a finite state machine to define the correct behavior.*

25.10 Embedding Commands In A TELNET Data Stream

The idea underlying TELNET is simple: whenever a client or server wants to send a command sequence instead of normal data, it inserts a special, reserved character in the data stream. The reserved character is called an *Interpret As Command* character (*IAC*). When the receiver finds an IAC character in its incoming data stream, it processes succeeding octets as a command sequence. To send an IAC as data, the sender *character stuff*s an extra IAC in front of it.

An individual command sequence can contain an *option request* or an *option reply*. A request asks the receiving side to honor (or not honor) a particular *TELNET option*; a reply acknowledges the request and specifies whether the receiver will honor it.

The protocol defines two verbs that a sender can use to form a request: *DO* and *DONT*. Like most items that TELNET defines, the protocol standard specifies that each verb and each option must be encoded in a single character. Thus, a request usually consists of three characters when it appears in the data:

IAC   verb   option

where *verb* denotes an encoded character for either a *DO* or *DONT*, and *option* denotes an encoded character for one of the TELNET options.

The *TELNET echo option* provides a good example. Normally, the server echoes each character it receives (i.e., sends a copy back to the user's display). To turn off remote character echo, the client sends three encoded characters that correspond to:

IAC   DONT   ECHO

25.11 Option Negotiation

In general, the receiving side responds to a request using the verbs *WILL* or *WONT*. The receiver sends *WILL* to specify that it will honor the requested option and *WONT* to specify that it will not.

A response to a request provides an acknowledgement to the sender and tells the sender whether the receiver agrees to honor the request. For example, at startup, the client and server negotiate to decide which side will echo characters that the user types. Usually, the client sends characters to the server and the server echoes them to the user's terminal. However, if network delays become troublesome, a user may prefer to have the local system echo characters. Before a client enables character echo in the local system, it sends the server the sequence:

IAC DONT ECHO

When the server receives the request, it sends the 3-character response:

IAC WONT ECHO

Note that the verb *WONT* refers to the option; it does not necessarily mean that the server rejected the request. In this case, for example, the server has agreed to turn off echo as requested.

25.12 Request/Offer Symmetry

Interestingly, TELNET permits one side of a connection to offer a particular option before the other side requests it. To do so, the side offering to perform (or not perform) an option sends a message containing the verb *WILL* (or *WONT*). Thus, a *WILL* or *WONT* either acknowledges a previous request or offers to perform an option. For example, UNIX applications like text editors often send special control sequences to position the cursor. They cannot use the network virtual terminal encoding because it does not support all possible 8-bit characters. Thus, the TELNET server from BSD UNIX automatically sends *WILL* for the *transmit binary* option whenever a client connects to it, offering to use 8-bit binary (unencoded) character transmission instead of NVT encoding. A client must respond by sending a command sequence that specifies *DO transmit binary* or *DONT transmit binary*.

25.13 TELNET Character Definitions

File *telnet.h* contains the definitions of constants used in the protocol:

```
/* telnet.h */

/* TELNET Command Codes: */
#define TCSB            (u_char)250    /* Start Subnegotiation          */
#define TCSE            (u_char)240    /* End Of Subnegotiation         */
#define TCNOP           (u_char)241    /* No Operation                  */
#define TCDM            (u_char)242    /* Data Mark (for Sync)          */
#define TCBRK           (u_char)243    /* NVT Character BRK             */
#define TCIP            (u_char)244    /* Interrupt Process             */
#define TCAO            (u_char)245    /* Abort Output                  */
#define TCAYT           (u_char)246    /* "Are You There?" Function     */
#define TCEC            (u_char)247    /* Erase Character               */
#define TCEL            (u_char)248    /* Erase Line                    */
#define TCGA            (u_char)249    /* "Go Ahead" Function           */
#define TCWILL          (u_char)251    /* Desire/Confirm Will Do Option*/
#define TCWONT          (u_char)252    /* Refusal To Do Option          */
#define TCDO            (u_char)253    /* Request To Do Option          */
#define TCDONT          (u_char)254    /* Request NOT To Do Option      */
#define TCIAC           (u_char)255    /* Interpret As Command Escape   */

/* Telnet Option Codes: */
#define TOTXBINARY      (u_char)  0    /* TRANSMIT-BINARY option        */
#define TOECHO          (u_char)  1    /* ECHO Option                   */
#define TONOGA          (u_char)  3    /* Suppress Go-Ahead Option      */
#define TOTERMTYPE      (u_char) 24    /* Terminal-Type Option          */

/* Network Virtual Printer Special Characters: */
#define VPLF            '\n'    /* Line Feed                          */
#define VPCR            '\r'    /* Carriage Return                    */
#define VPBEL           '\a'    /* Bell (attention signal)            */
#define VPBS            '\b'    /* Back Space                         */
#define VPHT            '\t'    /* Horizontal Tab                     */
#define VPVT            '\v'    /* Vertical Tab                       */
#define VPFF            '\f'    /* Form Feed                          */

/* Keyboard Command Characters: */
#define KCESCAPE        035     /* Local escape character ('^]')       */
#define KCDCON          '.'     /* Disconnect escape command           */
#define KCSUSP          032     /* Suspend session escape command ('^Z')*/
#define KCSCRIPT        's'     /* Begin scripting escape command      */
#define KCUNSCRIPT      'u'     /* End scripting escape command        */
#define KCSTATUS        024     /* Print status escape command ('^T')  */
#define KCNL            '\n'    /* Newline character                   */

#define KCANY           (NCHRS+1)
```

```
/* Option Subnegotiation Constants: */
#define TT_IS            0        /* TERMINAL_TYPE option "IS" command    */
#define TT_SEND          1        /* TERMINAL_TYPE option "SEND" command  */


/* Boolean Option and State variables */
extern char    synching, doecho, sndbinary, rcvbinary;
```

Note that the file defines symbolic names for each of the characters TELNET uses, including verbs like *WILL* and *WONT* as well as option codes.

25.14 A Finite State Machine For Data From The Server

Figure 25.4 shows the principle finite state machine that specifies the TELNET protocol, including states that correspond to the option negotiation described above. Think of the machine as specifying how a client handles the sequence of characters it receives from the server.

The FSM diagram uses conventional notation. Each transition from one state to another has a label of the form α/β, where α denotes a specific input character that causes the transition and β denotes an action to be taken when following the transition. A label α/β on a transition from state X to state Y means: *if character α arrives while in state* X, *execute action β and then change to state* Y. The names of states and characters in the figure have been taken from the software. For example, file *telnet.h* defines constant *TCIAC* to correspond to TELNET's IAC character. As shorthand, the name *TCANY* denotes any character other than the transitions listed explicitly.

To understand how the FSM works, imagine that the client uses it whenever data arrives over the TCP connection from the server. When a character arrives from the server, the client follows a transition in the finite state machine. Some of the transitions keep the machine in the same state, but others transfer to a new state.

25.15 Transitions Among States

The client starts its state machine in the state labeled *TSDATA* when it begins execution. State *TSDATA* corresponds to a situation where the client expects to receive normal characters and send them to the user's display (i.e., the client has not begun reading a command sequence). For example, if character *q* arrives, the client remains in state *TSDATA* and executes the action labeled *K* (i.e., the client calls procedure *ttputc* to display the character on the user's terminal screen, and then follows the loop back to the same state).

If character *TCIAC* arrives when the FSM is in state *TSDATA*, the client follows the transition to state *TSIAC* and executes action labeled *E* in the diagram. The legend specifies that action *E* corresponds to "no operation." Once it moves to state *TSIAC*, the client has begun interpreting a command sequence. If the character following the *TCIAC* is a verb (e.g., *TCDO*), the client will follow a transition to one of the option processing states.

The finite state machine for TELNET only needs six states because interpretation of the protocol only depends on a short history of the characters that have arrived. For example, following a *TCIAC* character, the server could send one of the option requests or responses: *TCDO*, *TCDONT*, *TCWILL*, or *TCWONT*, or it could send an *option subnegotiation request*. Option subnegotiation permits the sender to include a variable-length string in the option (e.g., the option a client uses to pass a terminal type to a server uses subnegotiation so it can send a string that encodes the name of the terminal). Although subnegotiation permits variable-length command sequences, the FSM needs only two states to handle it because a 2-character sequence terminates subnegotiation. The client enters state *TSSUBNEG* when it first encounters a subnegotiation request. It moves to state *TSSUBIAC* when it receives character *TCIAC*, and moves out of subnegotiation altogether if character *TCSE* follows immediately. If any other 2-character sequence occurs, the FSM remains in state *TSSUBNEG*.

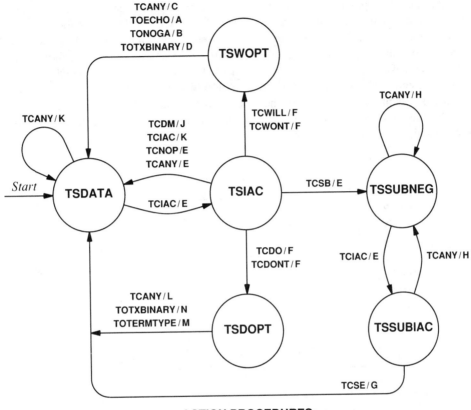

ACTION PROCEDURES:

A - do_echo   H - subopt
B - do_noga   J - tcdm
C - do_notsup K - ttputc
D - do_txbinary L - will_notsup
E - no_op   M - will_termtype
F - recopt   N - will_txbinary
G - subend

Figure 25.4 The finite state machine that describes how TELNET encodes command sequences along with data. State and character names have been taken directly from the software. *TCANY* stands for "any character other than those shown explicitly."

25.16 A Finite State Machine Implementation

Because it is possible to construct an efficient implementation of a finite state machine and because such machines can describe character-oriented protocols easily, our example code uses three separate finite state machines. One controls how the client responds to characters from the keyboard, another controls how the client handles characters that arrive over the TCP connection from the server, and a third handles the details of option subnegotiation. All three FSMs use the same type of data structures, making it possible to share some of the procedures that manipulate the data structures.

To make processing efficient, our implementation encodes the transitions of a finite state machine into a *transition matrix* as Figure 25.5 shows.

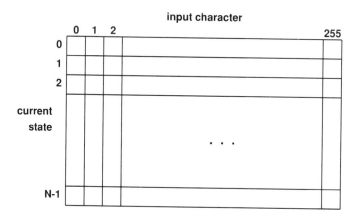

Figure 25.5 A finite state machine represented by a transition matrix. Each row corresponds to a state and each column corresponds to one possible input character.

At run-time, the client maintains an integer variable that records the current state. When a character arrives, the client uses the current state variable and the numeric value of the character to index the transition matrix.

25.17 A Compact FSM Representation

Writing C code to initialize a large matrix can be tedious. Furthermore, if each element of the transition matrix contains complete information about the action to take and the next state, the matrix can consume a large amount of memory. To keep the transition matrix small and to make initialization easy, our code uses a compact representation of a finite state machine.

In essence, the data structures chosen permit a programmer to create a compact data structure that represents a finite state machine and then arrange for the program to construct an associated transition matrix at run-time. File *tnfsm.h* contains the declaration of structure *fsm_trans* used in the compact representation:

```
/* tnfsm.h */

/* Telnet Socket-Input FSM States: */
#define TSDATA          0       /* normal data processing             */
#define TSIAC           1       /* have seen IAC                      */
#define TSWOPT          2       /* have seen IAC-{WILL/WONT}           */
#define TSDOPT          3       /* have seen IAC-{DO/DONT}             */
#define TSSUBNEG        4       /* have seen IAC-SB                    */
#define TSSUBIAC        5       /* have seen IAC-SB-...-IAC            */


#define NTSTATES        6       /* # of TS* states                    */


/* Telnet Keyboard-Input FSM States: */
#define KSREMOTE        0       /* input goes to the socket           */
#define KSLOCAL         1       /* input goes to a local func.        */
#define KSCOLLECT       2       /* input is scripting-file name        */


#define NKSTATES        3       /* # of KS* states                    */


/* Telnet Option Subnegotiation FSM States: */
#define SS_START        0       /* initial state                      */
#define SS_TERMTYPE     1       /* TERMINAL_TYPE option subnegotiation */
#define SS_END          2       /* state after all legal input        */


#define NSSTATES        3       /* # of SS_* states                   */


#define FSINVALID       0xff    /* an invalid state number            */


#define NCHRS           256             /* number of valid characters */
#define TCANY           (NCHRS+1)       /* match any character        */


struct fsm_trans {
        u_char  ft_state;               /* current state              */
        short   ft_char;                /* input character            */
        u_char  ft_next;                /* next state                 */
        int     (*ft_action)();         /* action to take             */
};
```

A compact FSM representation consists of a 1-dimensional array of *fsm_trans* structures. Each element specifies one transition. Field *ft_state* specifies the FSM state from which the transition begins. Field *ft_char* specifies the character that causes the transition (or *TC_ANY* to denote all characters other than those with explicit transitions). Field *ft_next* specifies the state in which the transition terminates, and field *ft_action* gives the address of the procedure to call that performs the action associated with the transition.

25.18 Keeping The Compact Representation At Run-Time

The example client does not copy all the information from the compact representation into the transition matrix. Instead, it leaves the compact representation unchanged and uses it to hold transition information. To do so, the software stores an integer in each element of the transition matrix. The integer gives the index of an entry in the compact representation that corresponds to the transition. Figure 25.6 illustrates the data structures:

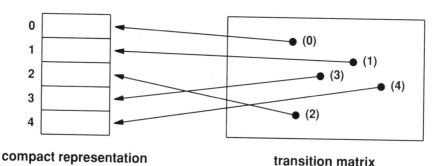

compact representation   **transition matrix**

Figure 25.6 The FSM data structures at run-time. Entries in the transition matrix contain an index that refers to an element of the compact representation.

25.19 Implementation Of A Compact Representation

File *ttfsm.c* contains an example compact FSM representation for the principle FSM shown in Figure 25.4:

```
/* ttfsm.c */

#include <sys/types.h>
#include <stdio.h>
#include "telnet.h"
#include "tnfsm.h"
#include "local.h"

extern int do_echo(), do_noga(), do_notsup(), do_status(), no_op(),
        recopt(), subend(), subopt(), tcdm(), ttputc(), will_notsup(),
        will_termtype(), will_txbinary(), abort();

struct fsm_trans ttstab[] = {
        /* State          Input          Next State     Action   */
        /* ------         ------         ----------     -------  */
        { TSDATA,         TCIAC,         TSIAC,         no_op       },
        { TSDATA,         TCANY,         TSDATA,        ttputc      },
        { TSIAC,          TCIAC,         TSDATA,        ttputc      },
        { TSIAC,          TCSB,          TSSUBNEG,      no_op       },
/* Telnet Commands */
        { TSIAC,          TCNOP,         TSDATA,        no_op       },
        { TSIAC,          TCDM,          TSDATA,        tcdm        },
/* Option Negotiation */
        { TSIAC,          TCWILL,        TSWOPT,        recopt      },
        { TSIAC,          TCWONT,        TSWOPT,        recopt      },
        { TSIAC,          TCDO,          TSDOPT,        recopt      },
        { TSIAC,          TCDONT,        TSDOPT,        recopt      },
        { TSIAC,          TCANY,         TSDATA,        no_op       },
/* Option Subnegotion */
        { TSSUBNEG,       TCIAC,         TSSUBIAC,      no_op       },
        { TSSUBNEG,       TCANY,         TSSUBNEG,      subopt      },
        { TSSUBIAC,       TCSE,          TSDATA,        subend      },
        { TSSUBIAC,       TCANY,         TSSUBNEG,      subopt      },

        { TSWOPT,         TOECHO,        TSDATA,        do_echo     },
        { TSWOPT,         TONOGA,        TSDATA,        do_noga     },
        { TSWOPT,         TOTXBINARY,    TSDATA,        do_txbinary },
        { TSWOPT,         TCANY,         TSDATA,        do_notsup   },

        { TSDOPT,         TOTERMTYPE,    TSDATA,        will_termtype },
        { TSDOPT,         TOTXBINARY,    TSDATA,        will_txbinary },
        { TSDOPT,         TCANY,         TSDATA,        will_notsup   },

        { FSINVALID,      TCANY,         FSINVALID,     abort       },
};
```

```
#define NTRANS (sizeof(ttstab)/sizeof(ttstab[0]))

int      ttstate;
u_char   ttfsm[NTSTATES][NCHRS];
```

Array *ttstab* contains *22* valid entries that each correspond to one of the transitions shown in Figure 25.4 (plus an extra entry to mark the end of the array). Each entry in the array consists of an *fsm_trans* structure that specifies a single transition. Note that *ttstab* is both compact and easy to define. It is compact because it does not contain any empty entries; it is easy to define because each entry corresponds directly to one of the transitions in the FSM.

25.20 Building An FSM Transition Matrix

The utility of the compact representation will become clear once we see how it can be used to generate a transition matrix. File *fsminit.c* contains the code:

```
/* fsminit.c - fsminit */

#include <sys/types.h>

#include "tnfsm.h"

#define TINVALID        0xff     /* an invalid transition index            */

/*-------------------------------------------------------------------------
 * fsminit - Finite State Machine initializer
 *-------------------------------------------------------------------------
 */
int
fsminit(fsm, ttab, nstates)
u_char                  fsm[][NCHRS];
struct fsm_trans        ttab[];
int                     nstates;
{
        struct fsm_trans        *pt;
        int                     sn, ti, cn;

        for (cn=0; cn<NCHRS; ++cn)
                for (ti=0; ti<nstates; ++ti)
                        fsm[ti][cn] = TINVALID;
```

```
for (ti=0; ttab[ti].ft_state != FSINVALID; ++ti) {
        pt = &ttab[ti];
        sn = pt->ft_state;
        if (pt->ft_char == TCANY) {
                for (cn=0; cn<NCHRS; ++cn)
                        if (fsm[sn][cn] == TINVALID)
                                fsm[sn][cn] = ti;
        } else
                fsm[sn][pt->ft_char] = ti;
}
/* set all uninitialized indices to an invalid transition        */
for (cn=0; cn<NCHRS; ++cn)
        for (ti=0; ti<nstates; ++ti)
                if (fsm[ti][cn] == TINVALID)
                        fsm[ti][cn] = ti;

}
```

Procedure *fsminit* requires three arguments. Argument *fsm* specifies a transition matrix that must be initialized. Argument *ttab* gives the address of a compact FSM representation, and argument *nstates* specifies the number of states in the resulting FSM.

Fsminit first initializes the entire transition matrix to *TINVALID*. It then iterates through each element of the compact representation and adds the state transition specified by that element to the transition matrix. Finally, it iterates through the transition matrix again and changes any transitions that have not been filled in so they point to the invalid transition at the end of the compact representation.

Most of the code in *fsminit* is straightforward. When adding transitions, however, *fsminit* must distinguish between an explicit transition and an abbreviation. To understand the code, recall that the compact representation uses character *TCANY* to denote all characters that have not been specified explicitly. Thus, when *fsminit* examines an individual transition, it checks the character that causes the transition. If the entry specifies character *TCANY*, *fsminit* iterates through all possible characters and adds the transition to any character that has not been initialized. If the entry specifies any character other than *TCANY*, *fsminit* fills in the transition array for that single character.

25.21 The Socket Output Finite State Machine

The finite state machine shown in Figure 25.4 defines the actions the client takes for each character that arrives from the server. A separate, and simpler, finite state machine describes how the client handles characters that arrive from the keyboard. We call the FSM associated with keyboard input the *socket output FSM*. The name may seem unusual. Figure 25.7 shows how the client software organization supports such a name.

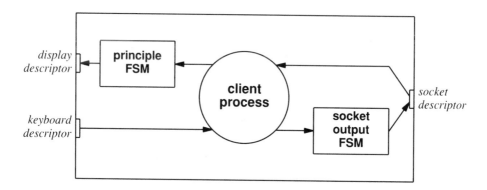

Figure 25.7 The client software organization. The central process reads data from either the socket or the keyboard and calls an FSM procedure to process it. The FSM that processes keyboard data is associated with socket output.

Figure 25.8 shows the socket output finite state machine:

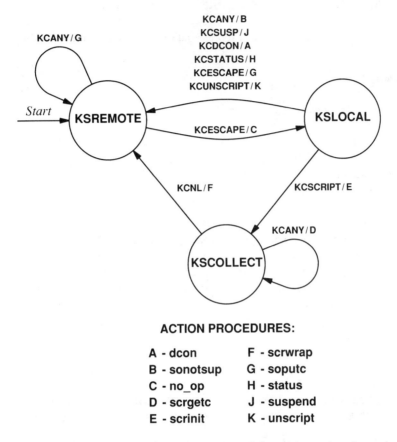

Figure 25.8 The socket output FSM used to define actions taken for each character the user types. The client sends most data characters to the remote server. However, the design permits the user to *escape* from the data connection and communicate with the local client program.

The socket output FSM begins in state *KSREMOTE*, which causes the client to send each character from the keyboard to the remote server. When the user types the *keyboard escape* key, the client enters state *KSLOCAL* where it waits for a keystroke. Most keystrokes that can follow the escape have no meaning, but a few cause the client to take action and return to state *KSREMOTE*. Only one, *KCSCRIPT*, causes the client to enter state *KSCOLLECT*, where it collects a file name to use for scripting.

25.22 Definitions For The Socket Output FSM

File *sofsm.c* defines the compact representation of the socket output FSM:

```c
/* sofsm.c */

#include <sys/types.h>

#include <stdio.h>

#include "telnet.h"
#include "tnfsm.h"

/* Special chars: */
char    t_flushc, t_intrc, t_quitc, sg_erase, sg_kill;

extern int      soputc(), scrinit(), scrgetc(), scrwrap(), unscript(),
                dcon(), suspend(), status(), sonotsup(), abort(),
                no_op();

struct fsm_trans sostab[] = {
        /* State          Input             Next State        Action  */
        /* ------         ------            ----------        ------- */
/* Data Input */
        { KSREMOTE,       KCESCAPE,         KSLOCAL,          no_op        },
        { KSREMOTE,       KCANY,            KSREMOTE,         soputc       },
/* Local Escape Commands */
        { KSLOCAL,        KCSCRIPT,         KSCOLLECT,        scrinit      },
        { KSLOCAL,        KCUNSCRIPT,       KSREMOTE,         unscript     },
        { KSLOCAL,        KCESCAPE,         KSREMOTE,         soputc       },
        { KSLOCAL,        KCDCON,           KSREMOTE,         dcon         },
        { KSLOCAL,        KCSUSP,           KSREMOTE,         suspend      },
        { KSLOCAL,        KCSTATUS,         KSREMOTE,         status       },
        { KSLOCAL,        KCANY,            KSREMOTE,         sonotsup     },
/* Script Filename Gathering */
        { KSCOLLECT,      KCNL,             KSREMOTE,         scrwrap      },
        { KSCOLLECT,      KCANY,            KSCOLLECT,        scrgetc      },

        { FSINVALID,      KCANY,            FSINVALID,        abort        },
};

#define NTRANS   (sizeof(sostab)/sizeof(sostab[0]))

int     sostate;
u_char  sofsm[NKSTATES][NCHRS];
```

Array *sostab* contains the compact representation, and variable *sostate* contains an integer that gives the current state of the socket output FSM.

25.23 The Option Subnegotiation Finite State Machine

Figure 25.9 illustrates the third FSM used in the client. It handles the sequence of characters that arrive during *option subnegotiation*. Because it only recognizes one possible option subnegotiation (terminal type), the FSM only needs three states.

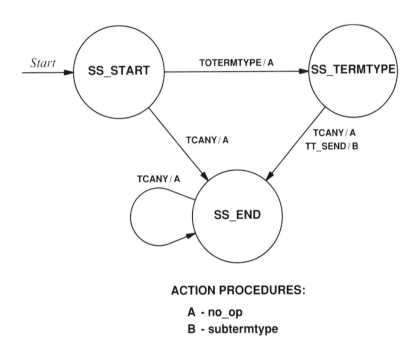

ACTION PROCEDURES:

A - no_op
B - subtermtype

Figure 25.9 The simple FSM used for option subnegotiation. The client reinitializes this machine each time it finishes an option subnegotiation.

The easiest way to think about subnegotiation is to imagine that it describes the interior structure of state *TSSUBNEG* in the principle FSM. While the main FSM operates in state *TSSUBNEG*, it calls procedure *subopt* to handle each incoming character. *Subopt* operates the subnegotiation FSM. As Figure 25.9 shows, the subnegotiation FSM makes an immediate decision that depends on the option. If it finds a terminal type subnegotiation, the machine moves to state *SS_TERMTYPE*. Otherwise, it moves directly to state *SS_END* and ignores the remainder of the subnegotiation string.

Once in state *SS_TERMTYPE*, the FSM checks the subnegotiation verb. It calls *subtermtype* if the verb is *TT_SEND*, and ignores the subnegotiation otherwise. The purpose and operation of the subnegotiation FSM will become clearer when we see how a client responds to the terminal type option.

25.24 Definitions For The Option Subnegotiation FSM

File *subfsm.c* contains the C declarations for the subnegotiation FSM:

```
/* subfsm.c */

#include <sys/types.h>

#include <stdio.h>

#include "telnet.h"
#include "tnfsm.h"

extern int      no_op(), subtermtype();
extern int      abort();

struct fsm_trans substab[] = {
        /* State          Input           Next State      Action   */
        /* ------         ------          ----------      -------   */
        { SS_START,       TOTERMTYPE,     SS_TERMTYPE,    no_op        },
        { SS_START,       TCANY,          SS_END,         no_op        },

        { SS_TERMTYPE,    TT_SEND,        SS_END,         subtermtype  },
        { SS_TERMTYPE,    TCANY,          SS_END,         no_op        },

        { SS_END,         TCANY,          SS_END,         no_op        },
        { FSINVALID,      TCANY,          FSINVALID,      abort        },
};

int     substate;
u_char  subfsm[NSSTATES][NCHRS];
```

25.25 FSM Initialization

At startup, the client calls procedure *fsmbuild* to initialize all finite state machines. As the code in file *ttinit.c* shows, *fsmbuild* calls *fsminit* to build the required data structure for each machine, and assigns each machine's state variable an initial state.

```
/* ttinit.c - ttinit */

#include <sys/types.h>

#include <stdio.h>

#include "tnfsm.h"

extern struct fsm_trans ttstab[], sostab[], substab[];
extern u_char           ttfsm[][NCHRS], sofsm[][NCHRS], subfsm[][NCHRS];
extern int              ttstate, sostate, substate;

/*------------------------------------------------------------------------
 * fsmbuild - build the Finite State Machine data structures
 *------------------------------------------------------------------------
 */
int
fsmbuild()
{
        fsminit(ttfsm, ttstab, NTSTATES);
        ttstate = TSDATA;

        fsminit(sofsm, sostab, NKSTATES);
        sostate = KSREMOTE;

        fsminit(subfsm, substab, NSSTATES);
        substate = SS_START;
}
```

25.26 Arguments For The TELNET Client

File *tclient.c* contains the code for the main program that executes when a user invokes the client:

```
/* tclient.c - main */

char    *host = "localhost";    /* host to use if none supplied          */

/*------------------------------------------------------------------------
 * main - TCP client for TELNET service
 *------------------------------------------------------------------------
 */
int
main(argc, argv)
int     argc;
char    *argv[];
{
        char    *service = "telnet";    /* default service name          */

        switch (argc) {
        case 1: break;
        case 3:
                service = argv[2];
                /* FALL THROUGH */
        case 2:
                host = argv[1];
                break;
        default:
                errexit("usage: telnet [host [port]]\n");
        }
        telnet(host, service);
        exit(0);
}
```

The user can supply zero, one, or two command-line arguments that the program parses. With no arguments, (*argc* = *1*), the client contacts a server on the local host and uses the *telnet* service. If one argument appears (*argc* = 2), the client takes the argument as the name of the remote host on which the server executes. Finally, if two arguments appear, the client takes the second to be the name of a service on the remote machine and takes the first to be the name of a remote host. After it has parsed its arguments, the main program calls function *telnet*.

25.27 The Heart Of The TELNET Client

File *telnet.c* contains the code that implements Algorithm *8.1*†:

```
/* telnet.c - telnet */

#include <sys/types.h>
#include <sys/socket.h>
#include <sys/time.h>
#include <sys/signal.h>
#include <sys/errno.h>

#include <stdio.h>

#include "local.h"

int     rcvurg();

extern int      errno;
extern char     *sys_errlist[];

#define BUFSIZE         2048    /* read buffer size      */

struct ttystate oldtty;

/*------------------------------------------------------------------------
 * telnet - do the TELNET protocol to the given host and port
 *------------------------------------------------------------------------
 */
int
telnet(host, service)
char    *host;
char    *service;
{
        int     s, nfds;        /* socket and # file descriptors */
        u_char  buf[BUFSIZE];
        int     cc;
        int     on = 1;
        fd_set  arfds, awfds, rfds, wfds;
        FILE    *sfp;

        s = connectTCP(host, service);

        ttysetup();
```

†See page 103 for a description of Algorithm 8.1.

```
        fsmbuild();       /* set up FSM's */

        (void) signal(SIGURG, rcvurg);
        (void) setsockopt(s, SOL_SOCKET, SO_OOBINLINE, (char *)&on,
                    sizeof(on));

        nfds = getdtablesize();
        FD_ZERO(&arfds);
        FD_ZERO(&awfds);
        FD_SET(s, &arfds);        /* the socket                 */
        FD_SET(0, &arfds);        /* standard input             */

        sfp = fdopen(s, "w");    /* to get buffered output      */

        while (1) {
                bcopy((char *)&arfds, (char *)&rfds, sizeof(rfds));
                bcopy((char *)&awfds, (char *)&wfds, sizeof(rfds));

                if (select(nfds, &rfds, &wfds, (fd_set *)0,
                            (struct timeval *)0) < 0) {
                        if (errno == EINTR)
                                continue;        /* just a signal        */
                        cerrexit("select: %s\n", sys_errlist[errno]);
                }
                if (FD_ISSET(s, &rfds)) {
                        cc = read(s, (char *)buf, sizeof(buf));
                        if (cc < 0)
                                cerrexit("socket read: %s\n",
                                            sys_errlist[errno]);
                        else if (cc == 0) {
                                printf("\nconnection closed.\n");
                                ttyrestore(&oldtty);
                                exit(0);
                        } else
                                ttwrite(sfp, stdout, buf, cc);
                }
                if (FD_ISSET(0, &rfds)) {
                        cc = read(0, (char *)buf, sizeof(buf));
                        if (cc < 0)
                                cerrexit("tty read: %s\n",
                                            sys_errlist[errno]);
                        else if (cc == 0) {
                                FD_CLR(0, &arfds);
```

```
                              (void)  shutdown(s, 1);
                     } else
                              sowrite(sfp, stdout, buf, cc);
              }
              (void)  fflush(sfp);
              (void)  fflush(stdout);
      }
}
```

Procedure *telnet* requires two arguments that specify the name of a remote machine and a service on that machine. The code begins by calling *connectTCP* to allocate a socket and form a TCP connection to the server. It calls *ttysetup* to initialize the local terminal parameters and *fsmbuild* to initialize the three finite state machines. It then calls the system function *signal* to establish a handler for urgent data. If TCP receives urgent data from the server after the call to *signal*, the system will invoke procedure *rcvurg* to handle it.

File *sync.c* contains the code for procedures *tcdm* and *rcvurg*:

```
/* sync.c - tcdm, rcvurg */

#include <stdio.h>

char    synching;        /* non-zero, if we are doing telnet SYNCH       */

/*------------------------------------------------------------------------
 * tcdm - handle the telnet "DATA MARK" command (marks end of SYNCH)
 *------------------------------------------------------------------------
 */
/*ARGSUSED*/
int
tcdm(sfp, tfp, c)
FILE    *sfp, *tfp;
int     c;
{
        synching = 0;
        return 0;
}


/*------------------------------------------------------------------------
 * rcvurg - receive urgent data input (indicates a telnet SYNCH)
 *------------------------------------------------------------------------
 */
/*ARGSUSED*/
```

```
int
rcvurg()
{
        synching++;
}
```

The TELNET protocol specifies that when urgent data arrives, the client must *syn-chronize* with the server. To synchronize, the client skips forward in the stream of data arriving from the server until it encounters the *DATA MARK* character. Thus, when an urgent data signal occurs, *rcvurg* merely increments global variable *synching* to place the client in synchronizing mode. While *synching* is set, the FSM action procedures discard incoming data without displaying it on the user's terminal. Later, when a *DATA MARK* character arrives, the client calls procedure *tcdm*, to set global variable *synching* back to zero and return the client to normal processing.

Once it finishes initialization, the client enters an infinite loop. At each iteration of the loop, it uses *select* to wait for I/O from the socket or from the keyboard (i.e., standard input associated with descriptor *0*). The *select* call will return value *EINTR* if the program receives a UNIX signal while the process is blocked. If that happens, the client continues with the next iteration of the loop. If the *select* call returns any other error code, the client prints a message to the user and exits.

If *select* returns normally, data can be available at the keyboard, at the socket, or at both. *Telnet* first checks the socket to see if data has arrived from the server. If so, it calls *read* to extract the data and *ttwrite* to write the data to the user's display. We will see below that *ttwrite* implements the principle finite state machine that interprets the incoming data stream and handles escapes and embedded command sequences.

After *telnet* checks for incoming data at the socket, it examines the descriptor for the keyboard. If data has arrived from the keyboard, *telnet* calls *read* to extract the data and *sowrite* to write it to the socket. *Sowrite* contains the code that executes the finite state machine for local escape processing. As a special case, the client interprets *end-of-file* to be a request to terminate the connection. If it receives an end-of-file (i.e., *read* returns *0*), *telnet* calls *shutdown* to send an end-of-file condition to the server. In any case, *telnet* calls *fflush* at each iteration to ensure that the output routines do not buffer the data that has been written. *Fflush* forces a call to the *write* system procedure.

25.28 Implementation Of The Main FSM

Procedure *ttwrite* implements the FSM from Figure 25.4 that interprets data as it arrives from the server. The code appears in file *ttwrite.c*:

```
/* ttwrite.c - ttwrite */

#include <sys/types.h>

#include <stdio.h>

#include "tnfsm.h"

extern struct fsm_trans ttstab[];
extern u_char           ttfsm[][NCHRS];
extern int              ttstate;

/*------------------------------------------------------------------------
 * ttwrite - do output processing for (local) network virtual printer
 *------------------------------------------------------------------------
 */
int
ttwrite(sfp, tfp, buf, cc)
FILE    *sfp, *tfp;     /* socket and terminal FILE ptrs*/
u_char  *buf;           /* buffer of data to send        */
int     cc;             /* # characters in buf           */
{
        struct fsm_trans        *pt;
        int                     i, ti;

        for (i=0; i<cc; ++i) {
                int     c = buf[i];

                ti = ttfsm[ttstate][c];
                pt = &ttstab[ti];

                (pt->ft_action)(sfp, tfp, c);
                ttstate = pt->ft_next;
        }
}
```

Ttwrite extracts *cc* characters from buffer *buf* one at a time. Each time it extracts a character, *ttwrite* uses the character and the current state (variable *ttstate*) to index the transition matrix. The transition matrix returns *ti*, the index of a transition in the compact representation (*ttstab*). *Ttwrite* calls the procedure associated with the transition (field *ft_action*), and sets the current state variable to the appropriate next state (field *ft_next*).

25.29 Summary

TELNET ranks among the most popular application protocols in the TCP/IP suite. The protocol provides for interactive character transport between a client and server. Usually, the client connects a user's terminal to a server across a TCP connection. Our example client software consists of a single process that uses the UNIX system function *select* to achieve concurrent transfer.

TELNET uses escape sequences to embed commands and control information in the data stream. To simplify the code, our example client implementation uses three finite state machines to interpret character sequences. One handles data that arrives from the server, another handles data that arrives from the user's keyboard, and a third handles option subnegotiation.

The example code in this chapter illustrates the implementation of the central client process as well as the data structures used to implement the finite state machines. The next chapter considers the details of the procedures that perform actions associated with transitions in the finite state machines.

FOR FURTHER STUDY

Postel [RFC 854] contains the standard for the basic TELNET protocol, including the network virtual terminal encoding. Postel and Reynolds [RFC 855] specifies the details of option negotiation and option subnegotiation. Details on individual options can be found in other RFCs. VanBokkelen [RFC 1091] specifies the terminal-type option. Postel and Reynolds [RFC 857] describes the echo option, while Postel and Reynolds [RFC 856] describes the binary transmission option.

Stevens [1990] describes UNIX's *rlogin* protocol, an alternative to TELNET, and shows an example of a simple client and server. Leffler *et. al.* [1989] discusses more about the details of UNIX terminal I/O.

EXERCISES

25.1 Compare a multi-process TELNET client to the design presented in this chapter. What are the advantages and disadvantages of each?

25.2 Read the *UNIX Programmer's Manual* to find out about UNIX terminal devices and device drivers. What are *cooked mode*, *cbreak mode*, and *raw mode*?

25.3 Write a program that disables *character echo* on the user's terminal. What happens to the echo parameter after the program exits?

25.4 Read the system documentation to find out about the UNIX command *stty*. What happens if one redirects the output from *stty* to a file? Why?

25.5   How does the code in *suspend.c* suspend the client process?

25.6   Rewrite the principle FSM to include states for option subnegotiation.

25.7   The example FSM implementation uses a compact representation to save space. Estimate the space required for the principle FSM using a conventional representation, and compare the estimate to the space required for the compact representation.

25.8   Under what conditions will *read* from a terminal return the value *0*?

25.9   Read the TELNET protocol specification to find the exact rules for synchronization. When does the sender transmit *urgent data*? Why is *synching* necessary?

25.10   A server can choose to send more data after the client sends an end-of-file. How does the client know when to terminate the connection to the server?

25.11   Rewrite *ttwrite* so it does not use an FSM. What are the advantages and disadvantages of each implementation?

25.12   In the example client, what happens if a *SYNCH* signal occurs while processing another *SYNCH*? Does this agree with the protocol specification?

26

A TELNET Client (Implementation Details)

26.1 Introduction

The previous chapter discusses the structure of a TELNET client and shows how it uses finite state machines to control processing. This chapter concludes the discussion by showing how semantic action procedures implement the details of character processing.

26.2 The FSM Action Procedures

Finite state machines implement most of the TELNET protocol details. They control processing, coordinate responses with requests, and map incoming command sequences to actions. Each time the client follows a transition in a finite state machine, it calls a procedure to perform the actions associated with the transition. Figure 25.4† shows the procedure names associated with transitions in the FSM that handles characters arriving from the server.

An action may be simple (e.g., discard the incoming character), or it may be complex (e.g., respond by sending a string that identifies the local terminal). Encapsulating each action in a procedure helps keep the machine specifications uniform and simplifies the code at the top level. However, dividing the software into a set of procedures for each action means that the relationship between procedures can only be understood by referring to the finite state machine that interconnects them.

---

†The figure appears on page 371.

The following sections each describe one of the action procedures associated with an FSM transition.

26.3 Recording The Type Of An Option Request

In state *TSIAC* (i.e., following the arrival of a *TCIAC* character), the arrival of *TCWILL* or *TCWONT* causes a transition to state *TSWOPT*. The FSM specifies that procedure *recopt* should be called. *Recopt* records the character that caused the transition so it can be used later. Similarly, the FSM uses *recopt* to record character *TCDO* or *TCDONT* during a transition to state *TSDOPT*. File *recopt.c* contains the code:

```
/* recopt.c - recopt, no_op */

#include <sys/types.h>

#include <stdio.h>

u_char  option_cmd;      /* has value WILL, WONT, DO, or DONT            */

/*------------------------------------------------------------------------
 * recopt - record option type
 *------------------------------------------------------------------------
 */
/*ARGSUSED*/
int
recopt(sfp, tfp, c)
FILE    *sfp, *tfp;
int     c;
{
        option_cmd = c;
        return 0;
}


/*------------------------------------------------------------------------
 * no_op - do nothing
 *------------------------------------------------------------------------
 */
/*ARGSUSED*/
int
no_op(sfp, tfp, c)
FILE    *sfp, *tfp;
int     c;
{
```

```
        return 0;
}
```

26.4 Performing No Operation

File *recopt.c* also contains code for procedure *no_op*. Because the FSM must have an action for all possible combinations of a state and an input character, procedure *no_op* can be used for those transitions that do not require any action. For example, a transition from state *TSDATA* to *TSIAC* does not require any action. Therefore, the FSM specifies a call to *no_op*.

26.5 Responding To WILL/WONT For The Echo Option

The server sends *WILL* or *WONT* followed by the *ECHO* option to inform the client that it is willing to echo characters or is willing to stop echoing characters. The FSM specifies that procedure *do_echo* should be called when such a message arrives.

```
/* do_echo.c - do_echo */

#include <sys/types.h>
#include <sys/ioctl.h>

#include <stdio.h>

#include "telnet.h"

char            doecho;              /* nonzero, if remote ECHO      */
extern u_char   option_cmd;

/*------------------------------------------------------------------------
 * do_echo - handle telnet will/won't ECHO option
 *------------------------------------------------------------------------
 */
int
do_echo(sfp, tfp, c)
FILE    *sfp, *tfp;
int     c;
{
        struct sgttyb   ttyb;
        int             ok, tfd = fileno(tfp);

        if (doecho) {
```

```
                    if (option_cmd == TCWILL)
                            return 0;          /* already doing ECHO           */
            } else if (option_cmd == TCWONT)
                    return 0;                  /* already NOT doing ECHO        */

        if (ok = ioctl(tfd, TIOCGETP, (char *)&ttyb) == 0) {
                if (option_cmd == TCWILL) {
                        ttyb.sg_flags &= ~ECHO;
                        ttyb.sg_flags |= CBREAK;
                } else {
                        ttyb.sg_flags |= ECHO;
                        ttyb.sg_flags &= ~CBREAK;
                }
                ok &= ioctl(tfd, TIOCSETP, (char *)&ttyb) == 0;
        }
        if (ok)
                doecho = !doecho;
        (void) putc(TCIAC, sfp);
        if (doecho)
                (void) putc(TCDO, sfp);
        else
                (void) putc(TCDONT, sfp);
        (void) putc((char)c, sfp);
        return 0;
}
```

The TELNET protocol specifies that the server can send a *WILL* or *WONT* to advertise its willingness to perform a given option or it can send such a message in response to a client request. Therefore, if the client has sent a request containing a *DO* or *DONT*, the message from the server constitutes a reply; otherwise, it constitutes an advertisement.

The client uses its current condition to decide how to respond. Global variable *doecho* contains a nonzero value if the client currently expects the server to perform character echo. If the server sends *WILL* and the client already has remote echo enabled, the client does not reply. Similarly if the server sends *WONT* and the client has remote echo disabled, the client does not reply. However, if the server sends *WILL* and the client currently has remote echoing turned off, the client uses *ioctl* to disable local character echoing. If the client has local echo disabled when a *WONT* arrives, the client assumes that the server has disabled the remote echo. Therefore, the client calls *ioctl* to enable local echoing. The client only sends a *DO* or *DONT* response if it changes the echo mode.

26.6 Responding To WILL/WONT For Unsupported Options

When the client receives a *WILL* or *WONT* request for an option that it does not understand, it calls procedure *do_notsup* to reply *DONT*.

```
/* do_notsup.c - do_notsup */

#include <sys/types.h>

#include <stdio.h>

#include "telnet.h"

extern u_char    option_cmd;

/*------------------------------------------------------------------------
 * do_notsup - handle an unsupported telnet "will/won't" option
 *------------------------------------------------------------------------
 */
/*ARGSUSED*/
int
do_notsup(sfp, tfp, c)
FILE    *sfp, *tfp;
int     c;
{
        (void) putc(TCIAC, sfp);
        (void) putc(TCDONT, sfp);
        (void) putc((char)c, sfp);
        return 0;
}
```

26.7 Responding To WILL/WONT For The No Go-Ahead Option

The client uses procedure *do_noga* to repond when the server sends *WILL* or *WONT* requests for the *no go-ahead option.*

```
/* do_noga.c - do_noga */

#include <sys/types.h>

#include <stdio.h>

#include "telnet.h"

extern u_char    option_cmd;

/*------------------------------------------------------------------------
 * do_noga - don't do telnet Go-Ahead's
 *------------------------------------------------------------------------
 */
/*ARGSUSED*/
int
do_noga(sfp, tfp, c)
FILE    *sfp, *tfp;
int     c;
{
        static  noga;

        if (noga) {
                if (option_cmd == TCWILL)
                        return 0;
        } else if (option_cmd == TCWONT)
                return 0;
        noga = !noga;
        (void) putc(TCIAC, sfp);
        if (noga)
                (void) putc(TCDO, sfp);
        else
                (void) putc(TCDONT, sfp);
        (void) putc((char)c, sfp);
        return 0;
}
```

As with other options, the client does not respond if the client's current setting for the option agrees with the server's request. If the server requests a change, the client reverses the current setting by negating global integer *noga* and sends either a *DO* or *DONT* response.

26.8 Generating DO/DONT For Binary Transmission

The server can send characters to the client either encoded, using the network virtual terminal encoding, or unencoded, using 8-bit binary values. Global variable *rcvbinary* controls whether the client expects to receive data as binary characters or NVT encodings. The client calls procedure *do_txbinary* to respond when the server sends a *WILL* or *WONT* for the binary option. Like the other procedures that handle options, *do_txbinary* has been designed so it can be called to request that the server send binary or to respond to an advertisement from the server. It uses the global variable *option_cmd* to decide how to proceed, and assumes that it contains an incoming request. Procedure *do_txbinary* tests to see whether the client expects the server to send binary, sets *rcvbinary* according to the incoming request, and responds to the server if *rcvbinary* changes.

```
/* do_txbinary.c - do_txbinary */

#include <sys/types.h>

#include <stdio.h>

#include "telnet.h"

char            rcvbinary;         /* non-zero if remote TRANSMIT-BINARY   */
extern u_char   option_cmd;

/*------------------------------------------------------------------------
 * do_txbinary - handle telnet "will/won't" TRANSMIT-BINARY option
 *------------------------------------------------------------------------
 */
/*ARGSUSED*/
int
do_txbinary(sfp, tfp, c)
FILE    *sfp, *tfp;
int     c;
{
        if (rcvbinary) {
                if (option_cmd == TCWILL)
                        return 0;
        } else if (option_cmd == TCWONT)
                return 0;
        rcvbinary = !rcvbinary;
        (void) putc(TCIAC, sfp);
        if (rcvbinary)
                (void) putc(TCDO, sfp);
```

```
        else
                (void) putc(TCDONT, sfp);
        (void) putc((char)c, sfp);
        return 0;
}
```

26.9 Responding To DO/DONT For Unsupported Options

The server sends *DO* or *DONT* messages to tell the client that it should enable or disable a specified option. The client responds by sending *WILL* if it agrees to honor the option, or *WONT* if it does not honor the option. As the FSM in Figure 25.4 shows, the client calls procedure *will_notsup* when it does not support a particular option.

```
/* will_notsup.c - will_notsup */

#include <sys/types.h>

#include <stdio.h>

#include "telnet.h"

/*------------------------------------------------------------------------
 * will_notsup - handle an unsupported telnet "do/don't" option
 *------------------------------------------------------------------------
 */
/*ARGSUSED*/
int
will_notsup(sfp, tfp, c)
FILE    *sfp, *tfp;
int     c;
{
        (void) putc(TCIAC, sfp);
        (void) putc(TCWONT, sfp);
        (void) putc((char)c, sfp);
        return 0;
}
```

Procedure *will_notsup* sends *WONT* to tell the server it does not support the option.

26.10 Responding To DO/DONT For Transmit Binary Option

When the client starts, it uses the network virtual terminal encoding for all data it sends to the server. Although NVT encoding includes most printable characters, it does not provide an encoding for all control characters. Servers operating on systems that support screen-oriented applications usually need the ability to transfer arbitrary character data. Therefore, such servers usually advertise their willingness to transmit binary data and request that the client also transmit binary data.

A server sends *DO* for the *transmit binary option* to request that the client begin using 8-bit, unencoded transmission. The client calls procedure *will_txbinary* when such a request arrives.

```
/* will_txbinary.c - will_txbinary */

#include <sys/types.h>

#include <stdio.h>

#include "telnet.h"

char            sndbinary;          /* non-zero if TRANSMIT-BINARY          */
extern u_char   option_cmd;

/*------------------------------------------------------------------------
 * will_txbinary - handle telnet "do/don't" TRANSMIT-BINARY option
 *------------------------------------------------------------------------
 */
/*ARGSUSED*/
int
will_txbinary(sfp, tfp, c)
FILE    *sfp, *tfp;
int     c;
{
        if (sndbinary) {
                if (option_cmd == TCDO)
                        return 0;
        } else if (option_cmd == TCDONT)
                return 0;
        sndbinary = !sndbinary;
        (void) putc(TCIAC, sfp);
        if (sndbinary)
                (void) putc(TCWILL, sfp);
        else
                (void) putc(TCWONT, sfp);
```

```
            (void) putc((char)c, sfp);
            return 0;
}
```

The client uses global variable *sndbinary* to control its transmission mode. If the request forces a change in the status, the client acknowledges the request by sending a *WILL* or *WONT*.

26.11 Responding To DO/DONT For The Terminal Type Option

Communicating the terminal type from client to server requires two steps. First, the server asks the client whether it honors the *termtype option*. Second, if the client agrees that it will honor the terminal type option, the server uses option subnegotiation to request a string that identifies the user's terminal type.

In UNIX, the client finds the user's terminal type by examining variable *TERM* in the process' *environment*. To do so, it calls the library function *getenv*, which finds the specified variable and returns a pointer to its string value.

When a request arrives for the terminal type option, the client calls procedure *will_termtype*. File *will_termtype.c* contains the code:

```
/* will_termtype.c - will_termtype */

#include <sys/types.h>

#include <stdio.h>

#include "telnet.h"

char    *getenv();

char            termtype;       /* non-zero if received "DO TERMTYPE"   */
char            *term;          /* terminal name                        */
extern u_char   option_cmd;

/*------------------------------------------------------------------
 * will_termtype - handle telnet "do/don't" TERMINAL-TYPE option
 *------------------------------------------------------------------
 */
int
will_termtype(sfp, tfp, c)
FILE    *sfp, *tfp;
int     c;
```

```
{
        if (termtype) {
                if (option_cmd == TCDO)
                        return 0;
        } else if (option_cmd == TCDONT)
                return 0;
        termtype = !termtype;
        if (termtype)
                if (!term && !(term = getenv("TERM")))
                        termtype = !termtype;    /* can't do it... */
        (void) putc(TCIAC, sfp);
        if (termtype)
                (void) putc(TCWILL, sfp);
        else
                (void) putc(TCWONT, sfp);
        (void) putc((char)c, sfp);
        if (termtype) { /* set up binary data path; send WILL, DO */
                option_cmd = TCWILL;
                (void) do_txbinary(sfp, tfp, TOTXBINARY);
                option_cmd = TCDO;
                (void) will_txbinary(sfp, tfp, TOTXBINARY);
        }
        return 0;
}
```

Procedure *will_termtype* behaves much like other option handlers. It uses global variable *termtype* to record whether the server has requested the terminal type option previously, and checks to see if the current request changes the status. If so, it calls *getenv* to obtain the value associated with environment variable *TERM*. If no such variable exists, the client responds that it will not honor the request.

A server requests terminal type information so applications can prepare output specifically for the user's terminal. For example, a text editor uses the terminal type when it generates the sequence of characters that clears the screen, moves the cursor, or highlights text. Thus, the client expects that once the remote application receives terminal type information it will send control sequences for the terminal. Because such sequences cannot be sent using the NVT encoding, *will_termtype* sends a *WILL* message that advertises the client's willingness to use binary transmission and a *DO* message that requests the server use binary transmission. Because functions *do_txbinary* and *will_txbinary* can be called from the FSM option processing code, they use global variable *option_cmd* to control processing. When calling the functions directly, other procedures must initialize *option_cmd* explicitly as if the client had received the appropriate *WILL* or *DO* message from the server before the call.

26.12 Option Subnegotiation

Once a client agrees to handle the terminal type option, a server uses option subnegotiation to request the terminal name. Unlike normal options which all have a fixed length, subnegotiation permits the sender to insert an arbitrary-length string in the data stream. To do so, the sender brackets the string by sending a subnegotiation header, the data for that particular option subnegotiation, and a trailer that identifies the end of the subnegotiation.

When the main FSM (Figure 25.4) encounters a subnegotiation command sequence, it enters state *TSSUBNEG*. Once in state *TSSUBNEG*, the client calls procedure *subopt* each time it receives a character. As the code in file *subopt.c* shows, *subopt* runs the option subnegotiation FSM to handle subnegotiation.

```
/* subopt.c - subopt */

#include <sys/types.h>

#include <stdio.h>

#include "telnet.h"
#include "tnfsm.h"

extern struct fsm_trans substab[];
extern int              substate;
extern u_char           subfsm[][NCHRS];

/*------------------------------------------------------------------
 * subopt - do option subnegotiation FSM transitions
 *------------------------------------------------------------------
 */
int
subopt(sfp, tfp, c)
FILE    *sfp, *tfp;
int     c;
{
        struct  fsm_trans       *pt;
        int                     ti;

        ti = subfsm[substate][c];
        pt = &substab[ti];
        (pt->ft_action)(sfp, tfp, c);
        substate = pt->ft_next;
        return 0;
}
```

26.13 Sending Terminal Type Information

The option subnegotiation FSM† calls procedure *subtermtype* to reply to a request for a terminal type. The server sends the sequence:

IAC SUBNEG TERMTYPE SEND IAC SUBEND

to request a terminal type. The client replies by sending:

IAC SUBNEG TERMTYPE IS term_type_string IAC SUBEND

File *subtermtype.c* contains the code:

```
/* subtermtype.c - subtermtype */

#include <sys/types.h>

#include <stdio.h>

#include "telnet.h"

extern char     *term;               /* terminal name, from initialization   */

/*------------------------------------------------------------------
 * subtermtype - do terminal type option subnegotation
 *------------------------------------------------------------------
 */
/*ARGSUSED*/
int
subtermtype(sfp, tfp, c)
FILE    *sfp, *tfp;
int     c;
{
        /* have received IAC.SB.TERMTYPE.SEND */

        (void) putc(TCIAC, sfp);
        (void) putc(TCSB, sfp);
        (void) putc(TOTERMTYPE, sfp);
        (void) putc(TT_IS, sfp);
        fputs(term, sfp);
        (void) putc(TCIAC, sfp);
        (void) putc(TCSE, sfp);
        return 0;
}
```

---

†See page 381 for a description of the option subnegotiation finite state machine.

The option subnegotiation FSM calls *subtermtype* after receiving the *SEND* request. Previously, the client must have replied positively to a request to honor the terminal type option, so global variable *term* must already point to a string that contains the terminal type. *Subtermtype* sends the reply by calling *putc* to send the individual control characters and *fputs* to send the string that contains the terminal type information.

26.14 Terminating Subnegotiation

When the principle FSM shown in Figure 25.4 encounters the end of option subnegotiation, it moves back to state *TSDATA*. Whenever it does so, it calls procedure *subend*. *Subend* simply resets the option subnegotiation FSM to its start state so it is ready to handle the next subnegotiation. File *subend.c* contains the code:

```
/* subend.c - subend */

#include <sys/types.h>

#include <stdio.h>

#include "tnfsm.h"

extern int              substate;

/*------------------------------------------------------------------------
 * subend - end of an option subnegotiation; reset FSM
 *------------------------------------------------------------------------
 */
/*ARGSUSED*/
int
subend(sfp, tfp, c)
FILE    *sfp, *tfp;
int     c;
{
        substate = SS_START;
        return 0;
}
```

26.15 Sending A Character To The Server

The client calls procedure *soputc* to convert an output character into the network virtual terminal encoding and send it through the TCP socket to the server. File *soputc.c* contains the code:

```c
/* soputc.c - soputc */

#include <sys/types.h>

#include <stdio.h>

#include "telnet.h"
#include "local.h"

/*------------------------------------------------------------------
 * soputc - move a character from the keyboard to the socket
 *------------------------------------------------------------------
 */
/*ARGSUSED*/
int
soputc(sfp, tfp, c)
FILE    *sfp, *tfp;
int     c;
{
        if (sndbinary) {
                if (c == TCIAC)
                        (void) putc(TCIAC, sfp); /* byte-stuff IAC     */
                (void) putc(c, sfp);
                return 0;
        }
        c &= 0x7f;      /* 7-bit ASCII only */
        if (c == t_intrc || c == t_quitc) {     /* Interrupt          */
                (void) putc(TCIAC, sfp);
                (void) putc(TCIP, sfp);
        } else if (c == sg_erase) {             /* Erase Char         */
                (void) putc(TCIAC, sfp);
                (void) putc(TCEC, sfp);
        } else if (c == sg_kill) {              /* Erase Line         */
                (void) putc(TCIAC, sfp);
                (void) putc(TCEL, sfp);
        } else if (c == t_flushc) {             /* Abort Output       */
                (void) putc(TCIAC, sfp);
                (void) putc(TCAO, sfp);
```

```
        } else if (c >= ' ' && c < TCIAC)          /* printable ASCII only */
                (void) putc(c, sfp);
    else
                switch (c) {
                case VPLF:
                case VPCR:
                case VPBEL:
                case VPBS:
                case VPHT:
                case VPFF:
                        (void) putc(c, sfp);
                default:
                        break;   /* invalid character */
                }
        return 0;
}
```

When transmitting in binary mode, only the *IAC* character needs to be character stuffed. That is, *soputc* must replace each *IAC* character with two *IAC* characters. For any other character, *soputc* merely calls *putc* to send it.

When transmitting in normal mode, *soputc* must convert from the local character set to the network virtual terminal character set. For example, if the character that arrives corresponds to either the UNIX *interrupt* character or the UNIX *quit* character, *soputc* sends a 2-character sequence:

IAC IP

It checks explicitly for each of the special characters that NVT defines as well as for printable ASCII. *Soputc* must also handle characters for which no NVT encoding exists. Following the protocol specification, the code ignores such characters. The consequence should be clear: if the server does not request that the client use binary transmission, the client will discard most control characters that the user types.

26.16 Displaying Incoming Data On The User's Terminal

Data that arrives over the TCP connection from the server can either be unencoded (if the server has agreed to transmit binary) or it can consist of characters encoded according to the rules for an NVT. The client calls procedure *ttputc* to display an incoming character on the user's terminal.

```
/* ttputc.c - ttputc */

#include <sys/types.h>

#include <stdio.h>

#include "telnet.h"

/*------------------------------------------------------------------------
 * ttputc - print a single character on a Network Virtual Terminal
 *------------------------------------------------------------------------
 */
/*ARGSUSED*/
int
ttputc(sfp, tfp, c)
FILE    *sfp, *tfp;
int     c;
{
        static  last_char;
        int     tc;

        if (rcvbinary) {
                (void) xputc(c, tfp);     /* print uninterpretted */
                return;
        }
        if (synching)                     /* no data, if in SYNCH */
                return;

        if ((last_char == VPCR && c == VPLF) ||
            (last_char == VPLF && c == VPCR)) {
                (void) xputc(VPLF, tfp);
                last_char = 0;
                return;
        }
        if (last_char == VPCR)
                (void) tcout("cr", tfp);
        else if (last_char == VPLF)
                (void) tcout("do", tfp);
        if (c >= ' ' && c < TCIAC)        /* printable ASCII      */
                (void) xputc(c, tfp);
        else {                            /* NVT special          */
                switch (c) {
                case VPLF:                        /* see if CR follows    */
                case VPCR:      tc = 1; /* see if LF follows    */
```

```
                                        break;
                        case VPBEL:     tc = tcout("bl", tfp);
                                        break;
                        case VPBS:      tc = tcout("bc", tfp);
                                        break;
                        case VPHT:      tc = tcout("ta", tfp);
                                        break;
                        case VPVT:      tc = tcout("do", tfp);
                                        break;
                        case VPFF:      tc = tcout("cl", tfp);
                                        break;
                        default:
                                tc = 1;
                                break;  /* no action */
                        }
                        if (!tc)                    /* if no termcap, assume ASCII */
                                (void) xputc(c, tfp);
                }
                last_char = c;
        }
```

If the server has agreed to send binary data, *ttputc* calls *xputc* to display it. File *xput.c* contains the code:

```
/* xput.c - xputc, xfputs */

#include <stdio.h>

extern FILE     *scrfp;

/*------------------------------------------------------------------------
 * xputc - putc with optional file scripting
 *------------------------------------------------------------------------
 */
int
xputc(ch, fp)
char    ch;
FILE    *fp;
{
        if (scrfp)
                (void) putc(ch, scrfp);
        return putc(ch, fp);
}
```

```
/*-----------------------------------------------------------------------
 * xfputs - fputs with optional file scripting
 *-----------------------------------------------------------------------
 */
int
xfputs(str, fp)
char    *str;
FILE    *fp;
{
        if (scrfp)
                fputs(str, scrfp);
        fputs(str, fp);
}
```

Xputc differs from the conventional UNIX *putc* because the client provides a *scripting* facility. If scripting has been enabled, *xputc* writes a copy of the output character to both the terminal and to the script file. Otherwise, it only writes a copy to the terminal.

If the server is not sending binary data, *ttputc* must translate from the NVT encoding into an appropriate character sequence for the user's terminal. Two cases arise: the client can be in normal mode or in *synchronize mode*. The client enters synchronize mode when it receives a TELNET *SYNCH* command. While in synchronize mode, the client reads and discards all data. The client returns to normal mode when it encounters a TELNET *DATA MARK*.

The server sends the SYNCH command as *urgent data*. When urgent data arrives at the client, UNIX sends signal *SIGURG* to the client, causing the client to execute the signal handler, *rcvurg*. *Rcvurg* sets global variable *synching* to cause the client to enter synchronize mode and seek to the next *DATA MARK* character in the data stream. The client discards all input in synchronize mode and does not display it. Thus, *ttputc* checks variable *synching* and drops the output character if *synching* is nonzero.

Once it has checked for synchronize mode, *ttputc* must interpret the remaining characters using the NVT encoding. Because some NVT encodings consist of a 2-character sequence, *ttputc* keeps a copy of the previous character in global variable *last_char*.

First, *ttputc* handles *carriage return* (*CR*) and *linefeed* (*LF*). It recognizes either of the 2-character sequences *CR-LF* or *LF-CR* as an end-of-line, and translates them to the single character *LF* that UNIX uses. Of course, if either a carriage return or line feed character occurs alone, *ttputc* performs the action associated with that character. To do so, it invokes procedure *tcout*, specifying a cursor movement operation as the first argument. For example, if it encounters a linefeed, *ttputc* calls *tcout* with the string argument *do*, which stands for *down*.

Ttputc calls *xputc* to print any of the printable ASCII characters directly. Otherwise, it handles the special characters. For example, if the character to be displayed is an NVT *BEL* character (*VPBEL* in the code), *ttputc* calls *tcout* with the code *bl*.

26.17 Using Curses To Control The User's Terminal

Procedure *tcout* takes a standard *curses* terminal capability name and a terminal's output file pointer as arguments. It uses function *getenv* to extract the terminal type from environment variable *TERM*, and then calls procedure *tgetstr* to look up the needed sequence of characters that will achieve the specified effect on the user's terminal. Finally it calls *xfputs* to write the resulting character sequence to the terminal.

```
/* tcout.c - tcout */

#include <stdio.h>

char    *getenv(), *tgetstr();

#define TBUFSIZE        2048

/*------------------------------------------------------------------------
 * tcout - print the indicated terminal capability on the given stream
 *------------------------------------------------------------------------
 */
int
tcout(cap, tfp)
char    *cap;
FILE    *tfp;
{
        static init;
        static char    *term;
        static char    tbuf[TBUFSIZE], buf[TBUFSIZE], *bp = buf;
        char           *sv;

        if (!init) {
                init = 1;
                term = getenv("TERM");
        }
        if (term == 0 || tgetent(&tbuf[0], term) != 1)
                return 0;
        if (sv = tgetstr(cap, &bp)) {
                xfputs(sv, tfp);
                return 1;
        }
        return 0;
}
```

26.18 Writing A Block Of Data To The Server

Telnet calls procedure *sowrite* to write a block of data to the server.

```
/* sowrite.c - sowrite */

#include <sys/types.h>

#include <stdio.h>

#include "tnfsm.h"

extern struct fsm_trans sostab[];
extern int              sostate;
extern u_char           sofsm[][NCHRS];

/*------------------------------------------------------------------------
 * sowrite - do output processing to the socket
 *------------------------------------------------------------------------
 */
int
sowrite(sfp, tfp, buf, cc)
FILE    *sfp, *tfp;     /* socket and terminal FILE ptrs*/
u_char  *buf;           /* buffer of data to send        */
int     cc;             /* # characters in buf           */
{
        struct fsm_trans        *pt;
        int                     i, ki;

        for (i=0; i<cc; ++i) {
                int     c = buf[i];

                ki = sofsm[sostate][c];
                pt = &sostab[ki];

                if ((pt->ft_action)(sfp, tfp, c) < 0)
                        sostate = KSREMOTE;    /* an error occurred     */
                else
                        sostate = pt->ft_next;
        }
}
```

Sowrite iterates through each character in the specified block and runs finite state machine *sofsm* to process each character.

26.19 Interacting With The Client Process

Like most TELNET client programs, our implementation permits the user to interact with the client process. To do so, a user types the *keyboard escape character* followed by a *command*. The table in Figure 26.1 lists the possible commands that can follow an escape character along with their meanings:

Symbolic Name	Character Typed	Meaning
KCSUSP	↑Z	Suspend the client process temporarily.
KCDCON	.	Terminate the TCP connection to the server.
KCSTSTUS	↑T	Print status information about the current connection.
KCESCAPE	↑]	Send the escape character to the server as data.
KCSCRIPT	s	Begin scripting to a specified file.
KCUNSCRIPT	u	Terminate scripting.

Figure 26.1 Keyboard input characters that the TELNET client interprets as commands when they follow *KCESCAPE*. The notation ↑*X* refers to the character generated by holding *CONTROL* and typing *X*.

File *telnet.h*† contains symbolic definitions for each of the keyboard command characters. For example, it defines the keyboard escape character, *KCESCAPE*, to be ↑] (i.e., the character with octal value 035).

When the client encounters the keyboard escape character, it changes the state of the socket output FSM from *KSREMOTE* to *KSLOCAL* and interprets the succeeding character as a command. Because most commands consist of a single character, the socket output FSM usually moves back to state *KSREMOTE* and executes an action procedure associated with the command. For example, if the FSM encounters character *KCDCON* following *KCESCAPE*, it calls procedure *dcon*.

---

†File *telnet.h* appears on page 368.

26.20 Responding To Illegal Commands

If the user types an unrecognized character following a keyboard escape, the socket output FSM calls action procedure *sonotsup* which prints an error message. File *sonotsup.c* contains the code:

```
/* sonotsup.c - sonotsup */

#include <stdio.h>

/*------------------------------------------------------------------------
 * sonotsup - an unsupported escape command
 *------------------------------------------------------------------------
 */
/*ARGSUSED*/
int
sonotsup(sfp, tfp, c)
FILE    *sfp, *tfp;
int     c;
{
        fprintf(tfp, "\nunsupported escape: %c.\n", c);
        fprintf(tfp, "s  - turn on scripting\t\t");
        fprintf(tfp, "u  - turn off scripting\n");
        fprintf(tfp, ".  - disconnect\t\t\t");
        fprintf(tfp, "^Z - suspend\n");
        fprintf(tfp, "^T - print status\n");
        return 0;
}
```

26.21 Scripting To A File

Our example TELNET client has one novel feature not found in most other clients: it permits the user to dynamically create a script file that contains a copy of all data being sent to the user's display. The idea underlying scripting is that a user may need to keep a record of all or part of a TELNET session.

Scripting is *dynamic* because the user can start or stop it at any time. Furthermore, the user can change the file into which the client writes the script. Thus, to capture the output of a single remote command, the user can log into the remote system with scripting disabled, then enable scripting and issue the command or commands for which the output must be kept, and finally, disable scripting. The script file will contain a copy of everything that the client displayed on the user's terminal while scripting was enabled.

26.22 Implementation Of Scripting

The socket output finite state machine illustrated in Figure 25.8 defines how the client handles scripting. If the user types ↑]s (i.e. character *KCESCAPE* followed by character *KCSCRIPT*), the socket output FSM calls action procedure *scrinit* and enters state *KSCOLLECT*. Until the user types an end-of-line character (i.e., *KCNL*), the FSM stays in state *KSCOLLECT* and calls procedure *scrgetc* to collect a string of characters that form the name of the script file. Once the user terminates the line of input, the FSM calls *scrwrap* to open the script file and move back to state *KSREMOTE*. The following sections each discuss one of the action procedures associated with scripting.

26.23 Initialization Of Scripting

When the socket output FSM first encounters a request to begin scripting, it calls action procedure *scrinit*.

```
/* scrinit.c - scrinit */

#include <stdio.h>

#include "telnet.h"
#include "local.h"

extern int              scrindex;
extern struct ttystate  tntty;

/*------------------------------------------------------------------------
 * scrinit - initialize tty modes for script file collection
 *------------------------------------------------------------------------
 */
/*ARGSUSED*/
int
scrinit(sfp, tfp, c)
FILE    *sfp, *tfp;
int     c;
{
        struct ttystate newtty;

        if (!doecho) {
                fprintf(tfp, "\nscripting requires remote ECHO.\n");
                return -1;
        }
        if (scrfp) {
```

```
            fprintf(tfp,"\nalready scripting to \"%s\".\n", scrname);
            return -1;
    }
    scrindex = 0;
    ttysave(&tntty);                          /* save current tty settings   */

    newtty = oldtty;
    newtty.ts_tchars.t_intrc = -1;            /* disable interrupt    */
    newtty.ts_tchars.t_quitc = -1;            /* disable interrupt    */
    newtty.ts_ltchars.t_suspc = -1;           /* disable suspend      */
    newtty.ts_ltchars.t_dsuspc = -1;          /* disable suspend      */
    ttyrestore(&newtty);

    fprintf(tfp, "\nscript file: ");
    (void) fflush(tfp);
    return 0;
}
```

Scrinit first verifies that the client is using remote echo (i.e., that all characters being displayed are coming from the server and not from the UNIX device driver). It also verifies that the user does not already have scripting enabled. *Scrinit* sets global variable *scrindex* to zero. Another procedure will use *scrindex* to count characters as it reads the name of the script file. Finally, before it prints a prompt, *scrinit* changes the mode of the user's terminal so the local terminal driver will print the characters of the file name as the user types them.

26.24 Collecting Characters Of The Script File Name

The socket output FSM uses action procedure *scrgetc* to read a sequence of characters that will be used as the name of a script file. File *scrgetc.c* contains the code:

```
/* scrgetc.c - scrgetc */

#include <stdio.h>

#include "local.h"

#define SFBUFSZ        2048      /* script filename buffer size  */

struct ttystate tntty;
FILE            *scrfp;
char            scrname[SFBUFSZ];
int             scrindex;

/*-----------------------------------------------------------------------
 * scrgetc - begin session scripting
 *-----------------------------------------------------------------------
 */
/*ARGSUSED*/
int
scrgetc(sfp, tfp, c)
FILE    *sfp, *tfp;
int     c;
{
        scrname[scrindex++] = c;
        if (scrindex >= SFBUFSZ) {        /* too far */
                fprintf(tfp, "\nname too long\n");
                ttyrestore(&oldtty);
                return -1;
        }
        return 0;
}
```

Each time a character arrives, the client calls *scrgetc*, which appends the character to string *scrname*.

26.25 Opening A Script File

When the client encounters an end-of-line, it calls procedure *scrwrap* to open the script file.

```
/* scrwrap.c - scrwrap */

#include <sys/file.h>

#include <stdio.h>

#include "local.h"

extern struct ttystate  tntty;
extern char             scrname[], *sys_errlist[];
extern int              scrindex, errno;

/*------------------------------------------------------------------------
 * scrwrap - wrap-up script filename collection
 *------------------------------------------------------------------------
 */
/*ARGSUSED*/
int
scrwrap(sfp, tfp, c)
FILE    *sfp, *tfp;
int     c;
{
        int     fd;

        if (scrindex) {
                scrname[scrindex] = '\0';
                scrindex = 0;
                fd = open(scrname, O_WRONLY|O_CREAT|O_TRUNC, 0644);
                if (fd < 0)
                        fprintf(tfp, "\ncan't write \"%s\": %s\n",
                                scrname, sys_errlist[errno]);
                else
                        scrfp = fdopen(fd, "w");
        }
        ttyrestore(&tntty);
        return 0;
}
```

Scrwrap adds a null terminator to the string that has been collected, resets global variable *scrindex* so it can be used again, and calls *open* to open the script file. If it successfully obtains a new descriptor for the script file, *scrwrap* calls *fdopen* to create a standard I/O file pointer for the script file and places the pointer in global variable *scrfp*. Before it returns, *scrwrap* calls *ttyrestore* to reset the terminal modes to the value they had before *scrinit* changed them.

26.26 Terminating Scripting

When the user decides to disable scripting, the socket output FSM calls action procedure *unscript*.

```c
/* unscript.c - unscript */

#include <sys/types.h>
#include <sys/stat.h>

#include <stdio.h>

#include "local.h"

/*------------------------------------------------------------------------
 * unscript - end session scripting
 *------------------------------------------------------------------------
 */
/*ARGSUSED*/
int
unscript(sfp, tfp, c)
FILE    *sfp, *tfp;
int     c;
{
        struct stat     statb;

        if (scrfp == 0) {
                fprintf(tfp, "\nNot scripting.\n");
                return 0;
        }
        (void) fflush(scrfp);
        if (fstat(fileno(scrfp), &statb) == 0)
                fprintf(tfp, "\n\"%s\": %d bytes.\n", scrname,
                                statb.st_size);
        (void) fclose(scrfp);
        scrfp = 0;
        return 0;
}
```

Unscript prints an informational message to tell the user that the client has stopped scripting, uses the UNIX system function *fstat* to obtain information about the resulting script file, and prints a message that gives the size of the script file. Finally, *unscript* closes the script file and clears the global file pointer, *scrfp*.

26.27 Printing Status Information

The user can obtain status information about the current connection by using the *KCSTATUS* command following a keyboard escape. The socket output FSM calls action procedure *status* to print the connection status.

```
/* status.c - status */

#include <sys/types.h>
#include <sys/socket.h>
#include <netinet/in.h>

#include <stdio.h>

extern  char    doecho, sndbinary, rcvbinary;    /* telnet options */
extern  char    *host, scrname[];
extern  FILE    *scrfp;

u_short ntohs();

/*------------------------------------------------------------------------
 * status - print connection status information
 *------------------------------------------------------------------------
 */
/*ARGSUSED*/
int
status(sfp, tfp, c)
FILE    *sfp, *tfp;
int     c;
{
        struct  sockaddr_in     sin;
        int                     sinlen;

        fprintf(tfp, "\nconnected to \"%s\" ", host);

        sinlen = sizeof(sin);
        if (getsockname(fileno(sfp), (struct sockaddr *)&sin,
                        &sinlen) == 0)
                fprintf(tfp, "local port %d ", ntohs(sin.sin_port));
        sinlen = sizeof(sin);
        if (getpeername(fileno(sfp), (struct sockaddr *)&sin,
                        &sinlen) == 0)
                fprintf(tfp, "remote port %d ", ntohs(sin.sin_port));
        (void) putc('\n', tfp);
```

```
     if (doecho || sndbinary || rcvbinary) {
            printf("options in effect: ");
            if (doecho)
                   fprintf(tfp, "remote_echo ");
            if (sndbinary)
                   fprintf(tfp, "send_binary ");
            if (rcvbinary)
                   fprintf(tfp, "receive_binary ");
            (void) putc('\n', tfp);
     }
     if (scrfp)
            fprintf(tfp, "scripting to file \"%s\"\n", scrname);
     return 0;
}
```

Procedure *status* prints information such as the name of the remote host, the local and remote TCP protocol ports used for the connection, and a list of the options in effect.

26.28 Summary

Our example TELNET client uses three finite state machines to interpret sequences of characters that arrive from the server or from the user's keyboard. Each incoming character causes a transition in a finite state machine. When the client performs a transition, it calls a procedure that implements the action associated with the transition.

This chapter describes action procedures for the three finite state machines that comprise the example client. Some actions are trivial while others are complex. The chief disadvantage of organizing the client software as action procedures for the finite state machine lies in readability. The resulting code can be difficult to understand because one cannot ascertain the relationships among the procedures without referring to the finite state machines.

FOR FURTHER STUDY

A series of RFCs document the details of TELNET options and contain protocol standards for each of the options handled by the example code. Postel and Reynolds [RFC 858] discusses the go-ahead option, while Postel and Reynolds [RFC 857] discusses character echo. Postel and Reynolds [RFC 856] describes the option that controls 8-bit binary transmission. Finally, VanBokkelen [RFC 1091] discusses the terminal-type option and the associated option subnegotiation.

EXERCISES

26.1   Some terminal types support multiple emulation modes, making it possible to have a set of terminal type names for a single terminal. Read RFC 1091. How can a client use a list of terminal names when it negotiates the terminal type with a server?

26.2   Read the protocol standard to find out exactly when a server must switch from sending data encoded using the network virtual terminal encoding to sending 8-bit binary data. In particular, how does the server handle transmission after it volunteers to transmit binary data but has not received an acknowledgement?

26.3   Does a client send *WILL* or *DO* when it requests the server to perform a given option? What does the server send when it requests the client to perform an option?

26.4   What does the mode argument *O_WRONLY|O_CREAT|O_TRUNC* mean in the call to *open* found in procedure *scrwrap*?

26.5   Instrument the client to print a message when it receives an option request. Use the modified client to contact a variety of servers. What option requests do they send automatically?

26.6   What happens if the client sends *DO ECHO* and the server sends *WILL ECHO* simultaneously?

26.7   What happens if a client sends *DO ECHO* to a server that already has *ECHO* enabled?

27

Practical Hints And Techniques For UNIX Servers

27.1 Introduction

The example server code throughout this text has been written to provide a clear, tutorial illustration of the concepts that will help the reader understand the fundamental design principles. Thus, the code omits many of the details needed in production software.

This chapter describes some of the techniques and conventional practices that professional UNIX programmers follow when building production server programs. The techniques presented make the code more robust and easier to debug. They also isolate the server from the process that starts it, and permit the server to follow conventions for safe operation in a UNIX environment. While none of these techniques is required to make a server correct, professional programmers recognize them as highly desirable.

27.2 Operating In Background

UNIX allows a process to execute in *foreground* or in *background*. The easiest way to understand the difference is to imagine a user typing commands to a command interpreter. Normally, each command executes in foreground, meaning that the command interpreter creates a process to execute the command, and then waits for the command process to complete before issuing a prompt and reading another command.

However, if the user specifies that a command should execute in background, the command interpreter creates a process to execute the command, and allows the new process to continue concurrently while it prompts for another command. To find out whether a background process has completed, the user must check its status. Background execution is convenient for tasks like printing because it permits the user to continue interactive execution of other commands at the same time.

Most servers operate in the background because they run forever. A server begins execution when the operating system starts, and executes in background waiting for requests to arrive. Usually, the initial process in a UNIX system starts each server when it runs the system startup script (*/etc/rc* on many systems). The startup script consists of commands that the system interprets exactly as if they had been typed at the console.

Although it is possible to program the startup script to place each server process in background, most production servers put themselves in background quickly and automatically. To understand why speed is important, consider the execution sequence. Imagine the startup script executing a sequence of steps that each start one server. If a server moves to the background quickly, the startup script can continue to execute and start more servers. If a server delays before moving to background (e.g., does not move to background until it finishes executing initialization code), the process running the startup script must wait for the server, so subsequent servers will be delayed.

Building a server that automatically moves to background also helps make system startup less prone to error. Consider what happens if a particular server, *S*, does not move to background automatically and the system manager accidentally fails to specify background execution for *S* in the startup script. The bootstrap process executes the sequence of startup commands until it reaches the command to start *S*. The startup process runs the server in foreground, waiting for it to complete before going on. Unfortunately, because a server runs forever, the entire bootstrap process will block waiting for a command that will never complete.

27.3 Programming A Server To Operate In Background

UNIX programmers uses the term *daemon* for any process that performs a service in background. Transforming a server into a daemon is straightforward. The technique consists of having the server call *fork* to create a new process, and then arranging for the parent process to exit. To do so, the server executes the following code almost immediately after it starts execution:

```
i = fork();
if (i < 0) {          /* less than zero means error occurred*/
        fprintf(stderr, "error when forking: %s\n",
                sys_errlist[errno]);
        exit(1);
}
if (i) {              /* nonzero is parent                    */
```

```
            exit(0);    /* normal process exit                */
    }
    /* child continues execution here and becomes the server */
```

The call to *fork* can produce three possible results: a negative value that means an error occurred (e.g., the system had insufficient memory to create a new process), a positive result that means the call succeeded and the process is the parent, and a zero result that means the call succeeded and the process is the newly created child.

In the example code, if an error occurs, the server prints a message on the *standard error* output stream and calls *exit* to terminate with an exit code of *1*. By convention, a nonzero exit code indicates an *abnormal process termination*.

If the call to *fork* succeeds, the *if* statement uses the return value to distinguish between the parent and child processes. The original parent process exits normally, while the child continues execution and becomes the server. It is easiest to visualize what happens from a user's point of view. Imagine that some server, *Q*, contains the above code. To run the server, a user types the server's file name as a command. When the user enters the command, it appears to complete almost instantly, and the user receives the prompt for another command. However, if the user requests a list of processes, it will show that the server has created a copy of itself and that the copy continues to execute in background.

The above code also handles a minor detail: it completely detaches the daemon from its parent. At any given time, each UNIX process has a *parent*, and the action taken by some UNIX system functions depends on the parent–child relationship. After the call to *fork*, the server's parent exits, leaving the newly created child temporarily *orphaned*. Whenever a process becomes orphaned, UNIX designates that the *initial system process* (*init*) becomes the parent. We say that the orphaned child has been inherited by *init*†. Although such inheritance is a minor detail, it means that the server can exit cleanly because *init* calls the UNIX system call *wait* to terminate each of its children.

27.4 Open Descriptors And Inheritance

A UNIX process inherits copies of descriptors for files or sockets that the parent had opened at the time the process was created. Thus, the set of descriptors that a server process inherits depends on how it was started.

Because UNIX uses a reference count mechanism for files and other objects, keeping descriptors open can use resources unnecessarily. For example, suppose a parent process opens a file, and then executes a server that forks and moves to background. Even if the parent closes its copy of the file descriptor, the server will still have a copy open and the file will not be closed. As a result, the file cannot be removed from the disk until the server exits.

---

†See section *8* of the *UNIX Programmer's Manual* for a description of the *init* process.

To summarize:

> *A server must close all file descriptors it inherits to prevent it from consuming resources unnecessarily.*

27.5 Programming A Server To Close Inherited Descriptors

To close all inherited file descriptors, a server executes the following code after it starts:

```
for (i=getdtablesize()-1; i>= 0; --i)
        (void) close(i);
```

Because the number of descriptors available to a process varies among UNIX systems, the code does not contain a fixed constant. Instead, it calls function *getdtablesize* to find the size of the process descriptor table. The descriptor table is indexed starting at zero. After it finds the maximum number of descriptors, the code iterates from the descriptor table size minus one down through zero, calling *close* on each descriptor. Once it finishes, the server will have closed all the open descriptors it inherited; calling *close* on a unopened descriptor has no effect.

27.6 Signals From The Controlling TTY

Each process in UNIX inherits a connection to a terminal that has been designated as its *control terminal*. UNIX calls the control terminal a *controlling tty*. UNIX makes the association with a controlling tty to permit the user who started a process to control it (e.g., to send the process a *hangup signal* when a user who is logged in over a dialup line hangs up the phone).

Unlike most processes, a server should not receive signals generated from the process that started it. In fact:

> *To ensure that signals from a user's terminal do not affect a server running in background, the server must detach itself from its controlling terminal.*

27.7 Programming A Server To Change Its Controlling TTY

The code required to detach a process from its controlling terminal consists of only three lines:

```
fd = open("/dev/tty", O_RDWR);
(void) ioctl(fd, TIOCNOTTY, 0);
(void) close(fd);
```

The call to *open* returns the descriptor for the controlling terminal, and the call to *ioctl* specifies that the process should be detached from that controlling terminal. Finally, the call to *close* releases the file descriptor, making it possible for the server to reuse the descriptor for other I/O (e.g., for an incoming connection).

27.8 Moving To A Safe And Known Directory

A server process should always execute in a known directory. Among other things, doing so guarantees that if the server aborts for any reason (or if the system manager decides to terminate a server that misbehaves), the manager will know the location of the resulting *core* file. Furthermore, all servers should execute in standard system directories, not the directory in which they are started. To understand why, consider what happens if a system manager notices that a server has failed and restarts it. If the manager is running a command interpreter in his or her home directory and forgets to change to a system directory before starting the server, it will execute in the manager's home directory. Having a process executing in a directory prevents any system management activities that require the file system to be unmounted. For example, it may be impossible to perform a routine file system dump. To summarize:

A server must move to a known directory where it can operate indefinitely without interfering with normal system management.

27.9 Programming A Server To Change Directories

To change into a known directory, a server calls system function *chdir*. For example, a server that needs to execute in the root directory makes the following call:

```
(void) chdir("/");
```

Choosing an appropriate directory can be difficult because no single directory works best for all servers. For example, a server that sends electronic mail might change to the directory where the system stores outgoing e-mail (*/usr/spool/mqueue* on many UNIX systems). However, a server that monitors idle terminal lines might change to the directory where all the terminal devices can be found (usually */dev*).

27.10 The UNIX Umask

Each executing process has a UNIX *umask* that specifies the protection mode for the files the process creates. The umask is an integer in which the low-order 9 bits provide a mask for the 9-bit file protection mode. Whenever UNIX creates a file, it computes a protection mode for the file by performing a bit-wise *and* operation of the mode specified in the *open* call and the bit-wise complement of the process' umask. For example, suppose a process has umask *027* (octal). If the process tries to create a file with mode *0777* (readable, writable, and executable by everyone), the system arrives at the correct file mode by computing the bit-wise *and* of *0750* (the complement of umask *027*) and *0777* (the requested mode). As a result, the file mode will be *0750* (readable and executable by the owner and the file's group, writable only by the owner, and not accessible by others).

Think of a process' umask as a safety net that prevents accidental creation of files with too many read, write, or execute privileges. Such protection is important because servers often execute as super user, so files they create are owned by the super user. The point is:

> *No matter what protection modes are specified in a call to* open, *the system will not provide more access privilege to a file the process creates than the creating process' umask specifies. Thus, restricting the umask at the beginning of a server prevents problems that might arise from incorrect mode specifications.*

27.11 Programming A Server To Set Its Umask

The server code required to restrict file creation modes is trivial:

```
(void) umask(027);
```

The call sets the server's umask to the value specified. The umask remains in effect unless the process makes another call to *umask*.

27.12 Process Groups

UNIX places each process in a *process group*. The notion of process group allows UNIX to treat a set of related processes as a single entity. Often, users think of a process group as a single *job*. In particular, if a user creates three processes interconnected by pipes, the command interpreter places them in a process group so that a termination signal sent to them will reach all three.

Usually, each server operates independently from other processes. Thus, it should not be a part of any group and should not receive signals sent to its parent's group. In summary:

Every process inherits membership in a process group. To avoid receiving signals meant for its parent, a server must leave its parent's process group.

27.13 Programming A Server To Set Its Process Group

The code required to place a server process in its own, private process group is trivial:

```
(void) setpgrp(0, getpid());
```

The call to *getpid* returns the process id of the currently executing process (i.e. of the server), and the call to *setpgrp* requests the system to place the specified process in a new, private process group.

27.14 Descriptors For Standard I/O

Many library routines expect three standard file descriptors to be open and available for I/O: *standard input* (*0*), *standard output* (*1*), and *standard error* (*2*). In particular, standard library routines like *perror* (which prints error messages) write to the standard error descriptor without checking it. If any of these descriptors is open and the server calls a library routine to read or write on it, I/O may occur to a terminal or file. To be safe, programmers usually open the standard descriptors and connect them to a harmless I/O device. Then, if any routine in the server attempts I/O using a standard descriptor, the server will not perform unintended I/O. In summary:

Because many library routines assume the three standard I/O descriptors are open, a production server usually opens all three descriptors and connects them to a harmless I/O device.

27.15 Programming A Server To Open Standard Descriptors

The code required to open standard I/O descriptors after they have been closed consists of three system calls:

```
fd = open("/dev/null", O_RDWR);    /* stdin  */
(void) dup(fd);                    /* stdout */
(void) dup(fd);                    /* stderr */
```

The call to *open* specifies the special UNIX file name */dev/null*, which corresponds to a device. The device associated with */dev/null* always returns an end-of-file condition on input and discards all output. Thus, reading or writing to */dev/null* has no effect; no data accumulates on any storage device.

The calls to system function *dup* duplicate an existing file descriptor. By convention, UNIX assigns file descriptors sequentially, starting at *0*. Once the server has opened */dev/null* and obtained a descriptor for it, the calls to *dup* provide a copy for standard output (descriptor *1*) and standard error (descriptor *2*).

27.16 Mutual Exclusion For The Server

For most services, only one copy of the master server should exist at any time. If concurrent execution is needed, the master server should handle all concurrency. Restricting server execution can be especially important if multiple individuals have privilege. For example, suppose two system programmers both notice that a given server has failed, and they both restart it simultaneously. Unless the managers coordinate their activities, both copies of the server could attempt to execute, and the results may be unpredictable. As a rule:

> *Only one copy of a server program should start execution at a time; all concurrency should be handled by the server.*

27.17 Programming A Server To Avoid Multiple Copies

We say that multiple copies of a server are *mutually exclusive* and that the server must invoke a mechanism that guarantees *mutual exclusion* when it begins execution. In UNIX, most processes use a *lock file* to achieve mutually exclusive execution. Each server uses a separate lock file. For example, a server that provides line printer service might use the file */usr/spool/lpd.lock*, while a white pages server might use the file */usr/spool/wp.lock*. When a copy of the server begins execution, it attempts to establish its designated lock file. If no other process is holding the lock, the attempt succeeds; if another copy of the server has already locked the file, the attempt fails.

The code required to implement mutual exclusion consists of a few system calls:

```
/* Acquire an exclusive lock, or exit.  Assumes    */
/* symbolic constant LOCKF has been defined to be  */
/* the name of the server's lock file.  For example, */
/*        #define LOCKF /usr/spool/lpd.lock        */
/*                                                 */
lf = open(LOCKF, O_RDWR|O_CREAT, 0640);
if (lf < 0)             /* error occurred opening file */
        exit(1);
```

```
if (flock(lf, LOCK_EX|LOCK_NB))
        exit(0);       /* could not obtain a lock      */
```

As the comment suggests, the example code assumes symbolic constant *LOCKF* has been defined to be the name of the server's lock file. The call to *open* obtains a descriptor for the lock file, creating the file if necessary. Note that the file does not contain any data: it merely needs to exist so the server can hold the lock. The call to *flock* requests exclusive use of the lock file. *Flock* returns zero if successful and nonzero if the attempt fails. If the server cannot obtain an exclusive lock, it simply exits because another copy of the server must already be running. Although it is possible to use other mechanisms to obtain mutually exclusive execution (e.g., creating a lock file that has mode *000*), the chief advantage of using *flock* arises because it automatically releases the lock after a system crash. In fact, a process only holds a lock established by *flock* while it executes. If the server crashes or the system reboots, the lock will be released. Servers that use file creation to guarantee mutual exclusion require the system to remove the file before restarting the server after a system reboot (or no copies of the server can execute).

27.18 Recording A Server's Process ID

In most production environments, system managers need a quick way to find a server in case it misbehaves or crashes. Although it is possible to list all processes in the system, doing so on a heavily loaded machine can take considerable time. To avoid having the system manager search for a server process, most production servers record their process identifier in a well-known file. When managers need to find a server process, they look in the file for the server's process identifier.

Which file should a server use to hold its process identifier? The most obvious choice is the server's lock file. There must be one lock file for each service, and the lock file normally has no other useful contents.

27.19 Programming A Server To Record Its Process ID

Once the server opens a lock file and obtains a descriptor, using the lock file to record the server's process identifier is trivial. The code consists of:

```
char    pbuf[10];   /* an array to hold ASCII pid */

/* Assume the lock file has been opened and its   */
/* descriptor has been stored in variable lf as   */
/* the code in the previous section shows          */
```

```
(void) sprintf(pbuf, "%6d\n", getpid());
(void) write(lf, pbuf, strlen(pbuf));
```

To make the file easy to read, the code calls *sprintf* to convert the process id from a binary integer to a printable string that contains the equivalent decimal value. It then calls *write* to write the string into the lock file. Because the file consists of readable text, the manager can find the process id by displaying the file; no special tools are required to read or format it.

27.20 Waiting For A Child Process To Exit

When a UNIX process exits, the system cannot complete the process termination until it informs the parent process. The parent must call the system function *wait* before termination can complete. Meanwhile, the terminating process exists in a *zombie state* and is sometimes called a *defunct process*.

27.21 Programming A Server To Wait For Each Child To Exit

We said earlier that when the server forks and the parent exits, the child process will become a child of *init*. Because *init* calls *wait* repeatedly, its children all terminate cleanly. Thus, if the main server process ever exits, no problems will arise.

Processes the main server creates become its children, not children of *init*. Thus, any server that creates processes must call *wait* when the processes terminate. The code in Chapter *11* illustrates how a concurrent server can arrange to wait for children that terminate. It shows that the server receives a signal for each terminating child and can arrange code in the signal handler to call *wait*.

27.22 Extraneous Signals

Even if a server detaches itself from its controlling terminal, it may receive signals. In particular, any system manager or privileged process can send a signal to the server. Often, a manager sends signal *SIGKILL* (9) to terminate the server. A programmer may decide to use one or more signals to control the operation of the server. For example, the programmer could arrange for the server to reinitialize itself upon receipt of a *HANGUP* signal (*1*).

27.23 Programming A Server To Ignore Extraneous Signals

Most production servers arrange to ignore all signals except for the few signals used to control them. To do so, the server either executes calls to the system function *signal* or to the system function *sigvec*. For example, to ignore the *HANGUP* signal, a server calls:

```
(void) signal(SIG_IGN, SIGHUP);
```

27.24 Using A System Log Facility

27.24.1 Generating Log Messages

Servers, and to a lesser extent clients, generate output intended for system programmers or system administrators. During construction, of course, most of the output consists of messages intended to help the programmer debug the code. Once the server begins production service, output is usually restricted to error messages generated when the server finds unusual circumstances or unexpected events. However, even production software may emit output regularly. For example, a server can be programmed to keep a log of each connection request or each transaction. To help maintain system security a server can be programmed to record information each time it rejects a connection request from an unauthorized client.

Many early servers recorded all their output on a console log. The idea arose from early computer systems on which the console terminal printed its output on paper. If a program wrote information on the console, it became part of the permanent system log that could be reviewed later if needed. On such systems, when a server began operation, it opened an output descriptor for the system's console terminal and used that descriptor when writing log messages.

27.24.2 The Advantage Of Indirection And Standard Error

The chief disadvantage of arranging for servers to write log messages to the console terminal is inflexibility. While the programmer constructs and tests server code, the programmer must walk to the system console to see the log. Furthermore, system administrators frequently move copies of client and server software to new machines. Because some machines do not use a hard-copy device as a console, server software must be changed to write log messages to a file before it can be moved to such machines. Usually, changing the destination of log messages means recompiling the source code.

UNIX introduced an interesting convention by providing each process with a file descriptor for *standard error* output (descriptor *3*). When a UNIX programmer writes server software, the programmer does not need to know whether the server will send error messages to the console printer or to a file. Instead, the programmer writes all error messages to the standard error descriptor, and relies on whoever starts the server to attach its standard error descriptor to a file or the system console. In essence, the notion of standard error provides a level of *indirection* that isolates the source program from the run-time environment: the source program references the standard error descriptor without knowing whether it will be bound to a file or to a terminal.

The flexibility gained through the use of the standard error descriptor becomes evident when one considers a site that has multiple copies of a given brand of machine, with each running a copy of a given server. One machine may use a console printer to log error messages, while another uses a file. A system administrator can run the same server code on both machines without recompiling because UNIX permits I/O redirection when starting the server.

27.24.3 Limitations Of I/O Redirection

While the use of a standard error descriptor makes server code more flexible than code that writes messages to a specific device or file, it does not solve all problems. A programmer, or the system administrator, may decide to have a server send some (or all) of the error messages to a user's terminal. Or the programmer may arrange to forward error messages to a machine other than the one on which the server executes (i.e., to send messages to a computer that has a printer).

UNIX's standard error descriptor mechanism does not provide sufficient flexibility to handle all possible destinations because the system does not allow one to redirect output to an arbitrary program or to a network connection. Instead another, more powerful mechanism is needed.

27.24.4 A Client-Server Solution

Not surprisingly, system designers have found that they can use the client-server paradigm to build an error logging mechanism with more flexibility than I/O redirection offers. In essence, each participating computer operates a *log server* that accepts and handles messages intended for the system's log. The log server can be programmed to write the messages it receives on the computer's console terminal, write them to a file, send them to a system administrator's terminal, or even send them to the log server on another machine.

When a running program needs to write a message to the system's log, it becomes a client of the log server. The running program sends its message to the log server and then continues execution. The log server handles the message by writing it to the system's log.

If the system manager decides to change the way a system handles error messages, the manager only needs to change the log server. For example, the manager can configure a log server so it prints all log messages on the system console. Later, the manager can change the log server so it appends all log messages onto a file.

Notice that a log server provides indirection much like the standard error descriptor described above. A program only has information about the log server compiled into the code; it does not know how the log server will handle each message. Furthermore, the address of the log server can be represented using the special name *localhost*, allowing a compiled program to find the log server on its machine without knowing the machine's address.

27.24.5 The Syslog Mechanism

BSD UNIX includes a log mechanism that uses the client-server approach described above. Known as *syslog*, the mechanism includes code for a log server (*syslogd*) as well as library routines that programs use to contact the server and send it messages.

The syslog mechanism provides two important features: (1) it groups messages into classes and (2) it uses a configuration file to allow the system administrator to specify how the server should handle each message class. Because *syslog* separates the handling for each message class, the system offers considerable flexibility. For example, the system administrator on one system might choose to send a message to the system manager whenever a serious error occurs, but choose to place low priority (informational) messages in a file without informing anyone. The system administrator on another system can make a different choice.

Because *syslog* uses a configuration file to allow a system administrator to specify how to handle each message class, the system is convenient to use. To change how *syslog* handles error messages, an administrator only needs to change a configuration file; the client and server software remain unchanged.

27.24.6 Syslog Message Classes

Syslog divides message classes in two ways. First, it partitions programs into groups, with each group known as a *facility*. Second, it subdivides messages from each facility into eight priority levels.

27.24.7 Syslog Facilities

The table in Figure 27.1 lists the facilities that *syslog* defines and their meanings.

Facility Name	Subsystem that uses it
LOG_KERN	The operating system kernel
LOG_USER	Any user process (i.e., a normal application program)
LOG_MAIL	The electronic mail system
LOG_DAEMON	System daemons that operate in background
LOG_AUTH	The authorization and authentication system
LOG_LPR	The printer spooling system
LOG_RPC	The RPC and NFS subsystem
LOG_LOCAL0	Reserved for local use; names LOG_LOCAL1 through LOG_LOCAL7 are also reserved

Figure 27.1 The facility types defined by *syslog*. Each log message must originate from one of these facilities.

As the figure shows, *syslog* has a facility for each major subsystem. For example, programs associated with e-mail belong to the *LOG_MAIL* facility, while most servers that run in background belong to the *LOG_DAEMON* facility.

27.24.8 Syslog Priority Levels

Syslog defines eight priority levels as Figure 27.2 shows.

Priority	Description
LOG_EMERG	An extreme emergency; the message should be broadcast to all users
LOG_ALERT	A condition that should be corrected immediately (e.g., a corrupted system database)
LOG_CRIT	A critical condition like a hardware error (e.g. disk failure)
LOG_ERR	An error that requires attention but is not critical
LOG_WARNING	A warning that an error condition may exist
LOG_NOTICE	A condition that is not an error, but may need attention
LOG_INFO	An informational message (e.g., a message issued when a server starts execution)
LOG_DEBUG	A message used by a programmer for debugging

Figure 27.2 The eight priority levels defined by *syslog*. Each log message must have one of these priority levels specified.

Priority levels range from *LOG_EMERG*, which is intended for the most severe emergencies, to *LOG_DEBUG*, which programmers use when they need to log debugging information.

27.24.9 Using Syslog

Whenever a program uses *syslog* to handle a log message, the program must specify a facility and a priority level for the message. To make *syslog* easier to use, the library routines permit a programmer to specify a facility when the program begins and to have *syslog* use that facility for successive messages. To specify an initial facility, a program calls procedure *openlog*. *Openlog* takes three arguments that specify an identification string, a set of handling options, and a facility specification. *Syslog* prepends the identification to all successive messages that the program writes so they can be found in the log. Usually, a programmer chooses the name of the program as its identification string. *Openlog* initializes logging and stores the identification string and facility for later use. For example, a programmer who is testing a private program can call:

```
openlog("myprog", LOG_PID, LOG_USER);
```

to specify identification string *myprog*, logging option *LOG_PID*, and facility *LOG_USER*. Option *LOG_PID* requests that *syslog* record the program's process identifier with each log message.

When a program needs to send a log message, it calls procedure *syslog*. Syslog sends the message to the *syslogd* server on the local machine. Procedure *syslog* takes a variable number of arguments. The first specifies a priority for the message and the second specifies a *printf*-like format. As in *printf*, arguments following the format contain values referenced in the format. In the simplest case, a program can call *syslog* with a constant string as a message. For example, to record a debugging message on the system log, a program can call:

```
syslog(LOG_DEBUG, "my program opened its input file");
```

Once a program finishes using *syslog*, it can call procedure *closelog* to close the log file (i.e., terminate contact with the server). *Closelog* terminates the log file connection and releases the I/O descriptor allocated for it. Thus, it can be important to call *closelog* to deallocate the log file descriptor (e.g., before a call to *fork*).

27.24.10 An Example Syslog Configuration File

Much of the flexibility in the *syslog* mechanism arises because it uses a configuration file to control the server. The configuration file uses patterns to allow the system administrator to specify how to handle each combination of facility and priority.

The *syslog* configuration file, */etc/syslog.conf* on most systems, is a text file that contains specifications, one per line. A specification consists of a pair of strings separated by white space. The left string specifies a *pattern* that matches some combination of facility and priority. The right string specifies a *disposition* for messages that match the pattern. For example, the specification:

```
lpr.debug    /usr/adm/printer-errs
```

contains a pattern that matches all messages with facility *lpr* and priority *debug*. Because the disposition string begins with a slash, *syslogd* interprets it as a file name. Thus, if it encounters the above specification, *syslogd* will send debug messages from the *lpr* facility to file */usr/adm/printer-errs*. *Syslogd* interprets an asterisk as a disposition string to mean ''broadcast the message to all users.'' It interprets other disposition strings that do not begin with a slash as the login name of users who should receive the message.

An example configuration file will clarify the concept and show how system administrators can specify logging behavior. The following is a sample configuration file used on one system:

```
*.err;kern.debug;auth.notice                          /dev/console
kern.debug;daemon,auth.notice;auth.info;*.err;mail.crit /usr/adm/messages
lpr.debug                                             /usr/adm/printer-errs
mail.debug                                            /usr/spool/mqueue/syslog
*.alert;kern.err;daemon.err                           operator
*.alert                                               root
*.emerg                                               *
```

Pattern matching is a powerful mechanism because it permits a system administrator to represent specifications without writing down individual combinations of facility and priority. For example, the configuration file above uses the pattern *.*err* to mean, "messages at the error priority of any facility."

27.25 Summary

Production servers employ a set of techniques that make them easier to manage and debug, more robust, and less susceptible to errors. This chapter discusses the motivation for such techniques, and shows the code required for each. The particular techniques discussed include the following conceptual operations:

- Operate the server as a background process (daemon).
- Close inherited file descriptors.
- Detach the server from its controlling TTY.
- Move the server to a safe, known directory.
- Set the UNIX umask.
- Place the server in a private process group.
- Open the three standard I/O descriptors.
- Guarantee mutually exclusive execution.
- Record the server's process identifier.
- Wait for child processes that terminate.
- Ignore extraneous signals.
- Use *syslog* to handle error messages.

FOR FURTHER STUDY

Many of the rules UNIX programmers follow when implementing servers come from unwritten conventions and heuristics; often programmers learn techniques by reading existing programs. Stevens [1990] discusses how to write daemon programs and describes some of the techniques outlined in this chapter.

EXERCISES

27.1   Build a procedure, *daemonize*, that includes the code from this chapter.

27.2   Read about signals in the *UNIX Programmer's Manual*. Which signals cannot be ignored? What happens if a server receives one of them?

27.3   Some programmers arrange for a server to terminate gracefully if it receives a special signal (e.g., *SIGHUP*). Doing so allows the system manager to terminate a server by sending the designated signal. How can the manager send such a signal if the server has detached itself from the controlling terminal?

27.4   In the previous question, is it possible for an unprivileged user to terminate a server by sending it the designated signal?

27.5   Our example code closes all file descriptors and then opens standard input, output, and error again. Some servers leave these three descriptors with the values inherited from their parents. What are the advantages and disadvantages of doing so? (Hint: think about logging error messages).

27.6   Most servers execute with root privilege (in UNIX, root privilege means absolute privilege). Why might a server choose to run with less privilege? How can it do so?

27.7   Write a server that uses the UNIX system function *creat* to provide mutual exclusion. (Hint: the technique is well-known and widely-used, especially in older UNIX programs).

27.8   Compare mutual exclusion using *creat* (see the previous exercise) to mutual exclusion using *O_EXCL* in a call to *open* and to mutual exclusion using *rename*. Which of the three techniques is preferable? Why?

27.9   Examine the source code for a production server. What techniques from this chapter does it use? Does it use other techniques?

27.10   Read the UNIX manual pages for *syslogd*. How can a system administrator change the configuration after the server has begun? Can you suggest an alternative?

Appendix 1

System Calls And Library Routines Used With Sockets

Introduction

In BSD UNIX, communication centers around the socket abstraction. Applications use a set of socket system calls to communicate with TCP/IP software in the operating system. A client application creates a socket, connects it to a server on a remote machine, and uses it to transfer data and to receive data from the remote machine. Finally, when the client application finishes using the socket, it closes it. A server creates a socket, binds it to a well-known protocol port on the local machine, and waits for clients to contact it.

Each page of this appendix describes one of the system calls or library functions that programmers use when writing client or server applications. The functions are arranged in alphabetic order, with one page devoted to a given function. The functions listed include: *accept, bind, close, connect, fork, gethostbyaddr, gethostbyname, gethostid, gethostname, getpeername, getprotobyname, getservbyname, getsockname, getsockopt, gettimeofday, listen, read, recv, recvfrom, recvmsg, select, send, sendmsg, sendto, sethostid, setsockopt, shutdown, socket,* and *write.*

The Accept System Call

Use

retcode = accept (socket, addr, addrlen);

Description

Servers use the *accept* function to accept the next incoming connection on a passive socket after they have called *socket* to create a socket, *bind* to specify a local IP address and protocol port number, and *listen* to make the socket passive and to set the length of the connection request queue. *Accept* removes the next connection request from the queue (or waits until a connection request arrives), creates a new socket for the request, and returns the descriptor for the new socket. *Accept* only applies to stream sockets (e.g., those used with TCP).

Arguments

Arg	Type	Meaning
socket	int	A socket descriptor created by the *socket* function.
addr	&sockaddr	A pointer to an address structure. *Accept* fills in the structure with the IP address and protocol port number of the remote machine.
addrlen	&int	A pointer to an integer that initially specifies the size of the *sockaddr* argument and, when the call returns, specifies the number of bytes stored in argument *addr*.

Return Code

Accept returns a nonnegative socket descriptor if successful and *–1* to indicate that an error has occurred. When an error occurs, the global variable *errno* contains one of the following values:

Value in errno	Cause of the Error
EBADF	The first argument does not specify a valid descriptor.
ENOTSOCK	The first argument does not specify a socket descriptor.
EOPNOTSUPP	The socket is not of type SOCK_STREAM.
EFAULT	The pointer in argument 2 is invalid.
EWOULDBLOCK	The socket is marked nonblocking and no connections are waiting to be accepted (i.e. the call would block).

The Bind System Call

Use

retcode = bind (socket, localaddr, addrlen);

Description

Bind specifies a local IP address and protocol port number for a socket. *Bind* is primarily used by servers, which need to specify a well-known protocol port.

Arguments

Arg	Type	Meaning
socket	int	A socket descriptor created by the *socket* call.
localaddr	&sockaddr	The address of a structure that specifies an IP address and protocol port number.
addrlen	int	The size of the address structure in bytes.

Chapter 5 contains a description of the *sockaddr* structure.

Return Code

Bind returns 0 if successful and *–1* to indicate that an error has occurred. When an error occurs, the global variable *errno* contains a code that specifies the cause of the error. The possible errors are:

Value in errno	Cause of the Error
EBADF	Argument *socket* does not specify a valid descriptor.
ENOTSOCK	Argument *socket* does not specify a socket descriptor.
EADDRNOTAVAIL	The specified address is unavailable (e.g., an IP address does not match a local interface).
EADDRINUSE	The specified address is in use (e.g., another process has allocated the protocol port).
EINVAL	The socket already has an address bound to it.
EACCES	The application program does not have permission to use the address specified.
EFAULT	The *localaddr* argument pointer is invalid.

The Close System Call

Use

retcode = close (socket);

Description

An application calls *close* after it finishes using a socket. *Close* terminates communication gracefully and removes the socket. Any unread data waiting at the socket will be discarded.

In practice, UNIX implements a reference count mechanism to allow multiple processes to share a socket. If n processes share a socket, the reference count will be n. *Close* decrements the reference count each time a process calls it. Once the reference count reaches zero (i.e. all processes have called *close*), the socket will be deallocated.

Arguments

Arg	Type	Meaning
socket	int	The descriptor of a socket to be closed.

Return Code

Close returns 0 if successful and *–1* to indicate that an error has occurred. When an error occurs, the global variable *errno* contains the following value:

Value in errno	Cause of the Error
EBADF	The argument does not specify a valid descriptor.

The Connect System Call

Use

retcode = connect (socket, addr, addrlen);

Description

Connect allows the caller to specify the remote endpoint address for a previously created socket. If the socket uses TCP, *connect* uses the 3-way handshake to establish a connection; if the socket uses UDP, *connect* specifies the remote endpoint but does not transfer any datagrams to it.

Arguments

Arg	Type	Meaning
socket	int	The descriptor of a socket.
addr	&sockaddr_in	The remote machine endpoint.
addrlen	int	The length of the second argument.

Chapter 5 contains a description of the *sockaddr* structure.

Return Code

Connect returns zero if successful and *–1* to indicate that an error has occurred. When an error occurs, the global variable *errno* contains one of the following values:

Value in errno	Cause of the Error
EBADF	The first argument does not specify a valid descriptor.
ENOTSOCK	The first argument does not specify a socket descriptor.
EAFNOSUPPORT	The address family specified in the remote endpoint cannot be used with this type of socket.
EADDRNOTAVAIL	The specified endpoint address is not available.
EISCONN	The socket is already connected.
ETIMEDOUT	(TCP only) The protocol reached timeout without successfully establishing a connection.
ECONNREFUSED	(TCP only) Connection refused by remote machine.
ENETUNREACH	(TCP only) The network is not currently reachable.
EADDRINUSE	The specified address is already in use.
EINPROGRESS	(TCP only) The socket is nonblocking and a connection attempt would block.
EALREADY	(TCP only) The socket is nonblocking and the call would wait for a previous connection attempt to complete.

The Fork System Call

Use

retcode = fork ( );

Description

Although not directly related to communication sockets, *fork* is essential because servers use it to create concurrent processes. *Fork* creates a new process executing the same code as the original. The two processes share all socket and file descriptors that are open when the call to *fork* occurs. The two processes have different process identifiers and different parent process identifiers.

Arguments

Fork does not take any arguments.

Return Code

If successful, *fork* returns 0 to the child process and the (nonzero) process identifier of the newly created process to the original process. It returns *–1* to indicate that an error has occurred. When an error occurs, the global variable *errno* contains one of the following values:

Value in errno	Cause of the Error
EAGAIN	The system limit on total processes has been reached, or the per-user limit on processes has been reached.
ENOMEM	The system has insufficient memory for a new process.

The Gethostbyaddr Library Function

Use

retcode = gethostbyaddr (addr, alen, atype);

Description

Gethostbyaddr searches for information about a host given its IP address.

Arguments

Arg	Type	Meaning
addr	&char	A pointer to an array that contains a host address (e.g., an IP address).
alen	int	An integer that gives the address length (*4* for IP).
atype	int	An integer that gives the address type (AF_INET for an IP address).

Return Code

Gethostbyaddr returns a pointer to a *hostent* structure if successful and *0* to indicate that an error has occurred. The *hostent* structure is declared to be:

```
struct hostent {              /* entry for a host          */
        char  *h_name;        /* official host name        */
        char  *h_aliases[]; /* list of other aliases       */
        int    h_addrtype;   /* host address type          */
        int    h_length;     /* length of host address     */
        char **h_addr_list; /* list of addresses for host */
};
```

When an error occurs, the global variable *h_errno* contains one of the following values:

Value in h_errno	Cause of the Error
HOST_NOT_FOUND	The name specified is unknown.
TRY_AGAIN	Temporary error: local server could not contact the authority at present.
NO_RECOVERY	Irrecoverable error occurred.
NO_ADDRESS	The specified name is valid, but it does not correspond to an IP address.

The Gethostbyname Library Call

Use

retcode = gethostbyname (name);

Description

Gethostbyname maps a host name to an IP address.

Arguments

Arg	Type	Meaning
name	&char	The address of a character string that contains a host name.

Return Code

Gethostbyname returns a pointer to a *hostent* structure if successful and *0* to indicate that an error has occurred. The *hostent* structure is declared to be:

```
struct hostent {              /* entry for a host         */
      char  *h_name;          /* official host name       */
      char  *h_aliases[];     /* list of other aliases    */
      int    h_addrtype;      /* host address type        */
      int    h_length;        /* length of host address   */
      char **h_addr_list;     /* list of addresses for host */
};
```

When an error occurs, the global variable *h_errno* contains one of the following values:

Value in h_errno	Cause of the Error
HOST_NOT_FOUND	The name specified is unknown.
TRY_AGAIN	Temporary error: local server could not contact the authority at present.
NO_RECOVERY	Irrecoverable error occurred.
NO_ADDRESS	The specified name is valid, but it does not correspond to an IP address.

The Gethostid System Call

Use

$$hostid = gethostid ( ) ;$$

Description

Applications call *gethostid* to determine the unique *32*-bit host identifier assigned to the local machine. Usually, the host identifier is the machine's primary IP address.

Arguments

Gethostid does not take any arguments.

Return Value

Gethostid returns a long integer containing the host identifier.

The Gethostname System Call

Use

retcode = gethostname (name, namelen);

Description

Gethostname returns the primary name of the local machine in the form of a text string.

Arguments

Arg	Type	Meaning
name	&char	The address of the character array into which the name should be placed.
namelen	int	The length of the *name* array (should be at least *65*).

Return Code

Gethostname returns *0* if successful and *–1* to indicate that an error has occurred. When an error occurs, the global variable *errno* contains the following value:

Value in errno	Cause of the Error
EFAULT	The *name* or *namelen* arguments were incorrect.

The Getpeername System Call

Use

retcode = getpeername (socket, remaddr, addrlen);

Description

An application uses *getpeername* to obtain the remote endpoint address for a connected socket. Usually, a client knows the remote endpoint address because it calls *connect* to set it. However, a server that uses *accept* to obtain a connection may need to interrogate the socket to find out the remote address.

Arguments

Arg	Type	Meaning
socket	int	A socket descriptor created by the *socket* function.
remaddr	&sockaddr	A pointer to a *sockaddr* structure that will contain the endpoint address.
addrlen	&int	A pointer to an integer that contains the length of the second argument initially, and the actual length of the endpoint address upon return.

Chapter 5 contains a description of the *sockaddr* structure.

Return Code

Getpeername returns 0 if successful and *–1* to indicate that an error has occurred. When an error occurs, the global variable *errno* contains one of the following values:

Value in errno	Cause of the Error
EBADF	The first argument does not specify a valid descriptor.
ENOTSOCK	The first argument does not specify a socket descriptor.
ENOTCONN	The socket is not a connected socket.
ENOBUFS	The system had insufficient resources to perform the operation.
EFAULT	The *remaddr* argument pointer is invalid.

The Getprotobyname Function Call

Use

retcode = getprotobyname (name);

Description

Applications call *getprotobyname* to find a protocol's official integer value from its name alone.

Arguments

Arg	Type	Meaning
name	&char	The address of a string that contains the protocol name.

Return Code

Getprotobyname returns a pointer to a structure of type *protoent* if successful and *0* to indicate that an error has occurred. Structure *protoent* is declared to be:

```
struct protoent {          /* entry that describes a protocol  */
      char  *p_name;       /* official name of protocol        */
      char **p_aliases;    /* list of aliases for the protocol */
      int    p_proto;      /* official protocol number         */
};
```

The Getservbyname Library Call

Use

retcode = getservbyname (name, proto);

Description

Getservbyname obtains an entry from the network services database given a service name. Clients and servers both call *getservbyname* to map a service name to a protocol port number.

Arguments

Arg	Type	Meaning
name	&char	A pointer to a string of characters that contains a service name.
proto	&char	A pointer to a string of characters that contains the name of the protocol to be used (e.g., *tcp*).

Return Code

Getservbyname returns a pointer to a *servent* structure if successful and a null pointer (0) to indicate that an error has occurred. The *servent* structure is declared to be:

```
struct servent {          /* one service entry        */
     char  *s_name ;       /* official service name    */
     char **s_aliases;     /* list of other aliases    */
     int    s_port;        /* port used for this service */
     char  *s_proto;       /* protocol used for service */
};
```

The Getsockname System Call

Use

retcode = getsockname (socket, name, namelen);

Description

Getsockname obtains the name for the specified socket.

Arguments

Arg	Type	Meaning
socket	int	A socket descriptor created by the *socket* function.
name	&char	A pointer to an array of characters.
namelen	&int	The number of positions in the *name* array; returned as the length of the name.

Return Code

Getsockname returns *0* if successful and *–1* to indicate that an error has occurred. When an error occurs, the global variable *errno* contains one of the following values:

Value in errno	Cause of the Error
EBADF	The first argument does not specify a valid descriptor.
ENOTSOCK	The first argument does not specify a socket descriptor.
EBOBUFS	Insufficient buffer space was available in the system.
EFAULT	The address of *name* or *namelen* is incorrect.

The Getsockopt System Call

Use

retcode = getsockopt (socket, level, opt, optval, optlen);

Description

Getsockopt permits an application to obtain the value of a parameter (option) for a socket or a protocol the socket uses.

Arguments

Arg	Type	Meaning
socket	int	The descriptor of a socket.
level	int	An integer that identifies a protocol level.
opt	int	An integer that identifies an option.
optval	&char	The address of a buffer in which the value is returned.
optlen	&int	Size of buffer; returned as length of the value found.

The socket-level options that apply to all sockets include:

SO_DEBUG	Status of debugging information
SO_REUSEADDR	Allow local address reuse?
SO_KEEPALIVE	Status of connection keep-alive
SO_DONTROUTE	Bypass Routing for outgoing messages?
SO_LINGER	Linger on close if data present?
SO_BROADCAST	Permission to transmit broadcast messages?
SO_OOBINLINE	Receive out-of-band data in band?
SO_SNDBUF	Buffer size for output
SO_RCVBUF	Buffer size for input
SO_TYPE	Type of the socket
SO_ERROR	Get and clear the last error for the socket

Return Code

Getsockopt returns *0* if successful and *−1* to indicate that an error has occurred. When an error occurs, the global variable *errno* contains one of the following values:

Value in errno	Cause of the Error
EBADF	The first argument does not specify a valid descriptor.
ENOTSOCK	The first argument does not specify a socket descriptor.
ENOPROTOOPT	The *opt* is incorrect.
EFAULT	The address of *optval* or *optlen* is incorrect.

The Gettimeofday System Call

Use

retcode = gettimeofday (tm, tmzone);

Description

Gettimeofday extracts the current time and date from the system along with information about the local time zone.

Arguments

Arg	Type	Meaning
tm	&struct timeval	The address of a timeval structure.
tmzone	&struct timezone	The address of a timezone structure.

The structures that *gettimeofday* assigns are declared:

```
struct timeval {        /* structure for storing time    */
    long tv_sec;        /* seconds since epoch (1/1/70)  */
    long tv_usec;       /* microseconds beyond tv_sec    */
};

struct timezone {       /* structure for timezone info   */
    int  tz_minuteswest;/* minutes west of Greenwich     */
    int  tz_dsttime;    /* type of correction to apply   */
};
```

Return Code

Gettimeofday returns *0* if successful and *–1* to indicate that an error has occurred. When an error occurs, the global variable *errno* contains the following value:

Value in errno	Cause of the Error
EFAULT	The *tm* or *tmzone* arguments contained an incorrect address.

The Listen System Call

Use

retcode = listen (socket, queuelen);

Description

Servers use *listen* to make a socket passive (i.e., ready to accept incoming requests). *Listen* also sets the number of incoming connection requests that the protocol software should enqueue for a given socket while the server handles another request. *Listen* only applies to sockets used with TCP.

Arguments

Arg	Type	Meaning
socket	int	A socket descriptor created by the *socket* call.
queuelen	int	The size of the incoming connection request queue (usually up to a maximum of *5*).

Return Code

Listen returns 0 if successful and *–1* to indicate that an error has occurred. When an error occurs, the global variable *errno* contains one of the following values:

Value in errno	Cause of the Error
EBADF	The first argument does not specify a valid descriptor.
ENOTSOCK	The first argument does not specify a socket descriptor.
EOPNOTSUPP	The socket type does not support *listen*.

The Read System Call

Use

retcode = read (socket, buff, buflen);

Description

Clients or servers use *read* to obtain input from a socket.

Arguments

Arg	Type	Meaning
socket	int	A socket descriptor created by the *socket* function.
buff	&char	A pointer to an array of characters to hold the input.
buflen	int	An integer that specifies the number of bytes in the the *buff* array.

Return Code

Read returns zero if it detects an end-of-file condition on the socket, the number of bytes read if it obtains input, and *–1* to indicate that an error has occurred. When an error occurs, the global variable *errno* contains one of the following values:

Value in errno	Cause of the Error
EBADF	The first argument does not specify a valid descriptor.
EFAULT	Address *buff* is illegal.
EIO	An I/O error occurred while reading data.
EINTR	A signal interrupted the operation.
EWOULDBLOCK	Nonblocking I/O is specified, but the socket has no data.

The Recv System Call

Use

retcode = recv (socket, buffer, length, flags);

Description

Recv obtains the next incoming message from a UDP socket.

Arguments

Arg	Type	Meaning
socket	int	A socket descriptor created by the *socket* function.
buffer	&char	The address of a buffer to hold the message.
length	int	The length of the buffer.
flags	int	Control bits that specify whether to receive out-of-band data and whether to look ahead for messages.

Return Code

Recv returns the number of bytes in the message if successful and -1 to indicate that an error has occurred. When an error occurs, the global variable *errno* contains one of the following values:

Value in errno	Cause of the Error
EBADF	The first argument does not specify a valid descriptor.
ENOTSOCK	The first argument does not specify a socket descriptor.
EWOULDBLOCK	The socket has no data, but nonblocking I/O has been specified.
EINTR	A signal arrived before the read operation could deliver data.
EFAULT	Argument *buffer* is incorrect.

The Recvfrom System Call

Use

retcode = recvfrom (socket, buffer, buflen, flags, from, fromlen);

Description

Recvfrom extracts the next message that arrives at a socket and records the sender's address (enabling the caller to send a reply).

Arguments

Arg	Type	Meaning
socket	int	A socket descriptor created by the *socket* function.
buffer	&char	The address of a buffer to hold the message.
buflen	int	The length of the buffer.
flags	int	Control bits that specify out-of-band data or message look-ahead.
from	&sockaddr	The address of a structure to hold the sender's address.
fromlen	&int	The length of the *from* buffer, returned as the size of the sender's address.

Chapter 5 contains a description of the *sockaddr* structure.

Return Code

Recvfrom returns the number of bytes in the message if successful and −1 to indicate that an error has occurred. When an error occurs, the global variable *errno* contains one of the following values:

Value in errno	Cause of the Error
EBADF	The first argument does not specify a valid descriptor.
ENOTSOCK	The first argument does not specify a socket descriptor.
EWOULDBLOCK	The socket has no data, but nonblocking I/O has been specified.
EINTR	A signal arrived before the read operation could deliver data.
EFAULT	Argument *buffer* is incorrect.

The Recvmsg System Call

Use

retcode = recvmsg (socket, msg, flags);

Description

Recvmsg returns the next message that arrives on a UDP socket. It places the message in a structure that includes a header along with the data.

Arguments

Arg	Type	Meaning
socket	int	Socket descriptor created by the *socket* function.
msg	&struct msghdr	Address of a message structure.
flags	int	Control bits that specify out-of-band data or message look-ahead.

The message is delivered in a *msghdr* structure with format:

```
struct msghdr  {
        caddr_t   msg_name;       /* optional address      */
        int       msg_namelen;    /* size of address       */
        struct iovec *msg_iov;    /* scatter/gather array   */
        int       msg_iovlen;     /* # elements in msg_iov */
        caddr_t   msg_accrights;  /* rights sent/received   */
        int       msg_accrghtslen;/* length of prev. field */
};
```

Return Code

Recvmsg returns the number of bytes in the message if successful and −*1* to indicate that an error has occurred. When an error occurs, the global variable *errno* contains one of the following values:

Value in errno	Cause of the Error
EBADF	The first argument does not specify a valid descriptor.
ENOTSOCK	The first argument does not specify a socket descriptor.
EWOULDBLOCK	The socket has no data, but nonblocking I/O has been specified.
EINTR	A signal arrived before the read operation could deliver data.
EFAULT	Argument *buffer* is incorrect.

The Select System Call

Use

retcode = select (numfds, refds, wrfds, exfds, time);

Description

Select provides asynchronous I/O by permitting a single process to wait for the first of any file descriptors in a specified set to become ready. The caller can also specify a maximum timeout for the wait.

Arguments

Arg	Type	Meaning
numfds	int	Number of file descriptors in the set.
refds	&fd_set	Address of file descriptors for input.
wrfds	&fd_set	Address of file descriptors for output.
exfds	&fd_set	Address of file descriptors for exceptions.
time	&struct timeval	Maximum time to wait or zero.

Arguments that refer to descriptors consist of integers in which the ith bit corresponds to descriptor i. Macros *FD_CLR* and *FD_SET* clear or set individual bits. The UNIX manual page that describes *gettimeofday* contains a description of the *timeval* structure.

Return Code

Select returns the number of ready file descriptors if successful, *0* if the time limit was reached, and *-1* to indicate that an error has occurred. When an error occurs, the global variable *errno* contains one of the following values:

Value in errno	Cause of the Error
EBADF	One of the descriptor sets specifies an invalid descriptor.
EINTR	A signal arrived before the time limit or any of the selected descriptors became ready.
EINVAL	The time limit value is incorrect.

The Send System Call

Use

retcode = send (socket, msg, msglen, flags);

Description

Applications call *send* to transfer a message to another machine.

Arguments

Arg	Type	Meaning
socket	int	Socket descriptor created by the *socket* function.
msg	&char	A pointer to the message.
msglen	int	The length of the message in bytes.
flags	int	Control bits that specify out-of-band data or message look-ahead.

Return Code

Send returns the number of characters sent if successful and *–1* to indicate that an error has occurred. When an error occurs, the global variable *errno* contains one of the following values:

Value in errno	Cause of the Error
EBADF	The first argument does not specify a valid descriptor.
ENOTSOCK	The first argument does not specify a socket descriptor.
EFAULT	Argument *buffer* is incorrect.
EMSGSIZE	The message is too large for the socket.
EWOULDBLOCK	The socket has no data, but nonblocking I/O has been specified.
ENOBUFS	The system had insufficient resources to perform the operation.

The Sendmsg System Call

Use

retcode = sendmsg (socket, msg, flags);

Description

Sendmsg sends a message, extracting it from a *msghdr* structure.

Arguments

Arg	Type	Meaning
socket	int	Socket descriptor created by the *socket* function.
msg	&struct msghdr	A pointer to the message structure.
flags	int	Control bits that specify out-of-band data or message look-ahead.

The page that describes *recvmsg* contains a definition of structure *msghdr*.

Return Code

Sendmsg returns the number of bytes sent if successful and *–1* to indicate that an error has occurred. When an error occurs, the global variable *errno* contains one of the following values:

Value in errno	Cause of the Error
EBADF	The first argument does not specify a valid descriptor.
ENOTSOCK	The first argument does not specify a socket descriptor.
EFAULT	Argument *buffer* is incorrect.
EMSGSIZE	The message is too large for the socket.
EWOULDBLOCK	The socket has no data, but nonblocking I/O has been specified.
ENOBUFS	The system had insufficient resources to perform the operation.

467

The Sendto System Call

Use

retcode = sendto (socket, msg, msglen, flags, to, tolen);

Description

Sendto sends a message by taking the destination address from a structure.

Arguments

Arg	Type	Meaning
socket	int	Socket descriptor created by the *socket* function.
msg	&char	A pointer to the message.
msglen	int	The length of the message in bytes.
flags	int	Control bits that specify out-of-band data or message look-ahead.
to	&sockaddr	A pointer to the address structure.
tolen	int	The length of the address in bytes.

Chapter 5 contains a description of the *sockaddr* structure.

Return Code

Sendto returns the number of bytes sent if successful and –*1* to indicate that an error has occurred. When an error occurs, the global variable *errno* contains one of the following values:

Value in errno	Cause of the Error
EBADF	The first argument does not specify a valid descriptor.
ENOTSOCK	The first argument does not specify a socket descriptor.
EFAULT	Argument *buffer* is incorrect.
EMSGSIZE	The message is too large for the socket.
EWOULDBLOCK	The socket has no data, but nonblocking I/O has been specified.
ENOBUFS	The system had insufficient resources to perform the operation.

The Sethostid System Call

Use

(void) sethostid (hostid);

Description

The system manager runs a privileged program at system startup that calls *sethostid* to assign the local machine a unique *32*-bit host identifier. Usually, the host identifier is the machine's primary IP address.

Arguments

Arg	Type	Meaning
hostid	int	A value to be stored as the host's identifier.

Errors

An application must have root privilege, or *sethosid* will not change the host identifier.

The Setsockopt System Call

Use

retcode = setsockopt (socket, level, opt, optval, optlen);

Description

Setsockopt permits an application to change an option associated with a socket or the protocols it uses.

Arguments

Arg	Type	Meaning
socket	int	The descriptor of a socket.
level	int	An integer that identifies a protocol (e.g., TCP).
opt	int	An integer that identifies an option.
optval	&char	The address of a buffer that contains a value (usually *1* to enable an option or *0* to disable it).
optlen	int	The length of *optval*.

The socket-level options that apply to all sockets include:

SO_DEBUG	Toggle status of debugging information
SO_REUSEADDR	Toggle local address reuse
SO_KEEPALIVE	Toggle status of connection keep-alive
SO_DONTROUTE	Toggle bypass routing for outgoing messages
SO_LINGER	Linger on close if data present
SO_BROADCAST	Toggle permission to broadcast messages
SO_OOBINLINE	Toggle reception of out-of-band data in band
SO_SNDBUF	Set buffer size for output
SO_RCVBUF	Set buffer size for input

Return Code

Setsockopt returns *0* if successful and *−1* to indicate that an error has occurred. When an error occurs, the global variable *errno* contains one of the following values:

Value in errno	Cause of the Error
EBADF	The first argument does not specify a valid descriptor.
ENOTSOCK	The first argument does not specify a socket descriptor.
ENOPROTOOPT	The option integer, *opt*, is incorrect.
EFAULT	The address of *optval* or *optlen* is incorrect.

The Shutdown System Call

Use

retcode = shutdown (socket, direction);

Description

The *shutdown* function applies to full-duplex sockets (i.e., a connected TCP socket), and is used to partially close the connection.

Arguments

Arg	Type	Meaning
socket	int	A socket descriptor created by the *socket* call.
direction	int	The direction in which shutdown is desired: *0* means terminate further input, *1* means terminate further output, and *2* means terminate both input and output.

Return Code

The *shutdown* call returns *0* if the operation succeeds or *-1* to indicate that an error has occurred. When an error occurs, the global variable *errno* contains a code that specifies the cause of the error. The possible errors are:

Value in errno	Cause of the Error
EBADF	The first argument does not specify a valid descriptor.
ENOTSOCK	The first argument does not specify a socket descriptor.
ENOTCONN	The specified socket is not currently connected.

The Socket System Call

Use

retcode = socket (family, type, protocol);

Description

The *socket* function creates a socket used for network communication, and returns an integer descriptor for that socket.

Arguments

Arg	Type	Meaning
family	int	Protocol or address family (PF_INET for TCP/IP, AF_INET can also be used).
type	int	Type of service (SOCK_STREAM for TCP or SOCK_DGRAM for UDP).
protocol	int	Protocol number to use or 0 to request the default for a given family and type.

Return Code

The *socket* call either returns a descriptor or *–1* to indicate that an error has occurred. When an error occurs, the global variable *errno* contains a code that specifies the cause of the error. The possible errors are:

Value in errno	Cause of the Error
EPROTONOSUPPORT	Error in arguments: the requested service or the specified protocol is invalid.
EMFILE	The application's descriptor table is full.
ENFILE	The internal system file table is full.
EACCESS	Permission to create the socket is denied.
ENOBUFS	The system has no buffer space available.

The Write System Call

Use

retcode = write (socket, buf, buflen);

Description

Write permits an application to transfer data to a remote machine.

Arguments

Arg	Type	Meaning
socket	int	A socket descriptor created by the *socket* call.
buf	&char	The address of a buffer containing data.
buflen	int	The number of bytes in *buf*.

Return Code

Write returns the number of bytes transferred if successful and *–1* to indicate that an error has occurred. When an error occurs, the global variable *errno* contains one of the following values:

Value in errno	Cause of the Error
EBADF	The first argument does not specify a valid descriptor.
EPIPE	Attempt to *write* on an unconnected stream socket.
EFBIG	Data written exceeds system capacity.
EFAULT	Address in *buf* is incorrect.
EINVAL	Socket pointer is invalid.
EIO	An I/O error occurred.
EWOULDBLOCK	The socket cannot accept all data that was written without blocking, but nonblocking I/O has been specified.

Appendix 2

Manipulation Of UNIX File And Socket Descriptors

Introduction

In UNIX, all input and output operations use an abstraction known as the *file descriptor*. A program calls the *open* system call to obtain access to a file or the *socket* system call to obtain a descriptor used for network communication. Chapters *4* and *5* describe the socket interface; Chapter *23* describes UNIX descriptors and I/O in more detail. It points out that a newly created process inherits copies of all file descriptors that the parent process had open at the time of creation. Finally, Chapter *27* discusses how production servers close extra file descriptors and open standard I/O descriptors.

This appendix describes how programs can use standard I/O descriptors as arguments, and illustrates how a parent rearranges existing descriptors to make them correspond to the standard I/O descriptors before invoking a child. The technique is especially useful in multiservice servers that invoke separate programs to handle each service.

Descriptors As Implicit Arguments

When the UNIX *fork* function creates a new process, the newly created child inherits a copy of all file descriptors that the parent had open at the time of the call. Furthermore, the child's descriptor for a given file or socket appears in exactly the same position as the parent's. Thus, if descriptor *5* in the parent corresponds to a TCP socket, descriptor *5* in the newly created child will correspond to exactly the same socket.

Descriptors also remain open across a call to *execve*. To create a new process that executes the code in a file, *F*, a process calls *fork* and arranges for the child to call *execve* with file name *F* as an argument.

Conceptually, file descriptors form implicit arguments to newly created processes and to processes that overlay the running program with code from a file. The parent can choose which descriptors to leave open and which to close before a call to *fork*, and can choose exactly which descriptors will remain open across a call to *execve*.

UNIX programs often use descriptors to control processing instead of explicit arguments. In particular, a UNIX program expects three standard I/O descriptors to be open when the program begins: *standard input* (descriptor *0*), *standard output* (descriptor *1*), and *standard error* (descriptor *2*). The program reads input from descriptor *0*, writes output to descriptor *1*, and sends error messages to descriptor *2*.

Choosing To Use A Fixed Descriptor

A server can also use descriptors as implicit arguments if it invokes a separate program to handle a given request. For example, a slave program that is part of a connection-oriented server can be written to expect descriptor *0* to correspond to a TCP connection. The master server establishes a connection on descriptor *0*, and then uses *execve* to execute the slave. The master could also be programmed to use an arbitrary descriptor and to pass an argument to the slave that specifies which descriptor corresponds to the connection. However, using a fixed descriptor simplifies the code without sacrificing any functionality. In summary:

> *Processes use descriptors as implicit arguments in calls to* execve. *Master servers are often programmed to use a single descriptor as an implicit argument for the slave programs they invoke.*

The Need To Rearrange Descriptors

If a master server calls the system function *socket* to create a socket for connectionless communication or calls *accept* to obtain a socket for connection-oriented communication, the server cannot specify which descriptor the call will return because the operating system chooses a descriptor. If the slave expects descriptor *0* to correspond to the socket used for communication, the master cannot merely create a socket on a random descriptor and then execute the slave. Instead, it must rearrange its descriptors before making the call.

Rearranging Descriptors

A process uses the UNIX system calls *close* and *dup2* to rearrange its descriptors. Closing a descriptor detaches it from the file or socket to which it corresponds, deallocates any resources associated with it, and makes it available for reuse. For example, if a process needs to use descriptor *0*, but it is already in use, the process calls *close* to make it free. Appendix *1* describes how a server can close unnecessary file descriptors when it begins.

A process calls function *dup2* to create a duplicate copy of one file descriptor in another. The call has two arguments:

```
(void) dup2(olddesc, newdesc);
```

where *olddesc* is an integer that identifies an existing descriptor and *newdesc* is an integer that identifies the descriptor where the copy should appear. If *newdesc* is currently in use, the system deallocates it as if the user had called *close* before duplicating *olddesc*. After *dup2* finishes, both *olddesc* and *newdesc* refer to the same object (e.g., the same TCP connection).

To "move" a socket from one descriptor to another, the program first calls *dup2* and then calls *close* to deallocate the original. For example, suppose a master server calls *accept* to obtain an incoming connection, and suppose *accept* chooses to use descriptor *5* for the new connection. The master server can issue the following two calls to move the socket to descriptor *0*:

```
(void) dup2(5, 0);
(void) close(5);
```

Close-On-Exec

A server can choose to close unneeded file descriptors before executing another program. One approach requires the server to explicitly call *close* for each unneeded file descriptor. Another approach uses a system facility to close descriptors automatically.

To use the automatic facility, a server must set the *close-on-exec* flag in each descriptor that it wants the system to close. When the server calls *execve*, the system checks each descriptor to see if the flag has been set and calls *close* automatically if it has. While it may seem that automatic closing does not make programming easier, one must remember that in a large, complex program the purpose of each descriptor may not be apparent at the point of the call to *execve*. Using *close-on-exec* permits the programmer to decide whether a descriptor should remain open at the point in the program where the descriptor is created. Thus, it can be quite useful.

Summary

Processes use descriptors as implicit arguments when creating a new process or when overlaying the running program with code from a file. Often, servers that execute separately compiled programs rely on a descriptor to pass a TCP connection or a UDP socket.

To make programs easier to write and maintain, programmers usually choose a fixed descriptor for each implicit argument. The caller must rearrange its descriptors before invoking *execve* so that the socket used for I/O corresponds to the descriptor chosen as an implicit argument.

A process uses the *dup2* and *close* system calls to rearrange its descriptors. *Dup2* copies an existing descriptor into a specified location, and *close* deallocates a specified descriptor. To move descriptor A to descriptor B, a process first calls *dup2(A,B)* and then calls *close(A)*.

FOR FURTHER STUDY

The *UNIX Programmer's Manual* contains further information on the *dup2* and *close* system calls.

EXERCISES

A2.1 Read about the UNIX command interpreter and find out which descriptors it assigns before executing a command.

A2.2 Sketch the algorithm a command interpreter uses to handle file redirection. Show how it moves file descriptors before calling *execve*.

A2.3 Modify the multiservice server from Chapter *14* so it uses descriptor *0* as an implicit argument and calls *execve* to execute a slave program.

A2.4 Read about the 4.3BSD program *inetd*. How does it use descriptors as implicit arguments?

A2.5 What does the call *dup2(n, m)* do if n already equals m? Write a version of *dup* that works for arbitrary values of n and m.

Bibliography

ABRAMSON, N. [1970], The ALOHA System – Another Alternative for Computer Communications, *Proceedings of the Fall Joint Computer Conference.*

ABRAMSON, N. and F. KUO (EDS.) [1973], *Computer Communication Networks,* Prentice Hall, Englewood Cliffs, New Jersey.

AHO, A., B. W. KERNIGHAN, and P. J. WEINBERGER [1988], *The AWK Programming Language,* Addison-Wesley, Reading, Massachusetts.

ANDREWS, D. W., and G. D. SHULTZ [1982], A Token-Ring Architecture for Local Area Networks: An Update, *Proceedings of Fall 82 COMPCON,* IEEE.

AT&T [1989], *UNIX System V Release 3.2 – Programmer's Reference Manual,* Prentice Hall, Englewood Cliffs, New Jersey.

BACH, M. [1986], *The Design Of The UNIX Operating System,* Prentice Hall, Englewood Cliffs, New Jersey.

BALL, J. E., E. J. BURKE, I. GERTNER, K. A. LANTZ, and R. F. RASHID [1979], Perspectives on Message-Based Distributed Computing, *IEEE Computing Networking Symposium,* 46-51.

BBN [1981], A History of the ARPANET: The First Decade, *Technical Report,* Bolt, Beranek, and Newman, Inc.

BBN [December 1981], Specification for the Interconnection of a Host and an IMP (revised), *Technical Report 1822,* Bolt, Beranek, and Newman, Inc.

BERTSEKAS D. and R. GALLAGER [1987], *Data Networks,* Prentice-Hall, Englewood Cliffs, New Jersey.

BIRRELL, A. and B. NELSON [February 1984], Implementing Remote Procedure Calls, *ACM Transactions on Computer Systems,* 2(1), 39-59.

BOGGS, D., J. SHOCH, E. TAFT, and R. METCALFE [April 1980], Pup: An Internetwork Architecture, *IEEE Transactions on Communications.*

BOLSKY, M. I. and D. G. KORN [1989], *The Kornshell Command And Programming Language,* Prentice-Hall, Englewood Cliffs, New Jersey.

BORMAN, D. [April 1989], Implementing TCP/IP on a Cray Computer, *Computer Communication Review,* 19(2), 11-15.

BROWN, M., N. KOLLING, and E. TAFT [November 1985], The Alpine File System, *Transactions on Computer Systems*, 3(4), 261-293.

BROWNBRIDGE, D., L. MARSHALL, and B. RANDELL [December 1982], The Newcastle Connections or UNIXes of the World Unite!, *Software – Practice and Experience*, 12(12), 1147-1162.

CERF, V. and E. CAIN [October 1983], The DOD Internet Architecture Model, *Computer Networks*.

CERF, V. and R. KAHN [May 1974], A Protocol for Packet Network Interconnection, *IEEE Transactions of Communications*, Com-22(5).

CERF, V. [October 1989], A History of the ARPANET, *ConneXions, The Interoperability Report*, Mountain View, California.

CHERITON, D. R. [1983], Local Networking and Internetworking in the V-System, *Proceedings of the Eighth Data Communications Symposium*.

CHERITON, D. R. [April 1984], The V Kernel: A Software Base for Distributed Systems, *IEEE Software*, 1(2), 19-42.

CHERITON, D. [August 1986], VMTP: A Transport Protocol for the Next Generation of Communication Systems, *Proceedings of ACM SIGCOMM '86*, 406-415.

CHERITON, D. and T. MANN [May 1984], Uniform Access to Distributed Name Interpretation in the V-System, *Proceedings IEEE Fourth International Conference on Distributed Computing Systems*, 290-297.

CHESSON, G. [June 1987], Protocol Engine Design, *Proceedings of the 1987 Summer USENIX Conference*, Phoenix, Arizona.

CLARK, D. [December 1985], The Structure of Systems Using Upcalls, *Proceedings of the Tenth ACM Symposium on Operating Systems Principles*, 171-180.

CLARK, D., M. LAMBERT, and L. ZHANG [August 1987], NETBLT: A High Throughput Transport Protocol, *Proceedings of ACM SIGCOMM '87*.

COHEN, D. [1981], On Holy Wars and a Plea for Peace, *IEEE Computer*, 48-54.

COMER, D. E. and J. T. KORB [1983], CSNET Protocol Software: The IP-to-X25 Interface, *Computer Communications Review*, 13(2).

COMER, D. E. [1984], *Operating System Design – The XINU Approach*, Prentice-Hall, Englewood Cliffs, New Jersey.

COMER, D. E. [1987], *Operating System Design Vol II. – Internetworking With XINU*, Prentice-Hall, Englewood Cliffs, New Jersey.

COMER, D. E., T. NARTEN, and R. YAVATKAR [April 1987], The Cypress Network: A Low-Cost Internet Connection Technology, *Technical Report TR-653*, Purdue University, West Lafayette, Indiana.

COMER, D. E. [1991], *Internetworking With TCP/IP Vol 1: Principles, Protocols, and Architecture*, 2nd edition, Prentice-Hall, Englewood Cliffs, New Jersey.

COMER, D. E. and D. L. STEVENS [1991], *Internetworking With TCP/IP Vol 2: Design, Implementation, and Internals*, Prentice-Hall, Englewood Cliffs, New Jersey.

COTTON, I. [1979], Technologies for Local Area Computer Networks, *Proceedings of the Local Area Communications Network Symposium.*

CROWLEY, T., H. FORSDICK, M. LANDAU, and V. TRAVERS [June 1987], The Diamond Multimedia Editor, *Proceedings of the 1987 Summer USENIX Conference,* Phoenix, Arizona.

DALAL, Y. K. and R. S. PRINTIS [1981], 48-Bit Absolute Internet and Ethernet Host Numbers, *Proceedings of the Seventh Data Communications Symposium.*

DEERING, S. E. and D. R. CHERITON [May 1990], Multicast Routing in Datagram Internetworks and Extended LANs, *ACM Transactions on Computer Systems,* 8(2), 85-110.

DENNING, P. J. [September-October 1989], The Science of Computing: Worldnet, *American Scientist,* 432-434.

DENNING, P. J. [November-December 1989], The Science of Computing: The ARPANET After Twenty Years, *American Scientist,* 530-534.

DIGITAL EQUIPMENT CORPORATION., INTEL CORPORATION, and XEROX CORPORATION [September 1980], *The Ethernet: A Local Area Network Data Link Layer and Physical Layer Specification.*

DION, J. [Oct. 1980], The Cambridge File Server, *Operating Systems Review,* 14(4), 26-35.

DRIVER, H., H. HOPEWELL, and J. IAQUINTO [September 1979], How the Gateway Regulates Information Control, *Data Communications.*

EDGE, S. W. [1979], Comparison of the Hop-by-Hop and Endpoint Approaches to Network Interconnection, in *Flow Control in Computer Networks,* J. L. GRANGE and M. GIEN (EDS.), North-Holland, Amsterdam, 359-373.

EDGE, S. [1983], An Adaptive Timeout Algorithm for Retransmission Across a Packet Switching Network, *Proceedings of ACM SIGCOMM '83.*

ENSLOW, P. [January 1978], What is a 'Distributed' Data Processing System? *Computer,* 13-21.

FALK, G. [1983], The Structure and Function of Network Protocols, in *Computer Communications, Volume I: Principles,* W. CHOU (ED.), Prentice-Hall, Englewood Cliffs, New Jersey.

FARMER, W. D. and E. E. NEWHALL [1969], An Experimental Distributed Switching System to Handle Bursty Computer Traffic, *Proceedings of the ACM Symposium on Probabilistic Optimization of Data Communication Systems,* 1-33.

FCCSET [November 1987], A Research and Development Strategy for High Performance Computing, *Report from the Executive Office of the President and Office of Science and Technology Policy.*

FEDOR, M. [June 1988], GATED: A Multi-Routing Protocol Daemon for UNIX, *Proceedings of the 1988 Summer USENIX Conference,* San Francisco, California.

FEINLER, J., O. J. JACOBSEN, and M. STAHL [December 1985], *DDN Protocol Handbook Volume Two, DARPA Internet Protocols,* DDN Network Information Center, SRI International, Menlo Park, California.

FRANK, H. and W. CHOU [1971], Routing in Computer Networks, *Networks,* 1(1), 99-112.

FRANK, H. and J. FRISCH [1971], *Communication, Transmission, and Transportation Networks,* Addison-Wesley, Reading, Massachusetts.

FRANTA, W. R. and I. CHLAMTAC [1981], *Local Networks*, Lexington Books, Lexington, Massachusetts.

FRICC [May 1989], *Program Plan for the National Research and Education Network*, Federal Research Internet Coordinating Committee, US Department of Energy, Office of Scientific Computing Report ER-7.

FRIDRICH, M. and W. OLDER [December 1981], The Felix File Server, *Proceedings of the Eighth Symposium on Operating Systems Principles*, 37-46.

FULTZ, G. L. and L. KLEINROCK, [June 14-16, 1971], Adaptive Routing Techniques for Store-and-Forward Computer Communication Networks, presented at *IEEE International Conference on Communications*, Montreal, Canada.

GERLA, M. and L. KLEINROCK [April 1980], Flow Control: A Comparative Survey, *IEEE Transactions on Communications*.

GOSIP [April 1989], *U.S. Government Open Systems Interconnection Profile (GOSIP) Version 2.0*, GOSIP Advanced Requirements Group, National Institute of Standards and Technology (NIST).

GRANGE, J. L. and M. GIEN (EDS.) [1979], *Flow Control in Computer Networks*, North-Holland, Amsterdam.

GREEN, P. E. (ED.) [1982], *Computer Network Architectures and Protocols*, Plenum Press, New York, New York.

HINDEN, R., J. HAVERTY, and A. SHELTZER [September 1983], The DARPA Internet: Interconnecting Heterogeneous Computer Networks with Gateways, *Computer*.

INTERNATIONAL ORGANIZATION FOR STANDARDIZATION [June 1986a], Information processing systems — Open Systems Interconnection — *Transport Service Definition*, International Standard 8072, ISO, Switzerland.

INTERNATIONAL ORGANIZATION FOR STANDARDIZATION [July 1986b], Information processing systems — Open Systems Interconnection — *Connection Oriented Transport Protocol Specification*, International Standard 8073, ISO, Switzerland.

INTERNATIONAL ORGANIZATION FOR STANDARDIZATION [May 1987a], Information processing systems — Open Systems Interconnection — *Specification of Basic Specification of Abstract Syntax Notation One (ASN.1)*, International Standard 8824, ISO, Switzerland.

INTERNATIONAL ORGANIZATION FOR STANDARDIZATION [May 1987b], Information processing systems — Open Systems Interconnection — *Specification of Basic Encoding Rules for Abstract Syntax Notation One (ASN.1)*, International Standard 8825, ISO, Switzerland.

INTERNATIONAL ORGANIZATION FOR STANDARDIZATION [May 1988a], Information processing systems — Open Systems Interconnection — *Management Information Service Definition, Part 2: Common Management Information Service*, Draft International Standard 9595-2, ISO, Switzerland.

INTERNATIONAL ORGANIZATION FOR STANDARDIZATION [May 1988a], Information processing systems — Open Systems Interconnection — *Management Information Protocol Definition, Part 2: Common Management Information Protocol*, Draft International Standard 9596-2, ISO, Switzerland.

JACOBSON, V. [August 1988], Congestion Avoidance and Control, *Proceedings ACM SIGCOMM '88.*

JAIN, R. [January 1985], On Caching Out-of-Order Packets in Window Flow Controlled Networks, *Technical Report*, DEC-TR-342, Digital Equipment Corporation.

JAIN, R. [March 1986], Divergence of Timeout Algorithms for Packet Retransmissions, *Proceedings Fifth Annual International Phoenix Conference on Computers and Communications*, Scottsdale, Arizona.

JAIN, R. [October 1986], A Timeout-Based Congestion Control Scheme for Window Flow-Controlled Networks, *IEEE Journal on Selected Areas in Communications*, Vol. SAC-4, no. 7.

JAIN, R., K. RAMAKRISHNAN, and D. M. CHIU [August 1987], Congestion Avoidance in Computer Networks With a Connectionless Network Layer. *Technical Report*, DEC-TR-506, Digital Equipment Corporation.

JENNINGS, D. M., L. H. LANDWEBER, and I. H. FUCHS [February 28, 1986], Computer Networking for Scientists and Engineers, *Science* vol 231, 941-950.

JUBIN, J. and J. TORNOW [January 1987], The DARPA Packet Radio Network Protocols, *IEEE Proceedings.*

KAHN, R. [November 1972], Resource-Sharing Computer Communications Networks, *Proceedings of the IEEE*, 60(11), 1397-1407.

KARN, P., H. PRICE, and R. DIERSING [May 1985], Packet Radio in the Amateur Service, *IEEE Journal on Selected Areas in Communications*,

KARN, P. and C. PARTRIDGE [August 1987], Improving Round-Trip Time Estimates in Reliable Transport Protocols, *Proceedings of ACM SIGCOMM '87.*

KENT, C. and J. MOGUL [August 1987], Fragmentation Considered Harmful, *Proceedings of ACM SIGCOMM '87.*

KLINE, C. [August 1987], Supercomputers on the Internet: A Case Study, *Proceedings of ACM SIGCOMM '87.*

KOCHAN, S. G. and P. H. WOODS [1989], *UNIX Networking*, Hayden Books, Indianapolis, Indiana.

LAMPSON, B. W., M. PAUL, and H. J. SIEGERT (EDS.) [1981], *Distributed Systems - Architecture and Implementation (An Advanced Course)*, Springer-Verlag, Berlin.

LANZILLO, A. L. and C. PARTRIDGE [January 1989], Implementation of Dial-up IP for UNIX Systems, *Proceedings 1989 Winter USENIX Technical Conference*, San Diego, California.

LAQUEY, T. L. [July 1989], *User's Directory of Computer Networks*, Digital Press, Bedford, Massachusetts.

LAZAR, A. [November 1983], Optimal Flow Control of a Class of Queuing Networks in Equilibrium, *IEEE Transactions on Automatic Control*, Vol. AC-28:11.

LEFFLER, S., M. MCKUSICK, M. KARELS, and J. QUARTERMAN [1989], *The Design and Implementation of the 4.3BSD UNIX Operating System*, Addison-Wesley, Reading, Massachusetts.

LYNCH, D. C. and O. J. JACOBSEN (PUBLISHER and EDITOR) [1987-], *ConneXions, the Interoperability Report*, Interop Company, Mountain View, California.

LYNCH, D. C. (PRESIDENT) [1987-], *The Interop Conference*, Interop Company, Mountain View, California.

MARZULLO, K. and S. OWICKI [July 1985], Maintaining The Time In A Distributed System, *Operating Systems Review*, 19(3), 44-54.

MCKUSICK, M., W. JOY, S. LEFFLER, and R. FABRY [August 1984], A Fast File System For UNIX, *ACM Transactions On Computer Systems*, 2, 181-197.

MCNAMARA, J. [1982], *Technical Aspects of Data Communications*, Digital Press, Digital Equipment Corporation, Bedford, Massachusetts.

MCQUILLAN, J. M., I. RICHER, and E. ROSEN [May 1980], The New Routing Algorithm for the ARPANET, *IEEE Transactions on Communications*, (COM-28), 711-719.

MERIT [November 1987], *Management and Operation of the NSFNET Backbone Network: A Proposal Funded by the National Science Foundation and the State of Michigan*, MERIT Incorporated, Ann Arbor, Michigan.

METCALFE, R. M. and D. R. BOGGS [July 1976], Ethernet: Distributed Packet Switching for Local Computer Networks, *Communications of the ACM*, 19(7), 395-404.

MILLER, C. K. and D. M. THOMPSON [March 1982], Making a Case for Token Passing in Local Networks, *Data Communications*.

MILLS, D. [September 1991], On the Chronometry and Metrology of Computer Network Timescales and Their Application to the Network Time Protocol, *Proceedings of ACM SIGCOMM '91*, 8-17.

MILLS, D. and H. W. BRAUN [August 1987], The NSFNET Backbone Network, *Proceedings of ACM SIGCOMM '87*.

MITCHELL, J. and J. DION [April 1982], A Comparison of Two Network-Based File Servers, *Communications of the ACM*, 25(4), 233-245.

MORRIS, R. [1979], Fixing Timeout Intervals for Lost Packet Detection in Computer Communication Networks, *Proceedings AFIPS National Computer Conference*, AFIPS Press, Montvale, New Jersey.

NAGLE, J. [April 1987], On Packet Switches With Infinite Storage, *IEEE Transactions on Communications*, (COM-35:4).

NARTEN, T. [Sept. 1989], Internet Routing, *Proceedings ACM SIGCOMM '89*.

NEEDHAM, R. M. [1979], System Aspects of the Cambridge Ring, *Proceedings of the ACM Seventh Symposium on Operating System Principles*, 82-85.

NELSON, J. [September 1983], 802: A Progress Report, *Datamation*.

OPPEN, D. and Y. DALAL [October 1981], The Clearinghouse: A Decentralized Agent for Locating Named Objects, Office Products Division, XEROX Corporation.

PADLIPSKY, M. [1983], A Perspective On The ARPANET Reference Model, *Proceedings of the IEEE INFOCOM Conference*, San Diego, California.

PARTRIDGE, C. [June 1986], Mail Routing Using Domain Names: An Informal Tour, *Proceedings of the 1986 Summer USENIX Conference*, Atlanta, Georgia.

PARTRIDGE, C. [June 1987], Implementing the Reliable Data Protocol (RDP), *Proceedings of the 1987 Summer USENIX Conference*, Phoenix, Arizona.

PARTRIDGE, C. and M. ROSE [June 1989], A Comparison of External Data Formats, in *Message Handling Systems and Distributed Applications*, E. STEFFERUD and O. JACOBSEN (EDS.) Elsevier-North Holland.

PETERSON, L. [1985], *Defining and Naming the Fundamental Objects in a Distributed Message System*, Ph.D. Dissertation, Purdue University, West Lafayette, Indiana.

PETERSON, J. and A. SILBERSCHATZ [1985], *Operating System Concepts*, 2nd edition, Addison-Wesley, Reading, Massachusetts.

PIERCE, J. R. [1972], Networks for Block Switching of Data, *Bell System Technical Journal*, 51.

POSTEL, J. B. [April 1980], Internetwork Protocol Approaches, *IEEE Transactions on Communications*, (COM-28), 604-611.

POSTEL, J. B., C. A. SUNSHINE, and D. CHEN [1981], The ARPA Internet Protocol, *Computer Networks*.

PRESOTTO, D. L. and D. M. RITCHIE [June 1990], Interprocess Communication in the Ninth Edition Unix System, *Software – Practice And Experience*, 20(S1), S1/3-S1/17.

QUARTERMAN, J. S. [1990], *The Matrix: Computer Networks and Conferencing Systems Worldwide*, Digital Press, Digital Equipment Corporation, Maynard, Massachusetts.

QUARTERMAN, J. S. and J. C. HOSKINS [October 1986], Notable Computer Networks, *Communications of the ACM*, 29(10).

REYNOLDS, J., J. POSTEL, A. R. KATZ, G. G. FINN, and A. L. DESCHON [October 1985], The DARPA Experimental Multimedia Mail System, *IEEE Computer*.

RITCHIE, D. M. and K. THOMPSON [July 1974], The UNIX Time-Sharing System, *Communications of the ACM*, 17(7), 365-375; revised and reprinted in *Bell System Technical Journal*, 57(6), [July-August 1978], 1905-1929.

ROSENTHAL, R. (ED.) [November 1982], *The Selection of Local Area Computer Networks*, National Bureau of Standards Special Publication 500-96.

SALTZER, J. [1978], Naming and Binding of Objects, *Operating Systems, An Advanced Course*, Springer-Verlag, 99-208.

SALTZER, J. [April 1982], Naming and Binding of Network Destinations, *International Symposium on Local Computer Networks*, IFIP/T.C.6, 311-317.

SALTZER, J., D. REED, and D. CLARK [November 1984], End-to-End Arguments in System Design, *ACM Transactions on Computer Systems*, 2(4), 277-288.

SCHWARTZ, M. and T. STERN [April 1980], *IEEE Transactions on Communications*, COM-28(4), 539-552.

SHOCH, J. F. [1978], Internetwork Naming, Addressing, and Routing, *Proceedings of COMPCON*.

SHOCH, J. F., Y. DALAL, and D. REDELL [August 1982], Evolution of the Ethernet Local Computer Network, *Computer*.

SNA [1975], *IBM System Network Architecture – General Information*, IBM System Development Division, Publications Center, Department E01, Research Triangle Park, North Carolina.

SOLOMON, M., L. LANDWEBER, and D. NEUHEGEN [1982], The CSNET Name Server, *Computer Networks* (6), 161-172.

STALLINGS, W. [1984], *Local Networks: An Introduction*, Macmillan Publishing Company, New York.

STALLINGS, W. [1985], *Data and Computer Communications*, Macmillan Publishing Company, New York.

STEVENS, W. R. [1990], *UNIX Network Programming*, Prentice-Hall, Englewood Cliffs, New Jersey.

SWINEHART, D., G. MCDANIEL, and D. R. BOGGS [December 1979], WFS: A Simple Shared File System for a Distributed Environment, *Proceedings of the Seventh Symposium on Operating System Principles*, 9-17.

TANENBAUM, A. [1981], *Computer Networks: Toward Distributed Processing Systems*, Prentice-Hall, Englewood Cliffs, New Jersey.

TICHY, W. and Z. RUAN [June 1984], Towards a Distributed File System, *Proceedings of Summer 84 USENIX Conference*, Salt Lake City, Utah, 87-97.

TOMLINSON. R. S. [1975], Selecting Sequence Numbers, *Proceedings ACM SIGOPS/SIGCOMM Interprocess Communication Workshop*, 11-23.

WARD, A. A. [1980], TRIX: A Network-Oriented Operating System, *Proceedings of COMPCON*, 344-349.

WATSON, R. [1981], Timer-Based Mechanisms in Reliable Transport Protocol Connection Management, *Computer Networks*, North-Holland Publishing Company.

WEINBERGER, P. J. [1985], The UNIX Eighth Edition Network File System, *Proceedings 1985 ACM Computer Science Conference*, 299-301.

WELCH, B. and J. OSTERHAUT [May 1986], Prefix Tables: A Simple Mechanism for Locating Files in a Distributed System, *Proceedings IEEE Sixth International Conference on Distributed Computing Systems*, 184-189.

WILKES, M. V. and D. J. WHEELER [May 1979], The Cambridge Digital Communication Ring, *Proceedings Local Area Computer Network Symposium*.

XEROX [1981], Internet Transport Protocols, *Report XSIS 028112*, Xerox Corporation, Office Products Division, Palo Alto, California.

ZHANG, L. [August 1986], Why TCP Timers Don't Work Well, *Proceedings of ACM SIGCOMM '86*.

Index